TOWARD A CHRISTIAN CONCEPTION OF HISTORY

EDITED AND TRANSLATED BY

**Herbert Donald Morton
Harry Van Dyke**

Institute for Christian Studies
and
University Press of America,® Inc.
Lanham · New York · Oxford

Copyright © 2002 by
Redeemer University College, Ancaster, Ontario, Canada

University Press of America,® Inc.
4720 Boston Way
Lanham, Maryland 20706
UPA Acquisitions Department (301) 459-3366

12 Hid's Copse Rd.
Cumnor Hill, Oxford OX2 9JJ

All rights reserved
Printed in the United States of America
British Library Cataloging in Publication Information Available

Copublished by arrangement with the Institute of Christian Studies

Library of Congress Cataloging-in-Publication Data

Smit, Meijer C. (Meijer Cornelis), 1911-1981.
[Selections. English. 2002]
Toward a Christian conception of history / M.C. Smit ; edited and
translated by Herbert Donald Morton, Harry Van Dyke.
p. cm
Includes the author's 1950 dissertation, The relation between Christianity
and history in the present-day Roman Catholic conception of history.
Includes bibliographical references (p.) and indexes.
1. History—Philosophy. 2. Providence and government of God. I. Morton,
Herbert Donald. II. Van Dyke, Harry. III. Smit. Meijer C. (Meijer Cornelis),
1911-1981. Verhouding van Christendom en historie in de huidige
Rooms-Katholieke geschiedsbeschouwing. English. IV. Title.

BR115.H5 .S6513 2002
231.7'6—dc21   2002018108 CIP

ISBN 0-7618-2140-6 (paperback : alk. ppr.)

♾ The paper used in this publication meets the minimum
requirements of American National Standard for Information
Sciences—Permanence of Paper for Printed Library Materials,
ANSI Z39.48—1984

TABLE OF CONTENTS

Editors' Foreword vii

PART ONE/ Catholic Conceptions of History

Preface 3
Introduction 7
   I/ Nature and the supernatural 14
   II/ Fall and redemption 35
   III/ Christianity and history 51
   IV/ Dualism and connection 70
   V/ World history and progress 91
   VI/ The problem of Christian philosophy 121
   VII/ The problem of Christian historical science 140

PART TWO/ Toward a Reformed Conception of History

   1/ Protestant conceptions of history 169
   2/ The current crisis in Catholic thought 185
   3/ Calvinism and Catholicism on church and state 189
   4/ Nationalism and Catholicism 202
   5/ The divine mystery in history 223
   6/ The character of the Middle Ages 247
   7/ Culture and salvation 260
   8/ The sacred dwelling place 281
   9/ A turnabout in historical science? 305
   10/ The meaning of history 318
   11/ New perspectives for a Christian conception of history? . . . 327
   12/ The value of history 341
   13/ The time of history 347
   14/ Approaches to the Reformation 358
   15/ The first and the second history 363
   16/ Toward a reordering of knowledge 380

Bibliography 399
Index of Names 421
Index of Subjects 425

EDITORS' FOREWORD

MEYER CORNELIS SMIT (1911–1981) taught history and philosophy in the Free University at Amsterdam for a quarter century. This volume presents the harvest of his scholarly output. The selection focuses on Smit as a thinker who struck out for paths of his own through penetrating analyses of a wide range of literature. The sustained discussions and polemics with other thinkers illustrate not only the breadth of his knowledge and interest but also the evolution and transitions of his own thought. Reared in the intellectual milieu of Neo-Calvinism and one of its cultural products, the Reformational school of philosophy spearheaded by Herman Dooyeweerd and Dirk Vollenhoven, Smit worked only sparingly with the technical apparatus of the school but drew all the more from its basic religious assumptions, such as the utter dependence of all reality on the Creator, the cosmic scope of redemption in Christ, and the pivotal function of the heart at the core of all human activity, including thought, reason and science. In consequence, he shared the school's critique of the alleged autonomy of rational thought, its repudiation of the dichotomy of fact and value and fact and interpretation, its careful delimitation of the nature of scientific analysis as it abstracts aspects of things and phenomena from their embeddedness in integral wholes as experienced in everyday life, and its emphasis on the law-like, orderly, reliable character of created reality as sustained by a faithful God. Receiving fresh accents in Smit's developing conceptions, however, are an unqualified avowal of the thoroughly historical nature of things without acceding to historical relativism, and an unreserved celebration of the multiformity and restlessness of all reality, whose only unity and point of rest lie in the orientation to its transcendental Origin. Meyer Smit may be regarded as the foremost thinker about history to come out of this intellectual milieu.

Smit's approach centered on the theme of God and history—the latter taken in the twofold sense of events and the discipline that studies events. It was certainly no coincidence that the inaugural oration with which he accepted his university appointment in 1955 wrestled with the question how one must see the relation between God and history. In the years that followed he was to apply a large portion of his mental energies to the problems inherent in articulating that relation in a manner consistent with Christian belief.

Smit's distinctive approach first took shape in his encounter with Roman Catholic thought, or, more precisely, with the modern Catholic mind that discovered history. His doctoral dissertation contains his report of this encounter, together with his attempt to formulate a response along the lines of the Reformational tradition. Interwoven with careful analysis of the position of others are many passages in which Smit developed his own views on important philosophical and theological issues in history.[1] Reviewing the published work, Berkouwer remarked that "a glow of enthusiasm lies over this study," which he called "the mature fruit of years of meticulous research."[2] The dissertation was to remain Smit's only book-length publication. As a record of the development of his thought and as a statement of what would become the main theme of his scholarship, its integral republication as Part One of the present collection would seem fully justified. Among Catholic reviewers of the book, Schoonenberg noted that "an enormous amount of research has gone into this skillful exposition"[3] and Congar congratulated the author on his skill at "perceiving the different currents, choosing his references, and giving objective expositions of views he does not share, ... grasping them at their deepest roots."[4] While later developments in Catholic thought have further elaborated the themes assessed in this study by a Reformed thinker, the work remains instructive in its analysis of some of the seminal issues and critical shifts that were debated prior to Vatican II. It is our hope that its publication in English translation will further contribute in this new millennium to a greater mutual understanding of two historic branches of Christianity.

Subsequent to the dissertation Smit wrote essays and presented papers in which he worked at fuller articulations of his own position as he interacted with Christian thinkers from a variety of faith communities. Sixteen of these pieces are included, in chronological order, in Part Two of this volume. Together they form a remarkable document of a conscientious intellectual journey in which the author seeks to account for the integral unity of human experience in doing *history*, *science* and *philosophy* even while enjoying free interplay with *knowing*, *loving* and *believing*, in single-hearted service of God in all of life's dimensions.

Meyer Smit was born on a farm near Haastrecht, a modest town in the dairy heartland of central Holland. The home he grew up in was Calvinist in religion and Kuyperian in outlook, hence marked by biblical piety, active church membership, and keen interest in social and political issues. Parents and grandparents, he fondly remembered, fostered an awareness of one's historical heritage and providential calling. Meyer learned to milk cows, handle the punt, stack hay, groom horses. His true passion, however, was books. How elated he was when given permission to continue his education! For six long years he attended the City Gymnasium of Gouda, an hour's cycling away, while on Saturday afternoons the headmaster of the local Christian elementary school

---

[1] Cf., e.g., pp. 71–76, 79–82, 84f., 89f., 91–93, 97f., 117–20, 134–39 and 150–57 below.
[2] G. C. Berkouwer, in *Anti-Revolutionaire Staatkunde* 20 (1950): 135f.
[3] Piet Schoonenberg, in *Streven; Katholiek Cultureel Tijdschrift*, Oct., 1950.
[4] Yves Congar, in *Revue des sciences philosophiques et théologiques* 34 (1950): 654.

tutored him in church history, Reformed doctrine, and Neo-Calvinist social and political thought.

Towards the end of these years, a column in the Anti-Revolutionary daily *De Standaard* caught his attention and fired his imagination. Written by Professor Vollenhoven of the Free University, it argued that higher education was a challenging field for Christian service, not just in the form of theological studies but in terms of "scholarship *tout court*." When Meyer Smit matriculated in 1932 his choice of university was clear, if not his area of study. With two other students he rented rooms in Amsterdam and enrolled in the Faculty of Theology. The following year saw him registered in the Faculties of Law and Letters as well. Mornings were spent attending a wide variety of lecture series; on late afternoons his roommates would regularly find him standing behind a tall desk near the window, working his way methodically through a volume of the *Propyläen-Weltgeschichte*. The oratorical society A.G.O.R.A. greeted in him a shy and pensive yet congenial new member.

Certain professors in particular attracted him. There was A. Anema for constitutional law, A. A. van Schelven for the history of Calvinism, and A. Goslinga for modern history. Meyer Smit developed a distaste, however, for the dogmatics of Valentine Hepp, whose elaborate syllabi, full of the minutest distinctions, finally kept him from taking the examination for candidacy in theology. By contrast, he very much loved the weekly classes with Herman Dooyeweerd, who taught philosophy of law but allowed himself many excursions into general philosophy. Before long, Meyer was caught up in the young, vigorous movement for the development and dissemination of a distinctively Reformational school of philosophy; he participated in the summer camps at Lunteren and devoured the publications by Dooyeweerd, Vollenhoven, and kindred spirits. Throughout these formative years he also made a habit of attending the Sunday worship services and Wednesday evening Bible classes led by *dominee* S. G. de Graaf. This preacher's critical and radical expositions carried a distinctively covenantal and theocentric thrust in their sustained elaboration of the biblical story line that human life has forfeited God's favor yet is restored through grace in Christ to service in his kingdom, a kingdom that encompasses the entire created world.

At the end of the 1930's Meyer Smit passed the examinations for candidacy in Law and in Letters (the latter *cum laude*). The German occupation interrupted his formal education, but in 1946 he sat for the qualifying examination in History (again sustained *cum laude*), whereupon he accepted a position in The Hague as librarian with the Kuyper Institute, the research center of the Anti-Revolutionary Party (since 1980 headquarters of the Christian Democrats).

In preparation for an academic career he now began to work on his doctoral dissertation. The choice of topic had come about indirectly. During the war years, when he had lived at home again, he had renewed his acquaintance with the principal of a local preparatory seminary, a Franciscan brother with whom he had many amicable discussions especially about a growing body of Catholic literature on the nature of history and historical study. One day it flashed upon him that this new and exciting intellectual current was the very thing he had been looking for as a subject for his dissertation. For one thing, it would engage his interest in the problems of Christian faith as applied to learning; for another, it would offer a splendid opportunity, for purposes of comparison and critique, to try his hand at articulating a Reformational view of history. Charting both frontiers, the dissertation, entitled *The Relation Between Christianity and History in the Present-day Roman Catholic Conception of History*, was completed and successfully defended on 17 February 1950. The work instantly established Dr. Smit's academic credentials, but it was to be some years before a coveted chair at his alma mater became vacant.

September 27, 1955 was a memorable day in the life of the 43-year-old scholar, as he inaugurated his teaching career at the Free University with a bold oration on "the divine mystery in history." The stirring address had the ring of a manifesto: historians cannot hope to say much that is truly meaningful about history if they systematically ignore its relation to God. One reviewer expressed his gratitude to Professor Smit for indicating, "not just for the practice of historical study but for the pursuit of science and scholarship in general," a way of embracing a scientific method that differs internally from that of "neutral" scholarship, namely a scientific method that unreservedly incorporates faith: "Faith is not an ornament added to knowledge acquired in another way; nor is it a subjective prejudice that the historian is never quite able to shake. Faith, rather, when oriented to God and divine Revelation, is a conscious ingredient of the scientific method that the researcher employs to open up his 'field.' "[5]

Eagerly Smit now set to work. Medieval History and Theory of History comprised his dual teaching assignment. The first year set the pattern for the next quarter century: the lectures in history centered on topics rich in metahistorical implications; the lectures in theory drew heavily on current debates among practicing historians. Invariably the lectures would be based on a steadily mushrooming personal filing system for which he methodically gleaned and processed scores of professional journals in history, philosophy, theology and archeology, published in Dutch, German, English, French and Italian.[6] While thus appearing obsessed with breadth, he also insisted on depth and imposed upon himself the highest demands of original reflection. A perfectionist by temperament, he ended by publishing very little. As he once explained, "I prefer to work through my students."[7]

---

[5] J. P. A. Mekkes, in *Anti-Revolutionaire Staatkunde* 25 (1955): 312, 316, quoting from the oration; cf. below, p. 233.

[6] The library and the literary remains of M. C. Smit are now lodged with the Institute for Christian Studies, 229 College Street, Toronto.

[7] Until the dramatic increase in enrolment during the seventies, the average incoming class, in the history and philosophy departments combined, ranged between twelve to fifteen students. Over the years, in addition to giving individual oral tests after each course, Professor Smit was mentor and guide for the writing of a score of *doctoraalscripties* (qualifying theses).

Foreword

Smit, who never married, made his home in Aerdenhout, a quiet town near Haarlem, close to the train station, from where he would commute to Amsterdam, always working as he traveled. For recreation he cycled through the dunes, daily except Sundays. There was a restlessness about him; he walked with rapid steps and seemed to be forever going somewhere. Yet he could also ignore the clock and be a gracious, relaxed host. He was genuinely interested in the people he met, in their lives, their experiences, their joys and sorrows. Though an informed observer of national politics and international affairs, the everyday concerns of the local community held an almost equal fascination for him. A man of books, he never owned a radio or television set, preferring to "read all about it" in the dailies. His students remember him as a friendly and gentle man, unassuming, given to formality yet not aloof, a teacher who surprised them with personalized reading lists and many helpful suggestions.[8] They were impressed by his erudition, intrigued by his universal outlook and interests, and inspired by his pre-occupation with the mystery of history. The private seminars held in his upstairs study on Friday evenings were the favorite of many and were talked about for years afterwards.

The rest may be summed up in dates. In 1963 Professor Smit was cross-appointed in the Philosophy Department, which he joined full-time in 1970 when his teaching load was expanded with philosophical propaedeutics for all incoming students in both history and art history. His illness manifested itself in the fall of 1980 and after months of hospitalization, on 16 July 1981, he fell asleep in Christ.

The teaching assignment that M. C. Smit accepted at the Free University in 1955 involved history itself (the medieval period) and thought about history (theory and philosophy of history). No accidental combination, the assignment corresponded to the appointee's own wishes: he publicly expressed the hope that it would enable him to demonstrate in practice the interrelationship between the scientific method of the discipline on the one hand and his view of life and history on the other.

---

[8] Four doctoral dissertations were prepared under the supervision of Professor Smit. They are, in chronological order:

Eduard van den Brink, *Rooms of katholiek; de opvattingen van Christopher Dawson over kultuur en religie* [Roman or Catholic? The views of Christopher Dawson concerning culture and religion] (Groningen: V.R.B. Drukkerijen, 1970).

Sander Griffioen, *De Roos en het Kruis; de waardering van de eindigheid in het latere denken van Hegel* [The Rose and the Cross: The appreciation of finitude in the later thought of Hegel] (Assen: Van Gorcum, 1976).

Jan Davidse, *Beda Venerabilis' interpretatie van de historische werkelijkheid* [The Venerable Bede's interpretation of historical reality] (Groningen: V.R.B. Drukkerijen, 1976).

Jan Aertsen, *Natura en Creatura; de denkweg van Thomas van Aquino*, 2 vols. (Amsterdam: VU Boekhandel, 1982). Eng. trans. by Herbert Donald Morton, *Nature and Creature: Thomas Aquinas's Way of Thought* (Leiden: Brill, 1988). Studien und Texte zur Geistesgeschichte des Mittelalters, no. 21.

Practically all the writings from the university period, here included in Part Two, date from the years 1955 to 1970. Strictly speaking, only four of these (numbers 4, 6, 7 and 8) can be said to be in the field of historical writing. They illustrate not only his breadth but especially his sustained endeavor to give concrete substance to the theme of the divine mystery in human life and its formative power for culture.

Certainly he entertained ideas of broader projects in this area. He toyed with the thought of writing a "history of the city," for example, and collected much material for such a study; the lecture notes (number 8) provide an indication of the direction he might have taken had he made any further forays into that field. That there were none is due importantly, beyond any doubt, to the demands made on his energies by the problems of philosophy of history. Perhaps his move in 1970 from medieval history to medieval philosophy was made after reaching the conclusion that it was impossible for him to do justice concomitantly to both parts of his teaching assignment. In any case, theoretical questions regarding history continued to absorb most of his attention.

Though steadfast in his basic conviction, Smit was reluctant to settle on very many final answers. The accent in the last decades of his life was entirely on seeking and inquiring. The writings in the field of philosophy of history which appear here were not (with the exception of numbers 13 and 14) published during his lifetime. Most of them are papers that were given between 1962 and 1970 (numbers 9 to 14). The text from 1970 (number 15) served as a discussion starter for a graduate seminar; it bears the fragmentary stamp of such texts while faithfully depicting the stage of his thought at that point in time. Calvin Seerveld has said of these essays that they show "the process, the struggle of ideas, and the unfinished vitality which a movement of Christian scholarship can have that is trying to be obedient to the Lord in academic work [through] careful, probing thought [and] philosophically responsible, straightforward wrestling with our complicated cultural world . . ." [9]

The volume now before us reflects the central questions that engaged Meyer Smit: the question of the influence of faith and worldview on the practice and appreciation of history; the question of the meaning of history as an answer to the *geschichtslosigkeit* or a-historical-mindedness that distinguishes our culture; the meaning of time as a way for academic historians to leave the inexhaustible richness of historical reality intact by relating historical reality in all its diversity to its divine Origin. By seeking to comprehend historical reality within the framework of temporality and transcendental origin, Smit, for all the restlessness and hesitancy that characterize his thought, found a basic conviction which he held to the end of his life: scholarship must be open to the active presence of the Origin of all things shimmering just beneath the surface of phenomena. It was not given him to elaborate this keynote for general philosophers or to make it operational for working historians. In his last piece (number 16), composed in

---

[9] In *Calvinist Contact*, 24 April 1987, p. 24.

Foreword

1980 but picking up a theme first broached in 1955, Smit came full circle. Here he not only gave voice to a radical critique of the reigning theory of knowledge and philosophy of science, but he also made a passionate plea for complete openness, when studying the world, to what comes at us from the metahistorical realm. It was a fitting close to a thoughtful career of one whose humanity, charity, and religious faith were never in doubt.

Preparations for a collection of Meyer Smit's writings date back to 1979, three years before his scheduled retirement. A committee composed of colleagues and friends in the philosophy and history departments of the university—Jan Aertsen, Jan Davidse, Sander Griffioen, Gerben Groenewoud, Jacob Klapwijk, Donald Morton, Michiel van Os, and Arie van Dijk—conceived the idea of marking the occasion of their mentor's official retirement with the publication of an anthology of his writings in English translation. The Free University's Board of Directors approved the necessary funding. Roger Henderson contributed extensive bibliographical research. The initiative enjoyed the full approval of Professor Smit himself, and he made an active contribution to its realization. His illness and death in the summer of 1981 cast a melancholy shadow on the project, though the long delay of its completion was due to other factors, now irrelevant.

For the text of Part One we have followed the published version of the dissertation after making a few minor corrections based on the original manuscript. The texts in Part Two follow the manuscripts, or their published versions where available; where noted, we have inserted a few subheadings. All manuscripts are deposited in the archives of the Institute for Christian Studies in Toronto.

We are pleased to be able to present this selection from Professor Smit's scholarly output for the international public who have shown an interest in it. The writings of Meyer Smit contain ideas and motifs that are of fundamental significance to anyone concerned with the problems of philosophy of history in our time.

HERBERT DONALD MORTON
International School of Amsterdam
Amstelveen, The Netherlands

HARRY VAN DYKE
Redeemer University College
Ancaster, Ontario

Earlier versions of Part Two, essays 2 to 15 and an excerpt from essay 16, appeared in M. C. Smit, *Writings on God and History*; Volume I: *Selected Studies (1951–80)*, edited by Harry Van Dyke and translated by Herbert Donald Morton (Jordan Station, Ont.: Wedge Publishing Foundation, 1987).

PART ONE

Catholic Conceptions of History

PREFACE

IT MAY SEEM TOO BOLD an undertaking to attempt to offer, already at this point in time, a more or less comprehensive survey of the relation between Christianity and history as viewed from the Roman Catholic side. Would such a work not inevitably be outdated before it appeared? An almost unbroken stream of studies in theology of history is seeing the light, and we may soon expect to see important new publications about the relation of Christianity and history. Leading Catholic thinkers have not yet taken a clear position on the question, even though they have been engaged frequently, and intensely, with the category of history—I have in mind the Christian existentialists in particular. But within the foreseeable future they too will demand consideration for their particular way of looking at the relation between Christianity and history. Moreover, the conceptions to be examined in the present work represent provisional positions. The various authors write from strong convictions yet appear to be still searching and open to new solutions. Even those who seemed to have made a definitive choice in the debate are prepared at times to make substantial revisions. It is beginning to look as if Catholic thought has broken loose from its moorings, set adrift in the direction of history and religious mystery. Who at this stage would dare to predict where Catholic philosophy and theology of history will end up?

And yet, amid rapid developments and heightened tensions the basic structure of Catholic thought remains clearly visible. This basic structure is what concerns us here, rather than a detailed description of a large number of conceptions and their historical links. Otherwise this study would indeed be premature.

The relation between Christianity and history remains a fascinating and pressing problem. To a high degree it represents a challenge today for Catholic thought, but no less for the Reformational conception of history. One can attempt to resolve the problem in two ways: either directly, by unfolding the rich implications of one's own worldview, never mind what those of other minds have written; or indirectly, by learning from the difficulties encountered by those who proceed from a different set of assumptions. The latter way is the safest, but it is not without danger, precisely because it is the easier of the two: negative criticism can make one forget the need for positive elaboration. This danger threatens here especially, since every Christian historian knows that an authentic Christian conception of history—a view of history in terms of the Christ who is both God and man, both crucified and risen—requires an all but superhuman effort.

Still, we shall follow the second, indirect method, for two reasons. In the first place, it will be good to focus attention on questions which, although they are currently being debated by Catholics, have as yet aroused scant attention among Reformational thinkers about history. Furthermore, the rich variety of present-day Catholic thought about the relation between Christianity and history presents an excellent opportunity for testing the correctness of a *point of departure* that differs significantly from our own, with the added benefit of clarifying and enriching our own understanding of the issues. Meanwhile, in articulating our critique from our own standpoint we hope to keep in mind as well that the relation Christianity-history contains a problem that can never be fully fathomed or satisfyingly resolved.

The organization of this study speaks for itself but it may be useful to make a few remarks about it. Since the word "history" has two principal senses: history as events, and history as the science of events, we distinguish two main problems with regard to our subject: (1) What is the relation of Christianity to historical reality? (2) What is the significance of the Christian religion for the acquisition of knowledge of this historical reality?

We shall deal with both questions against the background of general trends in the current Catholic outlook (Introduction), and against the background, further, of a number of key problems in philosophy and theology, problems that are current in Catholic conceptions of history and that reflect characteristic features of recent trends (chapters I and II). By proceeding in this way we can grow accustomed to the intellectual climate in which the problem is being discussed today. To achieve our objective as fully as possible, these opening chapters will canvass not only the *leading* ideas being advanced but also any *dissenting* views if these are helpful for gaining an impression of the turnabout that is taking place.

Upon arriving, then, at the heart of our subject, we make the acquaintance of a number of more or less divergent conceptions of the relation between Christianity and history (chapter III). These date mainly from the period since 1930. Our survey, though far from exhaustive, affords an impression of the rich variety of aspects that the problem poses for Catholicism.

In the next two chapters we go on to analyze various elements of the conceptions introduced thus far. Chapter IV deals directly with the central problem raised by the influence of Christianity on history. Time after time our analysis encounters an irresolvable dualism, which turns up in every new theory in a different form, to generate a latent or open tension within it: for example, the tension between the incarnation and the cross, or the tension between the indirect and the direct action of God in history.

Chapter V constitutes a transition to the relation between Christianity and history as a problem for historical science. It examines how the Christian conception can be applied to certain questions that are of profound concern to historical study and philosophy of history. Are the idea of the unity of world history and the idea of progress inextricably linked to Christian belief? That question is explored in four successive sections—in the last of these in all its complexity.

Since few Catholic scholars assign our topic to *philosophy* of history, these first five chapters deal mainly with *theology* of history. Two remaining chapters now inquire into the possibility of both a philosophy and a science of history in the Christian spirit. Although the turnabout in Catholic thought described thus far has affected practicing historians less than the theoreticians, our study culminates in the question: To what extent can one speak of Christian history-writing from a Catholic perspective, first of all philosophically but no less professionally?

While chapter VI, then, discusses the idea of a Christian *philosophy* of history, the term itself appears there only infrequently, for the simple reason that not much has been written on the subject. The problem of the relation of religion and *general* philosophy, in contrast, has received widespread attention. Hence we deal extensively with that problem as it has arisen in recent decades, in the conviction that this is the issue that determines to what extent Catholic thinkers can contribute meaningfully to an integrally Christian philosophy of history.

Chapter VII, finally, is devoted to the idea of a Christian historical *science*. Here the lines of the entire work converge. In particular we take up again the problems that engaged us in chapter V and now inquire with heightened interest: Is there a deeper and more intrinsic connection, beyond mere harmony, between a Christian conception of history and the scientific discipline of history as practiced by Christians?

A study such as this would not be complete unless it examined still a third aspect. In the fields of historical research and writing, Catholic scholars have a prominent place. It would be interesting to investigate how they, with or without theorizing about it, integrate Christianity and history in their works. When I set out to summarize the material I had gathered for this purpose, however, it soon became apparent that it was of such a scope that a separate work would be required for it. Some of this material is now appended to chapter VII to give at least an indication, however brief, of what practicing Catholic historians are doing in terms of writing history in a Christian spirit.

*

At the conclusion of my academic studies, my gratitude goes out to God for all he has given me. Throughout my years of study at the Free University, begun in high expectations, his unfailing nearness strengthened me. In part by means of often difficult circumstances, God opened my eyes to the wonderful task that awaits those who would pursue scholarship in the service of Christ.

Warm feelings of gratitude fill me when I consider what many professors in the Free University have meant for my academic training. It is due in large measure to their scientific work that Christian scholarship is to me not merely an attractive slogan but a reality. I am indebted to Professor Smitskamp for supervising the writing of this thesis. His keen interest in the problems addressed by my research confirmed me in the hope that my work, which required such lengthy preparations, might perhaps not be without some significance for the framing of a Reformational conception of history.

With a certain satisfaction, but not without nostalgia, I think back upon the many conversations I was privileged to have with friends and acquaintances about questions that so greatly concern us all. With special gratitude I mention here the name of dominee S. G. de Graaf of the Gereformeerde Kerk of Amsterdam, who in the course of many years had a profound influence on my thinking.

A word, finally, to those whose ideas are challenged here. I trust that in and behind my critique they will detect not only an effort on my part to enter into their minds, but above all a desire to dialogue with them—may it be in the not too distant future—about a possible conception or practice of history that differs from the one their own worldview allows.

INTRODUCTION

IF ONE WERE TO ASK why it is that the relation of Christianity to history was put on the agenda of Roman Catholicism in such a short time,[1] the answer would not be long in coming. The course of our civilization compels reflection on its foundations. The secularization of Western culture entered an acute stage after two world wars. Reason enough to ponder deeply, and without delay, the connection between the Christian religion and history!

This and similar considerations are undoubtedly important for the thinkers who devote their attention to the problem in question. Some of their conceptions are even inconceivable apart from this background. Maritain, for example, proceeds consciously from the fact of the secularization of our culture since the end of the Middle Ages, a process that leads him to search for a new possibility of Christian civilization.

Yet one must guard against overestimating the influence of the circumstances of the times. The fact that even in the current critical phase of our culture Catholic conceptions of history exhibit a predominantly optimistic streak should give us pause. In some of these conceptions one detects but little of the crisis that has been affecting the Western world ever more profoundly for decades now; when it does play a role, the crisis is often not a reason for pessimism but rather a passage to hitherto unsuspected possibilities for Christian forms of civilization. This fact alone suggests that from the outset we must focus on the distinctive character of Catholic thought and seek the reason for its new interest in history first of all in the internal development of Catholicism itself.

The theological, philosophical, and scientific situation within present-day Catholicism is extremely complex and therefore difficult to analyze. What can be established with certainty, however, is that the last seventy years have seen far-reaching changes and that current trends point not to consolidation but to a new, dynamic development. Surveying the stages of Catholic thought from the closing years of the nineteenth to the first half of the twentieth century, we see an unmistakable shift of focus: from the abstract to the concrete; from the static to the dynamic; from the immutable and essential to the progressively evolving and historical; from the dialectically rational to the "mysterious" and religious; from the distance between the natural and the supernatural to a synthesis of the two. I deliberately say *shift* of focus, for what we have here is a slow but steady process in continuity, a process that is not likely to end in a denial of what was

---

[1] See Aubert, "Les grandes tendances théologiques entre les deux guerres"; Daniélou, "Les orientations présentes de la pensée religieuse"; Congar, "Tendances actuelles de la pensée religieuse." [Note: for full descriptions of publications, see the Bibliography below.]

presupposed at the outset. True, we do come across such a denial in one or two thinkers, but they are not typical of present-day Catholic thought. What makes us listen with fascination to the often passionate debates is the endeavor to maintain the abstract, the static, the rational, the natural, and to reconcile it with newly discovered, or badly neglected, dimensions. The difference between Catholic thought today and Catholic thought at the end of the nineteenth and beginning of the twentieth century is mainly one of accent, yet such that many a problem is affected to the core.

While there appears to be only an external connection between the categories that are drawing attention nowadays, there is in fact an inner connection between them, though not in the sense that one of them could be said to be the most original category. Together, in mutual coherence, the concepts of the concrete, the dynamic, the mysterious, and so on, are being affected by the general evolution of Catholic thought. Initially these concepts were treated with the greatest possible reserve, or at least were not strongly accented; but of late they are increasingly being acknowledged as indispensable elements of the Christian worldview.

In the first place, there is a noticeable interest in the concrete. Here, realism itself is at issue. In the formation of knowledge, the focus is less on the abstract essence of things and more on their full, concrete reality. The thinker endeavors to "think along with" the things, to commune with them, in order to find out what they really are. A purely conceptual method can uncover the static structure of reality, the fixed order of things and phenomena. But reality entails more than that. One who begins with the essence of things will be inclined towards a static conception of reality in which dynamism and development are of secondary importance. But one who directs his attention first of all towards the concrete will encounter dynamism there from the very outset.

Proceeding from this opposition, Catholic thought has sought new access to the phenomenon of history. Once it had understood that the dynamism of things involves something essential, it could no longer be satisfied with a conception of history as something accidental. This has given birth to one of the most difficult and controversial problems for contemporary Catholic theology and philosophy: How does the becoming, in particular the historical becoming, of things relate to their unchanging, non-temporal being?

This problem has until now been of particular concern in the areas of theology of history, of dogma, and of salvation history. The so-called New Theology or *théologie nouvelle* is marked in the first place by the emphasis it puts on historical development in these areas. But while it endeavors enthusiastically to make its discovery of the "new dimension," history, fruitful for theological thought, it does not lose sight of the constant factors that operate in history. We are confronted here by a remarkable phenomenon that leads some to assert that a radical turnabout is taking place in theology and others to maintain that it is a question of ideas that were always present in any sound theology. In any event, both aspects of history are generally acknowledged: the constant and non-temporal, and the dynamic and evolving. The latter has been worked out in the notion that historical forms are subject to limitations and in need of something more, but for the time being this interrelationship remains in the "clair-obscur" of the debate.

In close connection with the "discovery" of history as an essential element of concrete reality stands the *rediscovery of the religious dimension* of reality. Luigi Sturzo even holds, as we shall see, that history in particular testifies of the supernatural and makes us aware of religion as the factor that integrates and synthesizes the whole of human life.

Yet can there be a question of a turnabout in Catholic thought with regard to the religious dimension when that thought has always esteemed the supernatural according to its true nature? What is taken ill of past generations is not, however, that they did not uphold the real, irreducible supernatural as such, but that since the sixteenth century they have assigned it too modest a place. In the current development of theology of history and philosophy of history it is no longer possible to be satisfied with a parallelism and harmony of nature and the supernatural, or with a conception of reality in which the natural is the passive substratum of religion. In the period after the First World War, Catholicism slowly and timidly accepted the idea of a nature that on all sides is intimately connected with religious reality. With that, Catholic thought faced a new challenge and one that is difficult to satisfy, since the supernatural, no matter how deeply it may penetrate human life, must still acknowledge a boundary between the natural and itself. The difficulty, obviously, stems from the dualism of nature and grace. On both sides of the equation, however, the boundary is experienced as a hindrance. There are theologians—still few in number, it is true—who do not hesitate to reduce the natural to the supernatural. There are also those who refuse to accept this solution but nevertheless take their own evolutionist thought so far, that the real distinction between the natural and the supernatural spheres threatens to be lost in a gradual transition of the former to the latter.

While in the nineteenth century the accent fell on the distance, on the yawning gulf between nature and grace, in the twentieth century, especially since 1930, the concern has become the synthesis and intimate union of the two. At the same time, however, most Catholic thinkers affirm the distance. Here lies the source both of the polarity and the infinite variety of their conceptions.

The question of the relation between Christianity and history acquired further relevance for Catholicism as a result of a remarkable phenomenon that emerged in Germany soon after the First World War and in France since the end of the thirties. I am referring to the mounting interest in the "laity." Not only is there an effort to give the faithful a more active role in the life of the church, but the question is also posed with ever greater urgency: What is the proper Christian vocation of the layman in the "secular" world? There is a call for an authentic lay spirituality, for a *vita christiana* that does not imply world-renunciation. Neither philosophy nor theology of history has been remiss in seeking to satisfy this desire, which fills so many of the laity.

It may seem odd that, in a study which deals with history, relatively little is said about the connection of the modern Catholic conceptions of history to those of earlier times. However, the far-reaching changes that are occurring within Catholicism render the question of the historical background extremely complex. Thinkers ignore or downplay former ties and seek to link up with forgotten or neglected conceptions. The situation has grown so complicated that the question of the historical roots of the problem of the relation of Christianity and history requires a separate study.

I point here to just one aspect. If one compares present-day Catholic thought about history with that of the first half of the nineteenth century, the differences are immediately apparent. At that time it had a much more theocentric character, while today it is decidedly Christocentric. A century and a half ago the emphasis was on the organic ties with what had historically come to be; in the newer conceptions what dominates is the idea of advancing towards new dimensions, and history is viewed more as a growing towards new values. Now then, is this the result of an abrupt turnabout? If so, when did it occur? In any case, post-1918 Catholic thinkers about history feel increasingly alienated from those of the nineteenth century. It is striking just how sporadically one finds today, at least in the writings of the French theologians of history, any mention of such names as De Maistre and Friedrich von Schlegel. When they do refer to earlier conceptions of history, they prefer the Patristic writers, at times to the complete neglect of the medieval Scholastics. Again a number of questions arise. What are the causes of this shift? Is present-day Catholic thought beginning to take distance from Scholasticism? What are we to make of the putative opposition between the Scholastics and the Church Fathers? In appealing to the Fathers, is sufficient distinction made between the various perspectives that divided them as well?

To these and many other questions no answer can be given within the scope of this study. It is also not possible to refer to one or more works from which one might acquire a clear picture of the historical background of present-day Catholic theology of history and philosophy of history. Nonetheless, we can make a number of general observations.

If many today are not very favorably disposed towards Scholasticism, then this pertains exclusively or mainly to the Scholasticism of the Late Middle Ages or of Early Modern Times. Post-Tridentine theology especially bears the brunt. It is accused of lacking respect for the mystery, of overestimating the apologetic method in theology. It especially is held responsible for neglecting the idea of the church as the Body of Christ, and for the fatal separation between nature and grace that has come to permeate the Roman Catholic worldview.

Yet we need to remember that the period of the Counter-Reformation was only one phase in a process that took its rise centuries earlier. According to some it dates from the heyday of Scholasticism, after the conflict with Berengarius of Tours, when theology acquired that analytical and apologetic streak that turns its attention away from the mystery.

In the meantime, the alienation of some present-day currents from the theology and philosophy of Thomas can hardly remain hidden from view. The controversy over Thomism is and remains an interesting phenomenon that has various facets and also offers various possibilities. There is, for instance, the quest for a closer connection with Duns Scotus—encouraged especially by the revival of the idea of the *desiderium naturale* as a positive orientation of nature towards the supernatural, and the search for a more Christocentric theology and ethics—or else for a closer connection with Bonaventure and other medieval thinkers influenced by Augustine.

But even when scholars continue to proceed from Thomism—and most Neo-Scholastics still do—they read Thomas's works differently today than they did just twenty years ago. Then they viewed the philosopher Thomas above all as a student of Aristotle, but today they emphasize the important Platonic elements in his philosophical system and admire the grand synthesis he brought about between Platonism and Aristotelianism. For many this is not to say, however, that Aristotle's influence on Thomas was of less significance than was once assumed: they point out that Thomas drew not only on the works of the mature Aristotle but also on his earliest writings in which he was still a thoroughgoing Platonist; it was precisely through these writings that Platonism entered Thomas's world of thought.[2] Thomas in this way adopted from Plato, so it is said, not just this or that implicit notion, but the core of his philosophy, the idea of *participation*. Anyone who knows just how important a place the idea of participation has acquired in a very short time in Neo-Scholasticism will understand the importance that must be attached to the Platonic influence in present-day Catholic thought.

The appraisal of Thomas as a Platonist smooths the way, for many, to the Church Fathers. It is well known that early Christianity was more attracted to Plato than to Aristotle; the synthesis with Platonism can be traced step by step insofar as the first centuries of Christendom and even the Early Middle Ages are concerned. Is it any wonder that present-day Catholic thought, which has a growing interest in Platonic principles, should orient itself more and more to Patristic and pre-Thomist philosophy and theology? Many thinkers manage to incorporate Thomas's doctrine into the development of their thought, but others look to a "patristic revival," outside Thomas if need be.

---

[2] For the genetic development of the philosophy of Plato and Aristotle, see D. H. T. Vollenhoven, "The Course of Plato's Development" [and H. Evan Runner, *The Development of Aristotle Illustrated from the Earliest Books of the Physics* (Kampen, 1951)].

If we ask about the underlying reasons for the "return to the Fathers," then we need not remain in the dark for long. It is believed that what many people are looking for today can be found in the Fathers. The revival of patristic studies is the most striking phenomenon in the present-day historical reorientation of Catholicism. We cannot analyze this important fact further here, but a number of remarks do need to be made in clarification of what has just been observed.

In the first place, it must be noted that not all of the Fathers are studied with equal interest, and that in recent years the Greek Fathers are found more attractive than the Latin Fathers, while before 1930 it was Augustine who drew attention.

Secondly, the shift to the Greek Fathers underscores once again that the current study of Patristics is not a product of purely historical interest. People are finding in the Church Fathers a sensitivity for the concrete, for coherence, for synthesis. The Fathers tended to accept the interrelationship of things without analysis, even at the price of being left with a less precise knowledge of reality.³ They endeavored to know things in their integrality and totality; not after their (formal) structure, but as such, in the way they are given in concrete reality.

That is why the intellectual atmosphere they created was so favorable for the development of historical consciousness. In contrast to Scholasticism, which would endeavor in the first instance to ascertain truth in its validity independent of place and time, the Patristic systems were based on the idea of history. For the Fathers, Christianity was essentially history. They expressed with the concept "figure" or "type" what people today say with the concept "evolution." Dominant in them is the notion of a "progressive economy," of the education of humankind until they are ready to receive the Word.⁴

This must all be viewed in connection with the chief motive for the return to the Fathers. For a long time already, a passionate struggle has been in progress about the nature of theology. The core of the debate is the place of reason in theological thought. The objection of many to traditional theology is that it assigns much too large a role to human understanding and restricts the divine mystery to the furthest extent possible. The Fathers, so it is said, can point the way out: they sought the enrichment of theology not by means of conclusions based on already established truths, but through intimate communion with the sacred sources—for them Holy Scripture, for us both Holy Scripture and the Fathers, along with liturgy. They let the mystery be mystery.

Present-day theology of history endeavors earnestly to transport history back into the mystery—more precisely, into the mystery of Christ. The attempt to make Christ the central theme is not limited to reflection on history; in dogmatic and moral theology, too, people are developing a more Christocentric approach. The objection to Scholasticism is that it caused theology to lose too much of its Christocentric character. People are no longer satisfied with a theology in which Christology is an isolated head of doctrine, nor with a moral doctrine in which

---

³ Congar, "Tendances actuelles de la pensée religieuse," 44f.
⁴ Daniélou, "Les orientations présentes de la pensée religieuse," 10.

Introduction

the imitation of Christ is understood as purely external. They are demanding a theology in which Christ and his fellowship of grace are the controlling center throughout. Now then, it is in regard to this "Christocentrism" that the return to the Greek Fathers is most telling. For the return is not to the Christology of the Greek Fathers in general, but in particular to their views of the incarnation. I shall return to this subject, but let me note here that transporting history back into the mystery does not imply for everyone an acceptance of the peculiar doctrine of the incarnation associated with the Greek Church Fathers. Nor does everyone view the patristic revival without reservations. Jean Daniélou, for instance, stimulates powerfully the return to the Fathers[5]; on the other hand he is afraid it will encourage people "to ignore the tragedy of personal destiny and to neglect the interior life." The optimistic perspective of the Greek Fathers must be complemented, as he sees it, by another, that of sin. Thus theology (of history) must follow at once both the Greek Fathers and Augustine.[6]

---

[5] [In 1944, Jean Daniélou, with his mentor Henri de Lubac, launched the series *Sources chrétiennes*, featuring critical editions of patristic writings (Paris: Éditions du Cerf). By the end of the century over 450 titles had been published.]

[6] Ibid., 11, 15f.

I / NATURE AND THE SUPERNATURAL

§ 1. Nature

Being, according to Scholastic philosophy, is the first known (*primum notum*). It is indefinable since the definition can refer to nothing other. It is possible to clarify being only by describing it from within. Or in other words, since the notion of being has as its primary mark transcendentality, which is to say that it implies everything that is, the whole of reality in all its aspects, therefore this one idea of being denotes all judgments and all knowledge.[1]

Being is the fundamental unity of everything, to which all diversity relates. The means *par excellence* of appreciating this unity and rich diversity alike are the two concepts of participation and analogy. We will not go into these concepts just yet, but shall soon return to them at length because of their significance for the conception of history.

If one desires to appreciate the richness of the idea of being, not by adding new concepts to the concept of being—this avenue, as we saw, is closed—but by proceeding to determine being more closely from within, then this can be done in two ways. "For in the concept of being are implicit both the marks that are related to the specific manner in which being is attributed to the various things as well as the marks that are related to being as such." [2]

In the case of the latter, one arrives at knowledge of being in its generalness, that is, at knowledge of the so-called transcendental basic concepts, or transcendentals; in the case of the former, one arrives at knowledge of the ten categories or predicaments, which are not applicable to all beings but only to certain groups.

The transcendentals subtract from being nothing of its generalness. They share in this generalness and transcendentality.

Numbered among the transcendental determinations of being are unity, truth, beauty, and goodness. They do not determine being in an accidental way but are fully identical with it. They belong to every being because they are proper to being as such. But just as each thing has being in its own way, it will have goodness, truth, and so on, in its own manner.

---

[1] This and the following sections are based chiefly on publications by Angelinus, Boyer, De Raeymaeker, Geiger, Kreling, A. Mercier, Peters, and Soukup, as listed in the Bibliography.

[2] Angelinus, *Algemene Zijnsleer*, 252f.

The transcendental determinations of being belong to things not in an identical but in an analogical way, since being itself is of an analogical nature.[3]

Just as being cannot be defined, neither can action and potency, which belong to the first principles of being. They can be understood only in their mutual relation. "Their complete determination consists in nothing but their interconnections."[4] This transcendental relation is the appropriate means of giving account of the problem of change as a transition from being in potency (*ens in potentia*) to actual being (*ens in actu*).

The principle of the relation action-potency is applied in various ways. It is applied, for example, in the doctrine of generation, in the doctrine of the four causes (material, formal, efficient, and final cause), in that of the relation of essence and existence, and, not least, in the doctrine of the categories.

Being is determined more closely by the predicaments or categories. We have seen that these differ from the transcendentals. The categories form the basis for distinguishing being of ten kinds. The first category is that of substance. It is the category on the basis of which it exists *in itself*—notice: not *of itself*—and not in something other. This is what distinguishes substance from the other categories, which typically exist in something other. Substance determines a thing according to its essence; the other predicaments concern only the accidents, of which substance is the bearer: these can thus never exist apart from the latter.

Among the accidents Scholastic philosophy counts the categories of quantity and quality (which are attributable to substance in itself); of relation—that is, the predicamental relation, which must be distinguished from the transcendental relation, as in, for example, the transcendental relation between act and potency; that of time and that of place (these categories exist entirely outside substance, for they are only an external measure); that of position; action; passion; and, finally, that of habitus.

Till now we have mentioned analogy a number of times just in passing. For purposes of the present study, our brief survey of a few of the fundamental concepts from the Neo-Scholastic doctrine of being will suffice; but there are two basic concepts, those of participation and analogy, that require more extensive discussion.

Even if one does not, with Przywara, elevate the doctrine of the analogy of being to the "essence of Thomism," it must still be acknowledged that this doctrine occupies an important place in the Roman Catholic worldview. The question of the *analogia entis* has become acute not only because there has been opposition to it from non-Catholics, but also because the doctrine of partici-

---

[3] Ibid., 273, 278.
[4] De Raeymaeker, *De metaphysiek van het zijn*, 265.

pation has within a short time become such a focal point. The question has been raised whether old concepts, including that of analogy, do not require rethinking in terms of participation. But before looking into the significance of analogy for the relation of God to finite things, we must first explain a number of pertinent terms.

A distinction is made between univocation, equivocation, and analogy. One speaks of univocation if two or more things agree in having the same nature. The term man, for example, may be used in entirely the same sense for Peter, John, and James, whatever else may distinguish them: what is implied in the concept man is nothing more than the nature that is found in all three.

A term is equivocal if it can be applied to a number of things having entirely different natures. Thus the word lion is used for two entirely different concepts, animal and constellation, which in reality have nothing in common.

Between univocation and equivocation stands analogy. A term is analogical if, when applied to a number of things, it has a multiplicity but likewise a certain unity of signification.

Within analogy one must distinguish between the *analogia proportionalitatis* or analogy of proportionality and the *analogia proportionis* or analogy of attribution.

In the case of the analogy of attribution, the term is applicable to "a multiplicity on the basis of a relation to one and the same, to which it is attributable in its main sense."[5] For example, animal, medicine, and color are denominated healthy, but all three cannot be denominated healthy in the same sense. The animal is healthy on account of the condition of the body, medicine because it improves the health of the animal, and color because it is a sign of the health of the animal. Thus the term healthy is attributable to the color and the medicine on the basis of their relation to the animal.

The analogy of proportionality is involved if the question is one of a relation of proportions, if there is an equality of proportions. This equality of proportions occurs in its pure form only in mathematics—from which the term analogy of proportionality is borrowed—where the proportions 2:3 and 4:6 are equal. In metaphysics, however, there is only a *similarity* of proportions, an *analogical* equality.

Two example may clarify the concept *analogia proportionalitatis* further. The eye sees, and the understanding sees: there is a similarity in the relation of the understanding to the soul and in the relation of the eye to sensory vision. Christ and the human head are both called head, for Christ is to the church as the human head is to the body. Applying these distinctions to the doctrine of being, in particular to the relation God-creature, we are immediately confronted by what seems a minor controversy yet which proves helpful for understanding the concept of nature in Catholic thought.[6]

---

[5] Boyer, *Handboek der Wijsbegeerte*, 1:76.
[6] Thomas's view of the *analogia entis* has been interpreted in different ways. While some,

The largest number of adherents belong to the school of Cajetan, including the Dutch Capuchin schoolman Angelinus. According to him, the analogy of attribution is not without value linguistically, but philosophically it is of little significance.[7] For what is the case?

If being were analogous only through the analogy of attribution, perfection would belong only to the *princeps analogatum* (or *analogum analogans*, that is, to the subject in which the perfection of being is found). In the other analogates it would not be intrinsically present—in which case the analogy would have no meaning, for being belongs *intrinsically* to all that is. If the proponents of the analogy of attribution appeal to its being intrinsic, then there is a conjunction with univocation or with the *analogia proportionalitatis*. These objections of the school of Cajetan expressed through Angelinus against the *analogia proportionis* remain valid, of course, when this analogy is considered in its principal application, namely, to the relation of God to finite things.[8]

In opposition to the analogy in question, Angelinus posits the *analogia proportionalitatis*. Only it, he writes, can afford insight into the nature of being. The analogates may simply all be different, for each participates in its own way in being, but the analogon is equal in all, that is to say, proportionally equal.

The *analogia proportionalitatis* means for the relation God-creature that God relates to his Being just as the creature relates to its being. There is in God something that is at the same time also in the creature: the relation of possessor to possession (that is, the possession of being). God *is*, has *divine* Being; the creature *is*, has *finite* being. In God the possession of being is *Self-possession*, for God is Being in identity; but in the case of the creature, the possessor and the thing possessed are different, since essence and existence are not identical in creatures.[9]

Cajetan's opponents do not reject the *analogia proportionalitatis*—at least, Kreling does not. But the *analogia proportionis* is the primary, all-controlling analogy.[10]

The objection of his opponents to the effect that the *analogia proportionis* really deprives natural theology of all significance, Kreling cannot accept. True, this analogy gets no further than a similarity between God and creature, but with the *analogia proportionalitatis* one arrives just as little at a precise determination of this similarity. A closer determination is simply not attainable. Kreling

---

including G. Manser and A. van Leeuwen, believe that Thomas was always fully consistent in the defense of the *analogia proportionalitatis*, others, including P. Kreling, are disposed to see in Thomas different elaborations of the doctrine of analogy; cf. Van Leeuwen, "L'Analogie de l'être," and Kreling, "De beteekenis van de analogie in de kennis van God," 45f.

[7] Angelinus, *Algemene Zijnsleer*, 219f; idem, "De eenheid van het analoge zijnsbegrip," passim.

[8] Angelinus, *Algemene Zijnsleer*, 238–44.

[9] Soukup, "Teilnahme an Gott," 158f.

[10] Kreling, "De beteekenis van de analogie in de kennis van God," 41.

points out again and again that our knowledge of God via analogy will always remain very defective.

Kreling attributes the antipathy of Cajetan's followers to the *analogia proportionis* where the relation of God and creature is concerned to a misunderstanding apropos of this analogy. That there are cases of the *analogia proportionis* in which the predicate is essentially present in only one subject is not to say that this always holds for this analogy or that, upon finding the predicate in more than one subject, recourse must necessarily be had to the *analogia proportionalitatis*. According to Kreling, the entire problem of whether a predicate belongs properly to a subject has nothing to do with analogy as such. If one were to ask whether the predicates wise, good, true, and beautiful are said of God literally, one could not reply by referring to the analogical relation between God and creature. At issue is a predicate of God and not a commonness of statement about God and creature. This brings Kreling to the very important assertion that the main problem of the knowledge of God lies outside the problem of analogy.[11] Kreling believes thus to have shown that if the *analogia proportionis* has but little significance for the knowledge of God, this is no less true of the *analogia proportionalitatis*, since knowledge of God via the *analogia entis* can only be limited.

We come now to the positive elaboration that Kreling gives of the *analogia proportionis* as applied to the relation of God and creature. There exists between God and creature a causal connection; this implies a certain similarity between Cause and caused, since the latter cannot be entirely alien to its Cause: for causing always implies imparting and being caused, receiving and participating. The similarity between God and creature consists, however, not in an agreement according to nature and essence—as between father and son—but in a similarity that exists between maker and made. This is the reason why it is possible to speak of a similiarity or analogy between God and creature.[12]

According to Cajetan and his adherents, the coherence of being between Creator and creature has two aspects: not only is there a common moment in the relation of both to being (the *analogia proportionalitatis*); there is at the same time a similarity in virtue of the causal connection in which the Creator stands to his creature (*analogia proportionis*).[13]

To summarize, the concept of analogy expresses two things about the Creator-creature relation: on the one hand, infinite distance; on the other hand, intimate connection, common moment. From the difficulty to define the connection some may infer that distance predominates; but then I would direct them to what W. J. Aalders says: "When Thomas . . . employs the *analogia entis,* it is clear that both terms, singly and together, must be given full weight. They are deep and loaded. Being is the miracle before which Thomas halts and which drives

---

[11] Ibid., 42–44; see also 51–54.
[12] Ibid., 33f.
[13] Soukup, "Teilnahme an Gott," 159–62.

him to his knees . . . Being (*ens*) is in Thomas something more and other than in Aristotle, a maximum, not a minimum, not just philosophically, but theologically; because all nuances and relations of the word find their ground and form in the divine being (*esse*), with which they are in some way connected." [14]

The concept of analogy in no way is intended to deprive the unity of being between God and creature of its force. On the contrary, it is a fitting means of expressing God's immanence in finite beings while at the same time maintaining God's infinite transcendence above all created things.

The *analogia entis* has its positive and its negative sides. The positive side, however, is better expressed by participation than by analogy.

The concept of participation has conquered the scholarly world very rapidly. Although little was heard of it in Neo-Scholastic metaphysics a decade ago—Rosenmüller in 1936 still expressly distinguished a realm of analogy that belongs to the natural domain from a realm of participation that essentially differs from the first in belonging to the supernatural life[15]—after 1940 some go so far as to see in the doctrine of participation in being "the most pertinent core" of Thomist philosophy.[16] The higher esteem for Platonism in modern Catholic philosophy is evident not in the last place in the emphatic way in which participation in the Thomist synthesis is being pushed to the foreground.

For a correct assessment of the renewed interest in the idea of participation and the conclusions that are being drawn from it, it is of importance to note that with participation in being, no essentially new aspect of being is discovered. What that concept expresses was already implied in the idea of being and especially in that of analogy. Participation, writes Peters, "teaches us no new facts from the world of our experience; this remains what it is, *yet for all that, the world is seen entirely differently* now that clarity is obtained about the connection, the ubiquitous contact, with the Transcendent and Absolute." [17] The proper means for understanding the *value* of being is the perspective offered by participation.

The concept of being is a transcendental idea, which is to say it encompasses everything and is susceptible of no addition; being is universal and concrete and permeates the whole of reality. The value of being is therefore absolute, because nothing is opposed to it. There is, of course, a multiplicity of beings which in virtue of their own determinateness stand opposed to each other, but being is not restricted to finite beings: it transcends them all and unites them in the one absolute value of being.

---

[14] Aalders, *De analogia entis in het geding*, 48f.
[15] Rosenmöller, "Die übernatürliche Belebung der natürlichen Ordnungen," 15.
[16] Peters, "De wijsgeerige waarde van Sint Thomas' participatieleer," 31.
[17] Ibid., 48 (ital. added).

Accordingly, opposite the unity and identity of being stands the multiplicity of finite beings, of the modes of being, since one being by itself can never actualize being fully. Value of being and modes of being are distinguished from each other in this way, but not separated. For the modes of being are opposed to each other insofar as they are mutually incommunicable, yet at the same time they are characterized by relativity, by being-connected-to-each-other, since they are united in the one, absolute being. The being that is given us is not identical with being, but it *does partake of the fullness of being;* every mode of being has being only in a particular way.

Here emerges the core of the problem of participation. Being is one, universal, absolute and transcendent. The modes of being, on the other hand, are many, restricted, and relative. How, now, is it possible that finite being participates in the absoluteness of being and yet is not itself absolute; that it participates in the unity of being and yet is itself nothing more than a restricted, individual mode of being, since it is taken up in an order that implies multiplicity? In short, do participation—hence restrictedness and relativity—and absoluteness, universality and unity of being not mutually exclude one another?

The doctrine of creation fully resolves this problem, as De Raeymaeker explains. For creation means absolute causality: every creature in its entire reality depends fully on its Creator. He is absolute Being, and the modes are not modes of being of absolute Being, for the latter would then fall prey to relativity. Only if one keeps in mind the absoluteness of the First Cause does one obtain the explanation. Finite beings may be independent with regard to each other because they do not have the principle of their existence outside themselves in other beings, but they are dependent on their creating Cause. In Him all particular beings meet. In this way they owe to the absolute divine Cause, on the one hand their autonomy, their ontological value, and on the other hand their relativity in the order of beings, which in its own turn is relativized with regard to the Creator.[18]

Thus finite being participates in God through its total dependence with regard to its Creator. In the relation of creation God has established for himself a *causal presence*.

Participation and analogy express *that* and *how* God stands in relation to the world, and that there is unity and distinction between the two. God gives all creatures his Being. Finite being, as the caused of the cause, includes God, not as part but as principle and end. And at the same time God wraps himself in infinite transcendence above all created beings: God has being in fullness, the creatures only as participants, in dependence and in imperfection.[19]

De Raeymaeker saw the following question as the core of the problem of participation: How is it to be reconciled that finite, restricted being, relativized

---

[18] De Raeymaeker, *De metaphysiek van het zijn*, 375–80.
[19] Peters, "De wijsgeerige waarde van Sint Thomas' participatieleer, 45.

in a multiplicity of diverse beings, nevertheless partake of the absolute ontological value? He believed the complete solution is found at the level of creation. For particular beings all rest on the same foundation and have the same ontological value; their essential relativity reveals the Absolute.[20]

We fail to see, however, how the twofold thesis that the absolute value of being is present in particular beings, and that these beings are nevertheless relativized in a multiplicity, is justified by the doctrine of creation. Sometimes De Raeymaeker and Peters appear to regard the connection of causality between God and finite beings as a religious one. Yet even if that were the case, the two parts of the thesis would remain mutually exclusive. The doctrine of participation, applied to the fundamental relation of God and creature, introduces an intrinsically antinomian element into the idea of being: it ascribes something to created being which belongs solely to the Creator and which, once it is ascribed to the creaturely, cannot be reconciled with creatureliness. What is absolute cannot be attributed—not even by analogy—to Creator and creature alike. Being is, in the Thomist conception, the fundamental unity of everything; it embraces both Creator and creature, even though via analogy and participation the infinite distance is likewise upheld. But to relate God and creature to the same unity of being can only be done at the expense of God's transcendence of the creature, precisely via analogy and participation, and by introducing an antinomy between absolute being and particular modes of being.

Evidently, it is difficult for Catholic thought to understand the connection between God and creature otherwise than as an ontological one, that is, as a relation *within* the unity of being. The emphasis on God's transcendence is but an attempt to avoid relativizing the Absolute.

The unity of being between God and creature is a preconception of Catholic thought. It is a presupposition of natural reason and not of scriptural thought—as Schoolmen no doubt will acknowledge: they make no claim that the idea is found explicitly in the Word-revelation.

But does rejection of the idea that the fundamental relation of God and creature is ontological in character not mean the denial of an enduring relationship between the two? Are we not left, if we regard the intimate presence of the First Cause in the creature as being in conflict with a pure idea of God, with just God's infinite transcendence of the creature? And will the world and its history not be despoiled of all meaning, since God must be entirely *alien* to it and separated from it by an unbridgeable gulf?

These questions would all have to be answered in the affirmative if, with the denial of an ontological relation of the world to God, every relation between the two were denied. Natural thought of itself does have the capacity to construct an ontological relation or a unity of being, but it can never conceive the idea that Creator and creation are connected with each other in any other way than in unity of being. Scholastic philosophy believes that the ontological relation is

---

[20] De Raeymaeker, "Le Climat doctrinal chrétien et la philosophie," 458.

understandable to natural thought through analogy. To abandon the ideas of being and analogy does not mean, however, that the relation of God and creature becomes shrouded in impenetrable darkness. For in the turning of our entire existence towards God, our knowing is directed to the Word-revelation. This teaches us to understand the connection of the creature to the Creator as a *religious,* not further analyzable, *relation of origin,* and as a *religious* orientation to, or apostasy from, God.

The application of the doctrine of participation to the fundamental relation of God to his world created, as we just saw, a tension within the idea of being. Naturally, this tension will make itself felt amongst its adherents as well. Having accepted the doctrine, they can still work it out in different directions.

Henri de Lubac, to whose theory we shall return later, does not view the spirit as primarily an autonomous center of capacities and forces; *as participation* of the divine Spirit, it remains always but a divine reflex which will never belong to itself as an independent nature. In the writings of de Lubac the accent falls so strongly on God's being interwoven into a unity with the human spirit that the question can be posed whether he does not allow nature to be swallowed up entirely by the supernatural.[21]

Others, in contrast, use the doctrine of participation precisely to establish a certain degree of independence for man with respect to God. The spirit, as created being, is dependent on God, to be sure, but it is also spiritual and free, for it is precisely in the human spirit that God communicates something of his own sovereign independence.[22]

This opposition, which we can do no more than indicate here, is exceedingly important for the development of Catholicism—not so much because de Lubac and company like to appeal to the Fathers and his opponents to Thomas, but because this divergence of interpretation must lead to unbridgeable differences. Just recall the profound influence it has had in recent years on the problem of the relation of nature to grace.

To sum up, the ontological way of thinking deprives not only sin but also redemption of its radical character. The fall, because of the loss of grace, only wounds nature. Nature as such does not need to be restored through Christ's work of redemption.

§ 2. *The supernatural*

It is common to begin defining the supernatural *negatively* as that which surpasses nature (*quod naturam superat*), which immediately raises the question: In what respect does the supernatural surpass nature? In the *positive* definition of the supernatural an important component is always "participation." As we

---

[21] De Lubac, *Surnaturel,* 431–38.
[22] On this, see Malevez, "L'Esprit et le désir de Dieu," 27.

have encountered this concept before, in the doctrine of being, we begin to suspect that participation is spoken of in two ways.[23]

By nature—a word with very many meanings—one commonly understands in current Catholic thought a being's "inner structure" whereby it is capable of acting in accordance with its character, or a being's "substantial ground" from which its action arises.[24]

A. Mercier has attempted to distinguish nature and the supernatural using the concept of participation. According to him, essential to the concept of nature is the relation of creature to Creator. By nature he understands all existing and possible *created* beings. The relation in question is one of cause and effect, such that with regard to his creatures the Creator is no more than the *causa efficiens et exemplaris*, and the creature no more than effect and copy. Participation at the level of nature thus says nothing more than is implied in the creaturely relation; that is to say, it is participation under the aspect of causality.

Yet the supernatural, too, is defined with the help of the concept of participation. Sometimes the supernatural is taken to mean the supernatural in itself, which, as such, excludes any elevation to a higher order and, likewise, any participation; in this sense only God's exalted nature can be called supernatural. Generally, however, the word is used to mean something else: then it indicates not something that surpasses man, but something that surpasses human nature. In that case, according to Mercier, we are considering something that transcends the creaturely relation. Supernatural participation is more than effect and copy alone, and God, at this level, is more than Creator and Cause. At the supernatural level God no longer communicates himself as First Cause, but as he is in himself. And God does this by uniting with the creature, which is to say by becoming its constitutive and intrinsic principle. The positive definition of the supernatural therefore reads: it is a participation in God's own Being, resulting from his uniting with the creature.[25]

With the supernatural, no new substance is infused into man but a new principle, from which new life arises that partakes of the divine life and transcends natural existence. This new, divine life presupposes, however, nature as bearer and subject: it is implanted into it, added to it in an accidental way.

Applying the distinction between nature and the supernatural once more to God, we can infer that in God, too, it is necessary to distinguish between nature and the supernatural.[26] On the one hand, God is the author and ultimate end of the natural order, and He communicates himself to the creature via causality; on the other hand, God is also the origin and ultimate end of the supernatural order, and here he communicates himself as he is.

---

[23] This section is based on De Raeymaeker, *De metaphyiek van het zijn*, A. Mercier, "Le Surnaturel," and Michel, "Surnaturel," as listed in the Bibliography.

[24] De Raeymaeker, *De metaphysiek van het zijn*, 220.

[25] Mercier, "Le Surnaturel," 131, 136f.

[26] Ibid., 134.

Consequently, one may view God from two angles. With these correspond two ways of knowing God. God can be known through natural reason, as First Cause. Alternately, God is known only via the Divine Word-revelation, initially in faith, later in glory, when man shall behold God face to face. "What a difference between the natural order and the supernatural order, between the God of the philosophers and the God of the Christians!" [27]

§ 3. *Nature and the supernatural*

Now that we have considered the natural and supernatural orders each in its own right, our attention must be directed to their mutual relation. This is a dual relation. We distinguish a relation of nature to grace and one of grace to nature.

One of the most remarkable phenomena in Catholic thought since 1920 is its great interest in the question of nature and grace. If we want to know more about the development of that thought we can do nothing better than note the conceptions that have been held regarding this question. An outsider may easily think this is just another of those notorious disputes between theologians. Yet one who takes the trouble to probe more deeply into the question of nature and grace will realize rather quickly that the issue is a doctrine of the utmost importance, and that the subtle arguments with which people often try to convince one another simply have to be accepted as part of the bargain.

First, we shall have to look at the relation of nature to grace, taking up each of the leading conceptions in turn. Not only will we be able in this way to form a clear idea of the direction in which a solution to the problem is being sought, but we shall be able at the same time to acquire some sense of the tensions currently dominating Catholic theology and philosophy. This theology and philosophy no longer exhibit the uniformity of a half century ago. Particularly in the theory concerning the relation of nature to grace a strong divergence and rapid evolution is evident. Though a lull seemed to set in around 1940, since then new interpretations have been defended that have caused the conflict to flare up afresh.

The relation of the natural order to the supernatural finds its focus, in Catholic thought, in the natural desire for the vision of God (*desiderium naturale ad Deum videndum*). Between grace and the life of glory, which is to say between grace and the beatific vision of God's Essence, there is no essential difference. Some writers make a distinction by saying that grace is glory in its inception. But, again, the supernatural life undergoes no *essential* change as grace develops towards the vision of God.[28]

The sixteenth century was decisive for the doctrine of the *desiderium naturale ad Deum videndum*. At this time, the doctrine began to follow a different course. On the Catholic side this change is generally viewed as a reaction to the Reformation doctrine regarding nature and grace. The condemnation of Baius

---

[27] Michel, "Surnaturel," col. 2854.
[28] Romualdus, "Het wezen van het genade- en glorieleven," 54.

in 1567, it is believed, was also of some influence.[29] In my view, however, the new orientation can hardly be ascribed solely to reaction. New paths were being sought in the sixteenth century not just with regard to the natural desire: with regard to other doctrines, too, the whole spirit of theology was changing. We can observe the same phenomenon in today's theology: generally speaking, there is an inclination to take distance from post-Tridentine theology. Hence we need not be surprised by the fact that, since 1920, sixteenth-century ideas pertaining to the *desiderium naturale* have been held in less esteem.[30]

Cajetan († 1534) in particular has been the target of criticism. It is objected that he solved the question of the natural desire towards the beatific vision all too smoothly by eliminating the natural character of that desire. Cajetan taught that man cannot, by nature, desire God, since nature does not incline towards that which is not naturally attainable. But nature does desire the vision of God once it is elevated to the supernatural order. The concept natural in *desiderium naturale* can therefore no longer be used in a literal sense: the expression can be maintained only because nature is the active subject of the supernatural desire.[31]

Opposed to Cajetan's interpretation of natural desire stood that of Sylvester Ferrariensis († 1528). The former supernaturalized the desire, the latter negated the supernatural character of its object. Ferrariensis therefore had no difficulty with the adjective. For the desire is directed, according to him, not at the vision of God's Essence but at seeing God insofar as he is *Prima Causa*. Such a desire arises from the knowledge of natural effects, which leads to the conclusion of a First Cause: this man desires to behold, since there dwells in him a natural desire to know the *what,* the *quid est,* of the cause.

To Cajetan and Ferrariensis, every notion of a positive inclination of nature to grace was foreign. This had been the prevailing idea in the thirteenth and fourteenth centuries, and it was still found in the centuries that followed, but gradually it was abandoned for the minimal interpretation of the *desiderium naturale* as "non-repugnance" to the supernatural.[32] The grace which God gives us does not correspond to a positive inclination of our nature, but will arouse in us a new desire that is only fulfilled in blessedness. According to this conception, the term *desiderium naturale* denotes no more than this, that nature is suited to receive grace if and when God grants it as a free gift of love: nature is but the passive substratum of this gift.

---

[29] Baius taught that man before the fall enjoyed the full right to the vision of God, that grace was "owed to unfallen nature." This view was condemned by the bull *Ex omnibus afflictionibus* of Pope Pius V.

[30] For the various theories of the natural desire for beatitude, one may consult Doucet's article in *Antonianum* (1929); Meyer, *De eerste levensvraag in het intellectualisme van St. Thomas van Aquino en het integraal-realisme van Maurice Blondel*; Bastable, *Desire for God: Does Man Aspire Naturally to the Beatific Vision?*; and De Lubac, *Surnaturel*, 431–38. These writers all belong to different schools of thought on the subject.

[31] Cajetan has few adherents today—a sign of the times! The best known perhaps is the Spanish theologian Mario Cuervo, who around 1930 repeatedly attacked rival conceptions.

[32] Doucet, "De naturali seu innato supernaturalis beatitudinis desiderio," 202.

At the end of the nineteenth century appear the first signs of a reaction to the ideas prevalent in the preceding centuries. C. M. Schneider in 1895 espoused an *appetitus innatus* for the beatific vision of God, but for many years he remained a rather solitary figure. Then, in 1908, P. Rousselot took his side with a work on *L'Intellectualisme de S. Thomas*: the human intellect, by virtue of its dynamic structure, inclines to the vision of God and finds its highest fulfillment in it.

It is only after the First World War, however, that the controversy over the natural desire for the vision of God's Essence flared up in earnest. The occasion was the appearance, between 1924 and 1928, of articles by Guy de Broglie in *Recherches de Science Religieuse* and by G. Laporta in *Ons Geloof* and in *Ephemerides Theologicae Lovaniensis*. After 1935 the debate subsided again. The new conceptions of nature and grace had already begun to consolidate when the book *Surnaturel* by Henri de Lubac appeared (1946). The writer, who is the foremost representative of the so-called *théologie nouvelle*, is certainly not of the opinion that the question involves just an isolated problem; on the contrary, the new conception of nature that he advocates marks a break with Counter-Reformational theology as never before.

Although it was de Broglie who launched a new phase in the conflict about the doctrine of natural desire and who has played a prominent role in it ever since, it would not appear to be his views that Catholic theologians will finally settle on. Various signs indicate that in the future the tone will be set by those who have gone on to draw the logical conclusions from de Broglie's conception.[33] The debate of many years was brilliantly summarized by Anselm Stolz, a promising Benedictine scholar who died young. In the superb closing pages of his article of 1936 he demonstrated the fundamental inadequacy of the doctrine of the *desiderium naturale*.[34]

Maréchal and Sertillanges arrive, though by a different route, at the same result as Laporta and Stolz. Both are strongly under the influence of Blondel, whose philosophy is so pervaded by the idea of the *desiderium naturale* that people sometimes name his entire philosophy after it. His ideas, which are often difficult to follow, have recently been gaining increasing support. In some conceptions of the relation of Christianity and history Blondel's influence is clearly in evidence.

The "newer" conceptions concerning nature and grace [35] have in common that they reject every notion of nature as a purely passive substratum of the supernatural. They reject both a co-ordination and a subordination of nature, because neither suggests the intimacy of the relation that nature has to grace, and neither gets beyond a demand for *harmony* between the two. It is precisely this notion of no-more-than-harmony that the newer perspectives object to. For it is

---

[33] E.g., Balthasar, Doucet, Laporta, and esp. J. E. O'Mahony, *The Desire of God in the Philosophy of St. Thomas Aquinas* (Th.D. thesis; Louvain, 1928).

[34] Stolz, "Natur und Gnade," 120–23; see also his *Anthropologica Theologica*, 4:23f.

[35] I leave undecided whether these conceptions agree with Thomas's doctrine. If the appeal is accredited, then the word "newer" is not entirely appropriate here.

seen to imply a fundamental dualism of two self-contained realms, a dualism that is by no means overcome by the notion that nature can be perfected by grace.[36]

Against all this is asserted the philosophical thesis of a positive ordering of nature to grace. But as writers work it out they part ways in what might be called a static and a dynamic direction.

The first proceeds from the presupposition that all being is essentially imperfect. But what is imperfect desires in some way the perfection corresponding to its essence. For every created being has by nature an inner, essential relation and ordering to its perfection. Earthly goods may be the *tentative* end of natural striving but never the true end, since they just evoke new desires and new endeavors. The desire that resides in nature will come to rest only when it directs itself to a final end located outside the natural order, and when man shall have attained his final perfection, the beatific vision of God. The natural desire to see God as he is must therefore be understood as an innate, ontological—hence positive—ordering of nature to the supernatural.[37]

This ontological orientation does not, however, entail any restriction with respect to the freedom of God, which is to say that God is not bound to respond to this desire. The natural desire is not sufficient to put nature in possession of the supernatural goods. To speak with Blondel, man's desire for an answer from another, divine realm is comparable to the concentric ripples or "waves" caused by a stone cast in the water, which expand and broaden yet never reach the shore. A counter-wave from God's side is necessary. The supernatural end is unattainable in a natural way, even though man is by nature inclined to it. To attain it we need grace, bestowed upon us according to God's free decree.

Those who oppose Laporta, Stolz and others of their view have accused them of confusing nature and the supernatural. They are said to have created a "contradiction" by confusing the efficient order and the final order: the latter is supernatural, so the former must be also, hence the "contradiction." [38]

Stolz concedes that there is a certain "duality" present here, but that is not the same as a "contradiction." A certain "disproportion" is undeniable, Stolz explains, precisely because man's "spiritual nature" is ordered to a higher end than it can attain of itself.[39] Laporta calls the disproportion between the end and the natural ordering and natural powers to attain that end an *antinomy*.[40]

---

[36] Stolz, "Natur und Gnade," 116.

[37] Ibid., 116, 119; idem, *Anthropologia Theologica*, 4:32; Doucet, "De naturali desiderio," passim; Laporta, "Natuur en genade," passim.

[38] See, e.g., Koster, "Natur und Übernatur. Die Christliche Gesamtordnung," 18. This article is instructive for the controversy surrounding the nature-grace problem. Koster defends the idea that nature is "a substrate capable of perfection" and subordinate "without contradiction" to the supernatural.

[39] Stolz, "Natur und Gnade," 117, 119f.

[40] Laporta, "Natuur en genade," 442f.

We cannot resist pointing to a hopeful element in Stolz's thinking. Twice he observes that the problem of the relation between nature and grace is at bottom apologetic. We would have liked to see the entire discussion governed by the tension Stolz feels between the apologetic and the theological approaches. On the one hand, there is the natural desire, which does not find its source in grace but is an enduring inclination of nature, even after its wounding by the fall. Yet on the other hand, that fall teaches us something else about human nature: we have to do in theology not with a nature pure and simple but with a nature affected by sin; and the cross of Christ reveals, not what nature strives after according to its inclination, but what road it has actually chosen to travel.[41]

Here the religious conception breaks through. Central to it is the cross. Only in light of the cross do we see how deep human nature has fallen, and how great is salvation. Stolz writes: "The Cross alone interprets the whole of reality, and gives the true link between nature and grace. Hail, O Cross, our only hope!"[42] Nevertheless, within "the whole of reality" there still are those who desire to be enriched by the fruits of Christ's suffering and death but who do not themselves wish to travel the way of the cross. Here it is evident once again that the ontological and religious conceptions of the basic relation of God and man are mutually exclusive. The former always involves some restriction of the latter, and the religious conception will not admit of restriction, precisely because of its integral character. An ontological view is not excluded, however, if it but rests in a religious view and is not applied to the relation of God and man (and world).

The "newer" doctrine concerning the ordering of nature to grace likes to appeal to Duns Scotus. It also numbers Thomas among its authorities—yet its opponents do the same; thus the exegesis of Thomas is severely tested.

In an entirely original way, however, the idea of the natural desire has been worked out by one of the greatest philosophers of contemporary France, Maurice Blondel (1861–1949), whom we venture without reservation to call the principal representative of the dynamic school in regard to the doctrine of the *desiderium naturale*. This doctrine is in fact the central theme of his extensive philosophical *oeuvre*. Even when he seems to be addressing entirely different subjects and digresses into countless excursions, the problem of nature and the supernatural continues to preoccupy him. To gain an idea of what Blondel teaches concerning the *desiderium naturale* it is sufficient to indicate some of the basic lines of his philosophical conception.

Blondel desires to be a realist, but not in the manner of the (Neo-) Scholastics. If only they were realists! Their stance is too abstract and conceptual. One must learn to apprehend the true nature of things in a different way, namely through involvement with them; insight into the concrete is acquired only

---

[41] Stolz, "Natur und Gnade," 122f.
[42] Ibid.

through practice. Blondel therefore calls his philosophizing a "practicing philosophy," a "philosophy of the concrete," or "integral realism."

Now then, when we actually become involved with things and live with them, we discover that their essence is dynamism, or "action." They are constantly seized by movement and becoming, by restless renewal and renovation.

Involvement with the concrete teaches us a second basic rule: the concrete reveals coherence, interconnectedness, interdependence, integration. For "all things hang together" (*tout tient à tout*). All is interconnected with all, to such an extent that if we were to know a part in all its interrelationships and influences, we would know the whole.

But the dynamism that pervades the whole of reality, all things and all men, reveals something else as well. Becoming means leaving what one already was, leaving one thing and becoming something else. Dynamism means coming to be, which entails breaking up and disintegrating.

All things desire unity, want to be connected, but at the same time all things break apart. Scarcely is a new, individual entity formed before its "essential incompleteness," its "normal deficiency" manifests itself. To be able to live on, it has need of something else. It must *become*, it must constantly *change*, otherwise it dies. Hence the deepest essence of the concrete is "deficiency," "insufficiency." Yet the nature of reality is at the same time a yearning for permanence and unity. For a moment it may seem that these are realized, in individual things, but it is immediately evident that every one of them is frail (*caduc*) and insufficient.

In the universe, too, the insatiable desire of things can find no rest, for that would mean remaining in an eternal cycle of welling up, flowing, and discharging.

And then Blondel writes these remarkable words: "God must not be left out of our affirmation of the concrete."[43] The dynamism and insatiability that have gripped all beings pervade all thought, being and action. In them are manifest the three aspects of the *desiderium naturale,* of the ascent of beings towards their destiny.

Thought: the more thought unfolds, the more it senses its shortcomings: our thought, "like the world itself, and more than the world, is in constant labor to give birth—ever a miscarriage— to unity."[44] God propels thought towards satiety, but in none of the many possibilities granted to thought can it attain satisfaction.

Being: it is no more successful than thought in attaining the object of its desire within this universe. All beings participate in being yet continue to desire being, since never and nowhere do they find the fullness of being.

And finally, action: it expresses itself in nine concentric "waves" which broaden as they move away from their center: man looks for the meaning of his

---

[43] Blondel, *L'Action*, 1:433.
[44] Blondel, *La Pensée*, 2:12.

action and desire, first in the cultivation of matter, then in the cultivation of himself, that is, in the forming of his own personality, next in the cultivation of family relationships and the broader communities—but even the ultimate, broadest wave of his action fails to reach the shore.[45]

Wherever we look, we are confronted by shortcomings, insufficiencies, voids, unsatisfied desires. The incompleteness of things, of the universe, is not of a psychological nature but is ontological. Blondel understands the *desiderium naturale* as an "ontological tendency" an ontological yearning for completeness; in virtue of a dynamic order the universe pursues completion beyond its own limited existence.

As in Laporta, O'Mahony and Stolz, the *desiderium naturale* in Blondelism is ontological in nature. But one acquires insight into the "entitative incompleteness," so Blondel maintains, only when one is initiated into the dynamism whereby things are propelled towards their completion. The original contribution of Blondelism to the doctrine of the *desiderium naturale* lies in the unique link it makes between a dynamic view of reality and the idea of the natural desire for the vision of God.

But can the natural desire attain its completion in and of itself? If it were located within the universe, yes. But we need be under no illusion: our final goal does not lie within reach of our natural powers. Happily, the dynamism conceals divine wisdom; it is no blind force that drives us onward.

The attainment of our final goal far surpasses our natural powers. And yet philosophy can close in the mood of Advent.[46] There is room for supposing that God will, in a counterwave, fulfill human desire. It is certain that God *can* let us reach our final goal.

Further than that natural thought does not bring us. Philosophy leads us to the threshold of the sanctuary. Not philosophy but religion reveals to us the answer to our questions, the satisfaction of our desire for God and the beatific vision.

One of the foremost concerns of those who regard the natural desire as an "ontological tendency" or "ontological ordering" is to be mindful of the boundary between nature and grace. To hold that nature can attain its supernatural destination of its own inclination and in its own strength would be to violate that boundary. That being the case, writers assure us—especially when they deem it necessary to ward off suspicion—that the natural desire is "inefficacious" with respect to grace, which is to say that attainment of the final goal wholly exceeds the capacity of nature.

Moreover, if God created in human nature such a drive towards supernatural completion, would that not result in nature making a demand of grace? Theologians sensed that an affirmative answer would shortchange the gratuity of grace,

---

[45] Blondel, *L'Action*, 2:177f.
[46] Maes, "De stelregels van het Blondélisme," 92.

would imply a restriction of God's free disposal. Even so, the idea of such a "demand" was so compelling that some theologians were able to free themselves of it only with great difficulty and barely escaped the charge of Baianism. The Augustinians Noris († 1704), Bellelli († 1711), and Berti († 1745) attempted to avoid the difficulty by inferring from nature's desire for grace not an absolute demand but a moral one. Blondel occasionally spoke of a "necessity" of the supernatural, and of a "demand" that human nature makes with respect to grace, but in later works he scrupulously avoided such suspect expressions.

The difficulty regarding the gratuitous character of grace will no doubt remain unresolvable. We would have asked no consideration for it here if the question of the "demand" had not been brought to an acute stage by the theory of de Lubac, who claims to have "exorcized the monster of the 'demand'." [47]

The doctrine of the *desiderium naturale* is tied very closely to the idea of being in general and to the doctrine of participation in particular. As we pointed out when discussing the idea of participation, many Roman Catholic theologians and philosophers part company here. Some use the concept of participation to stress the autonomy of nature as opposed to religion, while others use it to in fact dissolve nature in the supernatural order. In the first school of thought, moreover, many nuances occur as well. I hope to demonstrate that a strong emphasis on the autonomy of the natural order by no means constitutes an obstacle to seeking an approach from nature to the supernatural order—witness Blondel, Maritain and Malevez.[48]

To obviate incorrect conclusions, it should be noted that although de Lubac is one of the leading figures of the New Theology, his particular conception of the *desiderium naturale* does not define the school. His conception does, however, illustrate one endeavor that is characteristic of the *théologie nouvelle* as a whole, namely, to orient theology in all its parts to the Fathers.

De Lubac agrees with the Thomists to the extent that he, too, considers nature's desire for the beatific vision inefficacious, that is, nature desires something of which it is radically incapable. Or, to keep more to the terminology of Thomas, who used *non-sufficienter* instead of the more modern term *in-efficax*, de Lubac also says that nature is ordered to the supernatural final goal with an ordination that is "still insufficient." There is thus a disproportion between natural desire and natural capacity.

Nevertheless—and here de Lubac dissents from current conceptions—the natural desire for God is unconditional. A conditional desire for God would mean that its satisfaction not only fully exceeds our capacity, but, moreover, that it is entirely up to God's free decision whether or not to satisfy that desire, which requires a second divine act entirely independent of the first whereby God created that desire in us. De Lubac attacks this view. He does not deny a new act on God's part—for the natural desire is inefficacious—but he holds that the

---

[47] De Lubac, *Surnaturel*, 486.
[48] See below, chapter 6.

gratuity of the grace whereby God meets us and satisfies the desire of our spirit, which is to say the gratuity of God's second act, is not distinguishable from that of God's act whereby he awakens and sustains the desire within us. The desire whereby we reach out for God is thus at once "inefficacious" and "unconditional" or "absolute." [49]

De Lubac was not spared criticism for this thesis. For if the desire for God is absolute, what then remains of the gratuity of grace? Moreover, de Lubac entangles himself, some opponents say, in an inner contradiction: on the one hand he asserts the insufficiency of the desire, on the other hand he contends that it is absolute—two positions that are mutually exclusive.

De Lubac's conception of the absolute character of the natural desire cannot be explained, however, from the fact that he wants to find a way out of the impasse that the doctrine of the *desiderium naturale* has gotten into. The way out that he indicates can only be understood as an integral part of his theology. His book contains an observation that sheds significant light on the direction of his theological thought. Thomas, in whom he believes he can find the notion of the absolute character of the desire for the beatific vision, remained substantially faithful to the Fathers, de Lubac explains. But Thomas used Aristotle's categories for the traditional doctrine. This has caused much grief. For Aristotle, nature was "a center of properties and a source of activity that was strictly delimited and enclosed within its own order"; for the Fathers, however, the spirit was never more than the Image of God, "a divine reflection whose nobility is perpetually borrowed, a creation of the Spirit that never solidifies in an independent 'nature.' For the Fathers, there was no *nous* without an anticipated participation, ever gratuitous and ever precarious, in the unique *pneuma*." Thomas did try to fuse the two conceptions (the Aristotelian "nature" and the Fathers' "image"), but however great his powers of synthesis may have been, not even Thomas managed to combine them into a perfect unity.[50]

De Lubac desires to follow the Patristic conception. The spirit should never be severed somehow from the transcendental relation with the Creator and then declared autonomous. With the Fathers we should the human spirit as a participation in the divine Spirit. Our nature is permeated by a desire that is not its own but that belongs from moment to moment to God. Man's natural desire is not granted him as an autonomous possession but "emanates" constantly from God, so that when God answers, he meets his own will. What objection in that case could one still have to speaking of a "demand" that our spirit makes of God? For it is a demand, is it not, that God himself asserts? [51]

---

[49] Ibid., 484: "... we maintain that the desire for God is absolute—the most absolute of all desires. To desire the divine communication as a free gift, as a gratuitous initiative, is to desire it with a desire that is inefficacious of itself; but that is not to say, as some do, that one has only a platonic, conditional and conditioned desire for it."

[50] Ibid., 484; cf. 431–35, 436–38.

[51] Ibid., 435, 483–91. Cf. esp. Malevez's formulations as he presents de Lubac's theory in his article "L'Esprit et le désir de Dieu."

De Lubac's theory of the desire for God means a radical departure from the Thomist doctrine of the autonomy of human nature. It also means that the entire problem of the relation between nature and grace is so radically resolved that nature is entirely lost to view. Supernaturalizing nature would seem to have eliminated the nature-grace problem.

Cajetan also supernaturalized the natural desire, but he left nature as nature —on the Catholic view—intact; only, the desire was in fact deprived of its natural character. De Lubac, however, supernaturalizes *nature,* and with that, both nature and the *super*natural disappear.

§ 4. *The supernatural and nature*

Concerning the relation of the supernatural to nature we can be brief here, since this question will constantly require our attention below. We confine ourselves at this juncture to a few general remarks.

As in the case of the *desiderium naturale,* here too the effort is being made to advance beyond a merely harmonious order between the supernatural and nature. A corollary of the idea of nature as the purely passive substratum for grace was the notion of nature as a self-enclosed order. This amounted to a sharp distinction between natural and supernatural reality and served as the point of departure for a separation of philosophy and religion. Here we have one of the sources of the secularization of culture.

Catholic thought is engaged in emancipating itself from such conceptions. The emphasis today is on the transformation that grace brings about in nature. Natural life remains what it is in itself, but a new principle is implanted in it.

The transforming operation of the supernatural order on nature has as its consequence, first of all, that only in this way can nature attain full development in its own order. Thus natural reason—to take just one example—will see the creation ordinances more clearly than when dependent entirely upon natural light.

Yet the transformation goes much deeper. A positive sanctification of natural life through the life of Christ now becomes man's portion. This is the true elevation: the supernatural, implanted in nature, lifts it up to itself. In beatitude God will complete the transformation of nature: then God will be all in all.

These few remarks are meant to provide no more than an impression of the direction present-day Catholic thought is taking. There is still room for richly nuanced elaboration—elaboration that will inevitably be accompanied, however, by sharp tensions, which have their source in another tension, that of nature and grace. This makes the conflict about the relation between Christianity and culture, Christianity and politics, Christianity and history, so fascinating and engrossing.

Many are the ways in which an effort is being made to overcome the dualism of nature and grace. Yet one must be cautious about drawing conclusions from this fact for the philosophy and conception of history. An authentic Christianization of culture and of thought about history requires more than a recognition of the ordering of nature to grace, or of the elevation of nature by grace.

II/ FALL AND REDEMPTION

§ 1. *Sin*

One who studies Catholic treatises on sin quickly discovers that sin is regarded primarily as something negative: the seriousness of sin lies in that it *deprives* human nature of a great treasure. This deprivation is at once the punishment of sin, while one of its consequences is the disruption of nature.

The essence of original sin, according to the Roman Catholic conception, lies in the loss of sanctifying grace and, with it, of the supernatural virtues and the gifts of the Holy Spirit. To gain a correct view of the wounding of nature that results, one must notice the loss of the extranatural gifts. This belongs not to the essence of sin—for that is exclusively the deprivation of sanctifying grace—but to the consequences and punishments of sin.[1]

By extranatural gifts Catholic theology understands qualities with which grace adorns nature without their being strictly ascribable either to the supernatural or to the natural sphere. Included among these "extranatural" privileges are ethical integrity, bodily immortality, and the state of perfect beatitude.

These gifts were of no little consequence: they eliminated the shortcomings that come with nature as such. Deprivation of the extranatural gifts as a result of the loss of grace involved a deterioration of human nature, inasmuch as the inner dichotomy between matter and spirit then became manifest.

For according to the Catholic conception a tension obtains in human nature between soul and body. The body is material, the soul is not. The body has its sensual, the soul its spiritual desires. The body is mortal, the soul immortal. This tension, this deep opposition, was already there before the fall, but then it was elevated to a harmony of matter and spirit, in that the latter ruled the former and the sensual was ordered to the spiritual as the lower to the higher. The lusts of the flesh were fully subject to the spirit: thus man was free from every sinful desire (ethical integrity). It is true that the human body was subject to change and decay, but God allowed it to share in the privileges of the spirit (the extranatural gift of immortality). These two privileges entailed a third: negatively, man was free from suffering, sickness, and so on; positively, he enjoyed a permanent state of happiness and joy.[2]

Thus besides the dualism between nature and grace there is a second dualism in Catholic theology: one within nature, between matter and spirit. This second dualism is closely connected to the first.

---

[1] Van Hove, *De Erfzonde*, 245. [Cf. G. Vandervelde, *Original Sin: Two Major Trends in Contemporary Roman Catholic Reinterpretation* (Amsterdam, 1975; repr. Washington, 1981).]

[2] Luyten, *De Schepping*, 309f.; Van Rooyen, *De Genade*, 437f.

Now when, with the supernatural, the extranatural gifts were lost, man became a prey of the division, the disharmony which had hitherto remained barely hidden in his nature. To be sure, the soul after the fall remained spiritual, immortal, and endowed with understanding and will; but, severed from the order and harmony into which the extranatural gifts had brought the higher and lower, a struggle now ensued between the two, a struggle to which they were consigned by the primal opposition within human nature. As a result of the great struggle between the higher and the lower passions, the rational will is weakened. Reason is dragged down by the lower passions to the material, so that its understanding is necessarily clouded.

To this extent, sin consists not only in loss but means at the same time a deterioration of human nature, commonly called "wounding." In this sense Catholic theologians too will speak of our "corrupted" nature.[3] But then they do not mean by this the radical corruption as understood by the Reformers. For—and here the typically Roman Catholic doctrine of sin and grace stands out in bold relief—however devastatingly sin may have gone to work, and however much damage the evil will may do, the disposition to the good, the receptivity to grace, is not destroyed. It is only weakened. Nature's orientation to its perfection cannot be destroyed: God's work was good and remains good, even in the fall.

Appropriate to this view of human nature after the fall is a certain optimism, which one might almost want to call characteristic of the Roman Catholic worldview. Yet one must not overlook that some writers are extremely pessimistic about the power and consequences of sin. Such pessimism, however, by no means includes a denial of nature's orientation to grace.

§ 2. *Why the incarnation?*

If a Scotist were to cast a glance at the organization of this chapter, he would certainly object to treating the doctrine of Christ after that of sin. He would immediately suspect that a disciple of "hamartiocentric" theology was at work here.

For centuries a controversy has been waged over the question, *Utrum si Adam non peccasset, Verbum incarnatum fuisset*: If Adam had not sinned, would the Word have become flesh? One encounters this dispute already in the writings of the Church Fathers; think, for example, of the attention Athanasius devoted to it in his work on the Word become Flesh. It is only in medieval Scholasticism, however, that the positions become clearly delineated. The foremost camps are named after the Thomist and Scotist views.

In the view of Duns Scotus, typically, the incarnation would have happened even if sin had not entered the world. There is no creation without incarnation. All creatures are ordered to Christ, not just after they became sinners, but already as creatures. Even without the fall the creation needs Christ: before all else he is its reformer and finisher and, ultimately, also its restorer. Christ must therefore

---

[3] Van Rooyen, "De Genade," 438n.

Fall and Redemption   37

have the first place in the order of the decrees of God. Sin and salvation can alter nothing in the incarnation as such. It is true that the *circumstances* under which the incarnation finally occurred were changed: Christ now had to come as the suffering Messiah. Upon him rested not only the reformation and consummation of the entire creation, but likewise its redemption.[4]

From the Thomist side there has always been criticism of the speculative character of the Scotist doctrine. Thomas wanted to shift the question from the realm of dialectical thought to that of faith. Only Scripture is able, on his view, to inform us of the motive of the incarnation. Well then, it always associates it with the fall.

Reading the subtle argumentation with which people attempt to convince each other, one could gain the impression that we are concerned here only with the order of the divine decrees. There is, however, something far more important at stake. It concerns the meaning of the incarnation, the relation between incarnation and cross, the universal primacy of Christ.

Below, we shall observe a certain tendency in Catholic theology to define the meaning of the incarnation in terms of the cross. In recent decades leading Thomists like D. Feuling[5] and Michael Schmaus[6] have abandoned the Thomist view of the motive of the incarnation and have begun to marvel at the grand perspective Scotus opens for them. This indicates a shift of emphasis in Catholic theology from the cross to the incarnation, a shift that is also apparent in the latest developments in theology of history.

Noteworthy in this connection is the way in which the Dominican father Charles-Vincent Héris attempts to resolve the question. He endeavors to do justice to contemporary tendencies in Christology but at the same time to uphold Thomas's view. This he does by distinguishing between the motive and the result of the incarnation. If we study Scripture we will discover that it does speak of the primacy of Christ, but not that this primacy predetermined that the Word should become flesh. Surely one reads everywhere that Christ came in the flesh for our sin and salvation. The *motivum incarnationis* is hereby clearly indicated in Scripture. But the *result* of the incarnation was twofold, involving both man's salvation and Christ's glory. That Christ is the Head of humanity and of the universe is not in itself sufficient to establish that this was the motive of his incarnation.[7]

Thus it has gradually emerged that the universal primacy of Christ plays an important role in the debate about the *motivum incarnationis*.

On the Scotist side, of course, no one has any difficulty with the primacy of Christ. It is independent of the fall. It is *absolute*. And Christ is so much the first

---

[4] For an extensive discussion of this question from a Scotist perspective, see Bonnefoy, "La Place du Christ dans le plan divin de la création."
[5] Feuling, *Katholische Glaubenslehre*, 427.
[6] Schmaus, *Katholische Dogmatik*, 2:25f. et passim.
[7] Héris, "Le Motif de l'Incarnation," 24f.

in the creaturely order that no creature escapes his influence. The primacy of Christ is therefore also *universal*.

The question of the primacy is more difficult for Thomists. They themselves emphasize again and again that Christ's kingship is universal in creation and that absolute primacy belongs to him in the order of nature and grace.[8] Yet Thomists, who do not accept the Scotist view of the motive of the incarnation, will always view the primacy of Christ against the background of grace and of the transfiguration, of which Christ is the *causa meritoria et exemplaris*.

According to Féret, Scotists and Thomists agree that Christ is the absolute Head and universal King in creation as it actually exists. But Thomists would want to stress, more than is their custom—and this is where they differ from Scotists—that salvation through his death on the cross is an essential element of Christ's primacy. Thomists always have to keep in mind, so Féret continues, that Christ, who possesses absolute primacy, is not only the incarnated Word but also the Crucified one.[9] Unfortunately, Féret does not elaborate. But by seeing an unbreakable connection between the cross and the primacy of Christ, Féret, like Héris, upholds the necessary connection of the incarnation to the cross. That does not yet decide the question, however, whether a certain significance is to be attributed to Christ's incarnation independent of his suffering on the cross.

One would expect the Scotist theory to have been the starting point of many grand speculations about history. Yet that is not the case. Although one senses that it forms the background of many a reflection in theology of history, very seldom do Scotists venture to see history in the grand perspective that is opened up by their conception of Christ's primacy. Oswald Holzer gives us a sample of a Scotist "philosophy of history,"[10] but it suffers from too much pathos and too little substance to justify further mention here.

§ 3. *Incarnation, cross, and resurrection*

In the Word's becoming flesh is effected the great miracle of the union of the human and divine natures in a single person. We stand here before the mystery of the hypostatical union, or—what for Roman Catholic theology is practically the same[11]—the miracle of the perichoresis. By perichoresis is meant that the divine nature so penetrates or permeates the human nature that the divine prerogatives are made the possession of the human nature, such that it comes to partake in the glory, wisdom, and power of the divine nature.

The doctrine of penetration is indispensable for an understanding of Roman Catholic Christology and the Roman Catholic conception of grace.

One must begin by distinguishing two kinds of grace accruing to the man Christ. First, there is the uncreated grace or the holiness of the hypostatical

---

[8] Ibid., passim; Féret, "A propos de la primauté du Christ," 70.
[9] Féret, "A propos de la primauté du Christ," 71.
[10] Holzer, "Hamartiozentrische oder Christozentrische Theologie?", passim.
[11] Janssens, *Het menschgeworden Woord*, 174f.

union. By it, the humanity of Christ is substantially holy. The *unio hypostatica* suffices by itself for his holiness.[12] Union with the Word is a grace for the human nature, and Thomas accordingly also calls it the "grace of union." In actuality, this coincides with the *unio hypostatica* itself.[13]

A distinction must be made between the uncreated grace and substantial holiness of Christ and the created and accidental grace with which Christ was infused. Certainly, Christ's sanctifying grace also flows from the hypostatical union, though not in the way in which a branch grows from the trunk that nourishes it, but "by one of those debts of honor which the sovereign Wisdom is always pleased to respect."[14] Malmberg puts it even more strongly:

If, therefore, "the end of grace is union of the rational creature with God" (*finis gratiae est unio creaturae rationalis ad Deum*), or — what amounts to the same thing — if grace, by virtue of its very essence, means union (at least an inchoate union) of the rational creature with God . . . , then it cannot be otherwise than that all other graces in this historical order effect their respective union with God in total and intrinsic dependence upon *the* grace of union. Thus in this historical order no other grace can exist, unless necessarily and essentially connected to the *gratia unionis Christi*.[15]

By virtue of the hypostatical union and as the object of God's good pleasure, Christ's humanity possessed the absolute fullness of grace.

For the highest conceivable supernatural union of a creature with God, which is what the *unio hypostatica* is, cannot but include the highest conceivable accidental manner of supernatural union of a creature with God, the highest conceivable accidental grace.[16]

In this way, the grace of Christ, which accrues to him in plenitude, can be the fountain of the graces that flow to the saints. That Christ possesses the overflowing fullness of grace is meaningful only if grace as *gratia 'Capitis'* accrues to him, that is, as the Head of humanity, of the angels, and of the rest of creation. By this grace Christ is Head of the church, and the riches of grace accrue to the church only because Christ is its Head. In principle, the entire life of grace of the church was already present from the moment of the incarnation.[17]

The divine life was in Christ in such abundant measure that it had to overflow, as it were, the limits originally set for it. This it did in the resurrection and ascension. Then it broke through in his holy humanity and from and through that, in his church. Grace was "stopped" as long as Christ was still subject to

---

[12] Timp, *De Verlosser*, 372f.
[13] Vugts, "De vereenigingsgenade van Christus in de theologie van S. Thomas en diens tijdgenooten," 358f.
[14] Hugon, *Le Mystère de l'Incarnation*, 218; cf. Graham, *The Christ of Catholicism*, 194.
[15] Malmberg, "Onze eenheid met den Godmensch in de Kerk," (1942): 362.
[16] Ibid., (1942): 378; cf. (1947): 244, note 115.
[17] Ibid., (1942): 384.

suffering and death. Jesus, by his sacrifice on the cross, gained resurrection and ascension for his human nature, and, for those who are given to him, eternal divine life.

We have seen that the Scotist conception of the motive of the incarnation, which is shared by leading Thomists, opens the possibility of ascribing a particular significance to the incarnation distinct from the crucifixion. Catholic theology arrives at this point in yet another way as well. It does not halt before the idea that the incarnation announces the coming of the Savior. An element of salvation is present in the very act of becoming flesh, not in the sense that salvation is about to become a fact—meaning that reconciliation and restoration, for which many centuries have longed, is now imminent, but in the sense that in the very incarnation of the Word contact is established between the divine and the human. Salvation does not converge fully in the suffering and death of Christ on the cross, for the union of the divine and the human is in itself already an element in the process of salvation. Through his incarnation Christ possessed the fullness of grace and was in a position to make humanity partakers in the divine life. His passion and resurrection were a necessary sequel, however, since life could not flow to humanity until sin was atoned and the ransom paid. In this way, incarnation and cross remain necessarily connected to each other, but in point of fact the emphasis has shifted from the death on the cross to the moment of incarnation.[18]

This tendency to divide salvation, in its dual effect of acquiring and causing divine life and reconciliation, over the incarnation and the cross cannot remain restricted to Christology. The union of the divine and the human acquires a particular function in the doctrine of the church *qua* extension of the incarnation. If Christ in the incarnation has drawn all men to himself, then the human race and every member of it, "from the mere fact of the Incarnation, must have an altogether special relation to God the Son." [19]

These words suggest that an incarnation doctrine of this type will not remain restricted to ecclesiology either. Dividing salvation over incarnation and cross is a characteristic feature of many Catholic reflections on history. It is a real problem for Catholic theology of history to know whether to proceed from the incarnation or the cross. Thus if one calls Christ the center and turning point of history, the question remains which fact of salvation one has in mind. It seems more obvious, and easier, for theology of history to proceed from the incarnated Christ. Yet if theology of history would do full justice to the way of the cross traveled by Christ, it must ask itself whether the incarnation, when taken in the sense of Catholic theology, can still be united with the cross without creating inner tensions.

---

[18] Cf. e.g. Fortmann, "Enkele gedachten over Menswording en Verlossing," 321–23; Durand, "Incarnation et Christocentrisme," passim.

[19] Malmberg, "Onze eenheid met den Godmensch in de Kerk," (1943–45): 246.

§ 4. *The church*

Christ's suffering on the cross is not only the cause of the transfiguration of his humanity in the resurrection, it is likewise the active cause (*causa in actu*) of grace for all those given him by the Father. From this time on, the new life can flow to them from Christ as the Fountain. Because they are recipients of the fullness of the grace of Christ, they become partakers in the divine life, and their souls are elevated to the level of that life.[20] Yet not as individuals: the Holy Spirit infuses the life of Christ into a community, the church, and it is as a member of this community that an individual comes to partake of it.[21]

It is not the case that Christ earned grace and then left it behind as a treasure when he ascended into heaven. The divine life cannot be separated from him. So where grace is, there Christ is also. This can give us some idea of the intimate connection of Christ as Head with the church as his Body, that is, with the community that is infused with his life.

In the communication of grace to the church, Christ's humanity fulfills an important function. It is the instrument of the Godhead, and is able to be so because of the fullness of grace, which flows through it and elevates it as a result of the hypostatical union. Christ's human nature thus has life-giving power, not of itself, but as instrument.

Thus grace accrues to man with the help of the human nature of Christ, not only in the sense that it has fulfilled an instrumental role in earning grace but also in the sense that wherever grace operates there a mysterious contact is made with Christ's humanity. Such contact is possible for that humanity because, in the transfiguration, which became its portion on Easter morning, it was set free from the laws of space and time.[22]

The doctrine of Christ's humanity as *instrumentum coniunctum divinitatis* has enjoyed the lively interest of theologians in recent years. This is no doubt a result of a renewed emphasis on the church as the mystical body of Christ.[23]

---

[20] Thomas defines grace as "quaedam participatio divinae naturae" (*Summa Theol.*, I, ii, 112, 1), or circumscribes it as "anima Christi [i.e. of the Christian] fit divina per participationem quae est secundum gratiam" (ibid., III, 7, 1 ad 1). See further, among others, Malmberg, "Onze eenheid met den Godmensch in de Kerk," (1943–45): 48f; and Weyers, "In Christo Jesu," 508.

[21] Schmaus, *Katholische Dogmatik*, 3.1: 54.

[22] Ibid., 55–57; Malmberg, "Onze eenheid met den Godmensch in de Kerk," (1943–45): 61–63; Graham, *The Christ of Catholicism*, 196. On the different conceptions concerning the way in which the mysterious contact originates, see Schmaus, *Katholische Dogmatik*, 3.1:56.

[23] Tschipke, *Die Menschheit Christi als Heilsorgan der Gottheit*, passim. To account for interest in the instumental character of Christ's humanity, still another factor can be mentioned. It is thought to be possible in this way to maintain the truly human in Christ's activity and thereby to have a defense against the charge of monophysite tendencies. The Scotist camp especially criticizes contemporary Catholic theology for failing to do justice to the reality of Christ's humanity. Karl Adam ("Jesu menschliches Wesen im Licht der urchristlichen Verkündigung," 114) even speaks of "covert apostasy" from the Chalcedonian position and of "incipient monophysitism," the result of carrying too far the fusion of the human nature with the divine. Against an exaggerated apotheosis of the human nature, the so-called Assumption-Homotheology of De Basley, Gaudel and Seiller stresses that the hypostatical union did not influence the human

The church is invisible as to its internal supernatural life; it becomes visible, however, in its external organization. The essence and goal of the church is to carry on the salvific work of Christ; to this end it is furnished with sacerdotal, doctrinal, and administrative powers.

We have seen what a prominent place the incarnation occupies in the whole of Catholic theology, and in ecclesiology in particular. In current Catholic theological terminology one encounters statements like the following: "The Church is the continuation of Christ's work of salvation." "The Church is the prolongation of the Incarnation." "The Church is the appearance of Christ on earth." "The Church is the continuing presence of the personal union of God with a human nature."[24] The Church not only prolongs the work of creation but is the Incarnation itself "in its very constitution."[25] And in the encyclical *Satis Cognitum* (1897) Christ is called the model (exemplar) of his church. The incarnation-as-model is not restricted to the church, though it does manifest itself there first and foremost, in its prolongation. The union of the divine and human in Christ is primary and unique, to be sure, but it stands at beginning of a long journey.

Catholic theology is certainly conscious of the difference between the divine and the human in the historical and risen Christ and in his mystical body. Authors note that the church has received only in a derived and communicated way what Christ has received in fullness in an original way, through the hypostatical union. And in the encyclical *Mystici Corporis* (1943) the pope accents the difference thus: salvation is *earned* by Christ but *applied* by the church.[26]

It is usually conceded, however, that the church cannot be called the "prolongation of the incarnation" in the strict sense. Some theologians would even prefer to avoid such designations altogether, partly in reaction[27] to those who go so far as to accept an *unio hypostatica* between the church and the Son of God and in this way arrive at a real identity of Christ and the Christian. Yet the term "prolongation of the incarnation" expresses too deep and too rich a reality to be sacrificed from fear of misinterpretations or excesses. Christ unites himself with his mystical body differently than he does with his physical body, that is, not in a hypostatical but in a "pneumatical" union. Such terminology, it is believed, successfully expresses the distance, the true difference.

On the one hand, Christ is so intrinsically connected with the church that it partakes superabundantly of one and the same divine life of the "God-man," and that the same Holy Spirit, as the principle of divine life, dwells in Christ and in the church. This provides no basis, of course, for calling the union between Christ and his mystical body a hypostatical union, since the two clearly remain

---

nature intrinsically, and that Christ's humanity is by no means simply an instument of the divine initiative. On this point, see among others Ruding, "Het begrip Persoon in de leer omtrent de hypostatische vereniging" and Seiller, *L'Activité humaine du Christ selon Duns Scot.*

[24] Schmaus, *Katholische Dogmatik*, 3.1: 54.
[25] Michel, "Jésus-Christ," col. 1360.
[26] *Mystici Corporis Christi*, sec. xx.
[27] E.g., Cordovani, "Per la vitalità delle Teologia Cattolica," 143.

separate persons. Nevertheless one can speak of an identity. This identity is not unqualified, and it is mysterious, but it is real none the less. Expressions like "mystical identity," "mystical identification," and "mysterious identity" are beginning to gain currency in theological discourse.[28] One also finds it said that the Christian and Christ together form a "mystical subject."[29] An effort is being made to find a terminology that expresses both the distance and the intimacy.

Although I have endeavored to clarify the various aspects of the relation of Christ to his church, I am mindful that because of its brevity this endeavor has been only partially successful. My aim is not completeness, however, but elucidation of certain concepts that recur again and again in theology of history, together with an understanding of the background against which the relation of Christianity and history is to be viewed. For this reason I should like to take a brief look at the *corpus mysticum* doctrine in its historical development. To get a good sense of the changes this doctrine is undergoing we must go back several centuries.

We will leave the Middle Ages aside, however important they may have been for the development of the doctrine of the Mystical Body. Recent studies[30] have shown that during the heyday of Scholasticism a profound change came about in the understanding of the relation between church and sacrament, and that already at that time ecclesiology acquired an apologetic and analytical tendency.

Generally, in present-day Catholic theology a dim view is taken of post-Tridentine theology, the so-called *théologie baroque*. The theological thought of recent decades amounts to a grand effort to get beyond the problems that occupied "baroque theology." In particular the theology of the Counter-Reformation had a negative effect on ecclesiology. As a mitigating circumstance, of course, it is noted that at that time people had been put on the defensive by the Reformation, Jansenism, and other misconceptions. Theology has retained its apologetic tendencies ever since, well into the twentieth century. The predominance of apologetics dates from the Late Middle Ages. Against Gallicanism, the Conciliarist theories, the spiritualism of Wycliffe and Huss, the Reformation, Jansenism, and later against absolutism and modernism, it was continually necessary to defend the hierarchical order, papal primacy, and the prerogatives of the church. The result was—we continue to present the view of many contemporary Catholic theologians—that the church came to be seen mainly as a *societas perfecta,* as a hierarchical order under the primacy of the pope, and that treatises on the church dealt almost exclusively with its visible, hierarchical side.[31] This ill-fated development was not interrupted until the

---

[28] Malmberg, "Onze eenheid met den Godmensch in de Kerk," (1947): 228; Lialine, "Une Étape en ecclésiologie: reflexions sur l'encyclique *Mystici corporis*," 304.

[29] Malevez, "La Vision chrétienne de l'historie," 248.

[30] E.g., De Lubac, *Corpus Mysticum. L'Eucharistie et l'Église au moyen âge* (1944).

[31] Congar, "Bulletin d'Ecclésiologie," 77f; Lialine, "Une Étappe en ecclésiologie," 137.

nineteenth century, by J. A. Möhler and a number of other theologians. They took into account once again both aspects of the church, the visible and the invisible. Möhler's influence is clearly noticeable at the Vatican Council (1870). Yet while the dogmatic commission defined the church as *corpus Christi mysticum,* the Council did not adopt this formulation.[32]

In recent decades the doctrine of the *corpus mysticum* has become the focus of attention as people have tried to make it fruitful for asceticism, morality, and the liturgy. The central question in all this concerns the place it should have in ecclesiology. The days when the church was looked at exclusively in its hierarchical, institutional aspect seem to be over. Today the accent falls on its intimate communion with Christ and on the activity of the Holy Spirit. That does not yet imply, however, neglect of the human aspect of the church.

Some understand by the term *corpus mysticum* the church as such, that is to say, as embracing not only its supernatural life but also its visible, hierarchical aspect. Or in other words: the church as institute is the form of existence of the *corpus mysticum*; it is the instrument for realizing the mystical body of Christ.

Others, in contrast, believe that the term *corpus mysticum Christi* does not define the church but only expresses its mystical aspect, since by the term "body of Christ" Scripture never means the hierarchical institute of the church but exclusively the mystical identity of believers with Christ.[33]

In our discussion of the church we have placed the mystical communion with Christ in the foreground while relegating the visible aspect of the church to the background. Purposely so: it is a distinguishing feature of present-day theology of history to see the church mainly as *corpus mysticum Christi.* One must not suppose that by stressing the mystical aspect we have presented a distorted picture: Catholic theology indeed holds that it is only via the mystical identity of Christ and his church that its institutional, hierarchical aspect can be properly understood. Interpretations of this identity may vary widely, Berkouwer notes, but there is one point about which there is definitely a *communis opinio*: "the absolute authority following from this variously interpreted identity."[34] Hierarchy and papal primacy first acquired a solid basis in the doctrine of the *corpus mysticum*.[35]

§ 5. *The sacraments*

By what channels does the stream of life from Christ reach the church? In what way is the mystical body of Christ built? The answer to these questions must be provided primarily by the doctrine of the sacraments.

---

[32] See on his point Lialine, "Une Étappe en ecclésiologie," 138–49.

[33] For the controversies, see esp. ibid., passim; Congar, "Bulletin d'Ecclésiologie," 77–96; Tromp, *Corpus Christi quod est Ecclesia*, vol. 1.

[34] Berkouwer, *Conflict met Rome*, 34f [Eng. trans., 25].

[35] On this point see Schmaus, *Katholische Dogmatik*, III/1:43f.

Fall and Redemption

The sacraments are instruments by which God pours supernatural life into his church. Thus however important the function of the sacraments in the church and in the Christian life may be, there would be no reason to discuss them specifically here were it not for the fact that, already shortly after the First World War, sacrament and history were so intimately connected by some theologians that an entirely new school in historiography could arise, with its own view of the "essence" of the Early Christian Period and the Middle Ages and their mutual relation. And most recently, especially as a result of the influence of De Lubac's book on *The Eucharist and the Church in the Middle Ages*,[36] the relation of church and sacrament has become a subject of renewed inquiry.[37] It is not too hazardous to predict that this will produce new problems for theology of history. But we shall pass over in silence this latest phase of the discussion of the relation between *corpus mysticum* and *corpus eucharisticum,* since its importance for theology of history is not yet clear.

The link between sacrament and history has been put on the agenda in a startling way by the "mystery theology" of Odo Casel, a monk from the Benedictine abbey of Maria Laach. We shall limit ourselves here to presenting the main lines of this theology. How it has been worked out for history by Casel's adherents and coworkers is examined briefly in an appendix to chapter VII.

The Christian cult is in its essence "Mysterium." We are accustomed to giving the word "mystery" the sense of a "secret." *Mysterium,* however, is in its primary sense the "effectuation in the present" or the "re-presentation" of the "original salvation event." It is important to keep this primary meaning of "mysterium" in mind, for if one were to look first at the notion of secrecy or hiddenness, which is undoubtedly associated with it, then one might forget that it is something very real. It is a reality, but one having a particular character: "mysterium" means that that which it conveys is not present in its historical concreteness but according to its *aevitern* character.[38]

Now apply this to the sacrament, particularly to the eucharist. Here the matter is not one of subjective remembrance of the objective saving work of Christ, but one of *re-presenting* that work itself, not in its historical particulars but in what constitutes the core of it. The work of Christ in salvation, the "original mystery," comes to presence *per modum substantiae*. In the eucharist Christ's incarnation, passion, resurrection, and so on, do not actually re-enter our time and space in their historical sequence but in their convergence. The entire saving work of Christ converges in the *transitus,* the transition from death to life, from Good Friday to Easter. There is a multiplicity of successive salvation events, but they are all manifestations of the one (original) *mysterium*.[39]

---

[36] See note 30 above.
[37] Cf. e.g. Journet, "Définition synthétique de l'âme créée de l'Église," passim.
[38] Herwegen, *Kirche und Seele*, 8–10.
[39] Söhngen, *Der Wesensaufbau des Mysteriums*, 18.

Casel thus seeks the core of Christ's saving work in the *transitus*. Here we have a characteristic element in mystery theology. The salvation won by Christ was not yet finished with his passion and death; this was not accomplished until the resurrection, when the sacrifice was accepted by God.[40] According to Casel, the resurrection is a necessary complement of Christ's saving work, without which Christ's sacrifice is not a perfect sacrifice. By dividing salvation through Christ into two phases, whereby the resurrection comes to function as the definitive acquisition of salvation, the entire saving work of Christ enters a different atmosphere. Attention has to be divided between suffering and glory. Salvation acquires from the outset something festive: the accent is shifted from the cross to the open grave. This whole approach has given rise to critical discussions about (among other things) the relation between church and kingdom of God, and the significance of the Middle Ages: Herwegen, for example, contrasts the early church's image of Christ as the glorified victor[41] to the exaggerated attention of the Middle Ages for Christ the crucified one.[42]

In the eucharist the historical salvation act from incarnation to ascension is really present, yet not as spread out over historical events but *in mysterio,* in a sacramental way. The matter here—to say it one more time—is a real presence, be it of a particular sort, namely, a sacramental one, which is to say, in Casel's phrase, "beneath the veil of sacred rites and symbols."

Not a few objections have been raised against Casel's mystery theology, which appears to deviate considerably from prevailing interpretations of the sacrifice of the mass.[43] The criticism is directed not so much at the term "*re-presentation*," which is considered useful enough provided the *quod* of the mystery is given another meaning (something that Casel's position scarcely allows). But what Casel's critics resist is the idea that the salvation events as such—if not in their concrete particulars—come to presence, or are re-actualized, in the *mysterium* of the cult and can become effectual only in this way. Casel likes to appeal to the Fathers, but according to his critics, who appeal to Thomas, the "*re-presentation*" in the mass can only mean that "the mystery of the salvation

---

[40] Casel, "Mysterienfrömmigkeit," 107.

[41] Herwegen, *Kirche und Seele*, 17.

[42] On the importance of Christ's resurrection for salvation, see Van der Ploeg, "De verlossende kracht van Jezus' Verrijzenis," 263–65, where he takes issue with W. Grossouw; cf. Grossouw, *In Christus*, 35: "We all know that Easter, the high feast of Jesus' resurrection from the dead, is the foremost feast of the liturgical year, but why this is so, few are able to say. Most will confess, if they are honest, that Christmas is more appealing to them. This is because western Christendom has in large measure lost the sense of the resurrection of Christ as a *saving* factor, very much to the detriment of a vibrant and joyous Christianity." Both Grossouw and Van der Ploeg (ibid., 265) relate the differing appreciations of Easter to the difference between eastern and western theology: in the latter, the accent in connection with salvation is on the atoning death on the cross, while in the former it is on the resurrection.

[43] In general I refrain from supplying references for Casel's teaching, since it has been summarized and discussed so often that one may presume it is widely known. Casel's most important work is *Das christliche Kultmysterium* (1932; 3rd ed., 1948).

act of Christ is symbolically present in the sacrament and is effectual by virtue of this symbolical re-presentation in the present: to put more into the concept the clear teaching of Aquinas does not allow."[44] According to these Thomists, then, the presence of the passion of Christ in the sacrifice of the mass is purely spiritual: not the salvation act itself, but its effect is present in the sacrament.

Casel's school puts all the emphasis on the objective character of the *cultusmysterium:* Christ's sacrificial death and resurrection are sacramentally present, independent of any cooperation on the part of believers; they are present prior to any effect they bring about.[45] On this important point G. Söhngen, with the approval of many of Casel's opponents, has attempted to correct mystery theology by tying the coming to presence of the salvation act directly to the "effect of the sacrament in us."[46] The sacramental re-presentation, according to Söhngen, is not a reality that stands *between* the historical salvation and its realization in the soul of the believer: Christ's work of salvation enters into us *owing to* our "internal co-operation," as Söhngen and his adherents are fond of saying. Casel, of course, has to reject this interpretation of his mystery doctrine, since it relativizes the objective character of the "presence of the mystery."

Advocates of mystery theology cherish high expectations for the future. The *mysterium* in the authentic sense offers us the central element of Christianity. The mystery doctrine is accordingly not presented as just another theory of the sacrifice of the mass, but as an entirely unique, freshly rediscovered total view of Christianity based on the Church Fathers.[47] The incarnation is the core of the Christian religion. In the sense of the saving work of Christ it finds its cultic expression in the *cultusmysterium*.[48] Now it is of course the case that Christ's historical work of salvation can be really present only in the eucharist, and that there can be no thought of a cultic presence in the other sacraments or sacramentals, but these are to be regarded as the "setting" of the eucharist, as having an inner connection with it and sharing in its fruits.[49] Ultimately the entire life of the Christian is connected with the *cultusmysterium* and is incorporated into the "sacramental structure of Christianity."[50]

Winzen observes that mystery theology has not yet been developed in every area and that its effects are just *beginning* to be felt.[51] He is referring, no doubt, to strictly theological questions in the first place. Yet the goal of mystery theology is to bring the whole of life into proximity with the mystery.

---

[44] Poschmann, "'Mysteriengegenwart' im Licht des hl. Thomas," 68.

[45] [Cf. Berkouwer, *The Sacraments* (Grand Rapids, 1969), 205: "already before the use of the elements"; more on Casel in ibid., 196, 261–63, 268.]

[46] Van der Putte, "De Mysterietheologie en de scholastieke opvatting van de Oeconomia Salutis," 61.

[47] Winzen, "Note complémentaire et résponse à quelques critiques," passim.

[48] Dekkers, "De mysterieleer van Maria-Laach," 139.

[49] Dekkers, "Het Mysterium middelpunt van het Christendom," 17f.

[50] Dekkers, "De mysterieleer van Maria-Laach," 151.

[51] Winzen, "Note complémentaire et réponse à quelques critiques," 111.

§ 6. *Church and kingdom of God*

The kingdom of God and the church, God's kingdom and (world) history—here are two relations that must be of uncommon interest to us. For the moment we shall restrict our attention to the former. Only in light of the first relation can the second be understood correctly.

The Roman Catholic conceptions of grace and church suggest a very close relation between church and kingdom of God. In fact, one wonders whether it would not be better, strictly speaking, to talk of an *identity* rather than a relation.

Catholic theology has often had to resist an overidentification of church and kingdom of God. A recent example of this is Anscar Vonier, for whom the church and the kingdom of God for all intents and purposes coincide.[52] The life of the church, Vonier explains, is not so directly connected with the life and suffering of Christ on the cross as it is with his resurrection and transfiguration. That is not to say that the suffering and death of Christ for the church are not of infinite importance. But the church never was, and never will be, in the state of humiliation and death: Christ alone underwent death for sin. Now when Christ saved his own body from death, he also saved his mystical body. Christ is now the Christ of glory, and his church now shares in all respects in his transfiguration. The church is an essential element of the transfiguration of Christ. In the church, the *mysterium* of the *gloria Christi* is consummated, so perfectly that the church is a definitive reality, a province in the kingdom of Christ's glory. Thus the kingdom of God is already with us. What Christ has foretold of his coming and what the prophets have proclaimed about the glory of the Kingdom has already been fulfilled in the present age. The coming of the Holy Spirit at Pentecost meant the emergence of the church and therein the fulfillment of all the promises of Christ.[53]

Grosche has called attention to the one-sidedness of Vonier's view and given it the necessary amplification. He too recognizes that the kingdom of God has "dawned" and is really present on earth in the church—but not in glory. The kingdom of Christ cannot be any more than what Christ was before his resurrection: it forges its way not in glory but in *hiddenness*.[54]

In Vonier we encounter the same tension between Christ's suffering and resurrection that we noticed in the preceding section apropos of mystery theology. Grosche, opposing Vonier, stresses that the church is still not the *ecclesia gloriosa* but the *ecclesia crucis,* because as the suffering church it must still pass through the depths of humiliation. As long as the church is the *ecclesia crucis* the kingdom of God cannot appear in its full glory, no matter how much it may

---

[52] Vonier's conceptions are akin to Casel's, although important differences remain: for Vonier the *quod* of the "re-presentation" is the *Christus passus*, for Casel the *passio Christi*.

[53] Vonier, "Vom Mysterium der Verherrlichung Christi," 211–18 (paper at the Salzburger Hochschulwoche of 1934). [Abbot Anscar Vonier, O.S.B. (1875–1938) was born in Germany and studied in Paris and Rome before settling in England, where he rebuilt Buckfast Abbey.]

[54] Grosche, "Reich Gottes und Kirche," 47f.

already have been realized (in hiddenness) in the *tempus medium* of the church on earth.[55]

On the other hand, Grosche is forced to acknowledge that the tension between suffering and resurrection, between church and kingdom of God, has its source not just in the one-sidedness of the mystery theology but also in Roman Catholic teaching itself: because the Catholic church must take the resurrection seriously, it is constantly threatened by the danger that its children forget that the glorification has not yet come.[56]

Most Catholic theologians hold to a real distinction between church and kingdom of God. The relation between them, however, is clearly difficult to determine. One attempt was made by Charles Journet.[57] His ideas agree in large measure with Grosche's. From their writings one can form a fair picture of present-day Catholic thinking about the relation between church and kingdom of God.

Scripture says, on the one hand, that the kingdom of God is already present and, on the other hand, that it is coming: we are partakers of the glory of Christ, but that has not yet been revealed. The *gloria* is present, but in hiddenness. The kingdom of God must thus pass through two phases, the earthly and the heavenly.[58] There is a parallelism here with the life of Christ, with the king and the kingdom. That both king and kingdom must pass through the phase of the hiddenness of the *gloria*, which is in reality already their portion, is related to the road of suffering and humiliation they have to follow. Decisive for understanding the relation between the church and the kingdom of God is the relation between the passion and the resurrection of Christ.

The kingdom of God realizes itself in two ways. The first realization is in time, during which it is in the "state of movement and growth." The second is that of eternity, when it attains the "state of completion and perfection." [59]

Yet in both, the kingdom of God remains essentially the same, since what is primordial, grace, remains the same. There is thus a continuity between the *ecclesia crucis* and the *ecclesia gloriae,* a continuity of development from seed to flower.[60] Maritain calls the church the "chrysalis" of the kingdom. So long as Christ has not returned in glory, the kingdom continues to be realized in passing and veiled forms, and is to that extent an eschatological notion.[61]

---

[55] Ibid., 55, 59; see also 52f.

[56] Ibid., 60f.

[57] Journet is a kindred spirit of the philosopher Jacques Maritain, who joins Journet's precise expositions of the kingdom of God; cf. his *Humanisme intégral*, 112n [Eng. trans., 93n].

[58] Grosche, "Reich Gottes und Kirche," 47; Cerfaux, "Le Royaume de Dieu," 649.

[59] Journet, "Les Destinées du Royaume de Dieu," 71.

[60] Ibid., 71f.; Grosche, "Reich Gottes und Kirche," 52–59.

[61] Maritain, *Humanisme intégral*, 112f. [Eng. trans., 94].

Yet does this emphasis on the state of humiliation in which the kingdom still finds itself not mean a failure to appreciate Christ's resurrection? Not at all, for the glory of the church is nothing other than the cross of its Lord.[62]

---

[62] Grosche, "Reich Gottes und Kirche," 59.

III/ CHRISTIANITY AND HISTORY

§ 1. *History as apostasy from God: Bauhofer*

Oskar Bauhofer has adopted an extreme position with respect to the relation between Christianity and history.[1] His view is unique in Catholic theology of history, for he radically distinguishes the *corpus mysticum Christi* and profane history yet fully emphasizes the profoundly religious meaning of the historical process.

Bauhofer does not wish to deny that there is such a thing as profane history in a technical methodological sense, but he does want to deny the possibility of its existence in a metaphysical sense. He wants to rescue history from the alienation it has suffered by leading it back into the mystery. There alone one can understand what history is. There alone history has come home.[2]

History begins where the original, pristine being-as-man was lost through guilt. Pristine being-as-man is "being unto God" (*Sein zu Gott*), but history is the realization of another possibility: "being unto death" (*Sein zum Tode*); what was once mere possibility became the sole reality. Before suspecting that Manichaeism is involved here, one should note that historicity (*Geschichtlichkeit*) is not coeval with creation and has something to do, in a mysterious way, with salvation: there is a portal of hope for man.[3]

Through the fall, man's situation has become one of "there-being in need" (*Dasein im Mühsal*). Man has become destitute. To survive, he must do the works of the world, and therefore he can no longer be "constant unto God."

Thus, metaphysically, the status of historicity means first and fundamentally a "being *delivered up* unto the world," a "being necessarily preoccupied with *its* work and not our proper work, which is being able to be unto God."[4]

Is there no escape from this being-consigned-unto-death? History itself does not offer it, since history, as being-delivered-up-unto-death, leads never upward but always downward, toward the abyss. In certain times and places it can move on an ascending path, to be sure, yet even then—metaphysically speaking—the

---

[1] Following his conversion (around 1930) to Roman Catholicism, Oskar Bauhofer quickly became one of the leading figures of Roman Catholicism in Central Europe. As a philosopher of religion and culture, he had great influence on the laymen's movement among Catholic academics, especially at their annual Salzburger Hochschulwochen. Before his conversion he was sympathetic to dialectical theology, traces of which, as of Heidegger's ontology, are unmistakably present in his book of 1935, *Das Geheimnis der Zeiten*. For Bauhofer's relation to Barth, see Berkouwer, *Karl Barth*, 178ff.

[2] Bauhofer, *Das Geheimnis der Zeiten*, 11f.

[3] Ibid., 38f.

[4] Ibid., 51f.

matter is one of progression towards destruction: "historicity" is a state of being perpetually "in collapse." [5]

And yet for history, too, there is an end. What has been said about history thus far, about its not "being able to be unto God," pertains to its "intrahistorical meaning." It has still another meaning, which is external to it: the "other-worldly meaning of historicity." This is the true meaning of history. For its real, full meaning is triumph over history and *salvation from* history.[6] Now, in the incarnation of the Logos, history has attained its end. And in this way, metaphysically —not temporally—Christ is the end of history.

In Christ Jesus, God from all eternity appointed an end to historicity. Therefore he is not only the Last but also the First in history and its mysterious way, because he abolishes the being-forsaken-of-God by dying a death that is alien to him and thereby overcoming the historicity that is alien to him.[7]

The church, which is the Body of Christ, is the place where the "being-delivered-up-unto-death" of the historical person comes to an end, as he is incorporated into the church as a member. In the mystical Christ, what happened to Christ in incarnation, death, and resurrection happens to the historical person.

The church stands outside history. In its innermost being the church no longer even bears the signs of historicity, as its historicity is overcome and fulfilled in its sacramentality. Nevertheless the sacrament is a temporal "phenomenon." Thus the church is involved in two orders: on the one hand, it is located in time and space; on the other, it constitutes the order of sacramentality. Hence the church is "the repose of the ages." Time arches over it as an invisible core.[8]

As members of the mystical body of Christ we are brought back to God out of the "dispersal to the world." Yet with our corporeity we remain in the region of history. Our there-being still bears all the traits of historicity. This means we have been rescued only in an *inner* way from being-unto-death. Only in the hereafter our poor body, now still *corpus humilitatis nostrae,* will become like unto the glorified body of Christ: *configuratum corpori claritatis suae.*[9] This process of "configuration" commences, however, in the present, namely, in the "transformation [*Umgestaltung*] of our corporeity into sacrality." The type for this on earth is the saint, just as the hero is the personification of the "intrahistorical meaning" of history.[10]

But does this summary do justice to Bauhofer's theology of history? Has adequate account been taken of the development of his thought? Is it not the case that in *Das Geheimnis der Zeiten* [The mystery of the ages] there are traces of Barthian and existentialist influences which recall the period before his conversion to Catholicism? Did he not, shortly thereafter, overcome the radical

---

[5] Ibid., 56.
[6] Ibid., 60, 71.
[7] Ibid., 69.
[8] Ibid., 79.
[9] Ibid., 76.
[10] Ibid., 139–61.

dualism between history and the *corpus mysticum Christi*? One has to acknowledge immediately that the tone is different in his article of 1936, "Abendland und christliche Kultur" [The West and Christian culture], and in his book of 1937, *Die Heimholung der Welt* [Homecoming of the world]. Here the synthesis of nature and grace, the "servitude" of culture to grace, is in the foreground. Bauhofer sharply opposes those who interpret the notion that the church is the real creator and bearer of the idea of the West to mean that the church did no more than provide the technical apparatus for shaping the western world after the fall of the Roman Empire. The meaning of the church, Bauhofer explains, consists precisely in this, that its universality, which is of its essence, is carried over into the worldly realm as the unity of the West. The western order is a reflection, be it *suo modo* and imperfectly, of the true universality and unity of the church. And this is possible because the essence of western culture is a synthesis of nature and grace.[11]

Nevertheless, despite this positive tone Bauhofer has clearly remained true to his basic position as developed above. The dualism between culture and the supernatural is as sharp as ever. Nowhere after the fall can nature any longer be ordered purely in keeping with the supernatural: the synthesis is broken again and again by nature's "resistance." On earth, therefore, *the* Christian culture will never be realized. At most there was, and is, *a* Christian culture, that is, the *attempt,* the risky venture, the responsibility of an "incipient synthesis" of nature and the supernatural, or of an "incipient transfiguration."

If *the* Christian culture will not be realized in the *interim* between paradise lost and the transfiguration to come because the synthesis of nature and grace is a prescription, never a description, then in an *absolute* sense the whole concept of Christian culture is a paradox, and even meaningless. As soon as Christian culture in the absolute sense appears—and this can only be the new heaven and the new earth—it abolishes itself: culture is a human achievement, but the full penetration of nature by the supernatural, the new heaven and the new earth, is God's doing; here, human responsibility is abolished.[12]

The gulf separating history from the mystical Christ is deep. Precisely when taken in their proper senses, the two exclude each other. To be sure, there is warrant for believing that a hidden beginning of the transformation of culture is even now taking place, originating from the mystical body, and that a prospect is opening up of a "homecoming of the world" from its alienation, at least in the doing of "small things."[13] But in actuality only the inner man is freed from "historicity." The church—so Maximilian Rast writes correctly—touches the profane world with its fingertips only, to avoid contaminating itself.[14]

---

[11] Bauhofer, "Abendland und christliche Kultur," 38–44; *Die Heimholung der Welt*, 13ff.
[12] Bauhofer, "Abendland und christliche Kultur," 45f.
[13] Bauhofer, *Die Heimholung der Welt*, 176.
[14] Rast, "Zur Theodizee der Geschichte," 6.

Although it is perhaps not his intention, Bauhofer's dualism between Christ and history is accentuated once more when he tries to read Heidegger's *Sein und Zeit* as an existential ontological commentary on the "historicity" of fallen man. He does, however, raise a fundamental objection to Heidegger: the latter has not perceived that his "existential ontology" applies only to the state of man after the fall (*status hominis post peccatum*); there are also the *status innocentiae* and the *status gratiae*.[15]

For all that, Bauhofer overlooks two things. Human existence, even in its fallen condition, does not yield to understanding and analysis from the standpoint of apostasizing thought—no matter how closely it may be bound to such thought. Human existence becomes transparent only in the light of the Word-revelation. Furthermore, the *status post peccatum* may not be simply juxtaposed to the *status gratiae*. Immediately after Adam's fall, God in grace and favor took pity on his world. Even the continued operation of sin in the world is impossible apart from grace.

§ 2. *Sacred history as total history: Daniélou*

If Christ is the end of history to Bauhofer, to Jean Daniélou Christ is its only possibility.[16]

These two theologians of history hold strongly opposing views with respect to the idea of history. Father Daniélou is a leading figure among those who repeatedly call attention to the fact that historical consciousness has its origin in the Christian religion. "The historical way of looking at things," he writes, "originated with Christianity."[17] Christianity, according to Daniélou, not only incarnates itself in the cultures, but is itself historical in nature; antecedent to any incarnation in culture, it is itself already tied into history. That is why Christianity is essentially history.

Now, what is the nature of the relation between sacred and profane history? Daniélou distinguishes a dual relation here. On the one hand, Christianity is in history; on the other, history is in Christianity. Taken together, the two aspects mean that sacred history forms the *total* history within which profane history fulfills a particular, chiefly preparatory function.[18]

It repays to examine this dual relation more closely. In the first place, then, Christianity is in history. Daniélou calls this the incarnation of Christianity in the

---

[15] Bauhofer, *Das Geheimnis der Zeiten*, 33f (esp. note 1).

[16] Jean Daniélou (b. 1905) is currently one of the most prominent French theologians and a leading spokesman of the *théologie nouvelle* in particular. He takes a special interest in the question of history [cf. his *The Lord of History* (1958)]. His views concerning the place of history in the Christian religion have been strongly influenced by the Protestant theologian Oscar Cullmann and his book of 1946, *Christ and Time*. Daniélou is captivated especially by Cullmann's idea that God's revelation is at its deepest a historical event. [From 1941 Daniélou taught in Paris. He was made a cardinal in 1969 and died in 1974.]

[17] Daniélou, "Christianisme et progrès," 401. [Cf. *The Lord of History*, 93: "... the historical approach to reality was originally a Christian discovery..."]

[18] Danielou, "Christianisme et histoire," 175f.

cultures. This incarnation is a duty: here the church follows Christ, who was a man in a particular country with a particular culture in a particular time. Christianity may not, however, allow itself to be identified with any particular form of culture: alongside the call to "incarnation" stands the call to "detachment." If a culture embodying Christianity is destroyed, then this affects only Christianity's periphery, not its essence. The church, once clad in the cultures, must cast them off as old garments. This does not mean the old forms were not good; it means they are no longer suitable to a Christendom that is forming itself anew.[19]

Daniélou must accordingly reject the ideal of a new Middle Ages—an ideal that Maritain, too, no longer accepts, since its realization no longer seems possible in the present circumstances. Yet the background in Daniélou's case is different from that in Maritain's. Maritain does not definitively relinquish the ideal of the restoration of the Christian order on the medieval model; he only regards it as impossible of realization in the coming era. In contrast, Daniélou works the Middle Ages into his "incarnation–detachment" schema: Christianity incarnates itself in a particular culture and then leaves it for good to incarnate itself in other cultures, or actualizes itself in one period in a different fashion than it does in the next. Thus Daniélou is able, fully in line with his idea of incarnation, to appreciate bourgeois Christianity, or to be fascinated by the grandeur of the classical centuries.[20]

Nevertheless Daniélou regards the second aspect as even more important: profane history returns to sacred history. Here I think is the heart of Daniélou's view of the relation of Christianity and history. Religious history is the total history; the profane plays only a particular role in it. Daniélou believes this to be the perspective in which the Christian thinkers of the first centuries after Christ viewed world history. This is the way to grasp the religious unity of history.

Daniélou senses that difficult problems remain whenever the connections between sacred and profane history, between *ecclesia* and economy and so forth, must be specified more closely. And indeed, Christian thought, upon arriving at this point, has gone on to follow various paths. With the resurrection of Christ a new, *"future* world" dawned, and through his ascension Christ bore his humanity into the sphere of the trinitarian life. The future world has already come, but it has not yet been made manifest; it is present only in mystery, in the sacrament of the eucharist. This is the mystery of the church: the union of God and man.

Yet the "old world" remains, too. The present situation of the Christian is that he belongs to both worlds, which are juxtaposed and which coexist. The one is to succeed the other, but during the delay—from Christ's resurrection until his

---

[19] Ibid., 176–78; see also his "Orientations présentes de la pénsee religieuse," 20; "Christianisme et progrès," 401f.; and *Le Mystère du salut des nations*, esp. ch. 4, "Incarnation et transfiguration." [Cf. *The Lord of History*, 24–26.]

[20] Daniélou, "Christianisme et histoire," 176; idem, "Christianisme et progrès," 402. [Cf. *The Lord of History*, 25–27, 94.]

full revelation—they exist side by side, since the old world outlives itself while the world to come is already present in anticipation.

Again Daniélou poses the central question: What is the fate of profane history during the interim? The old world is granted a moratorium of sorts, so that it can complete its appointed task: to bask humanity to greater ripeness for the reception of grace.

Thus there is a profound link between sacred and profane history: the growth of humanity furnishes the church with the material which it transfigures by grace. In a figure borrowed from Irenaeus, Daniélou reiterates: world history is the vine on which the fruit of the church grows; when the fruit is ripe, the vine is left behind and discarded.[21]

Daniélou has gained great renown as a theologian of history in just a few short years. People listen to him. This is the more remarkable since the basic thrust of his conception has very little to offer that can be regarded as new in principle. What he has done is to find new ways of expressing it. But the real significance of his theology of history lies in his having asserted, against both the notion of the autonomy of the temporal and the idea of western history as a prolongation of the incarnation, that religious history is total history, in which profane history fulfills only a subordinate role. In doing so, however, Daniélou only revives an old tension in theology of history, while his solution, the correlation of incarnation and sacrifice, is unsuccessful.[22]

§ 3. *World history as the space for sacred history: Delp*

Upon comparing Alfred Delp's theology of history with Daniélou's, one is struck by the similarities as well as the differences.[23] Daniélou does not really know what to do with profane history; it has no intrinsic value or goal. Delp, in contrast, begins by positing that world history has a twofold goal. For Daniélou, history is primarily religious (salvation) history; for Delp, it is first of all world history. Moreover, whenever Delp uses the term "world history" he does not do so to detract from history in the sense that salvation history renders world history valueless and abolishes it. World history has a positive significance with respect to salvation history, although not such that one could speak of continuity.

---

[21] Daniélou, "Christianisme et histoire," 181–84; at 172 he uses the same illustration to elucidate the inevitable breaks between historical periods and the incorrectness of a purely linear conception of religious history.

[22] See further ch. IV, § 4, below.

[23] The theologian and philosopher Alfred Delp (1907–45) was receptive to many contemporary philosophical influences. He was keenly interested in the question of the meaning of history. Besides the article I have used, he wrote a book about the subject in 1943, *Der Mensch und die Geschichte*, which I have not, however, been able to consult. Philipp Dessauer defended ideas in his *Der Anfang und das Ende* (1939) that bear a strong resemblance to Delp's. [Delp was executed by the Nazis just before the end of World War II.]

As I have said, for Delp world history has a twofold purpose. First, history is the actualization of the general ordinances into the "fullness of reality." History's task will be done when the present world is destroyed and everything that was "this-worldly" is consumed in the apocalyptic fire. Secondly, one can discover the meaning of history by considering it from a human perspective. History is then a proving ground or "place of testing" where man, in transcendent faithfulness, must order things aright, to the glory of God.[24]

While world history thus has its own meaning apart from salvation history —its "this-worldly" goal—man is concerned with salvation, a goal that lies outside history. On the one hand, he must remain within history in order to fulfill the meaning of history; on the other hand, he must leave history in order to encounter the absolute, which is salvation. The relation between history and salvation Delp calls "distance-proximity" (*Distanznähe*).[25]

And yet, this is not the situation in which the world finds itself. God has summoned the world "in the order of immediacy to God." For salvation is the "encounter of immediacy to God." Hence the question now reads: What is the relation between history and the "encounter with God"?

Grace is a new spiritual state of being, fellowship with God, and is therefore disengaged from history. And yet grace is historically real and active: there is a *real* salvation history. Time and again God broke into history, not to resolve historical tensions in a direct manner or to abolish the laws of history, but to prepare the new order (by electing a holy nation, sending prophets, etc.).

The first period of salvation history consisted of supernatural—that is, suprahistorical—events *within* history. But the new salvation order too—Jesus Christ—is an order that has entered into history, and thereby salvation history has become real history.[26]

Does this mean that the two histories, world history and salvation history, run parallel, each pursuing its own goal?

Two things are certain in any case. First, although a new order, the "encounter with God," has entered into history, history itself is not abolished. Second, world history is the *one* history. Yet we saw that salvation too has its historical journey to travel. Salvation history has its center in the incarnation; world history rests upon the fact of the creation. It would seem that they must necessarily diverge. By putting the problem in this way, Delp clearly has left himself little chance of bringing salvation history and world history together in an inner unity of ground and goal. World history continues to run its own course: its meaning is twofold or, rather, world history has a single meaning with a dual aspect, namely, to be the "fullness of reality" and the "place of testing." Salvation history likewise pursues its own goal: its meaning is salvation. Nevertheless there is but one history, world history; and the whole of salvation history is but

---

[24] Delp, "Weltgeschichte und Heilsgeschichte," 250.
[25] Ibid., 251.
[26] Ibid., 252.

history as incarnation, which is to say, as an insertion in the history of the created world.

In constantly changing formulations Delp seeks to convince us that salvation history and world history are one single, unified history; but he is unsuccessful in hiding the dualism between the two. When his expositions at last converge in a final determination of the relation between salvation history and world history, he is able to do no better than posit an *external* connection: the meaning of world history in relation to salvation history is simply that it is the "space for the encounter with God." Its meaning cannot be salvation but the forming of "ever new possibilities to pass the test unto salvation."

Thus the meaning of salvation history is salvation and not creation. The world, and with it world history, persists in its old competency, and the new order of salvation creates no new historical situations. If the church were to do that, the unity of history, the unity of creaturely reality, would be broken. With respect to real historical happenings the church has no other task than to be "cooperative." [27]

If one compares the theories of Bauhofer, Daniélou, and Delp, one can detect important shifts.

In the first place, the inherent value of history is acknowledged in increasing measure. Delp and Daniélou are both far removed from Bauhofer's negativistic conception of history. Delp manages to give world history a twofold meaning even apart from the link to salvation history, and Daniélou has profane history furnish the stuff that will be sanctified by the new world to come.

In the second place, the three have differing views of the connection between grace and profane history. Bauhofer knows only a contradiction; for Daniélou and Delp, in contrast, profane history is a vehicle for grace, but they differ again in that, for Daniélou, history flows into the future world, which is already present in anticipated form, whereas Delp arrives at a parallelism.

Nevertheless—and this is the principal result of our investigation of the theories of Bauhofer, Daniélou, and Delp—not one of them has been able to discover an *intrinsic* value in Christ's work of salvation for the events of "profane" history. Maritain's and Thils' criticisms of contemporary theology of history begin precisely here. The importance of their work is that they exercise all their powers to get beyond the merely external relation of the so-called profane values to Christ and to reintegrate those values into their deep, living source, salvation through Christ. They turn against a juxtapositioning of the "wholly profane" and the "wholly Christian."

A remarkable shift is also evident in the field of theory. Whereas Bauhofer and Daniélou think mainly theologically, Delp values philosophy of history, while Maritain attempts to resolve the problem of the relation between Christianity and history at a level that is almost entirely philosophical. Where

---

[27] Ibid., 252–54.

Maritain differs from Delp is not unclear. For Delp philosophy of history is merely natural knowledge; for Maritain it is that too, but the light of revelation that rational thought receives via theology is nevertheless so important that he does not hesitate to call his philosophy of history a *Christian* philosophy.[28]

§ 4. *The idea of sacral and profane Christendom: Maritain*

Elementary for Jacques Maritain is the concept of "Christendom." By it he understands a culture that has arisen under the influence of the Christian view of life. A Christian culture or civilization, a "Christendom," materializes in time because it arises as a result of the penetration of Christian values into temporal, profane life.[29] The concept of Christendom distinguishes itself sharply from that of the church, in that the church belongs to the supernatural, supra-cultural values. "Christian civilization, the world of Catholic culture, remains a civilization, a world, the specific end of which, although ordained to eternal life, is itself of the temporal order." [30]

This implies that a variety of forms of Christendom are possible. One of these is already a reality, or rather, once was—the Christendom of the Middle Ages. Its distinguishing characteristic was its consecration or sacrality.

It is clear that for many centuries now there has no longer been such a sacral or "consecrational" Christendom. Why was such a thing possible in the Middle Ages? Life then manifested itself in an organic unity that excluded neither diversity not pluriformity. Its center lay in the spiritual order: sacral Christendom had its basis in a unity of belief, which was accompanied by a unity of outlook on life and the world.[31]

But what was the most characteristic trait of medieval Christendom? That its unifying center lay in the spiritual order. This meant that the temporal order had in the first place to play a role of *service* to the spiritual. Maritain speaks of the "predominance of the *ministerial* role of the temporal order in relation to the spiritual." Human institutions stood entirely in the service of God and of things divine. The sacral put its stamp on everything. The historical ideal of the Middle Ages came to expression in the concept of the Holy Roman Empire.[32]

Yet all that is now a thing of the past. In a process of centuries the Middle Ages have perished—engulfed in what Maritain calls an anthropocentric humanism. Does this mean, now that sacral Christendom has passed away, that Christendom has had its day once and for all? Or is it possible for it to assume other forms? Maritain's remarkable solution to this problem constitutes his original contribution to a Christian philosophy of history.

---

[28] Maritain, *Humanisme intégral*, 257 [Eng. trans., 237]. For this question, see further chapters VI and VII, below.

[29] Ibid., 144 [Eng. trans., 126]; cf. idem, *Du régime temporel et de la liberté*, 116f.

[30] Maritain, *Religion et culture*, 56 [Eng. trans., 37].

[31] Maritain, *Humanisme intégral*, 159f. [Eng. trans., 140–42].

[32] Ibid., 156, 159, 161 [Eng. trans., 137, 138, 142].

We have now arrived at the heart of our inquiry. Our question throughout has been: Is there, on the Catholic view, an intrinsic connection between Christ's work of salvation and so-called temporal, profane life? It is precisely this problem that Maritain and his closest kindred spirits have focused on. We follow their search for a solution in hope and fear. In hope, because a satisfying result would be of inestimable value to the whole of Christendom. In fear, because the Roman Catholic theme of nature and the supernatural (to which Maritain wishes to be faithful and which he accepts as the starting point for his philosophy of culture) will make it extremely difficult to leave Christian values their original force in the temporal sphere.

One of the peculiar traits of Maritain's philosophy of history is that familiar Scholastic terms frequently turn up in it only to acquire a meaning of their own. This is true in the first place of the concept of analogy. When Maritain introduces it into his philosophy of culture, he refers explicitly to St. Thomas. Thomas applied it to the diversity of political systems, or "cities"; Maritain applies it to the types of culture and Christian civilization. In the formation of culture the principles never change, nor do the highest practical rules for human life, but it is wrong always to apply them in the same way. With respect to the problem at hand this means that the principles that apply are the same for every Christian civilization, but that in every "new Christendom" they have to be realized "in terms of a new *analogue*." [33]

The very fact that civilizations are caught up in the stream of time signifies that they cannot be started over again. However, there is more. Decline was not the only feature of the modern age. In forsaking God, man devoted more attention to himself. In the modern, anthropocentric period the mind, through introspective self-examination, became ever more "conscious of itself." It discovered a truth, and it is our task to free that truth from its captivity and integrate it into a new form of Christian civilization.[34]

But even apart from this the restoration of sacral Christendom will turn out to be impossible. Its basis, the unity of faith, is no longer present. Maritain has given up the ideal of a return of the Middle Ages. He has found a new possibility of Christian cultural formation in the idea of a *profane Christendom*.

The Middle Ages play an important role in Maritain's philosophy of history. In his earlier works they were to him a model for our time. But ever since his ideas about a succession of forms of Christian civilization have ripened, he sees the ideal of the Middle Ages as one that is tied to a particular historical period.[35]

Maritain's conception and estimation of the Middle Ages are shared by many. What they find attractive in his perspective is the fact that the medieval world retains its full value and could remain the ideal if only circumstances were

---

[33] Ibid., 148 [Eng. trans., 131].

[34] Ibid., 149–51 [Eng. trans., 134–36] and *Religion et culture*, 30 [Eng. trans., 16].

[35] One can trace the development of Maritain's conceptions from his *Primauté du spirituel* (1927) through *Religion et culture* (1930) and *Du régime temporel* (1933) to *Humanisme intégral* (1936).

favorable, yet that no return to it is necessary in order to embark on a journey to a new Christendom. What Maritain has said with the concept of analogy has been expressed by Yves Congar in terms of the relation of substance to modality. On this view, the church has a mission with respect to the world: this mission belongs to the (nontemporal) *substance* of the church. The form in which this mission is fulfilled, however, is a historical *modality*: in the Middle Ages that was the *respublica christiana*.[36]

Whatever the mode of expression and whatever the philosophical terminology, it is becoming clearer every day that within Catholicism the attitude toward the Middle Ages is changing. Thus Congar is not exaggerating when he says, "We have managed . . . to disengage ourselves intellectually and pastorally from medieval Christendom." [37]

It is not only in France that these ideas are alive; one encounters them elsewhere too—without being able to establish just yet whether they must be traced to Maritain's influence. Consider, for example, August Zechmeister's words, "We realize better all the time that our situation is post-medieval." [38]

Following this excursion into the place of the Middle Ages in Catholic philosophy of history,[39] we return to Maritain's notion of a profane Christendom. A new period in history is announcing itself, according to him, a period which has barely begun but which has been in the making for some time. How long it will last no one knows. The new Christendom will not bring a golden age, but it will bring a new regime, that of integral humanism or, as Maritain likes to call it, the *humanism of the incarnation*.[40]

What will be the marks of profane Christendom? In it, too, the temporal remains subordinated to the spiritual, and then in a twofold sense. In the first place, the temporal may not contradict the spiritual. The difference from sacral Christendom cannot lie here, however. To determine that, Maritain again employs Scholastic concepts, namely, those of secondary principal cause and instrumental cause. A "secondary principal cause" produces an effect that corresponds with its specific grade of being, although it is subordinate to a higher cause. An "instrumental cause" produces an effect that is superior to its specific grade of being. Now, apply this to the medieval and future Christian civilizations: in the former, the temporal mainly had a *ministerial function*, for it was the instrumental cause with respect to the sacred, which is to say it could fulfill its proper causal function only *insofar as* a higher cause (namely, the sacral) used it to attain its own end. The meaning of the profane was exhausted in its being a means for the sacral.

---

[36] Congar, "Tendances actuelles de la pensée religieuse," 48.

[37] Ibid., 39.

[38] Zechmeister, *Das Herz und das Kommende*, 119 (cited in Congar, "Tendances actuelles de la pensée religieuse," 48). See also Aubert, "Quelques études récentes sur la place du laïcat dans l'Église," 690.

[39] See also Gurian, "On Maritain's Political Philosophy," 15f.

[40] Maritain, *Humanisme intégral*, 259f. [Eng. trans., 239].

How entirely different things will have to be in the new Christendom! To be sure, the temporal will still have to rank beneath the spiritual and remain subordinate to it—yet no longer as mere instrumental cause, but as secondary principal cause. That is to say, the profane may no longer be considered a mere means for the sacral: it must be once more what it is by nature, an intermediate or "infravalent" end. While the subordination of the temporal will be real, so also will its being not merely an instrument.[41]

The grand conception and reality of the Middle Ages can be spellbinding, but one must not shut one's eyes to that period's disparagement of the profane, its underestimation of the proper value of the temporal. From the thirteenth century onwards, however, a process of "restitution to the profane" took place. Thomas was providentially placed by God at the hinge between the Middle Ages and Modern Times. He accepted the restitution and laid its deeper foundations. Prior to Thomas, earthly things were valued almost exclusively for their relation to the supernatural. While Thomas and his followers did not lose sight of this relation, they drew special attention to the purely natural ends of the creature.[42] In a process of centuries, profane life became *autonomous* with respect to the sacred. The rise of false ideologies may cast dark shadows over this development, but something has been gained, which must be preserved.

In summary, it is possible to establish two characteristics of modern, profane Christendom. The temporal will be *autonomous*. But the temporal will not contradict the spiritual, indeed, will even be ordered or *regulated* by it, albeit as more than just a means.

Now, how does Maritain conceive of the relation between these two characteristics? Do autonomy and regulability not exclude each other? If Christianity is supernatural it can never *as such* enter into culture; it must of necessity transcend every culture. Accordingly, any real influence of Christianity in culture would seem out of the question. Yet Maritain still sees a way by which Christian values can reach profane life. His thought is superbly summarized by Theeuws when he writes: "A culture can be tied to Christianity in the sense that it arose and persists under the inspiration of Christian thought—a temporal expression in human history of evangelical principles, *a transposition of religious values into the temporal.* Christianity has become a leaven, a ferment that enters the social and political life of the nations . . . [it has become] a power that penetrates profane life, a nourishment even for the temporal ideal in human society."[43]

One or two examples may clarify what is to be understood by this transposition (called a "translation" by some writers). In the spiritual order the Gospel tells us that we are called to the liberty of the children of God; transposed to the natural order this means we shall seek freedom for humanity by liberating people

---

[41] Ibid., 190 [Eng. trans., 170].

[42] Ibid., 190n [Eng. trans., 170n]; Congar, "Pour une théologie du laïcat," 208f., 215f.; de Lagarde, *La Naissance de l'esprit laïque au déclin du moyen âge*, 3:86.

[43] Theeuws, "Sacrale en profane Christenheid," 268 (emph. added).

from slavery and oppression. Again, in faith we know the unity of the human race: all are children of one Father, and Christ died for all; for this reason we must work in society for a proportional equality of human rights.[44]

Enough has been said to afford some insight into Maritain's Christian philosophy of history. It draws the base lines for a new Christian culture. What is needed, though, is a more precise account of the relation between the supernatural and the temporal. This is provided by Gustave Thils, whose main work has become widely known (and hotly debated) in just a very short time. Its title has even become the name of a separate branch of theology: the "theology of terrestrial realities." [45]

By bringing Maritain's and Thils' theories into such close juxtaposition I do not mean to imply that they share each other's views in every respect. Thils lacks the broad historical perspective of a Maritain but is superior in his theological elaboration. Maritain's vision is distinguished by its strong dynamic, evident particularly in the idea of development from sacral to profane Christendom. Thils, more than Maritain, seeks the unity of the spiritual and profane orders, and so stands closer to the Christian ideal of the Middle Ages.[46] Maritain stresses the fact that Christian culture can be realized in a plurality of ways and expresses this with the Scholastic concept of analogy. Thils, however, is in search of the theocentric attitude toward life, in light of which differences of time and place are of merely secondary importance. He too employs the principle of analogy, but in a different sense from Maritain.

From what follows it will be clear that the differences between Maritain and Thils should not be exaggerated. As a matter of fact, Thils has reinforced Maritain's influence. Maritain's Christian philosophy of history and Thils' "theology of earthly realities" express what lives in the hearts of many. In a short time they have generated an influential movement within Roman Catholicism.

Viewed from the perspective of the present-day Roman Catholic conception of history, Thils' theology forms the transition from Maritain's humanism of the incarnation to Malevez's idea of progress as prolongation of the incarnation.[47]

Thils was profoundly impressed by the disintegrating effect of the postmedieval dualism between God and the world. The "theology of earthly realities" intends nothing other than to abolish this dualism and to restore the harmony between Christ and humanity, the unity of religion and life.[48] The great question, then, is this: Can the terms "salvation" and "elevation to the supernatural order," which are applied to rational creatures, also be applied to the profane

---

[44] Maritain, *Christianisme et démocratie*, 50 [Eng. trans., 53]. For this and other examples see the chapter "L'inspiration évangélique et la conscience profane," 39–52 [Eng. trans., 42–56].

[45] Thils, *Théologie des réalités terrestres*, 2 vols. (1946, 1949).

[46] Ibid., 1:112f.; idem, *Christendom en menschelijke instellingen*, 36f.

[47] This comes out strongly in Thils' *Théologie de l'histoire*; see also his *Naar een nieuwe voorstelling van de Katholieke zedenleer*, esp. 31–41.

[48] Thils, *Théologie des réalités terrestres*, 1:29.

—to institutional and cultural realities? (Notice that once again the question of the reintegration of earthly realities into Christ boils down to the question of the relation of the sacred and the profane.) When one says that culture, technology, and so forth must be Christian, that does not yet imply that they can be Christian in the same way that a person can be. In the case of the former, Thils explains, salvation in Christ must be understood analogously, in terms of the *analogia proportionalitatis*. In the case of man, however, God imparts himself by bestowing upon man his life. Man becomes like God, even though—such is the mystery of the supernatural life—man remains man. Now then, this encounter of God with man is the *prototype* of that between God and profane realities. They are taken up into a higher order of affairs without their partaking of the divine life.[49] (Salvation and elevation accordingly have different meanings, depending upon the different realities to which they pertain.)

At this point Thils introduces the familiar theological distinction between ontological and formal glorification of God. Institutional and cultural realities glorify God and partake of salvation through Christ "when they enjoy an internal order or inner perfection, which is in addition more or less elevated. They suffer from a sinful disorder when that order is disturbed and that perfection affected. They are redeemed when they are restored to the ideal perfection that makes them fit the Christian regime."[50] The transformation, the spiritualization, will be attained when the creation is given—as it is said today—"its full dimensions, its full maturity."[51]

§ 5. *History as prolongation of the incarnation: Malevez*

We come now to a conception of history that presents itself as a "philosophy of progress." For that reason it would seem to invite treatment not here but in the section of this study devoted to progress. We discuss it here because Léopold Malevez, one of the representatives of this philosophy, is concerned with a more general problem in theology of history than that of progress alone. He raises a question which is attracting growing interest in Catholic circles.

For Maritain and Thils the relation of Christianity and the profane world means integration of the latter into the former. But the "philosophy of progress" asks specifically, What value does the progress of profane history have for the kingdom of God? Malevez and company mean something quite different here from Daniélou. For Daniélou, world history provides the church with the material that must be consecrated through grace; the idea of progress is a fortress in which man holds out against God. Nor is Congar exactly sympathetic towards the "philosophy of progress"; he sees the value of progress for church and kingdom in that favorable conditions are created for the Christian life, and that

---

[49] Ibid., 80, 87–89.
[50] Ibid., 84.
[51] Congar, "Pour une théologie de laïcat," 217, and Aubert, "Quelques études récentes sur la place du laïcat dans l'Église," 689.

the creation receives its "full dimensions," since, when the kingdom of God is revealed at the end of the age, the world will have to have attained to full maturity.[52]

What is special about the "philosophy of progress" is that the development of history, and even the evolution of the universe, is seen as having Christological and soteriological meaning. The cosmic scope of salvation extends not only to sin but at the same time to the antinomy of flesh and spirit.

Malevez bases his optimistic view of historical development on the incarnation as the central event. By taking human nature upon himself, the Word transformed human nature, and even His body, so that it was elevated to the state of a glorified body. This effect of the fullness of grace, which was in Christ by virtue of the hypostatical union, was not "released" until after salvation was won by his death on the cross. From that time onward he was no longer bound by the spatial and temporal limitations of the natural body. Furthermore, by the radiation of his grace all human bodies and the whole earth are transformed. And in the consummation of the ages the universe itself will be transfigured. For "the physical universe is a member of the mystical Body of Christ, which is to say, it is impossible that it should *not* feel the effects of the diffusion of the grace of Christ. . . ."[53]

Is this transformation of the universe postponed until the consummation of the ages, and is it thus eschatological in the strict sense of the word, or is it already revealed beforehand? Malevez's answer is that if the grace of Christ is indeed real and contemporary, then so too is the transformation of the universe, at least in some measure, and in that case it develops and grows as Christianity spreads over the earth.[54] The facts themselves bear this out, Malevez believes. Living conditions are improving, control over nature is increasing, and technology, economics, and political institutions all share in this progressive evolution.

Noteworthy about this progress is that it arose and spread in the West—that part of the world where Christianity unfolded most abundantly. If it should be objected that many of the West's cultural goods had their origin not in Christianity but in pagan Rome, then it should be remembered that Rome had a unique, providential mission to fulfill: Rome was called to make possible the first diffusion of grace. Thus history itself points to an intimate connection between historical progress and Christianity. Malevez does not hesitate to regard the prized achievements of the West as a "prolongation of the incarnation." Present-day dominion over physical matter, political organization, art, thought

---

[52] Congar, "Pour une théologie du laïcat," 206, 213–17; cf. Rast, "Zur Theodizee der Geschichte," 9.

[53] Malevez, "La Philosophie chrétienne du progrès," 377f. Malevez obviously uses the term *Corpus Mysticum Christi* in a broad sense; in doing so he joins other theologians, who have extended it to the universe on the basis of the relation of Christ to the creation: He is its Head and Lord (see Malevez, "La Vision chrétienne de l'histoire," 260, 261n).

[54] Malevez, "La Philosophie chrétienne du progrès", 378.

and technology *"complete the Christ and therein glorify Him."* [55] It is via the church as the prolongation of the incarnation that Malevez extends the concept of the incarnation to the whole of profane history. Here the true Christian "philosophy of progress" discovers "an *intrinsic* aspect of the total Christ and the slow and mysterious elaboration of 'the new heavens and the new earth.' " [56]

Malevez is well aware that his conception of history has little in common with tendencies in modern thought and, in particular, that a deep chasm yawns between this philosophy and the theology of Karl Barth.[57] The fact of the incarnation, however, is decisive: whoever accepts that God took on our flesh can no longer dismiss the intrinsic value of history for the kingdom of God. The matter is for Malevez not just one of a conflict with Barth but it is part of the whole conflict between Catholicism and the Reformation.[58]

The "philosophy of progress" is strongly reminiscent of certain currents in Eastern Orthodoxy. Berdyayev, Bulgakov, and before them Solovyov, attempt to overcome the dualism between God and the world in this way. The influence of Russian Orthodox immigrants is palpable in Catholic theology, though it should not be exaggerated: Malevez's "philosophy of progress" as well as Teilhard du Chardin's evolutionism (see chapter v below), are able to draw upon a doctrine of incarnation indigenous to Catholic theology itself. The eastern and western churches alike view the incarnation as a universal cosmic principle, the only difference being that Catholic thought handles the idea "with more qualifications" than do a Solovyov or a Berdyayev.[59] Nevertheless one may say that the doctrine of the church as the prolongation of the incarnation, or as the continuation of Christ's redeeming work, has become a commonplace in Catholic theology.[60] But to call the progressive evolution of the western world, too, a prolongation of the incarnation of the Word goes too far even for many Catholic thinkers.

§ 6. *Sacrament and history: Michels and Pinsk*

The sacramental conception of history seeks the central fact of history in the incarnation of the Word. With equal justification, however, one might name the resurrection of Christ as the central event in this conception. Indeed the sacramental conception draws an especially close connection between incarnation and resurrection. Its vision of history is distinguished by the priority it gives to the glory of Christ, a glory that was already present in the union of the divine and the human but which first became manifest in the glorious resurrection.

---

[55] Ibid., 379 (emph. added).
[56] Ibid., 381, 383.
[57] Ibid., 384f.; cf. idem, "La Vision chrétienne de l'histoire," passim.
[58] Malevez, "La Vision chrétienne de l'histoire," 134. [Cf. below, essay 1.]
[59] Cf. Berkouwer, *Conflict met Rome*, 278, 281 [Eng. trans., 208, 210].
[60] Cf. Concilium Vaticanum I, Sess. IV: "The Eternal Shepherd and Bishop of our souls, for the purpose of perpetuating the saving work of redemption, decreed to found the Holy Church . . ." (Denzinger 1821).

The essence of the cosmos, writes Johannes Pinsk, one of the major spokesmen of the sacramental conception of history, is that it is order. That is to say, things do not exist side by side in isolation from each other but, on the contrary, they are interconnected. This implies at once that the union of the divine and the human in Christ as the divine-human form of life has a bearing, in principle, on the cosmos as a whole. For Christ's human nature is related to all people by virtue of the unity of the human race. Indeed, he is even connected with physical, earthly matter: was his body not formed of the dust of the earth? [61]

The real connection of Christ to the human race and to matter implies their elevation to the divine-human form of life from the moment the Word was united with human nature in Mary's womb, be it that at that moment this elevation only occurred "in embryo." [62] With the incarnation, the entire cosmos is taken up into the "Christ-life." Between the creation in its full dimensions and God there arises a relation far transcending the relation of the *analogia entis* which is based on the divine act of creation.[63]

There are no neutral terrains with respect to the salvation that Christ imparts to the world. World history—in its hidden nature, at least—is salvation history. The meaning of history, according to Thomas Michels, is the restoration of the original state of paradise. In principle, the *restauratio* becomes reality in the *incarnatio,* but the full restoration does not dawn until the resurrection of the Lord. Hence every professedly Christian conception of history must take its point of departure in the Easter event, not only because the *first day* of salvation then dawned, but above all because Easter is the *eternal day:* the perpetual repetition of Easter Day is the symbol of the eternal aeon that began in the transition from death to life.[64]

In the sacramental conception of history the emphasis thus shifts from incarnation to resurrection. The *reformatio* is already accomplished "at the root" by Christ's assumption of human nature, but the concrete appropriation of this reformation occurs in Christ's passion and resurrection.[65] The sacramental conception relativizes this distinction, however, inasmuch as all phases of Christ's redemptive work are said to converge in a single saving act, which comes to presence in each new historical situation in and through the sacrament.

Now, how does the "Christ-life" gain entry to the human race, to the cosmos and history? In the incarnation the cosmos is transposed *in secret* and *in principle*; but when the cosmos is being introduced into the sacramental realm by means of the great mysteries of the sacraments (mainly baptism and eucharist) and the sacramentals, then what happens is nothing other than this,

---

[61] Pinsk, *Die sakramentale Welt*, 18–21.

[62] Ibid., 20; Michels, *Das Heilswerk der Kirche*, 57f.

[63] Pinsk, *Die sakramentale Welt*, 22–24, at 24; Pinsk appeals to Eph. 1:10, Col. 1:16–20, and Rom. 8:19–21.

[64] Michels, *Das Heilswerk der Kirche*, 77; see also 16–19, 66, et passim.

[65] Ibid., 58ff.

that in the most widely divergent places "this being-possessed by the Christ-life is made *effectual* and *visible*." [66]

A single example will suffice to clarify what the introduction and elevation of the natural into the sacramental realm means. I purposely choose as an example not bread, wine or water, since these have special functions in the sacramental order, but light. One must begin by distinguishing between the idea of light as the giver of life and light in its empirical actualization where it is continually threatened and overcome by darkness. Now, in Christ the idea of light is fulfilled perfectly. He is the light of the world, and one day he will make the sun and the moon superfluous, when his glory fills Jerusalem. In the interim, however, the natural light is carried to completion, not, as in the case of bread and wine, by being filled with the divine life, but by the blessing and consecration of the sacramental church (think, for example, of the consecration of a candle).[67] Other examples in Pinsk are way, door, rest, sexual union, etc., etc. All evince a concrete connection between the realms of creation and salvation. These are not located alongside or above one another. Through the sacramental work of the church the natural realm is elevated. Yet the sacramental realm must never be regarded as definitive; it is only a transitional phase preparatory to the world's total transfiguration, which will dawn when creaturely participation in the glory of God, now still hidden in the sacramental order, shall be revealed.[68]

The restoration of the original state, having become a fact in the incarnation, is externally visible in history already in the here and now. This is the case above all in "consecrational dedication" which draws the earthly ordinances into the supernatural sphere of the church.

Michels and Pinsk both refer to the consecration of kings as an example of profane history "built into" the sacramental realm. Thus Michels' historical ideal is the medieval Empire, whose supreme representative received his lofty position through sacramental anointment.[69] The emperor was not granted spiritual power in the literal sense, nor did the temporal power fall to him only at the moment of anointment; but the earthly office, after *its* fashion and *its* form, was incorporated into the work of Christ and its continuation in the church. The sword, the crown, and the scepter were taken from the *altar* and anointed with catechumenal oil, precisely in order to signify that all power is of Christ, and that the king stands in a special relation of grace to him who has received the fullness of grace.[70]

The sacramental conception of history occupies a special place in theology of history. Yet the moment it claims to have resolved the dualism between the natural and supernatural orders in history, a protest is heard from another quarter

---

[66] Pinsk, *Die sakramentale Welt*, 183 (emph. added).
[67] Ibid., 192f.
[68] Ibid., 194–201,
[69] Michels, *Das Heilswerk der Kirche*, 37.
[70] Ibid., 37, 46f.; Pinsk, *Die sakramentale Welt*, 100–02.

against the undervaluation of the autonomy and intrinsic worth of historical reality. As Rast puts it, Bauhofer may have undervalued historical reality by placing it antithetically opposite grace, but Michels can assign no valid meaning to it either, for while he does value historical reality, he does so only from the perspective of supernatural reality.[71]

---

[71] Rast, "Zur Theodizee der Geschichte," 7; see also Dessauer's critique, "Wege und Abwege der Geschichtstheologie in der Gegenwart," passim.

IV/ DUALISM AND CONNECTION

§ 1. *Dualism and synthesis*
One who compares Bossuet's *Discourse on Universal History* with current Catholic conceptions of history will soon note an important difference. In Bossuet there is a heavy emphasis on God's direct intervention in both sacred and profane history. In particular, Bossuet traces God's providential protection of his church. Thus he is justly called the "theologian of providence."

In recent Catholic theology and philosophy of history many important problems have been addressed, but not that of God's direct intervention. To be sure, it is written about, and there is interest in it; yet it has been just a minor point of discussion. People consider God's direct guidance of history to be too heavily veiled in mystery to provide a solid basis for interpreting history.[1]

Instead, during the last thirty years another theme has been central: the relation of Christ to history. One could characterize the historical thought of the earlier period as more theocentric and that of present-day theology of history as more Christocentric, inasmuch as the main point at issue today is the relation of both the historical Christ and the mystical Christ to history. It is in this form that the theme of nature and grace becomes involved in the conception of history.

Although in the elaboration of the basic idea many nuances and even profound differences appear to be possible, all the thinkers we have thus far examined remain faithful, substantially, to the theme of nature and grace. At the same time, however, they endeavor to transcend the dualism inherent in the theme. Let me briefly summarize the various views:

1. History is opposed to God antithetically; Christ is its metaphysical end (Bauhofer).

2. Christianity incarnates itself in profane history, which in turn provides salvation history with the material to be consecrated by the church (Daniélou).

3. World history provides the space for the unfolding of salvation history (Delp).

4. The idea of a new Christian culture is to be understood as a transposition of (supernatural) Christian values into the temporal realm (Maritain) or as ontological glorification of God (Thils).

5. Human progress is a prolongation of the incarnation, a hidden transfiguration now, prior to the endtime (Malevez).

6. By means of the sacraments, the (natural) cosmos is elevated to the level of the divine life (Pinsk, Michels).

---

[1] See, e.g., Gilson, *The Spirit of Medieval Philosophy*, 374–78; Thils, *Théologie des réalités terrestres*, 2:40.

Dualism and Connection

Many of these theories contain elements which in themselves are quite acceptable and should be part of any Christian philosophy of history. Bauhofer has stressed anew, in the face of all optimism, the seriousness of the power of sin in history, denying all continuity between human effort and the mystical reality of Christ's church. Daniélou keeps warning against the dangers of the idea of progress, which people use again and again as a basis for arming themselves against God. Delp's contribution has been to accent the value of world history as the workplace for sacred history. Maritain has endeavored to extract the conception of history from the straitjacket of theology of history and to elaborate it into an original Christian philosophy of history.

However important these and other elements of truth in the theories before us may be, and however earnestly many may seek the meaning of Christ's redeeming work for world history, one must not lose sight of the fact that all this belongs to a universe of discourse that lacks something essential and involves a number of unacceptable presuppositions. Naturally, this assertion calls for an explanation.

The important questions that have occupied us thus far are these: Is there an intrinsic connection between Christ and history or do they merely touch each other externally? Whether intrinsic or extrinsic, how is it to be defined? I have put these questions to each new theory that we have examined, only to be disappointed every time. Either the connection is conceived in a purely extrinsic sense (Delp) or in an antithetical sense (Bauhofer), or else the boundaries between Christ and history threaten to be erased (Malevez, among others). Clearly, Catholic thought about history is confronted by an unacceptable yet inescapable dilemma. What is the *source* of this dilemma, which is driving theology of history and philosophy of history to opposite poles? Before we address that question it will be useful once more to examine closely the dualism in the different theories.

Bauhofer drew such a sharp dividing line between the corruption of history and the sacrality of the church that he barely escaped the charge of Manichaeism. His line of argument is this: creating culture bears primarily the character of sin, but salvation from sin and curse is possible—though only at the end of culture and history, since in the new heaven and the new earth there will be no room for what is human, as God will be all and in all.

Delp appears to promise more. Ostensibly, he would have nothing to do with a sharp division between nature and grace. Does he not take endless pains to show that world history and sacred history interpenetrate? Does salvation not acquire its own history through world history, which articulates the one saving event into a multiplicity of successive events? And is not this the deepest meaning of world history, that it is privileged to be the space for the unfolding of divine grace? Nevertheless, in Delp's conception the meaning of profane history for salvation amounts to no more than its being a substratum for redemption, or, to put it more in keeping with Delp's dynamic philosophy of history, to its being the bearer of salvation history: like a Christophorus, it will have the privilege of bearing Jesus, the mystical Christ, to the opposite shore, only to perish in the apocalyptic fire.

Our greatest disappointments were Maritain's Christian philosophy of history, Congar's theology of the laity, and Thils' theology of terrestrial realities. Whereas Bauhofer and Daniélou never knew how to esteem "the temporal" and "the profane" [2] in their proper significance but at best as means for the supernatural, these thinkers, in contrast, promised at least to take seriously the proper character of so-called profane history and its inner connection with redemption in Christ. But what remained of a Christian idea of history once the medieval idea of a sacral Christendom, in which the temporal was built into the sacral reality of the church and reduced to a mere means for the kingdom of God, no longer appeared practicable? All that remained was a purely temporal process, connected to the supernatural only with respect to its ultimate destination, and manifesting in its dynamics only a profane "transposition" or "translation" of Christian values and principles. To be sure, the profane continues to be ordered or regulated by the spiritual, which is on a higher plane; yet at the same time it jealously guards the autonomy it has won during the arduous course of many centuries.

Why have Maritain, Congar, and others not arrived at a deeper unity of Christianity and history? The reason is that they proceed from a strict boundary between a natural order and a supernatural order. The former may be regulated by the latter, and be peacefully and harmoniously connected to it; in reality there is a polar tension between the two, since what is actually rooted in each other is here first placed side by side and only *thereafter* brought into connection.

As a direct consequence of the tension between nature and grace, a certain fundamental restlessness pervades Catholic philosophy and theology of history. Sometimes the history of the kingdom of God is separated from profane history by a strict boundary that will not be abolished until the coming of the new heaven and the new earth, either through the destruction (Bauhofer) or else through the fundamental alteration (Maritain) of the profane world. At other times the distance between the natural and supernatural orders is lost sight of as historical progress is elevated to the heights of supernatural incarnation (Malevez and Pinsk).

The dualism of nature and grace is the reason why the glory of grace, the riches of Christ's redemption, cannot be deployed in world history in its full strength. Maritain is careful not to degrade the exaltedness of the supernatural sphere as it is brought down into the profane sphere, nor to violate the autonomy of the temporal order. Anything from Christianity's supernatural sphere that

---

[2] I use these and similar terms even though I regard them as unacceptable for a truly Christian view of history. They characterize Catholic thought about history too well, however, to be dispensable even to a critique which, like mine, takes a fundamentally different approach.

crosses the boundary to enter terrestrial reality can only be admitted after having undergone an *essential metamorphosis*.

In the school of Maritain the relation of sacral Christendom to profane Christendom is considered to be one of analogy; the relation between Christianity and the temporal was one of ends and means where medieval Christendom was concerned; and where the future profane Christendom is concerned, it is one of harmony. In fact, all these relations are governed by an open or hidden tension: in the Middle Ages (at least before Thomas) the proper value of the profane was depreciated in favor of Christian values, but in the new Christendom the originality of the Christian faith is sacrificed for the sake of the autonomy of the temporal.

Among Catholic philosophers of history the insight is growing that the Christian idea of civilization is not restricted to a single, ideal realization but can assume many forms. Yet a judgment seems to rest upon this richly differentiated Christian culture. Gains for the supernatural order entail losses for the temporal. To appreciate the temporal is to depreciate the sacred. And the more that temporal life directs itself towards supernatural reality, the more its autonomy is imperiled.[3]

And in cases where an inner connection is sought between historical progress and the kingdom of God, that same dualism leads to an underestimation of the full original meaning of the incarnation. For an original continuity between progress and the kingdom of God is insisted upon, despite their ontological discontinuity stemming from the absolutely gratuitous nature of grace and a certain positive resistance of nature to the supernatural.[4]

Surveying Catholic thought as a whole on the relation of Christianity and history, one finds it caught in an impasse from which it cannot escape as long as it insists on its starting point. Adventuresome or persistent thinkers may find it attractive to continue to attempt to sail between Scylla and Charybdis, but since all who seek a passage between them either run aground on the one or are swallowed up by the other, it would seem only sensible to look for another possibility. Catholic interpreters of history do keep informed about what others are writing on the relation between Christianity and history, but apart from their great interest in Orthodox theology it is striking that they are mainly aware of just two Protestant positions, both of which are excesses and hence objectionable to them. In the one, Christianity is humanized; in the other, the penetrating and transforming power of Christ's redemption is denied. Currently, opposition is being waged mainly against the latter peril, against the threat of the theology of Karl Barth.

---

[3] A good example of the problem is provided by Lefèvre's sharp critique of Maritain's secularizing of such fundamental Christian concepts as holiness, cross, humility, etc.; cf. "Une ascétique nouvelle," 7–21 (esp. 10f., 18f.). But how impressed are Maritain and Thils likely to be when Lefèvre (10, 19f.) immediately restricts the validity of supernatural principles to individuals and keeps them far removed from human communities and their leadership?

[4] Malevez, "La Vision chrétienne de l'histoire," 257, 260.

This limitation to a struggle on only two fronts is the more remarkable since Catholic scholars give every evidence of being aware of other currents of Protestant thought. Why do they not devote more attention to a philosophy of history that has developed from Reformational thought but which distinguishes itself sharply from both the liberal-modernist and the Barthian views of history? Is it not important? Or does it pose the problem of the relation between Christianity and history in such a way that there is no common basis for discussion?

I believe the answer to these questions must be sought in the fact that while there is indeed a deep gulf between the Catholic and Barthian conceptions of history, there is another very important point on which they are in agreement. Barth's thought is governed by the same basic theme of nature and grace that lies at the foundation of the Catholic worldview. When Barth seals off history and time against the fruit of Christ's redeeming work yet continues to speak of a "theology" of history, then he has already pressed it into a nature-grace polarity. To be sure, Barth's perspective on "nature" and "grace" differs greatly from that of Catholicism, but the character of their mutual relation, and the relation between salvation history and world history, is determined in principle by his denial of any actualization of God's grace in this world and in history. When Malevez reproaches "the Protestant conception of history" for getting practically no further than some "vague notion of a conjugation, or an association, poorly defined, of two entities," [5] then he may be striking a blow at Barth but he has not touched Protestantism. When a Roman Catholic opposes Karl Barth, the antagonists find themselves in a certain sense on the same plane. They have something in common in their basic theme. Yet it is precisely this theme that a Catholic theologian necessarily must lay aside if he would understand authentic Reformational historical thought.

Noting a cardinal point of agreement between Barthianism and Catholicism must not blind one to the fact, however, that the source of the nature-grace dualism is different in the two cases. For Barthianism, nature and grace are given concomitantly: "sin extends as far as the world extends," [6] and for this reason there is an unresolvable opposition of nature to grace. For Catholicism, however, nature is good and has remained so right through the fall. Thus here the dualism of nature and grace cannot be that of sin and grace. It can only be that of lower and higher; that is to say, nature participates in the *existence* of God, and the supernatural participates in the *essence* of God. The Catholic dualism corresponds, then, to a dualism between the "natural" and the "supernatural" in God.

With all this firmly in mind, one sees clearly that in Catholic thought both the conception of nature and the conception of grace are such that they cannot but lead to some form of dualism. It is likewise evident that in order to overcome this dualism another view of both nature and grace will be required. Opposition of nature to the supernatural becomes unavoidable the moment the former is

---

[5] Malevez, "La Vision chrétienne de l'histoire," 247.
[6] This and similar expressions recur time and again in writings of Barthian origin.

granted a certain autonomy and independence with respect to God while "the *religious* connection with God is recognized only as a *donum superadditum*, a supernatural gift to the 'rational nature.' "[7] The autonomy of nature (which includes history) is rooted in an ontological relation posited between God and the creature. This cannot but restrict man's religious connection with God. For an *ontological* relation between God and the creature cannot be at the same time a *religious* relation: the former involves either the autonomy (or else depreciation) of nature while the latter expresses the total dependence and surrender (or else apostasy) of the creature with respect to God. The religious connection with God, however, allows not only no ontological unity *within* itself but also none *next to* itself. Certainly, the isolation of the religious connection is a presupposition which has no support in Scripture. On the contrary, Scripture regards the whole of reality as fully dependent upon God, and it portrays every creaturely gesture of independence from the Origin as apostasy. The problem of the autonomy of the temporal is itself essentially a religious question.

Here we have reached the deepest point of disagreement between the Catholic and the Calvinist conceptions of history. Opposed to an ontological conception coupled to a religious approach stands the recognition of the absolute centrality of religion as *being oriented,* from the divine act of creation, *to the Origin and to service of God* throughout the whole of existence.

Reformed theology and Calvinist philosophy have groped for a suitable form of expression for the religious view of temporal reality *as a whole.* This endeavor has not been unfruitful. As a substitute for the basic theme of nature and grace, thinkers in the Reformational tradition have advanced the theme of creation, fall, and redemption. This threefold formula is not unfamiliar to Roman Catholic theology. Its distinctive usage in Calvinism becomes evident, however, when proper consideration is given the religious character of the creation, of the fall, and of redemption, and of their interrelations.

Opposing the Catholic idea of the analogical unity of being between God and the creature stands the Reformational idea of the (religious) connection and orientation to the Origin.

Opposing the idea of sin as a loss of supernatural communion with God stands the doctrine of the radical corruption of human nature. Instead of receptiveness and orientation to grace, Scripture teaches the inclination of man to do evil and the necessity of a reversal in orientation. In the fall, man remains man and nature nature, and the creature retains its creaturely mode of being: only, in the fall the creature has shut itself off from the living God.

Opposing the conception of salvation as the acquisition of supernatural divine life and the elevation of the natural, the Reformation speaks of salvation as a far greater event: the creature, which through man's pride turned away from God and his service, is reconciled in Jesus Christ and is opened to the re-creating

---

[7] Dooyeweerd, "De idee der individualiteits-structuur en het Thomistische substantiebegrip," 88.

work of God's Spirit. The effect of sin is radical and deep; deep and universal is likewise the effect of salvation in Christ.

It is from the religious theme of creation, fall and redemption, thus understood, that the difficult problem of the relation of Christ to history must be resolved. Only when we have apprehended the all-embracing and central character of the religious connection of the creature to God are we able to escape the dualism between autonomy of the temporal and total dependence in the supernatural, or to avoid a "lowering" of profane history to a mere means for salvation history.

§ 2. *Continuity and discontinuity*

One of the burning problems of present-day theology of history is that of continuity and discontinuity. At issue is a profound difference not only between Catholic and genuine Reformed thought but also between the various schools of Catholic thought. The concepts in question appear in various senses. Daniélou, followed by Thils and others,[8] employs continuity and discontinuity to express a relation between the various periods of the one great salvation event: on the one hand each successive period of salvation history carries forward what was essential in the preceding period, while on the other hand every new phase means a break with the past. Whenever difficulties arise regarding the concept of continuity in this sense, they pertain exclusively to relations *within* salvation history and to the nature of the periods relative to each other.

By the problem of continuity in theology of history, however, it is usually another question that is meant: Is profane history of any value to sacred history? Does human striving in the fields of learning, society and culture have any positive significance for the kingdom of God?

Malevez's answer to this question is affirmative. Union with the Word required "every greatness in the humanity of Christ," demanded a perfect man adequately "adapted to personalization in the Word." Jesus' humanity was brought into the required ontological disposition through the hypostatical union, or through the sanctifying grace flowing from it.

We meet here with a universal law, says Malevez. Wherever divine grace radiates out, it brings nature into a state conformable to its own excellence. By means of the civilizations, whose achievements are Christ's own work, Christ transforms us and brings us progressively into a state in which we can receive the fullness of his grace. In this way our human activities *prepare* us inwardly for the definitive kingdom of God. That kingdom already announces itself in the initial transfiguration. In this sense there is continuity between progress in the profane realm and the final reality (the kingdom of God).[9]

Malevez expressly maintains that profane culture can never by its own strength bring forth the kingdom of God, which is and remains entirely a free gift

---

[8] Thils, *Théologie des réalités terrestres*, 2:23–26; Daniélou, "Christianisme et histoire," 168, 170.

[9] Malevez, "La Vision chrétienne de l'histoire," 259–61.

of God. Hence the relation of culture and kingdom is one of authentic continuity and at the same time one of heterogeneity and discontinuity.[10]

Congar emphasizes the latter aspect: the kingdom is no fruit of human activity but is *given* through Christ. There is no continuity between them, although there is a relation: the faithful should promote favorable conditions for religion and the church, and they should strive to have all creation brought to full development when the purely eschatological kingdom of God arrives.[11]

Malevez and Congar are agreed in maintaining the entirely gratuitous character of the "final reality." Congar, however, places such strong emphasis on its heterogeneity that he is compelled to deny that the kingdom of God might in any sense be the fruit of human effort. This does not mean that Congar would dismiss all continuity between profane and sacred history, or between nature and grace. To understand this well it is useful to pinpoint where Malevez and Congar part company. The difference between the two pertains, in fact, to the influence of the incarnation and the transfiguration prior to the return of Christ in full glory.

To Congar, the kingdom of God is purely eschatological. Christ established his church for the interim and thus relegated the kingdom to the end of time. In the very act of doing so, however, Christ introduced a certain tension between church and world. The church bears no responsibility for the world—its task is only to bring people into contact, through faith and sacrament, with the kingdom to come. The world, in contrast, is to pursue its own course and see to it that it attains to full maturity before the kingdom descends.[12]

To Malevez, in contrast, the union of the divine and the human effected in the incarnation marks the beginning of a long road. Wherever in history divine grace radiates, it elevates nature to a higher plane. The continuity between human activity and the kingdom of God is thus based upon a real transformation during the interim. But this continuity rests upon still another one (a continuity that Congar does not dismiss, although he would prefer to avoid the term and speak instead of a link or connection, given the utter heterogeneity of the kingdom of God). Nature did not, as a result of sin, lose its radical receptiveness to the connection with the divine: supernatural reality could still link up with natural reality without any need of a radical turning to God.

A good illustration of this idea of connection is given by Justus George, who bases his conceptions on Rom. 8:19–22, where reference is made to "the earnest expectation of the creature" of the "glorious liberty of the children of God." Brother George interprets "creature" here to mean not angels and men but all created things, so that the passage says that the entire universe will be glorified.

---

[10] Ibid., 260.
[11] Congar, "Pour une théologie du laïcat," 194–218.
[12] Ibid., 195f.

But if the ineffable is to be creation's portion—so George continues—then certain "potentialities, certain threads of excellence" must be present in creation itself, awaiting actualization subsequent to the Last Judgment. The coming transfiguration has a basis in the universe itself, for George speaks, further on, of the glorification of the universe as *"arising from its very nature."* [13]

Here it is eminently clear that the ontological approach and the idea of transfiguration dovetail neatly: the excellence of nature—"the sacramental nature of being," as George calls it[14]—which constitutes the potential for the transfiguration to come, has its ultimate basis in a relation of the creature, namely, in the fact that the idea of being can be attributed to all being, to God or creature.

The point is not to charge that Roman Catholic theology would simply make the transfiguration an extension of nature or of temporal evolution; for it recognizes the qualitative difference between the two. Nature, however, even in its unelevated state, is conceived as being so wonderfully equipped that the heterogeneity of the divine and the creaturely fades into mere transition, and the distance between them to mere harmony and synthesis. In this way the incarnation of the Word loses every element of wonder and surprise: it does not initiate any new development but connects with one already in progress.

§ 3. The "dual" meaning of history

When one inquires of Roman Catholic writers what the meaning of history is, one does not receive a uniform answer.

Thomas Michels maintains that history moves towards a restoration of the original state, or towards the perfect rule of Christ.[15] According to Bauhofer, history itself can have no meaning, since it is apostasy from God; its meaning can only be that it will be abolished, which is accomplished by Christ. Christ will put an end to it, and so Christ is the hidden meaning of history.[16] Marrou defines historical meaning as follows: time will have reached its end when the mystical body of Christ has attained its full unfolding and perfection; hence the meaning of history is the progress of the church.[17] In contrast to these and others, writers like Herman Robbers and Franz Sawicki define the meaning of history as *"well*-being" or "human happiness." [18]

Thus history turns out to have meaning of two kinds. There is a meaning that philosophy of history arrives at via purely rational concepts, and there is a meaning that we learn from divine revelation. This is not to say, however, that the goal of history as discovered by natural philosophical thought would be purely immanent. The immanent has meaning only when connected to the transcendent: all political, artistic, scientific and technological developments

---

[13] George, "Transfigured Universe," 484f. (ital. added).
[14] Ibid., 491.
[15] Michels, *Das Heilswerk der Kirche*, passim.
[16] Cf. above, ch. 3, § 1.
[17] Marrou, "Existe-t-il une vision chrétienne de l'histoire?" 55f.
[18] Robbers, "De zin der geschiedenis," passim; Sawicki, *Geschichtsphilosophie*, 212–27.

acquire their deepest meaning only in the formal glorification of God. The ultimate meaning of history is Christ. However, philosophy as the inquiry of natural reason is incapable of pointing to Christ as the God-man.[19]

There is thus an immanent and a suprahistorical, a natural and a supernatural goal of history. It is true that neither can be conceived apart from the other. Ultimately, the natural goal of history is absorbed into the supernatural final goal. But profane history goes its own way—despite the profound influence of the supernatural factor—until, at the end of the age, it finally issues, after passing through an alteration of its character, into the kingdom of God. In the interim it has its own task to fulfill and retains its autonomy with respect to the higher, spiritual world.

It is patently clear that the idea of the dual meaning and destination of history is related to the basic theme of nature and grace. As a result of nature's *ontological* orientation to God, profane history has meaning even apart from the religious connection with God. Because the Catholic conception of history, in all its leading schools, proceeds from the autonomy of the temporal with respect to the higher spiritual order, it can continue to speak of meaning even when the *religious* orientation has been lost through sin.

The idea of a dual meaning of history offers advantages on two fronts. On the one hand, the extremely difficult question whether apostasy from God entails meaninglessness for history as a necessary consequence can be answered in the negative. On the other hand, in opposition to secularized thought which regards human culture as the ultimate objective of historical development, the idea of history's having a supernatural destination ensures the orientation of life in all its aspects to a supra-historical goal, thus making it possible to speak, not just with respect to salvation history but also as regards profane history, of a "Christian meaning of history."[20]

Yet there is a fundamental objection to be raised against distinguishing between a natural and a Christian meaning of history. One can speak of a natural meaning of history only if one ascribes to history a certain degree of independence with respect to God by exchanging the religious relation between Creator and creation for an ontological one, by virtue of which a degree of autonomy can be assigned to profane history.

That God placed himself in a dual relation—an "ontological" one and a "religious" one—to his creation is one of the assumptions of the Catholic nature-grace doctrine. Only when our eyes are opened to the fact that the whole of temporal reality, including history, is rooted in Jesus Christ as the new Head of the covenant, in whom God in his grace has had mercy on the world—only then will we discover meaning in history. It is only because Christ became its firm foundation and even now allows it to share in his triumph over the *civitas*

---

[19] Robbers, "De zin der geschiedenis," 246, 254, 256; idem, *Menschelijk weten over God en schepping*, 161.

[20] Cf., e.g., Haecker, "Über den christlichen Sinn der Geschichte," 481–500.

terrena that we are able to maintain, through all disappointments and fears and apparent meaninglessness, that the glorification of God is the meaning and purpose of all events.

History has retained its meaning not because its ontological foundation supposedly remained intact but because God gave the world, when it fell away from him, a new foundation in Jesus Christ. And even that broad and imposing life that is lived without God and against him retains its meaning because God compels it to be of service to himself.

The above implies the elimination of an ontological relation of history to God. This might appear to impoverish our historical vision. In reality it means the restoration of the only relation that history (including salvation history and world history) does have to God. Granted, on the Catholic view religion is never foreign to profane history, since the profane remains susceptible to supernatural elevation. But we have shown repeatedly that *in its essence* the profane remains inaccessible for religion.

If history thus finds its meaning exclusively in Christ, philosophy of history must appear in an entirely new light. Its first task will be to explore *in what way* the meaning of history, thus understood, expresses itself in created reality.

It will then very quickly be confronted with the problem of the relation between time and history. Catholic reflection on history has occupied itself intensively with this matter in recent years. It is no longer satisfied with the Scholastic conception, which excludes time from substance and regards it as an *external measure* of things. Various thinkers are trying cautiously to fit the "new-found" dimension of time, or history, into their systems. Most of them are well aware of the historicist and relativist dangers that would accompany any exaggeration of this dimension. Even when strongly emphasizing the value of history they hedge themselves about with so many reservations—the preceding may be sufficient evidence of this—that it is difficult to predict the direction in which they will finally seek the solution to the new problems of time and history.

But one matter is now irreversible: the place of history in created reality is back on the agenda. The struggle against modernism was for a long time an obstacle to open and thorough reflection on the problem of history. Now that the danger from that quarter is no longer regarded as so threatening, Catholic scholars have the room and freedom to discuss the question in all frankness, while the rest of the learned world looks on expectantly. Even today, however, especially in the controversy around the *théologie nouvelle*, one encounters warning after warning against historicism. And, indeed, holding this monster at bay remains one of the basic problems.

The danger of overestimating the historical does not lie in recognizing the fact that law, art, language, and even dogma have their histories. It lies in misjudging the true meaning of all these realities by believing that they are historical in nature.

One would not want to deny that Scholastic metaphysics provided a mighty bulwark against historicism, but it did so at the expense of time and history. And now the assault on the old concept of time has begun. It is of the utmost importance to Catholic metaphysics to bring the ontological problem of history to a satisfying conclusion. The question turns on one's view of created reality: Does one conceive history as a fundamental form of a reality that has a certain independence, or does one conceive it as a mode of expression of the total dependence of created reality on its Origin? The second possibility lies outside the sphere of natural thought, since it would mean the end of its autonomy. To accept the first possibility, however, is to face the perplexing task of reconciling the concept of history with the concept of substance.

§ 4. *Incarnation and cross*

The theme of nature and grace is not alone in obstructing insight into the full meaning of Christ's redemptive work for (world) history. A one-sided emphasis on the incarnation or the resurrection likewise causes tensions to arise in the various conceptions of history. I have already called attention in a number of places to a shift of focus away from the cross to the Word's becoming flesh and to Christ's resurrection from the dead. It should not be surprising that these tendencies are especially strong precisely in theology of history.

It is accordingly meaningful to raise the following question: What should be the point of departure for one's conception of history: incarnation or cross? The problem needs to be posed even more broadly: Should one's conception proceed from creation, from the fall, or from redemption? (By putting it this way I do not mean to suggest that Catholic conceptions of history attach themselves exclusively to the incarnation, or to creation, and so on.)

Perhaps some will object to questions of this sort, as presupposing the taking apart of what forms an intrinsic and coherent whole, while it is precisely the inner unity of creation, fall and redemption that should receive all the emphasis. I am persuaded, however, that there are factors in Catholic thought that weaken this unity, to say the least. In his article about the idea of individuality structures and the concept of substance, Herman Dooyeweerd writes:

> The ground-motive of the divine Word revelation, that of creation, fall, and redemption through Jesus Christ, is an *indivisible* unity. Whoever denies the *radical* character of the fall and redemption cannot but hold an unscriptural view of creation. The reverse is also true: whoever maintains an unscriptural view of creation cannot but arrive at a view of fall and redemption that shortchanges the Word revelation.[21]

Evidence of the correctness of these words is provided by Catholic philosophy of history. Its very conception of creation implies the dualism between ontological relation and religious connection. This dualism is carried forward into the

---

[21] Dooyeweerd, "De idee der individualiteits-structuur," 88.

doctrine of sin: nature as such cannot be affected by sin, since it partakes of the fullness of the divine being. The dualism is also extended into the doctrine of redemption: through the infusion of grace a new ground of life is added in an accidental way to the natural principle of life.

Because the basic theme of creation, fall, and redemption is intersected by another basic theme, that of nature and grace, every Catholic historian faces the question which of the three shall be his point of departure; and once this choice is made he faces the perplexing task of connecting the chosen factor with the other two. Bauhofer, in his theology of history, started with the fall, but the result was that he had to set history and church in virtual opposition to each other. Daniélou opted for another way: he began with redemption and ended by having profane history, to the extent that it has any value, absorbed into religious history. Delp followed two parallel lines, those of creation and redemption, and tried in vain to bring them into convergence.

This excursion into the relation of creation, fall, and redemption was needed in order to show more clearly that it is the conceptions of nature and of grace that disrupt the integrality and universality of Christ's redemptive work.

Malevez anticipates the criticism that there is no room for sacrifice and the cross in his conceptions of history as a prolongation of the incarnation and of profane values as a preparation for the body of Christ. His reply to this objection is that the theology of terrestrial realities in no way disputes the eschatological importance of the sacrifice, and that "perfectionism" does not necessarily forget the mystery of the cross. By "sacrifice" Malevez would have us understand that the physical, mental, and moral infirmities that everyone is given to bear must be accepted without rebelling insofar as it is not possible to overcome them with all the means afforded by the progress of civilization.[22]

If the theology of terrestrial realities and progress can manage to give no other meaning to sacrifice and the cross than this, then what is left of their proper meaning in the temporal realm? Daniélou, for one, finds himself compelled to register serious objections against such propositions. He points out that they fail to address the crux of the problem posed by sacrifice and the cross in the profane realm; for temporal values, he writes, have a tendency to claim absolute validity hence there will always have to be both the mystery of incarnation and the mystery of sacrifice.[23] Thus Daniélou perceives not only that the imperfect realization of the progress of culture means a sacrifice, but also that as a Christian one must distance oneself from the temporal especially because one is always inclined to seek in the temporal a solid ground for life apart from God and against God.

It is a pity, however, that Daniélou's precise intentions cannot be gleaned from his writings. He uses the term "incarnation" repeatedly, especially in *The*

---

[22] Malevez, "La Vision chrétienne de l'histoire," 262–64.

[23] Daniélou, review of Thils' *Théologie des réalités terrestres*, vol. I; in *Études* 255 (1947): 135.

Salvation of the Nations. Here he understands by it that just as Christ assumed our human nature with all its limitations of time and space, so does Christianity incarnate itself in the nations and cultures it encounters.[24] But what does he mean by sacrifice? Perhaps this: that Christianity cannot help but incarnate itself in the various cultures yet without becoming identified with any one of them; in due time it will leave them behind, like worn-out garments. Now it is curious that for this "disengagement" Daniélou uses the term "transfiguration." He sees a paradox: on the one hand transfiguration means the participation of our nature in the divine life, and on the other hand it means transcending all time and space and declining to be bound permanently to any one particular culture.[25] Is this what Daniélou has in mind when speaking of sacrifice and the cross?

Apparently, yes. But then it is clear that when he speaks of sacrifice he means two different things. Sometimes one has the impression that he wants to say that terrestrial values are not wrong in themselves and that the Christian ought to involve himself in them, provided he is careful at the same time to keep them at a distance lest they draw him away from God. At other times he so emphasizes the infinite elevation of supernatural values above terrestrial realities that the latter are deprived of all value: "they are secondary with respect to it [the supernatural life]—and in a sense abolished."[26] This indicates that in Daniélou the concepts "transfigured" and "abolished" are sometimes identical.

Daniélou deprives the entire concept of incarnation of its force. Malevez did the same with the concepts of the cross and sacrifice. In opposition to Malevez and Thils, Daniélou seeks to maintain the full religious meaning of sacrifice even in the temporal realm, as follows: incarnation in the cultures is simply necessary for Christianity if indeed it would reach the nations; yet if at all possible it must disengage itself from the temporal.

For Daniélou, taking sacrifice and the cross seriously means depreciating the temporal. Congar, too, sees no other possibility, unless one sharply separates the cross and the profane world from each other. There are two paths to God, according to Congar, that of world *renunciation* and that of world *renewal*. The first is the ascetic way; it consists of forsaking the world, including not only its evil lusts but also the world in the physical and cosmological sense. The church may not abandon the ascetic way, which has a legitimate place in it.[27] However, one who pursues world renewal does not forsake profane life but takes it as it is, ordered or regulated by God, to be sure, yet also having value in and of itself.[28]

From the above it is clear that the reality of the sacrifice on the cross is a real and perplexing problem for Catholic conceptions of history. In Malevez, what if anything remains not only of the profound humiliation and gravity but

---

[24] Idem, *Le Mystère du salut des nations*, 76 [Eng. trans., 57].

[25] Ibid., 81f. [Eng. trans., 62f.].

[26] Daniélou, review of *Théologie des réalités terrestres*, 135.

[27] Congar, "Tendances actuelles de la pensée religieuse," 40; idem, "Pour une théologie de laïcat," 212.

[28] Idem, "Pour une théologie de laïcat," 213.

also of the riches of the cross for profane history? And what remains of it in Maritain, who sees in the shedding of blood in the cause of temporal values an analogy of the shedding of Christ's blood on the cross? [29] Congar will not of course deny that Christ's sacrifice and the ascetic's withdrawal from the world yield benefits for the temporal, but beyond that, the realities of the cross and of the profane world remain isolated from each other. In contrast, for Daniélou, taking sacrifice seriously means detaching oneself from the temporal, and for Bauhofer it means the end of history.

The above suffices to show that in Catholic theology of history the cross and profane history are related to each other as polar opposites. To be sure, the cross of Christ is not without effect for history; the cross even makes history possible (Grosche). Humanity, even those living outside Christ, desire to reap the benefits of his suffering, but if it should ever want to take seriously the cross itself and "the fellowship of his sufferings" (Phil. 3:10), would that not render history impossible and entail the undoing of all earthly communities and their leaders?[30]

Given these tensions, the incarnation would appear to hold greater promise for a Christian theory of history. It speaks—at least to the Catholic mind—of harmony, contact, connection of the divine and human, elevation of natural events to the supernatural order. The cross, in contrast, speaks of humiliation and enmity, sacrifice and renunciation. Every conception of history that takes its starting point in the cross of Christ seems to become entangled in irresolvable difficulties. Jesus says in Luke 14:26 and 27: *"If any man come to me, and hate not his father, and mother, and wife, and children, and brethren, and sisters, yea, and his own life also, he cannot be my disciple. And whosoever doth not bear his cross, and come after me, cannot be my disciple."* Can one escape the force of these words by reading them in the light of Matt. 10:37: *"He that loveth father or mother more than me is not worthy of me"*; or by taking them to apply strictly to individuals or to certain groups? Nowhere in these words does one find a basis for such restrictions. Perhaps Christ never revealed more profoundly than here what the fellowship of his cross means for human life in all its relationships.

It is precisely when Christ's suffering on the cross is understood in its full significance for human life that it seems to be unable to offer a point of departure for Christian thinking about history. Surely the cross and involvement in history exclude each other, since the latter presupposes world acceptance rather than world renunciation?

I believe we can find a way out of the difficulties thus raised by considering the significance of the cross for "profane history" in terms of a fundamental *orientation*. In Christ's suffering and death, history was given another orientation. If after the fall history moved away from God and sought the world for its own sake, Christ's work of reconciliation and restoration effected the great

---

[29] Maritain, *Du régime temporel et de la liberté*, 204f.
[30] Cf., e.g., Lefèvre, "Une ascétique nouvelle," 19f.

reversal and reinstated the original movement toward God. The great turning point of history is not the incarnation as a union of the divine with the human but rather the incarnation as the advent of him who was to propitiate the offended justice of God and restore human life by giving it once again its original orientation to God.

The cross, taken in this sense, demands renunciation of the world—not of temporal life as such, but of the world in its development apart from God and in its imperviousness to Christ's redemption. The way of the cross means the end of history—to this extent one can agree with Bauhofer—but then of history as self-sufficient. The way of the cross and the way of history do not run parallel to each other: Christ's suffering puts an end to the autonomy and independent value of the temporal.

This is the awesome task for Christians: to remain in the world yet to live from the sacrifice of Christ. The historical record reminds us that Christians are not confronted with an impossible task, if only they go forth in the expectation of faith. There have also been periods in history, however, when the true Christian idea of world renunciation no longer commanded interest. At such times the idea would arise that worldliness could only be escaped by living in the margin of history, exposed to persecution, or sheltered in ascetic seclusion.

In a remarkable study of the problems of monastic life,[31] Agnès Lamy shows that after the Edict of Milan of A.D. 311, when people could be Christians without risking life or property and hence could belong to the supernatural and the temporal life at one and the same time, many withdrew into monachism, not primarily to earn merit, but *simply to be able to live as citizens of the heavenly polity*. It is a phenomenon that recurs over and over again throughout the Middle Ages: when worldliness reaches its peak an ascetic reaction sets in. The difficulty of living integrally from the life of Christ is felt the moment it becomes possible for Christians to participate without hindrance in the work of culture. Everyone who knows how difficult it is to live an authentic Christian life in the midst of the world will pause before criticizing the old monastic ideal; but one must likewise be mindful that living from Christ right in the middle of history has been made possible precisely *through the cross*.[32]

§ 5. *God's direct action in history*

In both Catholic and Reformational philosophy of history, the question of the "hand of God in history" continues to fascinate. The search for a satisfying solution has been carried on now for centuries. In the course of time people have grown cautious; arbitrary and speculative interpretations have made the Christian historian hesitant about pointing to God's special guidance in history.

---

[31] Lamy, "La Vie monastique et ses problèmes actuels. Introduction à Bios angelikos," *Dieu vivant* 7 (1946): 59–77.

[32] [Cf. below, Part Two, essay 7: "Culture and Salvation."]

That God's providence extends to everything in the world, every believer in the authority of Scripture will accept. The certainty that God rules this world sees the Christian through even the darkest periods of history with confidence in the future. No rationalist criticism is able to rob him of this comfort.

Difficulties and disagreements arise, however, the moment the attempt is made to show God's direct intervention in history concretely. The questions that arise in this area cannot be laid to rest by a general declaration that God's guidance embraces both history as such, and all particular events. There are many who refuse to be satisfied by such a general acknowledgment; in addition to such a general acknowledgment they accept a direct intervention of God in history, an intervention which presumably manifests itself in particular, usually striking, facts or developments. All that happens in history can be divided in this way into what God brings about *indirectly*, through means, and what he accomplishes *directly*, apart from all human activity. Or again, certain facts are sometimes abstracted from the stream of events and even though they may be products of human activity are elevated to the status of special signs from God.

Early in the nineteenth century, under the influence of Romanticism and the Historical School, the Christian conception of history equated God's government, the *gubernatio Dei,* with what had grown organically in history, and ascribed to it a higher value than anything in which human activity was clearly discernible. In the twentieth century the idea of God's providential guidance is wrapped in a new form of historicism, at least in certain Protestant circles: now it is no longer what has grown in the past that is normative, but we have rather to bow before the facts with which God confronts us from time to time: they are signals from God that we cannot ignore with impunity.

Since Catholic theologians have occupied themselves with the meaning of history for centuries, it is surprising that relatively little is being written at present about God's providential guidance. Certainly this is not attributable to any lack of interest. It is more likely a result of the fact that no new perspectives have been discovered that would place the problem in an entirely new light. As long as the ontological and religious conceptions of history are juxtaposed, it will be difficult to find a more satisfying solution.

Whenever Catholic philosophers of history address God's direct intervention in the historical process, they proceed with great caution, well aware of treading on dangerous ground. To date they have managed to steer clear, as far as I am aware, of the modern historicistic identification of concrete historical situations with the hand of God.

Sawicki, in his standard work *Geschichtsphilosophie,* deals extensively with the factors of history. Among these he numbers especially man, nature, and the cultural environment. These factors all belong to the creaturely realm. But he adds that besides these there are also transcendent forces or "supra-creaturely factors" at work in history. Divine Providence can assert itself in the historical process in two ways. God can guide events *indirectly,* by determining the innate character of the forces at work in the world order at the time he establishes it, and making this character an expression of his will. This functioning of the creatures in harmony with their nature is the usual form in which God guides world history in conformity to his plan. But God can also intervene *directly*, by giving things a different course than the natural historical process would lead one to anticipate.[33]

According to Sawicki, God's indirect providential guidance permeates the entire creation, from the brutes to the rational creatures. He appeals to the teleology discernible in the natural foundations of history and reflected in concrete historical events; the *telos* that is embedded in history will be attained, if imperfectly: the forces working in the right direction are so strong that humanity is advancing towards its ideal destination despite all forces that resist it. Supernatural influences in the historical process are suggested by both surprising coincidences and isolated events. As an example of the former Sawicki mentions the coinciding of the rise of Christianity and the Roman Empire and Hellenistic culture; and five centuries later when, as a result of the fall of the western empire Christianity's position seems particularly precarious, the church is already strong enough to educate the "barbarian tribes" to whom world dominion now passes.[34]

Bellon, too, who devotes just a few, albeit valuable, pages to the problem of God's direct intervention in history, is of the opinion that certain facts can be adduced, in religious history in any case, that suggest a supernatural intervention by God. He draws attention to the fact that the science of religion has as yet found no explanation for "the belief in God among the earliest civilizations" and that, particularly during the period of the rise of Christianity, events occurred that are not fully susceptible of explanation from natural factors.[35]

Thus far there is little in the views of Sawicki or Bellon that could be called specifically Thomist or Scholastic. It is not my intention, having said that, to say anything at all about the source of these ideas, but simply to observe that they are also advanced in this form by various Protestant writers. They too would take the examples cited, if with certain reservations, to be instances of God's special guidance. Disagreements usually arise the moment God's direct intervention in history is linked with a *concrete fact*. Not only will there be divergence between Catholics and Protestants; there will also be differences of opinion within these groups. And anyone who considers it futile to attempt to trace the *gubernatio Dei* can have a field day pointing out that a certain arbitrariness is involved in selecting certain coincidences and events as proofs of God's special guidance. More important than leveling such criticisms, however, would be to answer this question (and here I restrict myself once again to Catholic philosophy of history): Whence that distinction between God's indirect government and God's supernatural intervention?

---

[33] Sawicki, *Geschichtsphilosophie*, 173f., 183–87.
[34] Ibid., 178–80.
[35] Bellon, "Vrijheid, wettelijkheid en ontwikkeling in de geschiedenis," 74–76.

Sawicki indicates the source of this distinction when he raises the question of the "essential" relation of God to history. God does not enter into the temporal process, as pantheism would have it; rather, he calls the creatures into being out of nothing. The influence of God on the historical process can only be apprehended from the relation of the Creator to the creature: the creatures are proper substances and effective principles, but the course of events remains subject to the Creator's guidance. There are two ways for divine Providence to guide the flow of things: God works *through* nature, in the way just described, but God also works *upon* nature, by intervening directly in the world process.[36]

Sawicki's distinctions and explanations have to be viewed in the light of Scholastic philosophy. The idea of God's supernatural intervention in a historical process ruled by natural factors has its basis in this, that to the natural order is attributed a certain degree of independence with respect to its Creator. Even the relation between the natural historical process and God's supernatural intervention is ruled by the dualism of nature and the supernatural. In order to safeguard both the natural, autonomous character of profane history and the towering transcendence of God above the world process, the *direct* action of God is limited to a few striking, surprising and, in any case, not naturally explainable events.

The apparent irresolvability of the problem of special divine guidance in history stems, in our view, not so much from the limits of human knowledge as from a degree of independence that is ascribed to causal historical relations over against their Origin. One who limits the direct intervention of God to surprising, naturally unexplainable events may give the appearance of being careful not to mix, in an arbitrary and unholy fashion, the natural and the supernatural; but in reality he limits the mighty acts of God in this way to a select category of events.

Catholic philosophy of history generally provides ample treatment of the natural factors operative in the historical process while mentioning only briefly the supernatural factors. Without the latter, history is simply incomprehensible, yet philosophy of history cannot, as such, devote much attention to these factors, since they are really not accessible to natural thought. Dealing with the supernatural intervention of God in history carries one into the sphere of faith.[37] Thus an understanding of the historical process in its totality, in its internal and external coherence, requires both natural reason and faith.

The question now is whether the two form an inner unity. A second question is related to this one: Is the natural course of events, which is governed indirectly by God, knowable to natural reason? For the moment I shall let these questions rest. They arise again naturally in the context of the chapter devoted to the idea of a Christian science of history.

I conclude the following: as long as (Neo-)Scholastic philosophy takes its point of departure in its characteristic conception of nature, it will be able to find

---

[36] Sawicki, *Geschichtsphilosophie*, 186f.
[37] Bellon, "Vrijheid, wettelijkheid en ontwikkeling in de geschiedenis," 75.

only a limited place for the direct intervention of God in the normal process of history; such intervention, despite the blessing it can bring, remains an essentially alien force in the ordinary course of events. God's indirect and direct action in world history dovetail, and both propel history towards its appointed goal, but for all that, they lack a deeper unity.

I stated above that in recent years new directions have proved elusive in the matter of God's direct intervention in history. This statement needs some slight correction. In another field, paleontology, our problem was brought to a head by an attempt on the part of some Catholic biologists to resolve the old creation-evolution debate by accepting the notion of a "new creation." Hedwig Conrad-Martius has written some intriguing studies on the subject, in which she ascribes the regular appearance of new "fundamental types" in the history of life on earth to *Neuschöpfung,* the result of the supernatural intervention of God in natural events. Having once been introduced into natural history, such "fundamental types" are able to develop themselves further on their own.[38]

As in philosophy of history, one encounters here, too, in philosophy of the life sciences, the idea of a self-reliant nature, the normal development of which is regularly interrupted or deflected by a direct, creative act of God.[39]

The entire doctrine of a supernatural, divine intervention in the development of life and history has its source in the conception of nature: having once granted it a certain independence with respect to the Creator, one is forced to appeal to a "higher guidance" in order to explain the rise of new, naturally unexplainable forms of life and surprising turns in history.

Unity might be restored to the historical process by keeping the supernatural factor out of it and equating God's providential government of history with his *indirect* action. Such a solution is attractive because it seems consistent with the honor of God and puts an end to countless theoretical difficulties and idle speculations. Yet the objections to such a conception are even greater. The basic mistake in the theories of Sawicki and Bellon lay, we found, in their assumption of the autonomy of nature. As a corrective to their view they accepted the direct intervention of God, which they regarded as knowable, through faith. But anyone who denies the special guidance of God in history or, at any rate, regards it as unknowable, is in fact left with nothing but an autonomous nature or history and a merely general acknowledgment of God's providence in history.

But must we accept either of these standpoints? A thoroughly religious conception of history reveals still another possibility. It shows us history as a whole, including what is said to be governed only by the so-called natural factors, as effected directly by God. It does not limit God's wonders to surprising, striking events but sees reality in its entirety as dependent in the deepest

---

[38] See Conrad-Martius, *Ursprung und Aufbau des lebendigen Kosmos,* 329ff., and "Schöpfung und Zeugung," 801–26. [See also idem, *Abstammungslehre* (Munich, 1949), esp. 347–52.]

[39] [For a similar critique, cf. Jan Lever, *Creation and Evolution* (Grand Rapids, 1958), 206–08.]

sense on its Creator. In Deut. 3:3 Moses says, *"So the Lord our God delivered into our hands Og also, the king of Bashan, and all his people: and we smote him."* The passage should be read with the emphasis, "*so that* we smote him." The story relates a normal event of war; nothing is told us about any direct intervention by God. Yet the reality of God was so near to Moses and he lived in such deep dependence upon him that he attributed victory without reservation to divine "intervention."

Many similar examples could be mentioned. Scripture speaks very "naturally" about God's activity in history. When one's heart is but open to God's nearness, he discovers it everywhere, even in so-called profane history. The universal direct activity of God is and remains a profound mystery, which faith refuses to downgrade into a vague acknowledgment of a "higher guidance" but rather accepts *as* mystery. And precisely as mystery it can be the point of departure for radical Christian thought about history.[40]

---

[40] [Cf. below, Part Two, essay 5, "The Divine Mystery in History."]

V/ WORLD HISTORY AND PROGRESS

§ 1. *The Christian idea of world history*

The idea of universal history had its inception in Christianity. Yet in pagan Antiquity, notions of the unity and homogeneity as well as of the solidarity of humanity were not unknown. The basis of this unity was found in the rationality common to all men, which warranted expectations of the rise of a culture of humanity with the entire inhabitable earth as its stage.

These ideas are first encountered in an elaborated form in the Stoics, but the way was prepared for them in the cosmopolitanism of the Cynics. The man of wisdom, according to the Cynics, is not bound by historical ties or traditional political and social relations; his fatherland is the whole world. Among ancient historians more than one author endeavored to provide full descriptions of the peoples he knew about, and Polybius tried to give a coherent account of events by somehow relating them all to the growth and glory of the Roman Empire.

The new element introduced by Christianity was the perspective of an inner coherence in the fragmented course of history. The horizon of the ancient historian remained essentially limited to the diminutive world of his tribe or folk. And even when the Stoics brought the entire inhabited world into view, this did not result in the idea of world history as a meaningful whole embracing past, present, and future and unfolding under the guidance of a divine providence in a multiplicity of events and epochs. Both these notions—that the history of humanity coalesces into a meaningful unity, and that singular events and empires, phenomena and institutions all have historical significance, a particular task in the single process of world history—were the achievement of Christianity. For Christianity taught, by the light of God's Word, that the beginning of history is not to be sought somewhere in a vague mythical past, but in God as the Creator and Origin of all things. The Origin and beginning of history are, in faith, concretely visible. Moreover, Scripture teaches that all events are to be brought into connection with the coming of the kingdom—thus indicating the goal of history. And in the incarnation of the Word history acquires its new, meaning-bestowing center. It is from the incarnation that all peoples and epochs derive their value and meaning. The incarnation was the high point towards which all former ages had hastened, and it constituted history's point of departure toward the second coming of Christ. The entire world-historical perspective of Christianity is expressed by the biblical term "the fullness of time."

Creation, providence, redemption and the unity of the human race, and world history are intrinsically connected; to remove world history from this nexus is to deprive it of its meaning. The beginning, goal, and center of world history are mysterious, but accessible nonetheless to precise knowledge. World history accordingly does not lie enshrouded in myth but discloses itself for Christian faith.

The notion of a profound inner connection between world-historical consciousness and Christian belief appears regularly, in many forms, in Catholic historical, theological, and philosophical literature. In recent years especially, many thinkers have begun to point to the deep gulf between Christian and Greek thought about history.[1] These ideas have become very familiar outside Catholicism as well.[2]

In Catholic philosophy of history the Christian origin of world-historical consciousness has seemed so self-evident that in the years since 1918 very little has been written about the concept of world history. Yet there was occasion enough. For since as early as the middle of the nineteenth century, the idea of the unity of world history has threatened to dissolve into a purely external linking of particular histories, and into a pluralism of cultures. This process began already with the secularizing of the goal of history in the Enlightenment and in German Idealism. It is noteworthy that Hegel was unable to construe world-historical development as anything other than *dialectical*. Positivism of itself recognized only particular meanings of specific histories; that it nevertheless spoke of a goal of world history was possible only because it incorporated into its historical construction the ideal of progress, an idea which was intrinsically alien to it. The philosophy of life completed what positivism had begun: Dilthey and Troeltsch still have a vague sense that something universal lurks behind the many particular historical developments, but Spengler breaks even with this notion: in the place of the idea of world-historical connections he introduces the notion of a strict parallelism of cultural totalities. Western philosophy of history has not accepted this radical elimination of all world-historical thought, but neither has it returned to the idea of an inner unity of all historical events. It is quite likely that the concept of a single universal development will be replaced by the notions of chance "encounters" and random "contacts" between heterogeneous forces and world-historical situations.[3]

Given this development in modern philosophy of history, it seems remarkable that Catholic authors as a rule do little more than note the fact that world-historical thought is proper to Christianity. It is really the more remarkable when one recalls that in Antiquity, oddly enough, people were never able to advance

---

[1] Gilson, *The Spirit of Medieval Philosophy*, 383–402; Mounier, "Le Christianisme et l'idée de progrès," 191–93; Spiess, *Grundfragen der Geschichtsphilosophie*, 133f.; Haecker, *Der Christ und die Geschichte*, 94, 97.

[2] Cf., e.g., Freyer, "Die Systeme der weltgeschichtlichen Betrachtung," 11f.; Huber, *Glaube und Kirche*, 350; Van Schilfgaarde, *De zin der geschiedenis*, 2:291–95. For extensive reflections from a Calvinist perspective that have not lost relevance since their publication, see Woltjer, *Het Woord Gods en het woord der menschen* (1913), 87ff., 268ff.

[3] E.g., Freyer, "Das Problem der Einheid der Weltgeschichte," 181f.; cf. Toynbee, *Civilization on Trial*, esp. the chapter on "Christianity and Civilization."

to the notion of a universal connection or pattern in the history of the nations. This notion, one would think, should have come to them quite naturally. Ongoing historical scholarship indicates that fruitful intercourse and close relations existed between the many cultures of the Mediterranean Sea. The ancient observer was surrounded by world-historical connections yet did not perceive them in that way: they remained an enigma, or were explained in myths.

While the historical facts themselves thus point to an inner unity—indeed, point to it so strongly that one is astonished by Antiquity's inability to see it—these same facts speak also, however, of the opposite; they speak not only of the connection of cultures but also of historical diversity, fragmentation, discontinuity, and divergence. And the evolution of philosophy of history shows that belief is needed in order to discover in history unity, convergence, inner coherence, and meaningful progression towards a final goal.

Here we touch upon a problem that has received little attention thus far from Christian historians. The idea of the unity of world history is still too much a mere postulate of faith (which it primarily is, of course). In the background, however, hovers the difficult question *in what way* the individual, discrete cultures and events are gathered into a meaningful whole and an inner unity. The incarnation of the Word is *the* great turning point in world history, but how, concretely, are the cultures before and after this fact related to it?

Christian world-historical thought is threatened by a discrepancy between the postulate of faith, which holds that there is unity and coherence in history, and the results of historical research, which so far has failed—in the estimation of someone like Hans Freyer[4]—to bring to light any uniform tendency in world history. All the attempts that have hitherto been made to write a world history, writes Christopher Dawson, "have been in fact attempts to interpret one tradition in terms of another, attempts to extend the intellectual hegemony of a dominant culture by subordinating to it all the events of other cultures that come within the observer's range of vision." Why? Because history knows of civilizations and cultures, but not of civilization as such or culture as such. Thus if we rely on history alone we can never hope to gain insight into the inner coherence of history.[5]

I observed above that few attempts have been made on the part of Catholic writers to indicate the inner coherence of history concretely. Yet there are a number of thinkers whose contributions are significant enough to merit a brief discussion in the present context. Besides, they are characteristically Catholic in the way they attempt to solve religious questions in profane history.

Dawson came to recognize, as I stated, that as long as one remains within history it is impossible to resolve the problem of diversity. There is still another reality for Dawson, however: the church as the prolongation of the incarnation. Here we are confronted with a divine organism that is nevertheless a real his-

---

[4] See the reference to Freyer in *Stimmen der Zeit* 143 (1948): 151.

[5] Dawson, "The Kingdom of God and History," 200f. [in idem, *Dynamics of World History*, 273f.].

torical community, with a tradition of its own (the essence of all history), and with its own intellectual culture. Now then, the social traditions outside grace have their value for the supernatural community of the church. And what is more, every nation and every social tradition is consecrated in this high sphere:

And so we have the reception into the Church of Greek philosophy and scholarship, and of Roman law and leadership, until the whole civilized world found itself Christian. The vital thing was not the conversion of the Empire and the union of Church and State, but the gradual penetration of culture by the Christian tradition, until that tradition embraced the whole of the life of Western man in all its historic diversity and left no human activity and no social tradition unconsecrated.[6]

As regards its basic idea, Karl Thieme's conception is very similar to Dawson's. It is the church that welds the cultures together; the earlier stream of civilization flows into the church and thereby acquires a deeper meaning, while subsequent and future streams are likewise marked and consecrated by the church. Dawson and Thieme have the same thing in mind when the former explains *in what way* the church gathers history into an inner unity and the latter is willing to speak of a history of humanity only because Christianity has not remained a supra-historical factor but has exercised a formative influence upon the historical process in the direction of greater convergence. The real bearer of history, according to Thieme, is the history of the West. It is the *one* history, since eventually the historical development of the non-Western European peoples flows into it. Together with their entire tradition, they become a part of the one, western history—thus turning the latter into world history. Western history can fulfill this function because—and here Thieme picks up Dawson's notion—the history of the church, of the people of God, represents in a certain sense among the inhabitants of the earth "the primordial phenomenon, the same phenomenon in the large that Péguy came to see, in the relatively small case of the Dreyfus affair, as an *événement élu,* a chosen event." [7]

Our inquiry began with the question how Christ is to be conceived concretely as the inner unity and decisive turning point of world history. Dawson, Thieme, and, as we shall see, Ross Hoffman and Hilaire Belloc, give a decidedly clear and concrete answer: they point to the consecrated reality of the church, in which at one time or another all historical events converge. For the time being, it is enough to have raised this problem and to have indicated some approaches to solving it. I shall deal with these matters at a deeper level in chapter VII, after first having shown that a similar state of affairs exists in connection with the problems of periodization and progress.

In discussing Thieme's idea of the unity of world history, we unexpectedly encountered another question. Thieme speaks of world history and of the history of the "Occident" in a single breath. To him these concepts are either identical

---

[6] Ibid., 206; cf. 214, 215 [in *Dynamics of World History*, 278, 284, 285].
[7] Thieme, *Gott und die Geschichte,* 273.

or so intrinsically connected that the Occident (*das Abendland*) will be forever the center of world history.

In western culture, according to the Catholic conception, the church occupies the dominant position. It preserves the culture of Antiquity by absorbing and perfecting it in the Christian reality and so incorporating it as an essential ingredient of the western cultural community. The Christian Occident embraces more, however: the emanations of Christian civilization in the non-European continents also continue to be authentically western cultures, even after their external ties with Europe are broken.

In this way the concept of the Occident is freed of its restriction to Europe. Wilhelm Schmidt accordingly distinguishes two senses of the term: a primary one, which is the Occident proper and at the same time the origin of the second, and a secondary Occident, that of the non-European continents.[8]

The problem of concretizing the unity of world history is in fact resolved for various Catholic thinkers by means of the idea of the Christian Occident. Empirical reality may impress upon us the thought of an infinite number of events and discrete histories, but in the idea of the Christian Occident, they say, we have a means at our disposal for apprehending the deeper inner coherence (which far exceeds mere "influence"): historical development. And even though we know of many cultures that have had no relation at all with the Occident, not even an external one, yet once these come into contact with Christian culture and are permeated by it, they become, together with their entire past, world history. In this way the culture of the Occident grows into world culture. Even if it should expand to envelop the entire planet, or be driven from the territory where it first arose, world history will still always be the history of western Christendom.[9]

Thus there must be a truly unique relation between the Occident and Christian civilization. And that in a twofold sense.

In the first place, it is possible to identify a number of factors that were favorable to the rise of the Christian West-European cultural community. God surrounded the formation of the primary Occident with his special care, as it were. All those favorable factors were present in a particular historical arena and in a particular period, namely, the Western Europe of the Early and High Middle Ages. The new culture which originated at that time did not, according to Schnürer, have its center in the old Roman society: this had become too corrupt and rigid to bring forth new formations of culture. Nor could the initiative come from the Franks, since under the leadership of their kings they had become contaminated by the degeneration of Roman society. Eminent importance for the formation of Christian civilization was assumed by the Irish-Scottish church and the British Benedictines.[10]

---

[8] Schmidt, *Rassen und Völker*, 3:458.

[9] Thieme, *Gott und die Geschichte*, 273; see also Schmidt, *Rassen und Völker*, 455ff.

[10] Schnürer, *Die Anfänge der abendländischen Völkergemeinschaft*, 3f. [Cf. idem, *Church and Culture in the Middle Ages*, 188, 285, 335, 345.]

Benedict of Nursia in particular, adds Heufelder, rendered immortal service to the Christian Occident, in a way that certainly would seem most unsuited to the forming of a new cultural community. When all lay moldering about him, Benedict discovered new life by looking to the source from which all life springs: the reality of God. Benedict's primordial significance for the Occident lies in his having searched with all his strength for the *prime* source; to this end it was necessary to flee the world; only in this way could the world once more be firmly bound to God. God placed at the beginning of the Occident a man who was to give it a sure and lasting foundation. The true significance of Benedict and his followers does not lie in their having made important cultural contributions but rather in their having sought first the kingdom of God. In this sense, Benedict of Nursia may be called the "Father of the West." [11]

The spirit of Benedict was especially alive amongst the brethren of his order in Britain. There, and in the Irish-Scottish church, religious idealism and the idea of a Christian culture survived in purity. It was these brethren who saved the Frankish church from worldliness. Thus the real impulse to form a Christian Occident came from Britain. And then the peoples of the European continent understood their calling: under the leadership of Pope and Emperor they united to form a well-knit community. To be sure, it threatened to break up again and again as a result of the decentralizing tendencies so characteristic of the Germanic world, but neither were countervailing forces lacking to drive the peoples of the Occident together. Working in this direction, on the one hand, were their kinship and common Roman traditions, and, on the other, the threat of barbarian invasions from the east and north and from the world of Islam.[12]

But the unity of the Occident has still deeper roots, according to Schmidt. It had been in preparation for millennia. In the third millennium before Christ, the earliest Occidental entity took shape. At that time its basis was primarily economic: it was founded on the mutual interpenetration of a number of artisan and agrarian cultures whose bearers were pre-Indo-Germanic peoples. This economic integration made possible a cultural unity, for which two more millennia were required, to be completed with the unification of the Greek and Roman cultures. During the Middle Ages the Occident was unified for a third time, beyond a purely worldly entity or a universal empire like the Roman Empire, into a union of Faith. Geographically, the center of these three formations varied, but it was always located within the space of the primary Occident. By the High Middle Ages the formation of the western cultural community was completed and, Schmidt concludes, although it was severely mauled in the crisis of the sixteenth century it has been strong enough to beam Christian culture forth to other continents.[13]

---

[11] Heufelder, "Benedikt von Nursia und das Abendland," 131; see also Luigi Salvatorelli, *Benedikt, der Abt des Abendlandes*; idem, *Storia d'Italia*, 3:208–18.

[12] Schnürer, *Die Anfänge*, 2–4. [Cf. idem, *Church and Culture*, 197, 443.]

[13] Schmidt, "Werdendes Abendland," 9–12.

In the formation of the Occident the church had a grand task to fulfill: the cultural entity of the Greco-Roman world was preserved in the church, which was now called upon to salvage the centuries-old culture of Antiquity as the Roman Empire disintegrated.

In speaking of the relation between the church and the Occident, one has in mind, however, an even deeper connection. In the youthful western culture of the Middle Ages something materialized that was to be the *model* for all the periods that followed. It is not the case, as has sometimes been asserted, that the church with its international organization filled the vacuum that was left behind by the Roman Empire when it fell. That is the picture presented by a superficial "history of symptoms." [14] To call the church the source and bearer of the idea of the Occident is to say much more than that it disposed over the technical apparatus to create order and unity in the initially chaotic world of the West. In its very essence the church is universal. Its universality and unity, both supernatural in character, are the qualities that the church radiated into the worldly sphere, thus transforming it into a unified whole. The supernatural universality of the church continued in the profane sphere, be it *suo modo* and imperfectly.[15]

Many factors contributed to the unification of the Occident, but it did not attain its *inner* coherence until the world, in a process of centuries, was brought step by step into submission to God. On this view, the unique significance of the primary Occident lies in its having been the place where the synthesis of nature and grace was achieved. And in this synthesis the western cultural community is a model for the non-European communities.

§ 2. *The incarnation as the turning point of the ages*

World history presupposes continuity, while periodization is based on a certain discontinuity in historical events. World history appears to render every delimitation of historical phases, periods, or epochs illusory. That Ranke disliked periodizations while Huizinga grudgingly put up with them for pragmatic reasons would not seem to be inconsistent, therefore, with the proper character of world history.

And yet the belief will not be go away that the significance of dividing history into periods goes far beyond meeting practical needs, and that discontinuity is just as real in history as continuity. To go a step farther, not only is historical discontinuity a reality; the very nature of world history seems to demand division into periods. It is not when history advances in a uniform pattern leaving no possibility of discovering phases or periods that one can speak of world history, but precisely when combinations of developments are clearly distinguishable from each other and mere succession yields to growth or datable progression.

---

[14] Bauhofer, "Abendland und christliche Kultur," 43.
[15] Ibid., 41–43; Schnurer, *Die Anfänge*, 3.

The concept of world history thus implies two elements that appear to be opposed to each other but that in reality are connected: on the one hand, continuity; on the other, discontinuity, rupture or transition. The one makes it difficult to introduce caesuras into world history, the other renders it possible. The one enables us to regard history as more than mere transitoriness, the other commands our wonder at the diversity of world history.

The synthesis of continuity and discontinuity would seem to be the "transitional" period. Some people recognize little else. They are so impressed by the constancy of change in history that they give up searching for the high point of a period—the phase in which a period manifests its distinguishing feature most purely and clearly—and proceed to speak only of "transitions" and "transitional periods."

The concept of a period requires something in addition to continuity and discontinuity. A third element is needed for a period to be distinguishable from a single event or set of events: one can speak of historical phases, periods, or epochs only if they display their characteristic features during longer time spans.

Despite the judgment of Ranke and Huizinga, historians and philosophers have continued to search for the correct divisions in history. The most important question concerns the criterion to be employed in distinguishing or delimiting periods from each other. An additional issue is the question whether the criterion must have a bearing on everything that happens or only on what is of world-historical significance.

Upon examining the various principles of periodization, one discovers that they are intimately connected with the historian's worldview. Sometimes a fact or set of events that is considered to be of central importance is made the point of orientation; in other cases the achievement of an ideal, or of an ideal situation, comes to fulfill that role.

Thus the Christian conception of history since the days of early Christianity perceived an intimate connection between historical periods and the progression of God's work in creation and redemption. Such was the common point of departure. Differences arose only in the elaboration. In particular, no consensus could be reached on whether Scripture provides a more or less complete scheme of periodization or does little more than pinpoint a particular fact as the center of world history, a fact which is then to be taken as the point of departure for any further inquiry into the boundaries and defining features of the various periods.

In the period since 1900, H. M. Féret and Charles Journet have represented the first approach and Gustav Schnürer the second.[16] Féret, shaken by the events of 1940, has revived the old question how it is possible, despite the fact that Christ has won the victory, that Satan still wields such tremendous power in the

---

[16] Féret, *L'Apocalypse de Saint Jean*; idem, "Apocalypse, histoire et eschatologie chrétiennes"; Journet, *Introduction à la théologie*, 246f.; idem, "Les destinées du Royaume de Dieu"; Schnürer, *Über Periodisierung der Weltgeschichte*. Both Féret and Journet have been strongly influenced by Father Allo (1873–1945), who provided them with exegetical material in his well-known commentary of 1921 on the Apocalypse.

world. Féret believes he has found the answer in the Apocalypse: "*And white robes were given unto every one of them; and it was said unto them, that they should rest yet for a little season, until their fellow servants also and their brethren, that should be killed as they were, should be fulfilled*" (Rev. 6:11). History is there so that the number of saints may be complete. In Féret's words: "our world is a machine for making gods." [17]

In that same chapter, Féret goes on, reference is made to the main factors that determine world history. They are symbolized by the four horses: the white horse represents the victorious Gospel; the red, black and pale horses stand for war, famine and death. Then there follow in succession the prayers of the martyrs crying out for vengeance; great cosmic events; and the final judgment.[18] Given these main factors, Féret thinks it is possible to indicate the evolution of history. He claims to include history as a whole in his scheme, but from his elaboration it is clear he has mainly church history in mind, though he does make an effort to do justice to profane history as well.

In the light of the Book of Revelation, Féret distinguishes three periods. The first has already ended: it was the period of the struggle of the church against the Beast, the symbol of the Roman Empire. The time of the Beast ended with the fall of the Roman Empire: it is the manifestation of the first great victory of the Resurrected One in history.

The second period is that of the ten kings, who divided the Roman Empire amongst themselves and who were at the same time inspired by the kingdom of the Beast. This period, too, in which we are still living, will end with the victory of Christ and his saints.

Then a period dawns in which Christ and his law will exercise visible dominion over the nations. The struggle between good and evil will go on, but it will be confined to individuals. In the time of the burgeoning of Christian civilization, the civil and religious powers will enjoy peace and bring to expression the complete and everlasting victory of Christ. How long the third period will last no one can predict; probably it will last longer than the other two periods.

One last time, at the end of the age, Satan will be loosed. Then Christ will no longer tarry in exercising full dominion on earth. Satan will be cast out forever and there will be a new heaven and a new earth.[19]

Just how optimistic Féret is, in spite of the dark times through which he himself lived, can be discovered from a closer examination of the second period. It is marked by progressive improvement (admittedly there are many defects in the realization of ideals, but these pertain more to individuals than to institutions): in the feudal principle of personal fealty there is more evangelical truth than in Roman society with its slavery; there is more evangelical truth in the free corporations of the Middle Ages than in the serfdom of the feudal period; more

---

[17] Féret, *L'Apocalypse*, 162, 167 [Eng. trans., 93, 102].
[18] Ibid., 169 [Eng. trans., 105f.].
[19] Ibid., 309f., 320f. [Eng. trans., 204, 207f.]; see also Journet, *Introduction*, 247.

evangelical truth in the freedom for individual initiative introduced by liberalism than in the tyrannical restrictions of the old corporations, and so on.[20]

Féret has been opposed on numerous points by Joseph Huby. Huby has raised well-founded objections not only to his exposition of the Book of Revelation but also to the conclusions Féret draws from it for theology of history.[21] Huby finds in Revelation not so much a succession of periods as a synchrony throughout church history of the progress of Christianity and the world's continual resistance to it. That the dispute between Féret and Huby is not merely exegetical in character is clearly revealed by the closing words of Huby's review article:

So viewed, the Apocalypse appears to us as the book of witnesses: the witness of the glorified Christ about himself, crowning the witness he proclaimed here below; the witness tendered by his faithful, in heaven and on earth, to his sovereign kingship. A book of consolation because it assures us that good shall vanquish evil in the end, that Christ and his saints shall ultimately triumph over all the evil powers of man and the devil.[22]

Huby views the period between Pentecost and the second coming of Christ as filled by what John saw on the isle of Patmos, yet without its having been ordered chronologically by the apostle. Féret, however, believes the Apocalypse describes a chronological sequence of events. It is Roger Aubert who rightly asks whether "precisions" of this sort are not foreign to the true purpose of this book.[23]

This is, indeed, the principal objection to be made to Féret's conceptions. When Scripture is consulted in the way Féret and Journet consult it, something of reverence is lost, as Scripture is utilized to satisfy human curiosity. When Christ foretells what must come to pass in the period between his resurrection and his second coming, he warns repeatedly that he is not presenting the events to come in any particular temporal order. For it is precisely when we think we have securely pinned down a fixed order of events that Christ tells of the sudden, totally unexpected nature of his return. Every time we think we can go ahead and make our calculations, Christ focuses our attention on the power of sin, on his victory, but above all on the necessity of remaining *watchful*. All attempts at discovering a successive order in biblical prophecies—at least insofar as the period between the first and second comings of Christ is concerned—and to read into this a scheme of periodization for religious and profane history invariably prove disappointing; such schemes satisfy only for a short time, usually under the fresh impression of great historical events.

---

[20] Féret, *L'Apocalypse*, 303f. [Eng. trans., 201].
[21] Huby, "Apocalypse et histoire"; idem, "Autour de l'Apocalypse." The second article deals with the status of theology of history; see also his review of Journet's *Introduction*, 138f.
[22] Huby, "Apocalypse et histoire," 99f.
[23] Aubert, "Discussions récentes autour de la Théologie de l'histoire," 147.

From this it does not follow, however, that the passages of Scripture pertaining to the end time would be of no value for periodizing world history. What is needed, however, is a different point of departure from that of Féret and Journet. That brings us to a second method of dividing history on the basis of Scripture.

Quite naturally, interest in periodization increases towards the close of a century. Around 1900 a great deal was said about it in scholarly publications. Of abiding interest is Gustav Schnürer's rectorial address on the subject of the periodization of world history.[24] This oration attracted a great deal of attention and had considerable influence on Catholic historical writing in the ensuing years.

According to Schnürer, only historical peoples are eligible for inclusion in world history, and for the division of history only the developments of those peoples who have contributed to human culture in general. Its inception must be sought in the Near East; and the hub of today's flourishing culture is Western Europe.

In the Christian conception, Schnürer explains, Christ is not only the initiator of a new religion but also the founder of a new cultural ideal. The middle point or center of history is given in Christ, also insofar as the natural order is concerned. He is the great turning point of world history. Before Christ, the concept of culture remained limited and one-sided. It is Christianity that first teaches a world-historical way of thinking: Christianity is the bearer of an idea of culture that is valid in the same manner for all humanity, for all nations and classes. This difference in the concept of culture, says Schnürer, is in itself a sufficient basis for making a division between a "Pre-Christian Ancient Period," whose subdivisions pertain only to national cultures, and a "Christian Modern Period," which does admit of further periodization.

The latter, then, can be further divided. Until the nineteenth century there is an "Occidental Period," so called because the nerve center of world culture was Western Europe. But from this century onward, culture, in conformity with the command of Christ, diffuses in every direction and becomes world culture.

Within the "Occidental Period" a distinction must be made between an "Ecclesiastical Period" (the Middle Ages), a "Political Period" (the Modern Age), and a "Social Period" (the Nineteenth Century). The first of these must be so designated because the church was then the preeminent, authoritative agent in public and private life. In the following period, political objectives determined the course of developments, and political powers attempted to dominate religious and intellectual life, the legal order, the whole of culture. The third period brings better times for the church, for a new factor makes itself felt, the social; the instruments of ecclesiastical power are by nature not so much political as they are social: was it not through its social impact that the church triumphed over the Roman Empire?

---

[24] Schnürer, *Über Periodisierung der Weltgeschichte*; Freiburg, 15 Nov. 1900.

Periods of transition and preparation occupy an important place in Schnürer's periodization scheme. The first six centuries after Christ are merely a transitional phase leading to the Ecclesiastical Period. The name Christian Antiquity can be maintained for this period because it is the oldest Christian period and because Christianity allied itself with Antiquity at the time for the purpose of assimilating the cultural treasures of Antiquity in order to salvage them from the ruins of the Roman Empire.

The Political Period, too, had its time of preparation: towards the close of the Middle Ages the papacy, at the price of its independence and authority, sought the support of the political power of the king of France.

As for the Social Period, it is really nothing but a transition, namely, to the Age of World Culture.

Schnürer remains faithful to his insights in his later, major works, although he does go on, as the fruit of extensive study, to subdivide further and to characterize the periods more precisely. I have summarized his conception at some length because he has attempted to make a generally accepted Christian idea— that Christ is the center of history[25]—a point of departure for periodizing not only church history but world history as well. Schnürer is one of the few who have gone beyond an avowal that the incarnation of the Word is the all-controlling fact of world history, to a genuine attempt at orienting concrete historical events to it. The attempt is welcome, and it commands respect. It is not to be expected, however, that a problem so inherently difficult will yield readily to a satisfying solution, especially after the Christian point of departure has rendered it even more complex. In developing his approach Schnürer has encountered difficulties that are somewhat camouflaged by his fluent argumentation. He notes one such problem himself: the absence of sharp boundaries between successive periods would seem to render every scheme of division illusory.

For his periodization, then, Schnürer takes the incarnation of the Word as his starting point. In the sequel, however, this criterion does not remain exactly the same, for the church comes to take its place. From a Roman Catholic point of view this discrepancy will be of but little consequence, since incarnation and church exhibit strong continuity; but for those of another mind, Schnürer's scheme thereby becomes less acceptable. Furthermore, the second criterion, the church, is hardly adequate: it only works for the Ecclesiastical Period; the very next period already bears a negative relation to this criterion, and the Social Period is but remotely related to it: it is only towards the end of the nineteenth

---

[25] On the Calvinist side see Bavinck's chapter on revelation and history in *Wijsbegeerte der Openbaring*, 95–119 [Eng. trans., 113–41]; and Dooyeweerd, *Wijsbegeerte der Wetsidee*, 2:223 [*A New Critique of Theoretical Thought*, 2:295]: "Adam's fall into sin and Christ's incarnation, although both concern the *root* of the entire cosmos, also signify historical turning-points of all-deciding importance in the history of the world." In recent decades a similar idea has been expressed repeatedly by Catholic theologians and historians; besides Schnürer, see Bellon, "Vrijheid, wettelijkheid en ontwikkeling in de geschiedenis," 75f., and Sassen, "De opvatting van de geschiedenis bij de Scholastieken van de 12de eeuw," 55.

century that the inroads of the church on societal life gain momentum. The Modern Period may have a positive appellation, it is true, as Political Period; but it is meant negatively with respect to the criterion. I concede that there is no scheme of periodization in which this negative element can be avoided if a uniform criterion is applied throughout, but surely Schnürer's is inadequate at this point: it is precisely in the sixteenth and seventeenth centuries that religious forces were released which greatly enhanced Christianity's historical impact. Schnürer arrives at his unfavorable assessment of the Political Period because it stands out in such sharp contrast against the heyday of the Roman Catholic church, the High Middle Ages, and because he is not sympathetic to the age of the Reformation.

While the flaws and difficulties just noted—amongst which might also be reckoned the numerous transitional periods—are consistent with Schnürer's Catholic worldview, there is another difficulty which applies not just to his scheme but to every periodization based on the incarnation of the Word. When Schnürer calls the first six centuries a transitional period there is something less than satisfactory about such a label. Evidently, he was at a loss as to what to do with this period, and not just because he made the church his second criterion. Those first centuries, the first three in particular, do not seem to fit into any Christian scheme of periodization. If a division of history into periods is to be scientifically useful, it must not be imposed upon concrete historical development from the outside but must be suggested, as it were, by that development itself. Now then, Christianity confesses that Christ's advent on earth is the great turning point of history, but it takes centuries before Christianity becomes a power of world-historical significance, or, to put it in other words, until it effects an actual turnabout in the course of history. The world rushes on for several hundred years without appearing to pay much regard to Christ. The two touch incidentally, but not in such a way as to provide a guideline for periodization.

The main result of our inquiry into the problem of periodization is the same as the one we reached in connection with the idea of world history. In faith we know, as Christian historians, that the unifying center and decisive turning point of world history is given in Christ. However, when confronted with the need to show all this in history concretely, we face seemingly insurmountable obstacles. I would criticize Schnürer, not for failing to find a satisfying solution at the first attempt, but for thwarting our understanding of the difficulties by seeing solutions too quickly and too easily.

If I have raised many objections to the conceptions of Féret and Schnürer, I have done so not out of a desire to be critical but from a wish to discover what is essential in the problem of drawing up a Christian scheme for periodization. It is regrettable that not a single Catholic scholar has addressed this question in sufficient breadth and depth for at least the last half century.

§ 3. *Christianity and the idea of progress*

The times are inauspicious for the idea of progress. Yet this idea must have great hidden reserves of endurance. It has been much maligned in recent decades, and yet many have been unable to free themselves of it. And did it not once seduce an entire century?

Its acolytes are found in Christian circles too. So, also, are its adversaries. From this fact we may infer at once that ascertaining the relation between Christianity and the idea of progress will be no easy matter. On the one hand, Scripture teaches us the awesome power of sin until the end of time, and the expansion of the kingdom of Satan. On the other hand, it is no less certain that Christ *has* won the victory and that he propels history towards the full unfolding of the *Civitas Dei*.

Optimistic and pessimistic conceptions of history would appear not to exclude each other but to be reflections of the two realities: the power of sin, and the salvation won by Christ. Here if anywhere the theme of creation, fall, and redemption is particularly decisive for one's world-historical expectations. If evil is given with the world itself, it is well-nigh impossible to be left on this earth with any hope for this world; one's conception of history must in that case certainly be pessimistic. Conversely, if the world in its essence is regarded as not touched by sin, then the prospect can be hopeful in two respects: natural good has been preserved, and supernatural good can once again be granted through salvation.

With that, the two questions to be dealt with in this section are in a way already answered: How do people in Catholic circles regard the relation between the optimistic and pessimistic conceptions of history? And what is the basis for their optimism? Or to put it another way: Why does the Catholic outlook on history strike an outsider—and not him alone—as predominantly optimistic?

It would not be difficult, given the structure of the Catholic worldview, to give an immediate answer. However, to achieve a clearer picture I want to seek a solution to the questions via some of the newer theories.

In 1947 a remarkable article appeared on the "mediation of the Church" and the "mediation of History." [26] The excessive optimism of the author, Father Montuclard, may strike one as extraordinary; yet, recalling the customary expositions of the value of history for the kingdom of God, one suspects that many greeted the article with approval.

One can already tell from the title that there are two realities, Church and History, which work together to bring about the salvation of humanity.

History in Montuclard has the very broad meaning of profane activity. And this, now, is man's distressing problem: that he has been placed in both the profane realm and the church, and that these convey humanity as a whole in different, sometimes even contrary, directions.

---

[26] Montuclard, "La Médiation de l'Eglise et la médiation de l'Histoire."

Or is there still a possibility that history and church work together for the same salvation of humanity? The answer can be affirmative: history has its role to play in the *mysterious* fulfillment of the plan of salvation.[27] The church actualizes salvation directly and specifically, while history brings salvation only in an indirect manner. We are not forgetting, says Montuclard, that there is but one mediator of salvation, Christ; but the stream that springs from him is channeled into two beds, Church and History.[28]

But how, in that case, are the two related, and just how does salvation come to humanity through the "mediation of history"? In the first place, history has the providential function of opening man to the spiritual life and making circumstances more favorable for the blossoming forth of salvation. Montuclard calls this the "sociological role of history" and the "sociological preparation of salvation."[29]

In this sense, however, history is still no mediator of salvation. It becomes a mediator, properly speaking, only in providing those who have no religious affiliations with faith and hope in the form of the belief in progress. Granted, it is not salvation in the full sense that people receive in this way, but perhaps we stand before a new epoch in which the church will have to be alive above all to the meaning of the history that God has wrought outside the church, in other religions and in great cultural movements. "The Church's principal concern," Montuclard writes, "will be gratefully to *recognize*—in order to animate them *from within,* to rectify them, to reveal to them the dimensions of Christ—the stages by which the world and mankind have been marching towards Salvation, total Salvation, the Salvation of God in Jesus Christ."[30]

It was Daniélou who immediately challenged this optimistic view. Against Montuclard he argued that the belief in progress often entails the negation of every religion; that it is the great sin of our time; and that it has been an obstacle to many who might otherwise have come to God.[31]

There is another form of optimism that bears a resemblance at some points to Montuclard's conception of history: the evolutionism of Teilhard de Chardin.

In recent years, evolution has been one of the liveliest topics in Catholic circles. The views of Father Teilhard de Chardin in particular have attracted wide interest. Now, adherents of evolution and the evolution dogma usually do not restrict themselves to the natural sciences: they include the whole of reality in all its aspects in the development, which may or may not be progressive. Teilhard de Chardin, too, draws the whole universe into a unitary evolution.

Teilhard's break with earlier evolutionism accordingly does not lie in the scope but in the nature of the progressive development. He claims to have

---

[27] Ibid., 11, 15, 21.
[28] Ibid., 23.
[29] Ibid., 21.
[30] Ibid., 22, 31.
[31] Daniélou, "Christianisme et progrès," 399f. [Cf. idem, *The Lord of History*, 85–95.]

broken with the *materialistic* conception of evolutionism. Scientists made the mistake, so he says, of neglecting the "human phenomenon." Man appeared on the scene last, thereby becoming the "head" phenomenon; and that provides the key to solving the problem of evolution. Teilhard's conceptions all go back to the fundamental proposition that *the universe is evolution*. This evolution is marked by increasing complexity which at the same time involves ascending to greater consciousness and freedom: "evolution moves towards spirit." [32]

Evolution obeys the law of continuity, but within this continuity there are necessarily discontinuities—which is to say that every time evolution has progressed to a certain degree of complexity, the plan has to change and a transition takes place within the continuity: for example, from atom to molecule, from molecule to cell, from cell to lower organism, from lower organism to higher organism, and so on.

The "major discontinuity" produces the appearance of man, for with him, spirit established itself on earth. Did evolution come to a halt at this point? That would conflict with the evolutionary nature of the universe. Even less conceivable would it be for the process of evolution to reverse itself. Nor is that all. In every phase and in every synthesis, evolution conserves everything that previously existed. This means that in the synthesis now at hand, the freedom of the human personality that was gained with the appearance of the human spirit will be respected. To guarantee this will be a formidable task as the new synthesis is being formed to give birth, not to a superman (*surhomme*), but to "humanity." For at this stage the problem is: How can human personality be preserved in an all-embracing human community? Teilhard answers: Only through love; and only in an indirect manner, for the new synthesis will only be possible under the aegis of a supra-personal center that transcends the stream of evolution, namely, God. The transcendence occurs in such a way, however, that God is not an "ideal" center but one who "actively attracts" and who makes his activity felt from the outset.[33]

This supra-personal center is not merely the physical and organic Prime Mover; it is no less the psychical First Cause in a person-to-person relation. And so the "Christian phenomenon" presses upon us in the "human phenomenon." "Historically, from the time of the Man Jesus onwards," Bruno de Solages explains, "a phylum of religious thought has appeared in the human mass, a phylum whose presence has not ceased to exert influence, ever more widely and deeply, on the developments of the Noösphere."[34]

The incarnation is the culmination of the mighty movement from matter to spirit; Christ is the Alpha and Omega, the summit of the whole universe.

---

[32] Teilhard de Chardin, passim (the terminology remains consistent in all his works).

[33] De Solages, "La Pensée chrétienne face à l'Évolution," cxiii. This article by a disciple is a concise summary of Teilhard's oeuvre. For a specimen of Teilhard's speculative powers, see his article of 1937, "La Crise présente." [See today his *Christianity and Evolution* (New York, 1971).]

[34] Ibid., cxiv.

In this irresistible evolutionary movement towards the summit, scientific and technological progress also has its place. It contributes to the coming of the new heaven and the new earth. It guides humanity towards unity and universality. It liberates man from bondage to matter and makes the world, through evolution, more spiritual and more "pneumatic." Thus progress prepares the world for its glorification.

No doubt some people find Teilhard's ideas rather hard to digest at first. Such unbridled evolutionism and optimism are strongly reminiscent of the mental climate of the nineteenth century. Yet it would be a mistake to regard Teilhard de Chardin as an isolated figure. Philosophers, theologians and other scholars in Roman Catholic circles have found him very inspiring. One need only mention a few familiar names: Bruno de Solages, Charles Moeller,[35] Léopold Malevez[36] and Emmanuel Mounier.[37] Some follow him enthusiastically; others do so with reservations, and from a distance.

Teilhard and his adherents hope to achieve two things with their theory. On the one hand, Catholic scholars can now no longer be reproached for lagging behind in the evolution of science, since the tension between faith and science is hereby abolished, in the sense that scientific results can henceforth be integrated into the truths of faith. On the other hand, the idea of evolution can be upheld, needing only to be purified of its materialistic blemishes. The idea of a spiritual evolution is acceptable to Christian thought; it even leads to the supernatural.

Teilhard de Chardin's transformism may advertise itself as spiritual evolutionism, but it is still evolutionism. It may even wrap itself in Christian dress, but the evolutionary assumption cannot be disguised. For Teilhard, evolution is not a process of becoming and changing within individual structures and communities, but a continuous process overarching all structural differences. It is in the nature of all evolutionism to admit no limit to the stream of development. In reality the idea of a unitary evolution ruling the entire universe remains a phantasm. All particular evolutions, according to Teilhard, issue in the one, progressive development of the universe. The limited nature of any discrete evolution cannot be denied, even by Teilhard de Chardin, so he introduces the concept of discontinuity. Still, the concept of continuity dominates his theory; it is just that one cannot dispense with the concept of discontinuity if one wishes to do justice at all to the structural differences in created reality, and to render at all plausible the notion of a continuous development from matter to spirit, a notion that finds no basis in the data of experience.

Teilhard wants to proceed in a strictly scientific manner; that is, the phenomenal aspect of evolution is supposed to be capable of being understood

---

[35] Moeller, *Humanisme et sainteté*, 220f.
[36] Malevez, "La Philosophie chrétienne du progrès"; cf. above, chap. 3, § 5.
[37] Mounier, "Le Christianisme et l'idée de progrès," 196.

without reference to any metaphysical or theological conceptions!³⁸ He has no desire to deny the value of such conceptions, but they are to *follow* upon the ascertainment of facts, the establishment of a universal evolution. It eludes him, however, that with his discovery of an "evolving universe" and of a continuous-discontinuous progression from the atom to the "Cosmic Christ" he has not stumbled upon a pure, scientifically verifiable "phenomenon" but instead has enunciated metaphysical and religious preconceptions. There could be no objection to this if he were more conscious of the fact that he started out with presuppositions and that these control the rest of his inquiry and its results. He passes these presuppositions off, however, as scientifically verifiable facts, regarding which it is possible and even desirable *afterwards* to engage in metaphysical and theological reflection. Before the debate with Teilhard and his adherents about their transformism and progressism can begin, they will have to recognize that their ideas of an evolutionary universe and of continuous development from one structure to the next are nothing more than preconceived notions. For the correctness of their ideas they cannot appeal to scientific experience; if they wish to avoid creating the impression that these ideas are the result of subjective whim or of a calculated desire to gain scientific respectability, they will have to look for a deeper foundation than the facts as such can ever afford.³⁹

Teilhard de Chardin labors under the illusion that his idea of evolution can and must be accepted by Christians since spiritualism is its basis and the incarnation is incorporated harmoniously into it. But does Christianity admit of being neatly fitted into an evolutionary process without in any way shortchanging its uniqueness or its essential elements? In point of fact, in this evolutionism the idea of continuity overrules the full revelation concerning Christ and his work of redemption. And if something of it is still salvaged, it is because of Teilhard's lack of consistency in upholding the idea of continuous development.

The entire evolution is so natural and self-evident that the supernatural—the culmination of the total process in the Universal Christ—no longer surprises. The supernatural fits so harmoniously into the natural process that one can see in it only a new stage in the evolutionary ascent. The truly supernatural sinks away into the evolutionary process, faded and degraded beyond recognition.

We are happy to believe Bruno de Solages when he says that it is no longer a question here of "a dialectical demonstration from the evolutionary movement itself, but rather of finding out whether one might not discover, through a fresh look at total experience, a response to this appeal"; and we gladly take him at his word when he adds that evolution must not be lumped together with the Christian mystery, which transcends every natural scientific view of the universe.⁴⁰ However, it is possible to let the supernatural remain mystery in name,

---

³⁸ De Solages, "La Pensée chrétienne face à l'Évolution," cix.
³⁹ [For a similar evaluation, cf. J. J. Duyvené de Wit, "Teilhard de Chardin," *Philosophia Reformata* 29 (1964): 114–49; rpt. in Philip Edgcumbe Hughes, ed., *Creative Minds in Contemporary Theology* (Grand Rapids, 1966), 407–50.]
⁴⁰ Ibid., cxiii and cxiv–cxv.

and to elevate it above evolution in name, while at the same time having it dovetail so neatly with the natural order that in the end one cannot tell whether it is a mere extension of nature or whether it belongs to a realm inaccessible to any natural approach.

The tarnishing of the mystery is nowhere clearer than in connection with the work of God. The process of evolution proceeds so smoothly that God's continuous activity towards his creation is entirely overshadowed and reduced to a "final drawing" (*attirance finale*) and influencing.

The fact of the fall into sin does not appear in this evolution. Whatever is difficult to place in the development process or does not harmonize readily with its grandiose culmination is ignored. The evolutionist scheme has no room for the struggle of sin and grace, only for a tension between matter and spirit. The evolution is a *spiritual* evolution, one in which the incarnation fits well because (once it is understood as a union of the divine with the natural) it signifies continuity and culmination. Sin, however, and salvation through the cross, are not so easily worked into the idea of continuous development.

While calling attention to Teilhard de Chardin's substantial influence on Catholic thinkers, I must not fail to mention the criticism that many have leveled against his evolutionism and progressism. Henri Lusseau has voiced some of the same criticisms that I have just presented above.[41] Roger Aubert has expressed his objections in eloquent formulations: in this progressism there is an absence of true religiosity, of any sensitivity and respect for divine majesty and transcendence; the glorification of temporal values entails the danger of expecting everything from man's ability and of forgetting that it is God who draws us; finally, the fact that man is a sinner cannot but be relegated to the background.[42]

The rejection of Teilhard's ideas has not been the end of the matter. Some have looked for a positive solution to the question of progress that would not shortchange the supernatural. As he takes up the subject in *Progress and Religion* Dawson draws a sharp contrast between the secularized idea of progress and the Christian religion: though he would not deny the reality of progress, the true progress of history is a mystery that is "fulfilled in failure and suffering. . . ."[43]

Daniélou is afraid the idea of progress is a fortress that people retire into when confronted with God in order the better to resist him. Like Dawson, he regards progress—in its profane form at any rate—as a threat to the faith. This he wants to avoid even while preserving the notion of progress, since he regards it as belonging to the essence of the Christian religion. Montuclard and Teilhard may situate progress primarily in the profane, as a product of human effort, but Daniélou protests that Christianity—which is to say, the event of salvation with the incarnation as its center—is the primary form of history; civilization simply

---

[41] Lusseau, "L'Évolution spirituelle," 23–26.

[42] Aubert, "Les grandes tendances théologiques entre les deux guerres," 34f.

[43] Dawson, "The Kingdom of God and History," 216.

follows in the wake of the church. Profane progress, understood in a qualitative sense, must be consecrated in the church. Thus there is twofold progress: progress in Christianity and progress in the profane. The former is primary; the latter acquires meaning only through subordination to the former.[44]

According to Daniélou, progress has in fact retired into the supernatural order. Some have called Daniélou's conception "eschatological." I think this is less than accurate, since the progressive advance from creation to the consummation of the ages, at least in the course of salvation history, is very real to him. Nor can "eschatologism" be attributed to Marrou when he views the transfiguration as not taking place until *after* the resurrection. Marrou does not deny progress; what he denies is a harmonious continuity and natural transition between human effort and the transfiguration: between them falls the total reversal, the great catastrophe.[45]

Upon hearing Aubert, Daniélou, Lusseau and Marrou warn against "evolutionists" and "progressists," one wonders what is really at stake: the degree of optimism and its sources, *or* the negation or acceptance of the idea of progress? Aubert and others do not oppose the idea of progress as such, and they accept a moderate optimism. But the excesses of evolutionism they vigorously resist, believing that evolutionism, even if it does not explicitly deny fundamental truths of faith, nevertheless poses a serious threat to such truths and seriously degrades them. They anxiously wonder whether the idea of continuity associated with transformism is not dominant to such a degree that the otherness of the supernatural world is not lost in it, and whether this whole school of thought does not undermine the primacy that the supernatural should enjoy in the Christian life. Does it not underestimate the effects of sin and the great power of Satan?

Catholic thought rises in protest whenever the supernatural either threatens the natural order in its autonomy or is itself is made natural. By the same token it will oppose any conception of history that disturbs the balance between optimism and pessimism. The characteristic Catholic viewpoint is therefore represented neither by Teilhard de Chardin, who falls into excessive optimism by making the supernatural all too natural, nor by Daniélou, who depreciates the autonomy of historical development on the profane level. More typical of Catholicism is the position taken by Aubert when he concedes that Teilhard's conception contains much that is good and much that is true but at the same time fears it is dangerous because it contains too little of religion and too much of optimism.[46]

In summary, we may conclude that Catholic conceptions of history tend to be moderately optimistic and that while various important spokesmen for the idea of progress are found among Catholic thinkers they do not set the tone.

---

[44] Daniélou, "Christianisme et progrès," 401.
[45] Marrou, "Existe-t-il une vision chrétienne de l'histoire?" 62.
[46] Aubert, "Les grandes tendances théologiques," 34.

Far more important than the degree of optimism is the problem of the *source* or *sources* of optimism and progressism. By far the greater number of Catholic thinkers[47] hold two truths to be self-evident:

1. The world, nature, and culture are *still good,* despite sin and its grave consequences. The world has a built-in propensity to advance. As Haecker puts it, the world is *fortschrittlich.* And such it has remained, right through the fall into sin, since it has retained its orientation toward the good.[48]

2. The perspective opened by grace is richer. Nature as such may desire perfection, but it will never attain it through its own strength. Perfection is *granted,* as a free gift of God.

The distinctive feature of the Catholic idea of progress is not primarily its moderate optimism but rather its *dual* point of departure: nature, which is still good, and grace. The Reformational conception of history knows nothing of two sources of progress. When it speaks of progress in history, even when the formation of culture is guided by an apostate faith,[49] then it does not thereby mean to say that culture has remained essentially good or retained its *fortschrittliche* character. It bows before the mystery of God's favor: for Christ's sake God has mercy on his world and preserves temporal life from total disruption and disintegration, even when it is lived in disregard of him.[50]

§ 4. *Christianity and historical consciousness*

Ever since the 1930's Catholic thinkers have been very excited about their discovery of a new dimension—that of time or history! The excitement is the more astonishing since the concept of history had long been known, while the overemphasis on the idea of historical development had already precipitated the well-known crisis of historicism. Have Scholastic theologians and philosophers really lived a full century in splendid isolation from Western European thought? It is the more amazing that they should speak of "discovery" here, in view of the fact that for centuries the category of history had been by no means unfamiliar to Scholastic thought and had even occupied an important place in it.[51] What might possibly have occurred to necessitate assigning theology the immense task of "re-thinking" the various problems in terms of the category of history? [52]

Bernard Bartmann—to mention a more traditional thinker first—deals only briefly with the historical aspect of the church in his *Lehrbuch der Dogmatik.* The church is immutable with regard to its *essential* moments, though it is

---

[47] Cf., e.g., Mounier, "Le Christianisme et l'idée de progrès," 206f.

[48] Haecker, *Der Christ und die Geschichte,* 77. He adds, in the vein of Daniélou: the advancement of the creation is entrusted to man, but this precisely seduces him to *superbia* (77f.).

[49] [Cf. Dooyeweerd, *A New Critique of Theoretical Thought,* 2:309–25; idem, *Roots of Western Culture,* 99–107.]

[50] [Cf. S. G. de Graaf, *Promise and Deliverance,* 1:29–55, 242, 402; 2:111f., 215, 342; 3:178, 320; 4:57, 208, 267; et passim.]

[51] Cf., e.g., *Dialogue Théologique,* 40, 68.

[52] Congar, "Tendances actuelles de la pensée religieuse," 50.

subject to *accidental* changes, since it is an organism that undergoes development.[53]

More thought is devoted to the historical aspect of the church by Karl Adam and Michael Schmaus. As they are in agreement concerning the main idea, Schmaus cites Adam frequently, each time with approval.[54]

As against the transcendence of the church, these writers emphasize its historical reality. The church, after all, is always bound to space and time and caught up in a process in which it is constantly exposed to change and evolution.

Thus the church is necessarily subject to history, and one can ask: What does history bring the church? Gain, or perhaps also loss? Both. The church is a plenitude, but not everything can unfold in space and time at once. Now this aspect, then that aspect of church life enjoys special attention. Furthermore, all the peoples amongst whom the church is planted contribute something to its enrichment, enabling it to unfold in a multiplicity of cultural forms.

The very fact, however, that the church must enter history, the world, and culture, Adam observes, constitutes a serious threat to it. For in doing so, it gets entangled in human one-sidedness and sin. Given the variety in peoples and periods, there is always a manifest tendency to absolutize one characteristic of the church at the expense of others. If objectivity, order, authority and tradition were in the foreground with the Romans, the Germanic mentality tended, and tends, towards the subjective and individual. From the Hellenistic-Roman world of culture, the church derived a treasury of thoughts and forms that proved of inestimable value on its pilgrimage through the ages. However, over these acquisitions fell the shadows of power struggles and petrifaction. Germanic Christian religiosity nevertheless produced profound moral earnestness and a creative restlessness, though at the same time a polar tension between objective order and subjective experience. Writes Adam:

The process of historicalizing the gospel has grave consequences. Not only does it veil and conceal the pristine splendor, the luminary power of the Mystical Body of Christ, but it also inhibits and impedes its functioning, in fact it manages in the course of time to disfigure its forms and institutions to such a degree that these seem no longer to reflect the Spirit of Christ but rather an unchristian, even an anti-Christian spirit . . .[55]

In the face of this devastating power of history, however, Christ himself preserves his church. The threat posed by history necessitated special divine measures to keep the church from perishing. Thanks to supernatural protection, it is invincible. In fact, even the damage inflicted on the church by history is

---

[53] Bartmann, *Lehrbuch der Dogmatik*, 2:180.

[54] Schmaus, *Katholische Dogmatik*, III/1:110–27, frequently citing Adam, "Das Problem des Geschichtlichen im Leben der Kirche." [Cf. M. Schmaus, *Dogma*. Vol. 4: *The Church: Its Origin and Structure* (New York, 1972).]

[55] Adam, "Das Problem des Geschichtlichen im Leben der Kirche," 74f.; cf. idem, "Le mystère de l'Église," 44–46; Schmaus, *Katholische Dogmatik*, III/1:114–16.

turned to good by the work of the Spirit of Christ. Thus the storms that raged against a worldly papacy in the Late Middle Ages were a means in God's hand to restore it to a purely spiritual primacy. In the final analysis, history touches only the external, visible side of the church. The visible institute is but the instrument of the far more exalted mystical body of Christ. This, says Adam, is the heart of the matter when speaking of the church.[56]

In the conceptions of Adam and Schmaus about the historical aspect of the church, we are struck by two elements. History enriches the church, giving it the room and opportunity to blossom. Nevertheless, these writers accentuate the dangers that imperil it and the damage that it incurs in its contact with the world of culture; it is thanks only to the supernatural intervention of God that the ravages inflicted by the storms of history are not greater. History is *no essential element* of the church. In the church, changeless eternity is married to eternally changing time. The kingdom of God, the mystical body of Christ, remains forever exalted above history.

Challenging both views just described are new currents in Germany, France, and other countries. The New Theology in particular advocates a "re-thinking" of theology from the vantage point of history. Notably, Henri de Lubac, Jean Daniélou, and Bruno de Solages have made their mark on this score through their studies on the relation between history and Christianity.

A number of factors have led to this recent, rapid development. In the first place, there is the strong historical—even historicistic—streak in modern thought, which is closely related to the far-reaching and rapid succession of shifts in the cultural picture in the western and eastern worlds. Secondly, there are the efforts currently being made in Catholic circles to form a new historical ideal that will answer to the needs of our time, an ideal that deviates clearly from the sacral cultural ideal of the Middle Ages yet that is nonetheless authentically Christian. Finally, to mention no more, there is the influence of transformism or evolutionism—which presents itself as being spiritual in contrast to mechanistic and materialistic evolutionism: the idea of an "evolutionary universe" transforms the static relation between matter and spirit—between the natural and supernatural orders—into a dynamic, historical process.

The newer approach to history does not deny that historical development has often had a detrimental influence on Christianity. Nor would it contest that Christianity "incarnates" itself, or must "incarnate" itself, in the cultures with which it comes into contact. The objection of the newer history to earlier, more traditional conceptions, such as those of Bartmann, Adam, and so many others, is this: they exclude history on principle from the essence of Christianity; they fail to see that Christianity as such is historical in nature. Calculating the gains and losses of history for the church and demanding of the church that it enter the cultures leaves the main question of the relation of Christianity and history still

---

[56] Adam, "Das Problem des Geschichtlichen im Leben der Kirche," 76f., 80f.

unilluminated, namely, whether the church and Christianity are already tied into history *before* their "incarnation." [57]

Now, whenever this question is answered in the affirmative, history is understood as something more than a succession of events: what makes this succession *history* is the fact that it makes for progress, growth, the "acquisition of value." [58]

The concepts *history* and *historical consciousness*, it is averred, are known only to Christianity. Pagan Antiquity had cosmogonies, or myths of becoming, but it had no world history, because the idea of progress, of movement toward a grand goal from which all that transpires derives meaning and coherence, was foreign to it. Movement and change did command the interest of the Greek philosophers, but they regarded them as nothing but imitations of the unmoving and eternal world of the divine and of ideas. Antiquity regarded movement as cyclical: all that was and is and shall be returns again in the same order, in an eternal recurrence or repetition; the new is excluded on principle. In the cycle, the historical process participates in eternity.

For the person of Antiquity, history is no more than a *magnum carmen* (an epic poem) or a practical example, a series of events from which lessons can be drawn. For the rest, he strives to escape the world of occurrence and change and to rise to another world, one of unchangeable Being. The Greek sage never succeeded in developing a philosophy of history, although he did produce a physics of history: a number of constant factors were inferred from historical material for a restricted area and then, in accordance with these, laws were framed for politics.[59] When in Antiquity one really wanted to think historically, one resorted to the idea of circular periods, the *kukloi* or cycles. The characteristic expression of one's historical consciousness was the notion of a Great Cosmic Year. But this very idea is the opposite of historical thinking: it presupposes endless, monotonous repetition without unity or purpose. Periods of florescence do occur, but the cycle continues irresistibly towards a senseless close. The upshot of all this was a deep-seated pessimism in the Greek outlook on life, a pessimism that sharply distinguishes it from the Christian idea of a hopeful future.

How different everything is in Christianity! Absent here are the monotony of repetition, the fragmentation of evolution, and dismal destruction as the final outcome. Human history, Marrou reminds us, has a goal, a destination: it is heading for its consummation. From the beginning to the end there is progress, constant growth; the road is long, but it is marked by great salvation events, each of which in its own way brings about definitive change, ushering in something fundamentally new. History is guided by God's hand from the creation through the covenant with Abraham to the incarnation. And from here, as from its meaning-bestowing center, God directs history towards its completion, towards the

---

[57] Daniélou, "Christianisme et progrès," 401.
[58] Daniélou, "Les Orientations présentes de la pensée religieuse," 15.
[59] Marrou, "Existe-t-il une vision chrétienne de l'histoire?" 50.

full realization of his plan for the world, towards the ultimate goal of creation, the recapitulation of all things in Christ.[60]

Not all of this was equally clear at the outset to the Christian conception of history. To the present day, the Christian conception has not been able to free itself entirely of Ancient ideas. But the break in principle with Greek and Roman thought did come as early as the first centuries A.D. According to Daniélou, historical thought arose as early as Irenaeus, in whom one finds for the first time the notion of the progressive education of humanity. Irenaeus distinguished two stages: first man lives under the external discipline of the Law, but then comes the period of the Gospel, when humanity is educated for freedom.[61]

Despite this hopeful beginning, Christian philosophy of history in many respects remained tied to the world picture of Antiquity. Augustine did make a fresh breach in the cyclical idea by elevating the incarnation into the central event in history, but essentially he remained true to Antiquity's aesthetic interpretation of history, which saw little more in historical events than a *magnum carmen*.[62] Scholastic theology was acquainted with the idea of an immovable world, but not with the concept of history; in that sense, this theology was a reversion to the period before the Fathers.[63]

The notion that it was Christianity that first discovered history and that historical consciousness first arose in the Christian world will be found in many contemporary Catholic thinkers. Prominent theologians and philosophers have accepted it, be it upon the authority of others or not. I would mention only Étienne Gilson, Robert Grosche, Christopher Dawson, Régis Jolivet, Henri de Lubac, Jean Daniélou, Yves Congar, Anton Hermann Chroust, and Gustave Thils.[64]

Yet it would be incorrect to speak of a collective conviction. More than a few decline to accede to such representations. Some fear risks and cannot concede that history is an essential part of Christianity.[65] Others regard recurrence or repetition as belonging to the essence of history and are therefore less averse to Greek ideas about the relation between nature and history.

---

[60] Cf. ibid., 51.

[61] Daniélou, "Saint Irénée et les origines de la théologie de l'histoire," 228. [Cf. idem, *The Lord of History*, 5.]

[62] Grosche, "Natur und Geschichte," 52f.

[63] Daniélou, "Les Orientations présentes," 10, 15; on this issue see also *Dialogue Théologique*, 40, 68, 87.

[64] Gilson, *The Spirit of Medieval Philosophy*, 383–402; Grosche, "Natur und Geschichte"; Dawson, "The Kingdom of God and History"; Jolivet, "Le Christianisme et l'avènement de l'idée de progrès"; De Lubac, *Catholicisme*, 107–32 [Eng. trans., 67–82]; Daniélou, "Christianisme et histoire"; Congar, "Tendances actuelles," 49f.; Chroust, "The Metaphysics of Time and History in Early Christian Thought," and "The Meaning of Time in the Ancient World"; Thils, *Théologie des réalités terrestres*, 2:14–26.

[65] *Dialogue Théologique*, 40, 68, 87.

Particularly noteworthy on this score is Odo Casel, who on a number of occasions has explicitly addressed the problem of time and history.[66] Casel rejects the cyclical idea in its ancient form. But whereas Grosche locates the basic error of "the Greek conception of history" (to the extent that one can speak of such a thing) in history's being dissolved in nature, whereby it is robbed of its true and proper meaning,[67] Casel is for this very reason attracted to nature because its constant repetition, which occurs in it by virtue of its order, offers a reflection of eternity. Nevertheless, nature does lack something. The image of the circle, the symbol of nature, is simply not able to express perfectly the Christian idea of time. In the Christian life constant repetition does occur, but then each time on a higher plane. That which recurs is neither something absolutely identical nor something completely novel. Casel uses this image: the eternal, divine idea realizes itself in cyclical years which elevate themselves as a screw does with respect to an unmoving center and which therefore have in them something divine.[68]

Here Casel's conception seems to approach that of Daniélou, which recognizes both continuity and discontinuity between successive periods in the realization of salvation. The agreement is more apparent than real, however. Casel applies his conception of time to the liturgical year. It is not temporal development but divine realities that are involved here. The starting point is relative: Epiphany or Easter will serve equally well; or one can start with Easter and end with Epiphany. The temporal moments flow together in the fullness of the divine life. The natural year is a symbol of the divine year. Christ is the new year.[69] One can call Easter the first day, but also the eternal day, and the constant return of Easter symbolizes the eternal aeon.[70]

It is clear that this theology of mystery pays no regard to historical reality's own proper character. It is so engrossed with the divine that it never gives the problem of history and its meaning a fair hearing. It is not the course of history that is deemed of importance but the divine reality it contains. Theology of mystery would be able to gain access to history only if it applied the categories of time and history to the divine itself. And that it would consider outrageous.

Yet, to reject Casel's a-historical approach by no means implies that the newer conceptions of the relations of progress and history, etc., can command our acceptance. For is it correct to say that the Greek and Roman world lacked historical consciousness and that the idea of progress was entirely alien to it?

A review of the writings of those who espouse this position soon reveals that they make many exceptions. Grosche cites Theodor Haecker with approval,

---

[66] Casel, "Le Sens chrétien du temps"; idem, *Das christliche Kultmysterium*, esp. chap. IV on the liturgical year [Eng. trans., 63–70].
[67] Grosche, "Natur und Geschichte," 51, 58–60.
[68] Casel, "Le Sens chrétien du temps," 23.
[69] Ibid., 19, 20, 24.
[70] Michels, *Das Heilswerk der Kirche*, 77–79.

who in his work on Virgil as the "father of the West" shows that Aeneas is someone with a mission to fulfill, and that he knows it: Aeneas does not return home, unlike Homer's heroes. In Virgil's *Aeneid* one is confronted with history, in Homer's *Odyssey* with myth. Grosche attempts to dispense with the exception by (again following Haecker) promoting Virgil to the status of a forerunner of Christianity: in him lives the authentic Christian "virtue" of hope.[71]

Eugène Dupréel, to whom Gustave Thils appeals, points out that Greek thought of the fifth century before Christ was thoroughly permeated by the idea of progress and that in succeeding centuries the notion of a progressive development of humanity was much cherished in certain circles.[72] Emmanuel Mounier notes that the only instance in Antiquity of a "design of movement" occurs in Lucretius, who in the fifth book of his *De rerum natura* describes the history of a race of men that gradually raises itself from the savage state of nature to a life of order and juridical relations. This movement is not meaningful, however, since it obeys only the law of the conjunction and disjunction of atoms.[73]

Finally—to mention no more exceptions—Yves Congar states: "A new understanding [i.e., that things exist not just in accordance with their pure essences but also in temporal situations] was applied, one of which Antiquity had not been ignorant (Aristotle) but which it had scarcely cultivated: the historical understanding, in terms of genesis and development."[74]

In light of the above, the assertion of Daniélou, Grosche, and others that pagan Antiquity was unable to work itself up to the idea of progressive development is an exaggeration, to say the least—as some of them admit, be it indirectly and hesitantly. Herman Robbers, who devoted a separate study to this problem, likewise protests against all generalizations on this score.[75]

Two facts have now to be accounted for, however: first, the fact that the idea of repetition, of the Great World Year, is widely diffused outside Christianity and even predominates there; but, secondly, the fact that the idea of progress can apparently occur quite independently of any influence of Christian belief.

With regard to the latter point, it seems to me that Herman Dooyeweerd points the way towards a correct solution. He poses the question whether the unfolding of culture is possible when it is led by a faith that has turned away from God and, if so, how this unfolding is to be understood.

Dooyeweerd proceeds to argue that one can certainly speak of a radicalization or deepening in the process of apostasy. When this happens, idol worship goes beyond primitive nature religions or veneration of the impersonal and formless. The disclosure of faith caught in apostasy is to be regarded as a process of man's growth in self-awareness, in this sense, that man now apotheo-

---

[71] Grosche, "Natur und Geschichte," 53, citing Haecker, *Vergil, Vater des Abendlandes*, 91–104 [Eng. trans., 70–91].

[72] Dupréel, *Deux essais sur le progrès*, 16; Thils, *Théologie des réalités terrestres*, 2:20f.

[73] Mounier, "Le Christianisme et l'idée de progrès," 189.

[74] Congar, "Tendances actuelles de la pensée religieuse," 49.

[75] Robbers, "De eeuwige terugkeer der dingen"; idem, "De zin der geschiedenis," 237f.

sizes, instead of nature, his own "rational" functions together with science, art and morality. In this process of self-reflection he takes the liberty of projecting his own gods. He grows equally conscious of his freedom to shape his own future. Under the guidance of this process of disclosure within apostate *faith,* a corresponding process of disclosure now also occurs within *culture.*[76]

Thus Dooyeweerd's theory of the deepening of the historical process under the guidance of apostate faith reveals two things. On the one hand, the disclosure of culture and of thought is also possible in a state of apostasy. On the other hand, the deepening and unfolding of faith and of history are bound to the veneration of the creature so long as the process of increasing self-awareness is not illuminated by the divine Word revelation. Dooyeweerd's account makes plain that the idea of progressive development can also occur in a pagan culture. It likewise explains why this idea must encounter its characteristic limits in an apostate faith that is directed towards the creature.

It certainly was no coincidence that the idea of progressive development became widely accepted in the fifth century before Christ at the very time that Greek thought attained to philosophical self-reflection and Greek culture experienced its glorious unfolding.

Given the above, it will be clear that the antithesis is not between an idea of progressive evolution in Christian thought on the one hand and no inkling of it in non-Christian thought on the other. The antithesis can only be this: under the guidance of the Christian faith the idea of progress is focused on the true beginning and end as well as the meaning-giving center of world history; in Christianity the idea of progress thus embraces the whole of history, which it is able to do because it starts with God as the Origin and is focused on Jesus Christ as the Meaning of all history. Under the guidance of an apostate faith, in contrast, the idea of progress can derive its content only from the creaturely; there, if no remnants of the Word revelation have been preserved, it will be unable to discover the only Origin and Meaning of history. If it seeks an origin, it will have to be in the darkness of a mythical past; and if it pursues a goal, it will never be one beyond the horizon of the culture from which it has itself come forth.

As I see it, the view that the idea of progress is unknown outside Christianity and that historical consciousness can only arise in a culture that has been profoundly influenced by Christianity rests upon a confusion of historical and world-historical consciousness, or upon a failure to distinguish sharply between the idea of world history and that of progress. The consequence of this confusion is that, upon failing to discover world-historical consciousness in pagan Antiquity, observers go on to assert that the restricted horizon of Ancient thought likewise rendered impossible any consciousness of progress.

---

[76] Dooyeweerd, *Wijsbegeerte der Wetsidee,* 2:237–55 [cf. *A New Critique of Theoretical Thought,* 2:309–25; idem, *Roots of Western Culture,* 103–08].

It must not be forgotten, however, that apostate thought is capable of discovering certain moments of truth, even though in the very act it thoroughly falsifies them because it does not see reality in the light of the divine Word revelation. Now, the notion of progressive development is one of these partial, misconstrued truths at which Greek and Roman thought arrived. It is accordingly quite unnecessary to resort to strained explanations (such as those of Haecker, Grosche, and others) to account for those elements in the Greco-Roman worldview that point unmistakably towards a certain measure of historical consciousness (to the extent, at least, that this historical consciousness is connected with the idea of progress).

With this in mind, one will no longer regard the cyclical theory that occupied such a dominant position in pagan thought as a total contradiction of the idea of progress. Jolivet observes correctly that the very notion of eternal return implies a certain concept of progress.[77] The idea of eternal recurrence is definitely incompatible, however, with *world*-historical consciousness. Hence *historical* consciousness is indeed encountered outside Christianity, but no *world-historical* consciousness (as many mistakenly believe). There is an indissoluble connection between Christian belief and the idea of world history. That connection is so intrinsic that, given the ever deepening secularization of Western European thought, world-historical consciousness too is languishing and cyclical theories are gaining more and more ground.[78]

But why is it that the idea of world history stands or falls with Christian belief even though the idea of progress also occurs outside Christianity? The reason is that the first idea is a comprehensive idea: it presupposes a conscious knowledge of the true beginning and true end and of the all-determining center from which the myriad of events derives meaning and internal coherence. Once historical reflection has turned away from the divine Word revelation, which is faith's only true source for learning about the beginning, end and center of history, a certain degree of historical consciousness does remain a possibility, but then it will of necessity lack precisely those elements that can weld the bewildering multiplicity of cultures and episodes into a unity. World-historical consciousness does not require a knowledge of all that has ever happened or will ever happen—it may even pass over whole cultures and episodes if they are of no consequence for the development of *world* history—but it does require a belief in God, who, by orienting all history to himself, has fashioned it into a meaningful unity.

The acceptance of a plurality of parallel evolutions implies the denial, if not of every notion of coherence, certainly of unity of beginning and unity of goal. History in that case must break up into a multiplicity of developments lacking all inner coherence.

---

[77] Jolivet, "Le Christianisme et l'avènement de l'idée de progrès," 497.

[78] On the gradual rise of the theory of cultural cycles since Vico's *Scienza nuova* of 1725, see Wolf, *Wesen und Wert der Aegyptologie*, 16ff.

Certainly it is possible, in the absence of Christian belief, to write the history of individual peoples and countries. Apostate historical science, too, can discover connections and influences between particular cultures. In fact, striking differences between cultures, and their mutual contacts and influences, can well prompt apostate thought to search for some deeper unity and coherence. And some sort of unity and coherence can indeed be discovered, up to a point, independently of the Word revelation; pagan Antiquity provides the proofs. Yet all of this has not led, nor does it lead, to world-historical thought. Time and again the history of nations has been oriented to the history of one particular people, and some ideal order of affairs has been located in one particular period, at the price of depreciating all other periods or cultures. In the world-historical conception of Christianity, however, the history of every nation and of every age has its own, meaningful place in the divine world plan.

VI/ THE PROBLEM OF CHRISTIAN PHILOSOPHY

§ 1. *Historical orientation*

The question of a Christian philosophy began to attract attention in Roman Catholic circles as early as the close of the nineteenth century. At that time the question was approached not so much in terms of its own merits as in the context of related problems, such as the relation between faith and science, or between theology and philosophy. From before 1900 until about 1914, it was apologetics and the problem of the limits of human reason that kindled vehement discussions. Blondel's entrance upon the scene dates from this period, as does the heightened interest he stimulated among philosophers for the supernatural.

Only after World War I did the idea of Christian philosophy begin to arouse general interest. The polemics about a *desiderium naturale videndi essentiam Dei* had some bearing on the matter; yet the importance of this question for the problem of the possibility of a Christian philosophy must not be exaggerated, for while the *desiderium naturale* was the central theme for Blondel, it was not that at all for Gilson. And it was the latter who, in his writings between 1920 and 1930, again and again raised the question to what extent Revelation had influenced the shaping of the medieval philosophical tradition.

A heated debate flared up in 1928, and again in 1931, when Emile Bréhier, a professor at the Sorbonne, denied practically every influence of Christianity on philosophy.[1] According to him, it was only "by accident" that mental culture was so intimately connected to religion during the Middle Ages. Christianity has persistently tried to annex philosophy—Bréhier cites Augustinianism, Thomism, Traditionalism and, most recently, Blondelism as examples—but always to no avail: in the final analysis Christianity and philosophy are incompatible.[2]

Resistance to Bréhier's views was practically universal in Catholic circles. While he personally receded rather quickly into the background during the ensuing debate, the growth of interest in Christian philosophical thought was due in large measure to Bréhier. This interest reached its peak between 1930 and 1936. During these years the leading figures in the debate elaborated their conceptions in numerous works and many societies devoted a conference to it.[3] In

---

[1] Bréhier broached the subject in three lectures given in 1928 at the Institut des Hautes Études, Brussels, and in a work published in 1927, *Histoire de la philosophie*, vol. 1: *L'Antiquité et le Moyen Âge*.

[2] Bréhier, "Y a-t-il une philosophie chrétienne?" passim.

[3] I would mention the sessions (1) of the Société française de philosophie of 13 March 1931, keynoted by Jacques Maritain (the report of the debate, participated in by Gilson and Bréhier, appears in the *Bulletin de la Société française de philosophie* 31 [1931]: 35f); (2) of the Société des études philosophiques of 26 Nov. 1932 at Marseilles, keynoted by Blondel (a report

addition, a number of widely advertised and well attended international congresses found it an attractive theme.

It would be incorrect, though, to suppose that all this activity was meant simply to repel an attack. The commemoration in 1930 of Augustine's death unleashed an enormous flood of literature, a noticeable feature of which was a certain tendency to appeal to Augustine in support of a closer relation between the data of Revelation and the discipline of philosophy. This should not be surprising, however, given the increasing influence of this great church father on Catholic thought.[4] But in the end these were merely external and more or less coincidental factors that serve only partially to explain the interest of the foremost philosophers around 1930 in the relation between philosophy and the Christian faith. The entire internal development of Catholic thought had led up to this. Bréhier's attack and the Augustine commemoration merely provided the occasion. Following World War I, the nature-grace problem in particular had become acute, and the question of the possibility of Christian philosophy was just one aspect of it.

Between 1930 and 1936 three French philosophers, Gilson, Maritain, and Blondel, made their initial contributions to the solution of the central problem of this chapter. After that, the problem stayed on the agenda, but neither they nor anyone else was able to come up with any approaches that were really new.

France deserves to be called the classic country of Catholic Philosophy. Important studies of the subject have appeared elsewhere, as in Germany and America, but until now these have all been oriented to the original views of a Maritain or a Blondel or to the brilliant studies of a Gilson. I purposely say "until now," for since the Second World War the idea of Christian philosophy has been a focal point of interest in Italy. Here the results are to be found in the periodical *Giornale di Metafisica,* edited by Michele Sciacca, a philosopher strongly influenced by Blondelism. Moreover, the first three conferences of Christian philosophers at Gallarate (in 1945, 1946 and 1947) were largely devoted to the problem of Christian philosophical thought. It is not improbable that the Italian branch of Catholic philosophy will carry the problem into a new phase. It is also not impossible that the New Theology or the Christian existentialism of Gabriel Marcel will shed new light on the relation between theoretical thought and religion. I am satisfied simply to call attention to these currents, since it is not at all clear as yet

---

of the discussion appears in *Les Études philosophiques* 7 [1933]: 13–44; (3) of the Société thomiste of 11 Sept. 1933 at Juvisy, where A. Forest and A. R. Motte read papers and Gilson, A. D. Sertillanges, and others restated clearly their positions in the debate (for the proceedings, see *Journées d'études de la Société thomiste,* vol. 2: *La philosophie chrétienne*; (4) of the Vereniging voor Thomistische Wijsbegeerte of 14–15 April 1934, addressed by R. Huysmans, L. Steins Bisschop, and L. Buys (proceedings are in *Studia Catholica* [1934], Supplement). Then there were, for example, the Second International Congress of Thomists at Rome in 1936, keynoted by R. Garrigou-Lagrange, and the Eighth International Congress of Philosophers at Prague (1934), where E. Przywara read a paper entitled "Religion und Philosophie."

[4] See esp. the anthology *A Monument to Saint Augustine* (London, 1930), which includes contributions by the eminent Christian philosophers Gilson, Maritain and Blondel.

just where they will end up. I suspect their conceptions will amount to a complete revolution; it remains a question, however, whether they are not abandoning philosophy in favor of theology. Here I shall deal only with the most original and important figures in the debate about Christian philosophy. They are the thinkers after whom the various points of view are usually classified.[5]

§ 2. Pierre Mandonnet

In Mandonnet we find an extreme dualism between faith and philosophy.[6] Although Christianity transformed the world, Mandonnet does not believe it enriched philosophy. Progress in philosophical thought is not owed to Scripture but is the work of reason. The growth of learning is cumulative: each generation profits from what the preceding one has thought and said. With philosophy one finds oneself on a purely rational plane. To take seriously the idea of Christian philosophy would necessarily disrupt the unity of philosophical thought.[7]

Does this mean that Father Mandonnet and his supporters do not distinguish themselves at all, philosophically, from the strict rationalists? By no means; an important difference remains. On purely philosophical terrain, the Christian philosopher does take the truths of Christian faith into account, albeit not positively but negatively. To the Christian philosopher, faith or theology is the negative norm for philosophy; in other words, the revelation in Scripture is for the philosopher a beacon that keeps him from running aground. If there is no agreement between faith and philosophy, that is a sure sign that philosophy is off course. In the hierarchy of sciences, theology occupies the highest position; philosophy, placed lower, can go its way undisturbed so long as it is careful to live in harmony with theology.

Similar to Mandonnet's conception is that of the so-called Leuven School. This school is not, however, homogeneous. Fernand van Steenberghen stands closest to Mandonnet. The expression "Christian philosophy" has a valid meaning for him neither in the sense Maritain gives it nor in that of Blondel.[8] Only when it is taken to mean a philosophical activity engaged in by Christians can the expression be of any utility, but in that case the terminology—so the facts show—is a source of confusion. Still, being a Christian is not without significance for a philosopher; it enables him to devote himself to his research "with perspicacity, with prudence, with serenity." Decisive as well for Van Steenberghen is the notion of harmony: in the measure that philosophy is true

---

[5] For a more detailed account, see Baudoux, "Quaestio de philosophia christiana," passim. The classification Baudoux gives of the various positions is very brief indeed, but he refers to a great deal of literature for further orientation.

[6] Pierre Félix Mandonnet, O.P. (1858–1936) was a specialist in medieval philosophy and founder of the Société thomiste.

[7] The best source for Mandonnet's conception is *La Philosophie chrétienne*, the report of the discussion at the symposium on Christian philosophy held at Juvisy, 11 Sept. 1933, vol. 2 of *Journées d'études de la Société thomiste*, at 62–72.

[8] *Journées d'études de la Société thomiste*, 2:136f.

it will be compatible with and open to Christianity. But in a strict and formal sense, philosophy can never be called Christian.[9]

Léon Noël, one of the leading proponents of the Leuven approach, adopts an intermediate position between Mandonnet on the one hand and Maritain and Gilson on the other. He immediately distances himself from Mandonnet by accepting it as proven by Gilson that the development of medieval philosophy transpired under the decisive influence of Christianity and that this influence accounts for the progress in Western thought relative to Greek thought. But the central question for Noël is: How can Christianity exercise a decisive influence on philosophy without philosophy's ceasing to be philosophy? If Christian doctrines as such were to enter philosophical thought, philosophy would thereby abolish itself. What such doctrines can do is turn the mind of the believing thinker *in a new direction*. In that event, a moment will arrive in which something that was originally an object of faith can present itself as the result of rational thought. Although philosophical truths cannot incorporate any dogmas of faith, they can accord with them. The term "Christian philosophy" is acceptable provided one makes the proper distinctions, but in a formal sense philosophy remains fully autonomous and can never be Christian philosophy. "It is no more possible to speak of a Christian philosophy than of a Christian physics or chemistry or geometry." Only when a philosophical system is considered from the standpoint of its development may one speak, albeit less strictly, of Christian philosophy.[10]

§ 3. *Étienne Gilson*

I come now to one of the most confirmed and influential proponents of a Christian philosophy.[11] Even before Maritain laid the theoretical foundations for it, Gilson had converted many to his views under the impact of the wealth of material he had assembled from the history of philosophy. The study of history, not theoretical considerations, gradually convinced Gilson that a special relationship exists between Christianity and philosophy.[12]

Gilson's idea of Christian philosophy has as its unmistakable background the tension between Thomism and Augustinianism.[13] Sometimes he thinks the two "complete" each other, demonstrating the "infinite wealth" of religious

---

[9] Van Steenberghen, "La deuxième journée d'études de la Société thomiste et la notion de philosophie chrétienne," 554.

[10] Noël, "La Notion de philosophie chrétienne," 337, 340f.

[11] Étienne Gilson was born in Paris in 1884. He taught at the Collège de France beginning in 1931; since 1943 he has been associated with the Institut Catholique de Paris for the history of spirituality. He has earned his reputation principally as a historian of medieval philosophy. [In 1929 Gilson helped to establish the Pontifical Institute of Mediaeval Studies in Toronto, where he taught part-time till 1951 and full-time till 1968. Étienne Gilson died in 1978.]

[12] At a 1931 session of the Société française de philosophie devoted to the idea of Christian philosophy, Gilson related how he came to his position; cf. "La Notion de philosophie chrétienne," 72. [Cf. "What Is Christian Philosophy?" in *A Gilson Reader*, 177–91.]

[13] Ibid., 43, 45f. [Cf. *A Gilson Reader*, 68–81.]

reality.[14] At other times he sees a far-reaching disparity between them. Certainly there is also agreement, particularly as to the basic principles of the total dependence of the creature on God and of the real distinction between creature and Creator. Nevertheless, they go their separate ways in ontology (with respect to the doctrine of ideas), in anthropology (with respect to the relation of soul and body), and in epistemology (the doctrine of illumination in Augustine versus the theory of the *intellectus agens* in Thomas).[15]

The philosophies of Augustine and Thomas are both philosophies of the concrete, but they differ in their attitude towards it. Augustine takes the concrete as it presents itself in all its complexity, whereas Thomas analyzes it. That is why the concept of Christian philosophy poses no particular difficulties for Augustine: faith and reason are not two separate orders that have to be connected somehow; the two, while distinct, are nonetheless so much a unity that whenever a Christian philosopher truly expresses himself in his philosophy, that philosophy will be truly Christian philosophy. To Augustinianism belongs the honor of having always upheld the correctness of this expression. Thus Gilson can conclude, in agreement with Augustinianism, that a Christian philosophy will be integrally Christian and integrally philosophical, since one can never say: This is where philosophy stops and Christianity takes over.[16]

Gilson has worked this conclusion out more fully. He finds that the historical problems associated with Christian philosophy converge in this question: Can the systems of rational truths that we subsume under the rubric Christian philosophy be explained from the internal development of philosophic thought (Mandonnet's position), or are they incomprehensible unless one takes the influence of Christianity into account? If the latter view is correct, how can the nature of this influence be established more precisely? Can the significance that one philosopher had for another be put on the same plane as, say, the fertilization of medieval philosophy by Christianity?

Gilson grants that philosophy must avoid certain avenues because Scripture shows them to be in error. Thus he fully upholds the Word revelation as a negative norm for philosophy.

Yet the real meaning of the notion of Christian philosophy does not lie there. Nor is a philosophy Christian by virtue of the fact that it is compatible with Christian values; there are many elements in the thought of Plato and Aristotle that can be harmonized with Christianity, yet they have not a trace in them of Christian philosophy.

Christian philosophy appears only when Christianity plays an active role in philosophical thought, bearing fruit in systems of rational truths that are inexplicable without reference to Christianity.[17] In such a philosophy reason

---

[14] Gilson, "The Future of Augustinian Metaphysics," 309 [in *A Gilson Reader*, 99].

[15] Gilson, "Réflexions sur la controverse S. Thomas – S. Augustin," passim.

[16] See Gilson, as reported in "La Notion de philosophie chrétienne," 45f.

[17] Ibid., 48; cf. Gilson and Böhner, *Die Geschichte der christlichen Philosophie*, 1.

continues to occupy the central position, but it gladly accepts the Christian revelation as an "indispensable auxiliary to reason." For philosophy to deserve the name Christian "the supernatural must descend as a constitutive element, not into its texture, which would be a contradiction, but into the work of its construction." The various philosophical systems that have undergone the influence of the Christian religion remain species of the genus philosophy.[18]

In the process of influencing, Gilson distinguishes two possibilities. Christian philosophy can draw truths from Revelation and transform them into truths of reason. Or it can adopt concepts from ancient philosophy and assimilate and transform them, so that they acquire a Christian stamp and are "completed."

The most interesting but at the same time the most critical point in Gilson's theory is this: How does the transition take place from truths of faith to truths of reason? To this question Gilson replies: Revelation offers its truths to reason, which accepts, deepens, and transforms them into a "state of rationality." What was initially the insight of faith becomes, in the process of transformation, rational conviction; it becomes demonstrable to reason.

Gilson's book, *The Spirit of Mediaeval Philosophy*, provides a wealth of illustrations. One may suffice here. The notion of "creation" was unknown to philosophical thought before the coming of Christianity. It is Scripture that first enriched philosophy with it. This process of enrichment and reception required centuries, and in a certain sense it culminated in Thomas's attempt to offer a rational proof of creation.[19]

It is in this light that one must interpret Gilson's well-known expressions "revelation begetting reason" and "the rational fecundity of [the Christian] faith." Likewise, it is in this light that Gilson wishes to read Augustine's *credo ut intelligam* and Anselm's *fides quaerens intellectum*.[20]

The transformation process, however, remains obscure, even with Gilson's more precise explications. I cannot imagine just how truths of faith can be transformed into a "state of rationality." Gilson asserts that this process has occurred, and that it can continue, but he fails to show *how* it is possible. I am disposed to say against his position that Gilson places human thought before a task that is far beyond its capacities. Before reaching a final judgment, however, I want to examine the conception of Jacques Maritain, who was a kindred spirit of Gilson's and who further elaborated the ideas they both shared about the relation of Christianity and philosophy. Gilson always defended his insights with conviction and skill, but when the versatile Neo-Thomist Maritain offered him support in the form of a deeper theoretical grounding and a few corrections, he accepted it gratefully.[21]

---

[18] Gilson, *The Spirit of Mediaeval Philosophy*, 37.
[19] Ibid., 69–80; see also *La Philosophie chrétienne*, 63–72. For Gilson on the transformation process, see the discussion report "La Notion de philosophie chétienne," 47f.
[20] See Gilson, as reported in "La Notion de philosophie chrétienne," 48.
[21] Ibid., 72.

§ 4. Jacques Maritain

Gilson had observed that Christianity had had a profound influence on the history of philosophical thought. Maritain accepted Gilson's historical insights but did not wish to be satisfied with that.[22] He attempted to make the factual influence of supernatural truths on philosophical thought comprehensible by undertaking a theoretical analysis of the nexus of problems associated with the relation of Christianity and philosophy.

To clarify the problem, Maritain took as his point of departure the distinction between an "order of specification" and an "order of exercise," or, better, between the "nature" of philosophy and the "state" in which it exists.[23] He clarifies the difference in this way: Napoleon as victor and Napoleon as prisoner on St. Helena had the same individual *nature,* but the *state* in which Napoleon existed was different in the two cases.

Philosophy by nature cannot be called Christian, since it is dependent on the Christian faith for neither its objects, nor its principles, nor its methods.[24] However, when considering the essence or nature of philosophy one must not lose sight of the fact that one is dealing with an abstraction. It was the error of the rationalists and also of the Neo-Thomists that they invested this abstraction with a concrete existence. When considering philosophy in its concreteness one's assessment cannot be restricted to its "nature." Philosophy exists in a certain "state," which is dynamic in character and may be "Christian, pre-Christian or a-Christian." [25]

Nevertheless, between the nature and the state of philosophy there is an inner connection: without faith and Revelation[26] philosophy would not be able fully to meet its requirements. In its Christian state it receives, for the healing of its actual imperfection, help in the form of "objective contributions" and "subjective aids." In Maritain's phrasing, these are "the chief components of this *Christian state* of philosophy." [27]

The objective help consists of Revelation's presenting to philosophy truths that the philosophers failed to recognize even though they belonged to the field of philosophy, or else truths that were known to philosophy but were first cor-

---

[22] Jacques Maritain was born in Paris two years before Gilson. In 1906 he converted to the Roman Catholic Church. He soon became a prominent figure in Neo-Scholastic philosophy and, especially in recent decades, one of its leading thinkers. [He taught in Paris and Toronto (1932–48) and at Princeton (1948–60) and was among the intellectual fathers of the reforms of Vatican II. After his wife died he retired to a monastery in Toulouse, where he died in 1973. His work is carried on by the Jacques Maritain Center at the University of Notre Dame, Indiana.]

[23] Maritain, *De la philosophie chrétienne,* 27f. [Eng. trans., 11]; idem, "Le Catholicisme et la philosophie," 33.

[24] Maritain, *De la philosophie chrétienne,* 33 [Eng. trans., 15]. For a similar conception, see Joseph de Vries, "Christliche Philosophie," 7.

[25] Maritain, "Le Catholicisme et la philosophie," 33. [Cf. idem, *Science and Wisdom,* 79.]

[26] I often use the term Revelation without further qualification. From the discussions of Christian philosophy it is clear that authors mean primarily the special revelation of Scripture.

[27] Maritain, *De la philosophie chrétienne,* 39 [Eng. trans., 18].

roborated by Revelation. An example of the former is the notion of creation; of the latter, the validity of reason.

Maritain believes this positive help justifies Gilson's speaking of "revelation begetting reason," provided this is further defined. Closer definition is needed, first of all, because the expression may not be applied as strictly to philosophy as to theology. When applying it to philosophy one may not understand by Revelation the "entire revealed datum" or "the whole revealed deposit," but only "elements of the natural order" contained in it. Once philosophy has perceived these elements, it investigates them "according to its own order." [28]

In the second place, it must be remembered that the truths at issue here belong to the rational domain; thus they must in some way be present, if only "virtually" so, in mankind's philosophic treasury. One cannot pretend that prior to Revelation they were *"totally"* unknown; the early philosophers did not dwell in "sheer and total night" as regards the "revealed truths of the natural order." [29] Even in the case of essentially supernatural revealed data, one cannot speak of absolutely new concepts, for then who would have understood them? For example, the supra-philosophical idea of the Logos was long prepared by the philosophic concern with the idea of a logos, although there is an essential difference. It is more a matter of differences of clarity, albeit of differences that are very pronounced—: what used to dwell in shadowy regions was now placed in the full light of day.[30]

Besides objective contributions, philosophical thought receives from faith and theology "subjective aids," which is to say that the state of philosophy can also be changed with respect to "the vitality and deepest dynamism of the intellect." [31] On the one hand, the supernatural virtues and gifts represent a grade of perfection superior to that of philosophy—whereas for Aristotle it was philosophy that was uppermost—; on the other hand, they strengthen the lowlier virtues in their own order. For example, the virtue of faith enables the philosopher who accepts the existence of God on purely rational grounds to adhere to this truth with a firmer grasp; or again, the contemplative *habitus* spiritualizes the philosophical *habitus* within its own order, and in the light of theology metaphysical truths shine so clearly and distinctly that the philosopher's work is made easier. The phenomenon involves "synergy" and "vital solidarity," indeed even "dynamic continuity," not of "essence" but of "movement and illumination." [32]

Is this matter of any great importance? Whether a person is a queen or her minister does not change his or her human nature, but it does alter one's state and condition. Well, the advent of Christianity did, in a certain sense, dethrone

---

[28] Ibid., 40f. [Eng. trans., 19].
[29] Ibid., 41–43 [Eng. trans., 20f.].
[30] Ibid.
[31] Ibid., 54 [Eng. trans., 28].
[32] Maritain, *Science et sagesse*, 139 [Eng. trans., 80]; cf. *De la philosophie chrétienne*, 50–52 [Eng. trans., 26f.].

the wisdom of the philosophers by elevating theological wisdom and the wisdom of the Holy Spirit above it. Once philosophy recognizes this, its subjective condition is "thoroughly" altered. Philosophy in a Christian environment is orientated to a higher wisdom and is thus enabled to achieve a degree of self-detachment.[33]

In two different ways Maritain has brought out a fact of great importance. Philosophy was brought into an elevated condition by Christianity. And without violating its autonomy, faith now is philosophy's *stella rectrix*, or guiding star.[34]

As we ponder Maritain's conceptions we sense that, in spite of his lucid explanations, difficulties remain with respect to a synthesis. We are still not sure whether, or to what extent, the label "Christian philosophy" applies. The expression cannot be used, according to Maritain, for philosophy as such, in the abstract; but it can be used when philosophy is considered in a particular state. Yet the relation between Christianity and philosophy, so Maritain and Gilson both conclude, is not accidental but *intrinsic*, for it flows from the very nature of philosophy [35]—from its natural desire to know its objects as well as possible, and from the subjective and objective reinforcement that reason receives from faith and theology.[36]

Finally, Maritain looks at the problem in historical perspective. He distinguishes between an "organic Christian regime," which philosophy experienced when the Middle Ages were at their finest, and a "dissociated Christian regime," which fell to its lot in the centuries that followed. Western civilization was never free of Christianity: where it did not assist in building up philosophy, Christianity served as a stumbling-block. Today, philosophy may be intrinsically less Christian, but it is still full of Christian residues.[37]

Maritain's conception of the problem of Christian philosophy is shared by many in Roman Catholic circles, including Charles Journet[38] and Karel Bellon[39] as well as Reginald Garrigou-Lagrange, who acknowledges that through faith the transition from an incomplete to a complete state is possible for philosophy and that philosophy can be called "Christian as such," [40] and by Joseph de Vries, who deems the traditional doctrine of faith as a negative norm for philosophy to be decidedly inadequate since it fails to do justice to the entire reality we call "Christian philosophy." [41]

---

[33] Maritain, *De la philosophie chrétienne*, 53f. [Eng. trans., 27f.].

[34] Ibid., 54 [Eng. trans., 28f.].

[35] De Vries, "Christliche Philosophie," 13, formulates the matter thus: the influence of Christianity on philosophy is necessary, not to get it going but to have it "attain to the completion of which it is capable."

[36] Maritain, *De la philosophie chrétienne*, 55–57 [Eng. trans., 29f.]; idem, *Science et sagesse*, 166 [Eng. trans., 102].

[37] Maritain, *De la philosophie chrétienne*, 58 [Eng. trans., 31f.].

[38] Journet, *Introduction à la théologie*, 268f.

[39] Bellon, "Wijsbegeerte en theologie," 21–23.

[40] Garrigou-Lagrange, "De relationibus inter philosophiam et religionem," passim.

[41] De Vries, "Christliche Philosophie," 13.

After 1930 Gilson and Maritain became the leaders in the debate about the relation between Christianity and philosophy. Maritain's conceptions seemed to many to provide a satisfying solution to this difficult problem, at least for the time being. This stamps the development in Roman Catholic thought as a renewed orientation to the supernatural, an orientation that is only accentuated by the growing influence of Blondelism.

§ 5. *Maurice Blondel*

The most original and controversial position in the debate about Christian philosophy was undoubtedly taken by Blondel.[42] In certain respects he could go along with Gilson and Maritain and even the Leuven School, but he preferred to leave this agreement in the background since they had all obscured the fundamental problem of philosophy by accepting a "premature concordism" between natural and supernatural knowledge. In spite of that, they rendered an important service, Blondel allows, for they contributed, perhaps unawares, to posing the real problem: they helped prepare the distinction "of what remains incommensurable between the rational order and the supernatural order." [43]

Some—and here Blondel has Mandonnet and his circle in mind—never got beyond a "separated philosophy." The valuable and necessary distinction they make between rational and Christian truths is indeed one between two powers that are foreign to each other. But Blondel rejects with all possible force the idea that between philosophy and religion there might be only some kind of parallelism or superposition that would permit of no reciprocal influence.[44] Behind that idea lies the abstraction of a self-contained nature with a purely natural destiny.

Blondel devotes more attention to combating Gilson and Maritain. Many of his writings on "the problem of Catholic philosophy" open with an attack on what he labels "rational concordism" or "revived concordism." From the context it is clear that Blondel means not only Gilson, whom he mentions by name, but also Maritain.

In combating Maritain and Gilson, Blondel does not wish to negate in any way the historical influence of Christianity on philosophy. He values their implicit recognition of the insufficiency of philosophy. Nevertheless, by immediately transferring the problem of Christian philosophy to the historical domain and positing from the outset that through the ages Christianity has helped to shape the development of philosophical thought, the central problem of the relation between religion and natural thought is shunted to the sidelines. If philosophical thought were enriched by data from Revelation it would lose the awareness of its total insufficiency. Therefore, those who recognize the insuf-

---

[42] Maurice Blondel, born in Dijon in 1861, died in 1949, before the last part of his second trilogy was published. His best known work is probably his dissertation, *L'Action*, with which he shocked the scholarly world in 1893. From 1886 onward, he taught at Aix-en-Province.

[43] Blondel, "Le Problème de la philosophie catholique," 15, 17.

[44] Ibid., 15; idem, *La Philosophie et l'esprit chrétien*, 1:ix.

ficiency of philosophy but who do not accept a "philosophy of insufficiency" run the risk of arriving at a philosophy that is "separated, self-sufficient, and closed to every conception as well as every reception of the supernatural." [45]

There is another objection to such "philosophical historicism." It is unable to answer this question: When revelational data occur in a particular system, why did philosophy need them? And further: How must the support given by Revelation to natural thought be interpreted? History itself cannot answer these questions, since it cannot fathom the elevated reality that philosophy seems to have drawn on.[46]

Having rejected every kind of concordism, Blondel believes he can define the problem correctly. At bottom the question is whether, and, if so, under what aspects, the problem of Christian philosophy participates in the universal and permanent metaphysical restlessness.[47] An authentic and consistently upheld "philosophy of insufficiency" is at stake. We do not grasp this fully until we realize that the concept of "insufficiency" arises from "the total dynamism of the human being," that it is an expression of "the inborn and unforced desire in every created spirit." [48]

With that, Blondel has transposed the problem of Christian philosophy to the ambit of the *desiderium naturale* as he understands it. We saw earlier that his entire philosophical enterprise focuses on analyzing the "dynamism" that has taken hold of all beings throughout the universe. Philosophy has no other task than, by analyzing thought, being, and action, to make man aware of the ontological incompleteness of all things. In this way it will discover within itself the desire for the infinite. Natural means are no longer sufficient to make good the deficiency—are no longer adequate to come to know the full truth.

In this way philosophy is prepared to welcome light and support from the outside. There arises from it an ontological cry to the Transcendent, to Revelation. Reason has discovered "voids" within itself that can only be filled from regions that lie beyond the finite, natural world. Not that the Transcendent is obligated to respond to the ontological appeal—for the supernatural is granted us as a free gift of God—but it is God who oriented us to supernatural elevation.

The radical incapacity that pervades the whole of creation establishes an inner orientation of philosophy to religion. Hence philosophy is essentially Christian philosophy, regardless whether or not its content will be complemented by Revelation. Blondel would rather speak of "Catholic philosophy," however, since it is only in Catholicism that the one essential element, namely, the natural desire for God, has been kept pure.

---

[45] Blondel, "Pour une philosophie intégrale," 53; idem, "La Philosophie chrétienne existe-t-elle comme philosophie?" 89; idem, "Le Problème de la philosophie catholique," 17f.

[46] Blondel, "La Philosophie chrétienne existe-t-elle comme philosophie?" 89f.

[47] Blondel, "Le Problème de la philosophie catholique," 19f.

[48] Blondel, "Pour une philosophie intégrale," 53.

Yet philosophy carries out its task of locating the voids, the deficiencies, the incapacities, exclusively by means of natural reason. In doing so, it makes no use of direct supernatural participation:

So far from at once supernaturalizing, in a confused or presumptuous and perverse manner, the spiritual impulse of human consciousness, we shall always look for and *find in the activity of reason a positive and solid ground to cultivate*. . . . Into this ground must be inserted the authentic work of vocation, redemption, and elevation . . .[49]

It is by purely natural means that Blondel undertakes to establish reason's deficiencies. The "Christian contributions" will only offer an "escape from incapacities." In the entire process of philosophical thought in which its insufficiency is uncovered, the natural consciousness is assigned an "initiating role," one based on the "natural clarities."[50] It is precisely when philosophy remains fully autonomous that it can discern its radical insufficiency and its orientation to possible supernatural elevation. Philosophy does not cease to be itself when it encounters the mystery; it continues in its own "autonomous ways" even as the answer comes, from the mystery, to the enigmas in which philosophy got stuck.[51]

Philosophy ends in "enigmas," [52] but a solution is coming, from the mystery. In the midst of darkness a light shines. Not all uncertainties and enigmas are removed, to be sure, but the Christian religion does provide "solace" and "serenity."

The way of the philosopher is as follows. In search of answers to the great questions, he encounters enigmas that cannot be solved by reason alone. Into the formative process of rational doctrine, however, shines the light of faith. By this light of the Christian religion, philosophy broadens and deepens itself. In so doing, it discovers new difficulties beyond its earlier (always provisional) limits —difficulties, however, for which it again receives light. This "cycloidal path" spirals forward dynamically. Hence, Blondel calls his way of philosophizing the "cycloidal method."

From the expositions of Blondel, whose complex thoughts and numerous neologisms are not always easy to follow, it has gradually become clear to us that, in his conception, the relation of philosophy and religion has a dual aspect. On the one hand, there is the radical deficiency of philosophy, which directs it toward the mysteries of Revelation. On the other hand, there is religion, which does not leave reason's appeal unanswered but sends it the light of faith to illumine its toilsome path. Faith and reason are not opposed to each other on principle, nor do they share a relation of parallelism. What obtains between them

---

[49] Blondel, *La Philosophie et l'esprit chrétien*, 1: xiii (ital. added).
[50] Ibid.
[51] Ibid., 1:30.
[52] Ibid., 1:229. Blondel repeatedly uses the term "énigme" to express the idea implicit in the Greek philosophical term ἀπορία: "un embarras en cours de route, un sentier qui se perd, une chemin coupé" (a roadblock, errant path, blind alley).

is solidarity—this term taken in the Blondelian sense. Each is assigned an "original initiative." At the same time each prepares itself for "cooperation," and then of such a sort that it can best be compared to conjugal union. The intimate bond between philosophy and religion is most purely expressed by the term "symbiosis." Symbiosis is stronger than "connection," "union," "collaboration" or "cooperation": it denotes the "indispensable cooperation of two beings who, though of different species and each organically complete, need each other for their existence and their propagation." [53]

Despite this intertwining of faith and reason, the question remains whether Blondel has fully fathomed the relation of Christianity and philosophy when he presents it as "connection," "conjugal union," or "symbiosis." He is careful to guard the autonomy of natural thought. At the same time he guards with equal care the elevation of the supernatural order. He never tires of writing that a symbiosis obtains between the two, but a "symbiosis in incommensurability": there is "interpenetration" but no less "heterogeneity," an "indeclinable connection" but also "essential autonomy." [54]

Thus there need be no fear of any confusion of the natural and the supernatural, nor is there any occasion to suspect Blondel of minimizing the one for the sake of the other. Natural thought picks up rays from the "clair-obscur" of religion without in any way impairing the mystery of the supernatural world. What was always mystery remains so.

Never is the supernatural *as such* perceived by the consciousness or discerned by reflection. These are incapable of linking the anonymous facts of consciousness to the dogmatic aspect and the intimate action of grace. If there is a marriage of nature and Christ, it is always under a veil; and philosophy, so far from violating the protective obscurity, must preserve it.[55]

Thus there is indeed an intimate connection between nature and Christ, but "always under a veil." The supernatural appears shrouded in forms and shapes that are ordinary human categories.[56] It is quite beyond the capacity of philosophy to penetrate the supernatural.[57] On the contrary, we may well wonder whether the light that the autonomous reason receives from the "clair-obscur" of the mysteries of faith betrays its supernatural origin at all. I say this not so much because of the vague and cryptic terminology—"veil," "clair-obscur"—that is employed just at the moment when we eagerly await the resolution of the enigma of Christian philosophy; I say it more because of the many examples Blondel gives of cases in which the mystery of the Trinity is of central importance. It is precisely Blondel's elaboration of the trinitarian mystery as a

---

[53] Ibid., 2:x, note 1.
[54] Blondel, *Le Problème de la philosophie catholique*, 145.
[55] Blondel, "Pour une philosophie intégrale," 59 (ital. added).
[56] Robbers, *Wijsbegeerte en openbaring*, 118.
[57] Blondel, "Pour une philosophie intégrale," 51.

"fecund model" for the whole of life that raises numerous questions.[58] We look forward to the third volume of his trilogy, *La philosophie et l'esprit chrétien*,[59] but I cannot see how he is going to solve the difficulties into which his philosophy's presuppositions have carried him, unless he breaks radically with the idea of the autonomy of natural reason.

§ 6. *Autonomous philosophy or Christian philosophy: an evaluation*

Anyone who has followed the discussions about the possibility of a Christian philosophy for some time may well be disposed to ask, Why continue? The problem appears irresolvable while the differences between the various thinkers are slight. Maritain and Blondel both oppose a "separated philosophy" and both insist on the insufficiency and incompleteness of natural thought. Should we not concur with De Lubac and Robbers that Blondel's conception does not contradict but rather complements the theses of Maritain and Gilson?[60] Stronger yet, is de Lubac not correct when he sees no fundamental differences between Mandonnet and Maritain? Maritain may argue strenuously for recognizing an intrinsic relation between Christianity and philosophy, but does he not maintain a sharp dualism between revelation and natural reason? And when all is said and done, does Mandonnet ever deny the "subjective aids" that Christian philosophers experience in their work? And does Maritain not state that the truths of reason are also to be found, "virtually" at least, in pre-Christian philosophy?

If we were to concur in these negations of the fundamental differences between the different advocates, or between the advocates and the opponents, of a Christian philosophy, we would be guilty of gross superficiality. To start with, we would gravely underestimate the differences in the climate of thought of Maritain, Gilson, and Blondel. Nevertheless, the fact that a mistaken impression can arise so easily does raise the question whether there is not a certain element that Mandonnet, Maritain, and Blondel hold in common which at the same time drives them apart. Could it be, moreover, that this common element constitutes the heart of the problem in the controversy about the idea of a Christian philosophy, at least in Catholic circles?

Steins Bisschop stated, back in 1934, that many differences of opinion had been brought to light concerning the relation between Christianity and philosophy, *but that with respect to one point all were agreed: philosophy is an autonomous discipline,* with its own principles, its own method, and its own proofs; whatever its relation to Revelation may be, in its own proper domain philosophy enjoys autonomy and independence.[61]

---

[58] This theme is worked out most notably in Taymans d'Eypernon, *Le Mystère primordial. La Trinité dans sa vivante image* (1946). Particularly worthy of examination is the final chapter, where the influence of Blondelism is most clearly in evidence.

[59] [Published posthumously as *Exigences philosophiques du Christianisme* (Paris, 1950).]

[60] Lubac, "Sur la philosophie chrétienne," 240; Robbers, *Wijsbegeerte en Openbaring*, 111.

[61] Steins Bisschop, in his paper presented to the first general meeting of the Vereeniging voor Thomistische Wijsbegeerte, 14–15 April 1934: "Over het bestaan eener Christelijke Wijs-

I am inclined to agree with this assessment of the situation: the autonomy of natural thought has been the unquestioned starting point of both Maritain and Blondel, not to mention Mandonnet and his followers. It has also been the sticking point in the debate.

Blondel reproaches Gilson and Maritain for having resolved the problem of a Christian philosophy all too quickly and easily through "rational concordism." The one thing needed, according to Blondel, is to expose the absolute insufficiency of philosophy, which can only be accomplished if the autonomy of philosophy is fully preserved. This is no longer done when truths of faith from the supernatural sphere are admitted into natural thought, for then "voids" are filled and philosophy's total inability to be self-sufficient is obscured from view. The more philosophy maintains its autonomy, the better it will perceive its own incompleteness and the more receptive it will be to the answer from the mysteries of Revelation.[62]

Blondel has a second, no less fundamental, objection to Maritain. Maritain unreservedly maintains the autonomy of rational thought with respect to Revelation, and yet he has rational thought incorporate data from Revelation. Ostensibly, these are absorbed into the philosophical system in the same form in which they present themselves, namely, as mysteries of faith; in reality, however, they undergo a form of transubstantiation into human ideas. In this way Maritain's "concordism" compromises Christian truths by "forcibly robbing them of their supernatural originality": philosophical reflection "accepts them, handles them, tests them in its own natural, rational way."[63] Here, it seems to me, Blondel touches the jugular of both Maritain's and Gilson's conceptions of Christian philosophy.

Maritain and Gilson are well aware that they must not accept Blondel's objections. "Well-disposed souls are surprised," Maritain notes, that Blondel and he have not announced a cease-fire. But Maritain is too convinced of the irreconcilability of their respective starting points to be able to concede anything for the sake of a show of agreement. And as for Gilson, he notes that a philosophy that discovers incompleteness within itself and is open to the supernatural would certainly be compatible with Christianity, but that is still no reason to call it a Christian philosophy.[64] If it can be called Christian, Maritain adds, then that is not just because of its "voids." For how does it know its "voids"? Surely it recognizes what it lacks only when it has achieved a certain degree of perfection: ". . . and this degree of perfection which brings it to the knowledge of what it lacks is also the stage at which it knows the highest truths that it can attain: it only reaches this degree when aided by the light of faith."[65]

---

begeerte," 29.

[62] Blondel, "Pour une philosophie intégrale," 53f.

[63] See Blondel, as reported in "La Notion de philosophie chrétienne," 89.

[64] Gilson, *The Spirit of Mediaeval Philosophy*, 37. A similar critique of Blondel is found in Suenens, "Les controverses récentes autour de la notion de philosophie chrétienne," 402.

[65] Maritain, *Science et sagesse*, 146 [Eng. trans., 85].

Maritain thus opposes Blondel on the central problem of his philosophy. Philosophy can appreciate its lack of self-sufficiency only after it has allowed itself to be fructified by the data of Revelation. Maritain is afraid that Blondel, although he combats the Cartesian separation of faith and philosophy, has nonetheless retained the Cartesian conception of the autonomy of natural thought. For all that, Maritain's critique of Blondel's notion of autonomy does not imply a denial of the autonomy of thought as such. That must be maintained, though not as something absolute but as something that receives its independence from God. "The autonomy and liberty of speculative philosophy, far from being destroyed or reduced, are fortified by their union in the living subject with the light of faith." [66]

Besides the objection raised by Maritain to Blondel's idea of a Catholic philosophy, one can cite still another. Blondel correctly maintains that Maritain, in order to incorporate the data of Revelation into his philosophical system, robs them of their original force. Now, Blondel's own idea of a Christian philosophy has two sides to it: on the one hand the incompleteness of thought must be exposed, and on the other hand philosophy must permit itself to be fructified by the revealed mysteries. We have seen how Blondel conceives of this process of fructification. The details, however, remain hidden behind a veil. Once the result of the fructifying comes to light, the mystery appears in ordinary human form. Neither the character of the supernatural nor the autonomy of philosophical thought will allow the Revelational mystery as such to "cross over" to the natural domain. Hence, there must be a transubstantiation. Here Blondel's reproach that Maritain robs Christian truths of their "supernatural originality" recoils upon himself. The problem is more conspicuous in Maritain because he speaks openly of a "transformation" of supernatural truths into rational truths. In Blondel, however, the emphasis is on the deep mystery of the transit from the one order to the other.

The result of our inquiry into the actual meaning of the idea of a Christian philosophy in present-day Catholic thought is hardly encouraging. Whether we follow Maritain and Gilson or whether we follow Blondel, in neither case can we take the concept "Christian" in a strict sense. An awareness of the "insufficiency" of philosophy does not yet put one on the road to a Christian philosophy, not even in cases where the philosopher believes he has warrant to expect a "counterwave" from God's side to fill the voids. Even when the supernatural assumes some form in the philosophical domain through which it becomes accessible to natural thought, philosophy still cannot be called Christian, for that which becomes an ingredient of rational thought is not properly Christian but a transmogrification of it.

Modern Catholic thought seeks to maintain a philosophy that is at once autonomous and Christian. However, when it safeguards its autonomy it renders

---

[66] Ibid.

intrinsically Christian philosophical thought impossible; and when it takes seriously the input of faith it exorcises its autonomy. Autonomous philosophy and Christian philosophy turn out to be mutually exclusive. Gaston Rabeau sees the dilemma clearly when he writes, "The great difficulty blocking the idea of a Christian philosophy is philosophy's rationality— or, what amounts to the same thing, its autonomy." [67]

Catholic thinkers are serious in their quest for an integral Christian philosophy. Yet whenever they are confronted with the choice—and this choice cannot be avoided—of proceeding either from the autonomy or from the absolute religious conditionality of philosophy, they adopt the former of these two possibilities. There is something incomprehensible about this all-determining decision, for thereby they shut themselves off from truly critical reflection on their starting point as well as from a deeper grounding of theoretical thought and a more integral experience of reality.

Why Scholastic philosophers should cling to the autonomy of rational thought seems quite beyond human comprehension. Once one realizes, however, that the independence they attribute to natural life is deeply rooted in the Catholic worldview, one will have to acknowledge that the idea of an autonomous philosophy is neither an arbitrary mental choice nor an outcome of pure reasoning. Anyone, they think, who in any way at all would introduce the supernatural in all its original vitality into the presuppositions of his philosophical work would attack the very foundations of Scholastic metaphysics because it would mean incorporating an element essentially alien to it. Of course this danger is not taken too seriously either, since anyone who were to follow such a method would simply be disqualifying himself philosophically as he slipped into theology. De Lubac's attempt to make philosophy genuinely Christian by locating its inception in the midst of the mystery of the Incarnation has accordingly attracted little attention.[68] It is impossible to predict how the controversy about the idea of a Christian philosophy will unfold in the future, but at the present stage no transgression of the boundary between natural and supernatural cognition is tolerated.

It is not an arbitrary decision, so we observed, that Scholastic philosophers insist on the autonomy of natural thought. Scholastic philosophers consider themselves called to maintain the purity of philosophy. Moreover, they see no basis for dialogue with those of other persuasions unless they can rely for their arguments on reason alone. Thus reason must guard its autonomy by virtue of its own nature and in its own interest.

But autonomy has its obverse side as well. It is the "enfant terrible" not only of the problem of Christian philosophy but of all philosophy. The idea of autonomous thought is the foundation upon which the proud edifice of Scholas-

---

[67] Rabeau, "Communication, rédigée spécialement en fonction des positions de MM. J. Maritain et M. Blondel," in *La Philosophie chretienne*, 2:154.

[68] De Lubac, "Sur la philosophie chrétienne," 249.

tic metaphysics stands, but this foundation turns out, upon closer scrutiny, to be "autonomous" only up to a point. The autonomy of rational thought is never itself rationally demonstrable—more than a hundred years of controversy among Neo-Scholastics about philosophy's starting point have amply proven that. In point of fact, the autonomy of rational thought is no more than a postulate. In the name of the autonomy of thought Neo-Scholasticism rejects what are essentially *religious* presuppositions for science and philosophy, but in actuality it adopts as its starting point a purely religious idea of its own.[69] The difference between a Catholic philosopher and, say, a Calvinist philosopher lies in the fact that the latter self-consciously acknowledges that supra-theoretical, religious presuppositions belong to the very constitution of theoretical thought, while the former incorporates them into his system either unexamined, or as self-evident truths, or after transforming them into rational principles.

The postulate of autonomy is so intimately wrapped up with Catholic thought that for its sake even contradictions are accepted. Blondel discovers in all things and the universe as a whole an absolute lack of self-sufficiency, but he makes an exception for rational thought: although rational thought as such must be insufficient in view of the incompleteness of temporal reality as a whole, it is nonetheless sufficient to expose its own insufficiency, together with that of the world around it. Blondel is so caught up in the atmosphere of autonomous thought that this contradiction, which relativizes his conception, apparently eludes him.[70]

Maritain has discovered the Achilles' heel of Blondel's system and has gone on to seek a deeper basis for the autonomy of thought. At least, we encounter in him the idea (which, alas, he does not enlarge upon) that awareness of reason's insufficiency does not arise until reason is aided by the illumination of faith.[71]

With that, Maritain has brought the question of a Christian philosophy to the plane where it belongs. He links it here to the question of the philosopher's starting point, which has been so heavily contested and yet never resolved in Neo-Scholastic thought.

This insight is fairly rare. Ordinarily, Catholic thinkers make no direct link between these two questions. That is understandable, since the question of philosophy's starting point touches its direction and all its parts, whereas they believe the idea of Christian philosophy bears upon it only accidentally.

The principle of the autonomy of thought first demands that philosophical problems be pried loose from their original (religious) context and only afterwards permits a few refracted rays of Revelation to shine through. Proceeding from an autonomous realm of experience, natural thought must find its own way self-reliantly, and independently of the data of faith.

---

[69] On the religious nature of the idea of autonomy, see chapter I, above.

[70] [For a similar assessment, see S. U. Zuidema, "Maurice Blondel and the Method of Immanence," in idem, *Communication and Confrontation: A Philosophical Appraisal and Critique of Modern Society and Contemporary Thought* (Toronto, 1972), 227–62.]

[71] Maritain, *Science et sagesse*, 146 [Eng. trans., 85].

The principle of the independence of theoretical thought with respect to religion *controls* that thought in all its parts; the principles and values derived from Revelational data only *influence* it.

The idea of being and analogy, the notion of participation, the form-matter scheme, and ever so many other principles all bear the stamp of a self-contained universe. Thus the highest point that theoretical thought can still hope to attain is that of the analogical unity of being between God and creature. Yet it remains beyond the capacity of autonomous thought to ascertain if there is, indeed, an analogical unity of being between God and creature, since rational thought itself is permeated by that unity of being and since, so long as it maintains its autonomy, it can never step outside being in order to objectify it and so provide an account of it. Whenever the autonomy of reason is called into question, it turns out not to be based on rational principles itself but proves to be a suprarational presupposition in its own right. Likewise, whenever "proof" is sought for the analogy of being of God and the creature, or for the participation of the finite creature in the absoluteness of God, then the basis is always found to be simply a postulate that already fully incorporates the ideas of analogy and participation with respect to God. Thus the metaphysical principles of Catholic philosophy, which are presented as the results and requirements of human reasoning, turn out to be nothing other than nonrational preconceptions—or, more precisely, religious presuppositions, since they express something about the relation of God to his world and the relation of the creature to its Origin.

The position that Catholic scholars adopt with respect to the problem of Christian theoretical thought will not change until they acknowledge that their present starting point, the autonomy of reason, is an a-rational principle. Their academic integrity would in no wise suffer if at the basis of their theoretical work they were to place real Christian data that do not require to be transformed into rational principles. What is lacking is a recognition that it lies in the very nature of learning and scholarship to oblige the researcher to proceed on the basis of presuppositions in pursuing his philosophical and scientific work.

VII/ THE PROBLEM OF CHRISTIAN HISTORICAL SCIENCE

§ 1. *Louis Mercier*

Mercier's way of relating philosophy, theology and history is very simple.[1] Philosophy according to him obtains its results exclusively by the light of unaided reason. The moment it were to base its arguments on Revelation it would cease to be philosophy and turn into theology. Philosophy is characterized throughout as a rational discipline. And the science of history is no different. The first task of the historian is to "ascertain facts," and as he does so he must and can proceed in a purely objective way. Therefore there is no such thing as "Catholic history" in the sense of "research in, or teaching of history in terms of supernatural theology . . ." Historical science cannot and will not be anything other than a purely "rational discipline."[2]

The conclusion is startling. From the fact that it is the task of historical science to establish the historical facts objectively Mercier draws the conclusion, without thinking it necessary to justify it in any way, that history is perforce a "purely rational" discipline. We know there must be a Scholastic philosophical reason behind this facile conclusion, but to put the stamp of a "purely rational discipline" on a science simply because it declines to conduct its inquiries "in terms of supernatural theology" will be acceptable to no one of a critical mind without further justification. Mercier's single hypothesis "solves" countless problems that continue to vex a host of his colleagues.

Once the historian has ascertained his facts, Mercier continues, they have to be interpreted. This requires a principle by means of which events can be viewed in perspective, a principle, moreover, that gives us a view of historical reality as a whole. Now then, only philosophy can provide such a principle. Historical science therefore receives a necessary supplement from philosophical interpretation. Provided each observes their mutual boundaries, no tension need arise between them since both operate in a strictly rational and objective way.[3]

Mercier is well aware that the idea of a pure philosophy—"mere philosophy," free of every supernatural influence—no longer enjoys the sympathy of his younger colleagues. In fact, they yearn instead, he notes, "to be supernaturally and even mystically theological." Certainly the ideal of being a "mere historian"

---

[1] Louis J. A. Mercier (1880–[1953]) taught at Harvard, 1911–46. His special interest is in the philosophical and social backgrounds of literature. The article we cite served as an address to the annual meeting of the American Catholic Historical Association, 31 Dec. 1937.

[2] Mercier, "Current Crises and the Perspective of History," 258–60.

[3] Ibid., 260f.

or a "mere philosopher" no longer appeals. Although he would like to be accommodating of these notions Mercier feels he must insist on the pure autonomy of science and philosophy. Only in this way, he believes, can a correct view be gained of the relation between a philosophical interpretation and a religious vision of history. For so long as historical science and philosophy of history remain firmly objective or rational they cannot contradict theology of history![4]

Next to this negative relation of faith and history, however, there is also a positive one. Mercier leaves some room for a theology of history in the sense of Augustine and Bossuet. It must consist of religious "meditation" upon history.[5]

One other relation between faith and history that Mercier will admit is the following. Religion is a source of inspiration and comfort to the historian when he feels discouraged by the apparent triumph of evil in the world, or by the limits of our feeble human means to search after objective truth.[6]

All this is highly reminiscent of Mandonnet. Both Mercier and Mandonnet work with the idea of a parallelism and harmony between faith and reason —provided each restricts itself to its own domain and to its own method. The tide is running against them, however. It is difficult for Mercier to empathize with the mentality of many of his colleagues who, while maintaining the clear distinction between natural and supernatural knowledge, are restlessly looking for a synthesis, for something more than just harmony.

Many a Catholic philosopher or historian will arrive at conclusions similar to Mercier's, but in more than a few the argumentation and mood have changed. For example, H. F. Kearney (whom I discuss below) likewise believes history is an "autonomous form of thought" but precisely because such thought must do without religious knowledge it can have only "limited validity."[7]

§ 2. *Umberto Padovani*

Padovani's conclusion agrees in large measure with Mercier's, although their starting points are different.[8]

In Italian Catholic philosophy the question of the relation of religion and philosophy has engrossed many thinkers for many years. Since the end of the Second World War it has been highly topical. Padovani, whose position in the philosophical life of Italy is one of considerable prominence, has occupied himself with this very question throughout his career. Sometimes he reminds one of Blondel, yet there are profound differences between the two. Sciacca correctly calls him "a Thomist who does not reject Augustinian ideas."[9]

---

[4] Ibid., 267f.
[5] Ibid., 259.
[6] Ibid., 268.
[7] Kearney, "Christianity and the Study of History," 68, 70.
[8] Umberto Antonio Padovani (1894–[1968]) for many years occupied the chair for moral philosophy at the Catholic University of Milan, but in 1948 he transferred to the University of Padua.
[9] Sciacca, *Italienische Philosophie der Gegenwart*, 25.

Indeed, the interesting thing about Padovani is his incorporation of Augustine's theology of history into a modern conception of history. In the matter of the relation of philosophy and theology, however, he deviates from the Augustinian tradition. And it is precisely his views in this area that determine his understanding of the nature and interrelation of the science, philosophy, and theology of history.

Philosophy as such he regards as an autonomous, rational science that is no more able to be Christian than mathematics or biology. Philosophy, however, encounters—and here we arrive at the central problem Padovani poses—the power of evil in concrete life. The ratio can do no more than establish the existence of evil; to solve the problem of evil is beyond its capacity. This forces us to go beyond philosophy to religion and Revelation, which show us that evil is the effect of sin and that deliverance is possible in Christ. Thus natural reason has no access to the most important facts of concrete life. The real problems of life can only be solved with the Christian religion, in the supernatural realm.[10]

It is against this backdrop that one must view Padovani's idea of the divergence of the various disciplines that deal with history.

There is according to him an empirical history (*storia empirica*). This is the discipline practiced by the historian. It must of necessity remain incomplete, and it foregoes every metaphysical and transcendental element. It thereby leaves many fundamental problems unresolved, including those of the origin, development, and end of man, and of the function of evil in history. Empirical history may not, as happens all too often, admit or introduce philosophy of history. Should it do so, it would forfeit the name *storia empirica*.

The fundamental problems that empirical science leaves aside are the proper object of philosophy of history. This discipline strives to become "integral history" (*storia integrale*) by acquiring integral knowledge of the historical facts.

A unitary and universal vision of history on purely rational terms—that is to say, from the vantage point of philosophical history—is impossible, however, since the plan of history is *in fact* supernatural in character. Thus the fundamental problems of history find their solution not in philosophy but in theology, since the plan of historical development is knowable only in the light of Revelation. Yet it ought always to be remembered that although theology of history does give a universal vision of history, it is not itself, strictly speaking, scientific in nature, since its object is always the contingent and free.

Ultimately, historical science and philosophy of history merge in the theological vision of history. Only in theology are we able to explain the basic phenomena of historical becoming—sin and salvation. The modern conception of history, Padovani proposes, should link up again with Augustine, on two accounts. He was the first to articulate the supernatural character of the basic plan of history; and he was keenly aware of the elementary power of evil in

---

[10] Padovani, "Filosofia e religione," passim; see also *Giornale di Metafisica* 1 (1946): 208, where he presents a short and clear summary of his standpoint.

history. It is for this reason that the bishop of Hippo approached history not as a philosopher but as a theologian, informed by Revelation.[11]

§ 3. Ross Hoffman

A year after Louis Mercier had attempted to convince the American Catholic Historical Association of the chasm between historical science and theology of history, the society's president,[12] in a paper entitled "Catholicism and Historismus," endeavored to present the ostensibly autonomous development of history as an internal element of the church. In Hoffman, the boundaries between the disciplines that deal with history are blurred to such a degree that we are actually left in the end with nothing but theology of history and church history.

Hoffman introduces his ideal of Catholic historiography as an alternative to positivistic historical writing (which he calls "historismus").[13] Positivistic historicism began as early as Ranke, although the appellation positivist is applicable to him only in a limited sense. One does find in Ranke the notion that the historian must compose truthful and accurate narrative based on a critical study of the best contemporary documents and that he must abstain from value judgments. But Ranke was also filled with awe for the mystery of things and believed that the human mind would never fully comprehend the historical process. His mistake was to disregard the only real means by which the problems of history can be "probed to the bottom."[14]

If Ranke still knew and respected the mystery, the "philologist historians" who esteemed and emulated him conceived of historical reality as no more than a mechanically connected sequence of occurrences devoid of all mystery. Lost along with respect for the mystery was reverence for the past, since the element eliminated from history was precisely that which gave the historian a sense of oneness with the historical process.

The last decades of the nineteenth century witnessed a growing interest in the social, economic and cultural factors in history. Positivist historians fancied they could penetrate the truth more deeply by taking all these elements into account and thus approximating the ideal of an all-encompassing historical science. But it was precisely when they set out to do this, Hoffmann explains, that the inadequacy of their conception became evident. They failed to appreciate

---

[11] Padovani, "La teologia della storia," 483f; see also, especially for Augustine's importance for today, idem, La concezione cristiana della storia e "La Città di Dio" di S. Agostino.

[12] Ross John Swartz Hoffman (1902–[79]), teaches at Fordham University and is known for his studies in the fields of international politics as well as historiography. [Cf. *Some Aspects of History* (1957). Hoffman gave an account of his conversion to Roman Catholicism in his book *Restoration* (1934). He received the American Historical Association's George Louis Beer prize for his book *Great Britain and the German Trade Rivalry, 1875–1914* (1933; repr. 1969.]

[13] Hoffman, "Catholicism and Historismus," 401f.

[14] Ibid., 404f. [quoting Lord Acton, "German Schools of History," *English Historical Review* 1 (1886): 13].

that every generation is unique because it is of unique historical formation, alive on earth at a unique moment in a non-repetitive process. They failed to realize that we cannot understand the people of the past unless we "enter intuitively into them . . . We must know them from within, or we can never really know them at all." Today the twentieth-century historian stands before a debased past to which he has no access because of his own naturalistic way of thinking. He believes he can get closer to the truth by broadening his horizon and affirming ever more factors in the historical process. The positivist historian fancies he has once for all lifted the veil of mystery from history, only to be haunted by the suspicion that there is a remainder in history to which he has not yet had access. He is beginning to doubt whether historical science can know anything at all about the causal relations between events, and whether its representations of historical reality are anything more than "projections of subjective ideas." [15]

Historiography is in need of a radical turnabout. We must turn away from "historismus" and approach history with an intuitive knowledge of human nature and a deep spiritual insight into the life of the past. Real knowledge of the past is something we can acquire only if we *understand* it from the inside. It was the Italian philosopher Benedetto Croce who recognized this requirement; he was the first to show the inability of positivistic historiography to satisfy the appetite of the human spirit for historical understanding.[16]

The Catholic historian has an important task when it comes to entering into the mysteries of the past because he "is the one best equipped to offer some degree of satisfaction to this appetite." And what, specifically, equips the Catholic historian to enter into the *motio metaphysica voluntatis,* into the stirring drama of the spirit? The Catholic historian is the bearer of the "universal human memory," someone who knows as one who *remembers*, someone who is at one with the history of humanity, who in his memory has certainty about the past (and thus avoids "sinking into the morass of historical skepticism").[17]

One pressing question remains: Why is it the Catholic historian who is privileged with the "universal human memory" that opens up the mysteries of the past? It is because the condition for understanding history is the union of the mind of the historian with the mind of the church of Christ. For in the church lives the light and the wisdom of Him who "knew what was in man." And it is the church that knows and remembers the historical man of pagan antiquity, for she lived with him, baptized him, and gathered him into herself. She knows also every great event, every thought, every error, not from without or from afar but from the inside, since she experiences it all as something of her own.[18]

Such notions, which at first strike us as rather strange but which we will understand better if we keep in mind the opposition of many younger Catholic

---

[15] Ibid., 408f.
[16] Ibid., 403f.
[17] Ibid., 409f.
[18] Ibid., 409, 410, 412.

thinkers to positivistic historiography and "mere" history, can also be found in the well-known English writer Hilaire Belloc. Hoffman borrows several examples from him: the Roman Catholic historian, "in a way that no other man can," understands the Roman military effort, and also why that effort clashed with the gross Asiatic and merchant empire of Carthage, for he alone sees Europe "from within" rather than "from without," as do the Protestant, Jew or Mohammedan. "For the Catholic the whole perspective falls into its proper order." [19]

§ 4. *Luigi Sturzo*

In 1943 a work appeared in the United States which has remained almost unknown in Europe but which in my opinion ranks among the most important writings by Catholics about the problem of a Christian science of history. I mean Luigi Sturzo's book, *The True Life: Sociology of the Supernatural*.

When I say that this work is important and express my surprise at its neglect in Europe (Italy excepted), then I am referring in particular to the Introduction, which consists of only twenty pages. It is with this text that we shall be particularly concerned here, although not in isolation from other publications in which Sturzo speaks of a Christian sociology or a Christian historical science.[20]

The titles Sturzo gives his works are somewhat misleading. They create the impression that these works deal exclusively with sociology. Actually, his sociology is philosophical sociology and philosophy of history, albeit he rejects both these names for his works.[21] In Sturzo these two disciplines are so finely attuned to each other that the one cannot be understood apart from the other. Initially he called his theory "historicist sociology" but he abandoned the term because of the confusion it invited with German historicism. He now prefers the name "integral sociology" (*sociologia integrale*).[22]

The name "integral sociology" expresses what is distinctive about Sturzo's theory. What concerns him in the study of society is not an abstraction or a metaphysical entity, or even a moral standpoint whereby we judge what society should be. He is concerned, rather, with society as it is in the concrete.[23] True sociology is the science of society in its *concrete existence* and in its *historical development*. This is to say that if sociology is to fulfill its task it must take into consideration *all* factors that go to make up human life in concrete society. All this Sturzo would express with the term "integral sociology."

---

[19] Ibid., 411 [quoting Belloc, *Europe and the Faith* (London, 1920), vii–ix].

[20] Don Luigi Sturzo (1871–[1959]) was one of the leading figures in Italian political life between 1919 and 1924. He is best known as the founder of the first Christian Democratic party in Italy, the Partito Popolare Cattolico. In 1924 he was forced to flee from the fascist regime. In exile he wrote substantial works in philosophy, theology and, especially, sociology. His *Inner Laws of Society: A New Sociology* appeared in 1944, the year after *The True Life* had rolled off the press in America. The latter work was an English translation of a manuscript that he published after his repatriation under the title *La vera vita, sociologia del supranaturale* (1947).

[21] Sturzo, "History and Philosophy," 54.

[22] Sturzo, *La vera vita*, 25 [Eng. trans., 19].

[23] Ibid., 9 [Eng. trans., 3].

Up to this point there is no difference with other theories of society, for they would all endeavor to do justice to the various factors operating in the societal process. Thus Sturzo has something additional in mind when he employs this term. His criticism of other sociologists, and especially of the positivists, is that their theory cannot be integral.

The study of concrete society is only possible, according to Sturzo, if we view it in its fourth dimension, which is time. That is to say, we must investigate the formation of society from its most rudimentary beginnings down to the present day. Essential to the knowledge of society is history—not the external history of facts but society in its inner dynamism, in its perennial manifestation of novelty. Well then, it is according to Sturzo history in this sense that attests to *the supernatural fact inserted into the human process*.[24]

What history must lead us principally to discover—and what must remain hidden from philosophy since philosophy, being based on reason, stops at the threshold of the supernatural—is the divine and supernatural action in the world. This action has been operative from the beginning of Christianity, and even earlier, although it was then restricted to a single nation or to a dim reflection of the original revelation in pagan religions and morals.[25]

The first question that now arises is this: In what way can the divine or supernatural enter into the process of history? Although historical development, Sturzo explains, is a human process, extra-human or extra-historical factors can be absorbed into it and so rendered "historical," which is to say that they can become factors in human knowledge and action. In this way, for example, man's physical surroundings are absorbed into history by virtue of man's dominion over them and transformed into historical entities such as towns and estates.

Can the same be said of divine and supernatural factors? Can they too be "historicized"? Creatures are dependent upon God: this fact can be expressed rationally in an idea and thereby be made a factor in human action. In this sense one can say that God's action vis-à-vis his creation enters into history. In the same way the supernatural too enters into history by virtue of its being accepted or rejected in faith and thus made a dynamic force in history. There is still more: the supernatural as such enters into history, for God becomes man, and Christianity appears in history. All this is real history.[26]

By the supernatural in history Sturzo does not understand a separate sector in society, something juxtaposed to the natural. The supernatural implies a real transformation of human existence and activity. It is no less than the perfecting of the natural life as historically given. Concrete society exists entirely within the atmosphere of the supernatural; a societal life devoid of all supernatural influence has never been encountered anywhere.[27]

---

[24] Ibid., 11f. [Eng. trans., 5f.].
[25] Sturzo, "History and Philosophy," 59, 61.
[26] Sturzo, *Inner Laws of Society*, xxxii, xxxiii.
[27] Sturzo, *La vera vita*, 7, 8, 17, 24 [Eng. trans., 1, 2, 11, 18].

From this comprehensive function of the supernatural flow important consequences for the historian. The decisive element in Christian integralism is that in order to understand history it takes into account not only physical, biotic, economic and other such factors but also and especially the supernatural, since the supernatural, quite apart from the fact that it is requisite for the attainment of our final destination, enables nature to unfold according to its own order.[28]

"Positivist sociologists" too, it will be objected, have taken moral and religious phenomena into account in their investigations and done justice to them as factors in the historical process; thus demonstrating that subjective religious belief is not essential to recognizing the religious factor in history. But Sturzo vigorously rejects such an idea. Those sociologists do indeed affirm religion as a historical factor, but only after they have eliminated from it any notion of the supernatural and reduced it to pure "naturalism" or "moralism."[29] Consequently, Sturzo believes integral sociology can only be practiced by the faithful, since they alone have access to the supernatural world. Similarly, only a believing historian can penetrate deeply into the historical synthesis, since it is the supernatural that transforms and integrates, and thus synthesizes, concrete reality.[30]

Granted, the other kind of sociology can make important contributions to integral sociology, but it will be "abstractionist," "analytical" or "particular."[31] The same is true of non-integral historical science. People distinguish between "philological" and "philosophical" history and want to practice the former, without theoretical presuppositions, as "pure historians" observing historical "objectivity." Yet even in practicing "philological" history the researcher cannot possibly eliminate those general ideas from which one consciously or unconsciously proceeds, particularly one's views concerning the supernatural. It is fine to demand objectivity of the historian, Sturzo remarks, but I have yet to read an objective history of the French Revolution: everyone who has written about it has approached it from one point of view or another.[32] And if someone should object to Sturzo that his integral sociology introduces a dogmatic element into the knowledge of society and falsifies science which must be based on pure induction, the objection would not faze him in the least. At one time, so he tells us, he sought only to establish the natural facts about society, but simply studying their history, even though he did not proceed on the basis of a dogmatic preconception, impressed upon him the *factum* of Christianity in its supernatural character. If in the face of this given he were to remain on the natural plane and leave out the supernatural, or interpret it naturalistically as the result of material causes or emotional impulses or political and cultural influences, then, indeed, that which is essential to history would be fundamentally falsified.[33]

---

[28] Ibid., 7f. [Eng. trans., 2].
[29] Ibid., 10 [Eng. trans., 4f.].
[30] Ibid., 21–23 [Eng. trans., 15f.].
[31] Ibid., 21 [Eng. trans., 15].
[32] Sturzo, "History and Philosophy," 45–47.
[33] Sturzo, *La vera vita*, 19–21 [Eng. trans., 12–14].

When at the start of this section I emphasized the importance of Sturzo's theory I did not mean to imply that he has done pioneering work. "There is nothing really new in Don Sturzo's presentation of the Christian life . . . ," says William O'Connor in a review of Sturzo's book *The True Life*,[34] and I concur. Sturzo has expressed in a fascinating and lucid way what various Catholic historians today aspire to or have more or less successfully put into practice. Sturzo's writings will undoubtedly point the way for the future, since in Catholic circles the question concerning the place of the supernatural factor in historical research is being posed with increasing urgency. What Sturzo has done is sketch a few basic parameters, but trends among Catholic scholars suggest that more work will be done along these lines.

Considering Sturzo's conceptions for a moment apart from the dualism of natural and supernatural factors that informs his theory as well, we must acknowledge that he has shed light on an element of Christian historical science that must be of concern to every Christian historian: he has shown anew that the religious dimension, in all its originality, permeates the entire historical process, and that the historical *factum* can be understood as such in all its dimensions only if its connection with the religious order is taken into account. Nevertheless he has tied himself to a prejudice that prevents him from following through on his religious perspective. He is unable to answer satisfactorily an objection he himself anticipates. Some will detect a contradictory element in his "historicism": the historical process, on his view, is unified in the ratio—the divine and supernatural enter into that process as historical elements and are thus subject to "unification in rationality," yet surely as revealed mysteries they are inaccessible to reason. Sturzo supposes he can escape the bite of this objection by insisting that the mysteries lose nothing of their original character when inserted into the human process, since what is involved here is not rational comprehension of the mystery but "practical cognizance." One may speak of such cognizance when a mystery presents itself as such to the knower, who is certain that it will forever be beyond full comprehension. This phenomenon is encountered in other fields as well, for example, in the physical realm: is our natural knowledge of it not terribly limited? There is thus a great deal of reality, including historical reality, that is accessible to us only in its "practical rationality." [35]

Our account of Sturzo's theory makes clear that he considers the study of the supernatural in society, and of the transformation of the natural, to belong to the task of sociology. Integral sociology does not address the church, the mystical body of Christ, etc., as such, but studies them as elements of concrete society and historical development. Just as psychic or biotic factors are studied *as such* by psychology and biology but as historical factors by historical science, so the supernatural, to the extent that it influences society, belongs to sociology.

---

[34] In *Thought* 18 (1943): 749.
[35] Sturzo, *Inner Laws of Society*, xxxv, xxxvi.

There appear to be no further problems for Sturzo in this delimitation of the fields of inquiry: the ease with which he brushes aside the objection mentioned above indicates as much. Other Catholic thinkers, however, take this delimitation to be a genuine difficulty. Because of the importance of the matter we shall here take a brief look at the solution suggested by Maritain.

We leave aside differences in perspective between Maritain and Sturzo in order to concentrate our attention on Maritain's extension of his idea of Christian philosophy into Christian moral philosophy. Both thinkers agree that nature unfolds itself fully only in dependence upon the supernatural and that human existence and action are in fact tied to the supernatural order. Science must take this reality fully into account if it is to have any claim at all to adequacy in its own field of inquiry.

But both are now confronted by the question: Which of the sciences is to have human existence and action (be it in a fallen or an elevated state) as the object of its investigations? Is it to be theology, or is it to be a non-theological science? Both reject the first possibility, since theology studies only the supernatural as such, and not the supernatural as a historical or social factor. Sturzo goes no further than this, but Maritain proceeds to work the problem out in detail. He calls it the problem of Christian "moral philosophy," but then he takes "moral" in a very broad sense: when he speaks of moral philosophy he has in mind at the same time sociology, ethnology, economics, philosophy of culture, and so on and so forth—all the sciences that have human action as their of field of inquiry.[36] Now, where moral philosophy and its subordinate sciences are concerned, we are looking not at the problem of Christian philosophy in general but at a particular case. For here the distinction between "nature" and "state" pertains not only to philosophy as such but also to its object: "Here is a very special case, for we are face to face with an object which itself presents us with the distinction between *nature* and *state,* an object which is *natural* in its essence, yet whose *state* is not purely natural but dependent upon the supernatural order." [37]

Thus moral philosophy has an object which is natural in character but which at the same time has an inner connection with the supernatural order. Maritain now desires a moral philosophy that will be adequate to its object. He calls it a "moral philosophy adequately considered." [38]

A Christian moral philosophy will nonetheless have to be closely connected with theology: it remains philosophy, but as "subalternated" to theology.[39] The theological habitus taken in itself—which is to say, as a human activity—is natural, but "virtually and in its roots" it is supernatural. Moral philosophy, in contrast, is natural in itself and in its roots, but through its subalternation to

---

[36] Maritain, *De la philosophie chrétienne*, 70f. [Eng. trans., 38f.].

[37] Ibid.

[38] Ibid., passim. Despite criticism of this terminology Maritain still uses it in 1946; see, for example, his *Distinguer pour unir, ou les degrés du savoir*, page xii, note [Eng. trans., 5n].

[39] Maritain, *Distinguer pour unir*, loc. cit.

theology it receives a complement and perfection the origin of which is supernatural.[40] Moral philosophy, in order to be adequate to its object, adopts conclusions from theology, not in order to gain easy solutions to difficult problems but in order to *complement* and *perfect* its own solutions, which have been arrived at primarily by the light of reason. Thus the subalternation of moral philosophy to theology is not "radical and originative" but "completive and perfective." Via theology, various disciplines are supplemented with data derived from Revelation.[41]

Since 1933, the year in which Maritain first presented an extensive study of "moral philosophy adequately considered," the question of a Christian moral philosophy and of Maritain's conceptions in particular has often been a topic of debate. Both Maritain's defenders and his critics acknowledge that the problem is a real one, and that our times urgently require a solution to it. For all that, a significant breakthrough has yet to be heard of. Maritain's opponents[42] cannot accept that a moral philosophy that employs data from Revelation is still philosophy. To yield at all to such a notion is already to move into the field of theology.

§ 5. *The Catholic idea of a Christian historical science: an evaluation*

Having examined the theories of Mercier, Padovani, and so on, we now proceed to a critical evaluation of the Catholic idea of a Christian historical science. We shall start with the way in which Catholic scholars commonly view the relationship between the various disciplines that deal with history, or as I would prefer to say, with the historical. One must then distinguish four different ways in which one can approach the phenomenon called history.[43]

1. *Technical history.* Its task consists in establishing the historicity of events. This is the business of the real scientist, the "fact-finder," the practicing historian who endeavors to establish critically the value of the sources and tries in this way to learn if this or that happened thus or so.

2. *Historiography.* This builds on the "foundations" laid by the "fact-finder" but seeks to place the still isolated facts in a certain *provisional* causal pattern and in this way to construct a synthesis. But the historian who utilizes the data supplied him by the "fact-finder" does not, when constructing his synthesis, go beyond the realm of history; even when indicating a controlling factor in the facts such a scholar does not go beyond the phenomenal order.[44]

---

[40] Maritain, *De la philosophie chrétienne*, 149 [Eng. trans., 90].

[41] Ibid., 146–51 [Eng. trans., 86–92].

[42] See, e.g., Van Steenberghen, "La deuxième journée d'études de la Société thomiste et la notion de philosophie chrétienne," passim.

[43] Cf., e.g., Flahiff, "A Catholic Looks at History," 4–6; Thils, *Théologie de l'histoire*, 28f. Thils distinguishes just three ways, since he lumps the first two under the "physics" of history. The same term is used, though in a different sense, by Marrou, "Existe-t-il une vision chrétienne de l'histoire?" 50.

[44] Thils, *Théologie de l'histoire*, 28f.

3. *Philosophy of history*. This is where we transcend the phenomenal realm. Philosophy of history looks at history from the standpoint of principles and truths that are not present in historical reality itself but that have been introduced from the outside, in an attempt to answer the questions of the why, the what, and the how of the historical process, in short, the question of its meaning. Here, as in theology of history, there can be a wide variety of schools of interpretation, inasmuch as the questions admit of a wide variety of answers. As long as one attempts to explain history through nature and reason alone, one remains within philosophy of history.

4. *Theology of history*. This transcends philosophy—we find ourselves in an ascending order—albeit it should build on all the preceding disciplines. Revelation is its point of departure, proceeding from which it sheds light on the mystery of history, which, however—this in passing—will never be fully resolved, not even through Revelation. It is true that theology of history is concerned with supernatural realities such as God, sin, grace and salvation, but these are at the same time fundamental truths about human life on earth and thus objects of history, inasmuch as history has man in his earthly existence as its object of investigation.

Now then, to gain insight into the meaning and value of the Catholic idea of a Christian historical science,[45] we shall ascertain whether in the case of each of the four aspects of historical science—the concept of science thus taken here in the broad sense—this idea has any real and tenable meaning.

With respect to theology of history we can be brief. From the task assigned to it, it is at once evident that an authentic Christian conception of history, insofar as its theological side is concerned, is considered possible and regarded as embodied in a variety of theories.

The problem of a Christian conception of history is more difficult when its philosophical aspect is at issue. The consensus is that there can be no concept of a Christian metaphysics of history in the strict sense.[46] From what we observed in the preceding chapter about Christian philosophy this is immediately clear. Nevertheless, more than once we come across the expression "Christian philosophy of history." Here too, as in general philosophy, more than one meaning may be involved. Some take it to mean that none of the results of philosophy of history may conflict with what is known by faith, on pain of forfeiting its character as truth. Philosophy of history ought, in its thinking, to stay close to Christian dogma and, if possible, support it.

The term "Christian philosophy of history" can be used in yet another sense. Balduin Schwarz claims that Maritain's conceptions of history and culture, insofar as their philosophical articulation is concerned, have no tradition. Until

---

[45] Despite the fact that Roman Catholic writers tend to avoid the term, I do believe it is legitimate to speak of "Christian historical science" here, since the concept does play a significant role in their writings, as we will notice presently.

[46] At most there could be a philosophy of history which through its "surprising kinship" with Christianity would be easy for Christians to accept; thus Thils, *Théologie de l'histoire*, 31.

Maritain came along the conception of history, at least in Catholic circles, insofar as it was Christian, was purely theologically inspired.[47] The concept of a Christian philosophy of history has an unusual meaning in Maritain. He believes he can apply the adjective Christian to it because, even though it is based on purely rational insight, a transformation of supernatural values into temporal ones takes place within its field of inquiry.

Our problem is at its most complex where the establishment and synthesis of the historical facts are concerned. The facts are established and a synthesis is formed, according to the view prevalent among Catholic historians, by disciplines that work with natural means. Among the historical facts there are many that have a purely natural character. But alongside these, or among them, there also exist or operate supernatural facts and factors that are just as much objects of historical science. Moreover, historical science is confronted with a transformation of human existence that arises from the supernatural order. Now, this raises the question, given the totally disparate character of the factors in the field of historical inquiry, whether historical science, which aspires to a purely rational construction of knowledge, disposes over sufficient means to be adequate to its own object. How must historical science, which is in pursuit of natural knowledge, deal with supernatural data?

H. F. Kearney believes the inner life of the church, the essence in the supernatural fact, must escape the "historian's microscope." [48]

Standing in sharp contrast is the view of Alfred Feder and Luigi Sturzo, even though there is an important difference between them. While Feder believes that historical science cannot investigate the supernatural facts and factors in history without presupposing revealed truths and so positioning itself in the field of theology,[49] Sturzo maintains that the supernatural, taken in its full, original significance, is an object of investigation for sociology and historical science to whatever extent it appears as a factor in the historical process. It even forms the synthesis of concrete historical reality.

Feder's solution appears to be the more acceptable since he at least calls upon a discipline for the investigation of history that is adequate to very important historical factors. But Sturzo's construction remains unclear inasmuch as he wants to investigate purely supernatural givens by means of a science that works according to natural principles. On the one hand, according to Sturzo, historical reality is subject to "unification in rationality"; on the other hand it is the supernatural that forms its synthesis. Sturzo endeavors to salvage both "unification in rationality" and the integrity of the supernatural in history by invoking the concept of "practical cognizance" through which the nonrational mystery is supposed to be accessible. Sturzo gets caught in confusion here because he wants to uphold the natural basis of both history and historical

---

[47] Schwarz, "Jacques Maritain und die christliche Geschichtsphilosophie," 473f.
[48] Kearney, "Christianity and the Study of History," 72; see also 68.
[49] Feder, *Lehrbuch der geschichtlichen Methode*, 30.

knowledge, together with the unity of the sciences that deal with the historical. Feder acknowledges openly that this unity no longer exists and that the supernatural as a historical factor simply demands another form of cognition. Maritain succeeds in attaining the desired unity, but only after transforming the supernatural givens into ordinary human forms. The dualism in historical reality seems thus to frustrate any internal unity between the disciplines that go no further than establishing the facts and constructing a provisional synthesis, unless the supernatural allows itself to be reduced to a purely natural factor.

To sum up, in the view of many Catholic scholars the significance of the Christian religion for researching and writing history is not inconsiderable. The primary task of Christian historical science consists in establishing the facts. In this respect it is not yet distinguishable from non-Christian science. But it is exceptionally well equipped for this task, since it is better qualified to write about the supernatural factors and to assess also those periods during which Christianity had the preponderant influence on civilization. (The unbelieving historian will of course also pay attention to Christ's coming into the world, to the church and to miracles, but at the same time will denature these facts into ordinary phenomena.) Similarly, when constructing a synthesis Christian historical science will guard against overestimating economic life, for example, and will be able to indicate the predominant factor in each period. In short, the spirit in which history is researched and written, and the partiality with which a period or pattern of events is selected as a special field of study, will be one thing in the case of a believing historian and something else in the case of a non-believing historian. Even when the former is busy with periods in which there is no demonstrable Christian element, the approach to the material will be different: for in the case even of non-Christianized cultures, the Christian historian will accept the Providence of God.[50]

We saw that Mercier, Padovani, Flahiff, Sturzo, Feder and others define the task of historical science as establishing the facts and bringing them into a provisional synthesis. We can agree with this description of the historian's task, provided it can first be agreed what is to be understood by "the facts" and by "establishing the facts." For the Catholic historians or philosophers that we consulted, historical reality belongs largely to the natural order (this is accepted even by those who hold that history has its original meaning in religious history). Within this natural order, however, supernatural influences and factors play an important role—for cannot God's direct intervention in the evolution of history give it an entirely different direction?

Yet ordinary historical facts are natural at their core, according to them, even when the supernatural is taken to be the synthesizing factor in history, since within the supernatural wrapping, natural life carries on. The religious and

---

[50] Lousse, *Geschiedenis*, 62f.

natural elements in the historical realm are thus independent and, to a degree, separable quantities.

But is that ordinary, non-supernatural fact a "natural" fact? And do we indeed grasp its full reality if we attempt to acquire knowledge of it exclusively through a rational science without religious presuppositions? Do we, to echo Padovani, attain the "real history of the historian" if we dispense with every "metaphysical" and "transcendent" element? Flahiff retorts that if we seek the deeper meaning of historical facts in the light of other than purely historical principles and truths, we are no longer in the field of history, though the tie to it may be very close indeed; instead we are then involved in "history *plus*." [51] Now, I concede that a reflection on the deeper meaning of history is not an element of the fact under consideration. Yet meaning itself resides in the historical. To say that its deeper meaning is not accessible to us in so-called natural experience but only in the experience of faith is not yet to say that that meaning is a "plus" rather than an intrinsic element of the historical fact. What is this deeper meaning if not the relation of the historical fact, in its totality, to the Ground of all things, and to its involvement in the tension in which everything created is involved, namely, the tension between sin and salvation? Consequently, a historian who takes events or circumstances as purely natural is abstracting them from what is most elementary, from their connection to the ever present and yet transcendent Origin of all things. Such a historian consciously or unconsciously represses all that, and proceeds to write history *as if* the world rests and exists in itself.[52] Thus the "real history of the historian" is an abstraction, and either he or the theologian endeavors to heal the wound by incorporating into the *conception* of history, as elementary givens, the dependence of history upon God, and its sharing in the fall and redemption.

The dichotomy in Catholic thought between the science of history and theology of history stems not from a difference in their nature but from the fact that the former is concerned with an abstract, natural world and the latter with an integral, primarily religious world. In Catholic writings one often comes across complaints about this dichotomy. Aubert speaks of it in his fine summary of the debates surrounding theology of history: the technical historian is skeptical about theology of history (and philosophy of history); the latter may construct fine theories, but they do not touch him since they arise from *another* world that is *alien* to him qua historian; by the same token, the historical researcher often stands accused of concerning himself too exclusively with the "phenomena," to the neglect of theology or philosophy of history.[53]

---

[51] Flahiff, "A Catholic Looks at History," 3.
[52] Kearney, "Christianity and the Study of History," 68. Kearney sees no other possibility for the Christian historian, if he desires to remain objective, than to accept this reduced historical reality. The advantage the Christian historian has over his nonbelieving colleagues, according to him, is that he does not mistake this "reconstructed" history for the "real" world of history.
[53] Aubert, "Discussions récentes autour de la Théologie de l'histoire," 146.

This division between what is called "histoire phénoménale" and one's vision of history is evinced very strongly in the concrete problems of world history, of periodization, and of progress. In dealing with these I have repeatedly pointed out that in faith we know Christ to be the ruling center and his coming in the flesh the turning point of history, but that until now no one has succeeded in indicating concretely the unity of world history, and of its caesuras, according to purely Christian criteria.

I believe the dichotomy between theology of history and historical science will not be overcome unless the historian takes seriously the religious connection of history to its Origin. (This is not to say that one must accept uncritically the givens provided by Christian theology of history or philosophy of history, as these too can err.) The technical historian's realm of experience is not an autonomous historical reality. It is inaccessible to him through purely natural means. He has to acknowledge that it becomes understandable to him in its concreteness only by way of a supra-theoretical point of departure.

What I have just said could give rise to two misunderstandings. When I ask of the historian that he take fully into account the religious connections within which concrete history is situated, no one should conclude that I regard this task as easy or capable of execution in the short term. Equally objectionable, however, would be the conclusion that the issue is merely one of a confession of faith about historical reality, which, once stated, would allow the historian to go on and do history just like a colleague not sharing the same belief. I am convinced that the Christian historian is confronted here with a most difficult, well-nigh superhuman task. I do not reproach Catholic historians for having made but little progress in accomplishing this task, but rather for not sensing the urgency of the need for an *integral* Christian historical practice, commencing as they do by separating the historical facts from their most elementary connections. My critique of Mercier, Padovani and others is that they proceed from the autonomy of historical reality and only *afterwards* consider the relation of its dependence upon the Origin.

A second possible misunderstanding is the following. When the practicing historian is asked to take into account the religious relation of the facts to God, this is often taken to mean that he should undertake a detailed investigation into the operation of Divine Providence and that he should try to discover the plan of God for specific things, peoples, and cultures. That would, indeed, amount to a superhuman feat. It is not given to man to know God's purposes with particular historical configurations, not even when they have already run their course and passed on into new forms.

Thus the historian should not speculate about divine "causality"; in faith he will accept it. His concern is created reality, which is to say a historical world that is of divine origin. This religious presupposition entails the belief that the causal patterns in created reality are religiously determined. It is in this light that the problem of historical causality must be explored.

The modern historian endeavors to understand historical facts in their causal patterns. He is more aware than his nineteenth-century colleague, however, that knowledge of the factors determining a historical event will always remain very limited. For this reason, and for more profound philosophical reasons, various historians have proposed that the entire causality principle be eliminated from historical science and that, instead of seeking to "explain" historical events, historians should work to "understand" them in their full individuality. Remarkably enough, however, causal explanation has not been easy to repress. Even its avowed opponents continue all too often to work for the fullest possible knowledge of the conditionality of a historical circumstance or event. The situation in present-day historical science is now such that, in the absence of anything better, the historian continues to work with the concept of causality, but then with one that has been divested of its original naturalistic form.

So now that the concept of causality employed by the technical historian has been disconnected from the philosophical idea of causality oriented to classical physics, the Christian historian would seem to be justified in adopting it without objection as the basis of his research. He will speak of historical phenomena as arising and developing, as being connected, related, influenced, and so forth—all of them concepts that have something to do with causality—without interpreting them in terms of a naturalistic conception of reality. Yet should one ask such a historian about the nature of these concepts, he either will have no answer or will argue that this is a matter for philosophers, not historians. However, philosophy does not permit itself to be barred so easily from historical science. A historian may know numerous factors that have demonstrably conditioned the course of an event yet still not know in what intimate relation these factors stand to each other, or to the event, or which among them is of overriding importance. Historical research can provide indications that a relation exists between two particular facts or factors, but that tells us nothing about the nature of this relation or the extent to which the one fact determines the other.

From the side of Scholastic philosophers it may be objected that they at least are not content with a denatured, vague concept of causality; their concept of causality is built organically into the grand structure of their metaphysics. Our objection, however, is that the Scholastic concept of causality remains oriented to an autonomous view of reality: the points of connection for the countless host of causes are the "substances." In Scholastic philosophy the natural order of the causes, which is identified with God's indirect action in nature and history, is severed from the religious relation to God and made independent, in a speculative ontological relation. (In saying this I do not wish to ignore the fact that the reverse side of this independence is the ordering of the creature to God as First Cause.)

Some Catholic historians are conscious that the dichotomy of faith and science and the separation of the Christian and the historian make for an impossible situation, and that no satisfying solution is obtained by taking supernatural factors into account in doing historical research. The most radical solution is Ross Hoffman's proposal to elevate history in all its subdivisions to the proper life of the church, even when it has as yet had no known contact whatsoever with Christianity. Not only in Hoffman but also in many who go less far, it is the church that must bring to an end this dichotomy to which the historian is prey. Yet it will be clear that the concrete problems confronting the technical historian persist with undiminished force; the supernaturalization of historical reality can serve only to camouflage them. Moreover, such supernaturalization is at best only apparent: violence is done to the cultures by stamping them Christian; in reality they continue their autonomous existence; as to history, all that has happened is that it is now *thought of* as being overarched by the supernatural reality of the church. It continues to elude Hoffman, Belloc, and others that the religious dimension does not have to be imposed upon history from without; that history *as such* is religiously conditioned and dependent, and that it is the structure and coherence of *this* reality that the historian investigates.

More promising for the future than the excessive supernaturalism of Hoffman and Belloc is, I believe, the integralism of Sturzo and Padovani. This "Christian integralism" is one of the most noteworthy currents in modern Catholicism. Not only Sturzo and Padovani but Anselm Stolz and, in a certain sense, Blondel and Malevez as well, are looking for an integrally religious reality. Worthy of note in their endeavor, however, is the prominent place occupied by the concrete. "Abstract essences" and "natural reason" speak of self-sufficiency and autonomy, but the concrete has the religious dimension, evil and salvation. This contrast breaks the force of "Christian integralism." It persists in upholding the idea of a positive orientation of nature to grace even though concrete reality speaks quite a different language (Stolz); it continues to proceed from supposedly pure empirical research into history without taking transcendent elements into account, even though it knows that sin and salvation constitute the basic plan of history (Padovani). "Christian integralism" desires an integrally religious reality but is content with the dualism of the autonomous and abstract versus the religious and concrete.

APPENDIX/ Some Practicing Catholic Historians

1. *Gustav Schnürer*

Gustav Schnürer, though born a German, spent the greater part of his life in Switzerland. In 1889 he became a professor in the Catholic university at Freiburg, established that year, and remained so until his death in 1941.

Although he devoted the early years of his scholarly career mainly to the writing of monographs, there was no lack of effort during this phase to discover larger patterns in history. On one or two occasions he even ventured into the realm of philosophical reflections on history, as in his rectorial address of the year 1900 on "The Periodization of World History," but not until the interbellum did synthesis gain precedence. In five volumes he wrote the history of Europe from the days of the Roman Caesars to the French Revolution, while at the end of his life he was still working on a sixth volume. The first three volumes deal with *Church and Culture in the Middle Ages*; the two that follow are about *The Catholic Church and Culture in the Baroque Period* and *The Catholic Church and Culture in the Eighteenth Century*.[1] In these major works Schnürer was concerned with a particular aspect of history, the relation of church and culture. He was most successful with respect to the Late Roman and Medieval worlds. One senses in all his work that his heart goes out to medieval culture, in particular to the 12th and 13th centuries, during which the church had the leadership of the *vita Christiana*. In presenting his ideas about the influence of Christianity on western culture I confine myself to the period from 300 to 1300 and call attention only to his most characteristic conceptions.

1. When Christianity first appeared, Roman culture was ripe for collapse. Yet it contained many elements that could serve as the valuable seeds of a new cultural world. The problem was to preserve these through the catastrophe.

It was vital to the western culture that would now take shape that Roman culture as such should collapse. For Christianity could not blossom into a genuine Christian culture, in new and better forms, if the fossilized and decadent Roman society continued to exist: every new shoot would suffocate from lack of light and air.[2]

There was danger for Christianity not only in the decadence of Roman culture but also in particular elements in Hellenism and Judaism that could have deflected Christianity from its world-historical task. The ties with Judaism had to be broken before Christianity could become a blessing to all nations. The historical mission of Hellenism was completed when it brought Christianity and the intellectual culture of Antiquity closer together. And the Roman Empire had to vanish because it would have led Christianity onto by-paths: no sooner had the Roman emperors made the transition to Christianity than they did not scruple to extend their authority to the church. The newly converted rulers thought they had found in the church a means to enlarge their power and glory.[3]

2. True Christian culture—to Schnürer that is Catholic culture—is the bearer of a great moral force, although there is no guarantee that this will always remain at its peak. It too undergoes decline again and again, but it possesses the possibility and ultimate certainty that after periods of collapse and darkness it will arise and flourish anew. Thus in the Middle Ages there are times of deep decline followed by periods of powerful and wondrous recovery and a budding forth of what lay germinating through years of darkness.

Paganism does not possess the guarantee of moral regeneration. Once it has set out on the road to moral corruption nothing remains to preserve it from destruction. Heresy too has no such guarantee. For example, Arianism perished because in Christ it recognized not God but a creature, and so it crippled its own cultural force by rejecting the most precious truths of the Christian faith.

Schnürer's description of the struggle between "Catholicism" and Arianism for leadership in the religious and cultural spheres in the West is one of the best parts of his work on the Middle Ages. He sees clearly that this conflict was not of theological

---

[1] For full titles of the originals, see the Bibliography.
[2] Schnürer, *Kirche und Kultur im Mittelalter*, 1:19 [Eng. trans., 27].
[3] Ibid., 20 [Eng. trans., 28].

significance alone but that upholding the doctrine of the deity of Christ was of decisive importance for western culture. Not just because the difference in religion between Romans and Germans blocked the way to unification of their cultures (western civilization would never have arisen if the Germans had not embraced Catholicism, since a genuine cultural community can only be formed on the basis of religious unity), but also because the outcome of the struggle would determine if a *western* culture could emerge and if a *Christian* culture could survive and develop further. Had Arianism triumphed this would have been out of the question—that much is clear from the history of the Germanic kingdoms that remained loyal to Arianism: when they came into contact with the corrupt morals of Roman society they were carried along by the corruption without finding in their religion the power of renewal. The most telling example is that of the Arian Vandals who, having invaded Carthage, put an end to the worst immorality there but a half century later had become equally depraved. It was therefore not very difficult for the Byzantine general Belisarius to put an end to their domination in North Africa.[4]

Now take as a contrast the "Catholic" Romans. They too were not morally elevated; they threatened to be engulfed in the moral decay of ancient society. But, unlike the Arians, they had a solid ground below which they could not sink: among the Romans—at least among some of them—the belief in the deity of Christ lived on: "From here moral renewal could begin again, when the doomed Roman society, with its urban culture perverting both body and soul, had disappeared." [5]

Belief in Christ as the Son of God offers no assurance that a nation that has accepted the Christian faith will survive as a nation, but it does provide a nation with the means of lifting itself out of any moral depression and, "when one nation is dying, of calling forth, with all its energies, new life in another." [6]

It is not just the Roman world that provides an example of this. A similar process occurred in the Merovingian kingdom. Here too inner decay soon set in, as a result in fact of close contacts with Roman culture. Here too the church fell prey to the power of the king. One might therefore say: the Franks went over to "Catholic" Christianity and still they suffered moral and social decline—where, then, is the difference with the Arian kingdoms? It lies in the catholic character of the Frankish church. Thanks to its universality the church could receive help from without. Initially this help came from Ireland, later it was offered by the Anglo-Saxons, but in both instances it came from lands that lay far from Rome and had not been "contaminated with the corruption of Rome's superculture."[7] To be sure, it was from the Roman Empire that the island dwellers themselves had received Christianity and the fertile seeds of culture. With these, Britain and Ireland would now bless the European continent. Once again Schnürer sees this as a confirmation of his thesis that the Roman Empire had to fall before a new Christian culture could blossom forth, since this alone permitted the undisturbed growth of a young and powerful church and a Christian civilization that could liberate the European continent from the aftereffects of a decadent ancient society. It is therefore no coincidence that pope Gregory the Great sent the Benedictines not to the Frankish kingdom but to the Anglo-Saxons. In this way Gregory contributed indirectly,

---

[4] Ibid., 142, 157f. [Eng. trans., 190, 209f.].
[5] Ibid., 158 [Eng. trans., 210].
[6] Ibid.
[7] Ibid., 173, 183, 214f. [Eng. trans., 213, 242, 285f.].

without divining all the consequences himself, to the forming of the western cultural community.[8]

3. The history of Christian culture in the Ancient world and the Early Middle Ages is to be viewed as a preparation. At that time the seeds were planted that would come to maturity in the 12th and 13th centuries, when the Middle Ages reached their high point. It was the golden age of the Gothic but also of the Papacy and Scholasticism. The church acted as the leader of intellectual, economic, political and military life. It was the heyday of Christian culture.

Granted, there was a risk involved. The church might have become so absorbed in worldly affairs that it forgot to be not of this world. In the High Middle Ages, however, the church may have been caught in a field of tension with culture, but not yet in a contradiction between its supernatural character and its cultural work. For culture at this time still had an intimate tie with the church as a spiritual reality.[9] Not until the Late Middle Ages did the conflict arise between church and culture. Then the servants of the church were unable to stand up to the spirit of the world. This provoked counter-movements, which, however, quickly lapsed into excesses.[10] In the Gothic period, in contrast, idealism had been susceptible of harmonious union with a passion for realism.

Schnürer's conception of the 12th and 13th centuries stands in marked contrast to that of Herwegen and Mayer (see below), according to whom the Germanic spirit during this period refused to be bound any longer to classical forms and the Christian *mysterium* and dissipated itself in boundless subjectivism and ethicism. For Schnürer, the Gothic more than any other style was a product of the new community of the western peoples. The Romanesque style, too, was independent, but it was little more, really, than a continued development of the Roman basilica; thus unlike the Gothic it did not have Christian roots, since its ground-plan was derived from pagan architecture.[11]

Schnürer also praises—again contra Herwegen and others—the earnestness of religious feeling in the 12th and 13th centuries (as manifest, for instance, in the imitation of Christ by a Francis of Assisi). And he credits it to a deepening of Christian faith that henceforth Christ was generally portrayed as the Crucified one: no longer was the majesty of the King of the universe accentuated but rather the suffering of the Savior.[12]

In the Late Middle Ages, Schnürer continues, the tension that must always exist between the acceptance of culture and the idealist renunciation of earthly goods shifted to the detriment of the latter. The enjoyment of a refined "this-worldly culture" gained the upper hand in the Christian world. But then came the Age of Spain. From the 15th century onward Spain was able to assume the leadership of western culture because within its borders ecclesiastical idealism, respect for the church, and the spirit of the crusaders lived on. What had failed elsewhere succeeded in Spain: the valuable traditions of the Middle Ages were linked with the culture of the Renaissance.[13]

---

[8] Ibid., 259f., 270 [Eng. trans., 345f., 358].
[9] Ibid., 2:280, 286, 515f., 523.
[10] Ibid., 522; 3:8.
[11] Ibid., 2:506f.
[12] Ibid., 516f.
[13] Ibid., 3:8, 270f.

§ 2. Ildefons Herwegen, Anton L. Mayer and Johannes Pinsk

In the adherents of the sacramental conception of history the speculative element occupies such an important place that one hesitates to regard their works, in which they offer a synthesis of the Early Christian period or the Middle Ages and Modern Times, as history-writing proper. Yet their work is more than just a theological interpretation of the periods in question. They are quite intent on writing history, but then in such a way that both in the study of the details and in their synthesis they highlight the fact that in every historical period the dominant factor is the changed relation to the mysterium. These historians want to show that during the course of the Middle Ages the Christian life, in all its forms of expression, was deflected by the subjectivist and individualist tendencies of the Germanic spirit from its true end, the elevation to the supernatural order. One cannot deny the label history to this kind of historical writing, but it is history in which interpretation predominates.

The foremost representatives of these more recent interpretations of the "essence" of the Middle Ages are Ildefons Herwegen, Anton Mayer and Johannes Pinsk. They are all intimately connected with the Society at the center of the so-called Liturgical Movement, headed initially by Abbot Herwegen (1874–1946) and in later years by Odo Casel (1886–1948). The unmistakable background of the conception of history represented here is the "mystery theology" inaugurated by Herwegen and elaborated by Casel, the most original and profound theologian of the Liturgical Movement.[14]

Adherents of this theology contend that what constitutes the essence of Christianity is not dogma and ethics but the work, or rather the person, of Christ and the Holy Spirit's infusion of the divine life into the church.[15] The accent falls on being made rich in Christ through the sacraments, on being united with Christ in the *corpus mysticum*. The church is the recipient with respect to its Savior and Lord. The deepest reality of the church is expressed in the idea of being the Bride of Christ. The church is impregnated by Christ. Its origin and existence are not to be traced to the will of a man but to the Spirit of Christ that flows through it. Thus the Christian mystery, the re-presentation of Christ's work of redemption, includes two elements. First, the eucharist has an objective character; it is not primarily a matter of a subjective remembrance of the historical way of salvation traversed by Christ, but of an ontological fact, the effectuation in the present of the *oeconomia Christi*. No less important is the second element directly related to the first. The mysterium has community-forming, all-encompassing significance. When Christ's work of salvation is effectuated in the present according to its *aevitern* character, Christ enters into contact with the church and its whole life becomes of concern to him: the mysterious life entails an uninterrupted, ongoing sanctification and glorification of the church. Nor is it just the great fundamental goods of salvation that flow from the mysterium; the entire *vita christiana* is formed from and through it. Via the *mysterium*, life in all its expressions acquires a decidedly *theocentric* character and a sacramental and sacral stamp.[16]

It is in terms of these three aspects, the objective, the community-forming, and the theocentric, that Herwegen, Mayer and Pinsk view the historical process.

---

[14] Cf. above, ch. 2, § 5 and ch. 3, § 6. On the development of the Liturgical Movement, see Heitz, "Dernières étapes du renouveau liturgique allemand."

[15] See, e.g., Pinsk, "Germanentum und katholische Kirche," 361; Dekkers, "De mysterieleer van Maria-Laach," 139.

[16] Herwegen, *Kirche und Seele*, 9–11.

The first question they pose is this: How do the spiritual identities of classical Antiquity and Germanic culture relate to Christianity? [17] Postulating that the spiritual element is markedly different in each case, they seek to show that, as a result, the religious attitude and *vita christiana* of Christian Antiquity are wholly different from those of the Christian Middle Ages or of Modern Times.

Of decisive importance for the attitude of Ancient and Germanic people towards the spiritual were three factors: blood, soil, and seniority (of the tribal group in question). By far the most important factor in the spiritual identity of a people is the influence of the natural environment: man is one with it, he shapes it and it shapes him.[18] The person of Antiquity saw himself surrounded by sunny coasts, blue skies and flowering fields; everything invited him, as it were, to be absorbed into the cosmos. Such a cosmos awakened the appetite for the objective; the sunny environment inspired the idea of being and harmony, of harmonious being. Everything was assumed to possess a metaphysical perfection, which still had to be pursued, however, in the material world. Everything desired perfection, harmony, as its highest end. To some degree this elevated the products of culture, already in the here-and-now, to the eternal. In this way life in Antiquity had something permanent, something definitive about it. To be sure, things continued to have a goal and thus to remain in motion and development, but that was action striving for perfection, action *within* harmony and *within* perfection itself. Outwardly the dynamics was hardly noticeable; it consisted in a "progressive harmony of being." The life of ancient man was less a transition to the goal than the goal itself in ascending desire. Ancient culture strove after unity and rest, the elimination of unbridled dynamics and contradictions; it endeavored to attain this in symmetry, balance, clarity and monumentality (not of dimensions but of ideas).[19]

How totally different the spiritual world of the German! He saw himself surrounded by dense forests and inaccessible swamps, by rain, mist and snow, and he had to endure long dark winters. Nature terrified him, threw him back upon his own resources; it was a hostile power that had to be conquered. In the Germanic person all was restlessness, movement, dynamics and struggle. He turned away from the external world in order to look inward, but his internal restlessness drove him back again to the surrounding nature (here is the source of his subjectivism and individualism and his restless activity instead of contemplation). The crux of the spiritual world of the Germans lay in their ceaseless striving to give expression to what lived inside them. They valued things in terms of their importance for daily life. They were not drawn to the eternal but measured things by the moment. That is why they were always acting differently, afraid of repetition, focused on the concrete.[20]

The natural environment, therefore, ultimately accounts for the totally different spiritual attitudes taken by the Ancient and the Germanic person toward Christianity. For ancient man the highest reality was eternal, harmonious being; for the German it was the concrete, singular, transient or contingent.[21] All this made for a difference of direction in the religious attitude in Christian Antiquity and the Middle Ages. Early Christians endeavored to elevate the human to the divine; medieval Christians pulled

---

[17] Herwegen, *Antike, Germanentum und Christentum*, 10.
[18] Ibid., 13.
[19] Ibid., 14–17, 20, 66.
[20] Ibid., 17f., 67.
[21] Ibid., 26f.

the supernatural down to the human. The result was a difference in attitude toward Christ and the mysterium. In Christian Antiquity everything, even the most natural thing in the world, was viewed from the perspective of the mysterium, thus lifting all things out of their isolation. The whole of natural life was assigned an ordered place within the supernatural sphere.[22]

The cardinal question in the writing of history for Herwegen and kindred minds appears to be the relation of nature to grace. In Christian Antiquity these were still closely intertwined, via the mysterium; but during the Middle Ages, especially in Scholasticism, nature extricated itself, resulting in a clear separation of two "essentially alien" spheres, a natural and a supernatural, a temporal and a divine. No longer did the sacred realm radiate its glory over the whole of life.[23] From Antiquity to Modern Times there is a long evolution, at the end of which stands Luther. He denied any connection whatsoever between marriage, state, and so on, and the sphere of grace, because they belonged to a domain that is ontologically sinful.[24]

During the Germanic Middle Ages the Christian life underwent a profound transformation. No longer did it orient itself to the objective salvation event but it focused on the individual soul. The moral life, previously valued only as an "expression of the life of the mystery," now acquired a significance of its own.[25] The idea of the mystery was never entirely lost on the Germanic world, but it atrophied into an alien reality.[26]

This neglect of what is essential in Christianity is not, however, to be blamed solely on the Germanic spirit. What worked unfavorably as well was the fact that these were still young nations lacking all bond with the received idea of the mystery and living far below the cultural level requisite for such a high degree of religiosity.[27]

To clarify, let me cite two examples from the abundance of material adduced by Herwegen and Mayer in support of their assertions. The first is taken from art history. Early Christian mosaics were still entirely inspired by the "mystery liturgy" in which the one objective salvation event dominated. Medieval stained-glass windows, in contrast, featured detailed representations from the Gospels, the lives of the saints, and legends; such windows distracted worshipers from the essentials and scarcely separated them from the fleeting life of the world outside.[28]

Profound changes were likewise discernible in the world-picture. This can be seen very clearly in the concept of revolution. For ancient people revolution meant a *re*volving, which is to say, a coming round to renewed contact with the beginning, a reversion to a Golden Age. For modern people revolution means just the opposite: progress toward the unforeseeable new, antagonism to what once was. Accordingly, the idea of progress that came with the "breakthrough" of the Germanic spirit has not been one of periodic movement, of movement which by nature flows outward, symbolizing eternity, but one, rather, of unending, never completed development that acquires new dimensions and reveals new contents day after day.[29]

---

[22] Herwegen, *Kirche und Seele*, 13f., 22f.
[23] Ibid., 23; and idem, "Kirche und Seele: Eine Entgegnung," 240f.
[24] Herwegen, "Kirche und Seele: Eine Entgegnung," 241.
[25] Herwegen, *Kirche und Seele*, 15.
[26] Herwegen, *Antike, Germanentum und Christentum*, 51.
[27] Herwegen, *Kirche und Seele*, 16.
[28] Ibid., 22.
[29] Herwegen, *Antike, Germanentum und Christentum*, 38–40.

If the judgment of Herwegen (and of Pinsk and Mayer, as we shall see in moment) is not favorable where the religiosity and culture of the Germans is concerned, it is no better as to the way they adjusted to Christianity. This conclusion is so obvious as one reads their works that Herwegen anticipates the question: Is Christianity then antithetical to the Germanic spirit and identical to the Roman? His answer is a firm denial. He points to the great distance between every nationality and the essence of the Christian religion, and he reminds us of the only irreconcilable antithesis known to Christianity: sin and salvation.[30] In his booklet *Kirche und Seele* he defends himself against the charge of being prejudiced against the Middle Ages by explaining that he wishes only to offer a typology of two fundamentally different attitudes and not to pass a value judgment on medieval religiosity.[31]

Nevertheless, Herwegen does make a value judgment about both the early Christian and the medieval way of connecting the natural and spiritual realms. This is transparent in all his writings as well as in those of his supporters. At one point he says in so many words: "In Christianity, being (Logos) simply has precedence over becoming (Ethos)."[32]

And yet Herwegen's school does not idealize ancient civilization and early Christian culture to the extent that one might at first suppose. They regard the development as significantly richer in nuance than the examples suggest. Mayer in particular strongly emphasizes the nuances in the connection between the Christian religion and Germanic culture, and he ends by making a sharp distinction between Romanesque and Gothic.

Before going into that any further we must first broach another question that has attracted a great deal of interest in the circle around Herwegen and Casel: Why did Christianity first arise in the Greco-Roman rather than the Indic or Germanic world? Are we confronted here with a fact that was so willed by God, or with a more or less fortuitous coincidence? Thus the question arises once again: Is there a particularly close relation between the Romanitas and Christianity, and are the essential characteristics of the Germanic spirit little suited to assimilation to the Christian religion?

Pinsk takes a firm position. If the church is indeed the continuation of the incarnation, then it cannot but enter into a concrete cultural community. Now if God chose for this purpose the Roman-Hellenistic cultural world, then internal grounds must have made the difference. These can be indicated concretely. First, the characteristic religious attitude of Greco-Roman culture was expressed in the mysterium through which one connects with the life of the deity; the same idea is found in Christianity: of preeminence here is participation in the divine life through the sacraments. Secondly, the Roman Empire formed a world empire, just as the church was to do in the supernatural sphere; to the Romans the divine plan for a world church was self-evident, since a Roman was shaped through and through by the idea of world unity.

To these examples one might add many more, but enough to show that Pinsk, unlike so many others, is not concerned with the external advantages that (Greco-) Roman culture and empire offered the expansion of Christianity, but with an essential analogy and affinity between Roman Hellenism and the church—"if this expression is not too strong, in view of the infinite distance between the natural and the super-

---

[30] Ibid., 67f.
[31] Herwegen, *Kirche und Seele*, introduction.
[32] Herwegen, *Antike, Germanentum und Christentum*, 70.

natural."[33] This analogy does not exist between Christianity and the Germanic spirit. The core of the latter resides, according to Pinsk, in the willful and arbitrary, in the subjective and individual, in the passion for outward expression of innermost feelings. The symbol of the church, however, is that of the conceiving bride of Christ, an image that is foreign to the masculinity that marks the Germanic world. We cannot escape the impression, Pinsk remarks, that "the Germanic character at the core is less suited to the essence of Christianity than was the case with the Roman-Hellenistic world."[34]

The fact that Pinsk and Herwegen sense an inner affinity between Christianity and the Roman spirit does not blind them to the dangers implicit in the world of ancient thought nor to the significance that the Germanic spirit has had for Christianity. Placing a heavy emphasis on the eternal, absolute and objective entails the risk of atrophy, formalism and impotence in face of the concrete. This enables the Herwegen school to recognize what is valuable in the Germanic spirit: it knows how to translate the objective in Revelation into individual life, and, controlled as it is by energy and restless searching, it is less quickly satisfied and hence better disposed to penetrate to greater depths.[35]

With this in mind, one can understand the great appreciation with which Mayer speaks of the Romanesque. The cultural history of the Middle Ages—thus Mayer—was split in two by a deep rift. A spiritual revolution occurred in the medieval world, causing a separation deeper than that between the Middle Ages and the Renaissance. Throughout the Middle Ages the Germans were the bearers of culture, but in the period before 1100 (or before 1250, in Herwegen's view) the Germanic spirit remained bound to the norms and forms of the classical world.[36] During this period the Germanic ethos, with its individualism, gained access to the liturgy and to cultural expressions, but ultimately it reconciled itself to the primacy of the logos and the mysterium. The Romanesque—Romanesque art in particular—represents, historically speaking, a blend of the Germanic and the Ancient spirits. During the Middle Ages, till about 1100, a fascinating process took place: "Faustian man assimilated the heritage of Antiquity."[37]

The Romanesque is not the art of "serenity and peace," as A. Bäumler claims,[38] nor that of harmony, but is permeated by a tragic tension, which is perhaps nowhere so conspicuous as in the plastic arts. Here a tremendous vitality seems to want to free itself, but "the solemn regularity of liturgical discipline, the thought of supra-terrestrial harmony" guide this vitality into logical channels. A beautiful example is provided by the three-dimensional impact of the church of St. Peter at Moissac. Herein lies the grandeur of the Romanesque, that, while it can express and exhaust itself in an all but infinite wealth of forms, it nevertheless bows beneath classical order.[39]

On the one hand the Romanesque pointed to the Early Christian period, on the other to the Gothic. The conflict that was always latent in the Romanesque surfaced in the Gothic: the subjective extricated itself from its entwinement with the objective, the

---

[33] Pinsk, "Germanentum und katholische Kirche," 361f.; cf. Herwegen, *Antike, Germanentum und Christentum*, 68.

[34] Pinsk, "Germanentum und katholische Kirche," 17f.

[35] Herwegen, *Antike, Germanentum und Christentum*, 69f.; Pinsk, "Germanentum und katholische Kirche," 18f.

[36] Mayer, "Die Liturgie und die Geist der Gothik," 70.

[37] Mayer, "Altchristliche Liturgie und Germanentum," 80; see also 83, 86.

[38] Bäumler, "Bamberg und Naumberg. Über die Epochen des Mittelalters," 477.

[39] Mayer, "Altchristliche Liturgie und Germanentum," 81f.

individual element disesteemed the community, and the ethos no longer paid attention to the leading of the logos. Then the Germanic spirit manifested itself for what it was. According to Herwegen this growth toward independence by the subjective element began already in the time of the Carolingians, to gain the leading role in culture by the middle of the 13th century; according to Mayer "a deep rift split the age" as early as the beginning of the 12th century.[40]

The emancipation of the spirit occurred in every field, though primarily in art. The Gothic is not just an art style; it is also in an eminent sense a cultural style. Even in Scholasticism the individuality principle exerted its influence, for is it not typically individualistic to think that with one's own mental powers one can synthesize everything into a single system? Before this time there was "devout submission"; before the universalistic conquest of the problems of thought there was the "contented walk in the God-ordained ordo." [41]

Mayer's perspective necessarily also sets the relation between the Gothic and the Renaissance in a new light. Instead of a contrast he sees continuity between the two: both are permeated by subjectivism and individualism, albeit each in a different sense; the Renaissance is the southern parallel to the Nordic-Celtic development—an interpretation that tempers the basic premise of the Herwegen school. Other passages in Mayer also relativize the decisive importance of nationality for the inner nature of a spiritual culture, as in the following:

It is hard to tell whether everything can be traced exclusively to the Germanic as the driving element, whether much might not also have come about if the Germans had been different from what they were in fact, whether much did not result automatically from some process or other of cultural refinement, or from certain external exigencies such as the development of their own ecclesiastical system.[42]

In any case, the spirit of the Gothic is the spirit of Modern Times. Even post-Tridentine theology and piety and even the Counter-Reformation are implicated in the transformation of the Christian life, although they did provide one service: they weakened the subjectivist tendencies of the modern period by subordinating them to the hierarchy.

The Gothic, the Counter-Reformation and the Protestant Reformation have one element in common: they all turned away from the mysterium. This is clearest in the case of the Protestant Reformation, which can only be understood against the background of the catastrophic dualism that had become manifest in the High and Late Middle Ages. As long as the nations were willing to submit to Christ's vicar on earth their differences in character could be kept within limits, but when they ceased to recognize the God-given leadership there was no longer any rein upon their subjectivism and individualism.[43]

---

[40] Herwegen, *Kirche und Seele*, 16f; Mayer, "Die Liturgie und die Geist der Gothik," 69f.
[41] Ibid., 74–76.
[42] Mayer, "Altchristliche Liturgie und Germanentum," 95.
[43] Herwegen, *Kirche und Seele*, 30; idem, *Antike, Germanentum und Christentum*, 23f.

PART TWO

Toward a Reformed Conception of History

1/ PROTESTANT CONCEPTIONS OF HISTORY

IT IS AN UNDENIABLE FACT that Christian thinkers today continue to wrestle with the problem of a Christian philosophy of history. What the issues may be that frustrate the development of an integral Christian conception of history is a question as intriguing as it is important. The question has become pressing now that so many attempts at imbuing historical science and philosophy of history with the spirit of Christianity have proved unsuccessful. It is certainly the case that the question plays an important role in the background whenever Protestants today write about the meaning of history, although they often are not fully aware of it. And that is not surprising, since they are sometimes so fascinated by the results of their own thinking that they no longer pause to inquire whether it indeed bears an intrinsically Christian stamp.

The differences and nuances among modern Protestant conceptions of history are so great that a complete overview exceeds the scope of a paper.[1] We shall have to observe some restrictions, also because we could easily lose sight of the main lines if we tried to cover a large number of theories. Here we shall discuss only the views of Niebuhr, Barth, Van Ruler, Cullmann, and that of Reformational philosophy. Only the last is, strictly speaking, a Christian *philosophy* of history; the others are mainly theologies of history. Omitting numerous details, as interesting as these are in themselves, we shall in each case probe the fundamental premise and central idea. When we approach our task in this way we soon find that the various Protestant conceptions, with the exception of Reformational philosophy,[2] are all dominated by tensions between time and eternity, nature and grace, nature and spirit, God and creature. Further, attempts at resolving these polarities are made in terms of "dialectial relation" and "paradox" on the one hand and "analogy" and "sign" on the other, while the most radical solution is sought in reducing eternity to time.

While we must observe some restrictions, as we said, some extension of the terrain has also seemed desirable. Not just in Protestant but also in Catholic circles there is a growing interest in the question of the meaning of history. This fact invites a comparison. Roman Catholic thought too knows that tension between nature and grace. It must therefore be considered of some importance to ascertain at what point, given their agreement on a fundamental theme, Catholic and Protestant conceptions of history begin to diverge. I purposely do

---

[1] [This invited paper was read at a symposium for Catholic academics, 4–9 Sept. 1950; pub. in L. J. Rogier et al., *De zin der geschiedenis voor geloof en rede* (Heerlen, 1950), 217–46.]

[2] [In this early essay, the terms Reformational philosophy, Calvinist philosophy, and the Philosophy of the Cosmonomic Idea are used interchangeably.]

not say *the* Protestant conceptions, since Reformational philosophy does not have that polarity between nature and grace; thus there seems to be a way of escaping it.

Reinhold Niebuhr

An important representative of modern Protestant theology of history is Reinhold Niebuhr (1892–[1971]), a great-grandson of the famous German historian Barthold Georg Niebuhr (1776–1831). Initially an exponent of liberal theology, he went through a protracted spiritual crisis, to emerge after many years with a distinctive theology strongly influenced by Emil Brunner. His larger works begin to appear after 1930 and show the maturation of a consistent theological position. The main contours of his thought stand out most clearly in a work of 1937, *Beyond Tragedy*.[3]

For some years Niebuhr served as a pastor in industrial Detroit, where he became particularly interested in ethics, especially social ethics. This interest persisted after 1928 when he went to teach at Union Theological Seminary in New York. At the same time, like many other prominent theologians of his day, he devoted special attention to the phenomenon of history. History in fact forms the warp and woof of his entire theology. When his book *Faith and History* came out in 1949 it held little that we did not already know from his strictly theological works.[4] For Niebuhr, theology is primarily a Christian interpretation of history.[5]

Niebuhr's accent on history is no coincidence; it is implicit in the main theme of his theology: the paradoxical relationship in which man finds himself in his *deepest* essence. According to Niebuhr, man consists of nature and spirit. By nature he is finite, limited and restricted; in his spirit he transcends nature and is free and unrestricted. This makes for a dichotomy in human life. Aware of this, man lives in anxiety, conscious of the finite, contingent nature of his existence.

It will be clear at once that Niebuhr does not regard the paradox of historical existence as a result of the fall into sin, but rather as given with man. This notion is decisive for his conception of history. In this line of thinking the fall cannot have a historical origin. It is only a mythical form of the sin that is constantly present in every person's life. And history is, and always will be, ruled by the ambiguity of human existence.

Nevertheless, history is not meaningless. For despite the ambiguity from beginning to end, the creation is good, if not existentially, still potentially. The potential goodness of creation, and both human freedom and divine activity in creation, guarantee that history does not progress without meaning. History is

---

[3] Reinhold Niebuhr, *Beyond Tragedy: Essays on the Christian Interpretation of History*.

[4] Niebuhr, *Faith and History: A Comparison of Christian and Modern Views of History*.

[5] [Cf. George Hammar, *Christian Realism in Contemporary American Theology: A Study of Reinhold Niebuhr, W. M. Horton and H. P. Van Dusen* (diss.; Uppsala, 1940), 167–253.]

still the scene of the "completion and fulfillment of life." The latter, which constitutes the meaning of history, cannot, however, lie within history itself, since that would mean that something absolute could be found in history, which is impossible as history is by nature contingent and conditioned. History offers no more than the possibility of realizing fragmentary values and achieving only partial or provisional "fulfillments of life." The meaning of history is only achieved "beyond history."

This shapes Niebuhr's *eschatological* conception of history and of the relation between the kingdom of God and history. Although the kingdom of God is not revealed until the end of time, there is an intimate connection between that kingdom and the time of history: the latter is not the negation of the kingdom but its fulfillment. History is rushing toward its end in order to be set free from its contradictions, for its end, the kingdom of God, will see the "annihilation" of its paradoxes.

Bear in mind, however, that the word eschatological has its own meaning in Niebuhr. Eschatology does not mean for him the revelation of the "last things" at the end of time. "Last" here does not refer to something within the temporal order but denotes the very opposite: it means that these things fall *outside* time and history. If we relate them to our temporal order we have to take them symbolically. When the Bible speaks of the Last Judgment, for example, what is meant is simply a *sign* of the truth that history cannot save itself but that each of its moments issues in the judgment whereby God annihilates the evil in the world by taking it upon himself.

Niebuhr's theology of history is dominated throughout by the dialectical tension between time and eternity. Whatever in Scripture is expressly real but cannot be fitted into Niebuhr's dialectical scheme is devalued by him to a sign or symbol for realities beyond history. Neither the meaning of history nor the kingdom of God is present in history. Indicators, signs and symbols will have to do for us. This holds even for the cross and the resurrection; if they were purely historical they would be no more than contingent and conditioned facts.

Karl Barth

A peculiar stance in regard to history is adopted by Karl Barth (1886–[1968]). In his theology, too, history is a fundamental given, but he treats it with suspicion. He manages to see meaning in history only by defining history in an unusual way. This enables him to both appreciate and repudiate history.

Barth's theology revolves around the Word of God and the revelation of the Word of God in Jesus Christ. It is here that Barth encounters history, which plays an elementary role in the revelation of the Word of God. To understand his conception of history it is essential to note the core problem that pervades his dogmatics. Barth's point of departure can be summarized in two theses: (1) there is a strict equivalence between God and his Word, or, to put it differently, there is an absolute identity of the Word of God and the divine Person; (2) revelation occurs only where God himself is present.[6] This identity entails important consequences. Since the Word of God is the divine Person, hence God himself, it is *efficax*, omnipotent, and creative. That is to say, the Word of God brings about what it speaks, unlike the word of man, which lacks the power to realize what it speaks and thus does not make history. The God who speaks makes history because God's speech is identical with his action and not just an invitation or a command to man, for it brings man into the state which the Word speaks.

A second consequence, integral to Barth's theological system, is the freedom of the Word of God. Barth puts a heavy emphasis on this, which is of particular importance for his view of God's transcendence. God's freedom with respect to his world in consequence of his transcendence does not mean in Barth that God's relation to his creation is a purely negative one. Precisely in his freedom God can and will intervene in his world. If his transcendence necessarily separated him from the world, God would no longer be free. God therefore is free—free to penetrate his world; but in that penetration he retains his absolute freedom, free of every bond in created reality. Even when the Word of God enters the creaturely world, it never allows itself to be conditioned by it. This implies that it never becomes identified with a historical fact, which is always, if not completely, nevertheless partially conditioned. The Word of God does enter human history, yet at the same time always remains outside it, since it never becomes an element of it.

A third consequence of the identity of the Word of God is the "active presence" (*Aktualität*) of the Word of God. The Word is present only when God speaks and insofar as God speaks; when God no longer speaks, his Word is absent. Barth cannot acknowledge a perduring Word of God distinct and separate from the God who speaks. Thus the active presence of the Word implies the negation of God's immanence (unless one were to regard the interventions of the Word of God as his immanence). Barth knows only a fragmentary action of God in his world.

God reveals himself in a creaturely or sinful world. When God wishes to reveal himself he can only use actual creatures, for without these no contact with humans is possible. But here a paradox presents itself: the means God uses to reveal himself also conceal him; they are the only possible means for revelation to reach us but at the same time they are the veil that covers and conceals it.

And yet the creature reveals, namely when the act of divine re-creation takes place and the creature begins to reveal what it is not of and by itself. Revelation is always, ever and again, a "presently active" divine deed whereby the Word of God appears outside its concealment.

Barth knows only one revelation, the revelation of Christ Jesus. Even in Jesus the Word hid behind the form and required an "actively present" divine act to reveal the Truth there present. To be sure, there is a difference here with the

---

[6] [Cf. Jerôme Hamer, *L'Occasionalisme théologique de Karl Barth. Étude sur sa méthode dogmatique* (Paris, 1949), 25–47, 167ff.]

Word of God in Scripture and in the church's official proclamation, for in the case of Christ's human form the Word of God was directly and enduringly bound to God.

One cannot help but wonder why Barth can only accept a revelation in Christ, and why he can only see creature and revelation in a paradoxical relationship to each other. Here we have come upon a problem in Barth's theology that is of far-reaching consequence for his conception of history but that has so far not been clarified, despite the many pages he has devoted to it from time to time. I am referring to his view of *the relation between sin and creature*. The problem can be formulated thus: Does Barth identify creatureliness with sin and sinfulness? This cannot be his intention, since it would lead him straight into gnosticism and to the fringes of the Christian religion. Yet there are elements in his thought that push him in the direction of just such an identification. One is reminded here of Niebuhr, whose choice of starting point conveys him to a position where he is compelled to telescope creation and sin, however much he tries to escape this consequence with the subtle distinction that the anxiety gripping man because of the paradoxical tension in his nature makes sin, if not necessary, nevertheless inevitable.

The reason why the relation between sin and creatureliness is so problematic in Barth is that he defines the creature *qua* creature in such a way as to warrant no other conclusion than that the creature must be sinful by the mere fact of its being called into existence. For Barth, creaturehood as such marks a separation of God and creature. Not the fall but creation gave rise to the opposition between God and man, between eternity and time. Sin could only deepen the gulf. Barth's principle of separation does not just safeguard the boundary between God and creature but transforms that boundary into an antithesis from the beginning.

Despite all this it remains possible for Barth to acknowledge meaning in created reality and history. For although only God's purposes and acts are meaningful while everything non-divine is *in itself* bereft of all meaning, creation can nevertheless have meaning because it stands in a mysterious relationship to redemption in Jesus Christ. On this basis Barth can have a positive appreciation of the fact of creation.

When Barth speaks about that mysterious relationship he does not just have in mind a cognitive relation to creation, in the sense that both Creator and creation, owing to the awesome reality of sin, can only be known through faith in Jesus Christ. If Barth meant no more than that, his doctrine of creation would not have stood out in Protestant theology. What is distinctive about it is that it posits an *ontic* relation between Christ and creature. But even this formulation fails to bring out the uniqueness of his conception. Where he differs from others is in the further qualification of the ontic relation as an *analogical* one. Christ is the ground of creation in the sense that Christ is its "archetype," to which created reality is related analogically. Neither in whole nor in part can creation be understood in any other way than as signifying and referring to Jesus Christ.

Thus we can say nothing about creation apart from Christ; the texts of Gen. 1 and 2 must all be exegeted in terms of him. The christological nature of Barth's doctrine of creation appears at its starkest in his interpretation of Gen. 1:31, "*And God saw all that he had made, and behold, it was very good.*" Orthodoxy has never understood these words correctly, says Barth, because it separated them from Jesus Christ. The text does not pronounce on creation as it came forth from God's hand, but as it relates to Christ: creation is good because it was made *under this aspect*.[7]

By defining creation as good in this manner Barth gets into a peculiar difficulty. He calls this world good, even perfect, and yet shadows fall over this good world. There is a dark side to this world. How can these two sides of creation, which would seem to exclude each other, be seen as a unified whole? For Barth the problem is resolved in Christ. When we call creation good we do so not because it is good in itself but only because Christ can make use of it as his instrument and because it finds its ground and goal in him. That is enough to ensure that even in its negative, shadowy side creation can be called good, even perfect. The created world has two sides here, a bright side and a shadowy side; its perfection resides in its unity, because all this—the world in both its value and its nullity—points to Christ's suffering and death and to his resurrection. We may also turn it around. The world was created with a view to Christ and that is why from the beginning it has had two aspects, a bright and a shadowy side, as it has to point to the presence of both death and resurrection in the way of salvation. Thus in its very "duality" the world is good.

What Barth says here is in conflict with the Reformed confession. His statements leave no room for man's fall into sin as an historical event. Granted, his definitive position with respect to the historicity of the fall is not yet known, but to date his writings warrant the conclusion that what he says of creation holds for creation from the beginning, with no special role for a historical fall.[8]

This sheds light on Barth's view of profane history. God withdraws on high, away from the depths of our existence, leaving behind only signs, analogues, ectypes. But despite these positive things the primal opposition remains: the ectypes remain strictly human and worldly, but as such they are witnesses, pointers to God. In this function they are a demonstration of Christian hope, albeit no more than a demonstration.

Such is the meaning of history, and only to this extent may one speak of a meaning of history. By itself history constitutes an undefined chaos, yet in it one may encounter divine revelation; if history witnesses to God then only in its meaninglessness. However, into this human history in its original apostasy God has inserted another history, the true history. That is the history of Jesus Christ,

---

[7] Note that the analogy between creation and redemptive history (Christ) is here not just a sign of this relationship, but its very essence.

[8] [Since this was written (1951) Barth's writings have shown no change on this point. Cf. also S. U. Zuidema, "The Structure of Karl Barth's Doctrine of Creation" in idem, *Communication and Confrontation* (Toronto, 1972), 309–28.]

who became the center of history.⁹ Human, temporal history, even if it were without sin, is without meaning; but history *mirrors* the passion and death of Christ. Because history points to Jesus Christ, hence to something meaningful, it too has meaning.

A. A. van Ruler

We now come to the bold views of the theologian and cultural philosopher A. A. van Ruler.¹⁰ The name calls up the notion of theocracy, but however important this idea may be for Van Ruler,¹¹ to understand his conception of history we have to dig deeper. At the same time it is important for us to note his intellectual journey. Initially Van Ruler was strongly under the influence of Karl Barth and had the reputation of being an uncompromising proponent of Barth's most radical notions. Decisive in his move from Barthianism to his own system was his study of Abraham Kuyper (1837–1920) and his "idea of a Christian culture." In his book under this title¹² Van Ruler attacks Kuyper's theory of particular grace. According to Van Ruler, Kuyper recognized the presence of eternal life in the world but restricted it to the mystical hiddenness of the soul; and because of his (Kuyper's) realistic conception of the work of the Holy Spirit the renewal of man in Kuyper could only be a very restricted one, a renewal touching only the inner man. In conseqence Kuyper was unable—still according to Van Ruler—to appreciate renewal as an event touching the whole of creation.

Against Kuyper's doctrine of the reality of grace in the present world Van Ruler maintains that the *true* renewal is not a reality in this world. "Salvation is in heaven," he writes, and therefore it is purely eschatological. And yet Van Ruler holds that life is linked to salvation—not only the life of the soul but the whole life of creation in its length and breadth, not just internally but no less in its external shapes and forms. The gist of Van Ruler's own thought appears in an observation he makes in criticism of Kuyper's conception of culture:

> ... this is *too much* of particular grace in time, and therefore *too little*. In this spiritualization grace is not kept in heaven but lodged in the soul and therefore out of touch with external life. When grace is kept in heaven there is no fundamental difference between the body's and the soul's communion with salvation. In that case both are equally in need of the hidden, all-powerful work of the Holy Spirit, removing us to heaven to be linked with salvation. And then this work of the Spirit suffices equally for both. The Spirit does not have any greater affinity, and therefore relevance, for the soul than for the body. The Spirit is no mystic.¹³

---

⁹ Barth, *Die Kirchliche Dogmatik*, III/1, passim [*Church Dogmatics*, vol. III, pt. 1: *The Doctrine of Creation*].

¹⁰ [For Arnold A. van Ruler (1908–70), cf. Isaac Rottenberg, *Redemption and Historical Reality* (Philadelphia, 1964), esp. 161–85 and p. 217 n. 114; and the articles in a special issue of *Reformed Review* 26.2 (1973).]

¹¹ [Cf. Van Ruler, *Calvinist Trinitarianism and Theocentric Politics: Essays Toward a Public Theology*, ed. and trans. by John Bolt (Lewiston, NY, 1989).]

¹² Van Ruler, *Kuypers idee eener christelijke cultuur* (1940).

¹³ Ibid., 146.

It is not difficult to make out Van Ruler's intention from this quotation. By regarding the renewal of life as a *real* renewal, as a breakthrough of particular grace, one blocks the way to a truly Christian culture and postpones the christianized forms to the second coming of Christ. The quotation also shows—he elaborates this elsewhere—that the vision of a Christian culture can never be gained primarily from christology. It is the work of the Holy Spirit that enables one to see the kingdom of God in the flesh, here and now. Thus Van Ruler's idea of theocracy must be understood in terms of pneumatology. The word *idea*, however, does not clearly indicate the reality of theocracy; after all, it is already a *fact* today in European civilization, even if not yet in all its fullness.

Accordingly, it is the relation of christology to pneumatology that constitutes the core problem in Van Ruler's theology of history, and it is his view of the independent significance of the work of the Holy Spirit with respect to the work of Christ that determines the distinctiveness of his speculations. Directly related to this is the fact that Van Ruler, unlike the mainstream in current theology of history and especially in sharp contrast to Barth and Cullmann, does not think "from the center" but "from the end." In his case that does not necessarily mean that he thinks eschatologically, but he does think patrologically, not christologically: Van Ruler relates all of history not first and foremost to the God who *has come* in Christ but to the *coming* God; and this coming God is the Father. Now then, from the Father proceed both Son and Holy Spirit, both incarnation and pentecost. The one kingdom of God thus becomes manifest in the world under a twofold aspect, as kingdom of the Spirit and as kingdom of Christ, yet in such a way that the first takes precedence, since it is the reign of the Spirit that gives the reign of Christ consistency and extension.

The great work of the Holy Spirit consists in this, that he separates the first and second coming of the Messiah—that he sets the bounds of Christian existence: the ascension on the one hand and the parousia on the other. Although it is true that Christian existence has its being only in Christ, yet it is, like Christ himself, a creation of the Holy Spirit. "Christian existence" refers not only to the life of the individual but also to communal life. Thus the Spirit's work of setting the bounds of existence implies that he makes room for history, in fact creates history as such: it is the Spirit who slows down the irresistible advance of the kingdom of God in the second coming of Christ; the Spirit is the factor of retardation.

The space of the Christian centuries did not remain empty but was filled with the work of the Holy Spirit. This period is the dispensation of the Spirit, in which reality in all its parts is elevated to be a *sign* of the kingdom of God—a *filled* sign, inasmuch as the Holy Spirit enters into every aspect of reality, especially those that concern the state, justice, order, power and law.

Thus the Holy Spirit stands in a very intimate relation to history. He it is who creates the forms of the kingdom, notably in state and culture: the state is undemonized and culture is christianized. For the civic community is no more foreign to the Spirit than is the human heart, and in God's future—in terms of which we conceive the kingdom—we see before all else the kingdom, the *City of God*. This state and culture created by the Spirit places us squarely in history. To repeat, it is the Spirit who creates history. It is especially—in fact exclusively—in history that the Spirit becomes somewhat accessible to us. And that is why Van Ruler takes his leave of Barth, who can understand history only in terms of God's longsuffering. Van Ruler opposes this with the thesis that history can only be understood in terms of the work of the Holy Spirit.

Oscar Cullmann
The relation of time and eternity has become a real crux for modern theology of history. In Barth it takes the form of a sharp dualism and in Niebuhr it is dressed in dialectical garb, while in Van Ruler too it is the key to understanding his theory of the "filled sign" and his consignment of the reality of salvation to heaven. This debate about the problem of time and eternity is the backdrop of Oscar Cullman's study of Christ and Time.[14] Cullmann believes he can show from the New Testament that a polarity of time and eternity does not exist.

Cullmann (1902–[1999]) locates the core of the Christian message in the conception of time and history. Time is a key concept in the New Testament because God's revelation in Christ is always a historical event: the concepts time and history embrace the full reality of redemption. Thus it is of the utmost importance to arrive at a proper understanding of time and history. Our ideas about time, however, have been deeply infected by Greek thought. To arrive at a proper understanding we have to free ourselves from all philosophical concepts. Only then, says Cullmann, will we see that the difference between time and eternity is not of a qualitative nature. The only difference is that eternity is infinite duration—taking temporal duration in a linear sense—whereas time is finite duration.

Cullmann draws weighty conclusions from his conception of eternity as an "endless time line." He attacks the "dehistoricization" of Christianity. He posits, quite rightly I think, that there can be no Christianity without the historicity of the salvation events, and he attacks the devaluation of the essence of Christianity to philosophical, timeless verities. He states, for example, that when the historicity of the fall is denied all that remains is a "mythical description" of the sinful nature of man. Even though Barth and Niebuhr are not mentioned by name, it is clear that the difference between them and Cullmann is profound.

This conception of the relation between time and eternity cannot but shed new light on the concept of salvation history, or rather, on the concept of redemptive history in Christ. Basic to Cullmann's conception are the terms *kairos* and *aion*. Kairoi are the moments chosen by God to intervene; aiones represent delineated periods on the historical time line. The kairoi are all sharply

---
[14] Oscar Cullmann, *Christus und die Zeit; die urchristliche Zeit- und Geschichtsauffassung* [Eng. trans. *Christ and Time: The Primitive Christian Conception of Time and History* (1964)].

distinguished from one another; nevertheless they are linked in such a way as to form a continuous time line, the line of redemption.

The kairoi and the aiones are governed by one central kairos located at the midpoint of the time line: the incarnation of the Word and Christ's death and resurrection constitute history's center and focal point. Everything in history is related to this point, even the time before creation, and creation itself, while the time after the incarnation is the deployment of the incarnation in the church, by which Christ wields dominion over heaven and earth. In this way the time of the world is a "continuously christocentric history."

Cullmann cannot follow the often one-sided eschatological elaborations of current theology of history, because they ignore the fact that in Christ's resurrection the victory has already been won. The coming of Christ marked the decisive battle, which in some measure dethrones eschatology: the future can only reveal what has already been achieved. In this way Cullmann arrives at his important thesis that *it is not the end alone that determines the meaning of history*.

The central significance of the incarnation does not mean for Cullmann the devaluation of the other aiones. Precisely because no point on the time line can be replaced by another, every period has its own value and significance. Every phase before and after the incarnation is absolutely unique and has its own originality and its own charisma—the present age, for example, is uniquely gifted with the Holy Spirit. But every phase also has its own unique calling. We are not allowed to withdraw from the aion in which we live. Today we live in the aion between Easter and Parousia, an age that is full of strife, an age of proclamation and missions, not of contemplation and quietism.

Cullmann does not want his conception of history to be interpreted as a philosophy or theology of history in the accepted sense. What he gives can be read directly, so he believes, from the New Testament as its essential content. It is at this juncture that we can no longer follow Cullmann. His notion that the New Testament conception of time can be reduced to a strictly linear one, in which even eternity can be fitted, seems to me an unwarranted assumption. In any case one can point to 1 Tim. 1:17, where God is called the *basileus ton aionon*, the ruler of the ages. And how is the notion of eternity as an "endless time line" to be squared with the words of 2 Peter 3:8 that with the Lord one day is as a thousand years and a thousand years as one day? And how is it possible in a strictly linear conception of time to call Christ a central point from which meaning is bestowed on the whole of history?

By subsuming eternity under time Cullmann has introduced an inner contradiction into his theology of history. This prevents him from doing full justice to the New Testament revelation. He must have noticed the contradiction himself when he says that on the one hand God participates in the time modus and on the other hand rules over it. As long as this contradiction stands we cannot help but wonder whether the Scriptures have not been read here in terms of a philosophical bias. Contradictions have a habit of making their appearance whenever something in creation or within time is absolutized at the expense of some other reality.

A comparison with Catholic conceptions

Now that we have looked at a number of theologies of history by modern-day Protestants it would seem an appropriate moment to look back and draw some comparisons with Roman Catholic thinkers. One point of comparison appears to be the use of the concept of analogy. We have seen the important role it plays in Barthian theology, and it is of course known to be of fundamental significance for Catholic thought.

However profoundly the two may differ in the use of analogy, they agree in having it say something positive about creation. Beyond this formal agreement, however, the positive appreciation differs radically. Scholasticism uses the analogous relation between Creator and creature as a basis for the intrinsic excellence of the creature; or, more precisely (to highlight the contrast with Barth): the creature is good already by virtue of its creaturehood, it is good even apart from the relation to Christ, and the analogy serves as a methodological device for philosophically accounting for that goodness.

Barth's view of analogy is very different. He does not see in the creature anything in common with the Creator. Here in this created reality he sees only distance, which by virtue of the very act of creation means opposition. We find ourselves at bottom in a reality that is chaotic from the beginning, through sin. True, between the depths of the sinful world and the lofty heights of salvation in Jesus Christ there is a relation, but this relation expresses no more than a mirror reflection, a demonstration and a sign. This is the extent to which analogy has a place here. What can be said at best of created reality is that it is a sign of the eternal kingdom. According to Scholastic thought history has meaning simply in its natural existence, in its formal glorification of God; according to Barth history *qua* created reality is meaningless yet *acquires* meaning by *pointing to* something or someone that does have meaning. On this view, the meaning of history is always secondary and consists only in its referential function.

Having noted the sharp conflict between Barthianism and Catholicism with respect to the concept of analogy,[15] we can continue with our comparison.

Barth distinguishes between *Historie*, the temporal, horizontal history, and *Geschichte*, the real history, the history of Jesus Christ and of God's action in Jesus Christ. We have seen that the link between the two histories consists for Barth in the sign language that earthly history speaks concerning the archetype of all history. Action in history is therefore to be understood as symbolical action "with a view to Christ." At issue here is neither a system nor "isolated instances," but a "constant direction," a coherent pattern of "explications and

---

[15] [See today Henry Chavannes, *The Analogy Between God and the World in Saint Thomas Aquinas and Karl Barth*. Trans. from the French by Wm. Lumley (New York, 1992).]

applications." And then Barth gives us a series of examples of such analogous action. Suffice it to mention just one of these here, taken from the world of politics: The Spirit is one, but the one Spirit has endowed the Christian church with a diversity of gifts and tasks, *hence*—this is the operative word—in political reality the functions of the legislative, executive and judicial powers must be separated.[16]

On reading these expositions and examples one is reminded of the school of Jacques Maritain. The strong similarity between Maritain's examples of the realization of a new Christendom and Barth's is striking. Is this a coincidence, one wonders, or do Barth and Maritain to some extent share a common root (despite the profound differences between Catholicism and Barthianism noted above)?

Maritain acknowledges that the Christian civilization of the Middle Ages, when the profane was no more than a *means* for the sacral, is gone forever. When he goes on to pose the question whether there can be a Christian civilization different from that of the Middle Ages, he wants to answer yes. According to Maritain we are on the way toward new forms of Christian culture, forms that will no longer be mere means for the spiritual but which, now that the profane since the Renaissance has become autonomous, will be acknowledged in their own proper value. Yet this confronts Maritain with a thorny question. How is it conceivable, if the temporal is autonomous, to realize Christian values in it? The Christian religion is supernatural and so cannot *as such* (at least on the Roman Catholic view) enter into temporal life. It must necessarily remain transcendent to profane history. If Christianity is nevertheless to become united with it and permeate it, then that will only be possible if the temporal sphere becomes the place of a *transposition of supernatural values*. Maritain provides numerous examples to illustrate the reality of that transposition. To name just one, mankind's struggle to abolish the enslavement and exploitation of one human being by another is a transposition into the temporal sphere of the spiritual ideal of the freedom of the children of God, the liberation from the world of sin.

It is the dualism of nature and the supernatural that prevents Maritain from maintaining the Christian values in their full, original force as they enter the so-called profane realm. Only in a temporal, "translated" form is Christianity able to penetrate the natural domain. But in Barth, too, it is a similar dualism that separates the kingdom of Christ from temporal history. Barth sees the connection between the two worlds in the sign, the reflection, the reference from the world in the depths to the realm on high; Maritain makes the connection in the transposition, the transformation, the translation. To put it this way is to state at one and the same time the similarity and the difference between Barth and Maritain. The similarity lies in a dualism between temporal, natural reality and supernatural or divine reality; the difference stems from widely diverging

---

[16] Barth, *Christengemeinde und Bürgergemeinde* (1938), 163.

appreciations of the God-creature relation and is expressed in the concepts of reference and sign on the one hand, and transposition and translation on the other. Reflection and sign are terms that a Roman Catholic too may use, but from what we observed about the background of Barth's thought it should be abundantly clear in what special sense Barth uses these terms.

Reformational Philosophy

Thus far we have not yet spoken of a current within Protestantism for which a Christian conception of history is not identical with *theology* of history. This fact alone should catch our attention, since Protestant and Catholic thinkers alike usually deny the possibility of a Christian philosophy in the strict sense, hence of a conception of history that is independent of a theology of history and yet has an intrinsically Christian character. When Calvinist philosophy—for this is the school I have in mind—claims that philosophy can be Christian independently of theology it does not mean to say that in contrast to theology it can go its own way apart from Scripture and arrive at conclusions that bear a Christian stamp. To be genuinely Christian, philosophy must take its presuppositions and its point of departure from Scripture and proceed from there to investigate and reflect on reality. Taking Scripture into account at every turn allows it to determine the direction of philosophical studies, not in the sense that the results would be known in advance, but certainly that the presuppositions without which no philosophy can come to any conclusions are given from the start. As far as that is concerned, Reformational philosophy is not unique, since ultimately no scientific thought is possible without proceeding from pre-theoretical presuppositions.

That being the case, it will not be necessary to give a detailed exposition of the Calvinist philosophy of history. Here too, as in the other cases we looked at, everything depends on the principal theme or the starting point. Space does not permit comparing it here with the theology of Niebuhr, Barth and others, but I would like to briefly discuss *incarnation theology*, since it seems to contain elements that bear a strong resemblance to the Calvinist conception of history. To be able to make my case I must give a brief summary of this school.

Léopold Malevez, a leading representative of the "théologie de l'Incarnation," presents it as "the Christian philosophy of progress." What makes this theology so special is that soteriological significance is attached to historical development as such, in fact that the evolution of the universe is incorporated in the great christological event. This predominantly optimistic conception of history derives from the special meaning that Catholicism attaches to the incarnation. The importance of the incarnation is not just that the Son of God became flesh to save his people from the wrath of God by traveling the road of suffering, death and resurrection, but in particular that in Christ the union of the divine and the human took place that constituted a divine-human form of life. By assuming human nature the Word transformed Christ's humanity so that it was elevated to the state of a glorified body. The full effect of the union of the divine and the human in Christ did not take place all at once, for only after he had earned salvation by dying on the cross could it be "released" and flow through him.

By virtue of the unity of the human race Christ's human nature—still according to incarnation theology—stands in a relationship to all people. But this real connection with the human race and with physical matter implies their elevation to the divine-human form of life from the moment the Word was united with human nature in Mary's womb, be it only "in embryo." By the radiation of Christ's grace all human bodies and the whole earth are transformed; the grace of the incarnation has elevated the whole of mankind, as well as all of nature, to divinity, not just in a manner of speaking, but ontically.

In any event, the transfiguration of the universe will take place at the end of time. Does that mean it is purely eschatological? If grace is contemporary, then the transformation of the universe must be also, at least to a degree, growing and developing as it does with the spread of Christianity around the world. Even the *temporal evolution* of terrestrial realities is incorporated in the evolution of the spiritual, so that profane history too acquires a supernatural stamp. It is the facts themselves that point to an inner connection between Christianity and history: for it is precisely the Western world, the world in which Christianity flourished most richly, that has become the setting of progressive evolution in science and technology, economics and political institutions. And on the basis of the incarnation dogma and historical evolution alike Malevez is bold to conclude that the valuable cultural conquests of the West are to be considered a "prolongation of the Incarnation." Today's material, artistic and intellectual prowess "complete the Christ" and glorify him.

The philosophy of progress presents us with an approach to the problem of a Christian conception of history that differs markedly from Maritain's. In the latter, the nature-grace dualism, in spite of efforts at intimate union, remains in force, whereas in incarnation theology it seems to have been banished for good. This is of great interest to adherents of Calvinist philosophy, since their chief objection to Catholic conceptions of history has always been the open or latent dichotomy between nature and grace. Hence we ask, Has this new trend removed a rock of offense? Is this a definitive break with the notion of an autonomous natural domain *alongside* a religious reality? Is "profane" history imbued with religious significance?

Clearly, incarnation theology and Calvinist philosophy agree that the inner renewal of this world through redemption in Christ is a present reality and that to speak of "Christian institutions" and "Christian culture" is more than using symbolical language. Nevertheless a profound disagreement looms here as well.

Incarnation theology, particularly in Malevez, reduces the difference between the Catholic and Calvinist conceptions of history to the different answer each gives to the question of the meaning and value of profane history for the kingdom of God. In the Calvinist conception of history, it is alleged, political, moral and social endeavors are of no value to the future eternal kingdom, whereas in Catholic thought, at least in incarnation theology, the present dispensation does have value for the eternal realities, if not in the sense that profane culture can bring about the kingdom of God in its own strength—it remains a perfectly free gift of God—but certainly in the sense that through the transformation process in Christ we are progressively brought to a state in which we can receive the fullness of his grace. Our human work *prepares us inwardly* for the final reality: we are brought into a *disposition* for the definitive kingdom of God.

I too believe there is a difference here. But if we are to fathom fully the divergence between the Calvinist and the Catholic conceptions of history we will have to probe deeper, since our different evaluations of the significance of our earthly strivings for the kingdom of God arises from another difference, namely, in our evaluations of incarnation and grace.

Our summary of the philosophy of progress has made clear that its pivotal concept is not the cross but the incarnation as such. The accent falls on the union of the divine and the human as the possibility and starting-point for a Christian culture. In Calvinism, by contrast, the meaning of the incarnation, as we saw, lies primarily in the fact that now the Redeemer has come, who is going to bear the full weight of God's wrath, a mission that required the union of divine and human nature in one Person.[17]

This difference in interpretation of the incarnation is directly related to a profound contrast in the understanding of grace. For a Roman Catholic, grace is first and foremost an infused quality whereby a human being in principle comes to partake of the *divine nature* and whereby the whole of nature is elevated to a theomorphic state. For the Reformation, grace is first of all God's free favor and good will toward man, in which he forgives sin. The Reformation no less than incarnation theology acknowledges the universal significance of the incarnation and the cross—not, however, in the sense that creaturely life comes to participate in the divine life, but in the sense that the curse which covered the whole of created reality is lifted by Christ, as a result of which life in every one of its forms and expressions finds its restoration in him.

History's great event and mighty wonder is that both Christ's passion and his victory over death have given history a new direction. In the fall it moved away from God; in Jesus Christ it moves toward God once more. There is once again in this world a genuine—and not merely symbolical—obedience to the Word of God, and a true love of God that far transcends its analogue; there is once again the endeavor to restore the divine order. And there is, thanks to God's rule of grace over this world, not just a change of hearts but also a doing of God's holy will (Rom. 12). In that change of our hearts, and hence our entire lives, the kingdom is coming. In this way redemption and renewal do not withdraw into the inner life but, on the contrary, work their way through the length and breadth of history.

---

[17] [Cf. the wording in the Heidelberg Catechism, Q. & A. 15–18.]

Thinking about the meaning of history is governed by the question, How do you see creation, fall and redemption? We have learned that already with respect to redemption the Catholic and the Calvinist conceptions of history part company. We would find the same to be true with respect to creation and the fall. But Calvinist philosophy dissociates itself not only from Catholic but also from many Protestant conceptions of history. It rejects Barth and Niebuhr inasmuch as they, each in his own way, separate temporal reality and the meaning of history, and then afterward try to connect them again, via analogy or symbol.

It is plain that important issues are at stake in contemporary Christian thinking about history. To inquire after the relation between the kingdom of God and world history is undeniably to raise one of the most fundamental questions challenging Christian thought. Augustine wrestled with the problem and it has exercised the Christian world ever since. Especially in times when Christianity and culture threaten to grow apart, we see a heightened interest in the question of the religious origin and destiny of history.

Reformational philosophy[18] from the very first paid considerable attention to the question of the origin of history. It did not seek a solution by going back in time. With the confession of God as Origin of all that is it was able to recognize the meaning of history as the mode of being of created reality that finds no rest in itself.[19] It thus escaped historicism, which, by absolutizing the historical mode of being, had dissolved history into a normless and purposeless process embracing the whole of human reality. Reformational philosophy has had the distinction of demonstrating that the Christian worldview not only relates history to its ultimate meaning in Jesus Christ but also teaches[20] that the historical is but one mode of being among many.[21] This insight is of such decisive significance that whoever does not accept it, that is to say, whoever reduces non-historical reality to the historical, is no longer in a position to indicate a meaning of history that pervades history in all its parts and directs it toward its final end.

---

[18] [See note 2 above.]
[19] [Cf. Dooyeweerd, *A New Critique of Theoretical Thought*, 1:4, 11.]
[20] [The definition that follows in this sentence was later abandoned by the author.]
[21] [Cf. Dooyeweerd, *A New Critique of Theoretical Thought*, 2:192–229.]

2/ THE CURRENT CRISIS IN CATHOLIC THOUGHT

THERE IS A GENERAL FEELING that Roman Catholic theology and philosophy are basically unchanging quantities. No matter what theological or philosophical handbook one picks up, its content, it is generally thought, amounts always to the same thing; it is only in the form that one writer shows himself bolder and more original than another.

We strongly doubt the correctness of this notion, certainly in the case of current Catholic thought. In many areas of theology and philosophy Catholic thinkers are looking for new avenues. Sometimes the new insights gained are so surprising that one wonders whether they still really fit into the framework of the Catholic worldview. That tensions should arise is obvious. What we witness today is more than just resistance to a theory adhered to by a number of theologians. Rather, it is a reaction against a line that has been followed for centuries.

The impulse for renewal finds its strongest expression in the area of theology. In this regard people often think immediately and exclusively of the *théologie nouvelle*. However, it should not be forgotten that prior even to the rise of the New Theology a strong, dynamic development was observable in Catholic thought. The study of modern philosophical systems and of the early Church Fathers influenced Catholic thinking more profoundly than anyone at first had suspected. The result was twofold. Some remained faithful to Thomism and attempted to harmonize elements of modern thought with it. Others, by contrast, detached themselves from Scholasticism and either denied the possibility of a metaphysics which, insofar as the essentials are concerned, can be valid for all times; or else found in the writings of the Fathers deeper and richer insights than those available in traditional philosophy. From these remarks it will already be clear that the current development of Catholic thought is many-faceted. Even where the New Theology is concerned, we are involved not with one particular current but with a tentative convergence of often strongly divergent trends.

It gradually became apparent that, with the purity of Catholicism now beginning to be put at risk, the Pope would intervene in the clash of opinions, decisively and authoritatively. In August, 1950, Pius XII spoke clearly in the encyclical *Humani Generis*. That he regarded the situation as serious is evident from the heading of the letter: "Concerning Some False Opinions Which Threaten to Undermine the Foundations of Catholic Doctrine."

The encyclical contains too many elements for us to be able to deal with it here in its entirety.[1] We want to focus our attention on a single aspect. The fun-

---

[1] [This article appeared in *Mededelingen van de Vereniging voor Calvinistische Wijsbegeerte* (July, 1951): 7–9.]

damental thrust of the encyclical is that the Pope rises expressly to the defence of the value of human reason. When we read that, it immediately calls to mind the whole question of Christian philosophy, which has caused so much turmoil in Catholic circles in recent decades. Now, on the Catholic view that question entails two problems, that of the value of faith for natural thought, and that of the significance of reason for understanding Divine Revelation. The enduring value of reason for faith is the Pope's concern in *Humani Generis*.[2]

What compelled the Pope, really, to put such a strong emphasis on the value of human thought? In order to answer this question we might say something about the problems that have engaged current Catholic thought.

Traditional philosophy was reproached—especially after 1930—for aiming almost exclusively at grasping the abstract nature of things. If one wanted to know things thoroughly, one would have to meet and become familiar with them, it was now thought, in all their concreteness: then one would see that things are more than simple constancy, that things are part of a dynamic development. Dynamic development confronted theoretical thought so urgently that thinkers began to see it as the main problem of philosophy.

The renewed concern with concrete reality entailed two benefits. First, modern Catholic thinkers discovered something called history; the historical was known earlier, of course, but until now it had always been accorded a secondary place, at least in Scholasticism. Secondly, there was now a deeper realization that the supernatural was not merely a sector of reality but had to be "inscribed" in that reality, where it specifically manifested itself in dynamic development. One could still to speak of the "nature" of things provided one kept in mind that their reality was not exhausted in their immutable essential structure.

This reorientation gave rise to a most interesting problem: Was natural reason still to be considered capable of reaching this concrete, dynamic, religious reality, or were there elements in it beyond the command of rational conceptualization? The answer that was forthcoming was resonant with disdain for reason and contempt for the Scholastic way of thought. Catholic thinkers not only depreciated reason but at the same time turned away from Thomist philosophy as a philosophy of immutable essences and sought connections with more modern trends. They demanded attention for present-day philosophy which, more than the philosophy of the unmoved world-picture, was open to concrete existence and the dynamism of things. As they studied the Patristic Period and contrasted it with the Scholasticism of the Middle Ages, they developed ideas of their own. Thus a chasm opened up between modern Catholic thought and traditional Scholastic approaches.

---

[2] [Cf. *Humani Generis*, art. 29: "It is well known how highly the Church regards human reason, for it falls to reason to demonstrate with certainty the existence of God, personal and one; to prove beyond doubt from divine signs the very foundations of the Christian faith; to express properly the law which the Creator has imprinted in the hearts of men; and, finally, to attain to some notion, indeed a very fruitful notion, of mysteries."]

It is against this undisguised esteem for modern thought and for the Fathers at the expense of Thomas's philosophy of natural reason that *Humani Generis* is directed. Is this perhaps because the Pope perceived in the disparagement of human reason a failure to do justice to the Image of God? Yes, that too. Still, the core of the encyclical is located elsewhere. To devalue natural reason is to attack the very foundations of the edifice of the Catholic worldview. After all, the natural understanding has a most weighty function to fulfill with regard to faith. While remaining on a purely natural plane, man, in the Catholic conception, is capable of demonstrating at least the existence of God and the credibility of Christian Revelation.[3] Does this mean that certain matters are just as accessible to reason as to faith? Not only that; something even more important is at issue: *faith receives guarantees and certainties via the proofs of natural reason "so that faith is not a purely irrational leap into the totally unknown."* Reason reduces to a minimum the mystery that is the object of faith: whoever pulls the foundation of reason out from under faith sets faith atottering.

Matters being such, no disdain for reason can be tolerated by the Teaching Authority of the Church. What is surprising is that the Pope did not speak out earlier but allowed the evident danger to remain unchallenged for so long.

Now it also will be clear to us why the Pope once again imposed the study of Thomas's philosophy. For unlike modern thought, Thomism does not halt at the subjective and relative, at the mutable and fleeting. Rather, in Thomism the human mind has taken the turn towards the absolute. Through it man is able to discover immutable truths. And thus the conditions are met whereby the Thomistic synthesis is capable of affording faith the assistance it so urgently needs: "His [Thomas's] doctrine is *in harmony with divine revelation* and is most effective both for safeguarding the foundation of the faith and for reaping, safely and usefully, the fruits of sound progress."[4]

To the above we would add four critical observations.

1. If Catholics have not been able to arrive at an intrinsically Christian philosophy, the cause is to be found in this, that they are unwilling to relinquish the autonomy of rational thought. Our analysis has made it clear, however, that in terms of the Catholic view a genuine Christian philosophy is impossible on another account as well. Any philosophy that were to work with supratheoretical judgments—as intrinsically Christian thought always must—would precisely be unable, on that view, to offer faith the support it needs. Thus before Catholicism

---

[3] [Cf. *Humani Generis*, art. 27, where the Pope very explicitly admonishes "certain of Our sons who . . . belittle the reasonable character of the credibility of Christian faith." See as well art. 2: ". . . human reason by its own natural force and light can arrive at a true and certain knowledge of the one personal God, who by His providence watches over and governs the world, and also of the natural law, which the Creator has written in our hearts, . . ."; and art. 4: God has given "many wonderful external signs which are sufficient to prove with certitude, by the natural light of reason alone, the divine origin of the Christian religion."]

[4] Ibid., art. 31; italics added.

can arrive at Christian philosophical thought in the strict sense, and before it can break with the autonomy of the natural realm, it will have to acquire a different view of faith: it will have to recognize that faith by itself is perfectly certain of God and his Revelation. The question at issue reveals once again how profound is the opposition Reformation-Catholicism and how it assumes the proportions, at least insofar as the so-called natural realm is concerned, of an antithesis.

2. The Pope says here—in keeping with the accepted Catholic conception—that Thomas's doctrine is in harmony with Divine Revelation. But by what standard must or can such a harmony be established? By a religious standard, perhaps? But in that case harmony is impossible, for how can the Divine Revelation in Jesus Christ ever harmonize with thought that is self-sufficient with respect to Him? Shall the standard then be of a natural-rational character? But, then, what can autonomous reason say about the religious, which irrevocably and totally destroys all autonomy?

3. The encyclical opposes trends which not only are dangerous for Catholic thought but which because of their affinity to modern secularized thought jeopardize the entire Christian worldview. At the same time, however, it cuts off a very promising development. Various Catholic writers exhibit a yearning to return to the Sources. By that they mean the Church Fathers in the first place, but let there be no mistake about it: on their own testimony they hope by this route to find their way back to the true Source, Scripture. Granted, the Pope does not radically condemn this undertaking; he even encourages people to continue along this path. But there is a profound disagreement between Pius XII and those he reproves as the "advocates of novelty." [5] The latter no longer want to read the Fathers and the Bible in the light of Scholastic theology and philosophy. As was stated recently by Jean Daniélou, a scholar whose mind has been formed entirely through the study of the Patristic writings: Theology has suffered from a progressive desiccation since the thirteenth century, when its divorce from exegesis turned it into an autonomous science: it is time the Scriptures regain their central function in Christian thought.

4. The contrast between Calvinist and Catholic philosophy has been sharpened by the appearance of *Humani Generis*, not because the encyclical contains any particularly new elements pertaining to the relation of faith and reason, of theology and philosophy, but because it emphatically directs Roman Catholic thought back to the Thomistic synthesis. We shall have to reckon with the fact that the Teaching Authority of the Catholic church has spread its guardian wings over this synthesis and that when we critique the idea of the autonomy of natural thought we oppose that authority itself, unable as it is, precisely because of the Roman Catholic view of faith, to admit of any recognition of the religious conditionality of theoretical thought. This encyclical compels us—and that is the gain it can bring us—to focus the conflict on the deepest point of disagreement between Reformation and Scholasticism.

---

[5] Ibid., art. 18: "rerum novarum studiosi."

3/ CALVINISM AND CATHOLICISM ON CHURCH AND STATE

EVEN LONG BEFORE THE SECOND WORLD WAR there was a rapidly increasing interest in the attitude of Roman Catholicism toward civil and political liberties.[1] At issue from the outset were in particular the freedoms of religion, of education, and of propaganda. Numerous factors can be adduced to account for this renewed interest. For some time the higher birthrate of the Roman Catholic part of the [Dutch] population had been a subject of attention; the development was all the more striking because since 1830 the number of Roman Catholics on a percentage basis had steadily declined until the upturn began in 1909. In the second place, mention can be made of the obstacles placed in the way of Protestants in predominantly Catholic countries such as Austria and Spain. A third noteworthy factor would be the great flight made by Catholic thought in philosophy and theology and by Catholic action in the socio-economic and political areas. It became ever clearer that by the turn of the century a power had arisen that was fully up-to-date and conscious of its potential to become a decisive factor in the ongoing scientific, social and political struggle. Once it would gain political dominance as a result of demographic and intellectual shifts, it had to be considered capable of immediately assuming leadership in public life in a manner that would be consistent with distinctly Roman Catholic principles.

Under these circumstances there arose in broad, non-Catholic circles a sense of concern, an often indefinable fear that no reassuring statement could allay in view of the fact that actual practices in a number of predominantly Catholic countries still resembled restrictions of religious liberty under Catholic regimes in former times. The facts indicated that no radical break had been made with former ideas and conditions.

However topical the question of toleration in a Catholic state might have become, there was too much resistance to be overcome to allow for a thorough-going dialogue about the matter between Protestants and Catholics prior to 1940. Only after the Second World War, when it became apparent that the resurgence of Rome's power had continued unabated, did people on both the Protestant and

---

[1] [This article, a translation of "Rooms-Katholicisme en verdraagzaamheid" [Roman Catholicism and toleration], *Anti-Revolutionaire Staatkunde* 21 (1951): 245–57, was occasioned by a public address by J. J. Loeff entitled *Katholicisme, verdraagzaamheid en democratie naar Nederlandse verhoudingen* [Catholicism, toleration and democracy in the Dutch context], published by the Catholic People's Party (KVP), The Hague, 1950; 22 pp.]

Catholic sides take up the question of toleration to any significant degree—to such a degree, in fact, that it became a favorite topic of discussion in the various Centers for Dialogue where people from different faith communities come together to gain a better understanding of one another's beliefs and outlooks on life.

However, despite all the opportunities and attempts to remove misunderstanding through friendly exchanges of thought, a basic distrust of Rome's stand on toleration has persisted. In vain, people on the Catholic side have pointed out that there is no reason to allow events of the past, when the context of action was entirely different, to obscure the outlook for the future. As an example of new historical possibilities they have pointed to Ireland, where in a predominantly Catholic country Protestants enjoy complete freedom, politically and religiously, and are called upon to serve in the highest functions of the state. Attention is likewise called to the fact that the situation is changing theologically and philosophically as well: have not prominent Catholic scholars— including Pope Pius XII himself—affirmed in recent times that every person has the right to live according to his or her own honest convictions?

For all that, both theory (in old encyclicals and in many a scholarly and popular treatise) and practice (in Spain, Columbia, etc.) pointed in another direction. The very fact that Rome appeared able to adopt two entirely different approaches, that of toleration and that of intolerance, fostered uncertainty about its ultimate position. It is accordingly understandable that keen interest was aroused when the Center for Political Education of the Dutch Catholic People's Party chose as the theme for the celebration of its 5th Anniversary, 2 September 1950, the subject of "Catholicism, Toleration, and Democracy." This interest only grew when it became known that the fundamental principles of the question would be dealt with by the secretary of the Roman Catholic church province of the Netherlands, Dr. J. J. Loeff, who, while he could not of course make official pronouncements, could certainly speak with something more than the authority of a learned scholar.

The desired relaxation of tension has not been achieved. Far from ending the debate, Loeff's address itself has become a subject of controversy. On the Catholic side people have left no doubt that Loeff reflects not *the* but *a* Catholic point of view. For while his main principle is the traditional Roman Catholic one, he adds a second principle to it which, even though it is quite consonant with the Scholastic conception of politics and history, is by no means generally accepted by his co-religionists.[2] What is of interest in Loeff's presentation is that he manages, while upholding familiar Catholic principles, to shed new light on the old problem of toleration.[3]

---

[2] The pamphlet in which Dr. Loeff's address has been published also contains the paper given by [the Catholic] Professor L. G. J. Verberne on the historical aspects of toleration. We shall not enter into his discussion here because his historical sketch is too beautiful for us to want to spoil the impression of the whole by critiquing some of its details.

[3] The manner in which I shall discuss Loeff's ideas may seem to suggest he is the first to

Intolerant, but not to the ultimate degree

Loeff begins by posing the problem as follows. Every individual, and every community as well, is obligated to serve God according to the truth revealed by God himself in Jesus Christ.[4] According to Catholic conviction, this divine truth can be found pure and complete exclusively in the Roman Catholic Church. If Catholics were to have the leadership in the State, then, assuming they did not waver before the consequences, this would lead necessarily to suppressing all other religions or to placing their adherents in an exceptional position. Furthermore, in civil society this would lead to an interpretation of civil liberties consonant with the Catholic conception of Divine positive law and natural law.

With that, Loeff thinks he has posed the problem sharply and clearly, and he believes that the ideas just described are acceptable to Protestantism, given its confession concerning the calling of the magistracy to remove and prevent all idolatry and false worship.[5] And was it not Dr. Abraham Kuyper who said, "There is not a square inch of life of which Christ does not exclaim, 'It is Mine'"?

The principle enunciated above Loeff calls the *totality principle*, "without however [he is quick to add] attaching to it all the consequences of a totality principle." A remarkable restriction, the implications of which become clear in what follows.

In his expositions of the toleration question, Loeff follows a method that is very often adopted in Catholic treatises on the subject. A writer will begin by positing the totality principle, from which he then draws the conclusion that it entails intolerance towards dissidents; but he will immediately go on to assure the reader that religious liberty will not be threatened since other principles and practical considerations necessitate moderation. In this manner a contradiction is created between different principles. It is thus of great importance to acquire a proper understanding of the totality principle formulated above.

The totality principle contains two elements. In the first place the civil authority is dependent upon the Church with regard to knowledge of the common good, which the State has the specific task of promoting. To be sure, the natural norms by which civil life must be guided are clear in themselves and knowable to natural reason, but pronouncements by the teaching authority of the Church are still necessary since the natural understanding, while not darkened by the fall

---

advance them. In reality they can be found earlier, at least to some extent, in the works of Catholic writers abroad, especially in France.

[4] Loeff, *Katholicisme, verdraagzaamheid en democratie*, p. 6.

[5] [The allusion is to the Belgic Confession of 1561, one of the doctrinal standards of the Reformed churches in the Netherlands. Article 36, on Civil Government, reads in part: "Their office is not only to have regard unto and watch for the welfare of the civil state, but also to protect the sacred ministry *and thus remove and prevent all idolatry and false worship*, that the kingdom of the antichrist may be destroyed and the kingdom of Christ promoted." The words here italicized were retracted in 1905 by the Synod of the free *Gereformeerde Kerken*; the national *Hervormde Kerk*, the older and much larger denomination, has never removed them.]

into sin, is nonetheless disturbed to such a degree by the revolt of the baser inclinations against reason that error is possible. The teaching authority of the Church must protect the civil authority against deviating from the natural order and at the same time enrich it with ideas which of themselves belong to the natural order but which the natural understanding is capable of discovering only by the rays of light that fall from the supernatural. Thus the Church is indispensable for knowledge of the State's purpose or end because the Church is entrusted with the pure interpretation of natural and revealed ethics.

Yet the Catholic totality principle contains a second element that is closely related to the first. Although the end of the State is only of a natural and temporal character, the supernatural good of the subjects cannot be excluded from the concern of the civil authority. Now, if the immediate end of the State, the *temporal* good, is not fully and correctly knowable in a natural way, then certainly the task of civil government as it pertains to the *supernatural* cannot be known without the help of the teaching authority of the Church. There is more at stake here, however, than correct knowledge of the task of the State. The civil community does not itself need to pursue a supernatural goal, it is true, but individual human beings do. The Government should support them in this, first in the negative sense of removing any obstacles to their pursuit, but also, and especially, by promoting all that might assist them in their quest for eternal salvation. In the encyclical *Immortale Dei* (dated 1 November 1885) Pope Leo XIII states that the weightiest contribution civil society can make to man's attainment of the highest and imperishable good is "to take care to preserve religion holy and inviolate, for the practice of religion binds man to God." [6]

From this statement the Pope then draws practical conclusions with regard to political liberties. Of prime interest to us is what he has to say about freedom of education, since next to freedom of worship this freedom is the most contested. We read then, in the encyclical *Libertas* (dated 20 June 1888), that "freedom of education," insofar as it claims the right to teach whatever it pleases, without restriction, is "in conflict with reason and tends only to sowing utter confusion in men's minds—a liberty which the State cannot grant without failing in its duty." [7]

When decisions of such great importance to man's eternal salvation are made in profane life the Church, on the Catholic view, cannot be indifferent to what happens there. Granted, she has no direct jurisdiction over temporal affairs. Yet in an indirect way she does have a say, to the degree that there is some connection with grace. Ecclesiastical authority can thus in principle be extended to all created things, since they are all, at some time or in some way, associated with grace or else can be an external condition for the attainment of the supernatural good. [8]

---

[6] *Immortale Dei; On the Christian Constitution of States*, art. 6.

[7] *Libertas; On Human Liberty*, art. 24.

[8] On the totality principle see F. J. F. M. Duynstee, *Het glazen huis* [The glass house]

From the above we can draw three conclusions. I shall mention them here and then have more to say about them later, in my critical assessment. First, the totality principle, given the Catholic interpretation, contains two elements which in their mutual coherence must lead to absolute intolerance towards non-Catholic religions and which cannot but threaten religious liberty, in the broader sense, for dissenters. In the second place, it is patently clear that the Catholic totality principle is not oriented to the basic religious relation between God and his world but to the Church. Now, whenever there is talk of a totality of some sort, the cardinal question is: What determines this totality? In this case it is not the lordship of Christ over all things, but the Church of Rome as Christ's Mystical Body. That brings me to my third conclusion. The Catholic totality principle is not really totalist, nor can it be, since the natural life will continue to insist on a certain independence for itself vis-à-vis the overarching totality community, the Church. The autonomous natural order will never allow itself to be assimilated completely into the totality: it will give rise to unremitting protests against the totalist claims of the supernatural order and elicit the desire for moderation, the plea for toleration.

Toleration, but with reservations

To the extent that they consider our analysis of the totality principle correct, Catholics will say that unless more is added, what we have here is an extremely one-sided presentation of their standpoint. For Catholics, in point of fact, espouse a totality principle without, curiously, "attaching to it all the consequences of a totality principle." [9]

The numerous reservations that are held with respect to an unlimited implementation of the totality principle can be divided into two groups—which have in common, however, that neither can any longer be harmonized with the totality principle as such and that both give the impression of opportunism, to say the least, in the delimitation of religious liberties. Opportunism and tactics are at their most blatant wherever *practical* considerations lead to a tolerant posture towards dissidents. Catholics point out that especially today the possibilities in any given country of acting as one would like are limited by world public opinion and predictable international reactions, all of which must be taken into account when the interests of the State are in the balance.

Of still greater importance is the following consideration. One must not expect the rights of the minority to be restricted the moment Catholics have the majority in any given country. Loeff puts the matter this way:

(1946); C. F. Pauwels, "Godsdienstvrijheid en gewetensvrijheid" [Freedom of worship and freedom of conscience], *Het Schild* 26 (1948/49): 145–53; P. Ploumen, *De Katholieke levensopvatting: het burgerschap van twee rijken* [The Catholic view of life: citizenship in two kingdoms] (1937); V. Cremers, *Kerk en Staat* [Church and State] (1927).

[9] Loeff, op. cit., p. 7.

No Dutch Catholic believes for a moment that if they should ever have an absolute majority in the Netherlands they would automatically proceed to apply this totality principle to every area of public life. . . . Even in case of a Catholic majority the constitutionally guaranteed rights of religious denominations, in particular as regards freedom of confession, proselytism, public worship, of association and assembly, of nurture and education, of social service programs, would be perfectly safe.[10]

Words like these, although they may sound reassuring, are more likely to reinforce than remove the distrust of those who hear them from Catholic spokesmen. For to say that a certain action would not follow "automatically" is to imply a reservation. And one finds a reservation of some sort or other in most Catholic treatises on the question of toleration. Thus another writer, while defending freedom of education, hastens to add:

[The State] must . . . not only see to it that no views are proclaimed that conflict with the temporal common good, but the community would also suffer if young people were raised in an atmosphere of aloofness, misconception, and rancor. It must require an adequate education for all future citizens, even if religiously they belong to the dissidents. If a country has not only a Catholic foundation but also a traditional Catholic culture, then access to that culture must be opened to all citizens through the schools. Therefore a certain vigilance on the part of the State towards minority schools is reasonable.[11]

Practical considerations compelling moderation accordingly do not bring us any further, since time and again the possibility is left open of eventually restricting the promised freedom under certain circumstances. The question now is whether the principles underpinning toleration can furnish a solution.

We cannot delve deeply here into the many views held on this point in Catholic circles. Some have advocated toleration on the basis of the Divine commandment that we should love one another. Loeff points out the inadequacy of this view and argues that love of neighbor is always transcended by love of God and, moreover, that it is precisely love of one's neighbor that may require restricting his freedom. A second argument for toleration receives even less approval in Loeff's eyes, namely, that evil may be admitted entrance or be allowed to persist in order to prevent a greater evil. Against this argument Loeff observes that when a Catholic majority cooperates in, for example, granting a subsidy to non-Catholic private education, the question is surely no longer merely one of "toleration."

We shall give no further attention to these views, but it repays to take a closer look at two approaches that have come to dominate the discussions about toleration in Catholic circles.

---

[10] Ibid.
[11] Pauwels, "Godsdienstvrijheid en gewetensvrijheid," 149.

The first of these goes back to the renowned French philosopher Jacques Maritain, who has exercised an influence on Catholic thought in the twentieth century that would be difficult to exaggerate and who for a number of years after the Second World War was the French ambassador to the Vatican. It is especially through Maritain that Catholicism has come to the realization that the Middle Ages are over, if not for good then at least for the foreseeable future. A new age has now dawned in history, the age of 'profane Christendom.' This period is distinguishable from the Middle Ages in that the religious unity has been lost. In the Middle Ages there was a unity of belief accompanied by a unity of outlook on life and the world. In an age when the civil community consisted almost exclusively of Christians, apostasy or heresy meant a disturbance of both the ecclesiastical and the public order. Hence it was the inescapable duty of the State to take measures against heresy, precisely or partly because the unity of belief, the very foundation of medieval society, was under attack.

Maritain goes on to say, however, that at the end of the Middle Ages and the beginning of Modern Times this state of affairs was terminated by the Renaissance and the Reformation. At that time the unity of belief was fundamentally ruptured, and it became unthinkable for the State to suppress error since to have done so would have been to make life in society impossible.

There was more, however—and now we come to an essential point in Maritain's position. When at the great turning point in European history modern man detached himself from the supernaturally ordered culture of the Middle Ages, he inflicted incalculable harm upon himself. Yet, at the same time he gained considerable benefit; for in turning aside from the supernatural he began to look at himself, to study and inspect himself thoroughly, as it were, and so he discovered himself. He now gained an awareness of the infinite value of human personality. While this had not been entirely lacking in the Middle Ages, it had been overshadowed by ever so many other elements. Thus humanism, which put man at the center, acquired or rediscovered something that ought never again to be lost. And it is for this reason that the grand task facing the builders of the new Christian culture is to incorporate into the profane Christian society of the future the gain made by anthropocentric humanism.

Now then, recognition of the value of the individual human personality involves the right of every person to live according to his own convictions. Pope Pius XII became the voice of the ideas just sketched, which are shared by many leading figures in Catholic circles, when in his Christmas message of 1942 he recognized the right of the private and public exercise of religion as a fundamental right of the human personality.

Loeff rejects Maritain's position as well, although he presents only a very short summary of it and does not mention Maritain by name. Maritain's criterion, Loeff feels, lacks clarity: respect for the human personality prohibits forcing a particular conviction on anyone—but does it also mean, he inquires, that everyone is to be left free to propagate his convictions?

By discarding one argument for toleration after another, Loeff has made room to advance a position of his own.

After rejecting the humanist doctrine of the will, he advances the Thomist doctrine of natural law as the point of departure for resolving the question of toleration. Whereas the natural law philosophers of modern times divorce the principles that are to guide civil authority from any higher order with its moral values and duties, making these principles instead entirely dependent on the human will, the Thomist approach, in contrast, holds that man has to discover these principles in the natural order, which is valid quite apart from the human will. It is man's task to glean from the natural order the ideas and principles in accordance with which institutions, including the State, are governed, and in this way to give the social order an "objective" existence.

At a certain moment in the history of a people they will become aware that the existing legal norms are no longer suited to keeping the indulgence of freedom within bounds and that stronger restraints are called for. This leads to the discovery of the *idée gouvernementale*, that is, the idea of restraint, of order, to rescue the ideal of freedom. Thus the matter is primarily one not of restraint as such, but of *freedom in restraint*.

It is this *idée gouvernementale,* above all other factors, that led to the rise of the State, a process that began in the Late Middle Ages, required many centuries, and is in fact not yet finished. The process evolved in such a way that in a given period circumstances invited, as it were, the formation of a modern state community, but the work could not be done in just any arbitrary fashion since the material from which the life of the State had to be constructed was derived from the natural order.

If for some time now we seem to have lost sight of the totality principle, that is only apparently so. For behind our discussion there is a particular question that demands our attention: What is the relation between the *idée gouvernementale* and the totality principle?

The legitimacy of a particular decision, Loeff explains, depends not on the number of votes but on the certainty that it conforms to the *'idée gouvernementale' as interpreted at a particular moment in a community.* Thus the *idée gouvernementale* is not a rigid quantity fixed once and for all time. Its content, while remaining fundamentally bound to the natural order, alters with the development of the leading ideas in a given national community. This very circumstance allows the totality principle to be linked with the *idée gouvernementale.* The totality principle obliges Catholics to give the *idée gouvernementale* a Catholic interpretation and a Catholic content. Thus the totality principle is always valid, but the possibility of bringing it to expression in public decisions increases with the growth of the prestige and influence of Roman Catholics in public life.

Political intolerance unavoidable, but normed

Why such long expositions of what is apparently an irresolvable problem, some readers may well ask. Will we on our part ever be able to advance beyond Catholic writers by asserting the totality principle on the one hand and urging moderation on the other, lest fundamental human values be trampled underfoot? Should we not show some restraint in our criticism of Catholic ideas on toleration in view of the fact that Calvinists, too, have been known to be intolerant in the past and, above all, because they, too, are no strangers to the totality principle, which is a threat to the freedom of those of other persuasions? We cannot dismiss this difficult question merely by asserting that matters of religious or ethical good and evil are none of the State's business.

Catholics are happy to start with the totality principle when debating with Calvinists. This is (seems!) a common starting point and an identical platform from which to carry on the discussion. Loeff, too, regards the totality principle as a point of agreement between Calvinists and Catholics. We are surprised, however, to find that Loeff, who is trained not only in law but also in theology, places the Catholic and the Calvinist totality principles simply side by side. We can think of an explanation for this incorrect view only when we recall that for a Catholic, Church and Christ are identical. In saying this I do not lose sight of the fact that a Catholic thinker would qualify his use of the term "identical." But the identification is so self-evident that where Kuyper says, "There is not one square inch of life of which Christ does not say, 'It is Mine,'" a Roman Catholic can simply read "the Church" in the place of "Christ." Indeed, the distinction between these two words expresses the deepest point of disagreement between Calvinism and Catholicism on the idea of toleration.

In the Reformational view there is an authentic totality principle, with Christ as its determining, direction-setting center. There is nothing in the created world that is withdrawn from his rule, and man, in subjection to God's commandments, has to bring to expression in the entire order of things the redemption won by Christ. Christ's work and rule are total and all-embracing, and there is no terrain that on the basis of some alleged autonomy can abridge Christ's absolute kingship. Because Calvinism confesses the religious nature of the whole of creation and can therefore acknowledge no autonomous, natural order—to which the State is supposed to belong—its totality idea is without reservation or restriction.

The Catholic totality principle, in contrast, entails restrictions, as indeed it must in view of the fact that it finds its point of departure in the Church which, unlike religion, cannot *permeate* the whole of creation but can merely *overarch* it. The Church spreads her wings over natural life and allows it to carry on as such, provided it does not come into conflict with the supernatural good of believers and provided it remains ultimately oriented to the spiritual order.

Remarkably, although Calvinism confesses the kingship of Christ over all creation in more absolute terms than Catholicism does, Catholicism is more suspect on the point of toleration than Calvinism. Many know intuitively, or from familiarity with the past, that Catholicism—although it recognizes a distinction between Church and State and will not confuse the supernatural and the natural—accepts no fundamental, immutable boundary between the Church and natural life. The moment the supernatural good requires it, ecclesiastical authority may step across the boundaries of the Church and, abetted or unabetted by the strong arm of Government, subordinate non-ecclesiastical life to itself. That any indulgence of religious liberties on the Catholic view is dependent more on circumstance than principle is tellingly illustrated in the encyclical *Libertas*. It states that if in view of extraordinary circumstances the Church acquiesces in certain modern liberties, then she does so

not because she prefers them in themselves but because she judges it expedient to permit them. And if ever happier times should arrive, she would certainly exercise her own liberty and zealously endeavor, as is her duty, by persuasion, exhortation and entreaty, to fulfill her God-given task, namely, of providing for the eternal salvation of mankind. One thing, however, would always be true: the liberty which is claimed for all to do all things is not . . . of itself desirable, inasmuch as it is contrary to reason that error and truth should have equal rights.[12]

From the preceding it will be clear, I think, that our view of the problem of toleration and intolerance should be governed by two principles, neither of which should be applied except in close connection with the other: (1) the totality principle; and (2) the mutual irreducibility of Church and State. On this basis we can now proceed to a further analysis of our problem.

The points of departure of both Reformed Christianity and Roman Catholicism evidently lead along similar paths to political intolerance towards dissidents. After all, Calvinists profess themselves to be called, in the administration of the State, to follow the will of God as it is made known in his revelation. And on the Catholic view, "not only the individual but also every human community and thus certainly the State [is] obligated to serve God according to the religion revealed by God himself in the person of Jesus Christ." [13]

This implies that whenever either Calvinists or Catholics control public affairs and can build on the convictions of the subjects, they will positivize principles that will be experienced by non-Christians and by Christians who do not share their convictions as a power alien to themselves. Here, beyond doubt, is an intolerant element in the administration of the State! As long, at least, as the citizenry is divided along lines of principle.

We can and must go farther. Those who in public administration are guided by the revealed will of God, or who are self-consciously dependent on the religion confessed by the Church, are not the only ones to be intolerant in some measure toward those of other persuasions. Those who acknowledge no Divine

---

[12] *Libertas*, art. 34.
[13] Loeff, op. cit., 6.

will, or at least regard it as unknowable for civil life, likewise obligate their believing or dissenting subjects to be guided by norms which the latter experience as in conflict with their convictions. Modern man does not like to be thought intolerant. Perhaps that is why people in the humanist camp are so blind to the element of intolerance in every public administration and generally notice it in, or in any case impute it to, the Opposition alone. How often have the parties of the Left [14] not dreaded limitations on the exercise of their freedom at the hands of a Christian administration while remaining almost blissfully unaware that if it were up to them to decide, the Christian life would be permitted to unfold only on a limited terrain!

In the meantime, there are factors that have a moderating influence on political intolerance. In certain cases differences of political philosophy will not lead to divergent policies. It is also possible that a group of a particular persuasion will no longer oppose a given development to which it initially offered (vigorous) resistance because it comes to the realization that the trend is irreversible anyway and ultimately concludes that there is something good in the results achieved— indeed, something that is in harmony with its own principles. I have in mind the evolution of Liberalism in the struggle for Christian schools.[15]

While political intolerance may thus be tempered to some extent, it will be clear from the brief remarks we have just made that the governance of a population lacking religious unity will unavoidably be attended by a certain measure of intolerance.

The fundamental delimitation of Church and State

Must we conclude from the above that because political intolerance is unavoidable it makes no difference at all for political toleration *which* worldview people hold?

Certainly not. For while we have argued that the Divine ordinance for the life of the State necessarily entails some form of political intolerance, we shall now defend with equal vigor the idea that this intolerance is restricted by a fixed, inviolable boundary. Here the difference between Calvinism and Catholicism on the matter of toleration comes to a head.

We must begin by distinguishing between two elements. On the one hand, there is the calling of Government to provide public justice for *believers and unbelievers, Christians and non-Christians*. Government's primary task is to afford legal protection to all its subjects irrespective of their religious persuasion. The issue is, purely and simply, that Government create room for human life as such, in order to preserve it. On the other hand, Government must be guided by what God requires of it.

---

[14] [The reference here is to the "non-confessional" parties of conservatives, liberals, and socialists.]

[15] [In the schools question—should secular and Christian schools enjoy equal rights, including government funding?—Dutch Liberalism evolved from a position of absolute intolerance in the 1840's to a markedly liberal policy after 1910.]

The first element contains the guarantee of religious liberty for the subjects. The second brings with it the intolerance inherent in all public administrations of religiously mixed populations. These two elements are not contradictory. Rather, they are intrinsically related in such a way that the second is the norm for the first: in providing legal protection to human life Government must let itself be led by the Divine will. But the Catholic principle leads to different consequences, since it inserts the *Church* between God's commandments and the civil community.

The Church is entitled to exercise discipline over her members and, when their conduct shows them to have no part in Christ, to excommunicate them if need be. Ecclesiastical discipline is determined by the fact that the Church ought to be a community of faith in Jesus Christ. Whereas the State must embrace believers and unbelievers alike, the Church, in contrast, may finally be forced to expel the latter if they persist in their unbelief. Thus the position of the Church toward her members is fundamentally different from the position of the State toward its subjects. This fundamental difference in position reflects the fundamental difference in nature and essence that obtains between Church and State.

Catholicism has turned a blind eye to this difference for centuries and remains congenitally hostile to it to this day. It may offer assurances just as often as it likes that ecclesiastical and civil power have well-defined limits (as in the encyclical *Immortale Dei*, art. 13); still, in virtue of its totality principle, it repeatedly takes norms that are of fundamental importance to the life of Christ's Church on earth and proceeds to extend them to civil life. When the State is made serviceable to the attainment of supernatural good to such a degree that it has not only, negatively, to remove obstacles, whereby the Church (in keeping with 1Tim. 2:2) acquires room for her work in obedience to Christ's commission, but has also, positively, to promote everything that might help man to attain the spiritual order, and when the Church consequently is granted indirect authority over everything that disposes people towards grace, then the Church has long since overstepped her bounds. Then she is engaged in imposing restrictions on the religious freedom of dissidents via the civil authority that far exceed what I have called the "unavoidable" measure of intolerance. The intolerance many fear from Rome arises from this, that in virtue of the Catholic totality principle a structure is ascribed to the State that is essentially foreign to it, and a mandate is given to the State that belongs to the Church alone. In this way the Church, via the strong arm of Government, can exercise a form of coercion to which she was never called (see Zech. 4:6: *"Not by might, nor by power, but by my spirit, saith the Lord of hosts"*) and for which she was never given the instruments by her King, Jesus Christ.

The fallacy of the totality principle as interpreted by Catholicism is obvious from the fact that it conflicts with other elementary principles: the commandment to love one's neighbor, the recognition of the dignity of the human personality, and so forth. In Catholic circles people sometimes sense that they have a problem here. For example, Professor Van Melsen speaks of reconciling two "almost contradictory principles." [16]

People might conclude that where toleration is concerned, two contradictory principles are a better starting point than a totality principle alone. Yet we must not underestimate the potentially grave consequences of a merely external reconciliation. However well-intentioned, the school of Maritain remains unable to get beyond making the idea of toleration dependent on the tension between two mutually exclusive principles. Ultimately, all depends on how this tension will be resolved when Roman Catholicism gains the majority in any given country: which will predominate, the value of the individual human personality, or the medieval conception of the relation of Church and State? In the matter of toleration, Maritain leaves us uncertain and apprehensive.

Despite all this, it is Loeff's standpoint that I regard as the more dangerous. Admittedly, the religious liberty of non-Catholics will not be curtailed the very moment Catholics have gained the majority. Nevertheless, the totality principle is intended to penetrate the *idée gouvernementale* and to determine its content, not suddenly or unexpectedly, but in the long run. Suppose the *idée gouvernementale*, having that principle as its content, shall have become the leading idea in the civil community: what guarantees will then be left for the preservation of the liberties of those of other persuasions? In the end it does not make a great deal of difference whether religious liberty succumbs to democratic decisions based on fifty percent plus one or to internal developments within a so-called *idée gouvernementale*.

Many futile attempts have been undertaken by Catholics to allay Protestant fears. Loeff's effort, too, was bound not to succeed. His views contain too many elements that nourish rather than moderate our apprehensions.

---

[16] A. G. M. van Melsen, "Reflecties van een 20e eeuwse Nederlandse Katholiek over de tolerantie" [Reflections of a 20th-century Dutch Catholic on toleration], *Wending* 4 (1949): 246f.

4/ NATIONALISM AND CATHOLICISM

ANYONE WHO OCCUPIES himself for any length of time with the study of a historical phenomenon[1] is likely to have the surprising experience that deeper knowledge of that phenomenon does not lead initially to clearer insight but instead to a confusing multiplicity of questions. Of course, such a result need not be surprising, since one of the foremost aims of scientific study is to gain a knowledge of things and of events in their many aspects. And with that, a rich source of problems is tapped. For the matter now becomes one of understanding these many aspects in their mutual relations and also of understanding the things and phenomena as such in their manifold connections. Undoubtedly there already exists in pre-scientific insight a surmise of the complexity of phenomena. The scientist, however, experiences it as an inner law of life that he not be satisfied with such a surmise but instead focus all his attention on the apparently confusing multiplicity of patterns in which things occur.

If anyone think this is an exaggerated picture of the complex character of research into historical phenomena, it will be enough to point out to him the divergent interpretations that have been given of nationalism. After years of intensive study and discussion of the function of the state, language, race, and so on, in the development of national consciousness, the extent to which language and nation, state and nation, and so forth, are interrelated remains an open question.

People have not always been conscious of the complexity of the concept 'nation.' To read Bossuet, for example, is to gain the impression that the concept is a rather straightforward affair. Especially during the last hundred years, however, the conviction has grown that a multiplicity of factors have played a formative role in the evolution of nations. Above all, people have become conscious that in this whole process the function of worldviews—though at times latent—would be difficult to overestimate. Numerous intellectual currents can be identified that have been of such decisive importance that they form a basis for classifying various stages in the rise and flowering of national consciousness in Europe. In this regard it suffices to mention Romanticism.

When we reflect more deeply upon the eminent role played by such intellectual currents as Humanism, Enlightenment, Romanticism, Roman Catholicism, etc., we are struck by the remarkable fact that they all contributed to the growth of national consciousness. Each current contributed particular elements to the national idea, yet each in its own way also reached beyond national particularities towards a universal community. Is this not one of the reasons why Roman-

---

[1] [Text of a paper read to the Gezelschap van Christelijke Historici in Nederland; pub. in W. P. Keijzer, ed., *Christendom en Nationalisme* (The Hague: Van Keulen, 1955), chap. VI.]

ticism continues to be of perennial interest? After many generations devoted to anything called "national" had allowed themselves to be guided by the ideas of Romanticism, it turned out that Romanticism was also amply suited to contributing to the ideological foundations in an age committed to the construction of *supra*national communities. Humanism, Enlightenment, Romanticism, etc., have all been retired without their having arrived at an inner reconciliation of the national and the universal.

Catholicism too has known, and still knows, this tension. And here especially we must inquire into its origin. Is it perhaps implicit in Christianity? But Scripture knows nothing of this tension. To continue our line of questioning: Is it to be attributed to a confluence of Christianity with originally non-Christian currents? Or, still another possibility: Does the conflict of the national with the supranational perhaps find its origin not in some particular worldview but in the national itself? We will not be able to go into these problems extensively within the scope of this essay, but we shall have to keep them very much in mind.

The national versus the universal

A great deal has been published on the Catholic side about the national idea, but very little attention has been paid as yet to one aspect: the relation between Catholicism and nationalism in its historical dynamics. To mention one example, there is still no thorough study of the role played by genuine Catholicism in the development of national consciousness under French absolutism. Interesting material is to be found in Bossuet and the eighteenth-century Catholic philosophers of history who came after him and depended upon him. However, it has been left unexamined thus far.

Given this state of affairs, it is not possible for me to trace the importance of Catholicism for nationalism in a few broad lines. I shall have to confine myself to touching on Catholic influence in a few phases of the history of the development of nationalism in Western Europe.

Nationalism did not become a major factor in European history until the states formed themselves into historical entities. This happened in a long process that varied from country to country but that almost everywhere received powerful impulses from Humanism.

Humanism acquired great significance for the formative process of the modern nations not least through its extraordinary esteem for history. For the nations did not acquire form only in that a state became unified under able rulers or in that religious, cultural, and economic elements within a certain territory were focused on the political center of the evolving national entity. The course of development of national consciousness reveals clearly that however powerful and wise a ruler may have been, and however favorable to national unification the geographical location may have been, there was still always something artificial about the young nation if the many elements of which it was constructed were not melted together by the binding power of history: the national unity could be formed or deepened by prolonged dwelling together, but also by communally invoking a distant—sometimes mythical—shared past. In the Renaissance and in the immediately preceding period which resists precise delimitation, the modern nation evolving around the ruler acquired its initial form and was then integrated into a national entity by religious and other factors. But in Humanism there were powers that could bring this development to completion, at least provisionally: it was especially the Humanists who harked back to some earlier "national" greatness or who provided the often still shaky political entity with a historical basis. In the dim past, it was thought, the ideals had already once been exemplified; all that was necessary was their rebirth or revival. The conceptions of the Humanists about the historical background of the nation were often divergent. In many instances there was agreement between the stories from different countries while the conceptions within any one country could differ strongly. Yet almost all of them had the same tendency: to promote national unity and glory.

Among the creators of these fantastical and speculative theories there were also Catholic writers. Together with those of other persuasions, they enhanced national consciousness in Western Europe and were co-responsible for the excessive notions then already in vogue with respect to national greatness. There is something surprising in this course of development in view of the fact that the Roman Catholic church, in virtue of its essential structure and its historical roots in the medieval supranational culture, should be little favorably disposed towards any cultural and political differences that derived from national antitheses and were often divisive in their effect on the unity of the church. Thus Carlton J. H. Hayes is quite correct when he says that the Pope and the bishops recognized the principle of nationality and made concessions to it, but that as the builders of an international, if not a cosmopolitan, culture they "vigorously withstood anything which might savor of nationalism." [2]

The Catholic founders and rulers of national states and their lackeys were often scarcely conscious of this serious conflict between the national and the universal. It is instructive to consult the theologians and philosophers of the time. Among the philosophers, the Spanish scholastic Suarez († 1617) took a lively interest in the question. Among the theologians, it is Bossuet who invites attention. In his *Politique tirée des propres Paroles de l'Écriture Sainte* he devotes extensive attention to the concept 'nation' and related problems. To our mind, his views still lack a certain desirable complexity. Like so many writers before and after him in the modern period, Bossuet fails almost entirely to appreciate that the concepts 'nation' and 'fatherland' confront human thought with problems that are perhaps irresolvable. Bossuet sees no serious difficulties here. True, the rise of a nation depends on meeting certain conditions, but in Bossuet these are fulfilled as a matter of course. This impression is fostered especially by his all too abundant use of "proof texts" from the Bible.

---

[2] Carlton J. H. Hayes, *Essays on Nationalism* (1926), 38.

According to Bossuet human society is divided as the result of two causes: human passion; and the various nations (which, as it happens, were necessary given the growth in population). The fragmentation, which was unavoidable even apart from sin, was effected by the confusion of tongues at Babel, which befell people as a punishment for their pride. And then it seems, he continues, that those who possessed greater conformity in language were led to choose the same area of habitation—"to which kinship also contributed a great deal." [3] Voilà, the various factors required to form a nation worked felicitously together.

Yet all this is still not sufficient, as Bossuet well appreciates. There are the human passions. They tear society apart. And only one power can avert this, the authority of a strong government.[4] The will of all converges in the will of the prince, and so the forces of the nation meet in one person, thereby strengthening the hand of all. In a variation of *"l'état c'est moi,"* Bossuet can say that the fatherland is the prince: "The whole state is in the person of the prince. In him resides the power, in him resides the will, of all the people." [5]

It is God, Bossuet continues, who placed us in a particular nation, but it is also God who bound us to all people in a single universal society, who caused all people to be brought forth from one, and who gave all people the same goal: Himself. The bounds that God determined are therefore not intended to bring division but to enable people to help each other.[6] There is no conflict between love of man and love of country. If one must love all men, it follows *a fortiori* that he must love his fellow-citizens—for all his love for self, for family, and for friends combine in love of country. Therefore banish the sowers of division! [7]

We encounter various elements in Bossuet's conceptions that are the common property of the genuine Roman Catholic national idea. For Bossuet, two elements are typical. Although the nation, as he sees it, rests upon strong pillars, it still needs the state—and the state in its absolute form at that—to hold it permanently together. Here the national idea is joined to the state absolutism of Bossuet's master, Louis XIV. On this score Bossuet had many followers, but he also drew sharp criticism from fellow Catholics.[8]

Yet another accent makes Bossuet interesting to us. As a philosopher of history he was the "philosopher of Providence," and he supplies us with a beautiful, worked-out sample of that in his national idea. It is God who guides the entire process of the forming of nations, it is God who overrules human actions and passions to establish the many conditions for the rise and survival of nations, and it is God who causes everyone to be born in his own country.

---

[3] J. B. Bossuet, *Politics Drawn from the Very Words of Holy Scripture* (1709), I, ii.

[4] For this point, too, Bossuet, ibid., I, iii, appeals to numerous Scripture passages, *inter alia* Judg.17:6 ("In those days there was no king in Israel, but every man did that which was right in his own eyes").

[5] Bossuet, *Politics*, VI, i.

[6] Ibid., I, i and v. [Cf. Acts 17:26–27.]

[7] Ibid., I, vi.

[8] Cf. H. A. Rommen, *Die Staatslehre der Franz Suarez* (1926), 268.

Bossuet's doctrine of the origin of the nations in God's providential decree finds its complement in the perspective he develops, especially in the *Histoire des variations des églises protestantes*, according to which the decline of the church must necessarily entail the decline of the state as its consequence.

To appreciate how much the two ideas thus sketched were part of Catholic thought in Bossuet's days, it is instructive to read with an open mind the still too little studied writings of his adherents from the seventeenth and eighteenth centuries, such as Charles Rollin († 1741) and René Louis d'Argenson († 1757). To an even stronger degree than Bossuet, if that is possible, these authors relegated all so-called secondary causes to the background, in favor of the Providence of God as the all-determining factor in the whole of human history.

The secularization of nationalism

Still another line runs through the eighteenth-century Catholic conception of history and the state. Though it, too, finds its starting point in the Christian worldview, it is so overshadowed by the ideology of the Enlightenment that its Christian origin is largely lost to view. It was Jean-Baptiste du Bos († 1742) in whom the transition was effected from the Christian but unproblematical ideas of Bossuet to the Enlightenment. Du Bos differed from Bossuet precisely with regard to the two aspects that were characteristic of the latter's approach. This did not mean that Du Bos did not remain Roman Catholic; he was sometimes fiercely so, and he remained hostile to Protestantism. But while Bossuet and his followers endeavored to view things in the light of religion, Du Bos detached them from the integral supernatural order and considered primarily their dependence on external circumstances. With that, the climate was created for a drastic change of perspective within eighteenth-century French Catholicism. Following in the footsteps of Du Bos, people no longer regarded the flowering of the nation as something dependent upon the maintenance of the Catholic religion but rather as something dependent on various non-religious factors—factors which, so it seemed, were favorable precisely to the Protestants.

The Enlightenment, because of its cosmopolitan character, seemed to promise little good for the national consciousness; and yet it powerfully stimulated the growth of nationalism in Europe, and it provided France with an important part of her national ideology. The inner connection that arose between the cosmopolitan and national elements in the rationalist and empiricist thought of the eighteenth century was possible because the national idea had already been detached from the religious order. Bossuet and his closer adherents had proceeded on the assumption that whatever nation God has assigned to a man is his fatherland, even if it was an inferior one. But the Enlightenment reversed that: one could call a country (read: state) his fatherland only when it made its citizens happy, in the Enlightenment sense of guaranteeing freedom and equality.

These notions concerning fatherland and nation did not arise from Christianity—or if they did, it was by way of the long course of secularization—yet they found a sympathetic audience amongst many in Roman Catholic circles, not least amongst the clergy. Alphonse Aulard cites some startling instances in his book on French patriotism from the Renaissance to the Revolution.[9] The patriotism of the clergy bore all the trademarks of Enlightenment ideas but at the same time retained the connection with the Christian religion. One of the most interesting illustrations of the synthesis I have just sketched is provided by the speech delivered by Dom Ferlus, a Benedictine of Saint Maur, in the assembly of the Estates of Languedoc on the eve of the Revolution, which he published under the telling title, *Le patriotisme chrétien*.[10] Ferlus is of such interest to our subject because he turns against the philosophers and pins his hope on religion. For all that, his ideas about the *patrie* are no less revolutionary. Originally, Ferlus argues, people lived as one family, ruled by a *patriotisme divin*, but in a process of increasing pride, egoism, and division, people were gripped by a *patriotisme humain* that shattered even time-honored religion into a plurality of cults.[11] But it is in the *patriotisme chrétien* that people recover the original *patriotisme divin*: it is religion which restores to people, or at least to a portion of mankind, the *patrie* by bestowing liberty and happiness upon them. Ferlus makes clear the sense in which he takes religion, freedom, and happiness when he writes: "The Christian religion did not impose duties on man that were alien to him. The Gospel is but the sublime commentary of natural law. . . ."[12]

Aulard believes Ferlus's patriotism to be "after the manner of Bossuet and Fenelon."[13] In light of the development in religious and national consciousness within French Catholicism described above, this construction is untenable; but Bossuet did continue to have his followers. We again mention Rollin and d'Argenson, but now add another name, Jean-Jacques Lefranc de Pompignan, Bishop of Le Puy, who published a celebrated *Pastoral Instruction* in 1763 on the "so-called philosophy of modern unbelievers."[14] No more than Bossuet does Le Franc de Pompignan see a contradiction between everyone's having been created of one blood and their being bound to each other in one love to one end, and the attachment to the fatherland. Love of country is but one of the many forms of love; it is rooted in a special attachment, in virtue of which we will love our fellow citizens "by preference above all other men."[15] In his ongoing polemic with "le citoyen de Genève" (Rousseau), the bishop seizes upon the deepest

---

[9] François-Alphonse Aulard, *Le Patriotisme français de la Renaissance à la Révolution* (1921), 46–83.

[10] Dom François Ferlus, O.B., *Le Patriotisme chrétien. Discours prêché aux États du Languedoc en 1787*. A few years later Ferlus played an active role in the French Revolution.

[11] Cf. Ferlus, ibid., 22, 23.

[12] Ibid., 22.

[13] Aulard, *Le Patriotisme français*, 80.

[14] J. J. Lefranc de Pompignan, *Instruction pastorale sur la prétendue philosophie des incrédules modernes* (1763). Although he was among the strongest antagonists of Voltaire and Rousseau, when the Revolution broke out the bishop allowed himself to be swept along: he became president of the National Assembly. He died the year after, in 1790.

[15] Pompignan, *Oeuvres complètes*, col. 164.

difference that divides them: a person's fatherland is not the country that gives him the highest happiness but the country in which Providence places him.[16]

The influence of Romanticism

When one studies the history of the national idea especially in its Catholic form he is struck by the dominating place of God's providential decree. Yet this belief does not recur in every new phase without modification. Time and again it absorbs new elements and becomes itself a formative power in the historical phenomena. If people of the sixteenth and seventeenth centuries regarded the action of God pertaining to the origin of the nation and the state as an overpowering *intervention*, as a calling into being, after Romanticism they perceived divine Providence as permeating and becoming visible in the great *flux* of history. The Romantics and those who followed in their train, the champions of organic conceptions, drew near in silent awe to history, to the market places of the past, also to its precious product, the nation: for in order to be a nation, a folk community surely must have its origin in a region of mystery in a distant past.

Romanticism, however, bore within itself many a contradictory notion. At the very moment when Romantics, bewitched by the profound language of the flux of history, threatened to be swept away in the current, they would break the spell and revolt against all tradition in order to enter upon a vast, unknown world. The Romantics were never able to overcome the polarity in their attitude toward history. Closely related is their ambivalence toward nation, fatherland, and folk community: everything in them draws them, on the one hand, towards the security of the nation, and on the other hand, towards the universal world. Guardini has said of the true Romantic that no one experiences as much homesickness as he, the "wanderer who yearns for home"; but no sooner has he returned than everything about home seems too restricted and he wants to leave again. What he seeks but does not find in family, folk, or nation is unity—not the unity of many elements consigned to each other or held together by merely external connections, but a unity in which the manifold, infinitely varied shapes know themselves safe with each other through their common origin in a mysterious primordial ground. He seeks the wide world that would be entirely "inner," the limits of distances which guarantee at once full freedom of movement and intimate security.[17] Thus the Romantic will seek out the nation and in the next moment flee it for the universal world; he can be fanatical about Germany and at the same time be mindful of his calling with regard to Europe.

This inner ambivalence or dichotomy in the historical and national consciousness of Romanticism was not resolved in its symbiosis with Catholicism. Did not many of its Catholic representatives, like Friedrich Schlegel, Adam Müller, Joseph Görres and others, contribute importantly to shaping the abiding

---

[16] Ibid.
[17] Romano Guardini, "Erscheinung und Wesen der Romantik," in T. Steinbüchel, ed., *Romantik; ein Zyklus Tübinger Vorlesungen*, 242.

sentimental values of the impressionable new youth of German nationalism? To be sure, the European idea, the notion of a Christendom transcending national boundaries, remained alive in all of them. Many a Romantic, especially in his later years, was disposed to give it priority. Schlegel dreamed of a "collegially interwoven unity" of a free European "association of nations" encompassing all nations and states[18] and Görres dreamed of an "organically articulated" Europe in which each nation would represent a particular class.[19] Nonetheless, the polar contradiction between the national-individual and the universal remained, reconciled only in *appearance*: it is one nation—one's own nation—that forms a bridge between the two: the destiny of Europe depends on Germany[20]; through the nature of the German *Volk*, which strives for knowledge and justice, Europe acquires firmness and strength[21]; the German *Volk* is the organ of history.[22]

For Romanticism, the nation and humanity were co-original. This explains why Herder's early doctrine of the *Volksgeist* was not able to gain the upper hand at that time. Matters began to change, however, with the rise of the Historical Schools, since there the connection with the universal weakened as time went by. Yet this brought to the fore an irresolvable problem that had remained partially hidden in genuine Romanticism as a result of its universalizing of the national idea: if the history of every separate nation must be explained on the basis of some permanently unchanging national *Volksgeist*, how is it possible to account for the alien elements that a *Volk* assimilates and may even give priority? Because he accepted this heritage of Romanticism and the Historical Schools, the Roman Catholic historian Johannes Janssen was unable, in his *Deutsche Geschichte*, to deal satisfactorily with the influence of other cultures on German culture: thus he attributed signs of decline in German history at least in part to foreign influences, particularly to the reception of Roman law.

French Traditionalists

The Catholic national idea was more varied in the nineteenth century than we have indicated thus far. There were writers in whom the national idea was relegated entirely to the background in favor of universalism, be it in the ecclesiastical or in the European sense. There were also those who based their hope for the salvation of the West on a nation other than their own. Ernst von Lasaulx († 1861), for example, in his "fact-based" essay of 1856 in philosophy of history which is being read avidly again today, looked to the Slavs, not to the Germans, for the healing of Europe.[23]

---

[18] Friedrich von Schlegel, "Die Signatur des Zeitalters," *Concordia* (1820), as quoted in H. Finke, *Über Friedrich Schlegel und Dorothea* (1918), 61.

[19] Joseph Görres, *Europa und die Revolution* (1821); in *Gesammelte Schriften*, 12:253.

[20] Fr. von Schlegel, *Über die neuere Geschichte* (1810); in *Sämtliche Werke*, 11:268.

[21] K. J. Windischmann, *Das Gericht des Herrn über Europa* (1814), 274; see also 258ff.

[22] Thus Görres, albeit not in his Catholic period; for details see W. Schellberg, ed., *Joseph von Görres' Ausgewählte Werke und Briefe* (1911), 1: vi and following.

[23] Ernst von Lasaulx, *Neuer Versuch einer alten, auf die Wahrheit der Tatsachen gegrün-*

Yet there is still another, even more obvious sense in which the national idea varies from one Catholic thinker to another, namely, according to their respective nations. Among the most interesting clashes in this regard is the one between the Romantic Joseph Görres and the Traditionalist Joseph de Maistre. When they criticize each other and Görres defends the idea of the German Reich against De Maistre's attacks, then that is partly a result of the fact that they are of different nationalities and accordingly have different histories in their backgrounds. De Maistre finds his ideal in a particular system from the past and tries to restore it as an absolute entity: the most glorious phase in French history, he believes, occurred under the absolute rule of Louis XIV. Now it so happens that for the Romantics anything that is absolute is not organic and bears within itself the seeds of its own destruction[24]; for this reason they cannot aspire after the restoration of a historical period elevated to an absolute norm: in the national idea of Romanticism, history has an original function as organic historical becoming. In De Maistre, however, history primarily serves only those who are seeking an absolute norm. But this is not the only thing De Maistre has to say about the relation between the nation and history: the true "moral unity" of the nation, which is indeed present in principle at its inception, still has need of the stamp of historical evolution.

If a serious divergence of viewpoint persists between the Romantics and De Maistre with regard to the forming of nations, there is a strong agreement on a number of points between the latter and his co-religionist, Bossuet. Although De Maistre saw the rise of nations as more complex than Bossuet did, he has the same sense of the perfect naturalness of it all: the Creator has made the boundaries of the nations clearly visible on earth, so one sees each nationality seek out and occupy its appointed space or *réceptacle*. And in this "receptacle" the unity that is already implicitly present expresses itself in the course of history in the *unité morale*. "This unity manifests itself above all in language." [25]

Yet there is still another, weightier point where De Maistre approaches Bossuet: the predominantly statist feature of his nationalism. It is in sovereignty that the nation finds its well-knit unity and center. A strong *raison nationale* must be formed, for this alone will guarantee national greatness; and it is the state's task to clear away all obstacles to the forming of the *âme nationale*. If the state is negligent in this regard, an individualistic and revolutionary spirit will undermine the foundations of state and nation. De Maistre reproaches the successor of Louis XIV for having given the Protestants free rein and thus having helped prepare the French Revolution.[26]

---

deten Philosophie der Geschichte (1856; repr. 1952), 167.

[24] Cf. Schlegel's work cited in note 18, pp. 51–54, as quoted in G. Salomon, *Das Mittelalter als Ideal der Romantik* (1922), 74.

[25] De Maistre, *Étude sur la souveraineté* (1794–96), I, iv; *Oeuvres complètes*, 1:325f.

[26] See De Maistre, *Mémoire sur la liberté de l'enseignement public* (1810); in *Oeuvres complètes*, vol. 8.

De Maistre senses no conflict with freedom here, since sovereignty and nation are equally original and natural and only the upholding of the *ordre intérieur*—in his sense—can guarantee the happiness and greatness of the people.

Forms of synthesis

Our description of the position on nationalism adopted by Catholicism since the end of the Middle Ages may show many gaps, but a number of characteristics have become unmistakably clear. Modern nationalism has already passed through many phases and assumed numerous shapes, but every time again, Catholicism and nationalism have managed to come to terms. Viewed in the abstract, Catholicism and nationalism are not mutually exclusive, and it might have been possible for Catholicism to have rendered its assistance without inner conflicts. Yet, both the historical forms of their collaboration and the philosophico-theological justification of the national idea by Catholic thinkers have always really had the character of a synthesis, which is to say of a matching together of elements which in essence do not match.

History is illustrative in this regard. Bossuet could not construct the unity of the nation without invoking the absolutism of the prince. In the eighteenth century the concept of nationhood acquired amongst many clergymen the utilitarian feature which also stamped "enlightened" philosophy. In the Romantic period the Catholic national idea had to deal with all the tensions inherent in the Romantic view of life. And in the days of National Socialism, Catholic thinkers joined in professing the special talent of a particular race for Christianity. In short, we can pose the question whether there has ever been any form of nationalism to which a Catholic thinker did not seek, and find, a way. This means that Catholicism sustained serious damage during the centuries in which nationalism was a factor of the utmost importance.

But history tells not only of damage. There have been Catholic thinkers who were aware of the menace of the virile national idea. Often, however, the spirit of the age was too powerful for them. Still, the belief that it is God himself who allots to everyone his fatherland and that God made all people of one flesh kept alive in them the consciousness that the nations are subject to divine norms and that their interdependence is a law of life.

The nation and the supernatural order

Has our cursory inquiry into the historical connections between Catholicism and national consciousness shown us the *essential* relation between the two? No. To be sure, the course of history, if our investigation had been deeper and broader, would have disclosed further indications about the place of the nation in the Catholic worldview as a whole. But indications; no more. For once we undertake to account for the significance the nation has in the order of things and in history, we are compelled to take the path of philosophical and theological reflection. Only in this way can the perspective revealed so far be deepened.

One can approach the concept 'nation' from many angles, and the many Catholic writers who have thought and written about the subject have done just that. In fact, some of them have selected the starting point for their conceptions in such a way that what is distinctive in Catholic ideas about the forms of community found in human society is relegated entirely to the background. I shall devote no further attention to these writers.

With that restriction, we now ask: Do all those Catholic ideas about 'nation' have anything distinctive about them? If yes, we immediately wonder: Does that distinctive quality serve at the same time as the defining aspect for every one of the elements contained in the concepts of 'nation,' 'national consciousness,' and so on? — Well, such a distinctive point of departure is indeed present in the Catholic worldview. It is found in the relation of the nation to man's ultimate destiny. For implicit in the relation of the natural datum, the nation, to the supernatural order are both the high value and the relative significance that Catholicism attributes to the nation and to national consciousness.

As we contemplate the richly unfolded life of man, we soon detect in it a multiplicity of communities. This communal life does not, on the Catholic view, exist for itself. Whatever group one takes, not one is an end in itself. The end served by all, rather, lies in the individual human personality. Whatever in created reality one considers, he encounters the creaturely as a means for the attainment of man's destination. The human personality has been so created that without the things around it, including the forms of community in particular, it is unable to blossom and come to perfection. The matter is one of values that can never be realized by the individual acting alone, but only in community. Catholics are so strongly convinced of the correctness of this view of earthly things as God-given means for achieving the ends of the human personality that even in the papal encyclicals no further evidence is adduced for it than the words of Paul in 1 Cor. 3:22–23, "... *all are your's; and ye are Christ's; and Christ is God's.*" [27] Thus we arrive both via natural reason and via revelation at the

---

[27] Thus *Divini Redemptoris (On atheistic communism)*, 1937, art. 30. [For the context, see the following extracts from articles 25–30, quoted from Joseph Husslein, ed., *Social Wellsprings*, vol. 2: *Eighteen Encyclicals of Social Reconstruction by Pope Pius XI*, 351-53:

"We have exposed the errors and the violent, deceptive tactics of bolshevistic and atheistic Communism. It is now time, Venerable Brethren, to contrast with it the true notion, already familiar to you, of the *civitas humana*, or human society, as taught by reason and revelation through the mouth of the Church, *Magistra gentium*, Teacher of the nations.

"Above all other reality there exists one Supreme Being: God, the omnipotent Creator of all things, the all-wise and just Judge of all men. The supreme reality, God, is the absolute condemnation of the impudent falsehoods of Communism. . . .

"In the Encyclical on *Christian Education* We explained the fundamental doctrine concerning man as it may be gathered from reason and faith. Man has a spiritual and immortal soul. He is a person, marvelously endowed by his Creator with gifts of body and mind. He is a true 'microcosm,' as the ancients said, a world in miniature, with a value far surpassing that of the vast inanimate cosmos. God alone is his last end, in this life and the next. By sanctifying grace he is raised to the dignity of a son of God, and incorporated into the kingdom of God, in the Mystical Body of Christ. In consequence he has been endowed by God with many and varied

same basic idea: all things are ordained to the perfecting of the human personality.

Now then, among the means to achieving that, the nation occupies a leading place. For the nation is a good which—we shall return to this point later—is intimately associated with the human personality. If on the Catholic view the nation is thus a good which fulfills an important function in the attaining of the individual human destination, then we must make some careful distinctions.

In the first place, the nation is a means to attaining man's *natural* end. At the same time it has a place in the ascent of human nature to its *supernatural* destination. Natural end and supernatural destination are intrinsically connected. The better natural perfection is realized in and through the national community, the better human personality can strive to achieve its supernatural destination. For while the common good that individuals work together to secure in and through the national community is not the cause of grace, it nonetheless creates a disposition, a receptivity to grace. The highest law of man's natural life in the natural communities, not least in the national community, is to order the natural functions and actions so conformably to man's nature that he places himself at the disposal of his supernatural destination.[28] And receptivity to the supernatural reaches its full depth when human nature, precisely through the attainment of its natural ends, becomes the more aware of its own deficiency, its deep need, and its insatiable yearning for its final destination beyond the natural order.

In the ascent of the temporal order to the supernatural destination, the national community has an eminently religious role to play. The nation itself

---

prerogatives: the right to life, to bodily integrity, to the necessary means of existence; the right to tend toward his ultimate goal in the path marked out for him by God; the right of association and the right to possess and use property.

". . . In the plan of the Creator, society is a natural means which man can and must use to reach his destined end. *Society is for man and not vice versa.* This must not be understood in the sense of liberalistic individualism, which subordinates society to the selfish use of the individual; but only *in the sense that by means of an organic union with society and by mutual collaboration the attainment of earthly happiness is placed within the reach of all.* In a further sense, it is a society which affords the opportunities for the development of all the individual and social gifts bestowed on human nature. These natural gifts have a value surpassing the immediate interests of the moment, for in society they reflect the divine perfection, which would not be true were man to live alone. . . .

". . . Man cannot be exempted from his divinely imposed obligations toward civil society, and the representatives of authority have the right to coerce him when he refuses without reason to do his duty. Society, on the other hand, cannot defraud man of his God-granted rights, the most important of which We have indicated above. Nor can society systematically void these rights by making their use impossible. *It is therefore according to the dictates of reason that ultimately all material things should be ordained to man as a person, that through his mediation they may find their way to the Creator.* In this wise we can apply to man, the human person, the words of the Apostle of the Gentiles who writes to the Corinthians on the Christian economy of salvation: 'All things are yours, and you are Christ's, and Christ is God's' (I Cor. iii, 23). While Communism impoverishes human personality by inverting the terms of the relation of man to society, to what lofty heights is man not elevated by reason and revelation!"]

[28] Cf. John Joseph Wright, *National Patriotism in Papal Teaching* (1943), 13.

belongs to the natural order and is thus not religious in essence, yet it is of significant religious value since it is a means—and certainly not the least—to open man up to supernatural riches and to provide him with means to attain his eternal destination.

This yearning for the supernatural destination unleashes the urge for natural perfection. The desire to bring the things of this world to the perfection willed by God bore fruit in periods of great historical florescence dominated by a culture of spirit and the supernatural.[29]

By now the question will have occurred to us: Suppose the national communities are a God-given means to the attainment of man's supernatural destination, in what particular respect is the nation so equipped? Surprisingly, confidence among Catholics about the nation as just such a means is balanced by vagueness about human nature's specific need to live in national communities. One of the few people to have concerned himself with this question is Father Hyacinthus Woroniecki, whose framing of the problem and whose insights[30] have been adopted by his fellow Dominican J. T. Delos, the well-known expert in international law.[31]

The nation, Woroniecki argues, has to educate the citizenry for a fuller, more perfect life which, left to themselves, they would be powerless to achieve. Man does not by nature possess the perfect capacity to guide his moral actions at all times. This he must acquire through education, which will train his disposition for performing the same actions with greater ease, skill and self-confidence. Morals, habits, customs, etc., assist in this great work. Well now, the nation is founded on this education for morality. The nation even takes precedence above the state, since it is the nation that gives internal unity to human society and in this way reinforces the moral powers of individuals; for morals contribute more to upholding the virtues than laws do. Nations are therefore more durable and of more importance to morals than states are. The national morality touches the human spirit more profoundly than do the laws of the state and consequently bear a more essential and immediate relation to man's ultimate destination.

The relative autonomy of the nation

Now that we have cast some light on various aspects of the religious value of the nation, we turn to the problem implicit in that peculiar relation of the national community, as a natural regime, to the supernatural.

---

[29] Cf. Ludwig Lenhart, "Christentum und Germanentum im Werturteil der letzten Jahrhunderte," *Beiträge zur christlichen Philosophie* 1 (1947): 29f.

[30] Cf. Hyacinthus Woroniecki, "Quaestio disputata de natione et statu civili," *Divus Thomas* (Freiburg) 29 (1926): 25ff; see also his contribution in M. Vaussard, ed., *Enquête sur le nationalisme* (1924), 286ff.

[31] Joseph Thomas Delos, *La Société internationale et les principes du droit public* (1950), 16ff.

Eugen Lemberg remarks in his *Geschichte des Nationalismus in Europa* (1950) that the birth of nationalism presupposed secularization, since national communities now began to form in which human energies no longer were devoted to a religious community as in the days when the Empire, through its orientation to the supernatural community of the Church, had itself acquired a religious character. The modern nation that was emerging was no longer anchored in the transcendent; to the European consciousness, the emerging national communities were not religious in character. Nevertheless—still according to Lemberg—in the course of its development the national idea was invested with religious content in that people came to regard the nations as created by God, inserted by him into his world plan, and furnished with a specific mission.[32]

However many correct elements Lemberg's sketch may contain, it is not entirely acceptable because, to begin with, he neglects religion as a factor in national unification since the Reformation. Furthermore, apart from other objections that could be raised against his interpretation, Lemberg does not do justice to the unique place of Catholicism in the rise of modern nationalism. Ordinarily, Catholics regard the Renaissance and Reformation as decisive factors in the process of secularization since the Late Middle Ages. In doing so, they fail to recognize that this secularization received powerful impulses as early as the heyday of Scholasticism, when Christian thought entered into a more intimate union with non-Christian, mainly Greek thought. True, they acknowledge that Thomist thought—for it is that in particular which we have in view—represented an incision within the Middle Ages, but they would be reluctant to call the break of Thomist philosophy with medieval Augustinian thought a form of secularization. After all, in Thomas the ordering of temporal life to the supernatural continued to be recognized, and was even essential! That it was essential is undoubtedly correct. For all that, it is here that the separation of the profane and transcendent worlds began—or continued in a more stringent form[33]—with the secularization of the national communities as the outcome. In the centuries prior to Thomas, people had valued worldly life almost exclusively as the *means* for the supernatural; worldly life consequently acquired a religious coloration, since it was enclosed on all sides by the relation to the religious even while in many respects it lacked religious value intrinsically.

With Thomas Aquinas all this changes. The temporal is no longer valued merely as a means for the supernatural but is also recognized for its own sake, independent of its relation to the religious. To be sure, it remains ordered to the supernatural, but in such a way that it is granted its own, autonomous existence. An irresolvable dualism is introduced into the temporal—between being ordered to the spiritual, on the one hand; and, on the other, having independence,

---

[32] Eugen Lemberg, *Geschichte des Nationalismus in Europa*, 77f.

[33] We use this rather unclear formulation advisedly in order to draw attention to the fact how precarious it is, given our present understanding of the structure of the medieval world, to establish when the process of secularization actually began.

freedom, and autonomy over against the spiritual. This Scholastic doctrine would now come to dominate the Roman Catholic position on natural life. Once Thomas had recognized the intrinsic value of the profane, the way was free for a long process. In the course of the centuries that followed, especially after the mid-sixteenth century, a dichotomy of the natural and supernatural orders was taught with ever greater emphasis. People tended in increasing measure to regard the profane as a self-contained, self-sufficient order. Yet the dualism within this order persisted, and with it vestiges of the medieval view of the natural: never was the awareness lost in Roman Catholicism that the temporal, despite its autonomy, remained a stepping-stone to the supernatural and therefore continued to require the concern of the church. Political theory in particular labored under the inner contradiction between autonomy and orientation to the religious.

To what purpose this lengthy excursus? Only against this background does our thesis become plausible that the secularization of the rising national consciousness found fertile soil in the genesis of Roman Catholicism. Once the national communities had been recognized for their own sake and put on an independent footing, the modern national ideology was acceptable for Catholics, even though it rather quickly lost any connection to the transcendent. The way was now prepared for accepting association with the many forms of nationalism. Was not the nation a good to be highly esteemed? Subsequent developments were to prove the truth of an observation once made by Father Daniélou: temporal values must be acknowledged in their significance, and the Christian may not withdraw himself from them, but they do have a tendency to assert themselves absolutely.[34] Indeed, Catholicism has not always managed to keep its distance when the nation presented itself as an absolute quantity or made excessive demands. There are numerous examples from the history of nationalism in which Catholics not only yielded to the spirit of the age but were active partners in overemphasizing the national community. Bossuet's glorification of absolutism—a necessary capstone of his national idea—is a frightful example of this.

Once Catholicism had recognized the nation in its own, independent value, there were still ways of ascribing religious meaning to it. Specifically, Romanticism brought the nation back into the religious sphere: the nation was brought into inner connection with divine Providence and furnished with a divine mission. Yet it should be noted that this did not impair its autonomy with respect to the supernatural order. Besides, the Romantics veiled it in a shroud of mystery. Its autonomy, far from being weakened, was accented, and the nationalism that took mystical forms no longer recognized any real limits. One of the most striking examples of mystical, inflated nationalism is afforded us in a leading figure of the Roman Catholic revival in Germany, K. J. Windischmann, who concludes his book of 1814, *Das Gericht des Herrn über Europa* (a predominantly pessimistic view of the development of the West) by confessing his faith in Germany as the "predestined arbiter of Europe," in the German spirit as a

---

[34] Jean Daniélou, in *Études philosophiques* 255 (1947): 135.

"Christ-bearer," and in the German character as the *logos spermatikos* for the "healing of Europe."[35]

The Roman Catholic view of the relation between the natural and supernatural orders likewise opened the possibility for a positive appreciation of the National Socialist revolution of 1933. Thus Karl Adam could at many points justify the breakthrough of "Volkish" nationalism before the forum of the Catholic worldview, although not without a certain qualification: nature and the supernatural presuppose each other; Catholicism protects the distinctive character of each *Volk* and imbues it with the leaven of the Gospel; "the supernaturalism of the Church by definition determines the nationalism of her missions and her faithful."[36] The nature-grace doctrine again allowed for an inner connection between the Germanic race and the Christian religion: the supernatural forces which God has placed in his Church have never come to such a magnificent revelation and fulfillment as in the Christianization of the Germanic world.[37]

We should not exaggerate the importance of Adam's view, however.[38] A remarkable process has been underway within Catholicism in recent decades that is characterized by a renewed attempt to see nature and the supernatural in a more intimate relationship. And on this basis the effort is being made to provide the national community with a deeper religious foundation, by esteeming it as a means in the process of the natural perfecting of human nature that causes it to orient itself all the more to its supernatural destination. We have seen that these ideas are interwoven in the very texture of the Catholic worldview.

The nation and moral ends

Having analyzed the basic structure and thrust of the concept 'nation' as entertained in Catholic circles, we now want to turn our attention to the various elements contained in the good that the nation represents for man. In regard to both the nature of these elements and their interconnections there are serious differences of opinion amongst Catholic writers. The conflict of opinions is primarily about deciding which elements are necessary determinants of the concept 'nation.' But even when one has taken a particular position on this matter, the question still remains which determinant should be given priority. To sum up: this debate shows that every social good that has ever served to bind people together into a nation is an occasion for disagreement; as the national bonding agent writers distinguish language, native soil, cultural and religious traditions, while likewise not denying the state a function in the growth of the nation.

---

[35] This epitome of Windischmann's final chapter ("The Healing Powers of Nature and of Grace in the German People") is by Heinz Gollwitzer, *Europabild und Europagedanke. Beiträge zur deutschen Geistesgeschichte des 18. und 19. Jahrhunderts* (1951), 200.

[36] Karl Adam, "Deutsches Volkstum und katholisches Christentum" [German folkhood and Catholic Christianity], *Theologische Quartalschrift* 144 (1933): 59.

[37] Ibid., 63.

[38] [Adam himself, in the very next year, was harassed by the Nazi authorities for denouncing the Volkish concept "German religion."]

In light of the above it will not surprise anyone that we should go on to concentrate, for now, on the religious traditions. It would be unnecessary for us after all the things that have already been said to add anything more about the religious traditions, were it not for the fact that in them we confront the main problem of the Catholic national idea. When the nation is a good that the individual cherishes for the sake of his own and others' temporal and eternal good, then the nation is somehow related to the moral law. For if the nation is to answer to its lofty purpose, it ought to be normed by moral principles. Yet the moral law necessarily presupposes God, and thus religion, for it is only in its association with religion that the moral law has full force. The upshot of this line of reasoning is that the national community needs religion. If the nation is to flourish and achieve greatness, people must conform to the moral law and respect religion. Recalling that the Catholic church is considered the consummate medium of religious life and the authentic interpreter of the moral law, one can see at once that on the Catholic view the church ought to occupy the central place in national life. The religious divisions that have afflicted the nations now for centuries are a source of woe and constitute an obstacle on the path to national greatness, the source of which, after all, is national unity.

When a people in its national unity and manifestation opens itself up, without reservation, to morality—as interpreted by Catholics—and to the Catholic faith, then its national heritage will eventually acquire a Catholic stamp.

Yet, a people can acquire a Catholic stamp via another, less conspicuous route, namely when in their national life they begin to recognize truths and submit to norms that admittedly are as such not points of faith but that flow from natural reason: for example, when a people acknowledges God as the first Cause and final Goal. This truth, it is said, is not specifically Catholic but one that is knowable and acceptable to all.[39] Granting natural reason and its truths their proper place does not make a people a Catholic nation, but it can become so, even while it remains in the natural order. For the natural truths may be present in the treasure houses of human wisdom, but Catholic believers are indispensable for a clear knowledge of them. According to many Catholic thinkers all people of good will can unite in a national entity on a purely national basis, but Catholics should be allowed to take the lead since, living in the light of the supernatural, they are better equipped to discover the divine natural order.

This stage is not ideal. The purely natural order is only to be accepted as a period of transition to a culture in which the spiritual will have the lead. Cooperation with those of other persuasions can be a duty for the sake of advancing the national well-being, which derives its importance, after all, from its function of guiding people towards their eternal destination.

---

[39] Wright, *National Patriotism in Papal Teaching*, 89; C. P. M. Romme, *Nieuwe grondwetsartikelen* (1943), 13; cf. P. Chanson, "L'Oeuvre des quatres derniers pontificats sur le plan social," in *La Continuité pontificale* (1935), 96.

But it is precisely the place occupied by the "common good" of the national community in the intertwinement of the natural and spiritual orders that drives people to transcend the association with "persons of good will" towards the supernatural fellowship of the church where are found the supernatural elements that can fulfill the needs of natural communities. No nation, no natural group whatever, can succeed without the divine things of the church.

But if the national good is so intimately associated with the treasures of the church, it becomes fully understandable why in Catholic literature, including papal encyclicals, the key notion is constantly reasserted that the flourishing of nations depends on the church. Leo XIII speaks forcefully when he opens the encyclical *Immortale Dei* (1885) with these words: "Wherever the Church has planted her feet she has at once transformed the face of things and ennobled peoples' manners with hitherto unknown virtues and a new civilization. All nations which have yielded to her sway have excelled in gentleness, a sense of justice and equity, and glorious deeds." [40] Thus the church, so we read in the encyclical *Inscrutabili* (1878), is "the patroness, teacher, and mother of civilization." [41] Hungary, Portugal, and ever so many other nations are the historical proof that the church is a guarantee of national greatness.

Yes, the peoples are indebted to Christianity for their national existence. Prior to the coming of Christianity, asserts Cardinal Faulhaber, the Germans, to the delight of their enemies, were divided, and no civilization could flourish amongst them, but Christianity hammered the many tribes into a nation, and a high level of culture was attained.[42] Faulhaber's view may seem overly simple, but it should not be overlooked that one encounters such notions repeatedly in writers, and that they are supported by papal pronouncements.[43] To Catholic

---

[40] *Immortale Dei (On the Christian constitution of states)*, art. 1.

[41] *Inscrutabili (On the evils affecting modern society)*, art. 5.

[42] Michael von Faulhaber, *Christentum und Germanentum* (1933), 13.

[43] Cf. the encyclical *Inscrutabili*, articles 7–10 [e.g., quoting from Étienne Gilson, ed., *The Church Speaks to the Modern World: The Social Teachings of Leo XIII*, 281–83:

"Again, if We consider the achievements of the see of Rome, what can be more wicked than to deny how much and how well the Roman bishops have served civilized society at large? . . . This apostolic chair it was that gathered and held together the crumbling remains of the old order of things; this was the kindly light by whose help the culture of Christian times shone far and wide; this was an anchor or safety in the fierce storms by which the human race has been convulsed; this was the sacred bond of union that linked together nations distant in region and differing in character; in short, this was a common center from which was sought instruction in faith and religion, no less than guidance and advice for the maintenance of peace and the functions of practical life. In very truth it is the glory of the supreme Pontiffs that they have steadfastly set themselves up as a wall and a bulwark to save human society from falling back into its former superstition and barbarism. . . . Unquestionably to the Roman Pontiffs it is that Italy must own herself indebted for the substantial glory and majesty by which she has been preeminent amongst nations. . . . [By their] exertions or protection Italy has escaped unscathed from the utter destruction threatened by barbarians; has kept unimpaired her old faith, and amid the darkness and defilement of the ruder age, has cultivated and preserved in vigor the luster of science and the splendor of art. To this, furthermore, bears witness Our own fostering city, the

thinking, as surely as a nation unfolds and elevates itself automatically when its members confess the Catholic faith, so national unity is unconditionally dependent upon religious unity. There is no national greatness without national unity, and there is no national unity without the religious unity of the nation. This, too, is a notion which has been the common property of Catholicism ever since the Middle Ages.

The shattering of Christendom

With that, we have arrived at one of the sources of severe criticism of the Reformation. Its consequences were allegedly fatal, not only in the sense that here and there religion was subordinated to the national interest—one need only recall the principle *cuius regio, eius religio*, "as the religion of the prince, so the religion of the people"—but more specifically because in the face of religious fragmentation, national life could no longer achieve its concentration in the supernatural. Apostasy from the one universal church necessarily entailed fragmentation and upheaval. The idea gained dominance in the Catholic worldview especially through Bossuet but it had already developed before him, in fact was implied by the Catholic view of history from the outset. According to De Maistre it was the Cartesian and Protestant spirit of free inquiry that spawned the individualistic mind and so undermined the foundations of the state.[44] With the Reformation, according to Johannes Janssen, began a period of rivalry between two mutually opposed religious ideas for the soul of the German folk: "From the rootstock of the Lutheran claims and demands arose the anarchy in the religious domain, and from this anarchy there followed . . . the moral degeneration of the nation." [45]

Not only did the Reformation lead to the undermining of national order and to the decline of morals; it inflicted even more serious damage upon the national communities. To appreciate the gravity of these consequences, one must view the development of national consciousness against the medieval background.

The Middle Ages have always remained the point of orientation for the Catholic conception of history, the more so as the European world has become estranged from them. Even today, when many Catholic thinkers have felt obliged to follow a new cultural ideal sharply distinguished from that of the Middle Ages, the old medieval world remains a highly desirable goal. What makes this world so extraordinarily fascinating is its coherence and universality. In medieval times there was one mind that embraced both the supernatural and natural orders. The spiritual and the temporal were but two sides of a single all-controlling, universal coherence. There was differentiation, infinitely variegated, yet all things particular were integrated in the universal. True, the

---

home of the Popes, which, under their rule, reaped this special benefit, that it was not only the strong citadel of the faith, but also became the refuge of the liberal arts and the very abode of wisdom, winning for itself the admiration and respect of the whole world."]

[44] See note 26 above.
[45] Johannes Janssen, *An meine Kritiker* (1891), 181.

destination lay beyond history, but in the *ecclesia universalis*, the universal church, the temporal was directed towards and bound up with the coming kingdom of God. In the one church were two powers—*in ecclesia sunt duae potestates*—the spiritual and the worldly, with respect to which the leading role did fall to the spiritual while only subordinate, temporal concerns were entrusted to the wordly, but then in such a way that its task contributed to the building of the kingdom of God on earth. Church and state were both universal in character and formed the one universal community of the West. The indispensable condition for this was the unity of belief and the unity of mind. Certainly there were differences in language, tribe, folk, and eventually even of nation, but these were just nuances within the universal culture. The many elements that would later converge in the national communities were already present but were dispersed over the many communities within Western Christendom.

Now, when the Reformation and its accompanying trends detached themselves from the supernatural guidance of the church, that spiritual unity was necessarily forfeit, and with it the unity of the West. To be sure, cleavages that separated the various national groups had intensified long before that, and owing to sects and heresies, stones had become dislodged from the edifice of medieval unity. But in its foundation it had remained unshaken. The common Christian faith was the strongest binding force of the Western universal community, and it was even capable of embracing the increasingly independence-minded nations. Yet, with the Reformation the Western nations' sense of solidarity, while it did not entirely vanish, was spiritually broken, and there was no longer any power capable of checking the "anarchy of nations." Now that the nations were no longer embedded in Christendom, the consciousness of their relativity with respect to mankind in general was lost.

To be sure, there are Catholic writers who perceived profound religious forces at work in the Reformation—Görres and Clemens Maria Hofbauer, for example, and numerous other modern thinkers. In general, however, the Reformation has been regarded as the source of the secularization of the West, or at least as a powerful impulse behind it. When the ideal of the medieval Christian West was powerfully reawakened in Romanticism, people at once associated it with the idea that the West's secularization and disintegration were somehow connected, and that both had some connection with the Reformation. Adam Müller, for instance, ascribed the demise of Christian Europe to the Reformation because it failed to appreciate the public law character of religion.[46] The return to medieval Christendom occurred in mystical forms in Müller's thought: in Europe he recognized a new revelation of the Mystical Body of Christ.[47] In many Catholic Romantics, the initial dialectic between national community and the West ultimately ended in a clear preference for the latter.

---

[46] Adam Müller, *Elemente der Staatskunst* (1808–09), lecture 10.//
[47] Ibid., lectures 34 and 35.

It is noteworthy that when a pan-Christian entity proved unfeasible, a Western idea of more limited scope arose. Thus, writers like Müller and De Maistre conceived of a European entity as a Catholic community under papal leadership.

Between the national and the universal

Have we become sidetracked by devoting so much attention to the Catholic view of Protestantism as apostasy from the West, and have we lost sight of the Catholic concept of nation? Not at all. The fact that Catholics see an inner connection between secularization, the betrayal of the West, the anarchy of nations and the Reformation should not make us forget that within Catholicism there is a dialectic between the universal and the national-particular. One cannot surmount this tension by pointing to the Middle Ages in which it was possible for national differentiation to unfold within the unity of the Western world, for the various elements which are mutually interrelated in the modern nation had not yet all reached their crystallization point. Only after the nation, in the modern sense, has been formed can the problem of the relation between the universal and the national-particular be posed in all its sharpness.

Yet at the same time the possibility must be faced that the problem thus raised is irresolvable. Should one not give precedence to national entities in times when conditions are favorable for their unfolding, and equally pursue the ideal of the West or of a Second West during periods in which history presses towards global or supranational communities? Or should one be reconciled to the impossibility of surmounting the dialectical solution of Romanticism? Or, perhaps, is there a way out in the collective conviction that every nation has a vocation, which elevates it to the rank of a "chosen People" but which at the same time causes it to seek the well-being of other peoples? [48]

All these questions remain caught in the tension between the national and the universal. For that reason alone they are unable to point us the way. We now pose a different question: Behind the relation of the national community to the supranational world is there not still another reality with respect to which both nation and world are relativized? Indeed, this question has never been far from the minds of Catholic thinkers. They believe that the absolute claims of the natural communities lose their force only against the background of the church, not just in the sense that the presence of the universal order of the church sets limits to every natural community of whatever sort, but above all because to their mind the church seeks its reflection in temporal things and thus makes visible in the worldly forms the mark of relativity.

---

[48] On this, see the important views expressed in a sermon delivered in Notre Dame Cathedral, 13 June 1937, by Cardinal Pacelli (since then Pope Pius XII) on "The Christian Vocation of France."

5/ THE DIVINE MYSTERY IN HISTORY

ESTEEMED DIRECTORS AND CURATORS of the Free University, Madam and Gentlemen Professors, Lecturers and Instructors, Ladies and Gentlemen of the Student Body, and all who honor me with your presence here today,[1] highly esteemed Audience:

In this very place a little over five and a half years ago, I was asked by a learned opponent in the course of the public defense of my doctoral dissertation[2] whether I did not entangle myself in contradictions. On the one hand I rejected every notion of a fragmentary, supernatural intervention of God in the natural course of events. At the same time I ventured to assert: "Although Robert Fruin has proved that the tale of a miraculous ebb tide in 1672 is a legend and the abnormally long ebb tide of 2 August 1673 had no influence on English invasion plans, this does not resolve the problem of whether the English decided against a landing in 1672 and 1673 as the result of 'supernatural' events." [3]

My reply to this objection was never completed, for I was cut off by the mace-bearer's *"Hora est!"* Today, after a long intermezzo, I should like to resume the debate about that contested thesis. Thus I ask you to consider for a few moments the problems pertaining to the Hand of God in history. Since the latter is usually interpreted in too narrow a sense, however, I have formulated my subject more broadly and called it: The Divine Mystery in History.

It will perhaps not be superfluous to say at the outset that I do not use the word "mystery" in the sense now fashionable. I use it in the New Testament sense, fraught with the ineffable that is in God.

My choice of topic must seem questionable. After all that has been written during so many centuries, who could still hope to add anything worthwhile to this perplexing subject? Should we not rather be glad that after centuries of fruitless debate about the demonstrability of God's Finger, people are now almost universally agreed that historical science (I restrict myself to that), including philosophy of history, must keep silence here? Is the question of God's Hand not a "religious" rather than a scientific or philosophical matter, whose

---

[1] [The occasion was the delivery, on 27 Sept. 1955, of an inaugural address upon assuming the office of Professor of Medieval History and Theory of History in the Free University at Amsterdam. An earlier translation of the main text appeared in the *Free University Quarterly* 5 (1958): 120–45. Subheadings have here been added.]

[2] M. C. Smit, *De verhouding van Christendom en historie in de huidige Rooms-Katholieke geschiedbeschouwing* (1950). [Eng. trans. in Part One of the present volume.]

[3] Thesis XVI, appended to the dissertation. Cf. Robert J. Fruin, "Over de dubbele ebbe in het jaar 1672" [On the double ebb tide in the year 1672], in *Verspreide Geschriften*, 9:161–72.]

mystery is best preserved by keeping it within the sphere of faith? Would it not be better, accordingly, to reserve reflections on God's concrete agency in history for a meditation in the evening of one's life, when one may have acquired a wealth of experience through prolonged scholarly study and the insight may at last have registered that we should speak of the things of God only with the utmost reserve?

There is a compelling reason for me to address the issue at this time, however, as I undertake to give an account of the spirit in which I hope to fulfill my office. Every historian, whether he realizes it or not, encounters the divine mystery in history. Although its full depth will always be ineffable, this mystery should descend into our knowledge and into our words. It is just possible that there is an intrinsic necessity to take up precisely those problems that have resisted solution through the years, not in order to solve them completely or to deprive them of their mystery, but in order to fathom the depths to which they reach and explore the remote places where they turn up. Is that perhaps one of the reasons why in every age thinking and believing people apply themselves to the question of God's Hand in history? There was a brief period, bounded roughly by the two world wars, in which people came to the conclusion, following many unsuccessful attempts at demonstrating God's Finger in history, that this cannot and should not be the historian's task since it is too high and too deep for him, and that he ought to confine himself instead to human relations. Remarkably, after a short period of such sober-minded insight a reaction has set in, not only among theologians—that would be understandable—but among philosophers and professional historians as well. I have in mind (leaving the foreign literature aside) the interesting discussions by G. C. Berkouwer and W. den Boer.[4] It took courage—for the historian at least—to defend the so-called theocratic view. This is abundantly clear from the sometimes vehement criticism leveled against Den Boer's ideas. So there is nothing resembling a collective conviction. Yet there are signs—Den Boer's piece is one of them—that things are changing. A look at the foreign literature would make that even clearer to us.

The old danger remains, however, that people will talk about God's Hand in history in terms of fragmentary divine acts rather than a sustained agency that controls and shapes the whole of history. Hence it is good to begin by considering the problems that have arisen in connection with God's guidance of history.

The problem in historical perspective

From the outset until today, Christianity has had a strong sense of the close link between God and history. Of course, there have been important differences in the way people have conceived this link. In the Early and High Middle Ages, again at the time of the Reformation, in the seventeenth and eighteenth centuries, and in the nineteenth century as well—think only of Groen van Prinsterer—

---

[4] G. C. Berkouwer, *De Voorzienigheid Gods* (1950), 190–228 [Eng. trans., *The Providence of God*, 161–87]. W. den Boer, *Benaderbaar verleden* [Accessible past] (1952), 60ff.

people had an eminently lively sense of direct divine action in history. In the Middle Ages until the heyday of Scholasticism, God was so much the focal point of people's sense of history that they really deemed every event an immediate act of God.[5] History became a series of divine acts and, correlatively, of human acts directly linked to divine Providence. Far from being regarded as neutral, these divine acts were regarded as charged with the justice of God. He chastened and he blessed. Prosperity indicated God's blessing and approval; adversity, sickness, and so on, were direct punishments for sin. God's Hand of retribution was especially visible in striking and surprising events. In the centuries that followed, and for many Calvinists both before and after the French Revolution, prosperity as blessing, adversity as punishment, and the striking and surprising persisted as the most salient elements of the conception of the Hand of God.

Undoubtedly, non-Christian religions, especially in Christian Antiquity and the Middle Ages, had a profound influence on these ideas. In the Germanic world, for example, the notion was widespread that the gods were responsible for immediate retribution in the human world; thus repeated crop failures would lead people to conclude that the divine force was no longer in the king. Here, however, we encounter an important difference from the common Christian view: in the Germanic world the constant divine presence was couched in magical and mythical notions in which the divine and human realms merged in the divine.

But the Germanic world was not alone in determining the medieval ideas. Medieval people also drew upon the Old Testament, or, to be more exact, upon certain portions of the Old Testament. Times without number they would appeal to Old Testament texts that directly link human deeds and divine judgments. In more recent centuries as well, the Old Testament remained the principal source for the defense of fragmentary acts of direct divine judgment in history.

Side by side with the view I have just delineated, however, one encounters a distinct hesitancy to identify the Hand of God in such simple terms, even among those who otherwise have no qualms about interpreting reverses suffered by enemy forces as divine chastisement. Otto of Freising and Bernard of Clairvaux—certainly not the least among those we could mention—would on occasion feel quite diffident in the face of the divine agency. Yet time and again such scruples were overshadowed. In light of the Old Testament many Christian writers found the purpose of the divine agency too plain to refrain from pronouncing judgment.

Augustine, however, halted before the mystery of God in history. True, he often spoke of it in terms at odds with language that we would consider consistent with reverence before a mystery. His conception of history is decidedly

---

[5] Cf. esp. Heinz Müller, "Die Hand Gottes in der Geschichte. Zum Geschichtsverständnis von Augustinus bis Otto von Freising" [The hand of God in history: on the understanding of history from Augustine to Otto of Freising] (unpub. Ph.D. diss.; Hamburg, 1949); and Paul Rousset, "La Croyance en la justice immanente à l'époque féodale" [The belief in immanent justice during the feudal period], *Le Moyen-Age* 54 (1948): 225–48.

theocentric, but how different from that of his predecessors and followers! Augustine was conscious of the limits of human knowledge and of the mystery in history precisely because history has to do with God. He loved to quote texts from the Bible that refer to God's incomprehensibility. Augustine had a lofty view of the divine gift of happiness: God grants happiness only to the good, but because the good are indifferent to this world's goods, the happiness that worldly possessions afford may fall to a person's lot (or not) without its being evidence of divine approval, if only because perfect happiness is attainable only in the other world. In his fine study, *Die Hand Gottes in der Geschichte,* Heinz Müller states correctly that in Augustine happiness is not so much devalued as it is "revalorized" (*aufgewertet*): happiness comes from God and, given the right spiritual attitude, returns to him again.[6] Not only is Augustine's conception richer in *content* when compared with the medieval and many modern, simplistic views; its *direction* is the one in which I believe the solution to our problem will have to be sought. The striking thing about Augustine is that he was conscious not only of the mystery in God himself but also of the mystery in this world and the indissoluble connection between the two. That is to say, he knew that the mystery in history has its origins in the mystery of God.

Incarnation, providence, and world-order

The belief in the direct identifiability of God's Hand in history was to become entangled in still other, no less serious difficulties. It is an undeniable fact that in theology of history a sometimes scarcely concealed tension exists between the direct intervention of God in history and the mystery of the Incarnation. This seems rather odd, because God's coming in the flesh surely is the supreme instance of divine intervention. The early medieval vision of history can help us discover where the difficulty lies. When a historical event is so heavily charged with divine judgment, and when God himself is the Sole Agent in history, Christ recedes into the background. Müller reports that in the sources he examined from the time of Salvianus to the days of the Investiture Controversy, little special mention is made of Christ.[7] True, the mystery of Christ had not vanished, but the way to a clear view of the relation between this mystery and the divine agency had been cut off. Nor were medieval people the only ones who failed to overcome this difficulty. Bossuet and other modern writers also struggled with it.

A related problem is the following. People in the Early Middle Ages were only marginally prepared, if at all, to regard history as an indivisible whole. Otto of Freising is the one who took a decisive step towards apprehending the unity of history, and he was able to do so precisely because he related history to the Incarnation.[8] No doubt this statement surprises you. Surely medieval historical

---

[6] Müller, 11.
[7] Ibid., 133.
[8] Ibid., 149.

thought was saturated with the idea of a single, universal history from Adam through Christ to the consummation of the ages? Indeed, but the medieval histories were often nothing more than a stringing together of facts. The very thing they lacked was insight into the interconnections of the facts and into the intrinsic relation of historical events to Creation and Redemption. Apart from their immediate cause and operation, the acts of God were commonly rehearsed in a loose fashion. The *perspective* of the one, total history was missing; what linked them was the constant presence of God in history.

Clearly, the idea of God's direct agency in history leads to an impasse, one that is not restricted to medieval conceptions. How is it possible to maintain the idea of the unity of history if historical events are to be attributed entirely or in part to direct acts of God? One might argue that this unity is given with God himself, since the very existence of world history, which is to say the reality of interconnections between the historical facts, is possible solely because all historical facts stand in relation to the One God. That the unity of history rests ultimately in God is clear, but how are we to understand the inner coherence of concrete events in the world? The usual solution is to approach the unity of world history with intra-mundane or inner-worldly concepts—while the connections between the striking and surprising acts of God remain an unsolvable and often even unperceived problem.

However interesting all these different aspects of the subject may be, they do not form the heart of our discussion. The heart of it is to be found in the relation of divine Providence to the divine world-order. Many are immediately disposed to speak of continuity and harmony in this regard, so perhaps they will be surprised to hear that from the earliest Christian times a latent or open tension, not to speak of a contradiction, existed between the two concepts. Again, to illustrate this I would refer to the Middle Ages. It is possible, of course, to equate the idea of the divine world-order with that of the providence of God. But if "providence" is taken to mean God's activity apart from the mediated agency of the world order—the immediate manifestation and assertion of his will in history —then it is clear that initially this idea was by far the predominant one in the Middle Ages and that it was not until the Investiture Controversy that the concepts of Providence and divine world-order begin to converge. A systematic elaboration of the relation between the two was accomplished by Scholasticism, in a form that has predominated in Roman Catholic philosophy to this day. On this view, divine Providence can assert itself in the historical process in two ways: *indirectly,* by making the forces and laws at work in the world-order expressions of the Divine will; and *directly,* through God's intervening immediately and supernaturally to give things a different turn than might have been anticipated in the natural course of events.[9] For that matter, in Protestant circles, too, the idea of a twofold divine action in history has had a profound influence.

---

[9] See F. Sawicki, *Geschichtsphilosophie* (1923), 173f, 183–87.

Protestant writers, too, gladly employ the direct-indirect scheme, at least to the extent that they accept the idea of a fragmentary (knowable) activity of God.

The limits of human knowledge

In our efforts to canvass the many baffling problems associated with the question of the Hand of God in history, we have already intimated the direction our critique will take. I shall mention just two reasons why I too find the traditional conception of the Finger of God in history unacceptable.

In the first place, our knowledge of the acts of God is thereby invested with something it cannot and may not have on earth. An immanent divine justice is ascribed to events—at least to certain ones—that anticipates God's final judgment. The advocates of the view in question like to appeal to the Old Testament, but it is precisely the Old Testament that pulls the ground out from under their conceptions. It is sufficient to cite the Book of Job and Psalm 73. In Job—such an important book for philosophy of history—God does not explain why he has visited so much misery on an upright and godfearing man, but in a lengthy revelation he discloses who he is; and Job, when he has experienced God from so nearby, no longer needs an explanation: "*I have uttered that I understood not; things too wonderful for me, which I knew not. . . . but now mine eye seeth thee*" (42:3,5). In these few words Job covers and uncovers the true gulf in knowing the acts of God. Likewise, in Psalm 73 the solution to the riddle of why the wicked prosper is found to lie not in any reasoned explanation but in acknowledging that God is God, and in appearing before God by going into the sanctuary (vs. 17). Not just the so-called 'acts of God' but the whole of history discloses its full, authentic meaning only when God reveals himself in his fullness. Therefore all events and all knowledge must be ruled by an eschatological desire to behold God as he is. This fullness remains hidden to this world, even to faith, although faith knows it exists and is kept for the Consummation.

The danger of dualism

There is still another, no less serious objection. The acceptance of some sort of supernatural divine intervention in the normal order of things entails acceptance of a split world-order and at the very least puts God in a dual relation to his creation. This objection applies only in some degree to the vision of history of the Early Middle Ages, since in that epoch's theocentric world-picture (clearly reflected even in the capitularies) there was scarcely any room for the notion of autonomous intra-mundane causal relations. The Middle Ages are an eye-opener in this regard. In an evolution that required many decades, in pamphlets and philosophical treatises, the notion arose that history can claim a certain independence, in the face of which God must recede into the background except insofar as he gives an indication of his presence through direct supernatural acts, in punishment and blessing. Eventually, on the mature Scholastic view, it was thought possible to distinguish within the cosmic order a part so well furnished by the Creator—is man's being not a finite participation in the divine Being? —that it could advance toward its goal in its natural, creaturely freedom along paths of its own, especially appointed, prepared, and maintained for it by God.

In later centuries and also in the Protestant tradition, this dual or, more accurately, dualistic relation of God to history via a mediated as well as a supernatural causality became increasingly common, with a result that was deplorable, as we shall see, on two counts: the process of history came to be viewed as autonomous; and the untenable pretension arose that in certain historical events God's judgment is discernible already today.

But, as I said, in both Catholic and Protestant quarters opposition arose to such speculative and dualistic conceptions of the Hand of God and especially to the unlawful intrusion upon the mystery of God. The writings of Van Schelven[10] and Bellon[11] are landmarks in the effort of modern Christian historians to turn historical science away from divine to human matters: historical science and likewise philosophy of history must no longer pay attention to "acts, plans, and thoughts of God" but must concern themselves instead with the historical order or with "human deliberations, human intentions, and human deeds." [12] With that, dualism and speculation have vanished—or at least so it seems.

For, the believing historian continues to acknowledge with all his heart that divine guidance is determinative for the whole of history, that world history has its origin and end in God and is given meaning from its center in Jesus Christ. Nevertheless, in his investigation of concrete historical facts and patterns, the believing historian derives little practical benefit from this confession of faith. If he works with it at all, the "gulf of blasphemy yawns before him," in the sense that he as a mere historian "attributes his fallible human judgment to a higher power." [13]

But another gulf yawns here as well, just as unbridgeable and no less alarming. It is the gulf inside a person (pardon my imperfect metaphors) between the judgment of faith and the judgment of historical science. On the judgment of faith, God guides all things and, although transcendent, is intimately present in all things and events. On the judgment of historical science, God is there all right, having propelled history on its way and ever guiding it, but to the human understanding he himself is very remote. Concretely, the historian cannot do a thing with God. The great danger is that God ends up hovering high above our heads as history goes its own way, according to its own laws and self-perception. For it must be acknowledged that if God is no longer regarded as *concretely* knowable in his acts, he recedes from our field of vision to the periphery of our existence, in spite of our *general* confession of his guidance. What we are left

---

[10] A. A. van Schelven, "Geschiedeniswetenschap en Voorzienigheidsgeloof" [Historical science and belief in Providence], *Almanak van het Studentencorps aan de VU, 1924*, 81–88.

[11] K. L. Bellon, *Wijsbegeerte der geschiedenis* (1953), 251–360.

[12] Van Schelven, 86n.

[13] J. H. Thiel, review of *Benaderbaar verleden* by W. den Boer, in *Tijdschrift voor geschiedenis* 66 (1953): 249.

with is the historical order, its laws and events, and its human agents—indeed, it is from the latter that guidance now comes, if we may go by our historical experience. God, however, has become a marginal figure, as unsearchable and inscrutable as ever, imponderable by historical science even as a mere factor.

Past and present, thinking, knowing and doing, sociology, economics, history and ever so many other sciences all converge in the same complex of problems, at the center of which is the presence of the divine mystery in reality. Important things are at stake, for the problems we have noted in the science of history likewise beset us, in a parallel and increasingly distressing way, in the ordinary practice of modern life.

And yet we ought to ask whether we do not touch upon problems here that are too high and too deep—whether we ought not to step back and remain silent about the connection between historical matters and the ultimate Why of God, a question that he alone can answer. But we have just seen what such scruples lead to: slowly but surely, the world of God and the world of man grow apart! If therefore the relation between God and history is disappearing from the scientific mind as a reality accessible to human knowledge, I should like to draw it back into the scholarly debate—despite the gulfs which then open—before the question is settled.

The God who is there

For that matter, is the situation really all that hopeless? Admittedly, we have been compelled to conclude that the answer to the ultimate Why is given only when one stands in the presence of God and hence presupposes the end of history. But that does not mean that in the interim God has remained silent about his presence. God has revealed himself, and he has done so in a time when we know in part; but proper to this time is faith, the very mode of cognition that is the correlate of Revelation in the interim. And Revelation has a lot to say about history. But what is no less important: the subject of what God says to mankind is always the relation of himself to his creatures. In other words, the Bible contains fundamental statements about what is essential in *all* creaturely relations. Sometimes the divine norm is imbedded in the simple story of a particular case. The Bible, as the common saying goes, is not a code of law—at least not in the modern technical sense—nor is it a textbook for any non-theological science. And that is correct. Yet having said this, one can still respond in two ways. Conceivably, the Bible may now remain a closed book where science is concerned. But it is also conceivable that people will give up the practice of looking for particular texts to fit particular cases and go on instead to try to understand how what is normative in any particular text applies to other particular cases.

But now, someone will object, you are forcing your way towards a facile solution. And someone else will object: the object of your study now becomes God himself, whereas science is supposed to be concerned with the things he created, with structures and concrete historical events. Of course you must proceed on the basis of the fact that God created all things and sustains all things in his Providence. But you should not study God himself. You should investigate his world. And then the end result will be a profound sense of awe at the mighty works of God.

There is a fundamental objection to be raised against all the conceptions I have related thus far—against the tendency among Christian historians to place the integral relation of God and man outside the terrain of scientific research and to assign it to faith. The objection is this: God is present in history. Historical science may be at a loss what to do with that fact and may relegate God to a mode of cognition beyond the pale of science, to faith; but that does not rid it of the reality of God in the field of history. Only if God had done no more than create the world and furnish it in such a way that it could get along without him, or only if God should do no more than sustain the world extrinsically, only then would it be feasible—yes, then indeed it would be possible—to imagine him as being outside history; and then it would make little difference whether we involved him in our conceptions and ideas of the world or not. But what if God is intimately present in this world? What if he acts in it from moment to moment and has related all things to himself? How then would anyone be able to say anything true about history while leaving God out of account, content with some merely general confession of his providential rule? Imagine someone writing a history of the Renaissance and systematically eliminating the aesthetic factor because it is too full of mystery: who would attach any value to the picture of the Renaissance that would emerge in that case? The analogy is faulty, I admit, but all the same, it makes a point. Every historian strives to do justice to all the factors that are determinative for a historical event. Why does he not show similar concern, then, for the Divine (which is more than a mere factor)?

There are historians who have struck a compromise in these perplexing matters. They do speak of God in their scholarship, but then of a God who is accessible to rational understanding. Such a God, the God of the philosophers, can then still have a certain function because he does not differ radically from what people suppose they actually encounter in the field of history. Following this line, a "part" of the truth will suffice for other concepts as well. One can then deal with, say, religious phenomena like the church not in their religious depth but in their mundane aspect, while their full reality is accessible only to faith.[14]

But the God who acts in history is not the God of the philosophers. He is not an abstraction, but the living God. The corollary to this is that all things related to God never appear in history except in their full religious dependence.

Our sense of history

If historical knowledge self-consciously abstracts from God's acts and the creature's response, then, as we are now amply aware, such a procedure has a

---

[14] See H. F. Kearney, "Christianity and the Study of History," *The Downside Review* 67 (1949): 62–73. [See also the editor's afterword, ibid., 73–75.]

profound effect on our historical experience. To abandon the traditional Christian notion of the perspicuity of God's ways in history means more than to cease to point out God's Hand in extraordinary events. The development of no one less than the historian Ranke is most illuminating here. It is well known that in his youth he harbored the desire to show the providential dealings of God concretely in history, to do his part in "deciphering the holy hieroglyph" (a metaphor that would have meant even more in 1820 than it does today).[15] Later, however, Ranke shrank from such statements, and although his consciousness of God's governance of the world remained strong his historical writings restricted themselves almost entirely to the "natural course of things" (*die natürliche Lauf der Dinge*) and their interconnections. Henceforth, what determined the course of history for Ranke were ideas and principles, intellectual elements and their underlying spirit, inscrutable inner forces, the inevitable course of affairs, the nature of the case, the natural trend of politics, and so on, and so forth.[16]

The transformation illustrated in Ranke is rather thorough. God continued to be background and, in Ranke's mind, the real actor. But once the dynamics of history could no longer be attributed to God concretely, he had to take recourse to some other agency. He began to invest the intra-mundane phenomena with powers that really belong to God, or that function only in the direct relation between God and the world. There is a lesson here. Reduce phenomena to mundane forms, and they have to shed their divine character and be re-thought as mundane realities, realities which for all that continue to betray their original force deriving from the divine sphere. The historian, after all, must carry on: when God vanishes from the concrete, much vanishes with him, and so, to prevent the historical process from disintegrating into a multiplicity of elements, the notion of natural processes based on immanent regularities is introduced as a stopgap. Thus there must be a close connection between divine and worldly matters after all. For as soon as the divine is eliminated, at least insofar as concrete human knowledge is concerned, a substitute is needed in the human sphere.

But might not our problem (which in the meantime has perhaps become clearer but also more complicated) be brought closer to a solution if we interpreted the acts of God somewhat more precisely as the work of God in the history of salvation rather than as his work of fragmentary intervention in the form of surprising and unusual events? For then we could speak with much greater clarity, namely, about God's coming in the flesh, about the guidance of the Holy Spirit, about the public presence of the Church on earth. Moreover, did Christendom in all ages not always regard the advent of Christ as the center of

---

[15] Leopold Ranke to his brother Heinrich, late March 1820; in W. P. Fuchs, ed., *Das Briefwerk* (1949), 18: "diese heilige Hieroglyphe [zu] enthüllen." [Hieroglyphic writing was not completely deciphered until 1822.]

[16] See F. Baethgen, "Zur geistigen Entwicklungsgeschichte Rankes in seiner Frühzeit" [Ranke's early intellectual development], in *Deutschland und Europa: Festschrift für Hans Rothfels* (1951), 337–53.

world history? Do we not find ourselves here upon the very ground of facts and patterns that are religious yet at the same time concrete?

No, the "clarity" thus provided will not do, even if we leave aside the unwarranted polarity created in this way between the Providence of God and the work of Christ. For we encounter precisely the same difficulties in connection with the centrality of the incarnation of the Word—in the absence of which no salvation history can exist or be known—as confronted us in identifying the Finger of God. Both involve the mystery of God; in both it is this mystery that imposes identical limits on our knowledge.

Whatever the angle of our approach to God, we encounter the mystery. Equally, whatever the angle of our approach to historical reality, we encounter the mystery; for God stands in such close relation to his world that as long as there is mystery in God there will be mystery in earthly existence. Think away the mystery of God, and the mystery of earth turns into a riddle. We shall let mystery be mystery.

In the end, then, have we no choice but to admit the impotence of our knowledge, or at least of our scientific knowledge? But the mystery has come down into mundane relations, has even entered into human knowing. This brings us to a crucial question, which I humbly submit: Has science not gradually withdrawn from the reality of God to such an extent that it no longer possesses the organ needed to integrate the relation of God to his world into the questions it formulates for investigation? Is this not the real reason for science's estrangement from the mystery in intra-mundane relations? Time and again, any knowledge of God's guidance in history is assigned to faith—presumably this guidance is knowable after all—while patterns of historical causality are considered scientific affairs. Thus if God's guidance were just a separate dimension of history, the combination of faith and science together would suffice to make history in its totality knowable. But God is by no means an added dimension, for he stands in relation to all of history. If then God is so intimately present in things, they can only be fully known when worldly knowledge embraces knowledge of the divine mystery. Is this mystery a prejudice? Not at all. Prejudice is a concept that arose to denote that which *precedes* rational thought. That which faith tells us, however, is an *integral part* of the fabric of scientific knowledge. Scientific judgment is therefore correct and true only to the extent that it also incorporates what is known in other ways, in this case the way of faith. Or more precisely, to obviate the impression that we are still thinking in terms of two distinct modes of cognition: faith is not an ornament added to knowledge acquired in another way; nor is it a subjective prejudice that the historian is never quite able to shake. Faith, rather, when oriented to God and divine Revelation, is a conscious ingredient of the scientific method that the researcher employs to open up his "field."

Christian thought often made the mistake of claiming the scientifically inexplicable part of the world for the domain of faith. This had fatal consequences.

Not only did the area commanded by faith shrink steadily before the triumphal progress of science, or at any rate come to depend on the scope of science. As well, it caused people to form an altogether erroneous notion of the object of faith, the divine and the intra-mundane mystery. Essentially, the mystery of faith vis-à-vis science came to be identified with what science had *not yet* disclosed. In this way, incalculable damage was inflicted on faith and science alike.

But why in the world exclude faith from the scientific attitude if the relations of this world are characterized by religion? Reality itself demands a congenial method of approach as a prerequisite for full disclosure. For example, several distinct and separate approaches are commonly taken to a concrete historical event: by historical science, and by philosophy of history, and sometimes also by faith or theology. In this manner students of history are certainly able to illuminate particular aspects of the historical event. But the problem is, how can the fragmentary results thus obtained ever reflect the full reality of the event?

Suffering in history

To save time, much of what I have said thus far I have simply posited, without adducing any further grounds for it. I believe, however, that a "re-ordering of the theory of knowledge,"[17] a theory that takes its starting point in the recognition of the fundamental unity of the special sciences, philosophy, and faith, offers a sound point of departure for acquiring a better understanding of the divine mystery in history.

It is worthy of note that in almost all great systems of philosophy of history attention is given to the problem of suffering. Suffering is manifest in history: the extinction of whole peoples, massacres, wars, and so on, have such a far-reaching influence on the life of the nations that they are necessarily granted a place in every conception of history. Yet it is astonishing in what matter-of-fact way this suffering is recorded. Sometimes a tragic situation is said to be brought about by "the course of circumstances" or "the unavoidable confluence of historical factors." At other times (this is the form in which suffering most often appears in philosophy of history) suffering is made to find its justification in the broader perspective of history as "the indispensable transition to a new age," for the happiness of future generations. Suffering has been granted its place, its meaning, in the totality of history and is caught in the nexus of phenomena and events. No sooner did historical science begin to secularize than an intra-mundane determination or meaning also had to be found for suffering. As Mircea Eliade says in his book, *The Myth of the Eternal Return,* where he devotes a number of excellent pages to the problem of suffering in history: "If no trans-historic meaning emerges from the extinction of so many nations, from the mass deportations and massacres of the present time, suffering can only be

---

[17] See J. Münzhuber, "Erkenntnis und Glaube" [Knowledge and belief], *Zeitschrift für philosophische Forschung* 3 (1948): 73. [Cf. essay 16 below.]

the resultant of the blind play of economic, social and political forces."[18] To pose the problem in its most acute form, I would add: How can a lonely individual bear the suffering generated by the operation of historical forces if he has lost the prospect of a trans-historic world?

Does the question I raise here not apply, however, to *all* of history, to world history in its entirety, irrespective of the suffering inherent in it? In the great systems of philosophy of history suffering is justified again and again in terms of some immanent historical purpose. But, similarly, in these same conceptions all antecedent periods are judged in terms of a period to come, or else one period derives its meaning from another period, from the following one or the preceding one. Generally, earlier periods are regarded as transitional phases or preparatory stages for later ones and ultimately for the ideal time that history is presumably advancing towards or that is about to "dawn." The achievements of earlier times are then assessed either negatively as darkness before the daybreak or positively as preludes, but in both cases they are measured not by the yardstick derived from the nation, culture or period to which they belong but by the significance they have for other times and cultures that sooner or later will set the tone in history.

It is the cyclical theory especially that has resisted this conception. On the cyclical view, every culture develops according to its own law, finding its standard and meaning not in the values of other cultures but entirely within itself. What is the result? Both the cyclical and historicistic approaches to world history fragment that world history in order to preserve for each culture its own proper value. Furthermore, these approaches can apprehend the substance of cultures other than those to which they are native only at the price of inner contradiction.

Now, this resistance to ascribing meaning to a part of history or to a historical event in terms of an ultimate meaning of history has contributed to a denial of the idea of world history as such, or at least to a denial of any trans-historical meaning by means of which the multiplicity of events and phenomena would be forged into an *intrinsically* coherent whole. Currently, every notion of a universal history whose inner coherence and meaning would be derived from metahistory is met by fierce resistance from many sides. People have committed themselves instead to the idea of the historical event or pattern that is determined exclusively by intra-mundane forces. They still grant the concept of world history a certain acceptance, but not in terms of a unity that transcends history. Rather, world history is conceived of as a plurality of cultural "encounters," as an arena for "dynamic interactions"[19] which admit of empirical discovery independent of theological and speculative philosophical preconceptions and

---

[18] M. Eliade, *Le mythe de l'éternel retour*, 222 [Eng. trans., 151].

[19] "*Wirkungszusammenhänge*"; cf. Hans Freyer, "Das Problem der Einheit der Weltgeschichte" [The Problem of the unity of world history], in *Philosophische Vorträge und Diskussionen. Bericht über den Mainzer Philosophen-Kongress* (1948), 180–84.

which present themselves to the technical historian in the specific form of "world-historical situations." Alternatively, the starting point is the unique historical fact whose meaning is not externally imposed by rationality but is internally present, radiating outward with irruptive force; so conceived, history itself forges unity from the world's events and forms the arena for the various "intersecting meanings." [20]

I am fully aware that a perplexing dilemma confronts us here. Thévenaz even speaks of a "Copernican revolution" in philosophy of history. The irreconcilable polar opposites appear to be the following. *Either* history derives its meaning from some trans-historic realm, or from a certain ideal age in which trans-historic meaning has already come to reside or towards which it impels its treasures to their full unfolding. On this view, the unity and coherence of world history are not guaranteed by factors external to it and consequently are not at every moment in jeopardy either (in fact, they survive ruptures and revolutions). However, the elements of history have to sacrifice their own intrinsic value as they must suffer themselves to be measured against trans-historic norms or immanent historic standards regarded as absolute. *Or,* alternatively, the rejection of every notion of world history, Christian or secular, does secure the intrinsic value of the historic event, culture, or period as such, but ignores the really crucial question how events ever come to be connected, how one fact is able to link up with another, how historical complexes are woven into a single, unified tapestry.[21]

Moreover, does the denial of trans-historical unity in world history truly rescue the intrinsic value of the periods and cultures? And if it does, if this unique, immanent historical meaning in the patterns and events themselves is indeed secured, can history then still be known? And can it be endured?

The terror of history

Our discussions of suffering and world history have clearly revealed the extent to which the recognition of a trans-mundane, divine world affects the conception of history. One of the main approaches being taken in contemporary philosophy of history is to rethink the problems of history in terms of intra-mundane elements exclusively. To be sure, this 'Copernican revolution' is an assault on rationalistic schemes of history in the first place, but it is certainly also aimed at the Christian belief in a trans-historical meaning in history.

But all these problems apply only to the *philosophy* of history, someone will say. They are of no concern to history as a special *science*. Of course philosophy of history has to deal with things divine at one point or another, but surely technical history is concerned with suffering and world-historical patterns only to the

---

[20] "*Sens entrecroisés*"; cf. Pierre Thévenaz, "Événement et historicité" [Event and historicity], in *L'homme et l'histoire. Actes du VIe Congrès des Sociétés de Philosophie de langue française* (1952), 217–25, esp. 224.

[21] At the same congress where Hans Freyer presented his ideas Nicolai Hartmann declared, not surprisingly, that he could not share the latter's optimism.

extent that these can be established and explained empirically. The professional historian today is able to note to his surprise and great satisfaction that a number of schools in philosophy of history have ended up precisely where historical science has been for more than a century: namely, at empirically verifiable patterns and concrete events whose meaning is completely self-contained and in no way dependent on the intrusion of some Absolute.

Now indeed, an important difference undoubtedly persists between historical science and philosophy of history in connection with the rejection of any trans-mundane meaning in history. Philosophers are moved primarily by considerations of principle while historians are prompted chiefly by methodological concerns. But let us have a look at the implications of the disavowal of trans-mundane meaning in the historical facts—regardless whether it originates in philosophy or in historical science—both for concrete historical facts themselves and for empirical patterns.

Mircea Eliade, in the work mentioned earlier, has spoken of the *terror* of history. Does he perhaps mean by it decay and transience; things changing beyond recognition; being constantly dislodged from one's familiar historical surroundings? Or is he alluding to the suffering of the nations? That too, to be sure; but in speaking of the terror of history he has in mind history as such, quite apart from the misery and devastation it brings. *Can man endure history if it is nothing more than an immanent historical process?* Eliade's question is pertinent and decisive. It might well have been posed in the nineteenth century—in fact it was posed then, but at that time people were still too preoccupied with a happy future, and too expectant of what the inner dynamics of history would bring forth, to dwell very long on such perplexities. Even when the "philosophy of life" captured the minds of many and unrestrained historicism began to pave the way for relativism, people still held on to their belief in some "creative formation" whereby one generation bequeaths an enlarged and enriched heritage to another. However, when, from whatever cause, the idea of progress lost its charm, people were left with nothing but complex yet bare facts and mere interconnections, world-historical in character or not. Modern consciousness was confronted by the very thing that historical science had produced via empirical methods—produced, that is to say, to the extent that historical science had observed its self-imposed limits. The resulting situation was soon reflected in the "philosophy of existence," which in many respects speaks a language in these matters that modern man can identify with for his own attitude toward history. Modern man feels more intensely all the time that he is pitted against history as against an alien power that threatens him even as it comes with promises of opportunity and progress. History no longer speaks to modern man, and he no longer identifies with it. Yet he cannot escape the flux of history, which is so intrinsically alien to him, because in essence he is history himself. At best, he can *try,* in the existential moment, to free himself from historical relativity for the sake of some absolute value. The flux of history is not eliminated, but it survives only as a secondary reality surrounding him like a prison.

An extremely complex situation has grown out of all this. In a process lasting decades, man has attempted to free himself of the trans-historical ties that determined the purpose of his life from without. But now that he has gained the freedom he desired, mundane reality bereft of trans-historical meaning frightens him. Granted, this feeling of being threatened by history is not universal. Yet one may not counter this assessment by pointing to the great love that many still have for history. No, what causes man so much anxiety is the fact that in his deepest being he himself belongs to history and no longer has the possibility of rising above it.

Historical science and alienation from history

Those who have closely followed our discussion of man's alienation from history, and have noted that the root of the problem is the dearth of a trans-historical meaning, might conclude that the perplexities and terrors of history are merely a problem for philosophy of history and not for historical science. That would be an obvious conclusion, especially given the technical historian's impression that it is the philosophers of history with their preconceived schemes who rack history on a Procrustean bed and put human personality in a quandary. Yet such a conclusion would be decidedly incorrect. The impasses and terrors of history also concern historical science. In fact, it is not impossible that technical history is at least partly to blame for the terror of history. For is it not remarkable that the immanent-historical events, which increasingly form the starting point of contemporary philosophy of history, bear a strong resemblance to the empirical data with which historical science has always worked? It is precisely in those concrete historical facts, established by an ever more sophisticated and perfected historical method, that the menace in history first accosts us. The menace in question could not emerge until the transcendent background of history, which was still present even in the secularized versions of Christian values, receded. As long as man still knew himself to be one with the ultimate ground of the universe, he could feel secure in history; he could trustingly surrender himself to its march even when the familiar course of things was interrupted.

History's threat to man arises from his having fallen prey to historicity and being alienated from history as the consequence of that reduction. Still, how can historical science possibly be held co-responsible for man's alienation from history? One often hears it said that historical science is concerned with establishing facts, and then not isolated facts but facts that are so interwoven that empirical knowledge of them necessarily entails a knowledge of their interconnections as well. Thus whenever a historian wishes to know a fact, he turns not to an isolated atom in historical reality but to a datum integrated by virtue of innumerable ties in a more comprehensive whole. He seeks to identify the causal relations of historical phenomena or, more broadly speaking, to account for their conditioned character. For according to the prevailing scientific view, such phenomena are determined by a great many factors and circumstances, determinants which do not exert their influence in a random or arbitrary fashion but which are themselves in turn integrated in well-ordered patterns or (as the more recent version would have it) basic "structures." Man is conditioned not only from without, by an intricate web of economic, political, social, religious, physical, and other causal factors, occasions, and influences, but also from within: his thoughts and actions are also affected, for example, by his psychic structure. Moreover, an historical event, conditioned in this way and having man as the agent, in turn exerts an influence on other circumstances and historical entities. Thus the conclusion arrived at by historical science (in collaboration with other sciences) is that things, events and people not only are determining factors in their own right but also are enclosed, integrated, and given direction by and in a formidable network of forces and powers, of structures and systems. Historians are extremely resourceful in their attempts to capture in words the conditioned character of historical events. To name just a few of the expressions in common use, how often do we not read: "because," "on account of," "the result being," "with the inevitable consequence that," and so on, and so forth.

Meanwhile, the world of history is not yet closed. In the twentieth century historians realize better than they did in the nineteenth that perfect understanding of life's extreme complexity is beyond the capacity of human knowledge. Historians often nurtured the optimistic hope that time would bring a solution for unresolved historical problems, such as the origin of the rise of towns in the Middle Ages or the causes of the Eighty Years' War. That is, they hoped that with the increase in source materials the patterns would become clearer to us. The outcome was often the reverse. The more comprehensive our knowledge of a historical phenomenon became, the more complicated it appeared to us, and as a rule the problems increased proportionately in number.

But historians have not just acquired a lively sense of the limitations of human insight into the conditioned character of historical phenomena. They hasten at the same time to reassure us over and over again that a nexus of historical causality does not function like a law of nature and that human freedom is not impaired by it. In fact, they claim that human freedom is gradually being enhanced, especially as the result of improving social conditions.

For all the sincerity of such words, they have not alleviated the gravity of science's predicament and man's plight. Following a purely scientific approach, scholars have come to the conclusion that man is caught in a web of factors, influences and systems, partly knowable and partly unknowable, partly rational and partly irrational.

This then, is the real threat posed by the course of history. This is the terror of which Eliade spoke. When a Christian looks at history, he too sees historical facts, their connections, their apparent inevitability; but he also senses, if only dimly, that there is no power in the historical facts themselves but rather that they are ordained by God and form part of his purposeful plan. In secularized thought, however, facts possess meaning and power by virtue of their mere existence. Granted worth in their own right, they acquire compelling force vis-à-vis other facts and even in regard to man himself. They are autonomous power plants furnished with equipment that belongs (I say it reverently) to God alone, powers that bear down upon people and things along avenues of causality and influence and in their mysterious anonymity overwhelm them and reduce them to subservience. We are not talking about disasters and calamities or excesses like despotism, tyranny, revolution, deportation. We are talking about ordinary, inconspicuous—morally, legally, juridically, socially, or economically warranted—facts, facts which may even spell prosperity and happiness. The terror of history does not arise from evil in the usual sense but from the fact that man is subject to the historical course of events.

Does this not entail a depreciation of the world-order? Is it not denied here that the things God made were good? Not necessarily; but once the elements of the world-order and the structures are removed from the relation to God, all one has left are the things themselves. Whatever worth and meaning they have is then self-contained; they are then entirely self-determined. And people increasingly experience a history furnished like that as an alien and hostile world.

Oddly enough, as the conviction gained ground in science that historical facts are intra-mundanely conditioned in character (a conviction that often went hand in hand with the idea that God cannot be known concretely in history), many failed to realize that the circle of influences and patterns nevertheless cannot be fully closed—that breaks occur in the continuity of historical reality. Some examples will suffice to make my meaning clear.

Few historians will deny that there was a causal relation between the assassination of the archduke of Austria and the outbreak of the First World War. There are differences of interpretation, but they pertain to the relation of this factor to other factors leading to the war. And yet, neither the assassination of the archduke, nor any other factor, nor yet all the factors combined, made World War I compellingly necessary. What remains inexplicable is precisely *the fact that* the assassination had that consequence. The empirically observed connection between cause and effect, between the elements of a pattern, could have been broken. *The question now becomes that of the ground of the possibility both of the rise of the pattern and of the pattern's being broken.* It is beginning to look probable that the connection between cause and effect, that the quality or state of being conditioned, in the broadest sense of the word, is wrapped in mystery—although many will contend that precisely at this point there is no mystery but at most incompleteness in our knowledge. As I see it, divergence in the explanations that are advanced for a phenomenon is able to arise because of the break between cause and effect. The diversity of opinions among historians is possible not only because of the complicated nature of a phenomenon but more especially because the lines that link the factors to the outcome pass through an area where cause is transformed into effect.

I want to refer to another example. In studying the Carolingian Renaissance we can ascribe its inception to many influences, but ultimately we shall have to ask ourselves in amazement how in the world it was possible that such a thing as the Carolingian Renaissance should ever have arisen. Here too, after all, the great problem is precisely the question how all these influences were able to give rise to this particular phenomenon.[22]

Summarizing, we conclude: in the transformation of cause into consequence, in the transition from influence to effect, lies the possibility for consequence and effect alike—I speak, as ever, anthropomorphically—of deliverance from the compelling force of circumstances.

Do the constant breaks in the patterns of history on the one hand, and deliverance from history's terror on the other, perhaps have something to do with each other?

The transcendental relation

Two things are simultaneously true of man: he is surrounded by and integrated in overpowering patterns of systems, structures, influences, and so on; and he transcends the intra-mundane relations. Man is elevated above the interplay of worldly forces by a transcendent power, by the Transcendent One, by God, and thus he stands in relation to the Transcendent One. In religion, understood as the relation between the living God and the creature, man cannot be touched by the relations of this world. There is something in man that transcends them. However much the facts may seem in man's eyes to be charged with divine power, or with transcendent forces transformed into the mundane, and however much they may seem in their self-contained meaning to hold sway over worldly relations, in reality man in one respect at least is permanently beyond their reach. It is in this region of transcending security in the relation to the Transcendent One that human freedom and responsibility reside. This transcending of the intra-mundane relations is valid and real both for those who believingly acknowledge the Transcendent One and for those who disesteem him or carelessly pass him by. *Even in rebellious apostasy man is kept by God in the trans-mundane relation* and can be called to account in it.

My formulations could give the impression that only a certain sector is beyond the reach of the mundane. Yet my position is not that at all. I hold rather that the total man, and in him the whole of history, is comprehended in the liberating transcendental relation.

None the less, is freedom in the transcendental relation, is release from the intra-mundanely conditioned nature of things not contradicted by the experience of common sense and science alike? Surely man remains entangled in intra-mun-

---

[22] Cf. Butterfield, *Christianity and History*, ch. 5: "Providence and the Historical Process."

dane relations and subject to irresistible historical facts; and are systems, institutions and powers not constantly expanding their sway over human life? The mere recognition that man transcends historical relations is therefore not an adequate solution. To escape the grip of the intra-mundane, to break away from the absolute conditionality of things, it is necessary to deprive the mundane of that which enables it in the first place to acquire power over this world and all it contains. Historical facts and the mundane must be deprived of that which makes them mundane and factual: their autonomy, their possessing power and meaning in and of themselves.

As God alone can lift man above the intra-mundane relations into the transcendental relation, so Christ alone can disarm things as such of the absoluteness with which they assert themselves. Piercing to the root, Christ speaks in the Gospels of breaking through the continuous, horizontal course of events and historical patterns, and of putting an end to the independent power of the facts. He does so in the Sermon on the Mount when he condemns the ordinary attitude of concern, of thought for the things that are so important to earthly relations, and in its place puts concern for the Kingdom. He does so, too, when he makes severing family ties and forsaking life's most intimate relationships conditional for entering the Kingdom.[23] People have often blunted Jesus' words by limiting their scope to a particular category of persons or to the private sphere. But Christ demands precisely that we forsake and hate the very things that play an elementary role in historical relations as well. People have also undertaken to deprive Jesus' words of their radical character by accommodating them to other passages in Scripture that speak of the claims of love and of cherishing life. Yet this interpretation too obscures what the Incarnation has brought clearly to light. Normally, people think of things as having value even apart from God, as they supply needs and give satisfaction. This is what Christ came to put an end to. The condition for coming to God is to forsake natural relations as these assert themselves as self-reliant and self-determining, independently of God.

Perhaps someone will object by pointing out that the world God made was good and that he preserved its ordinances through the Fall—including marriage and family (which the demand to hate father and mother seems to destroy). Yet this is precisely the fact that the ordinances have availed themselves of to constitute themselves independently of God and in defiance of him, to give man satisfaction and to supply his needs! It is not excesses in marriage and family or in any other human relations nor any overstepping of their bounds that Christ denounces, but mundane relations as they conform to the standards of organized society. Christ challenges their autonomy and self-sufficiency.

Things, historical relations, need constantly to constitute themselves anew, to emerge afresh, divested of that which was hitherto essential in them. And so historical facts and patterns reappear, emptied of their intrinsic self-importance and hence also of their tyranny over man. In passing from self-contained power

---

[23] Matt. 6:25-34; Mark 10:29, 30; Luke 14:26.

to divine mercy, the facts acquire a new orientation. Being oriented to God, says Augustine, defines the essence of man and rules the course of history: *Fecisti nos ad Te*—Thou hast made us for Thyself.[24] Christ's words indicate that this orientation to God does not bypass the ordinances and facts but rather appropriates them. That is why it was feasible for me to speak of historical things in anthropomorphic terms: their autonomy and self-constitutive capacity stems from their relation to man; yet in this same relation they are the object of divine renewal. If facts are indeed constituted only in the relation to the Transcendent One, then it is no longer possible to understand the intra-mundane relations without taking this relation into account.

The constituting of the facts

We have traveled a long route—a tortuous detour, some will say—to reach a conclusion that can be stated in a few words. History involves more than intra-mundane conditionality; it involves also the relation to God. That is stating it in terms that are too quantitative and too spatial, but it is a real question whether words will ever be able to express the depth to which the transcendental relation penetrates historical relations. To say that the transcendental relation is constitutive of the facts entails at least this: in their very state of being intra-mundanely determined the facts are at the same time, from within as well as from without, determined and given direction from the trans-mundane, divine world.

By way of a double denial—on the one hand, of fragmentary, supernatural acts of God; on the other, of a historical science restricted chiefly to mundane relations—we have arrived at historical facts and relations that do not constitute themselves except in their relation to God, whether negatively by asserting themselves as absolute[25] or positively by affirming, in the divine-human *metanoia*, the transcendental relation.

It is with such facts and relations that the historian is confronted, whether as a philosopher of history or as a working historian. It is the historian's task to rethink the philosophical problems raised by history in terms of the interlocking of intra-mundane and trans-historical reality. I have in mind problems such as the unity of world history, historical causality, historical periodization, and the role of great personalities in history—a question Huizinga brought to a new stage when [in answer to the question by what earthly standard we can take the measure of saints] he proposed measuring their influence, via the holy, against a superlunary yardstick.[26] Nor should we neglect to mention that Catholic thinkers too are poised to take a fresh look at these phenomena from the perspective of their relation to God and their transcendental orientation to the

---

[24] Augustine, *Confessions*, I, 1.

[25] To avoid all misunderstanding I want to emphasize that not just the Christian world but all peoples, cultures and historical phenomena are of importance to the Christian historian, for all are lifted above historical causality and kept in the transcendental relation—the Gentiles in spite of themselves (cf. Matt. 6:32 [*"For all these things do the Gentiles seek"*]).

[26] Huizinga, "Historische grootheid" [Historical greatness], in *Verzamelde Werken*, 7:217.

Absolute. Especially worthy of mention in this regard are the studies of Bellon and Kwant.[27] Common to their standpoint and ours is the rejection of any purely intra-mundane form of transcendence. Our ways part where they adopt a natural theology as background and the doctrine of participation as their starting point: we do not share the idea that the finite participates in the divine Being.[28] Furthermore, the transcendental relation as they deal with it is made fruitful too exclusively for philosophy of history; it is doubtful whether on their conception the special sciences, which investigate the actual coming to be [of phenomena], can do justice to the presence of a religious relation in created reality.

So it will not be enough for professional historians to heed the signs of the times and shift their emphasis from national history today to supranational and world-historical aspects tomorrow, or to transfer their attention from political to cultural and economic factors or to structures in history. However momentous such shifts may be and however importantly they may alter our picture of history in the long run, they are never anything more than intra-mundane relativizations of the sort we have so long been accustomed to and which generally result in setting up some recently discovered or newly appreciated factor as an absolute. No, what I have in mind are questions like these: What is implied in the fact that economic life is determined not just by intra-mundane but also by trans-mundane reality? And what does it mean, to suggest another question, that the national element—I do not say excessive nationalism—no longer holds autonomous sway?

Here problems are disclosed to which I wish to devote myself from now on. That will not be possible without a firm conviction and the glow of enthusiasm. But above all it will be necessary that God preserve me from love of the world, fear of difficulties, and premature satisfaction with any results obtained.

I know that the desire to practice scholarship in such intimate relation to God involves the risk of losing sight of the truly divine. Nevertheless, I adhere to Blondel's words: God must not be left out of our affirmations of the concrete.

[*The inaugural lecture, as is the custom, concluded with the following personal addresses:*]

Members of the Board of Directors: I am profoundly grateful for your willingness to appoint me to this office. It is a privilege and joy for me to be appointed in *this* university, which through its bond with the Christian religion creates the condition for pursuing scholarship *in freedom*. It fills me with great thankfulness that I can devote myself completely to scholarly studies from now on.

---

[27] Bellon, *Wijsbegeerte der geschiedenis* (see note 11); idem, "Onder welke voorwaarden is de wetenschap der geschiedenis mogelijk?" [Under what conditions is the science of history possible?], *Tijdschrift voor philosophie* 15 (1953): 163–78. R. C. Kwant, "De historie en het absolute" [History and the absolute], *Tijdschrift voor philosophie* 17 (1955): 255–305.

[28] [On the doctrine of participation, see Part One above, Introduction and Chapter I.]

From the lecture I have just delivered, the ideals with which I assume my office will be clear to you. You could hardly have assigned me a more attractive combination of disciplines. At the same time, I am well aware that the combination is a risky one and that I shall have to be careful to provide no occasion for suspicion. For more than a century now relations between historians and philosophers of history have been markedly poor, and although there have been some signs of rapprochement in recent years, the technical historian continues to be afraid that the philosopher will do violence to the facts and the philosopher of history continues to fear that the technical historian will ignore the deeper historical patterns that are not subject to direct empirical verification. Although to my way of thinking this old antagonism rests on a misunderstanding and historical science and philosophy are so intimately related that neither can be pursued in the absence of the other, I do take it seriously. I interpret your assignment to mean that I am to contribute to the best of my ability to the termination of this conflict.

Members of the Board of Curators: It is only now, at the start of my work here, that I realize more fully the responsibility you have laid upon me. If someone were to ask me what guarantee I have to prove myself worthy of the trust you have placed in me, my answer would be: neither this university nor myself have ever lacked the faithfulness and help of Almighty God.

Professors, of the Faculty of Letters in particular: It was your wish to see me in your midst as the successor to Professor Goslinga. Some of you are my former teachers; to some of you I am bound as well by ties of friendship. Not only from them, but from all of you, I will experience spontaneously the cordiality, helpfulness and cooperation I so very much need.

Esteemed Professor Goslinga: I am not your successor in the strict sense of the word, but my appointment was possible because you made room for it. I rejoice that you, my mentor, worked for my appointment and for the teaching assignment that satisfies my desires completely. *Noblesse oblige:* your meticulousness as a scholar and your intimate ties with the traditions of Calvinism impose upon me obligations that are not light but that I accept with joy.

Esteemed Professor Smitskamp: In you I greet my former thesis supervisor, my predecessor in this chair and, starting today, my closest colleague. The line dividing our respective areas of work is to be—I expect to the satisfaction of both of us—not 1648 but 1500. Across this new boundary we will extend hands in a cordial collegiality that will be sustained by a deeper spiritual unity even if our views should differ—and when does that not occur in the pursuit of science? Inexperienced as I am in organizational matters, I know I can count on you for guidance.

Esteemed Professor Vollenhoven: The second part of my assignment in particular, theory of history, will bring me into close contact with you. The way has been prepared in past years, when ties of friendship and trust developed between us. To you and to Professor Dooyeweerd I owe a great debt of gratitude, since you two especially were the ones who opened to me the prospect of the possibility of Christian scholarship.

Members of the Board of Governors of the Doctor Abraham Kuyper Foundation, Dear Dr. Groen: At my departure from the Kuyper Institute, there was a difference, as it turned out, in our evaluations of the manner in which I had conceived my task.[29]

---

[29] [As reference librarian for the membership and parliamentary caucus of the Anti-Revolutionary Party.]

I am pleased to think that in the future I shall have ample opportunity to bridge the difference then noted by helping to advance the purpose of the Foundation with the results of my study.

This day is also not without its shadow. Neither of my parents was permitted to live to see it. Mother passed away just a few months before the appointment was announced. But I fervently desire that what lived in them will live in me: warm love towards God, a strong sense of history, an interest in the deeper questions of life.

Ladies and Gentlemen of the Student Body: The days are evil for history. From many sides we hear of cavalier interpretation of the sources, of a critical decline in philological rigor, and of diminishing respect for historical facts. Moreover, the freedom of philosophy of history is in serious jeopardy because it is being chained to sociology or compelled to dabble in futurology. But what poses the greatest threat to history is the new idea of progress, which suggests we have arrived in an entirely new age, and the modern sense of the generation gap, which drives a wedge not only between past and present but also between teacher and pupil.

In spite of all these foreboding signs, or rather because I know a wealth of spiritual resources are at stake here, I ask for your trust, your unfolding interest, your youthful enthusiasm, your warm love for a past in which much lovelessness, injustice, and cruelty occurred, and lastly and above all, a spirited effort also on your part to pursue our discipline from the heart of the Christian religion.

My heart is filled with suspense. Will there always be, even at this university, that disinterested interest in both medieval history and philosophy of history which is an indispensable condition for the study of both? I consider it a point of honor for this University to pursue its own distinctive path in medieval studies, that is to say, in the study of a world from which it would seem on the surface to be separated by a greater spiritual distance.

Insofar as philosophy of history is concerned, you will surely not, and may not, expect me to force my insights upon you. My heart's desire is to make you aware of the great issues with which history confronts us and to be allowed to lead you to the place where the unassailable starting-point for our discipline is to be found.

Thank you.[30]

---

[30] ["The Divine Mystery in History" was reviewed, among other places, in *Trouw*, 8 Oct. 1955 (by G. C. Berkouwer); *Ad Fontes* 6 (1958/59): 2–8 (by H. Berkhof); *Antirevolutionaire Staatkunde* 25 (1955): 310–16 (by J. P. A. Mekkes); *Bijdragen voor de Geschiedenis der Nederlanden* 10 (1956): 249–50; *Canon Gestorum Scripturae* 8 (1956): 10–14 (by J. H. Harms); *Historische Zeitschrift* 184 (1957): 662 (by H. R. Guggisberg); *Nouvelle revue théologique* 79 (1957): 331 (by R. Mols, S.J.); *Sola Fide* 10 (1956/57): 17–22 (by K. J. Popma); *Tijdschrift voor Philosophie* 17 (1955): 738; and *Vox Theologica* 26 (1956): 160–61 (by J. Smit-Sibinga).]

6/ THE CHARACTER OF THE MIDDLE AGES

FOR MORE THAN ONE HUNDRED and fifty years now scholars have been busy exploring the medieval world.[1] Yet, despite an impressive stream of publications, Régine Pernoud was recently compelled to observe in her *Lumière du Moyen-Age* that this period is still the least known part of Western history.[2]

Think of it! More than one hundred and fifty years of intensive investigation and still, deficient knowledge. Is there an obvious explanation? Does medieval culture perhaps offer so much resistance that we cannot penetrate it?

I am disposed to answer this question initially in the affirmative. After all, the external approaches already are hard going. Few periods in history require such extensive study of the ancillary sciences. In the best known centers of European medieval studies, the youthful researcher is required to spend years practicing the ancillary sciences alone. Many medievalists devote practically their entire life to these auxiliary studies without getting to medieval culture itself. It must be conceded, though, that just by working in the ancillary sciences, where one deals with documents, calligraphy, old script, seals and the like, one can gain deep insight into the thought and aspirations of this culture.

There is another, stronger source of resistance. The medieval world is so utterly different from that of the nineteenth and twentieth centuries. The spirit of the two periods is altogether dissimilar. The Middle Ages afford a wide range of phenomena and are even rich in contradictions, but there is one characteristic common to the medieval world as a whole: it is religious through and through, even where it has been unable to give concrete shape to the religious "factor."

In contrast to this are the nineteenth and twentieth centuries. I do not want to argue now about whether they are a-religious. I simply want to observe—and it will not be denied—that the religiosity of these centuries is in many respects a different religiosity. Undoubtedly there is tremendous diversity in the religiosity of modern times, but the predominant feature is that religion—by which I mean the relation of the divine to this world—concerns a mere compartment of life. This is something that was unknown in the Middle Ages, when even humor, as Pernoud shows, was of a Christian cast because it found its source in the omnipotence of God.[3]

---

[1] [This essay was Professor Smit's contribution to one of the university-wide lecture series, *Interfacultaire Voordrachten*, for the academic year 1957–58.]

[2] Régine Pernoud, *Lumière du Moyen-Age* (Paris, 1944); Eng. trans., *The Glory of the Medieval World* (London, 1950), 5, 137, 181–93.

[3] Pernoud, *The Glory of the Medieval World*, 253–55.

The modern scholarship that is being brought to bear on medieval history is itself a child of its times, if only because it strives to purge itself of the religious element as much as possible, relegating it to its own compartment. How can a discipline that has self-consciously divested itself of a fundamental relation ever hope to learn the truth about a culture that is suffused with this relation?

Now, I do not want to overlook a change that may be taking place. Among active scholars there are a few who, in conscious resistance to the spirit of the nineteenth and twentieth centuries, have undertaken to stress the element of worldview in medieval attitudes.

When one places current works on medieval culture side by side and compares them—say, Pernoud's book and the works of Philipp Funk—one is tempted to ask, "Are they discussing the same culture?" We would soon be reassured, however, for they both talk about the Gothic and about courtly love and they both acknowledge that Pope Urban II died in 1099. And yet, how they differ!

This is far from being the only division between medieval historians. The field fairly bristles with diverging interpretations. But is that so unusual? When scholars are at work, are rival hypotheses and competing opinions not bound to emerge? No doubt, but I dare say that in the case of the medieval world the harvest has been exceptional.

And now I come to a third source of resistance. This one is not *originally* present in medieval culture. It is more in the nature of resistance to the way in which the modernist approaches it. Let me try to make this clear with a figure of speech. As a blossom closes for protection against coolly wafting evening breezes, so the Middle Ages wrap their garments close about them against the cold stare of alien spectators.

Of course, there are many ways of looking at the Middle Ages that reveal a lack of understanding in the beholder. Allow me to mention two: that of the person who judges history in terms of progress, and that of the person who measures it by its significance for his own time. Both attitudes exist. In both cases, the measuring stick is either one's own time or the future.

To be sure, we are often told that while the nineteenth century did think in categories of progress, that particular approach has long since become passé. Presumably, we now recognize that the world has reached an impasse and that modern man has given no better shape to his life than did the people of earlier, culturally less developed periods. But, if the belief in progress has indeed been overthrown, why do we keep on hearing expressions in which people put themselves above those dark Middle Ages, as in: "Cultural life in that region is still at a medieval level"? While we hear such expressions from the man in the street, we also read them in scholarly works, negatively and positively: "people had not as yet . . ." and "in that period people had already . . . ." So while I grant that modern man has weaned himself of the belief in progress as a *universal* principle, he still keeps it in reserve for limited use. As so much sinks away around him, it remains a last point of support in the general upheaval; it gives him a comforting feeling to know that "science advances."

Medieval culture, too, has been assigned a place in this progression. It is evaluated, and more often than not condemned, by the yardstick of progress or some ideal future.

Thus shaped, the modern picture is reinforced by still another factor. Among academic historians it has long been asserted that history must be rewritten in every age. Supposedly, every age approaches the past in its own way, accordingly takes a *different* position with respect to history, and naturally will interpret what has happened in the past in its own *distinctive* way. A glance at the scientific literature, however, reveals that not just every generation but every school of thought writes history anew. A plurality of approaches to history results, with the consequence that modern conceptions and methods are legitimized beforehand and then projected into the conceptual world of the period under study.

In summary, we have taken note of medieval culture's resistance to disclosure, and I hope the point will be taken when I say its resistance is to be attributed in a fundamental sense to the modern researcher, the person of the nineteenth and twentieth centuries. He asks if the Middle Ages have any *use,* and he asks if they still have anything to say to him in the *present*. He supposes that to understand the Middle Ages he should approach them with insights borrowed from the time in which he lives. In essence, the conflict between the hidden medieval man and his would-be modern discoverer comes down to the unwillingness or inability of the latter to take distance from his own inevitably limited world.

Many regard the Middle Ages as a period of barbarism and darkness, lacking in real culture. It was a time when individuals withdrew into lonely, bare monastic cells to practice a strict asceticism; when people built heavily fortified castles in which knights led boring lives and from which noblemen fought endless wars against their neighbors for the sake of a little distraction; when peasants eked out their days in slavery and serfdom, subsisting, but without comforts or cultural refinements. And what of art, the most exquisite cultural product of all? The Middle Ages cannot be said to have lacked aesthetic sense, but only towards the end did the period begin to rise above a primitive stage.

Disdaining this popular view, I shall proceed to speak about the *culture of the Middle Ages*. Thus we must assume that there was culture in those times, a culture still worth studying today.

To understand a culture, we must have something in common with it. And here our historical consciousness is put severely to the test, for are the centuries not steadily growing apart? And if we already have so much difficulty evaluating the period, say, between the two world wars, how much more difficult it must be to gain a proper insight into a distant millennium!

Medieval culture spans a thousand years—another obstacle! Can we deal with an age in an hour? Shall I speak about just one century then, a not uncommon approach? But which? The twelfth and thirteenth, the centuries of the great transitions? But then, the face of civilization changed earlier, in the eleventh century, when under the influence of the conflict *sacerdotium et imperium*—better known as the investiture controversy—the realms of the sacred and profane parted company. Or shall we select a particular character from these ten centuries and say, "He that has beheld this figure has looked upon *the* medieval person"? That has been tried repeatedly, and even recently, only to stir up protests more strident than usual in the scholarly world.

Let us draw one important lesson from all this. More than one hundred and fifty years of medieval studies have taught us that these "dark ages" were possessed of a strong dynamic. There was a wealth of ideas, currents, phenomena, as well as a multiplicity of contrasts. This makes it impossible to characterize the entire age in terms of one particular period, phenomenon or person. Perhaps I should add that the diversity and dynamism of a culture *can* be indications of its vitality—provided the fruit exhibits the soundness of the root, though there be some rust spots on the leaves.

One thing, at least, is imbedded deep in medieval culture from the outset. It is the problem of how man is to relate to what lies above or beyond this world. What has this world to do with the divine reality? This theme accompanied medieval man throughout the many centuries of his existence. He lived in this relation without always being consciously aware of its what and its how. Yet he felt so much at home in it that modern students of the period have often exclaimed without hesitation: *How theocentric were those times!*

I would dispute that last point. In the many centuries in which culture was granted him, medieval man undoubtedly had a lively sense of God's activity, but he often altered that into a consciousness of walking in proximity to *the divine*. And that is something quite different. Precisely because the divine, the sacred, pressed upon him so cloyingly—after he had framed it himself—his devotion to God and expectations of God weakened. Thus it would be more accurate, it seems to me, to characterize the Middle Ages not as theocentric but as a period in which people were *concerned with the transcendent*.

What did that mean for medieval culture?

At the beginning of the Middle Ages a phenomenon appeared that we can witness even today among nations that adopt Christianity. They generally do not restrict themselves to a bare acceptance of the Christian faith but perceive from the outset that the new religion cannot leave unaltered the relations in which they have hitherto lived. Whether that stems from the fact that the old religion, too, had an absolute character or from the fact that people apprehend at once something of the all-embracing nature of Christianity, we shall leave undecided here.

What interests us much more is the question of the form and substance of that desire and its realization. Michael Seidlmayer observes about medieval civilization that the postulate of making the world as such Christian—of a "Christian culture"—is a creation of the *Early* Middle Ages.[4]

The reserve that Christian Antiquity showed towards the postulate of a Christian culture was unknown to medieval man. He embraced the Christian revelation—it took him centuries to do so—but at the same time he held on to the culture around him: Germanic, Celtic, or Romance; and he reached back to classical culture as well.

By relinquishing none of these, medieval man in his youthful vitality made things extremely difficult for himself. In his cultural ambition he aimed at the absolute. He almost had it with him on earth. And when he thought he had disclosed and captured it, it escaped him, for it was not of this earth.

Yet the postulate survived: to bring all the aspects of life and every phenomenon of human existence *directly* into relation to transcendence: all is nourished by that relation and all returns to it again.

Now, two things must be kept in view. Early medieval people did not find themselves in a cultureless, empty world in which one had only to announce the program of a Christian culture. They were bound by countless ties to a non-Christian environment.

Nor was that the only thing. The young tribes that streamed into the established world of classical culture may not have lacked culture, but they had very little in the way of cultural goods. Yet they did not have very far to go to find them: they availed themselves—sometimes immoderately, sometimes mindlessly—of classical culture.

Thus was set the main problem that would confront the Middle Ages. Would it be possible to establish an inner bond between the enveloping culture—Celtic, Germanic, Romance, the culture of the classical world—and the Gospel?

Medieval man pursued this goal with all his might. In so doing, however, did he not take on too much? Remember, he was not just out to correct what was there, or to put a Christian veneer on it. Even less was he bent on pruning away heathen malgrowths. No, he had something very positive in mind: to form a Christian culture drawing directly on the transcendent.

I can already hear your objection: Did the Middle Ages not excel precisely in allowing heathen elements to survive in Christian dress?

We can enhance that objection with a telling example. The "Christian Middle Ages" were not content with an emperor who protected the church, or even with one who saw it as his task to help define dogma. No, they anointed the sovereign for his "worldly" role with holy oil and consecrated him with a consecration corresponding to a bishop's even in the details. They removed all boundary markers between the "temporal" and the "spiritual" by proclaiming the

---

[4] Seidlmayer, *Das Mittelalter. Umrisse und Ergebnisse des Zeitalters* (1949), 23–42, 47.

emperor "Vicar of Christ," "Image of God," "Type of our Savior," "King and Priest."

To their own mind, medieval people were striking out for the radically Christian. In reality, they continued to uphold many non-Christian ideas. So I ask, in attempting to assimilate classical culture into their surrounding culture in terms what is Christian and transcendental, did they not place themselves before irresolvable tensions, robbing them of light and joy? Certainly the synthesis they sought was never successful.

The main bearers of medieval culture were Germanic and Romance peoples. After the fall of the Roman Empire, which entailed the loss of the crystallization point for classical culture, Germanic tribes settled in the wide reaches of the West. To them, in association with other peoples, fell the task of being new crystallization points—a task for which they were by no means equipped.

One could compare Western European culture following the centuries of the barbarian migrations to a tree in winter. The most striking thing about such a tree and its surroundings is the bareness. Such a tree, anthropomorphically speaking, barely subsists. It has withdrawn into itself, into its inner core, bereft of every adornment. And yet, that bare tree in that winter landscape has vital force—as yet invisible.

Western culture was already in winter condition when the ancient world —for whatever reason—collapsed, and the Germanic world soon sank away into a veritable barbarization of life marked by ceaseless strife and bloodshed.

The nadir was reached around A.D. 740. Then came the reversal, ushered in by a Frankish mayor of the palace who inquired of the pope who should have the power, he who was king in name or he who possessed the real power? The pope's reply, that he who possessed the power should be king, cleared the way for the Carolingians to set Europe's political house in order.

A sturdy political system can be erected in a number of years, but to build a culture from the ground up requires centuries, unless people are not too proud to seek and accept help elsewhere. That is what the Carolingians did. The memory of classical civilization had never been entirely lost even in the days of the barbarians. It is worthy of mention, for example, that after A.D. 750 the type of architecture long in vogue was rejected in favor of a revival, at St. Denis, of the Early Christian romanesque basilica.

Yet it was not only in architecture that Antiquity and the Early Christian world provided the model. The past was revived in many fields. Nor was the resort to Classical Antiquity unique to the early medieval culture of the Carolingians. Medieval man faced the necessity of shifting his cultural plane time and again, and he indeed possessed the vitality to develop culture. But he did not have the capacity to give form and substance to it, all on his own, in a short space of time. To his mind, that was also not necessary: the past had modeled what he now merely had to recall to life.

Here we have a characteristic phenomenon of the Middle Ages, one that we are accustomed to referring to as a renaissance, restoration, renewal, etc. Initially, modern historical science restricted the concept of renaissance to what we call *the* Renaissance, that is, to the last two hundred years of the Middle Ages and the beginning of Modern Times. Gradually, however, the concept was applied to every important medieval movement for renewal. Thus one speaks of the Carolingian Renaissance of the eighth and ninth centuries, and of the tenth-century Renaissance, and of the Renaissance of the twelfth and thirteenth centuries. Note well, not one of these revivals occurred without the powerful influence of the ancient world.

One other thing. Bear in mind that while there was something obvious and natural in that appeal to classical culture, it was at the same time rather astonishing. To medieval people the ancients were pitiable pagans, and yet they drew upon their culture.

Ultimately, though—and the people of the Middle Ages were probably scarcely aware of it themselves—it was not the old culture as such that mattered, for that was not in itself their standard and model. What they wanted to return to was the divine world; and that, to them, was not just something in heaven but something realized again and again on earth: in the Old Testament dispensation, in the Roman Empire, and . . . also in the renewal of their own time. They saw classical culture not as a lofty, useful culture that happened to be at hand, but as one in which the divine model had appeared in a special sense.

To the medieval mind a renaissance did not mean the creation of something novel; it did not mean revolutionary reversal. On the contrary, it meant a return to normative olden times and a revival from decline and decay. Reduced to a formula: decline meant a falling away from the old, model age, and restoration consisted in calling this model back to life again.

The Germanic peoples—to mention the second component—were not merely bearers of medieval culture. They contributed numerous cultural elements of their own, including their many conceptions of life and religion. Yet these are often so overlaid by classical and Christian influences that they can be brought to light only by long and painstaking scholarly research.

But now the third component, Christianity. We shall have to dispense with the usual picture of a unified medieval ecclesiastical culture. It is an honest interpretation, and it is even understandable that people should have adopted it. Nevertheless, it misjudges the true character of medieval civilization. That medieval civilization was ecclesiastical is only partly true, and that it was a unified culture I would contest. The medieval world never succeeded in bringing *Romanitas*, *Germanitas* and *Christianitas* into authentic union.

Medieval culture developed from renaissance to renaissance, from renewal to renewal, during which the *Romanitas* invariably played a primary role. As often as the promise of a renaissance or renewal was fulfilled, however, a reaction set in. Immediately following the death of Charlemagne there was a distinctly "puritan" reaction, led by Benedict of Aniane († 821), against the cultural optimism and "worldly mind" of the Carolingian Renaissance. I cannot resist quoting several statements that put the situation in a stark light. The young Walafrid Strabo († 849) complains some years later in the renowned, culturally outstanding monastery of Reichenau: "Those who are in charge here do not like to see me making verses; all studies are slipping, and the light of wisdom is unloved and becoming scarce." No less to the point is the assessment of Smaragdus of Saint-Mihiel († c. 830): "There are soldiers of the world and soldiers of Christ—the former deliver themselves to eternal torment; the others gain eternal life." And in the twelfth and thirteenth centuries, when classical culture had again contributed to a new blossoming of worldly culture, resistance appeared in the form of a revival of the ascetic ideal.

I have cited only two specific reactions, but cultural history of the period A.D. 500–1500 has many more to offer. They confront us with the question how to account for them. What is their source? Why was there such chronic resistance to worldly culture, to the reception of classical elements, when the medieval world experienced such a great need of them? Was it perhaps because the worldly attitude no longer recognized any limits? To say that of the Carolingian Renaissance would be far-fetched; people objected, says Strabo, even to his writing poetry.

No, the problem lies deeper. I would prefer to formulate it differently, taking just one aspect, albeit one that contains the entire problem. The medieval West never came to terms with the ancient world. It was attracted to it since unable to do without it, yet repeatedly repelled by it. Seidlmayer compares the situation to an unhappy romance: ever and again, infatuation, followed as often by disappointment and repulsion.[5]

But with that I have only shifted the question, not answered it. What gave rise to the medieval world's restlessness, and why did it always end up rejecting Antiquity? However powerful its influence may have been in the Middle Ages, to medieval man Antiquity always remained an alien element, a *Fremdkörper*; it pressed in from the outside. A real synthesis was never achieved.

Was that because the Germanic mind could not tolerate the Romance mind? Perhaps, but there is no evidence for that. In any event, we must be careful not to underestimate the importance of the failure of this synthesis, a synthesis that is talked about so facilely. The Middle Ages acquired their distinctive character precisely from both the mutual attraction and repulsion of Antiquity and Christianity. From the outset the Middle Ages suffered from a deep-seated ambivalence unknown to non-Christian cultures.

Wherein lay that element of irreconcilability? To put it briefly, medieval man wanted to serve two masters. As a Christian traveling the *jenseitige*,

---

[5] Ibid., 31.

other-worldly road, he wanted to serve the transcendent Lord; as a person of culture here below, on the *diesseitige* road, he wanted to serve that which is of this world.

Many historians maintain there was nothing else he could do. After all, he had to live in social relations and build his life on a particular material culture. These could not be had along the transcendental route.

Furthermore—it will be objected—medieval man never experienced the culture of this world in detachment from the transcendent.

I would not contest that, but at the same time I maintain that the synthesis between classical culture and Christianity, between transcendence and profane culture, proved to be impossible in the Middle Ages. The entire period was marked by hostility to culture, disdain for the human body, depreciation of marriage—not just among the sects, but often by the most prominent representatives of the age.

That the Middle Ages remained profoundly ambivalent in their appreciation of culture is attributable at bottom to the period's perceptions of culture and transcendence alike. There is an antinomy involved here that is a feature of *medieval* Christianity and not of Christianity as such.

Certainly, medieval people saw all things in connection with the transcendent. However, that need not have issued in disparagement of the human body and of culture. And yet it did, because for medieval people, transcendence or living unto God was predominantly spiritualistic and ascetic in nature. It will be said, "Granted, this is the way the sects looked at it; this is the way the hermits and monks felt about life." But that restriction is by no means valid. To forsake the world with one's whole heart was the fulfillment of life for the average medieval person just as much as it was for the religious idealist.

Meanwhile, the average person knew that to renounce the world was not possible for him—or, at least, not for everyone. Condemned as he was to remain in the world, he fixed his gaze on the ascetic saint who had detached himself from the world on his behalf, as it were. Such saintliness was beyond his capacity, yet he could not get along without it. There might be saints in marriage and saints among kings, but they could not inspire him in anything approaching the measure of the ascetic saints, for they alone had forsaken the world.

Now we are able to comprehend what seems at first incomprehensible to us. Even the most wretched miscreant—and that would certainly include some of the Merovingian kings—revered only the person who fulfilled the Christian ideal of asceticism and who in doing so was his substitute.

However much the status of being pilgrims in the world may have been *the* medieval ideal, even medieval people could not deny that the human body is a reality, that the passions are unavoidable, economic requirements inescapable, and classical culture indispensable. This is precisely what produced the fascinating epic of medieval history. The ascetic ideal was held high, but people had to get along with their body, their passions, their world of culture—and what a body, and what a culture: one seething with youthful vitality and creative energy!

One common interpretation is that the church gathered all that worldly life into itself, just as Noah took the animals into the ark, and that it proceeded to focus that life on a transcendent goal—not the pure ascetic ideal now, but the salvation of souls. Thus all aspects of worldly life were enlisted in the service of other-worldly salvation. Presumably, the church was successful in that endeavor until the close of the Middle Ages, when art, science, politics, etc., began to disengage themselves from the embrace of the church.

That the former was the church's intention we shall not dispute, but that it succeeded during the Middle Ages in focusing culture on other-worldly objectives is another matter. From the outset there was a yearning, sometimes fervent and at other times dormant, to recognize so-called profane life and culture in their own right, albeit within the transcendent order.

Now, this is eminently understandable, for the idea of fleeing the world entailed nothing less than an outrage upon human life. Life broke through the restraints again and again. And these ruptures were not just isolated cases, rare occurrences of derailment. No, breaking with the ascetic and ecclesiastical ideal constitutes an essential feature in the cultural picture of the Middle Ages. Let me illustrate that with a few randomly selected concrete instances.

1. For the Germanic peoples, or at least for their elites, warfare and battle were an essential element of life. Medieval men went on fighting even though they sensed their actions were inconsistent with Christian morality. Still, the problem was resolved in a process of centuries. They dressed war up in the raiments of spiritual warfare. And thus were born the wars of extermination fought in the name of Christ against the heathens and heretics of this world.

2. An extremely dangerous situation was created by the ascetic ideal of world-flight and disdain for the body. Not everyone could subdue the natural passions, so that task was delegated to the ascetic, whose vocation it was to do so. Meanwhile, the ordinary person was left without any genuinely positive value to place upon the passions and so was left helpless before them. He could hate vehemently and be infinitely cruel to his enemies. The Middle Ages were not filled solely with cultural creations and religious idealism. What breach of faith was not known to the Middle Ages! What social hardness there was! What ingenuity in torture! Torture as a public festival to which even women came as spectators! What superstition! And were the Middle Ages not rampant in free love, as if, incomprehensibly, it was the most natural thing in the world? Nor was this evil restricted to some forgotten corner; it was found on the high road: the well-known medievalist Finke has determined that in the leading circles of the Middle Ages, the sanctity and permanence of the marriage bond were largely fictitious.[6]

---

[6] H. Finke, *Die Frau im Mittelalter* (1913), 62; as quoted in Seidlmayer, op. cit., 56.

3. Yet this was not the only peril. There was another, more humane, humanistic possibility. Throughout the Middle Ages one can detect a turn toward the things of polite society. One finds it in the culture of the Carolingian court, in the humanism of the Late Middle Ages. One finds it no less in the heyday of chivalry during the twelfth and thirteenth centuries, when from southern France through central and northern France and into Germany a fresh attitude toward life emerged, largely fixed upon this world and driven by an impulse to improve, decorate and refine the home, clothes, food, drink, forms of social contact (music, dance, games, etc.). In short, there was an appetite for worldly things, for things that had value also in their own right. No wonder the ascetics polemicized vehemently against the culture of chivalry.

Again, the Late Middle Ages in particular were exceptionally cruel centuries. They saw the rise of the Inquisition, and long before Machiavelli's day politics paid homage to the pursuit of personal advantage. Very little remained of "peace and justice" as the ideal of "Christian politics." Rather, great advances were made in the brutalities of war, especially in the form of a scorched earth policy for the helpless countryside. Indeed, all these evils, and more, belong to the normal pattern of events in the Late Middle Ages. Make no mistake, however. While these things were especially true of the Late Middle Ages, the darkness was only a little less deep in the centuries preceding. When we hear of the "Dark Ages," then, much of it is true.

On the other hand, medieval culture has always fascinated people, and many have attributed the decline of the West to a departure from the medieval *ordo*. On this view, the catastrophic development commenced with the disruption of the medieval worldview. By putting the matter in such terms people do indeed create a picture of the Middle Ages, but one that is badly oversimplified and lacking in certain essential features. Throughout the entire period the Augustinian ideal of *pax et justitia* continued to guide people, it is true, yet wars went on without interruption. The Middle Ages may be inconceivable without the power of the *ordo* idea, yet that did not prevent countless excesses of libertinism: I have mentioned free love, but the attachment to house and home seems to have been so tenuous for many that they simply left everything to wander through the land in bands.

Despite all this, Pernoud concludes that medieval culture knew a confidence in life and a joy in living that have no equal in any other culture. In philosophy, architecture, life-style, in everything, she writes, there was an exultant delight in existence, an energy that was nothing but positive.[7] This idyllic scene would be true to life, if the dark backdrop had not been omitted.

The Middle Ages failed. This in itself is not exceptional, since every historical period falls short. The Middle Ages failed because they had to fail. They aspired to a goal that can only be attained in heaven. In the cloisters of Cluny the monks sang praises to God like the redeemed in heaven, and in an

---

[7] Pernoud, *The Glory of the Medieval World*, 258f.

anticipatory way they realized eschatological peace by giving up all possessions, the source of all discontent.

The failure of the Middle Ages, however, was fraught with serious consequences. Medieval people sought above all else the absorption of worldly things into the transcendent. They were unsuccessful in many respects, but nowhere did they have as little success as in the economic and social areas. Towns were established, flourishing economic centers, with a church in the center and saints as guardian patrons of the guilds—and yet, that did not preserve the inner connection of religion to economic life.

What was the everyday reality? There was a Christian, transcendent superstructure, but it was suspended in space, without any inner connection to real, concrete economic life, which went its own way according to its own norms.

The burghers of these medieval towns were pious, even exceptionally pious. They lived in a multiplicity of religious forms. But all this was no longer attuned to the requirements of life. A unified ecclesiastical culture was never achieved in the economic field; from the outset, there was a duality. Whatever there was of religion in economic life consisted largely of an external framework.

But the divergence between religion and worldly life is not the only thing the Middle Ages have bequeathed us.

In the Gothic, a form of life is disclosed that was no less determinative for the centuries to come, down to the present day. In medieval culture, as in so many other cultures, houses were regarded as *dwelling places of God*. Only, the Middle Ages concentrated this idea upon the church edifice. The most exalted expressions of it were the Romanesque and Gothic cathedrals.

The Gothic churches point symbolically towards a supraterrestrial reality, for—despite their rational construction—the arches, the many windows, the light, the altars, the images, the polyphonic music, etc., are all designed to apprehend supraterrestrial reality, which is ungraspable as such, and to represent it to the senses and bring it into proximity upon this earth. Because worldly components faded into the background or were "enveloped as by the heavenly regions," the world as experienced by the faithful inside Gothic edifices was a transfigured, heavenly world.

Yet the Gothic did not succeed in conjuring up heaven by material, sensible means; nor did it succeed any better in enveloping naked terrestrial reality in celestial light. On the contrary, its bold identification of this world with a perfect world distracted people's attention away from the latter and focused it on the earthly paradise. In the Gothic, consequently, an authentic secularization of Christian values occurred. That is, these values were so fascinating in their earthly forms that their transcendent origin in heaven came gradually to be neglected. At the same time, in the medieval cathedral the *divine* is so embodied in the outward sacramental *sign* that it can be fully experienced there, and even taken hold of and borne away: its numerous altars, images, windows, spaces, niches, etc., each in its own way, bring one into direct contact with the divine.

Perhaps by now you will have some objections to my way of dealing with the Middle Ages. So many gloomy aspects have been mentioned that I shall perforce have to characterize the period as the Dark Ages after all, shall I not? We have heard of little else besides sins, unbridled passions, inner ambivalence, failure of the attempt at a cultural synthesis, and so on. But what of the bright side, you will say! Surely the culture of chivalry, although it lowered people's sights, was a unique phenomenon in world history; who would want to deny its greatness? Moreover, was not asceticism itself a cultural factor of the first order? In those periods in which cultural life declined—and there were many—was it not precisely the centers of asceticism that rescued culture from extinction and preserved it till the time arrived when the task could be left to other, worldly institutions? Did not the monasteries engage in cultural life even at the risk of forgetting the ascetic ideal? Is it not thanks to them that much of the classical heritage was preserved? And does the credit for land reclamation, as important then as now, not belong to the monastic orders? Were the foundations of much that we often take pride in, as being in contrast with those dark ages, not laid in that very period, so that all we had to do was build upon them? Did they not, in a word, bequeath to us a culture that still enriches our lives today: their chronicles with their world-historical perspective, their philosophy of history imbued with real human concern for suffering and transitoriness, their masterful satire, their priceless *evangelaria* and other illuminated manuscripts, their now classic Christian lyrics? And how little I have mentioned! Why, just in the last two years two works have appeared on the Middle Ages as the Age of Light. How clearly the light must have shined at that time. Surely the period must have been the Age of the Cathedral (what a misnomer to label it with the pejorative epithet *Gothic*!)—of the cathedral where light entered in a hundred ways, there to take possession of life?

For all that, we shall maintain our characterization of the Middle Ages as a period of profound ambivalence or fundamental dichotomy: on the one hand, being for God; on the other, being for this world; at one and the same time, drawing upon classical and Germanic conceptions, and living by the Gospel.

7/ CULTURE AND SALVATION

TO KNOW OR UNDERSTAND one's times it is of great importance to know what sort of things and problems our contemporaries find engaging. There are subjects that almost everyone suddenly has something to say about; for a while they hold everybody's attention, but then they are dropped again, and if one asks this person or that why no one takes an interest in it anymore he is likely to be told, "Oh, it's not so important after all," or "You can't resolve it anyway, we can make better use of our time." There is a note of fatigue in these remarks, but also of doubt concerning the value and utility of certain subjects.

There are questions, however, that do *not* disappear from discussion and that have even persisted for centuries. It is one of those questions that I would like to consider with you[1] tonight: Is there an intrinsic relation between *culture* and *heil* (salvation)? The experts know instantly what must follow: Is there a Christian culture, or what should a Christian's attitude be toward culture? Is it permissible to see an intimate connection between Christ and culture? What should a Christian think of progress in civilization? And—perhaps the most difficult question—does such progress (if it exists) have its origin in Christ?

These are questions that have been the subject of lively debate in recent decades, not least since the Second World War. The debate is not only lively; it is also surprising. Imagine that someone highly knowledgeable of the religious and cultural currents of the nineteenth and twentieth centuries took leave of Europe to go to a deserted island in 1935 or 1936, stayed there without any means of communicating with the rest of the world, and then ended his isolation just this year [1959] to find out what is stirring in the world of the theologians. Astonished, he would ask himself how it is possible that in such a relatively short time such profound changes have taken place in the thought of so many. The last one hundred years saw severe criticism of those who drew a close relation between Christ and culture and who have ventured to speak of a Christian culture. But today? To be sure, there are those who continue to take a strong stand against the possibility of a Christian culture, but this is not the group that attracts attention at the present stage of the debate: listening carefully, one finds little that is new in the objections being leveled against the idea of a Christian culture. A general enthusiasm has been aroused for renewed reflection on the positive implications of culture and history, in particular for the idea that the meaning of both can be approached or discovered only in terms of the passion and resurrection of Christ. We encounter this enthusiasm, however, not

---

[1] [This speech was given at the 35th Anniversary celebration of the student oratorical society A.G.O.R.A., of which Meyer Smit was an alumnus; Free University, 10 Nov. 1959.]

in the first place amongst those who have felt called to Christian cultural work but amongst those who previously, indeed who until very recently, emphasized almost exclusively the infinite qualitative difference between God and this world and who understood the lordship of Christ in an eschatological or individual-spiritual sense. The change in the climate of opinion is so thorough-going that a psychological explanation—for example, that people are hungry to escape the atmosphere of crisis and to take up life once again on the basis of positive values —must be considered inadequate.

Much of our surprise vanishes, however, when we examine developments in theology between 1920 and today more closely. Certain elements in the theological currents of this period go far to explain the unexpected shift from negative to positive attitudes regarding Christianity and culture. For a historian —and not only for him—the interesting question now becomes: Exactly why have developments, so surprising from a distance, taken this positive direction and why there is not a persevering in the negative attitude? A historian may have a predilection for such questions, resolve them he cannot; at most he can cast some light on them. He should be aware that a purely historical method, however excellent it may be, is inadequate for solving a problem like the one just described.

The matter that engages us this hour is not the framing of a historical problem but rather the relation between Culture and Salvation. But then, as it turns out, we cannot do without history. For history is indispensable to fathoming this relation, if only because of the fact that since the days of Jesus and the Apostles there has never been a period in which Christendom has not wrestled with the question of Christian culture. Simple wisdom teaches us to have recourse to history, to see how people in Christian circles have thought about culture. Yet this is not the only thing we can learn from history. History teaches us that we can never avoid the cultural question and that we shall always be confronted by the relation of salvation to culture: man lives permanently in this relation, consciously or not and whether he likes it or not. The main question is, *How* does he live in it?

We can understand this from Scripture. In the very first chapter of the Bible God himself gave the cultural mandate, and Christ alluded to it in the Sermon on the Mount when he explained the fundamental structure of the Kingdom. In general, the Scriptures are filled with statements pertinent to culture. They speak about it in such a natural way—in different terms than we use, but no less clearly for that—that it generally does not stand out. It may sound strange when I say that in the closing passage of Matt. 6 Jesus deals with the problem of culture in all its depth. Since receiving the cultural mandate, man has never ceased to live in culture; he cannot escape the mandate. But in his cultural labors it has been his experience time after time that culture can be to his salvation or to his grief. To mention a few examples: Moses forsook the treasures of Egypt (Heb. 11:26); food and clothing, says Jesus, are things the Gentiles seek (Matt. 6:32);

God's people are told that *"the ships of Tarshish shall be the first to bring your sons from far; they shall bring their gold and silver with them, to honor the name of the Lord, your God "* (Isa. 60:9).

Before looking more closely at the relation between culture and salvation, we should add a note here to avoid some misunderstandings. Often a treatise on the problem of culture commences with an explanation of what we are to understand by the concept of culture, including how it differs from civilization, history, and so forth. We shall not do so since that would wither the problem at the outset. Nor shall we start by defining the concept salvation (*heil*). I use both terms in a pre-theoretical sense, according to their meaning in everyday usage. Our intention in leaving the concepts open is not only to avoid a premature restriction of our discussion but also to be reminded from the outset that the intrinsic relation that salvation has to culture exists also between—to mention some examples—salvation and sexuality, salvation and history, and so on. In many instances where I use the word culture you may substitute the terms history, sexuality, etc., and sometimes I shall proceed to do so myself. That the problem can be transferred every time is not due to culture, history, etc., as such, but to salvation, which remains essentially the same in all relations whatsoever.

The ascetic ideal

I started by observing that the problem of culture is of lively interest in Christian circles nowadays and that there is a tendency to appreciate culture as something positive . . . in Christ, and therefore (it goes without saying) with an appeal to Scripture. There have also been times, however—and they are still continuing—in which people were apprehensive of culture, fearing too great a fascination for this world and a slackening in love for God. And Scripture provides support for such fears. In broad historical perspective, world acceptance and world renunciation again and again occur side by side, most often as reactions to each other: a period of cultural optimism is not infrequently followed by another in which world and Christian belief are kept far apart. This development makes us think of an unhappy love affair. Sometimes the Christian is drawn to culture—precisely because of his being a Christian. At other times, he tries to keep it at arm's length—again because he is a Christian. This game has been going on for centuries already. This image—which is happily somewhat defective, as we shall see—is helpful also because we believe the same problem is encountered in the relation sexuality-salvation as in the relation culture-salvation (I do not use the word sexuality in the current sense but in the sense of the male-female relationship).

Let us examine this unhappy love affair a bit more closely. What comes to mind immediately are monachism, eremitism, and asceticism. Since the early Christian era, their relation to culture has been strained; and yet monasteries were, and are, centers of culture as well. We cannot really imagine what might have become of Western European civilization if in the Early Middle Ages, a time of profound cultural decline, there had been no monasteries into which the ancient civilization could withdraw, as it were. Is the estrangement of culture and cloister, then, based on a misunderstanding? By way of introducing the answer to that question, let me recall an anecdote: Alcuin was a very important figure in the cultural reformation under Charlemagne, and to this end he kept to a cloister, but without practicing the ascetic life. He preferred to stay in the monastery even when his lord summoned him to follow in his retinue—not because he wished to be undisturbed in the experience of God's presence, but because he desired to pursue his studies without hindrance.

This story brings us naturally to the question of what is essential or, if you will, primary in asceticism. Much has been written on the subject in recent times. Does its essence lie in its *merit*, perhaps, both for those who practice asceticism as well as for those who did not have the opportunity to withdraw from normal life? Undoubtedly, the merits earned by ascetic life and thought played an important role: how often, for example, do we not detect in medieval sources a certain reassurance in the realization that the ascetic life of the privileged benefits those who have to be satisfied with a life in the world. Nevertheless, when we consult ascetic literature, especially from periods in which the practice of asceticism reached a peak, it becomes abundantly clear that the motives of merit, rigorous self-discipline, imitation of the sufferings of Christ were indeed of very great importance yet as a rule played only a subordinate role. The supreme motivating force behind asceticism is *love of God*.

Here we touch the core problem regarding the relation between culture and salvation. Someone unfamiliar with the history of asceticism may find it odd to learn that precisely love of God should have brought about strained relations with respect to culture. This tension between the Great Commandment and the world—in which culture is an integrating element—has left its traces in many legends and stories, and not only in those of opponents of asceticism. Let me relate one such story, as we find it in Albert Camus: Saint Demetrius was to meet God in the steppe, but as he hastened towards the appointed place he met a farmer whose wagon was stuck in the mud. The wagon was heavy and the mud deep, but after an hour the battle was won and Demetrius could hurry on to the place where God awaited him. But when he arrived, God was no longer there.[2] Stories of this nature have come down to us from every age. Simple and interesting, they contain an element of profound tragedy. People try to love God above all, and to serve him without reservation; but when they do so, things go wrong on earth: they neglect love of neighbor.

Not unintentionally, I will add a story from a non-Christian religion that reveals a similar tension in the practice of asceticism. Indra, in the Indian religion, retires to the mountains for an exceptionally demanding ascetic exercise because of the vanity of this world. However, he is unable to complete it because

---

[2] Albert Camus, *Les justes, Acte IV*, 123f; cf. G. Didier, "Eschatologie et engagement chrétien" [Eschatology and Christian engagement], *Nouvelle revue théol.* 75 (1953): 1ff.

to do so would endanger the world's *equilibrium*—for has Indra not had to abandon his wife and neglect his worldly duties?

Alternatively, one can look at the tension entailed in asceticism and observe that asceticism involves—the history of Western culture bears this out—a healing element, not only for the ascetic himself but also for his environment and the culture that is host to his cell. Now we certainly do not want to deny the tremendous influence that the practice of asceticism has had on culture; but to accentuate this aspect is to forget the tension in which the ascetic himself lived and the inner conflict that besets a culture the moment asceticism is required and practiced in order to partake fully of the love of God.

Is this tension, this inner conflict, not inherent in an integral Christian approach to life, and is distance with respect to the world and culture therefore not enjoined upon the Christian—if he would save his life? This is not just a question for a historian who would like to know precisely how things used to be; it is also a burning issue in a time when a Christian cultural optimism is gaining in influence. Here, historical and current problems converge. Present-day historians have a penchant for strongly emphasizing the differences between medieval and modern man, but all at once these two turn out to stand very close together in the face of the great problems of life. It is remarkable that just in our time, when many Christians are being carried away without resistance or reservations in the maelstrom of cultural development, numerous authors are presenting asceticism as a way to rescue the freedom of the Christian man. It is a curious thing that culture, which surely is not evil in itself, can begin to imperil Christian freedom. Apparently there is an inner connection between Christian freedom and being free from the world. When the ascetic seeks freedom in this dual sense and relates it directly to love of God, then he touches upon a commandment that is repeated over and over again in the Bible, too.

It is not entirely accurate to speak of *the* ascetic, for there is a rich variety of ascetic attitudes towards life. Some ascetics have carried their world renunciation to the verge of manicheism. We cannot here go into all the varieties of asceticism and monachism and must necessarily generalize; but it is fair to say that precisely the rigorous ascetic firmly believes God created all things good yet finds himself called to warn against this world, even to forsake it, because love of God renders this inevitable. And so these two come to oppose each other: love of God demands estrangement from the world, and love of God requires going out into the world, turning to the world in love.

To keep the question in its pure form, I want to make two comments. First, my exposition so far must not be countered with the observation that in historical reality this opposition has not been so serious after all. Take the order of Cluny. How strict were the rules of Bishop Odo (926–942)! Entirely in line with Pope Gregory the Great, he regarded monasticism as a "transcending of this world" (the *extra mundum* or "other-worldly" ideal). Yet, how offended Christians were to be at the turn of the eleventh to the twelfth century by the beauty and luxury that reigned in Cluny! Is it not clear from this example that somehow people always find a way from cloister and cell back to the world? The history of the order of Citeaux is even more telling in this regard. The order was founded to follow strictly the original Rule of St. Benedict, which meant absolute withdrawal, prayer, charity and penance. Yet it is precisely this strict order which, even before rigorous asceticism flagged and luxury set in, accomplished so much for the unfolding of medieval culture—for example in the reclamation of wasteland, improvements in the methods of agriculture, and so forth. Thus history seems to want to impress upon us that the tension at issue is not so serious after all. And indeed, to all appearances, that may be so. Yet the ascetic, the Christian mind, found it hard to come to terms with it. A single example may suffice. Gregory I, a pope who meant so much for the ascetic ideal of the Middle Ages, saw himself pulled to and fro between his calling in ecclesiastical affairs and the ascetic ideal of leaving this present world in order to enter already into the kingdom of eternal life.

Not only did the *connection* that was yet found along many avenues between world renunciation and world ministry have important historical consequences; no less did the *tension* which the ascetic never resolved between heavenly call and cultural calling put a permanent stamp on Western culture. The Middle Ages bequeathed asceticism as an irrepressible challenge not just to the Reformation but also to Humanism. I hope to say more about this.

My second comment relates to the first. One hears it said fairly often that the ascetic may think he can escape to some place far removed from the world but that the world pursues him right into his solitary cell; and that he may delude himself into thinking he has renounced culture but that in reality he remains culture-bound since life without it is possible for no one. Take the Cistercians. They built their monasteries far from the inhabited world, taking great care when selecting sites to insure the experience of the monastic ideal. But what do we see? Their buildings exhibit the style of their times: Romanesque—transition from Romanesque to Gothic—Gothic. With that, many regard the problem of asceticism as a dead issue; they simply write it off as an impossibility. To be satisfied with such a result, however, is to miss the heart of asceticism, as will be clear from what follows. I do not deny that asceticism is an impossibility, but what interests us here is the question *why* it is an impossibility. It seems superfluous to pose this question, since it is as transparent as can be. However, I feel it is worth our while to have a look behind this self-evident character of the case, in order to determine why man can never disengage himself from culture. In the interest of fairness to the ascetic—and for a good understanding of my argument —let it be noted once more: in the literature of asceticism it comes out again and again that the ascetic, too, is usually well aware that total world renunciation and an *extra mundum surgere*, a rising out above the world, are not possible, but he likewise knows that the world is not equally perilous for him at all points, or, more correctly, that worldly temptation is concentrated in certain institutions and phenomena, where its effect is multiplied, and that by holding these things at bay he delivers a blow to the world . . . in its perilousness.

But let us return to the basic problem that confronts every form of Christian asceticism. Does complete surrender to love of God not require of the Christian that he abstain from the world? To ensure a sound comprehension of culture and its meaning for salvation, I repeat: the ascetics—exceptions aside—maintained that God created this world good; and yet they believed they had to flee the things of earthly life because they saw in the world an obstacle to love of God and the attainment of perfection. To their mind, this world no longer understands itself as God's creation but as sufficient unto itself and hence tends to forget the love of God. This theme dominates the literature.[3] Thus suffering as such can not be the main point of asceticism (albeit there are many exceptions to this rule, since what was secondary often became the leading idea). The primary purpose of the ascetic life was deliverance from both the world and self. To live as a monk or hermit means to step out of worldly entanglements into the vastness of the love of God. The threads of the ascetic life come together in the *non-use of this world*. The negative—deliverance from the world—does not come first, but the positive: concentration upon God, placing oneself radically and totally at his disposal. Thus the negative is an implicate of the positive, and Christian writers expressed that by identifying love of God and the ascetic life. Theodoret of Cyr († 460) subtitled his history of monks: "History of the Love of God or the Ascetic Life."[4]

The thought suddenly occurs to us: Is the ascetic not "standing on Biblical grounds" here? He adduces numerous texts that often occur to us, too, when we hear the Messianic and apostolic message about forsaking the world. People have invoked the words of Jesus to the rich young ruler, *"If thou wilt be perfect, go and sell that thou hast, and give to the poor, and thou shalt have treasure in heaven: and come and follow me"* (Matt. 19:21). Here we find all the elements of our problem together: perfection—exactly what the world of the ascetics was all about; very well, you can only acquire it when you put the world behind you. But there are many more Scripture passages that one can cite in support of world renunciation: *"For our citizenship is in heaven"* (Phil. 3:20); *"Love not the world, neither the things that are in the world. If any man love the world, the love of the Father is not in him . . ."* (I John 2:15–17); and last but not least: *"Set your affection on things above, not on things on the earth. For ye are dead, and your life is hid with Christ in God"* (Col. 3:2–3).

One can object to all this and say, Yes, but there are other statements in the Bible which attest to the good that still exists in spite of sin, and to the Chris-

---

[3] Cf. Macarius the Great, *Hom.* 24, 1f (Migne, *Patrologia graeca*, 34:661 D).

[4] On this point, see Uta Ranke-Heinemann, "Die Gottesliebe als ein Motiv für die Entstehung des Mönchtums" [Love of God as a motive for the rise of monasticism], *Münchener Theologische Zeitschrift* 8 (1957): 289ff.

tian's calling in this world. Undoubtedly. We would not want to abridge the latter in any way. Yet it would be just as impermissible to empty the quoted passages of their meaning in order to force them into harmony with the rest of the Bible. In all these troublesome passages, so cherished by ascetics and monks, the issue is the meaning of life (perfection, salvation, etc.), namely, God: and to share in that meaning a condition is set that can in no way be deprived of its force: forsake the world and deny yourself. Asceticism (and the Bible as well) seems to place us before a dilemma: either proceed on the basis of the goodness of creation and find our calling in it in keeping with the great cultural mandate proclaimed by God himself, *"Replenish the earth, and subdue it"* (Gen. 1:28); or else give primacy to the mortal peril that is entailed in culture and flee from it accordingly.

The matter becomes considerably clearer when we pursue the ascetic line of thought further, or, to put it differently, when we throw some additional light on a no less essential feature of the ascetic conception of the love of God. It pertains to an aspect that receives considerable attention in current historical literature. I shall mention in this connection only Jean Leclercq's book about the love of learning.[5] According to Leclercq, the aspect in question was a constant in every period that asceticism was practiced. In the ascetic pursuit of the love of God, this world is *transcended* in what tends at the same time to be an eschatological sense. In monastic literature one finds numerous expressions or themes for this, including that of ascension, that of the *vita angelica*, and so forth. These expressions will not make very much of an impression on us at first, but upon closer scrutiny they will be seen to have a very distinctive content that we can best grasp by thinking of the "other-worldly" ideal: it involves a transcending, a stepping out of this world. The danger exists, however, that we can no longer comprehend today what that entailed, since the expression has undergone a great deal of erosion: the monk was dead serious about taking leave of this world. Leclercq states correctly that the entire conception of monastic culture must be judged according to the positive meaning of the *extra mundum*, that is, that the ascetic life is an anticipation of life in heaven, a real beginning of eternal life.[6] Something more is involved here than merely orienting oneself to the great eschatological future; the strictest ascetic knew that the heavenly life cannot be realized in its fullness on earth, but he did regard as possible a form of anticipatory participation, or what German commentators have called a *Vorwegnahme der Ewigkeit*, an anticipation of eternity. And just as the life of eternal blessedness is indescribable, so also must the monk's sojourn in solitude remain beyond the reach of human concepts and words, as an "inhabiting of the heavenly places."[7]

---

[5] Jean Leclercq, *L'Amour des lettres et le désir de Dieu* (1957). [Eng. trans., *The Love of Learning and the Desire for God: A Study of Monastic Culture* (1961).]

[6] Ibid., 67 [Eng. trans., 72].

[7] [Cf. Eph. 1:3, 20; 2:6; 3:10.]

Yet we are able to form some idea of this "anticipation of eternity" if we consider the positive objectives of life in the monastery according to the—oft renewed—Rule of St. Benedict: no marriage, no personal possessions. This all sounds extremely negative, but if we view it in the light of the "anticipation" we learn that in the very "detachment" elements of the heavenly life can be present on this earth. Ascetics diligently studied the Bible on this point, searching for the description of heaven. They read the words of Jesus, *"Ye do err, not knowing the scriptures, nor the power of God. For in the resurrection they neither marry, nor are given in marriage, but are as the angels of God in heaven"* (Matt. 22:29-30). Thus the injunction against marriage was ultimately motivated by anticipatory participation in eternity. This is also true of other monastic do's and don'ts. For the rule of silence, for example, appeal was made to Rev. 8:1, to the great silence during which all creatures stand before the Son of Man. And for the *laus perennis*, the never-ending praise that the monks were to offer God, they followed numerous Scripture passages.

Now, the danger exists that we will not take all this seriously enough and interpret away the real intention in monastic life by thinking of it in terms of some common expression like "a heaven on earth." I know that this is the predominant tendency in interpretation. For the medieval person, however, the *"new Jerusalem, coming down from God out of heaven"* (Rev. 21:2) was a present reality. As we shall see, the category of the "anticipation of eternity" had consequences for the history of culture that can be felt to this day.

Berkhof on Christ the Meaning of History

Let us now put asceticism aside for a few moments. No, I would ask one more question. We heard that even the most rigorous ascetics knew of the goodness of God's creation. But why, then, that detachment from this world, why that habitation of the "heavenly places" already now? We sense that everything turns on the meaning of "goodness." I hope it will become clear that our view of the relation culture-salvation depends on what we are able to discover in the concept of the good. To this end I want to look briefly at Berkhof's *Christ the Meaning of History*, which came out and went through three editions only last year.[8]

How different the world of this writer is from that of the ascetic! Berkhof's reflections pertain to history in the first place, but culture is such an important part of history that we can speak of Berkhof's theology of culture with as much justification as of his theology of history. The central feature of Berkhof's perspective is his approach to the whole of culture and the whole of history as analogies of the cross and resurrection of Christ.[9] Berkhof appears in this way to supply an answer to the age-old problem of how Christ is in a concrete sense the center of world history. That particular question we must leave aside here, in

---

[8] Hendrikus Berkhof, *Christus de zin der geschiedenis* (1958). [Eng. trans., *Christ the Meaning of History* (1966).]

[9] Ibid., chaps. 6 and 7 [Eng. trans., 101ff.].

order to concentrate entirely on the substance and meaning of the analogies. To understand them fully we would have to present an extensive survey of Berkhof's book, but of course we cannot do that here. (For that matter, we would have to do a lot more: we would have to study Berkhof's book against the background of current developments in theology of history, in Barthian and Catholic circles in particular. But let us return to those "analogies.") In Berkhof's conception, too, we encounter the currently popular but fortunately not yet generally accepted notion that history does not begin until Jesus Christ. Given this postulate, the perspective one will have on history is already decided. In the first place, it is immediately clear that Christian missions must excel all other forces in shaping history since "the missionary endeavor leads to freedom." It is equally clear that the freedom which missions confer is not the freedom that existed before Christ and which is proper to people of all times, but a freedom that liberates man from a deified reality: till then, man was bound to the (natural) powers that came to him as gods or that were filled with something godlike; he could not free himself of them: apart from them there was no point of orientation to be found for the construction of a new life. Sexuality, for example, was not a purely earthly datum or event but something understood as human participation in the divine creative life; what was not at stake, then, when man extracted himself from this process!

Now, on this view the decisive thing that came about in Christ was that man acquired freedom with respect to the world around him and for the first time was truly liberated from the cycle of naturalism. For the first time, through Christ's victory, it could now be revealed what is in man, in man as he came forth from the hand of God, as he was before he got caught up in the sacral order of life. In Christ's victory the dynamic of man's "becoming" was set in motion, manifesting itself in man's independence from nature. Against this background, technology and culture appear not as the ripe fruits of the ancient world but as products of the gospel and the kingdom.

Berkhof's interpretation of culture rides on his notion that the new order of life, the powerful manifestation of culture and technology, can also be the portion of one who accepts and experiences them outside their origin, outside Christ. The new salvation, whose riches are not really perceived until they are contrasted with the bygone, nature-bound, sacral order of life, comes to be shared in equally by those who remain far from belief in Christ. The lordship of Christ over this world has become so overpowering that non-Christians are often less attached to the old pattern of life and more devoted to building up culture than Christians are:

Countless people are in the service of Christ's dominion without knowing it or desiring it: scholars, artists, physicians, nurses, educators, social workers, engineers and technical assistants in underdeveloped countries, but also and no less the mothers at home who pass Christ's order of life on to their children. These and many others are in the service of Christ—who has compassion on the groaning creature that waits with earnest expectation for deliverance into liberty (Rom. 8:19–22). . . . Therefore what we call progress in the world also originates in Him, just as the entire concept came into the world only after and through Christianity.

This quotation is found in the chapter on "The Risen Christ in History."[10] For Berkhof, the resurrection power of Christ consists not only in the restraining of the power of sin; it is equally a principle that sets history in motion in good earnest, and shapes it. Our author speaks in this connection of "analogies" to Christ's resurrection, but his conceptions go far beyond simple analogical thinking.

Now, does the foregoing mean an unbounded optimism to Berkhof? No, for as he says, "Whenever freedom is awakened in this fallen world, there will also be a misuse of freedom." The very proclamation of liberty in Christ opens the possibility for man to use his acquired freedom apart from and even against God and thus to behave as an anti-god and the measure of things.[11]

Many of the nuances in Berkhof's interpretation had to be left out of our summary. Most of what I have cited thus far will be familiar to you, for it is in keeping with the theological thought of former ages and our own day. Berkhof's basic theme has appeared repeatedly, in various terminological guises, in the course of time. Thus the idea that salvation can fall to someone's lot independently of his personal attitude of faith is at once old and new; nowadays the phrase often used for it is "objectivity of salvation."

There is another notion in Berkhof that has become fashionable in recent decades; I mean "thinking from the center," that is, from Christ. It is especially with respect to this point that Herman Ridderbos and Jan Bakker have expressed criticism of Berkhof's way of thinking.[12] I shall return to this point later.

The perils of dualism

We have now assembled sufficient material to enable us to pick up the thread of our argument concerning asceticism as it pertains to the relation between culture and salvation. But, someone may caution us, are we now not comparing or assimilating conceptions that are far removed from each other and that betray entirely different universes of thought? At the risk of becoming bogged down in complications we will work our way through some highly divergent views.

We have already observed that the genuine ascetic attitude to life does not imply a manichean denial of the goodness of this world. Perhaps the very heresy of Manicheism saved nascent asceticism from open dualism. Still, the Christian ascetics often promoted so radical a renunciation and non-use of the world that, as the Catholic writer Joseph Ernst Mayer remarks, "a certain quiet propensity

---

[10] Ibid., 160f. [Eng. trans., 171].
[11] Ibid., 85 [Eng. trans., 92].
[12] Herman Ridderbos in *Gereformeerd Weekblad*, 5 Sept.–3 Oct. 1958; J. T. Bakker in *Homiletica* 17.3 (1958): 13–20.

toward dualism breaks through which then congeals, in popular piety, in a positively heretical, manichean form." [13]

It should be noted that Mayer's words pertain not only to the early Christian centuries but also to our own time. To the ascetic mind the goodness of the world and its independence with respect to God—and thus its non-usability—were two poles, albeit the former was often lost in the latter.

Perhaps we ask in great astonishment how this was possible: to have begun with a recognition of the goodness of God's world and yet before long to have ended with the demand to abstain from this world? To my mind this was possible because people grounded this goodness in the creation. At first blush this statement will seem obscure and even unacceptable. Even I, when I do not reason from the beginning, seem to start thinking from the center. Perhaps a few of you feel frustrated at the rather round-about way in which I am trying to extricate us from this tangle. Yet there are too many important things at stake for us to simply cut through the knots.

The ascetic acknowledges that God has made everything good but discovers that because of the Fall the world now seeks itself rather than God; he also discovers that love of the world resides within himself too. Up to this point we are in agreement with him. It is the ascetic's experience that the world proffers itself repeatedly, in all its desirability and fearsome seductiveness, even in his lonely cell and cloister. Yet he also knows divine deliverance, a place of refuge, namely, eschatological space, already present on this earth, in part at least, present as an anticipation of heaven. The ultimate aim of the cloister cell, Leclercq observes, is the translation, the transmission—still on this earth, in this sinful world—of eschatological values.[14]

To continue speaking in spatial categories: as a result of the estrangement of the world from God, access to the space of the good creation silted up, while the center of history, the cross and resurrection of Christ, seemed to afford entrance only to places where a foretaste of heaven and the heavenly future could be enjoyed. But what did the center of history mean for worldly things, for everyday life, for culture, for socio-economic affairs? When we consult the prevailing ideas and the commonplace expressions we can answer without hesitation: the effect of Christ's work at the turning point of the ages was enormous! Did it not, for example, stamp many centuries as the "Christian Middle Ages," as the "Theocratic Age" (700–1300)? I mention this example because it was at this time that asceticism also reached its peak. That being the case, were the blessings of cross and resurrection then perchance *not* restricted to th experiencing of heavenly values in monastic solitude and to the saving of souls? Could it be that instead the blessings flowed out over the full breadth of human life?

---

[13] J. E. Mayer, "Vollkommenheit in dieser Zeit" [Being perfect in our time], in *Seid Vollkommen* [Be ye perfect] (1955), 198.

[14] Leclercq, *L'Amour des lettres*, 59 [cf. Eng. trans., 66: "The monks delighted in using the new language they had created [in literary art] to translate the desire for Heaven . . ."].

Our problem displays so many facets that we are constantly in danger of distorting it. So I would like to say in passing that however critical we may be—as will appear shortly—of the notion of *Christian* Middle Ages, we fully recognize that Christianity had a powerful impact, despite all opposing forces and harmful conceptions, amongst which we include the monastic tendencies. And I do mean "despite," for humanly and unhistorically speaking, much more could have become of the Christianization of Europe if monastic theology had not in many ways restricted the meaning of the cross of Christ. Monasticism simply did not know what to do with this sinful world—it wanted to keep it at bay, even to overcome it by fleeing it, but in so doing it deprived itself of the possibility of orienting that world to Christ. To avoid the reproach that as Reformed Protestants we are poorly equipped to comprehend the true nature of medieval life,[15] I shall cite some Catholic authors, especially the well-known German medievalist Michael Seidlmayer:

The monastic life represents—and this is a second ancient catch-word (present already, for example, in the Rule of St. Benedict)—the *militia Christi*, life as military service for Christ. And to this ideal the layman, too—the Christian who is living in the world—insofar as he strives after true perfection, has to conform, as best (or as poorly as) he can. For all intents and purposes the Christian ethic of the Middle Ages amounted to a "monasticization of the lay world." Apart from the brief flowering of a class ethic in courtly chivalry, the Middle Ages were not able to work out (in any case not beyond a few fragmentary theoretical beginnings) a Christian lay ethic, an ethic that is erected upon an unreserved appreciation for life in the world with its tasks and its values and so is *grounded in itself*—which points up one of the essential respects in which the spiritualized (later) Middle Ages no longer did justice to their Christian mission. The layman remains, so to speak, the Christian "at the left hand of God." [16]

Other writers of recent times strike the same chords as Seidlmayer. Here I shall mention only Father Hendrikx[17] and the previously cited J. E. Mayer:

It seems to me that the Church's attempts so far to give the lay element its own proper form of Christian perfection were never very strong, and less so as history wore on. Granted, attempts to mold worldly Christians and laymen in a Christian fashion were made by Francis of Assisi, Francis of Sales, Ignatius of Loyola, yet it seems to me that today the problem is being addressed much more urgently and in much broader terms than before. For, surely, one cannot shake a certain uncomfortableness when one sees again and again how in the very theories and spiritual teachings of the masters, precisely because of their distance from the world, a certain quiet propensity towards dualism breaks through which then congeals, in popular piety, in a positively heretical,

---

[15] [Allusion to A. H. Bredero, "Een mythe der Middeleeuwen" [A myth of the Middle Ages], *Te Elfder Ure* 4 (1957): 40–55, 78–89.]

[16] M. Seidlmayer, "Religiös-ethische Probleme des italienischen Humanismus" [Ethico-religious problems in Italian humanism], *Germanisch-Romanische Monatsschrift* 39 (1958): 108.

[17] Ephraem Hendrikx, *Lekenspiritualiteit, een probleem in de geschiedenis van de kerk* [Lay spirituality: a problem in the history of the Church] (1959), passim.

manichean form. One cannot ignore that in many popular writings on the spiritual life one detects at least an aversion to vocation and marriage and the world which exceeds the proper measure and which somehow discovers in the essence of things, instead of eschatological relativity, evil itself.... Is Christian perfection a commandment for all Christians or only a counsel for the select, talented, charismatically gifted few? At issue is the opposite of Matt. 5:48 and Matt. 19:21.[18]

Numerous Catholic writers emphasize that the ideal of perfection (dying to the world out of love for God) has not, over the centuries, been restricted to the inhabitants of cell and cloister but has been held up to every Christian: every believer must *detach* himself from the earth in order to *attach* himself to God.[19] This requirement of every Christian appears repeatedly in Christian authors, notably in Chrysostom.[20] But it must be evident to us by now why "the Christian life" in its monastic sense could not be realized in the world of the laity.

That culture and morality in many respects failed to measure up to Christian standards in the "Christian centuries" is not just to be attributed, however, to the fact that the ideal or, if you prefer, the norm, was set too high, that it lay in heaven, really, and was no longer suited to this earth. They had to fail because people overestimated the Christian life. They also foundered, however, because they underestimated it. We are compelled to acknowledge with the ascetic that the deep tendency of the world is to keep us from the love of God, yet we must at the same time contradict him: there is a possibility of escaping the mortal peril of worldly temptation, not in world-flight, but in surrender to Christ. Christ himself set the requirement that man should detach himself from worldly things, in a most radical way at that: "*sell all that thou hast*" (Luke 18:22) and "*whosoever he be of you that forsaketh not all that he hath, he cannot be my disciple*" (Luke 14:33). Yet at the same time Jesus points back to the world: "*I pray not that thou shouldest take them out of the world, but that thou shouldest keep them from the evil*" (in the high-priestly prayer, John 17:15). Jesus detaches his own from the world and at the same time attaches them to it, because in him is perfect assurance that they can withstand the temptation of the world's self-sufficiency. In Christ, the non-use and the use of the things of this world coincide.

Thinking from the center
There is thus a way from Christ to history, to a positive appreciation of culture and the whole of human life in all its facets. This is the starting point for a new, optimistic interpretation of the history of culture after Christ, and apparently we have no choice but to adopt it.

Still, we sense difficulties. This time, however, it is a question of fine distinctions, and it is no easy matter to find just the right words; yet these distinctions have to be made, since they are ultimately decisive for our per-

---

[18] Mayer (see note 13), 197f.

[19] Cf. Leclercq, *L'Amour des lettres*, 69 [Eng. trans., 77].

[20] Cf. e.g. *In Mattheum homilia* 55.6 (Migne, *Patrologia graeca*, 58:548).

spective on the possibility of a Christian culture. Must we—to take one point—proceed "from the center" (Christ) or "from the beginning" (creation)? At first glance the question seems unimportant; yet theologians discuss it animatedly, and rightly so. Berkhof views both culture and history from the center and the end, while the significance of the beginning remains entirely in the shadows. Ridderbos, however, in his trenchant review[21] of Berkhof's book, remonstrates with the author that the Christian view of culture is more multifaceted and more complex, and that to ignore "the beginning" is to neglect a big part of reality.[22] In turn, Ridderbos is reproached for drawing two lines, one from creation and one from Christ, thus remaining caught in a kind of dualism.[23] He replies to his critics with a fine discourse on the convergence of the two lines in Christ as shown by Paul in the Epistle to the Colossians, but in the sequel he never quite escapes the two-line approach.

I can imagine that many will think something is wrong here after all, and that therefore a consistently Christological approach still seems preferable. Again, is the question really of any importance? This is not the place to elaborate on all the implications of thinking "from the center" or "from the beginning" or "from the end," but one thing strikes us immediately in those who actually choose one of the three possibilities: by doing so they are unable to do justice to certain important aspects of the whole question. Thus Berkhof devalues Greek and Roman culture in its significance for the making of Western civilization by having the disclosure of history take its inception in Christ. His picture of ancient culture, at least insofar as its essence is concerned, is rather unfavorable. To be sure, he is too keen a thinker to impose a rigid, naturalistic scheme on the pre-Christian cultures; and he notes that both historical research and philosophy of history have led to the insight that the last thousand years before Christ were a unique period in world history, a period of exceptional importance because "man no longer experienced himself as a function of the harmonious cycle of nature."[24] And yet Berkhof contends that although the Greeks more than any other people before them "discovered in man a being that transcends the events of nature," history to them did not in principle "stand above nature," with the result that the Greek world had "no room for history."[25] (It will be objected that Berkhof's view pertains to history, not culture. Granted; yet this objection cannot be admitted since it is of far-reaching importance for a view of culture whether the bearers of culture experience history as a cosmic natural process or as an event having a distinctive character and meaning of its own.)

---

[21] See note 12.
[22] In *Gereformeerd Weekblad*, 19 Sept. 1958.
[23] Ibid., 3 Oct. 1958.
[24] Berkhof, *Christus de zin der geschiedenis*, 14 [Eng. trans., 18]. Karl Jaspers refers to this period by the—now commonly accepted—term Axial Period [see his *The Origin and Goal of History* (1953), 1–6].
[25] Berkhof, ibid., 17 [Eng. trans., 21].

If thinking from the center brings Berkhof to an undervaluation of the pre-Christian cultures, it leads him no less to a schematization of the present cultural scene. After Christ, he explains, the powers in this world rage against God, especially the power of self-deification. It is certainly not the case that after Christ's victory on the cross freedom in Christ has become the salvation of all. On the contrary, Jesus' triumph is accompanied by apostasy from the Christian faith, by anti-Christian doctrines of salvation, by a Faustian pursuit of self-realization.[26]

Reading all this, we must admit that the power of sin and evil appears to be taken in all its seriousness here. Still, I hesitate to concede this, in view of the fact that Berkhof also advances the idea that people can come to share in salvation without having turned to the Fountain of salvation in personal conversion, and that they can be serving Christ's rule without knowing or acknowledging it. To my mind, he renders his words about the anti-Christian powers in the dispensation of Christ's lordship powerless by sublimating them to the notion that Christ's salvation is shared in by those who do not accept his cross or his rule.

It is not only interesting but also illuminating once more to compare Berkhof's way of thinking on one particular point with that of Ridderbos as well as Kuyper.[27] Berkhof proceeds from the center—with the result that the pre-Christian period fares badly at his hands. Ridderbos and Kuyper know, besides the center, also the beginning, the creation—and their assessment of ancient culture is more favorable. In this way, the assessment of the period between creation and incarnation becomes a touchstone of one's philosophy of culture and history.

With reference to what was said above I repeat: each of these interpretations entails a weakness. If one thinks only from the center, history before Christ seems to be inevitably shortchanged and the creation motif inevitably neglected. On the other hand, if one draws two lines, one from the creation and one from Christ, a certain dualism seems unavoidable. Moreover, both interpretations seem to entail a minimizing of the radical corruption of man and the power of sin and evil.

The relation to God

Is there no escaping this dilemma? As a non-theologian I shall not presume to indicate a way out, but I will attempt to cast some light on a few aspects of the problem that are at the same time of crucial importance for the relation of culture and salvation. Perhaps what I am going to say is implied in Ridderbos's exposition[28] of the connection between creation and Christ according to Col. 1:15 ("*Who is the image of the invisible God, the first-born of every creature*"); the

---

[26] Ibid., 85–87 [Eng. trans., 91–93].

[27] For Ridderbos, see note 12. For Abraham Kuyper, see *De Gemeene Gratie* [Common grace] (3 vols.; 3rd impr., 1931–32), 1:422–28. [See also S. U. Zuidema, "Common Grace and Christian Action in Abraham Kuyper," chap. 4 in his *Communication and Confrontation* (Toronto, 1972), 52–105, at 65.]

[28] In *Gereformeerd Weekblad*, 3 Oct. 1958.

reason I have my doubts is that in the same exposition as well as in other publications this connection once again recedes into the background. But to the point.

Throughout the entire discussion the little word "good" recurs repeatedly. To my mind the view of the relation of the creation to Christ and vice versa is governed by what people understand by "good." The word also occurs in the creation story: *"And God saw every thing that he had made, and, behold, it was very good"* (Gen. 1:31). Must we understand this to mean that all things had what they were supposed to have, that they were created to the purpose? Or must we search behind these apparently so neutral words and read them in the light of what precedes them: *"Let us make man in our image, after our likeness"* (Gen. 1:26a)? Without hesitating we choose for the latter. But then everything comes to turn on understanding these words correctly; and how many views have there not been about the "image of God"! Inspired in part by Berkouwer's very fine expositions of *Man, the Image of God*,[29] we hear in the familiar words of Gen. 1:26 that the most essential thing that can be said of man is that he stands in a *total* and *active* relation to God. This implies that anything further that can be observed in or about man cannot be understood except in terms of this relation to God. The image of God can thus never be exhausted in a mere relationship with God: everything in and about man, all he does and accomplishes, and the world in which he moves, is constituted from this *relatedness* to God; it is in the relation to God that the truth about human existence and the world is first disclosed. Calvin already expressed this: "Man never attains to a true knowledge of himself unless he has first contemplated the face of God, and then comes down from contemplating Him to look into himself." [30]

The light of the preceding is so clear that both the one line (from Christ alone) and the two lines (from both the creation and the incarnation) fade and another line comes into view, the *theocentric*. The matter can be put as follows. In human existence, yes, in all creation, the purpose is not man or the creature as such, but God. Everything revolves about him and moves towards him. This is what Gen. 1:26 principally teaches us. Now then, that is at the same time the essential, the real purpose of Christ's work, *the* meaning of the coming Kingdom, namely, the resumption of the original meaning of creation that was negated by man in his turning away from God. There is a great danger—strange to say—in the Christocentric approach, which often results in Christomonism or Christolatry, namely, that God is lost to view or relegated to the background. Christ himself, however, points always away from himself towards the Father. He came not for himself but for the Father. Jesus steps back so that the perfect wholeness (*heil*) and ultimate meaning, which were put into the creation by God,

---

[29] G. C. Berkouwer, *De Mens het beeld Gods* (1957). [Eng. trans., *Man, the Image of God* (1962).]

[30] Calvin, *Institutes of the Christian Religion*, I.i.2. In the same vein Dooyeweerd, *A New Critique of Theoretical Thought*, 2:560–65; and Berkouwer, *De Mens het beeld Gods*, 17–33 [Eng. trans., 20–36].

will now stand wholly revealed: "*I seek not mine own will, but the will of the Father which hath sent me*" (John 5:30; cf. 6:38ff, 4:34, etc.).

There is therefore harmony between the divine purpose in creation and the work of Christ. The new element that is revealed in the latter, namely grace, is an answer to the negative response from man's side.

Theologically, the entire religious relation of man and world to God now lies open to view. But—whenever this insight is to be made fruitful for culture and history, numerous difficulties arise, almost all of them stemming from the fact that somehow a stipulation is made whereby man is still guaranteed a certain independence in his worldly activities. The religious relation to God is acknowledged, to be sure, but the modifiers *total* and *active* demand just a little too much of a (Christian) person. Anyone who is not immediately persuaded of this should read Berkouwer's important discussion of freedom, in which he makes a serious attempt at understanding this concept entirely in terms of the relation to God and to exclude every notion of a more comprehensive formal concept of freedom.[31] Public reactions[32] suggest, however, that many find it difficult to embrace an integral religious idea of freedom. (The addition of the term "integral" to "religious" is really redundant yet appears necessary nonetheless).

I firmly believe there is a solution to the problem of culture as well as the problem of freedom. The solution lies in assimilating them into the intimate coherence between creation history and the revelation of the kingdom of Christ. We have already seen (from Gen. 1:26–31) that it is not possible to speak of the goodness of things in a neutral way, apart from the relation to God; only in being oriented to him are they good, purposeful, etc. Now then, in Jesus Christ the orientation of man and things is again what it originally was. The final words of Gen. 1 ("*everything that he had made . . . was very good*") are adopted, as it were, in the Sermon on the Mount, specifically in the closing passage of Matt.6.

Between Gen. 1 and Matt. 6 Christians often see a contradiction, or at least a different emphasis.[33] The first book has the cultural mandate; carrying it out requires entering into cultural life; and it is nothing less than a divine commandment. In the Sermon on the Mount we hear the opposite; here the commandment is to put away the world of culture: you think you need food and clothing— cultural goods if ever there were any—but mind you well: these are the things after which the Gentiles seek (Matt. 6:32). The upshot therefore seems to be that the Christian camp must necessarily split into two parties. The cultural optimists, who advocate a Christian culture and espouse an objective salvation in Christ and his supreme lordship in this world, remind us that God made things good

---

[31] Berkouwer, *De Mens het beeld Gods*, 346–89 [Eng. trans., 310–48].

[32] [Allusion *inter alia* to S. U. Zuidema's critical review of *De Mens het beeld Gods* by G. C. Berkouwer, in *Correspondentie-bladen van de Vereniging voor Calvinistische Wijsbegeerte* 22.1 (1958): 6–14; for a partial retraction, see ibid., 24.3 (1960): 1. Cf. A. Troost's favorable review of the same work in *Sola Fide* 11.1/2 (1957): 42–48.]

[33] On this controversy, see P. Schoonenberg, "Onderwerpt de aarde" [Subdue the earth], *Nederlandse Katholieke Stemmen* 52 (1956): 162–65.

and impress upon us the cosmic scope of Christ's saving work. Opposed to them are the genuine ascetics, who prize above all else the pure, unhindered love of God and who wish to call attention to the radicality of man's corruption and the world's tendency, given God's beautiful gifts, to forget God himself.

Shall we say that both are right? Shall we say to the ascetic: the cultural mandate has been given to us, and when we act upon it we are always safe? But the ascetic will—quite correctly—counter with the objection: you misjudge what culture has come to mean since the Fall. What is to be the solution? God tells us in the creation story and Christ explains to us in his sermon on "taking no thought": cultural mandate, acceptance of culture, well and good, but first remember that I am the meaning of all culture and that accordingly you can accept culture only when you desire my kingdom and love me more than yourself. See Matt. 6:33, *"But seek ye first the kingdom of God . . . and all these things shall be added unto you"*; see also especially Mark 10:28–31, where Jesus elaborates, as it were, upon the words just cited:

Then Peter began to say unto him, Lo, we have left all, and have followed thee. And Jesus answered and said, Verily I say unto you, There is no man that hath left house, or brethren, or sisters, or father, or mother, or wife, or children, or lands, for my sake, and the gospel's, but he shall receive an hundredfold now in this time, houses, and brethren, and sisters, and mothers, and children, and lands, with persecutions; and in the world to come eternal life. But many that are first shall be last; and the last first.

Here Jesus explains concretely that even in this life, houses, lands, etc., will, for his sake, fall to the lot of those *who believe in him,* provided they first give up everything for Christ. The tragedy of the ascetic was that he neglected to read the words "in this life," or exegeted them away, because he failed to understand that Jesus restores the things of this world to us if we have but once given them up for his sake.

The danger is not imaginary, however, that we will construe as self-evident for Christians the total and active relation—restored in Christ—of all culture to God in just as gratuitous a manner as Berkhof thinks "countless people are in the service of Christ's dominion without knowing it or desiring it." [34] In this way the very essence of a Christian culture would elude us.[35]

Culture and its discontents

What strikes us in Scripture and particularly in Gen. 1 and Matt. 6 is the nearness of all culture to God. That nearness culminates in the words of Gen. 1:26: *"Let us make man in our image, after our likeness, and let them have dominion . . . over all the earth."* This passage links man's cultural calling most intimately with his complete relatedness to God, for in the clause *"and let such have dominion over all the earth"*—which is a more literal translation of the

---

[34] See note 8.
[35] On this point, cf. J. E. Mayer (see note 13), 200ff.

Hebrew text—the word *such* denotes "these creatures, who possess the meaning of their existence in living before the face of God." Culture is carried on immediately before the face of God—even when man in his desire to be something in and by himself denies, disesteems or attempts to destroy this nearness and immediacy to God. Man can never slip out of the relation to God, not because he desires to remain in it but because God keeps him there.

We can claim to know many things about culture, about its forms and its unfolding, but the moment we inquire after its meaning or ask about its relation to salvation we stop getting answers so long as we remain within mundane dimensions. It is as if everything transpires in interaction with God, and about that only Scripture can make us wise. We must catch the light that falls here, which is not easy, if only because the Bible often speaks in other terms and about other matters than those with regard to which we consult it. Yet ultimately this is no obstacle, for Scripture always centers on the relation in which man and things stand to God. It often does so in a story or a detailed description, which is why the words of the Bible touch people and things that are centuries apart.

Thus Scripture speaks to us directly as we wrestle with the problem of culture. According to the creation story and the Sermon on the Mount, the immediacy of culture before God expresses the meaning of culture. Nearness to God is salvation, is the meaning of life in all its expressions.[36]

If this is true—if culture remains in immediacy to God under all circumstances so that its proper meaning can never be lost because God constantly manifests himself in it—then does it really make any difference whether or not people acknowledge the fundamentally religious meaning of culture in conscious faith? It almost seems as though Paul had foreseen this central question; in any case, in Rom. 1:18 he answers it directly: the truth can be held in unrighteousness—and is so held by those who stray from God and thus attempt to escape God's immediate nearness. Just as loving surrender to God and living in his nearness determines culture in its essence and external features, so also does the negation or misconception of the true meaning of all of life leave its imprint on culture. If life no longer finds its meaning in God, it must itself become meaning. Such an identification can take place in two ways: either by equating culture and the divine (or at least blurring the boundary between the two); or by attempting to locate the fullness of meaning or of salvation directly in culture, history, the state, sexuality. The former dominates in cultures that have not yet been touched, or touched but feebly, by Christianity, the latter in all cultures that have passed through Christianity and now offer resistance in increasing measure to God as the meaning of life.

The transference of meaning away from God's immediate nearness in the issues of life entails yet another very important consequence. It introduces a profound restlessness into culture, a restlessness that manifests itself in many

---

[36] Cf. the beautiful short essay, "De twee vormen van het geluk" [The two forms of happiness], in J. H. Bavinck, *Flitsen en fragmenten* (1959).

cultural forms. Whenever man seeks the meaning of life in culture he discovers that the form, the style, the cultural expression that he has invested with the meaning neither is nor ever can be that meaning. Psychologically and historically, the existential disappointment at the failure of a whole generation or an entire era will find expression in a lack of inner peace, in a reaction, in an intense search for a new style. Once again expectations run high. Will the new forms finally manifest the meaning that resides in all things? I do not know how long this expectation has dominated our culture. Perhaps it arose (again) in the Middle Ages; at least, the Gothic had such expectations when it substantialized the kingdom of God on earth. And as for Modern Times, in which the transcendental background of earthly things recedes ever more from view, they attempt to overcome the strain by identifying this world with a perfect world or with a secularized earthly paradise. For some considerable time now, the restlessness in culture has been on the increase. Modern man is able to discover ever more quickly that meaning cannot be here, so perhaps it is some place else. The hope of having the meaning of culture disclosed has become a matter of "moments." I cannot help but be reminded here of what is happening nowadays in the relation between the sexes: people expect the meaning of life to be revealed in this relation, but they demand of it what it can never give. Once more we face the dilemma: either drop all expectations, since salvation lies outside things and relationships anyway; or live in tension between the disappointing present and the still undisclosed, perhaps meaningful future.

In order to abide in the love of God the ascetic tried to get away from the world of culture, but he never succeeded. Understandably so, it will be said, for no one can live outside culture. Yet the cause lies deeper. Cultures may rise and fall, richly unfold or slowly petrify, but man can never step outside of them because he cannot distance himself from the meaning of his own existence.

Modern man restlessly turns from one cultural form to another, barely touching them. Culture does not give itself, however, when it is desired only for its external appearance. It opens itself only to those who want to understand it in its essence and deep meaning. But that demands from the man of culture the sacrifice of himself—loss of self in the Biblical sense described above.

We are going to close, perhaps to your disappointment, for it is just now that things should really begin to open up. Can we stop here without applying our reflections to the many practical and scientific questions that we continue to wrestle with—as well we should? And yet it is good that we can close here, for it happens so often that the religious background of our cultural problems is acknowledged, only to be taken less than seriously in practical life. What is urgently needed is that we again and again dwell a good while upon the perspective I have sketched above. One who does so will be able to understand that we conclude now in the spirit of Advent, since in God, who is the Meaning of all that is, the meaning of culture is very near to us.

8/ THE SACRED DWELLING PLACE

FOR ORIENTATION in the problem I would like to explore with you this year,[1] we shall first make an imaginary visit to various cities and edifices.

(1) EGYPT

Located at the entrance of the Fayum is the city of Kahun, the present name for Hetep-Senusret, which was built by Senusret II of the Twelfth Dynasty in about 2000 B.C. Only a part of this city has been preserved, namely, the northern part; the southern part was washed away.

The most striking thing about the layout of the city is the north-south orientation both of the city as a whole and of its individual houses, so that the streets run in an east-west direction. Moreover, a north-south wall divides the city into western and eastern parts. The western part was for the unfree workers. The eastern part was for the magnates; here were also the market and shops. The houses of the magnates make no mean impression; they had as many as eighty rooms and were situated against the northern wall of the city.

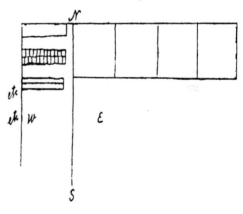

In addition, there are the temple buildings and the palace, for the city Hetep-Senusret (which means *May Senusret be gracious*) served at the same time as a residence of the king and his court.

The city is a small one, but all the important parts and aspects of life are present: economic, social, political, and religious life. Thus Kahun is not a sacred city in the strict sense of various other ancient oriental cities like Persepolis, Arbela, Loyang. Nor is it a place in which economic life dominates. It seems to be just a very normal, everyday city that owes its great fame to nothing but its well-preserved layout, a city therefore that can be regarded as an important source for our knowledge of Ancient Near Eastern urban structure. And yet this city raises a very important question: Why the precise north-south alignment? It is carried through even into the components,

---

[1] [This text is taken from a set of lecture notes for a course taught in 1960–61; the diagrams were prepared by Margaret Van Dyke after freehand drawings in the original.]

not in any geometrical sense but certainly so that every building (consistent with an organic harmony) has acquired a proper place in the social order, which in turn is itself incorporated into the north- south orientation.

I want to say more about this order. An organism arose whose laws were in turn determined by the requirements of climate, the social order, and religious conceptions. These three elements are inseparable, however, because according to the conceptions of the ancients, life is a unity. When they mention first one aspect and then another they do not mean to say that these aspects can be isolated from each other; their attention is merely focused for the moment on one particular aspect. For example, if the artisans were settled in the western part of the city, that was for more than one reason. There was a climatological consideration: the bad winds blew out of the west. But there was also a religious reason: evil came from the west. Furthermore, the homes of the magnates lay along the northern wall. Where the temple or temples may have been located at Kahun, however, is uncertain.

To form a correct notion of the Egyptian city and of the layout of Hetep-Senusret, we shall visit two other Egyptian cities. First, El-Amarna, not the renowned city of kings and temples but the so-called workers' city, which is no less famous, though only among specialists. Every pharaoh required a very large number of workers to build a city of his own, his tomb, and the temple complex that went with it. Usually, space was reserved for these workers in the temple city itself—think of Kahun—but in the case of Amarna a separate city was built for the workers to the east, happily so because it gave rise to one of the most remarkable cities in the world, remarkable not just for the model—not unknown, however, elsewhere in the world —but especially for the purity with which it was executed:

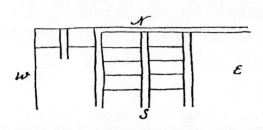

the whole is a quadrate, divided into western and eastern sectors by a wall in the middle. The western sector has one street and the eastern four, the streets running in a north-south direction parallel to the outer walls; all the houses on these streets are situated in an east-west direction. The result of such planning was a *checkerboard model*, without a single deviation since there were no public buildings. Many questions still remain to be answered. For example, what was the purpose of the wall that divided the city into eastern and western sectors? Yet the system is clear: it has a north-south alignment, parallel streets, and houses placed at right angles to the streets.

There is one further aspect of the Egyptian city that might be pointed out, and for that we go on to Thebes, the capital city of the Middle and New Kingdoms, situated on the Nile. At Thebes, too, we must content ourselves with probable boundaries, and then we find—insofar as we can make out at the moment—that the alignment this time is not exactly north-south but south-west to north-east for the long axis, an alignment oriented to the course of the Nile.

If we had time to look at every ancient Egyptian city that we know today, we would discover that almost without exception their perimeters have the form of a rectangle, or even a square. We would discover as well that the water of sacred pools, canals, or the Nile played an important role in the life of these cities. What significance should be attached to these facts?

Thebes was the capital of the Middle and New Kingdoms. Here the Nile flows in a north-easterly direction, and the bordering hills run further apart, widening the valley. The Egyptians call it Nu, the city; or Nu-a, the *great* city; or Nu-amon, the city of Amon. To the Greeks it was *Diospolis hè magalè*, the *great* city of the gods. The Latin name was *Diospolis Magna*. Today the area is one of villages: El-Uksor, or Luxor; and El-Karnak.

Thebes is very old, antedating the Middle Kingdom. It was destroyed in 661 B.C. by the Assyrians, later again by Cambyses, and in 24 B.C. by the Romans. Homer said it had a hundred gates. It is worthwhile to note the references in the prophet Nahum: "Art thou [Nineveh] better than populous No, that was situate among the rivers, that had waters round about it . . . ?" (Nahum 3:8). The particle *be* ("among" in the Authorized Version) can mean "on" or "between"; and in the Hebrew Bible *ye 'orim* is the plural (albeit for the Nile) of *ye 'or*, from the Egyptian word for the Nile.

The size of the city in various periods is uncertain, but in about 24 B.C. Strabo visited it and reported that traces of the city were discernible for a length of what would be about fourteen kilometers. That *could* mean the city was about that long, which is plausible in view of the fact that the probable length of Memphis was nine to thirteen kilometers. Strabo aside, if we take the present area of ruins we get nine kilometers by six kilometers, with the nine kilometers as the southwest-northeast axis and the six kilometers for the short axis.

Thebes raises countless questions. The present situation is as follows. Karnak and Luxor are on the east bank of the Nile, the Nile itself having lateral tributaries, not at right angles but branching from the Nile and then running parallel for a stretch; then there are more ruins on the right banks against the hills, and in the hills the royal tombs, with extensive empty spaces in between. Thebes as we know it today gives us no impression of the ancient city. That is not to say it was not there, for the street plan also shows us no city *between* the streams (see Nahum). In all likelihood the Nile flowed much more to the east four thousand years ago, east of Thebes' eastern wall, with artificial canals from the Nile protecting the southern and northern walls.

However many the probabilities, it is certain that the main directions of the city follow the course of the Nile (that is to say, the principal streets and the monumental buildings). As in Memphis, the waters of the Nile are diverted for the construction of canals, lakes, and the like. It is probable that one of these canals gave rise to the river's present course.

Speaking of lakes, one of them can still be accurately reconstructed. One kilometer by two kilometers in length, its axis parallel to the Nile, it was built by Amenhotep III in front of his palace, called Birket Habu today. Issuing into this lake at right angles was a kilometer-wide canal that most likely received its waters from the Nile.

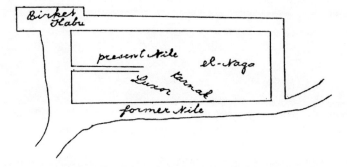

In summary, one can say the following about Egyptian cities:

a. The main direction is north-south, with larger or smaller deviations as required by the course of the Nile (see Thebes or Amarna) or by the terrain.

b. Palaces and houses of magnates are oriented towards the north (also at Tanis, for example, in the eastern delta); temples usually point toward the east.

c. The perimeter of the Egyptian city is predominantly rectangular, sometimes even perfectly square.

d. Egyptian cities were constructed according to certain ratios: 1:1; 1:2; 1:2.5; 1:3; 2:3; 3:5. These proportions were applied to items large and small.

e. Worthy of note is the important function of water in Egyptian life: the Nile itself, many canals, and also lakes and pools in urban life.

f. Certain deviations notwithstanding, the layout of the Egyptian city is plain; its straight, consistent forms even give it a modern look.

All this being so, we can only ask: What are the principles that govern it?

(2) INDIA

In recent decades the so-called Indus civilization has acquired great renown, especially through the publications of Ernest MacKay and Mortimer Wheeler.[2]

In the prehistoric period, or towards its close, a nation of conquerors (where they came from is not known) invaded the land and subjugated the indigenous population (circa 3000 or 2600 and 2500 B.C.). It is probable that this race was spared serious political turmoil and was able to develop its civilization for some thousand years. The question concerning contacts between this civilization and

---

[2] Ernest Mackay, *Die Induskultur. Ausgrabungen in Mohenjo-Daro und Harappa* (1938); idem, *Early Indus Civilizations* (1948); Mortimer Wheeler, *The Indus Civilization* (1953).

other civilizations has still not been answered. Especially interesting is the question of its relation to Mesopotamian civilization. It has been suggested—a very interesting point of view—that the Sumerian and Indus civilizations originated in the same region: the mountains and plateau situated between Mesopotamia and India. If that is true, the conditions for habitation there must have been far better than they are today, especially with regard to climate. Unfortunately, archeological data is still inadequate for providing a clear picture of how the land was inhabited.

The important settlements of the Indus civilization are Mohenjo-Daro in the Sind north of Karachi, on the Indus River; and Harappa, far to the north and east of the Indus, in the Punjab. In the former, we must have a look at the residential city. The city has something most remarkable: ten levels have been excavated representing ten urban periods yet with no essential difference between the levels. The levels reveal that the end came each time as a result of some catastophe, most probably natural, not political. The final demise occurred around 1500 B.C. through revolts or foreign invasions, and the civilization of Mohenjo-Daro and Harappa was destroyed. The Aryan invasions came some 200 years later, which explains why the Aryans adopted nothing of the indigenous culture. The intervening period is called that of the Dravidians. In contrast to the civilization of Mohenjo-Daro, the Veda civilization was purely agrarian, at least at the outset.

Mohenjo-Daro was spread over two hills, separated by a ravine some 250 meters wide, probably a branch of the Indus. Here, too, the streets ran north to south and east to west, without exception; the whole of the city was about 1100 meters by 1250 meters, its orientation to the four regions of the world. Three streets ran north-south more or less parallel to each other; and two streets ran east-west to the north and south of the western hill, which served as the citadel of the city with its own fortification. This plan divided the city into twelve major precincts, each in turn subdivided by broad or narrow streets, the whole being regular and oriented to the four winds. Here again there are palatial structures, albeit dominated by a confusing multiplicity of forms—the effect, in all likelihood, of later remodeling and joining of structures. The end result is a capricious whole. The size of these structures varies greatly: there is one with 112 chambers and there are many with eighteen.

The significance of the city plan at Mohenjo-Daro is enhanced by its great similarity to that of Harappa in the north. Here, too, the citadel is in the center of the western sector, the orientation is to the four points of the compass, and the regularity in construction does not extend to the houses themselves. One gets the impression that Mohenjo-Daro had a more economic and civilian character and Harappa a more military one.

The Veda civilization (1400–800 B.C.) evolved gradually. Initially agrarian, it saw the development of life in villages, fortified villages, fortresses, later also royal citadels, and really only in the fourth phase (1000–800) certain settlements encompassed by city walls. It was in this phase, we know, that the layout and construction of houses, palaces, and cities according to sacred rules became established. How far back these rules go and whether they still had some connection with the Mohenjo-Daro civilization is now beyond discovery. Failure to adhere to these rules, it was believed at the time, resulted in certain misfortune. The rules were compiled in books—for example, in the *Silpa Sastra*, which consisted of sixty-four books, some with instructions for architects and sculptors.

The *Silpa Sastra* stipulated the maximum dimensions for houses for the king, military chiefs and ministers, specifying length, breadth, height, and number of chambers, with each house strictly oriented to the four winds. Moreover, all this—especially the last requirement—was absolutely essential for the good fortunes of the house, its inhabitants, and all it contained!

From the *Silpa Sastra* it is more than clear that the rules governing the construction of the house were not just important technical, economic, and perhaps aesthetic considerations but, most decisively, religious-sacral ones. To be sure, there need not always be a clearcut distinction between the technical and the religious-sacral requirements—which might explain why these religious-sacral requirements elude us whenever we are confronted with archeological data unaccompanied by written sources.

The *Silpa Sastra* does not let matters rest with these general rules but goes on to provide detailed information concerning the religious-sacral meaning of its components. It is worthy of mention that this applies not just to religious edifices such as temples but equally to ordinary houses and settlements. For example, essential in the religious-sacral meaning are the location of the doors; the open veranda (on one or several sides, or a specified side of the house); the interior structure (in particular, the corners and the center); the forms; the measurements; and the building materials.

The same can be said of the construction of cities. Religious conceptions of the city are decisive. Orientation was to the four regions of the world; measurements and proportions were fixed. Especially important were the two principal streets. The longer east-west street was the royal street; the shorter north-south street was the broad street. As well, inside the city was a city ring or processional street; and in the center of the city was a mound where a temple tower or *stupa* might eventually be built. There were even various magic zones for various castes among the people.

In summary, house and city were conceived and constructed as the microcosmic epitome of the macrocosm and imbedded in nature and landscape and climate. Furthermore, house and city, settlement and dwelling were thereby placed in relation to the powers of the underworld and the world above. And it is precisely in this relation that house and city, etc., were directly linked to happiness or misfortune, blessing or curse (these concepts in their all-embracing, religious-sacral sense). That is the heart of the matter.

The writings I have cited, and others, stipulate that a house be built when the sun moves north (December to June) and the moon waxes: the latter assures prosperity, the former light and blessing. The construction site may not be salty, and there must be no thorns (probably in connection with infertility). Certain trees are not permitted to face the prevailing winds, on pain of premature death.

One who desires fame and power must make a door to the east, one who desires cattle and children a door to the north. In addition, numerous rites, including sacrifices and sprinklings, must be enacted before and after construction, or annually, in order to guarantee blessing for the house.

Also important was the location of the sanctuary in the city or village. The Siva temple was in the northeast, the Visnu temple in the west, the Suriqa temple in the east. The entrance to the first and last of these would face the rising sun and the center of the settlement. Sanctuaries dedicated to evil or dreaded powers, however, were perforce located outside the settlement. To the northeast lay the way to heaven, the place of victory.

Thus building construction and world-picture are interwoven, and they are grounded in the magical connection between the universe and the world of man. Buildings can properly fulfill their functions only when they are in harmony with the structure of the universe.

Now for an important question. The *Silpa Sastra* belongs to the phase 1100–800 B.C., which was Aryan, but what link did it have to the Mohenjo-Daro civilization? Are these conceptions strictly tied to the Aryans, and did they bring them with them?

Certain arguments can be advanced in favor of a link. (1) The Aryan conquerors came down from the northwest of India via the passes of Karakorum, etc., and the first settlements were restricted to the Punjab and Indus region, that is, to what had been the Mohenjo-Daro civilization sphere, whence they spread, though not until later, to the Ganges region and elsewhere. (2) When the Aryans arrived around 1400 B.C. they were an agrarian people who found city life distasteful; yet city life was well established by about 1100 B.C. (3) The *Silpa Sastra* suggests a long-established urban tradition and its precise rules can only stem from long practical experience. It is therefore legitimate to wonder whether in the Aryan conceptions of the city we are not witnessing a revival of the urban tradition of the bearers of the Mohenjo-Daro civilization.

(3) MESOPOTAMIA

We have seen that in Egypt a uniform type of city was practically ubiquitous. In the Land between the Two Rivers the situation was entirely different.

At Borsippa the ground plan is a quadrate, as is the temple. It is not known how the residential streets and civic buildings were situated. Apart from the perfectly square layout, we are struck by the fact that the streets, as far as our knowledge goes, did not run north-south and east-west, but that the diagonal is oriented exactly north-south in the case of the city as well as the main temple. Both diagonals intersect exactly in the center of the city and the center of the temple. Flowing through the city at right angles to the northern and southern walls and parallel to the eastern and western walls is the arm of a lake. (The same situation exists at Babylon, where it is the Euphrates that flows through the city.)

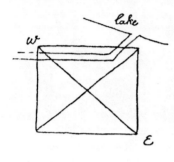

Borsippa is located south of Babylon and west of the Euphrates. The city is (almost) an (extended) quadrate of 250 hectares, an area 1,408 meters by 1,760 meters. The main temple is exactly in the center and is also a quadrate. The regularity in both quadrates is impressive. Moreover, the temple quadrate is also at right angles to the arm of the lake. Nor should we overlook the unit of measurement of 176 meters, which governs the proportions so that it is possible to construct a rather accurate table of ratios for the city as a whole:

1. of the temple quadrate $2a = 2 \times 176m =$ 352m
2. of the south side $3a + 3a + 2a =$ 1408m
3. total of one side $10 \times 176 =$ 1760m
4. total of the other side $8 \times 176 =$ 1408m
5. the gates, too, fit in; see, e.g., the four gates at 3 x 176 (there are actually seven gates in all)
6. that is not all: the temple quadrate is equidistant from all city walls: $3 \times 176m =$ 528m

Our enumeration does not exhaust the characteristic features of this type of construction. The diagonals are oriented to the four winds, or better, to the four regions of the world, and the palace is situated in the northeastern corner, along the lake. The civic arrangement of the city is not known, but according to one theory the arti-

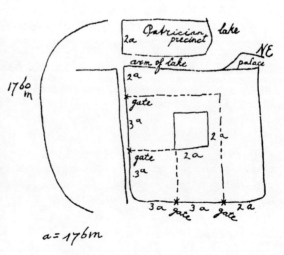

The Sacred Dwelling Place

sans' residences were inside the temple area, together with the market. As to its orientation, Borsippa was therefore both on the water (either at right angles or parallel to it) and, in virtue of its diagonals, on the four regions of the world.

Dur Sarrukin, to the north of Nineveh, was built between 713 and 707 B.C. Here too a proportional design was followed, one reminiscent of Kahun, suggesting possible Egyptian influence. The unit of measurement was sixty-one meters—for the basic layout of the city, the offset from the walls, etc. Again, there are the same tendencies towards proportional designs as in Egyptian cities.

We cannot deal with every Mesopotamian city, but we can note that Sumerian influences were important, as were Hittite, Kassite and Egyptian influences. But what is especially noteworthy about Assyrian and Babylonian cities is the following. Besides important external influences there was something indigenous as well. On the one hand there was an established ground plan, often rectangular or quadratic with diagonals and axes, subject to geometrical and rational rules; on the other hand, in the internal structures of the cities this plan was abandoned, creating an impression of disorder and lack of discipline. Both characteristics have been ascribed to the Semites—the latter feature purportedly reflecting the peculiarities of nomadic life; thus rectangular perimeters, but at the same time crooked streets. Additionally, the hilly terrain often influenced construction, causing striking irregularities, for example, in Nineveh and Assur.

However all that may be, what interests us in Mesopotamia, for a variety of reasons, is still another shape of city construction: the circular city.

Is a greater difference imaginable than between a circle and a rectangle or square? And yet, from the standpoint of urban planning and architecture, these forms actually have a great deal in common: a center, and a north-south orientation. It recurs countless times in the Near East, but also on other continents. Given the north-south line, one draws schematically fixed lines parallel to it as well as perpendicular lines, and the ground plan is finished. But one can also bisect the north-south line with the east-west line, with a circle forming the perimeter of the whole, and the city is divided into four equal quadrants.

I would emphasize that the city consists of four equal parts that meet in the center, and that the center is situated at the point where the four regions of the world meet. I would point out in addition—don't say this is self-evident—that the gates are located at the ends of the two intersecting main streets. This system appears in the Assyrian reliefs, such as the one in the palace at Kalach, where it pertains to an army camp that is so perfectly circular that the circumference can be drawn with a compass. Is this intended to be a pure representation of reality? That is not impossible, for the walls of the Hittite city Zendsjirli (c. 1300 B.C.), with a diameter of 700 meters, at the foot of the Amanus, had the strictly circular form. Later, similar cities are found among the Parthians, under the Sassanids. And then there is Baghdad, built under the Abbasids, the "round city of Mansur" (A.D. 762). The perimeter of Baghdad consisted of a double wall, in two concentric circles. Both walls were surrounded by a moat, and each had four gates situated at the ends of the two streets which intersected at right angles in the exact center, precisely where the palace of the caliph was located. Inside the inner wall ran a circular street that widened at each gate to form an open area.

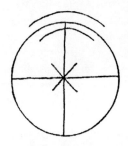

In light of this ground plan it is possible to regard the Assyrian army camp at Kalach, the Parthian cities Darabjird and Sassanid Firuzabad—all perfectly circular, as if drawn with a compass—as prototypes of the most perfect circular city to be found anywhere in the world: Baghdad.

An excursus on construction materials

There was little natural stone available in Mesopotamia, so people had to use materials made of clay, usually in brick form, e.g., 40 × 40 cm with a thickness of from 5 to 10 cm.[3] These were usually sun-dried only, though for facing walls they were baked more thoroughly and often glazed. The clay bricks in the core of a wall were laid with mortar of clay, but the outer masonry in baked stone was often laid with asphalt. Glazed reliefs of fired brick were first modeled in clay, then cut into brick-form pieces for firing and glazing. Where the glazed bricks were dismantled in the course of time for use in the construction of houses, the inner core of sun-dried brick was exposed to wind and weather and quickly reduced to a shapeless mound of clay.

The upper part of a wall would be built of less durable materials than the lower part, on account of the pressure. For example, the walls of the ziggurat up to a height of about 1.60 meters were made of fired brick, and above that level, of sun-dried bricks.

Houses from the time of Hammurabi consisted of dried clay mixed with reeds, in brick form or as a compressed mass.

At Dur Sarrukin (built by Sargon II between 721 and 705 B.C.), the city wall has been preserved to a height of up to 2.3 meters, of which 1.10 meters consisted of natural stone and the part above that of bricks.

Practically all the houses of the Indus civilization, including the very simple ones, were constructed of fired brick, doubtless with the heavy rainfall in mind, since unfired brick would have been reduced quickly to a mass of clay.

---

[3] See the publications of R. J. Forbes.

In Egypt, prior to the Third Dynasty, construction was of woven reeds plastered with clay, of unfired (thus sun-dried) brick, and of wood, but seldom of natural stone. Real stone architecture as well as buildings exclusively of natural stone, together with the first applications of the pillar, also of natural stone, date from the Third Dynasty. Excavations corroborate the statement of Manetho, a Greek-Egyptian priest, that it was Imhotep who invented the construction of monumental edifices from hewn natural stone.

(4) DENMARK

My earlier statement, that Baghdad is the "most perfect circular city to be found anywhere in the world," I shall have to retract. In the last twenty years settlements have become known that surpass the system of the circular city in mathematical exactness, in a region where one would hardly expect to find them. I want to travel with you outside the world of Islam, away from the Baghdad of 762, to the world of northern Europe, to Trelleborg and Aggersborg. The former is a Viking citadel three to four kilometers from the coast of West-Seeland, thus on the Great Belt; the latter, likewise a Viking fortress, is on the Limfjord.

A brief historical digression is necessary here for a good understanding. Excavations were begun in 1934 and the fortresses got their name in 1948 and 1949 when the excavators published their reports, Nørlund on Trelleborg and Schultz on Aggersborg.[4]

Nørlund advanced an historical interpretation of some plausibility: the fortresses were probably built shortly before A.D. 1000 and used until about 1050, when they fell into ruin. Nørlund associates them with the raids of King Sven Gabelhart (986–1014) into Western Europe. Both citadels lay on the sea routes there, Sven was the great organizer of the Viking raids, and from the fortresses' construction it can be shown that the assault on Britain was carefully prepared. Here were the assembly and embarkation points and, in case of failure, a safe haven. The fortresses were situated between two bodies of water, the outermost wall shielding them from the hinterland. Thus they were positioned on promontories surrounded by very little solid ground. Moreover, dividing the inner wall from the outer wall as well as the hinterland was a moat running the entire circumference of the two walls. The fortresses were exceptionally large, with estimates of up to a thousand men per garrison.

Undermining these conjectures is the fact that not a single artifact from Britain has been found at these sites, while there are many objects from the Baltic area. Were they perhaps royal garrisons, directly under royal command?[5]

---

[4] Poul Nørlund, *Trelleborg* (1948); Carl Georg Schultz, "Aggersborg," *Vikingelejren ved Limfjorden fra Nationalmuseets Arbejdsmark* (1949): 91–108.

[5] See Otto Höfler, *Der Runenstein von Røk und die germanischen Individualweihe* (1952), 371. [Cf. idem, "Die Trelleborg auf Seeland und der Runenstein von Røk," *Anzeiger der philologisch-historischen Klasse der Österreichische Akademie der Wissenschaft* (1948): 9–37.]

What accounts for the great scholarly interest in these fortresses? They are circular, but that was true elsewhere as well. Here, however, we are confronted with a strict mathematical system, with an exactness of execution which —insofar as is now known—made only one concession to the terrain or to geographical conditions. The two main streets are axial or portal streets that intersect at right angles, thus connecting the eastern gate with the western one and the southern gate with the northern one. The system as a whole resembles exactly the concentric cities of the Near East, but there is more. The two axial streets divide the fortress into four quadrants and within each quadrant there are four buildings, thus sixteen in all. The radius of the fortress is eighty-five meters, including the wall of earth and wood, which is seventeen meters thick, but eighty-five meters is also the distance from this wall to the outer ring of defense works, so that the diameter of the inner fortress is 170 meters, which is likewise the length of the radius from the outer wall to the center. I quote you these numbers in order to give you an impression of the mathematical precision with which people went about their work here. These measurements recur time and again, but the numbers 24, 12, and in particular 29.5 occur even more frequently, since the chosen unit of measurement was the Roman foot. For example, the length of the buildings is one hundred Roman feet or 29.5 meters, and the diagonal of the central square is the same.

Ah, yes, those buildings, about which so much has already been written! They are in the shape of an ellipse truncated at both ends. It is generally agreed that these buildings are to be regarded as models of ships. But what does this symbolism mean? Or did these buildings originally serve as shelters for the ships in winter, although later they did not, since they were eventually furnished as quarters for the crews? Nørlund and Schultz, the two people who know Trelleborg and Aggersborg best, both point out that the latest finds corroborate the hypothesis that it was the intention of the builders to imitate ships, which is to say that the seamen wanted to remain seamen even in their winter quarters.

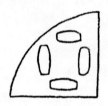

Just a comment yet about the number twelve. There is a strong similarity between Trelleborg and Aggersborg, but it may perhaps be important to note that the number twelve, usually in its multiples, plays a larger role in Aggersborg.

Another fact also deserves mention at this point, since it could well be decisive for the interpretation. Nørlund, upon further investigation, has come up with three additional discoveries. Beneath the excavations of 11th-century Trelleborg there is an older settlement—a temple, or else a chieftain's seat. This older settlement shows a striking similarity with the buildings of Trelleborg, or rather vice versa. And Trelleborg is situated precisely where the largest building (temple or whatever) of the older settlement once stood. This triple discovery refers numerous problems concerning Trelleborg to an earlier time. Regrettably, in preparing this study I have not been able to consult the results of further excavations.

Let us now move to the other side of the Danish peninsula. Fyrkat is located on a spit of land south of Limfjord, on the east coast of Jutland. By land it can be approached only along one road, as the surrounding area is marshy. Since the only other access is by sea, it can be defended easily.

There is not a shred of written source-material on this fortress. Here too the principal material for buildings and streets was wood, almost all of it now vanished as the result of fire, rotting, and so on. Nevertheless it is possible to reconstruct the ground plan and the buildings from the piling holes, now filled with some undefinable substance.

This citadel, too, was built according to the established geometrical system, similar to Nonnebakken in Odensee (on the northeast coast of Fünen), and both were constructed with absolute exactness. Once again they are circular, and surrounded by a wall and a moat. Again there are four openings in the wall, all at the ends of the four streets which intersect at right angles in the center of the camp, thus again creating four equal parts. Each resulting quadrant has four identical wooden houses (in Aggersborg there were three per quadrant), again in the shape of a truncated ellipse. Even the interior construction of the houses is identical, with the Roman foot as the unit of measurement, although there are a few differences in the characteristics of the details. The pallisade just beyond the outer ring of defense (see Trelleborg) is missing. All the emphasis here is on the main wall.

As to the measurements of Fyrkat, the diameter was 120 meters, and the wall was twelve meters [thick at the base] and probably about three meters high. The sixteen houses were 28.5 meters long (corresponding to 96 Roman feet), 7.5 meters wide in the middle, and approximately 5 meters wide at the ends. As at Trelleborg, their elliptical shapes always had one focus in common. The houses appear to have been divided into three rooms, a smaller one at each end of the ellipse and a large space exceeding eighteen meters. The purpose of the small chambers is uncertain, but the great hall was definitely for sleeping and living, since in the center of that space in some of the houses traces of a large fireplace have been found, and along the walls were probably wide sleeping berths able to accommodate at least fifty sleepers per hall. It is probable that some of the houses were used not as dwellings but as work places (for example, one was a smithy) or as storage sheds (one contained a great quantity of grain). Not everything can be established with certainty, for some traces of habitation may have been ploughed under.

There are deviations from the rigor of the system. The houses have four doors, one in each ellipse and two in the hall diagonally opposite each other. This is all uniform, but the two doors in the long sides have entryways as large as church doors and even resemble them. These portals are not always built with the same exactness as the houses, and the excavators are agreed that this is because they are not incorporated into the system. Such portals do not appear in other Viking houses.

Twenty-three graves have been excavated in the northeastern sector of the spit of land. The heathen graves contain funerary gifts and are recognizable because on the surface there was a fireplace for the ritual fire, while the adjacent Christian graves contain nothing but the bodies, fully decomposed.

Objects found at Fyrkat indicate that this fortress, too, was built or inhabited in the last decades of the tenth or early in the eleventh century.

Just a few general observations remain to be made about the four Viking citadels. It is generally agreed that they could not have been constructed just like that in a very short time, given the uncanny exactness of the constructions as a whole and the well-considered details. There is a difficulty, however: little evidence exists of centuries of preparation. They appear suddenly, and after a half century the development abruptly ceases. Scholars have therefore sought their prototypes elsewhere: in the geometrical camps of the Romans, the remains of which the Vikings would have seen in Britain (note that Roman foot!). But L'Orange contests this theory, for the Roman *castra* is rectangular, Roman military theory having forbidden circular camps unless the terrain required them.[6]

Therefore, our recourse must be to Antiquity.... The matter is extremely complicated and cannot be resolved without further excavations.

(5) PERSIA

We must leave the Danish citadels for a while and return to the Ancient Near East, this time to Persepolis. This city has become very familiar to us through the excavations and magnificent publications of Pope and Herzfeld, and especially through the work by Erich Schmidt, the first volume of which came out in 1953.[7]

Persepolis is rarely mentioned in Persian and Greek sources. Even Ctesias, who resided for a long time at the Persian court, is silent about the city. This silence in the non-Persian sources is the more surprising since Persepolis was unsurpassed in scope, opulence and grandeur. Xenophon says the kings divided their time between Babylon, Susa, Ecbatana; he does not mention Persepolis, even though it was the capital.[8] Perhaps it was too remote? But why then so many treasures bestowed on precisely this city, more than on any other? The king did go there, but the residence there seems to have had no political significance. The solution has been sought, naturally, in the idea that Persepolis

---

[6] See Hans-Peter L'Orange, "Trelleborg-Aggerbord og de kongelige byer i Osten," *Viking* (Oslo) 16 (1953): 307–31.

[7] [See *inter alia* Arthur Upham Pope, *A Survey of Persian Art from Prehistoric Times to the Present* (6 vols.; 1938–39), esp. vol. 1; idem, *Masterpieces of Persian Art* (1945); Ernst Emil Herzfeld, *Archeological History of Iran* (1935); idem, *Iran in the Ancient East* (1941); Erich Friedrich Schmidt, *Persepolis* (3 vols.; 1953–69).]

[8] [Xenephon, *Anabasis*, III, v, 15.]

may have been a luxury residence for the king and that such a grand city displayed royal power and gratified royal pride. Examples of such cities or residences are certainly not hard to find.

Yet Pope has subjected this entire interpretation to fundamental criticism, even though he is unable to construct a complete argument to support his own view. He sees Persepolis as a *sacred* city—like others to be found in the Ancient Near East, such as Arbela (which is not to deny that they were also meant to exhibit royal power). In accentuating the sacred character of Persepolis, Pope does not mean to say that the city had a normal urban life and that in addition to that it was sacred as well. Rather, the city was *intended* as a holy city, and this was decisive for the character of its buildings, its reliefs, its economy, etc., etc.[9]

Yet, is this so exceptional? Was not every ancient oriental city sacred in virtue of its temples, its processional streets, even its palaces and fortifications?

Religion and the ordinary

Here we have arrived at a point where it is necessary to look back over the route we have traveled. We can describe the cities in the customary way and never inquire into the deeper meaning of their existence. In an Egyptian city we find a lake, and we have the explanation ready at hand: water was urgently needed in Egypt for the economy and for hygiene, nor could cultic requirements dispense with it. But does that exhaust the meaning of water for the life of the city?

It is these and similar questions that should engage us. Their importance for understanding the history of the ancient Orient will not be lightly dismissed today. The studies of Lavedan have made a considerable impact.[10] In his entire *oeuvre* the idea is upheld that in the origin and life of cities, paramount importance must be attributed to religion, at least where Antiquity is concerned. Lavedan's work is cited approvingly with striking frequency. Yet it is no less striking that many scholars make little or no mention of the religious factor even in connection with the ancient oriental cities. Even a prominent specialist like Edith Ennen relegates the religious element to the background.[11]

By the religious factor in the construction of a city it is possible to mean the simple fact that a city has not only profane but also religious buildings. Temples, churches, but also palaces, fortifications, and even houses can be sacred edifices.

---

[9] [Cf. a later work by Pope, *Persian Architecture: The Triumph of Form and Color* (1965) 29f.: "The usual view that Persepolis was primarily a group of impressive palaces built in the capital city of a great empire in order to express political might and to gratify royal pride is Western thinking: factual, literal, rationalistic. It fails to comprehend the constellations of assumptions, attitudes, hopes that had descended from the ancient Orient with its ingrained reliance on emotions and symbolism. Persepolis . . . was, in fact, a sacred national shrine dedicated to a specific purpose: it would not only glorify the divinely sanctioned dynasty, proclaiming the political and religious unity of the state, but—even more important—it would also concentrate and heighten his [Darius's] empire's appeal to the powers of heaven for fertility and abundance, particularly at the spring festival of the new year."]

[10] Pierre Lavedan, *Histoire de l'urbanisme*; vol. 1: *Antiquité – Moyen Âge* (1926).

[11] See her well-known book *Frühgeschichte der europäischen Stadt* (1953).

Such sacred buildings occupied a larger place in the ancient and medieval worlds than they do in the cities of the present-day Western cultural sphere. Although these things no longer really need to be said, I may perhaps be permitted to point out as a sign of the times that it is just in the last decades that a great deal of attention has been paid to sacred buildings. Archeologists are no longer satisfied just to observe that a temple or palace show up in a city. Today they want to know in the first place what the function of these buildings was in the basic plan of the urban settlement. And it is not only the sacred buildings that are attracting attention. Scholars are also investigating the religious significance of the streets, lakes, fortifications, and so on. In the ancient Egyptian cities, for example, one would expect to find crooked, narrow streets, but instead there are broad avenues, ranging up to forty and even 120 meters in width. These are processional streets before all else—which serves to explain why they are so wide: full deployment of a procession required considerable space. Even in small cities, substantial space was left clear for processions. To mention a concrete example, in Amarna, well known through excavations, a straight street forty-eight meters wide was discovered running parallel to the river in a north-southerly direction. The other streets ran at right angles and/or parallel to this street, resulting in a city plan on the checkerboard model. Thus the design of the city was determined by a street of preponderantly religious significance: the processional street.

People have tried to prove the existence of such processional streets in medieval cities as well. I have in mind, for example, an essay by Noack on medieval town architecture.[12] While it is beyond doubt that the ancient oriental cities had their processional avenues, their presence is arguable where the Middle Ages are concerned. At issue are broad streets that some think were street markets but that Noack believes were processional streets from the period of the later Otto's. They would have been intended for the so-called *Festkrönungen*, occasions on which the king was crowned in the church and strode in full state to the main church for the mass; only the cities of the bishops had space enough for the elaborate ceremonial. As cities with such processional avenues Noack mentions Trier, Würzburg, Spiers, and several others.

It should now be clear what is normally understood by the "religious element" in city construction and urban life. Scholars can now—and they commonly do—describe urban life from economic or political or social or aesthetic vantage points, and likewise from the perspective of the religious aspect. And someone who takes a broad view will look at all these aspects in their mutual coherence, and in that way many a scholar, especially in recent years, has arrived at the insight of the dominating significance of religion in the urban civilization of the ancients.

---

[12] Ulrich Noack, "Stadtbaukunst," in *Festschrift für Kurt Bauch* (1957).

The Sacred Dwelling Place

Religion in a deeper sense

What I have in mind, however, when speaking of the "sacred" dwelling place and the "religious" meaning of cities, buildings and human settlements in the broadest sense, is not primarily temples, processional streets, churches, or any other such sacred structures. I use the word "religion" in connection with the concept 'dwelling place' in a much deeper and more universal sense. My intention is to raise the question whether the human dwelling place *as such*, whatever it may be, has religious significance.

Leaving modern times aside, let us direct our attention exclusively to Antiquity and the Middle Ages. I would emphasize that it is not my intention at this time to present the results of extensive research but rather to provide a few introductory reflections at the start of the investigation. Some such reflection is badly needed, for there is an obstacle to the unraveling of our problem that many take as a warning to venture no further. The apparently insurmountable difficulty is this: *the silence of the sources*. This seems an exaggeration; after all, the primary sources do speak of the sacral character of the human dwelling place. Indeed they do, but—let me put it this way: *What is the scope of what they say?* Is this universe of thought divulged only in vague outlines, and are the deeper-lying, truly motivating ideas suppressed? Must we strictly limit ourselves to what the source materials teach us in a direct way? The historian will prefer to adopt that method, accustomed as he is not to go beyond the sources. The phenomenologist of religion, in contrast, is easily disposed to look behind the sources, believing himself to have at his disposal sources of information which a historian would reject as speculative. Should we not choose the side of the historian? His method has a solid basis and leads to knowledge that is certain, does it not? It may just be, however, that ordinary sources will not reveal the very thing that is essential, that they will be silent about it, and that we will not even know why they keep silence. Yes, in that event the historian—not to mention the philosopher and phenomenologist—may venture upon extremely precarious paths and even deem these paths reliable, while the handbooks of historical method have not a good word to say about them. Let me bring my argument home to you with a few cases that have given rise to current controversies.

I have already mentioned Persepolis and the debate concerning it between Pope and others. Scholars as a rule try to understand Persepolis in terms of modern Western thought. They compare it with Versailles or with Hadrian's villa at Tivoli. The city then becomes an expression of a king's pursuit of power and grandeur. Accepted into the bargain are the inscriptions which dutifully proclaim that the buildings were erected by the grace of God and that kings are mediators between the divine and human worlds.

To my mind, one of the first conditions for acquiring an understanding of the dwelling place of the ancient and medieval worlds is an awareness that the natural presuppositions of modern Western science, with its exaggerated confidence in rationality and factuality, with its literalism and secularism, threatens to close off access to fundamental aspects of ancient Near Eastern civilization. Throughout the Orient, as Pope says, the religious motive was primary, and symbolism was the natural and universal form of thought.[13] Only when this is appreciated do we have a sound point of departure. Yet even that does not, at a stroke, solve all our problems and difficulties of interpretation.

To stay with Persepolis: its reliefs are celebrated and admired for their great aesthetic value. But let us have a closer look. On the reliefs there appears a bull that slays a lion, and a king that slays the bull. Is the meaning of all this that the king is mightier than lion and bull, or are we confronted here with a nature symbolism that was indispensable to the survival of life on earth? I am reminded also of the representations of the sacred mountain in the palaces of Persepolis: are they purely aesthetic depictions, or are they deeper symbols?

The sacred mountain played an enormous role in the Orient; beyond Mesopotamia, think of Angkor in Indo-China! Yet the portal had no less significance in the urban life of both East and West. The portal was preeminently the boundary between this world and another world. In Egypt especially, people reflected long and often on the meaning, the symbolism, of the portal and discovered in it the transition, the point of transition from death to life, the point where life conquers death, or more exactly, where life *rises* from death. And when we keep in mind, furthermore, that in symbolical thought the part usually stands for the whole, we can begin to gain some idea of what the Egyptians saw in the depiction of a portal.

In connection with it, too, the question presses: Did the portal in Egyptian life have technical and aesthetic significance only, and did it fulfill a symbolical function in religious contexts merely because it was eminently suited to do so? Or did the city gate in its religious meaning of transition from death to life have an irreplaceable and decisive significance in the life of the Egyptians?

We sense that this all comes down to the meaning of symbolical depictions as such in the lives of ancient peoples. The problem which I have concretized with these examples is essentially the same for the Middle Ages as it is for Antiquity.

(6) MEDIEVAL EUROPE

Huizinga asserts in *The Waning of the Middle Ages* that every aspect of the medieval universe of thought is thoroughly permeated by religious notions. This viewpoint has been formulated countless times, both before and since Huizinga gave expression to it: the Middle Ages are religious through and through, and even theocentric.

I am not convinced of very much of that, however—at any rate not when I go by the standard reference works on the subject[14] or the writings of great

---

[13] [Cf. Pope, *Persian Architecture*, 30.]
[14] E.g., the *Algemene Geschiedenis der Nederlanden* [History of the Low Countries].

medievalists like F. L. Ganshof. True, church and cloister, pope and priest occupy a very substantial place, but for the rest, life has a rather worldly, or better, secularized look such as we are familiar with today, and the idea that the medieval mind was thoroughly permeated by religious notions is a fine theory, but little is done with it in practice—I don't mean in the practice of medieval people but in the practice of present-day medievalist scholars (I do not say of *all* present-day scholars). People built cities. There they carried on an economic life and a social life, according to rules which still have validity. Naturally, there are important differences, but essentially there has been no change. Then as now, people acted rationally, in keeping with the principle of utility, and on occasion they would also act impractically. They built bulwarks around their cities for such obviously useful purposes as protection and security.

Perhaps someone will object: We cannot deny that this is the trend in our modern scholarly literature, but why are we to resist it? The medieval sources themselves are "worldly" and when we say that the Middle Ages were religious through and through then what we have in mind is the dominant position of church and theology.

To see whether this objection holds water I am going to comment briefly on a very recent article by Jacques le Goff. This writer is an authority in the field of medieval economic and social history and has made an important contribution to the question just posed in the form of an article that appeared in the *Annales*.[15] Here Le Goff argues that the concept of time in the ecclesiastical-religious sense differed fundamentally from the economic concept of time of the merchant of the High and Late Middle Ages. The average medieval person had no eye for the essential difference between the various historical periods; he was markedly indifferent to time. Or, as Marc Bloch has noted, in the Middle Ages there was an unmistakable flowing together of past and present, so that a second-century missionary, for example, was made a contemporary of Christ's. But now observe the merchant of the medieval towns, says Le Goff; his whole existence required an exact accounting of the measure of time: in economic life a minute can mean a fortune. Thus in sources pertaining to the economy, such as those for the annual fairs, great value is attached to correct time measures. One finds the same phenomenon in other contexts as well. In 1355 the governor of Artois set fixed hours for workers to arrive at their place of work. For the merchants, Le Goff concludes, an entirely new concept of time came into play. Time now became measurable and likewise *worldly*: it was the time for profane activities.[16]

Le Goff does not present very much that is new. Earlier research by Paul Rousset, Marc Bloch, Étienne Gilson and others had yielded the same results, at least insofar as the religious concept of time is concerned.

---

[15] "Au Moyen Âge: Temps de l'Église et temps du marchand," *Annales* 15 (1960): 417–33. [Reprinted in Jacques le Goff, *Pour un autre Moyen Âge. Temps, travail et culture en Occident* (1977); Eng. trans., *Time, Work, and Culture in the Middle Ages* (1980), 29–42.]

[16] Ibid., 424–28 [Eng. trans., 35–38].

And yet it is doubtful whether Le Goff's contrast is sound. In 1958 a dissertation appeared in Göttingen written by a Heinrich Schmidt dealing with town chronicles as "mirrors of late medieval burgher consciousness." [17] It attracted much attention in Germany. Schmidt gave the *Städtechroniken* an unusual reading. Reasoning along the line taken by Le Goff, one would expect to find in these Late Medieval town chronicles a modern conception of time; after all, merchants had been using it already in the High Middle Ages. Schmidt, however, arrives at the conclusion that in order to read these chronicles properly we must first forget our modern concepts: only then will we discover that, right along with all kinds of factual reports and legal documents, the chronicles present a picture of the world, of time and history, that is distinctively their own—confusing to the modern sense, but to the medieval sense having a deeper unity.

The most surprising finding of Schmidt's study, however, is the blurring of the conception of time in these chronicles. They shift the contemporary juridical status of the town back to the origin and bring the origin forward into the present —thereby abolishing all historical evolution, which is to say that the time measure, or the *value* of time, disappears.

I trust that this presentation of the controversy between Le Goff and Schmidt will have cast sufficient light on the path I want to take. Both authors devote insufficient attention to an important aspect of the problem of time in the Middle Ages, so that the controversy, especially in Le Goff's approach, cannot be brought to a satisfactory resolution. But we fully agree with Schmidt in maintaining that even when we come upon directly accessible notions in the sources, we must still first ask what they meant to the medieval mind. So, to bring the matter to a head and return to our subject: what does a *wall* mean to a medieval person, and why has he enclosed his cities with walls?

To be able to answer those questions, it will be worthwhile to take note of certain peculiar features of medieval thinking.

a. Pars pro toto thinking is strongly present in the Middle Ages. For centuries people imagined the city by thinking of its walls and/or gates and towers. In *De universo* by Hrabanus Maurus we read: *Murus autem ipsius civitatis inexpugnabilem fidei, caritatis speique firmitatem significat*: "The wall of this city signifies the invincible firmness of faith, love, and hope." [18] In numerous cases the walls are sufficient to represent the entire city.

b. For ancient and medieval people the city had a profound meaning, often expressed by means of symbolical devices. The city was the domain of justice and order, and the walls and towers were what enclosed and secured it. Through the *civitas* man was free, delivered from the peril and disorder that ruled the countryside. Justice reigned within the city walls, but injustice was a tyrant

---

[17] Heinrich Schmidt, *Die deutschen Städtechroniken als Spiegel des bürgerlichen Selbstverständnisses im Spätmittelalter.*

[18] In Migne, *Patrologia Latina*, 111, l. xiv, 384.

holding sway outside these bulwarks, in the wilderness.[19] Numerous illustrations bear out this interpretation. Also indicative is the representation of the first human pair being driven out of the city gate, out of the domain of divine civil order, into a desolate country devoid of justice. This motif is found in all phases of the medieval period. Thus the city was highly esteemed in the Middle Ages.

    c. To the medieval mind the ideal city was circular. Circularity was the image of perfection. (It could be objected here that a hexagon was the form of the perfect city—see especially the miniatures of the Early and High Middle Ages—but it should be borne in mind that the hexagon and the circle were closely associated in meaning.) People conceived of the heavenly city and eternal Jerusalem as circular—that is, perfect—cities. And so the earthly city, too, had to have a perfect form. From the twelfth century onward, to be sure, preference was given to the rectangular or square designs for smaller towns, probably for practical reasons; yet even then depictions of ideal forms reveal a continued preference for the circular city. Rome and Jerusalem, for example, continue to be circles, and on a seal of Louis of Bavaria dating from 1328 we find imprinted: *Roma caput mundi regit orbis frena rotundi*: "Rome, the capital of the world, controls the reins of the circular world." One could not imagine the form of the walls of Rome without a symbolical meaning.

    d. The symbolism goes even further. The walls had twelve gates. The heavenly Jerusalem had twelve portals. And Milan, before its destruction by the barbarians, was described as a city with twelve mighty gates. In the smaller towns especially, as late as the fourteenth century, people tried to divide the town's domain into twelve equal parts.

    e. There were many deviations and irregularities to which one might call attention, but behind them medieval people still saw the form of the ideal city, in intimate relation with the actual city. For example, there were fifteen gates in the third wall built around Florence, yet in some surveys of the city, as that of 1339, we read: *portas habens duodecim magnifice forme*: "having twelve gates of glorious beauty."

    f. For this entire subject we shall have to detach ourselves from modern conceptions. That is even clearer from the following example. A church in the Middle Ages was built after the model of another church, the ideal church. To the medieval mind they looked alike, but the modern reader wonders how they ever managed to see a resemblance. The medieval notion of representation, symbol, likeness differed entirely from ours. It did not involve the whole but was *limited* to a few choice *essential* elements. Only with the thirteenth century is there a shift toward efforts at reproducing visible aspects of the originals. By contrast, a modern representation, with its exactness in rendering the *entire* building and with its pursuit of absolute reliability, leaves out the *substance and meaning* of the edifice—the very *goal and essence of the medieval model or representation.*

---

[19] Cf. Günter Bandmann, *Mittelalterliche Architektur als Bedeutungsträger* (1951), 97ff.

To medieval people, exact imitation of the model was not essential. For instance, they often copied the Church of the Holy Sepulcher and are even known to have traveled to the Holy Land to take its measurements; yet to the modern eye it is difficult to discover similarities between the affiliated structures and the model church. The medieval person was concerned to imitate what he regarded as an *important*, and to him *meaningful*, feature of the model. For if such a feature were incorporated or worked into the building there would be an *inner, essential* relation between the old model and the new building, and this connection far transcended the copying of the external forms. That was the case, for example, with regard to numbers derived from the Church of the Holy Sepulcher. Eight was taken to involve the return of one; it was a symbol of new life, of regeneration (see, e.g., Candidus of Fulda). A great variety of interpretations was possible. Thus the measurements and imitations pertained only to particular parts or aspects. Yet these aspects placed the entire building in which they were applied, not just in relation to but *fully in the center of* the higher, ideal order. The medieval term for it was typical (*typice*) or figurative (*figuraliter*) construction.

Some concluding observations

I can understand that people have approached the life of ancient civilizations and of earlier times with modern notions in mind. In earlier times, too, people allowed themselves to be guided by considerations—even by the necessity—of self-preservation and utility, and when the sources tell about that naively we must not go on to look for too much behind it. We understand the sources so well and so immediately because in them human beings speak to human beings. To give a very concrete example: Must we look *per se* for deep religious motives behind the many feuds between cities?

With these questions—I concede at once—we have approached the most critical point in my presentation. I cannot even answer them adequately at the moment—happily not, for then I would already have reached the end of an investigation that will, I think, require many years.

It does, however, even now raise another question that has so far remained too much in the background. Is it really so important whether people used to see more in a city or some other human settlement than a rationally furnished dwelling place? People may have attached ever so many religious and symbolical notions to walls, portals, palaces, fortresses, yes even to hovels, but did all that symbolism not remain far removed from the humdrum, everyday life of society and politics? Anyone who would so assess the case would thereby show that he had not yet succeeded in disengaging himself from modern concepts.

Fortunately, there is a growing awareness that symbols in Antiquity and the Middle Ages were not yet weakened, let alone emptied of meaning, as they have been in recent centuries. Scholars are becoming much more conscious that in the mind of the ancients religious ideas did not lead the shadowy, marginal existence they are so often condemned to today.

A primary distinction in the history of religions is that between the sacred and the profane. This armchair distinction has far-reaching significance: it suggests a *split* that makes itself felt in all parts of life, a split that cuts through the homogeneity of space and thus affects the human dwelling place as well. The constant concern of the ancients was to maintain contact with the sacred and to remain within its ambit, since only what is sacred is real, and life arises from the sacred alone.

The sacred space had enormous significance in the lives of practically all peoples, for here communication could be had with the other world of divine beings and of the forefathers, with the world of divine forces. This accounts for the great concern of many peoples for the *opening*: the *opening* in the tent, in the *roof of the hut*. In this universe of thought, the portal too—the palace doors first of all, but no less the city gate—had a crucial function to fulfill.

The sacred space, in assuring contact with the source of life, is itself the point of intersection between the sacred and the profane. But communication with the other, cosmic, celestial world can take place in another way as well, namely, by means of the symbol. We shall have to disengage ourselves, however, from our idea of the symbol. In the conception of many peoples, the symbol was the unifying link between seemingly distinct realities. Finding oneself in the symbol meant participating in the symbolized reality. People remained aware of the distinction between symbol and reality but acted as if the two were identical. It is beyond our capacity adequately to express the relation entailed in the symbol. For that matter, the ancients never succeeded in doing so either. But the relation is essential none the less, for it is the way to linking the other existence with this existence; and to link them means to have this life participate in the divine, cosmic life. Whenever people built a model of the sacred mountain in the palace or the city, or even merely painted the sacred mountain on the walls, then the palace, city or fortress itself participated in the sacred mountain—which is to say that in the mountains were concentrated the mysterious forces of life that produced vegetation, from the mountains arose a renewing primordial force, and a simple depiction in the sacred space was basic to the survival of an entire nation.

By the same token, people took great care in selecting the site for a settlement. The ways in which the city could reflect cosmic relations were calculated with great precision. Primary importance in this regard was given to celestial direction, number, circular or rectangular model. The application of a cosmic number meant that people lived in cosmic relations here on earth. The imagination of the ancients was inexhaustible, ranging from the vague to the concrete. Symbolical thinking exhibits an elasticity that can drive a scientific researcher to despair.

One must keep in mind that something impossible was expected of symbolism in the ancient sense: the linking together of the sacred and the profane after they had first been separated from each other. This is the deeper reason why one and the same human dwelling place can be sacred one moment and profane the next, and why the street, portal or pillar can be nothing more than an ordinary avenue, entryway or technical support at one moment and at the next lose its contours and be absorbed into the transmundane reality it is meant to represent. Suger of St. Denis saw the pillars of his abbey church transformed into the twelve apostles—and he was not out of his senses when he saw it.

9/ A TURNABOUT IN HISTORICAL SCIENCE?

THE QUESTION MARK after the title of my paper [1] will suit many of you. I can answer the question both affirmatively and negatively myself. Many of you will wonder whether the changes in our picture of history are so drastic that we may speak of a turnabout.

True, our primary source material is growing very rapidly on the whole, and in various areas of historical science a reorientation has proved imperative. I mention just two instances: the discovery of the Dead Sea Scrolls, and the discovery of numerous philosophical and theological works from the Middle Ages. Yet all this—and I could mention a great deal more—is not sufficient to warrant speaking of a "turnabout" taking place in a discipline. That would require more than just an increase of source material and, thanks to it, improved knowledge of a historical phenomenon, of an institution, of a complex of events. We shall speak of a turnabout only when the *outlook* on history changes.

Generally speaking, a proliferation of source material and a change in *outlook* go hand in hand, yet this is not always the case. It happens not infrequently that old, familiar material that has seen little or no augmentation is interpreted differently, sometimes entirely differently, after the passage of time. Medieval studies in particular are rich in such reinterpretations. I mention as an example Heinrich Fichtenau's assessment of the primary sources for Charlemagne's coronation as emperor in 800. Fichtenau uses the old, familiar sources but arrives at new conclusions. Why, however, does he choose to accept the reliability of the *Annales Laureshamenses* while this is doubted by most experts? Does Fichtenau's interpretation deserve preference because it is scientifically more sound? His conclusion is accepted on those grounds, but when we examine it in the context of his picture of history, we say: his preference is in part a matter of *historical outlook*.[2]

My line of argument so far implies, however, that the *outlook* or *change in outlook* on history as a whole or on a particular event is determined not only by the source material but by a much more comprehensive background.

It will be necessary to set several limits on my presentation today. Obviously, it will deal primarily with views current in the present and in the recent past. To draw a line there, however, is more difficult. The number of

---

[1] Presented to the Gezelschap van Christelijke Historici in its session of 3 Sept. 1962.
[2] See H. Fichtenau, "Karl der Grosse und das Kaisertum," *Mitteilungen des Instituts für Österreichische Geschichtsforschung* 6 (1953): 257–334. [Cf. idem, *The Carolingian Empire*, trans. Peter Munz (Oxford, 1957), 74.]

phenomena pointing to a turnabout is exceedingly large, and it is impossible to deal with all of them in a single session. Nevertheless, the formulation of our subject promises completeness insofar as possible. Though less than satisfactory, a *choice* must be made from a large number of problems, and it will be up to you to judge whether I have made a happy selection.

I need not restrict myself to the *science* of history or to the *writing* of history or to the *view* of history, for from the use of the concept *historical outlook* it is at once obvious that our subject is the mutual relations of all of these within the single discipline of history.

Finally, I must, to my regret, set one other limit. I shall offer no *evaluation* of the questions to be discussed. Within the limited framework just indicated they can only be presented in outline; a searching discussion would require a separate study for each.

Uneasiness among historians

Prevalent among many practicing historians today is a strong sense of uneasiness. Note that I say *many*, and that I have not yet said *what* it is that so many feel uneasy about, for that is difficult to define. I believe, however, that I shall not be very far from the core of this uneasiness if I regard it as an expression of the feeling that the historical profession is not fulfilling its purpose. There is concern, in the first place, that all too many historians are preoccupied with isolated facts, with facts, moreover, that are viewed only from the outside or that have no essential value. Secondly, there is concern that history is gradually losing importance in our culture.

I said that many *historians* are troubled. It is important to take note of this. That *philosophers* of history have serious objections to the common way of doing history is a well-known fact, but this generally does not bother practicing historians very much.

Furthermore, it is *many* historians who are concerned, thus *not all*. There are others who are also not quite at peace but whose uneasiness is of an altogether different sort. Their complaint is that our source materials are still defective in many respects and that there is no prospect of filling in all the gaps in our historical knowledge. In addition, research techniques and methods of procedure are still far from perfect. But what grieves them the most is that preconceptions which by their very nature involve philosophy, theology, or worldview are being admitted into the practice of strictly scientific history. This group too will on occasion acknowledge history's loss of function in contemporary society, but they expect a recovery as soon as the present anti-historical storm has blown over—and is it not subsiding already? Or else they advocate as a remedy the writing of history once again in the grand manner of the great historians of former times who inspired entire generations through their creative powers. Or, again, they retreat from the impasse with the declaration that the true historian need not concern himself with the *usefulness* of his studies; he need only establish how things actually went in history. All that the professional researcher does, as it were, is to make the facts available (although it is not a matter of indifference to him into what edifice his bricks are ultimately incorporated).

Perhaps you are not happy with my portrait of this second group and would like to hear the actual words of someone who takes the position I have just described. Very well, listen to what Professor Enklaar wrote in a book review not too long ago: "[O]ur author shows himself to be more an aesthete than a historian, *the latter of whom is disposed, or has learned, to look at the course of world events, even in changing times, with neutral resignation, as from a distance.*"[3]

It would be difficult to express more sharply the controversy between the "neutrals" and the "concerned." The latter vehemently oppose this "neutral resignation." They complain bitterly, for example, that the historians' preference for remaining unimpassioned observers at a distance, passing their lives in strict scientific erudition with no relevance for life, is co-responsible for the fact that France in 1940 was easily trampled underfoot, forfeiting its leading position in the world.[4] Similarly, when human nature with its "confused, superstitious, and dark emotions, which can be marshaled by leaders under myths and symbols" allows dictators to rise to power, then the historian may not remain indifferent but must come out of his "ivory tower."[5] The present has hitherto been the "victim of the past," but from now on the present will exploit the past.[6]

Conyers Read, another of the concerned, has spoken in this connection of the "self-indulgence" of the historian.[7] With that, the background of the concern is clearly indicated: it is concern about *man*, who is shortchanged in traditional historical practice. Here we are confronted by an extremely complicated problem. I shall try, leaving various aspects aside, to present an analysis of it.

The focus on man

In the first place, we must not think here of the dilemma whether history is determined by the great personalities or ruled by suprapersonal, anonymous forces. It is a lingering legacy of the Renaissance, the 'new historians' declare,

---

[3] D. T. Enklaar in *Bijdragen tot de Geschiedenis der Nederlanden* 6 (1951/52): 240f.

[4] Thus Lucien Febvre in his *Combats pour l'histoire* (1953), in a review article of Marc Bloch's *Strange Defeat* (1949). [Eng. trans. in Peter Burke, ed., *A New Kind of History: From the Writings of Febvre* (1973), 27–43, at 42 note 2.]

[5] Thus Charles A. Beard and Alfred Vagts, "Currents of Thought in Historiography," *American Historical Review* 42 (1936/37): 460–83, at 460.

[6] Thus James Harvey Robinson, *The New History: Essays Illustrating the Modern Historical Outlook* (1912), 5. For this and the following paragraphs, see Fritz Fischer, "Objektivität und Subjektivität—ein Prinzipienstreit in der amerikanischen Geschichtsschreibung," in A. Hermann, ed., *Aus Geschichte und Politik* (1954), 167–82.

[7] Cf. Conyers Read, "The Social Responsibilities of the Historian," *American Historical Review* 55 (1949/50): 280: ". . . the ivory towers we have erected for our private enjoyment, if they are to survive, must be converted into research laboratories. Learning without reference to social living has no more claim upon social support than any other form of self-indulgence."

to focus attention primarily on the ruler, the artistic genius, the great man; it is up to us to debunk the great historical personalities and to focus our research on the common man, perhaps the anonymous individual in the masses. This is the demand of our anthropologically, or rather anthropo*centric*ally minded age.

The usefulness of scientific history in this view is made tangible, as it were, in the human interests it serves. Society in this century is undergoing progressive development on the way to a better and happier future. Man's task in all this is not that of an observer. Rather, he ought to participate fully through an ambitious program of social action. An important task is reserved for history. Though renamed an *auxiliary science*—the name is a token of its subordination and usefulness alike—history provides a service that is indispensable: it provides the raw material, the facts with which "to promote rational progress."

You have been listening to tones from a very influential circle of American historians, the *liberals*: Robinson, Becker, Beard, Read, and many others. Enlightenment thought, socialism in various forms, Marxism—these all had their influence on them, but no less so, in a more recent phase, the politics of the New Deal (which they influenced in turn). Of perhaps still greater influence, however, has been American pragmatism, according to which the social sciences have a direct stake in history because of the useful empirical source material it provides.

The "liberal" historians in the United States are not the only ones who put all the emphasis on the central importance of man for historical study. Various schools in Europe are doing the same thing. For instance, in the *Annales* circle (thus of Febvre, Braudel, and others[8]) we are told over and over again that history is about man, that man is the true subject of historical study. Human creative activity and the inexhaustible wealth of human potentials are of paramount importance, rather than the facts. If one deals primarily with facts, man will also be *determined* by the facts.

Following their line of argument further, however, we discover that they got stuck. Here we bump up against a peculiar difficulty, which occurs not only in the circle of the *Annales* but which is a topic of debate in numerous kindred schools. I see myself compelled to discuss our general problem at some length.

For a long time already historians have battled over the question what factors are at work in the historical process, what factors control it, or more generally formulated, what connections exist between the various factors (political, economic, psychological, geographical, natural factors, ideas). There is virtually no phenomenon in history that has not been subjected to the merry-go-round of factors. Many a historian is weary of this game—I have in mind the circle of the *Annales*, but no less Werner Conze, as well as the holists, the integralists, the structuralists in the broader sense (for the sake of convenience I am using labels). But, what is more important, they have come to the

---

[8] [Historians associated with the French journal founded in 1929 and continued after 1945 under the title *Annales: économies, sociétés, civilisations*.]

insight that the current way of practicing history can never achieve its objective. Historians start out from the isolated factor, from the isolated (preferably political) fact, and in so doing touch only the external side of historical events and can arrive at best at a synthesis.

Take good note of this word synthesis. It is the binding together of things in an external way, the combining of what was separated and remains intrinsically separated for lack of an *original* coherence. By taking their point of departure in components (the individualistic or "meristic" method, according to Othmar F. Anderle), historians are depriving themselves of the possibility of ever discovering what belongs originally together. This is the fate of "event history," of *l'histoire événementielle* (as the school of the *Annales* likes to call it). There is only one way out, believes Fernand Braudel, and that is to listen to the *histoire nouvelle*. This 'new history' is *l'histoire sociale*, but then not in the old sense of social history that focused on the social question or on social life. The new social history must be taken as a *histoire des structures*, which is to say that all aspects of a civilization, of a society, of a historical period penetrate each other, forming a true structure in which the many elements are genuinely intertwined in an original way and for a long duration.[9] Historians are to take their point of departure in a coherent organic whole—a period, a culture, etc. They are to think themselves into it, understand it as such at its deepest level, and only on that basis go on to describe its elements and the behavior of individuals. There is not a political history and an economic history and an art history. As Febvre once put it: there is only one history, and that is simply *l'histoire sociale*.[10]

We encounter *parallel* conceptions in the integralistic and holistic approaches advocated by, respectively, Romein and Anderle. Generally, says Anderle, historians proceed according to the meristic method, but by this route they never arrive at the real coherence; to reach that, they need a "reversal of methods": to descend from the whole, the *Ganzheit*, the totality, the structure, to the component parts, the constituent elements. The terminology is curious: Anderle says a "meristic" method works synthetically but the holistic-integralistic method analytically.[11]

To illustrate, I give three examples. First, a favorite one in *Annales* circles. In his study on "death in fifteenth-century art" Alberto Tenenti observes that the representations of death undergo a fundamental change in that century: instead of the so-called heavenly death, that is, serene death focused on the hereafter, there now comes a truly human representation of death, dominated by reason. But earlier historians have seen that too, have they not? Certainly, Tenenti explains; but what usually eluded them—Huizinga is an exception—is that this

---

[9] See F. Braudel, "Sur une conception de l'Histoire sociale," *Annales* 14 (1959): 308–19.

[10] Cf. Febvre, *Combats pour l'histoire*, 20.

[11] Othmar F. Anderle, "Arnold J. Toynbee und die Problematik der geschichtlichen Sinndeutung," *Die Welt als Geschichte* 20 (1960): 143–56, at 147.

drastic change in the representation of death conformed to the change of *structure* of the entire period, a change that manifests itself in all phenomena of this time.[12] Thus every period and every civilization has its own universe of feelings and thoughts, a *univers mental*. In this respect they are all distinct from other periods and civilizations, and this distinctiveness penetrates *to* and arises *from* the deepest level.

My second example is taken from Fernand Braudel. A civilization, the French for example, can undergo major upheavals and suffer great losses yet retain virtually all of its distinctives and points of originality as against other civilizations. Thus "the French Revolution is not a total break in the destiny of French civilization, nor the Revolution of 1917 in the Russian. . . ." [13]

Now a third illustration, from the integralistic-holistic historical writing of Anderle. The assassination of Wallenstein makes sense only in terms of a comprehensive whole in which the component parts are mutually dependent and non-interchangeable. In itself the death of Wallenstein is "fortuitous," but it acquires meaning in the entire complex of the Thirty Years' War, which in its turn acquires meaning only as a substructure of the Age of Spain, etc., etc., until we arrive at the last meaning-unit in this holistic regress: the framework of Western culture as a whole.[14]

Some critical questions

As announced, I shall not engage in criticism, but for the sake of what follows it is of importance to pose the following critical questions—though this certainly does not mean that we decide against the structuralistic and holistic method in favor of the prevailing way of writing history: the same critical questions can be posed with equal justice of the latter.

1) If in the various civilizations and periods we are dealing with totally irreducible worlds, each with its uniquely distinctive *univers mental*, how will we be able, in an authentic way, to get to know or understand other peoples, other styles, other universes of thought?

2) We must—so we are told—proceed from the whole or the structure in order to get to know the parts or the details. But how can we arrive at an intimate knowledge of this all-controlling structure if we are not permitted to traverse the way from below (from the component) to above (the structure, the civilization)?

3) The most important question is the following. One of the deepest tendencies of current historical science, as we saw, is consideration for man, even more for what is essential in him, his freedom. Historians have set out to save man from the determining powers, from the terror of history. With this program all the schools under discussion (the American liberals, the structuralists, the

---

[12] A. Tenenti, *La Vie et la Mort à travers l'art du XVe siècle* [Life and death in fifteenth-century art] (1952).

[13] Braudel, "L'Apport de l'histoire des civilisations," *La Table Ronde*, no. 137 (May 1959): 65f [Eng. trans., 210].

[14] Anderle (see note 11), 146.

integralists, etc.) have launched their campaign against the modern disciples of Ranke. And what has been the result?

Allow me to read you several quotations. Braudel, addressing himself to the *histoire des structures*, talks of "this silent and *imperious* history of civilizations": all the phenomena of time obey this history—at bottom in any case.[15] And what Febvre writes is almost disconcerting: ". . . human beings carry society within them to the depths of their individuality, an individuality for which society provides the definitive key and explanation."[16] And once more we hear Braudel: Individual lives and events are little more than specks of dust; "they pass across the stage of history like fireflies, scarcely glimpsed before they are swallowed up again by the night, often passing into permanent oblivion."[17] And all this has been written by those who have called *man* the true subject of history!

History and freedom

The problem is too comprehensive, however, to dispose of the criticism and the efforts of Braudel, Anderle, and others without further analysis. Placing the problem of structure and factors in a broader context, we want to note two points in particular. Both points hinge on the question: What is history, really?

1) In modern historical science it is repeated ad nauseam that its central concern is the individual, the unique, the unrepeatable. But does this stand on its own? Surely it is ordered in a coherence? I shall return to these questions.

2) When the school of the *Annales*, however inconsistently, makes the case for man, it has good reasons. One of its sympathizers, Professor Boogman, has censured the—still all too common—*finalistic* scheme, in which the past is viewed far too much as a preparation for the present and is reconstructed simply as a rectilinear, natural development.[18] Such an approach fails to acknowledge the originality, the uniqueness, but especially the intrinsic value of an event or a period. The tenth and eleventh centuries have often had to forfeit their uniqueness because they have been regarded almost exclusively as a preparation for the luxuriant blossoming of the twelfth century. In contrast, the old cyclical theory but no less the new *histoire des structures* made it their central doctrine that historical periods and cultures have their value within themselves.

---

[15] Braudel, "Les responsabilités de l'histoire," *Cahiers internationaux de sociologie* 10 (1951): 16.

[16] Febvre, "Pro parva nostra domo. Sur deux articles belges," *Annales* 8 (1953): 514.

[17] Braudel, *La Méditerranée et le Monde Méditerranéen à l'époque de Philippe II* (1949), 721 [cf. 2nd rev. ed. (1966), 2:223; Eng. trans., *The Mediterranean and the Mediterranean World in the Age of Philip II* (1973), 2:901]. But for a trenchant critique see Gerhard Ritter, "Zur Problematik gegenwärtige Geschichtsschreibung," in idem, *Lebendige Vergangenheit. Beiträge zur historisch-politischen Selbstbesinnung* (1958), 255–83.

[18] J. C. Boogman, *Vaderlandse geschiedenis (na de middeleewen) in hedendaags perspectief; enige kanttekeningen en beschouwingen* [Dutch (post-medieval) history in present-day perspective: some glosses and reflections] (inaugural lecture, Groningen, 1959), 4.

But I believe even more is at stake here. At stake is man, his freedom and responsibility. What is left of human freedom if history advances irresistibly and man imagines he is giving shape to events yet is himself at bottom determined by the sovereign course of history?

With that we have arrived at the theme of freedom in history, a key theme for both philosophy of history and historical science. It will be clear that the question of freedom refers not only to man in his relation to the State but also, in a far greater degree, to his relation to actual historical events, to history as such.

It cannot escape our notice that philosophers of history have been much more preoccupied with this question than working historians have been. Just think of Hegel, for whom the goal of history is "progress in awareness of freedom." Freedom is central in the thought of towering historicists like Dilthey and Troeltsch. And is human freedom not the main theme of the philosophers of existence? But even in the technical monographs of working historians, freedom time and again turns out to be the dynamic factor, and increasingly so in recent decades.

Yet the difference in approach remains. Why, and to what end? As I see it, the deeper explanation is that one can deal with history in two ways insofar as its essence is concerned (and I would add immediately that the line of division does not run between philosophers of history and working historians). Two diametrically opposite effects issue from history: on the one hand, an enriching effect, creative of meaning; on the other, an emptying effect, depriving of meaning. This polarity is as old as history itself, but the tension reached its high point in the second half of the nineteenth and first half of the twentieth centuries —an inevitable complement of the strong awakening of historical consciousness in this period.

It deserves to be noted, first and foremost, that the unveiling of history through historical research meant an unparalleled enrichment of human existence. For the first time man was in a position to see things in historical perspective, to see them in their becoming. Whole cultures, even worlds, opened up their riches to untiring investigation. Historical traditions, convictions, forms of life, myths and philosophies disclosed what had been concealed for centuries. Thus the last two centuries bear as much the stamp of history as they bear the mark of progress in the natural sciences. It is only natural that the working historian should first of all experience the enriching effect of history and that its depriving effect should generally make little impression on him. One who devotes himself lovingly to the facts of history is richly rewarded.

None of this, of course, has eluded the philosophers of history. Only, they (and some practitioners of historical science) have been equally impressed by the depriving effect of history. For, said they, if historical consciousness has thrown open the treasure chambers of history, it has at the same time unmasked every belief, every worldview, every phenomenon in all its historical conditionality and limitation, in all its relativity. Every religion, art form, philosophical insight, etc., is valid only in a particular time-bound period and can make no claim whatever to general validity.

In earlier times, too, people lived with transitoriness and mutability, but it did not touch historically existing man at the depth-level: precisely the depth, the essence, the substance, the core, the true nature of things were perceived as unaffected by the changing times. History was there, of course, but it touched only the exterior, the accidental. The new historical mode of thinking, however, has discovered man in his true nature, which is not substance but, on the contrary, *historicity*. "Man, as a type, dissolves in the process of history," said Dilthey, who elaborated extensively the theme of man as history; hence when man sees life's values and goals sinking away in the relativity and anarchy of the flux of history, then nothing is left to him in the midst of the treasures of past and present but the "pain of emptiness."[19] Indeed, pain; for it is no secret to historical thought that man has an urge to rise above his limitation and take up residence on higher ground, far removed from relativity. Nevertheless, historical consciousness deprives him of precisely that: it knows only of constant leave-taking, never again to find a permanent home.

Why does historicism take this gloomy road of deprivation rather than the path of enrichment that historical consciousness has equally opened up? Because historicism manages—in fear and trembling—to ascribe a positive meaning to it. Whoever travels this road *to the end* is rewarded with the *liberation of man*. Just listen: historical consciousness of the finiteness of every historical phenomenon or social condition, of the relativity of every sort of belief "is the final step in the liberation of man."[20] Man is no longer bound to one true faith, to one social or philosophical system. Accordingly, Dilthey can write, "The knife of historical relativism ... must also bring healing"—and that healing is freedom.[21]

Here, I believe, we have hit upon the deepest motive of historicism: the emancipation of the human personality and the recognition of its sovereignty.

When existentialism came to work out the freedom motif it did so entirely in agreement with historicism. If man were to receive deliverance as coming from the meaning of history, his emancipation would come to an end. Therefore man does not receive the meaning of his existence from metahistory, nor yet from the historical process, even less from the future, and thus he realizes his existential freedom. Yet where then does he find the meaning of his life, and how then can meaning still be ascribed to events? No longer from without, but through the fact that the well-spring of meaning lies in the event: the event has its meaning, its ordering power fully within itself, and man "projects" the meaning of his existence in terms of himself, in terms of his own sovereign autonomy. Naturally, the fundamental problem now becomes: How is history

---

[19] Wilhelm Dilthey, *Gesammelte Schriften*, 8:6,194.
[20] Ibid., 7:290; see also 5:9.
[21] Ibid., 8:234.

still possible if these meaning-charged monads (events and persons) may have no meaningful connection with one another?

A reaction to historicism
If the historicistic and existentialistic mode of thought has left its mark on philosophers and theologians as well as professional historians,[22] no less noteworthy is the vehement reaction to it by others.[23] The latter rebel against historical thinking as such, and they find support in the current revival of natural law. Now when they emphatically assure us that the most implacable resistance at the awakening of modern historical consciousness was offered in terms of *natural law*, then we suspect that an old, supposedly dead controversy has sprung to new and vigorous life. We observe a renewed interest in the *Ansichseiende*, in objective Being, in the elements of tradition, in the classical epochs, that is, in the peaks of history—peaks, Krüger explains, because they were relatively closer to *the* reality, to the *Ansichseiende*.[24] And Löwith turns from that which ebbs away in history to that which is enduringly human, to nature and the world as such: man must understand himself not as a historical being but as a member of the cosmos.[25]

In Löwith's view, history has become the "ultimate religion." [26] He traces the concept back, behind its secularization in modern times, to Judaism and Christianity with their discovery of the historical world and historical existence, whose meaning is located in the *telos* of the future.[27] But this turning to history was achieved only by turning away from the world and from nature, from what is enduring (*immer-während*), from what is constant.[28]

One wonders, what will become of history if its "most elementary form" is permanence, not a permanence sprung from some transcendent reality but from nature, from the cosmos? And yet, how understandable this reaction is!

The ultimate question: metahistorical convictions
Here I must break off my sketch in order not to impose upon your indulgence. In preparing it for publication I shall work it out. I especially regret that I cannot now take up the new approach to history from the side of such Christian

---

[22] E.g., Hofer, Smith, Michalson, Butterfield, Thévenaz, E. Grassi.

[23] E.g., Löwith, Krüger.

[24] See Gerhard Krüger, *Freiheit und Weltverwaltung. Aufsätze zur Philosophie der Geschichte* (1958), 125, 138, 140.

[25] Karl Löwith, *Der Weltbegriff der neuzeitlichen Philosophie* (1960), passim.

[26] Löwith, "Die Dynamik der Geschichte und der Historismus," *Eranos-Jahrbuch* 21 (1952): 217–54, at 244.

[27] Löwith, *Meaning in History* (1949), passim. In a similar vein Gerhard Gloege, "Vom Sinn der Weltgeschichte; Überlegungen zum Thema 'Heilsgeschehen und Weltgeschichte,'" *Lutherische Monatshefte* 2 (1963): 112–22; repr. in Gerhard Gloege, *Heilsgeschehen und Welt. Theologische Traktate*, vol. 1 (1965), 27–52.

[28] Löwith, "Natur und Geschichte," *Die Neue Rundschau* 62 (1951): 65ff.

historians as Wittram, Butterfield, Meinhold, Marrou, Dawson.[29] Nevertheless, I must not omit some kind of epilogue.

Perhaps the thought has occurred to you, or at least to some of you: What have all these ruminations to do with historical science? The topic was to have been the historical discipline in general, but all our attention has been absorbed by views of history. Well, one ought to keep the following in mind. With the exception of the structuralist and integralist approaches, what has developed in the *views* of history shows up as mere *tendencies* in the practice of historical science—tendencies, however, which are growing year by year.

In the inaugural lectures of Niermeyer and Boogman, for example, one can detect a budding sympathy for, respectively, social history in the new sense and the structuralist approach; yet both scholars are in the first instance professional historians. And is Butterfield's conception of history comprehensible apart from the existential philosophers? Is Marrou's? And what to think, in this connection, of the new integralists? And lastly—to leave it at that—preparations are afoot among German historians to write world-history again, though not from the standpoint of philosophy of history but on the basis of the results of the special sciences. But wait! now that they have begun to reflect on the *concept* of world-history the element our German colleagues are arguing about is the concept *world*. How the debate will end is still difficult to say, but it is certain that the old conception of world-history will not get a second chance. Instead, a lot of weight is being given to Löwith's idea of the relation between world and history, with primacy for the world.

These examples illustrate that theoretical and philosophical reflections do influence our work, although by the time they reach our discipline they have already lost much of their vigor and freshness; it is at most tendencies that are adopted. But has it ever been otherwise? Ideas have generally impregnated historical science in weakened form, but precisely in this way they have induced historians to embark on new roads.

And so I can return to the prologue, to that uneasy feeling, that inner uncertainty expressed by so many contemporary historians.[30] Where does it stem from? To clarify my answer I would recall for a moment several thoughts of Robert Fruin's, together forming a bit of philosophy of history, be it of simple construction. I refer to his convocation address, *The Significance and Value of History*, given at Leiden at the beginning of the academic year in 1867 and repeated in 1870 and 1872.[31] Fruin observes that in his time many people are interested in history, and he attributes this phenomenon "to the entire direction of our time, which may indeed be called the historical direction. . . ." Fruin then turns on the revolutionary mind:

---

[29] [See the paper of three years later, essay 11 below.]

[30] I would refer to statements by Postan, Caillois, Barraclough, Wedgwood, Heimpel.

[31] Fruin, "De betekenis en waarde der geschiedenis," in *Verspreide Geschriften,* 9:337–42.

Our time stands diametrically opposed in its mode of thought to the spirit of revolution with its propensity towards sudden change. . . . But above all we have gained the certainty that in the history of humanity . . . everything is interconnected . . . that nothing is immutable, that everything steadily transforms, not arbitrarily, but according to the nature of its essence. . . . From which it follows that the things that are, can only be properly known if the causes from which they issued are known.

Then comes the clincher as Fruin gives his own peculiar interpretation of the old adage *historia magistra vitae*, 'History is the schoolmistress of life':

The direction in which [the development of human society] is moving at the moment must allow itself to be determined by the direction followed until now . . . It shows where we have come from and where we are going. It shows us the goal. . . .[32]

And we listen as well, finally, to Lord Acton in his inaugural lecture at Cambridge in 1895. Facts can be established impartially, Acton assures us; methods of research can be improved, and so it can be ascertained precisely how things happened—to the end that men may acquire knowledge of the past as a "chart and compass" for the direction of our civilization, as an "instrument of action and a power that goes to the making of the future." For history is the story of how humanity has constantly improved and increased in knowledge, justice, and civilization. . . .[33]

The great historians, and many others with them, lived against a firm background. They plied their trade in faith, even as they brought to light events of seemingly little importance. They were unapologetic about expressing their ideas —sometimes only intuitive and very simple ideas—concerning the *meaning* of history and the *meaning* of their toil. Notice, however, that this background, this faith was *meta*historical in nature.

History in the grand style has always been practiced this way: with an intellectual-spiritual vision. The medieval history-writer would open his chronicle—even when it was only a city chronicle—with a sketch of sacred history starting with Adam, and then would follow the account of often disconnected facts. And Tillemont worked with the same metahistory as Bossuet, though his work is little more than a series of footnotes, which he regards, however, as footnotes to divine revelation. And so we could go on to mention many more.

History wants to be practiced against a metahistorical background, however rudimentary it may often be. There the historian finds the serenity for his concentrated toil and the certainty of doing meaningful work.

And then he may still be ever so much at a loss—Fruin, the chroniclers, Tillemont will have been too—when he is asked to show the connection between his metahistorical belief and the bare facts.

---

[32] Ibid., 338–40.
[33] Acton, "On the Study of History," *Lectures on Modern History* (1926), 17.

The crisis, the uneasiness, the uncertainty in our discipline arise from the fact, I am convinced, that the former metahistorical conviction has fallen into decay. What constituted the meaning of history in the nineteenth and early twentieth centuries, notably the idea of progress, lost its validity or charm for many in our time. Inevitably, the facts lost their *meaningful coherence* and now stand isolated, side by side, linked only by external factors. Time and again one encounters expressions like "the atomization of history," "the cult of the bare facts," and so forth. Even the European perspective can offer no relief.

There are signs, however, that the nadir is already past—prematurely, I fear—and that many are getting ready to place the historical phenomena in new meaningful frameworks. New? Is that really the case? In the conceptions I have discussed, as well as in others, a great deal is to be found that stems from the eighteenth and nineteenth centuries. I have in mind among other things the revival of the ideology of progress.

But it is noteworthy that in all these new efforts the word *meaning* is used so frequently. We hear of "meaningful frameworks," *Sinngebilde, Sinngefüge,* and so forth. Noteworthy too is the context in which the word is preferably employed: 'meaning' is no longer applied to history in its entirety; rather, a *culture*, a *period* is now a meaningful whole. Yet this is the sense in which the concept was employed already by Troeltsch and Dilthey, when the belief in world-history as a meaningful whole had perished in relativistic historicism—Troeltsch used it this way in his idea of the *jeweilige Kultursynthese*, "the obtaining cultural synthesis,"[34] and Dilthey used it in his notion that meaning is attributable only to the individual period as a *Wirkungszusammenhang*, a self-contained "dynamic system."[35] In a comparable way, it is the shared conviction of structuralists and integralists[36] that the "meaning of history" is always a structural coherence, an inner order, albeit not of world-historical character but an order proper to a period or civilization.

Accordingly, a *reduction* of *meaning*—but is this admissible? Can meaning be reduced without being destroyed? And so our epilogue issues in the problem of the meaning of history, but then as a problem in the first instance for the practicing historian.

---

[34] Cf. Ernst Troeltsch, *Gesammelte Schriften*, 3:71f, 175, 188.

[35] Cf. Wilhelm Dilthey, *Gesammelte Schriften*, 7:152–60, 172.

[36] For integralism, see esp. Jan Marius Romein, "Integrale geschiedschrijving" [On the writing of integral history], in *Eender en anders; twaalf nagelaten essays* (1964), 25–42.

10/ THE MEANING OF HISTORY

THERE ARE CERTAIN CONCEPTS that we use very easily but find difficult to define or even describe.[1] The very moment we say what we understand by *meaning* we sense that our definition misses the essence of it. Try as we may, all our attempts to approximate meaning more closely will fail. Why is that? Because *meaning* is of such a fundamental nature that no single verbal description has the capacity to express its true content. Much rather, it is only in the light of meaning that other concepts disclose their content.

Does history have meaning?
In recent decades there has been a veritable flood of writings bearing in their title: *the meaning of history*. The subject was addressed time and again in the nineteenth century as well, but then it was done in another way and in another climate. At that time, many knew from conviction what the meaning of history was. There was the reassuring certainty that history had a purpose and that one knew where it was headed. This reassurance provided a sense of security. History was not experienced as an *alien* power but as a power to which man could entrust himself. History had an anonymous course, true, but that course was meaningful.

This belief has been profoundly shaken in the twentieth century as a result, many say, of two world wars and a depression that brought to light the wickedness that man is capable of and the evils and horrors that history conceals. To my mind this explanation is too facile, too obvious, hence arouses suspicion. But whatever the cause may have been, it is certain that what in the nineteenth century had counted as *meaningful*, and had held a powerful fascination for people, lost its validity in the twentieth. I am thinking here in particular of the idea of progress.

If the question of the meaning of history is raised as persistently as it is today, then the reason is, I think, that people no longer know what its meaning is even though they realize man cannot exist outside the "meaning of history." And so we get the bizarre situation that in many circles there is a turning away from history—"Are we not living in a radically different age?"—while at the same time there is an intense desire to know whether history has any meaning. People are prepared to exchange scientifically established facts for mythical tales

---

[1] [This unpublished essay dates from around 1963. Preserved in impeccable manuscript, it may have been the start of a book in the series *Christelijk Perspectief* (27 vols.; Amsterdam: Buijten & Schipperheijn, 1962–80), for which Smit was scheduled to write a monograph on "the meaning of the question of the meaning of history." Subheadings have been added.]

if such a trade-in can resolve the all-decisive question concerning the meaning of history.

It is also noteworthy that the "meaning of history" is usually mentioned in one breath with the "meaning of human existence" and the "meaning of life." The meaning of life, to be sure, is also connected with the meaning of love, or the meaning of justice; but it is undeniable that modern man senses, as if by intuition, that the question concerning the meaning of life is answered in the meaning of *history*. This commands our full attention as it is precisely modern man who is disposed to turn his back on history yet when he wants an answer to the question of meaning he turns by preference to philosophy of history.

Thus a number of points are established. But why all this should be so is still unresolved. This we shall focus on next.

Meaning and origin

A historian is always asking *why* things are, but also *whence* they originate. This is also the way he deals with the *question of meaning*. In this he does not differ in principle from the non-historian. Only, he makes it his profession and devotes his entire life to it. The true historian is so obsessed with the questions of why and whence that for their sake he is prepared to lead an ascetic life. His concern in these questions—often without his being clearly aware of it—is the *meaning* of things. I believe there is an indication here that *meaning* and *origin* have something—yes, a great deal—to do with each other. In fact, could it be that the question concerning the meaning of life, the meaning of my existence here and now, is the same as the question concerning the origin? Should this be so, that is still not to say that the meaning of life arises from history, for it is possible to conceive of living from the origin while circumventing history. I say: it is conceivable, but is it also possible?

Let me put it succinctly. To find the meaning of history, or of life, I have to return to the origin of all meaning, for there is the source; but history is the means, the channel whereby I participate in meaning here and now.

If this be true, what power history has! And how extremely important is the work of the historian! Yet this also raises questions. If the meaning of living from the origin reaches us by means of history, are we not made utterly *dependent* upon history? In order to participate in what is to be cherished above all—in meaning—are we not made to live in *servitude*?

Here we may well have hit upon the source of modern man's ambivalence towards history. His enduring concern, even now in the latter half of the twentieth century, is with the meaning of life. But to attain it, is he obliged to let the whole past of thousands of years come over him with all its outmoded ideas and institutions, its false paths and failing solutions? Moreover, how shall history ever provide *meaning,* for is history itself not finitude, impermanence? Can we not somehow, so modern man inquires, circumvent history in order to discover and attain the meaning of life?

With our questions we have posed no *hypothetical, abstract* problems. Rather, we have provided a sketch of what deeply perturbs philosophy of history both in the nineteenth century and today. The whole problem pertaining to the meaning of history can be provisionally focused in the question concerning the *origin of meaning*.

Various positions are taken with respect to this supreme question. It is widely held that life, the entire course of history, does have meaning, but that this is more a matter of philosophical reflection, of subjective conviction, especially of *belief*, with which we can do very little in everyday life, least of all in science. Only the brash presume to speak about meaning with scientific certainty, and history has taught at least this, that not only *pride* but also *presumption* goes before the fall. Time and again you can hear it said, by Karl Jaspers[2] and Oskar Köhler[3] among others: How can we say anything valid about the meaning of history as long as the historical process has not yet reached its end, for only in terms of the end can it be known what has fundamentally determined the course of history.

Meaning, some protest, is a mystery, and to want to disclose it is to violate the mystery and to lose meaning. Therefore, humans can do little else (and historians in particular need to be mindful of this) than restrict themselves to the exterior, the surface, the contours of the phenomena; it is simply not given them to penetrate to their ground and reason of existence.

Now, a most remarkable thing happens with regard to this unquestioned view so widely held. Many of its adherents—I dare say all of them—are untrue to it. In an unguarded moment they do pose the question of meaning, and they are often extremely positive in their answer. This curious inconsistency should give us pause. It suggests to me, for now, that not a single question, nor a single historical investigation, nor yet a single historical phenomenon is able either to exist or to be known if meaning is excluded from the picture. Willy-nilly, we are thrown into the problem of meaning. That is why every person, certainly every historian, cares deeply about the meaning of history. Indeed, who would he be if he no longer cared about *this*?

Under the spell of history

Once we have recognized as an illusion the view that history has no meaning or that its meaning is unknowable to us, we can concentrate all our attention on the *where, the wherein, and the whence* of the meaning of history. Although we may now land in a veritable witches' cauldron of mutually contradictory opinions, happily these can be reduced to a few models.

---

[2] Cf. Karl Jaspers, *Vom Ursprung und Ziel der Geschichte* (1949). [Eng. trans., *The Origin and Goal of History* (1953).]

[3] Cf. Oskar Köhler's articles in the journal for world history: "Was ist 'Welt' in der Weltgeschichte?" [What is the meaning of the term world in world-history?] *Saeculum* 6 (1955): 1–9; and "Versuch Kategorien der Weltgeschichte zu bestimmen" [Toward defining categories of world history], *Saeculum* 9 (1958): 446–57.

The Meaning of History

In modern times—taken in the larger sense—the conviction has become predominant that the meaning of history is located in history itself and arises from it. To this type I also assign Hegel's philosophy of history.

From the Renaissance and the Enlightenment until today there has been almost unanimous agreement amongst modern people that the meaning of history is *progress*. Especially of late, many Christians have endorsed the idea of progress and have come to regard it as the fundamental difference between the Christian view of history and pagan *mythical* thought. I mention here only the 'progressistic' doctrine of evolution developed by Teilhard de Chardin and the great influence it has had in recent times. Let us examine this mode of thought more closely.

1) Its decisive point of departure is: meaning is *in* history, is *of* history, *arises from* history. This implies that man is to seek meaning in something which itself is limited, fleeting, finite, relative, which is to say in something that does not have the ground of its existence within itself. But the only sense of seeking meaning in history consists in finding something that is *exempt from relativity*, something absolute and abiding that can offer ultimate ground and rest to the fleeting-historical. Now then, the riches displayed by history may be ever so abundant, but it is a hallmark of history that it can never offer a place of refuge from transience and relativity. Thus understood, history repels meaning, even though modern man seeks meaning *in* history. To find meaning he will have to circumvent history. Yet there is no path around history but only a path through history.

In his quest for meaning, man is thus always thrown back again into the historical process. Who can fail to sense here the profound tragedy of modern man who in his wrestling with the meaning of history is driven by the injunction to remain faithful to history?

2) When meaning is sought *within* history, another no less serious difficulty presents itself. Hegel's philosophy of history can be used to demonstrate this (though what I am about to say applies equally to other conceptions).

The meaning of history, according to Hegel, lies in the fact that the World Spirit unfolds its entire rich content, its substance, in history. The Spirit employs historical manifestations, national spirits, states, great individuals, to demonstrate what is most essential in it, namely, its freedom. Reason strides through history, and in its sovereign course it works out—progressively—its own freedom. The nations, the great individuals may think that they pursue their own ends, hence that they are free, but in reality they execute the will of the World Spirit.

There it is: the nation, a people, the individual person is subservient to the will of *the spirit* (read: *the meaning*) of history. But suppose the individual, concerned above all with his personal freedom, withdraws from the sovereignty of the spirit: what happens then? In that case he places himself *outside the meaning of history*, whereupon his lot becomes a *meaning*less and *purpose*less existence.

Man cannot step outside meaning, upon penalty of landing in nothingness. But will he not gladly sacrifice his individual freedom, for what treasures does he not gain in exchange?

And so it has gone in the nineteenth and twentieth centuries with the idea of progress. Progress is a sovereign, anonymous power which endows individuals with meaning apart from their individual wills, since meaning is implied in the process itself. Why would one reject it, given the happiness, the fullness of life which it brings? Yet, however one looks at it, *man has been surrendered to and made dependent upon the flux of history.* Nor can he escape this even from a Christian standpoint by joining Teilhard de Chardin in proceeding from the unproven assumption that the universe brings forth consciousness, for here too man is subject to a supra-individual controlling principle.

Nevertheless, this whole mode of thought is so typical of the modern Western mind that most historians frame their questions in terms of it, even when these questions are purely scientific in nature. It is remarkable that a historian always desires to inquire into the *origin* of a phenomenon and almost always does so by looking for external influences. Few historians, for example, regard the courtly culture of the twelfth century as a spontaneously grown historical phenomenon: the majority of them are almost compulsively in search of the origins of this culture, its forms and ideas, either among the Cathari, or the Arabs, or in the West itself. Evidently, it is an ineradicable propensity of Western historians to understand historical events and persons in terms of historical development and to locate their meaning in their significance and consequence for later events and periods. Thus the ninth to eleventh centuries are valued as a *preparation* for the Renaissance, which in its turn is valued as the *foundation* of modern times. This is indeed history "under the spell of history" [4] —with as consequence that the significance of a historical phenomenon or period *in itself* recedes entirely into the background.

Our conclusion must be that both in philosophy of history and in historical science the *individual event*, the *individual person*, has become *subservient to the historical process*. He cannot circumvent it without *forfeiting the meaning of history. Man is fundamentally determined by history.* We have at the same time shown how essentially meaning is bound up with freedom. And most harrowing of all: there is apparently no way out.

History as emancipation

A way out has been passionately sought from under the overpowering force of history. The magic word for this quest is *freedom, liberation, emancipation.* Yes, but from what? Not from meaning, but certainly from the iron sway of the anonymous historical process. The basic question perforce has become: Is it possible to escape history and yet retain the meaning of life?

---

[4] [Allusion to P. J. Bouman, *In ban der geschiedenis* [Under the spell of history] (1961).]

This passionate struggle to emancipate man while retaining the fullness of meaning accompanied both philosophy of history and historical science in their heyday in the nineteenth and twentieth centuries, reaching its peak in recent years. It should accordingly not surprise us that the struggle for freedom is fought out in the field of philosophy of history no less than in the political and socio-economic fields. Hence Professor Schwarz of Vienna is not exaggerating when he says that there are at bottom but two attitudes towards history. Either history is seen as absolute Necessity, where the individual is no more than an organ in and through which this world process realizes itself; or history is experienced as Freedom, individual freedom in responsibility. And the motive force behind both attitudes, Schwarz claims, is concern about *the meaning of history*. Either people are glad to be nothing more than organs in the historical process, in order thus to participate in meaning; or else they want to be absolute freedom in order thus to actualize the *meaning* of their existence.[5]

For the moment I have said enough about the dominance of history. Now its counterpole, freedom.

Should we not put the matter as follows: There is no need to be so anxious about history's dominance. That is mere appearance. *History brings emancipation*. Is it not the essence of history to be *freedom*?

Consider the following paradigm. You find yourself in a particular situation, you are conditioned on all sides by *this* situation, which is to say you are *bound* by it; where in this situation is your freedom? Worse yet, this very situation is in turn fully determined by historical circumstances. And so I could regress ad infinitum. Everything speaks of *determination*. On the other hand, history itself appears to break all ties and thus to be freedom itself. After all, history is finitude while impermanence, complete independence while relativity. Is it not true that in history everything sooner or later *perishes*? History executes judgment upon itself by killing the buds or cutting short the blossoms. Nations groan under the yoke of a tyrant: have no fear, just be patient, some day the tyrant will vanish from the scene. Or, to stay with our model: In your situation you are bound in a hundred ways, but what happens? — The situation vanishes, it sinks away, and you are free. Granted, you do become the prisoner of a new situation, but this situation too must eventually release you. In short, history constantly throws its tentacles around the individual, but it can never hold him permanently. Scarcely is the individual bound before he is released again, as by a process, thanks to history's own rhythm.

Accordingly, freedom is guaranteed by history itself. But is this not necessarily accompanied by the loss of meaning? For *meaning* was said to reside *in* history and to arise *from* history alone, but on this view the individual person and the particular fact constantly detach themselves from history and from its meaning. From what source, then, can they still derive meaning?

---

[5] Cf. Richard Schwarz, "Die Frage nach dem Sinn der Geschichte," *Wissenschaft und Weltbild* 14 (1961): 161–79, at 177.

Because this sort of liberation causes *meaning* to perish, I mistrust this *liberation*. The way of freedom that I have just sketched is the way that has been recommended by historicism and by existentialist philosophy. They have shown that according to the prevailing view individuals, events and facts derive their meaning from without, from an intellective world, or from the immanent historical process; that historical things are thus subordinated to an outside power, to the tyranny of an outsider, an alien force—which may then ever so properly be called 'meaning.'

To counter this, historicism and existentialism have asserted: individual persons, things and events have their *meaning* in themselves and by virtue of this are at bottom *free*. They do not receive meaning from without, from some transcendent world or from the historical process. Meaning "springs" or leaps up from the particular person or event itself, and in this manner announces its own original existence and fullness.

The solution is astoundingly simple. Things are *free* and are *charged with meaning*, and they are so in an entirely original way.

From the existentialist side this outcome is proclaimed a *Copernican revolution* in philosophy of history, in particular in the *problem of meaning*.[6]

Only, one may claim that the individual person and the particular event have their meaning entirely within themselves and from nowhere else, but this is no more than a naked assertion. There is nothing whatsoever in the world that exists just like that, without some basis—not even meaning. Meaning must *arise from something*, or else meaning is a nothing. But now for a most remarkable turn: even according to the existentialistic conception meaning does arise from something after all! Just listen: *"the authentically existing man pro-jects his meaning himself, and the event brings forth its own meaning—on its own authority."* [7] Thus, independent of any center of history or eschatological goal, man actualizes himself, and so he actualizes the meaning of his existence and his autonomous freedom.

So what appears to have been the point to this positing of meaning? The point was to be able to assert man's absolute autonomy, his being entirely himself. And the last tyrant to be fended off was history.

In the final analysis, however, is this second view at all different from the first, which favors the superiority of the meaning of the historical process? In the one case, meaning derives from history; in the other, from the individual. Nevertheless, *both are enslaved: the one to the historical process,* the other to ... *himself*. The latter is constantly engaged in pro-jecting *himself*, caring for[8] *his freedom*, perpetually preoccupied with *self-interest*.

---

[6] Cf. Pierre Thévenaz, "Événement et historicité" [Event and historicity], in *L'Homme et l'histoire. Actes de VIe Congrès des Sociétés de Philosophie de langue française* (1952), 217–25, at 220. [An expanded version appeared in idem, *L'Homme et sa raison* (1956), 121–28.]

[7] [This quotation (by Thévenaz? Sartre?) could not be traced.]

[8] [The manuscript has: 'besorgen' (a term in Heidegger).]

I go still one step further. This entire historicistic and existentialistic position is impossible. For how could I ever have received my existence and with it the meaning of my existence except through history? Without history I would have no being. This is acknowledged, too, despite the inner contradiction. Bultmann, for example, admits to a basic "paradox." Only the individual face to face with God is of importance, he writes, whereas the cross of Christ is a mere historical fact hence without significance. "Paradoxically however," so he continues, how could anyone ever meet God without that cross of some two thousand years ago and without the transmission of the Gospel through the historical labors of the church? [9]

The redemption of history

I need not summarize. Every road we have traveled thus far robs us of meaning or of freedom or of both.

And still there is hope and we can close in the spirit of Advent—provided we allow meaning and freedom neither to issue from world history nor to spring from the "existing" person. Meaning and freedom alike can originate only in God.

In asserting this I must be sure to avert two fallacies and fatal errors.

1) The first argues that if the meaning of history is God, or the kingdom of God, then meaning has nothing to do with our terrestrial history. It is then far above us, entirely *supra-historical*. Only human *hubris* can involve it in our history—in which case its divine nature is at once compromised.

2) The second fatal error is the converse of the first. It concludes that God is co-mingled with history, even identical with it—in which case the historical process itself assumes a divine character.

When I maintain that *God is the meaning of history* I mean to say that history has meaning in that it is totally, in all its elements and phenomena, in all its subjects and agents, *related to, oriented to* God. He has created the world in relation to himself (and by relation here I do not mean some external connection but a relation such that one of its correlates finds its total fulfillment in the relation). History finds the ground of its existence exclusively in its *Meaning, which is God.*

That means for history not only fullness of meaning but also freedom, since for its meaning it is not dependent on the historical process, nor on the autonomous person. This meaning-relation was called into being by God himself *when he created man in his image.*

The creation mandate, the supreme historical commandment "*to have dominion over all the earth,*" cannot be primary. What takes precedence before all else is the reality of being created in God's image, of *being placed in relation* to

---

[9] Cf. Rudolf Bultmann, "Zur Frage der Entmythologisierung. Antwort an Karl Jaspers," *Theologische Zeitschrift* 10 (1954): 81–95, at 93f.

him. *And man can never fall from this relation, however deep he indeed may fall*, which is to say that man can never lose or escape the meaning of history.[10]

If, however, man thus receives the meaning of his existence *directly* from God, independently of history, then does that not do away with the importance of history, hence also with the meaning of history, and does history not remain of significance only for all kinds of earthly cares? Is the direct relation with God not purchased at the price of history? No, for history itself, in its total course and in its separate events, is comprehended or centered in this direct relation to God. Thus when *this* relation was disrupted by sin, all history fell, and when communion with God was restored, all history was saved.

Nevertheless I repeat my question: Does history still have a *meaning-full* function?

We come now to something unique in our conception of history, something that is only to be found in the Christian view:

The meaning of history was saved by an historic act, by a purely historical fact, and the meaning of history, thus upheld, *comes to the individual person and to the historical fact* as well with the aid of history.

To be sure, the meaning of our life is a matter directly between God and ourselves. Yet God still uses history for that purpose. There would be no communion with him without the historical suffering and resurrection of Christ and without the proclamation of the Gospel now for almost two thousand years.

History is the channel, as it were, along which meaning is conveyed. Meaning is granted directly, immediately, but again not without the means of history. And so we can say that every fact has a double origin, but that both "origins" are intertwined with each other.[11]

History comes to us because meaning comes to us, powerfully but not *over*poweringly. We are *confronted* by the past, which inescapably bears down upon us because it conveys meaning towards us; yet meaning does not realize itself apart from us.

Every generation, every individual is asked what he or she will do with meaning, and no one can get away from that by saying, "You have to go along with your times" or "It can't be helped." In this confrontation with the past, an awesome responsibility is laid upon *everyone*. It is from the past that one must receive the *meaning of life*, and nothing will change that, for there can be nothing greater in world history than the crucifixion and the resurrection of Jesus Christ. But then this *historical* meaning must be realized in every age and in every life in an *original* way.

---

[10] See Romans, chap. 1.

[11] [The theme of twin origins is elaborated in essay 15 below.]

11/ NEW PERSPECTIVES FOR A CHRISTIAN CONCEPTION OF HISTORY?

IN THIS PAPER[1] I propose to discuss to what extent a Christian view of history has received new impulses from a number of recent publications by Herbert Butterfield, Henri-Irénée Marrou, Peter Meinhold, Fritz Wagner, and Reinhard Wittram. Only three problem areas will be dealt with: (1) history and its knowability; (2) God and history; and (3) the individual and the universal in history. We shall not always be able to respect the boundaries between these areas; thus before long it will become clear that the first problem is present in the second and the third as well, that the third is present in the first, and so forth. Moreover, other problems no less fundamental in nature are involved as well, such as: history and freedom; whence does history constitute itself; how is history possible; the relation of continuity and discontinuity; history and nature.

There are reasons for not taking up these other questions. First, our authors do not intend to write philosophy of history but simply to reflect on the remarkable phenomenon that history *is* and that man remains interested in his past. Another reason for restricting ourselves is that the three problems mentioned have both a *foundational* and a *referential* character, hence belong together and presuppose each other. In thinking about history the successive problems are not isolated topics or separate chapters but are implicit once the foundations are laid.

With regard to a number of writers to be dealt with here, however, a serious problem arises, especially in the case of Marrou. They begin somewhere, but nowhere do they explain why they consider their chosen *point of departure* to be the correct one—perhaps because it seems to them to be self-evident, or because it is accepted by many historians and philosophers. The consequences of this omission are far-reaching because the choice of starting point also determines in part how the road will be traveled.

(1) *History and its knowability*
First we want to talk about history in an unproblematical sense and pose the question in a very general way: Is history knowable and, if so, *how*? For the moment we avoid raising the problem whether the *meaning,* the *essence* and the *goal* of history are knowable, let alone whether we can get the relation between God and history in focus. We shall see how long we can stay within the bounds of our questions.

---

[1] Presented to the Gezelschap van Christelijke Historici in its session of 4 Jan. 1965.

We must, indeed, set these restrictions if we wish to be able to listen attentively to Marrou, for it is with him in particular that we shall have to deal.

Naturally, Marrou too asks the question, What is history? But in posing this question he does not wish to concern himself with the essence of history, for the answer he gives is: "History is the knowledge of man's past." [2] Marrou chooses the word "knowledge" advisedly, he says, in order to exclude numerous misconceptions and to include the rigorously systematic methods of operation of this knowledge. Knowledge concerning the "essence" of man's past is not sought: that is done by the "philosopher of history"—"our worst enemy," Marrou adds.[3]

Why this hostility to the philosopher of history? For Marrou, the very mention of Hegel's name suffices, and he expresses alarm at the Hegel revival of our day. But why this alarm? Because the philosophers of history chain the historians to their "laws" and make use of the results of historical science without asking that science, *How* do you know? The philosophers of history, moreover, are without excuse. Did Hegel not live in the very age when the real scientific approach to history blossomed, as a result of the pioneering work of Niebuhr and Ranke? Yet notice how Hegel deals with that: he is familiar with Niebuhr's work but refers to it only in order to criticize it and heap sarcasm upon it. Hegel knew very well how to find the weak spots in Niebuhr's *Roman History,* but what escaped his notice was the true renewal represented by this "systematic application of critical methods to history." [4]

From Marrou's various writings it is clear that he is here not concerned with an isolated instance. Rather, Hegel's rejection of the awakening science of history reveals the basic defect of philosophy of history: its dogmatism.

Now it has not escaped Marrou—he often returns to the matter in his many writings—that historical science is experiencing difficulties in our day. It is believed that the historian can do anything and will defend anything with his material. In consequence, a skepticism regarding the results of historical science prevails as never before. Worse yet, historical science has descended to the level of erudition and history has vanished from people's everyday attitudes, so that there is a real gulf between the world of the professional historian and the life of culture and society.

But now the paradox. People are turning today to the solutions of "our enemy," the philosopher of history. However much Marrou may regret this, he finds it understandable. In our time people are more conscious than ever of *man's fundamental historicity, his confinement in history.* This accounts for the great place occupied by the question concerning the 'Meaning' of history, for the latter is not posed and pondered in some sheltered corner but arises from *angst,*

---

[2] H.-I. Marrou, *De la Connaissance historique* (Paris, 1954), 32 [Eng. trans., *The Meaning of History* (1966), 33].

[3] Ibid., 34 [Eng. trans., 35].

[4] Ibid., 18 [Eng. trans., 18].

from the existential anxiety of being delivered up to history. The vexed person of our time desires certitude, hence in the first place certitude about the *meaning* of history. Historical science, however, has grown *un*certain about the past, whereas philosophy of history has not. The philosopher offers his perspective and solutions, without concerning himself about the uncertainties of the historian's methodical, empirical inquiry.[5] Such, in a nutshell, is the background to Marrou's ideas about the inevitable sequence: confinement in history, anxiety born of that, the passionate search for the meaning of history, the inadequacy of scientific historical research, the intervention of philosophy of history—rejected by Marrou as a flight from authenticity into a dogmatic scheme.

Many of these terms are familiar to us, familiar from existentialism, but we also miss a few customary notes. Marrou edges towards existentialism, even embraces it, but then backs away. It seems to me that the best way to characterize his thought about history is to call it *existentializing*.

But is this not a question of terminology, which we could better leave aside? Not really; for Marrou himself often calls attention to his appreciation for existentialism. More importantly, however, the various difficulties that Marrou has encountered in solving the problems by which he sees himself confronted all converge, as it were, in the term 'existentializing.'

Marrou's ideas have been opposed by many scholars, but they have also been welcomed by many others with approval. The book *De la connaissance historique* has enjoyed great success; within a decade it saw three reprints. One may consider this surprising as it contains little that is original, but in seeking an explanation for its success one should keep two things in mind. First of all, Marrou is able to explain difficult, seemingly abstract problems in an arresting, often playful manner. I imagine many a reader must have thought: So much of what I have been thinking about for a long time is marvelously articulated here; in studying this book one constantly has the feeling: here at last is a historian who takes up *my* questions and those of our time. Secondly, Marrou's book has been so influential, I believe, because it is a French book. It has had enormous success in France—or better, in the Romance world. That German historical science required no such book will be clear from what follows.

I return to the question of originality. Marrou made no pretense to it, aware as he was of standing in a tradition, one which must be sought primarily in Germany: his authorities are Dilthey, Neo-Kantians like Windelband, Rickert, Simmel, but also phenomenologists, finally Jaspers and Heidegger. And then, as well, there are a few English and French thinkers. He calls attention especially to Raymond Aron—remarkable, as will become apparent. But indeed, it was Aron who, shortly before the Second World War, was the first to fully inform French historians and philosophers about that German tradition that we can characterize with the slogan: *the critique of historical reason*.

---

[5] Ibid., 17 [Eng. trans., 17].

Aron published his two theses in 1938. Their titles say a great deal: "Introduction to the philosophy of history: An essay on the *limits of historical objectivity*"; and "*Critical philosophy of history:* An essay on contemporary German theory of history." [6] The original labor of this critical philosophy of history was done in Germany by Dilthey and others, adopted by Aron in France, and accepted and elaborated by Marrou. In other words, Marrou does recognize a philosophy of history, in fact his book *De la connaissance historique* is filled with it. As he states, historians have suffered for too long from an inferiority complex with respect to philosophy.[7]

How can this be squared with Marrou's sally against "our enemy," against Hegel and company? Well, Marrou aspires to a "formal" or "critical" philosophy of history, one that incorporates a critique of historical reason, a justification of historical knowledge.

We have taken some time to trace Marrou's journey past both the rejection and the affirmation of philosophy of history because his entire critical philosophy, and with it his view of history, rests on the assumption that it is *possible*, indeed even mandatory, to account for history critically *without* involving "material" or "speculative" philosophy of history in the process. We follow Marrou with bated breath. Will it be possible to establish a critical philosophy after first having shown philosophy of history the door? For in so doing he also eliminated the question of meaning!

Marrou summarizes the result of his critical philosophizing, the substance of the *connaissance historique*, in a few pithy remarks and formulas: (1) history is a mixture, indeed an indissoluble *mélange,* of subject and object; (2) history is inseparable from the historian; and (3) history is a relationship between two *p*'s: between the past (i.e., the historical object) and the present (i.e., the present of the historian).[8]

At first glance these formulas appear quite innocent and they suggest nothing new. Every positivistic historian—to whom Marrou is fiercely opposed —could accept them. They mean, simply, that all knowledge of history presupposes a subject, someone who knows; and the act of knowing involves the present, the current situation in which the investigator of history finds himself. Historians have always known that however empirically and critically they may go about their work, subjective elements can never be avoided entirely. Only, they always seek to reduce the present to a minimum in their critical inquiry: such is the very purpose of historical criticism.

However, in his formulas Marrou says much more than all this. He sees it as his task—as the aim of critical philosophy—to open historians' eyes to the

---

[6] Raymond Aron, *Introduction à la philosophie de l'histoire. Essai sur les limites de l'objectivité historique* (1938) [Eng. trans. (1961)]; and *Essai sur la théorie de l'histoire dans l'Allemagne contemporaine. La philosophie critique de l'histoire* (1938; 2nd ed., 1950).

[7] *De la Connaissance historique*, 10 [Eng. trans., 11].

[8] Ibid., 37, 53, 229 [Eng. trans., 39, 54, 238].

subjective, personal element present in the *scientific* activity of the historian, not in order to *warn* against it but in order to furnish it its *legitimate* place.

We recall what is Marrou's greatest concern: that history is vanishing from the general outlook of contemporary man. Now, Marrou believes that the break with history can be repaired if the historian—followed by contemporary man—personally enters into history *with* what he has, not just to open himself to it—no, the historian actively forms and shapes it with both the limitations and the capacities of his mind. Although Marrou continues to use the term 'subjective,' the word *existential* expresses more satisfactorily that act of entering into history with one's entire intellectual baggage.

Marrou's critics have charged him with skepticism—which is just. He has defended himself—which is also just, for while history is undeniably a mixture of subject and object, he himself is on guard against overemphasizing the existential relation in the work of the historian; hence he beats an elaborate retreat and ultimately ends up at the prevailing scientific historical critique and its demand for objectivity. And if we observe the historian Marrou at work—if we read, say, his study of the troubadours[9]—we notice that little remains of the vaunted break with objective history.

Has the mountain brought forth a mouse, and can we lay Marrou's *Connaissance historique* aside for what it is, full of inner contradictions? No, we cannot do that either. He has chosen a safe middle course, it is true, but his sympathies are with the *existential* practice of history. It is from it that he expects the rehabilitation of history in our culture. Only in its existential function can history offer help to *anxious* man.

There is irony in Marrou's predicament. It was primarily with the help of Aron's theses of 1938 that he entered the lists against the old ideal of objectivity. But now observe what happens. Dismayed by the consequences of accentuating the subjective element in the formation of knowledge, he turns against the consequences, to wit: the excesses of a relativism that has assumed "delirious forms" and the prevalence of the "dissolution of the object."[10] In 1938 Aron felt called upon to stress the *limits* of *objectivism*; today Marrou seeks *guarantees* for objectivity, whereby the subjective element in historical interpretations is only a limited subjectivity after all.

Marrou's and Aron's problem is of concern to every philosopher and historian. Both Aron's conception (the limits of objectivity) and Marrou's (a middle course between the existential and objectivist attitudes) are solutions born of perplexity. We cannot here discuss the impasse fully, but we must raise the question: How did Marrou get into it?

We have characterized Marrou's point of departure as *existentializing*. He is fond of invoking the insights of existentialists, especially Heidegger's. Yet

---

[9] Cf. H.-I. Marrou, *Les Troubadours* (Paris, 1971); originally published in 1961 under the pseudonym Henri Davenson.

[10] Ibid., 234, 256, 262, 270 [Eng. trans., 243, 265, 271, 279].

existentialists do not know what to do with the "history of the historian" and depreciate it, for example, as a kind of secondary history. Marrou cannot follow them in this, yet what he finds valuable in existentialism he wants to make useful for historical science. In so doing, however, he throws up barricades for himself on the path to history, while his pretension is precisely to clear the way.

In essence we have here the same tension as in Dilthey. Through the method of *Verstehen* we gain access to alien cultures of the past and are enabled to explore them in depth and know their meaning. And yet, that is nevertheless impossible, since the act of *Verstehen* is altogether historically conditioned, which is to say that it is always the *Verstehen* of an individual subject, entirely bounded by a limited historical horizon.

Similarly in Marrou. He speaks of an immense gap between the real course of events and the way in which the historian gives form to this! There is a qualitative and structural difference between the present as it is experienced at the time, and "recovered time" as the historian brings this to life. What the historian resurrects is not history as it took place, for this is inaccessible; he encounters himself in history.[11]

For Marrou the basic question would have to be: If my human existence is so shackled to itself and its own present, how can I possibly gain access to that *other reality, which is not my existence, not my situation*? Aron has cautioned Marrou that more is at issue here than just knowledge of the past: the knowing process as such is at stake! Mistakenly, Marrou has shown little sympathy for this broadening of the question.

There is more. If the way to the past is blocked by my confinement to myself, does that not also sever all ties with my neighbors, *in casu* my fellow historians? Just listen to Marrou: "The image each historian gives of the past is so profoundly and so organically shaped by his own personality that the differing standpoints of historians are in the final analysis not so much complementary as mutually exclusive."[12] It is in this light that we must understand Marrou's statement, "I seek to convince *myself* of the truthfulness of *my* understanding of the past."[13] Yet for all that, Marrou protests that there is a real meeting of minds among historians, true dialogue, and so on, and he can assert this because he takes a saving leap into objectivity.

How remarkable! At least twice, the restoration of the connection (with history and with other historians) is expected to come, not from the existential approach but from the object.

Nevertheless, Marrou's *Connaissance historique* is extremely important. He has articulated what many have felt and he has formulated specific problems that beg solution. Many regard his middle course as a genuine way out. His

---

[11] Marrou, "Comment comprendre le métier d'historien?" [How to understand the historian's craft?] in Charles Samaran, ed., *Encyclopédie de la Pléiade*, vol. 11 (1961), p. 1468. Cf. also *De la Connaissance historique*, 90 [our trans.; cf. Eng. trans., 92].

[12] *De la Connaissance historique*, 231 [cf. Eng. trans., 240].

[13] Ibid., 229 [Eng. trans., 237]; emphasis by Marrou.

exclusive subjectivism and existentialism died an early death in his practice as a historian.

Still, our judgment cannot be milder than the following: Marrou has not gotten us one step closer to solving some of the key problems that have engaged both philosophy of history and the science of history now for more than a century. Could it be that Marrou has blocked his own view by excluding philosophy of history? From his standpoint he repeatedly raises the question—he even begins with it—*How do you know?* Should this not have been preceded by the question: *Who is the knowing subject?* A marvelous treasure would then have been discovered, in any case not that everlastingly-concerned-about-its-own-existence-and-confined-to-itself subject.

I was asked to speak about new perspectives for the Christian view of history. What have we gained thus far? Marrou certainly does make it difficult for us. As a Catholic historian he has addressed the problem on several occasions, for example, in an address of 1948 entitled "Is There a Christian View of History?" [14] And later he repeatedly returns to this theme, though not—this is telling—in his *De la connaissance historique*. In Marrou's eyes, theology of history on the one hand and critical philosophy on the other are two separate worlds. In terms of the Catholic worldview, that makes sense: the *connaissance historique* belongs to the temporal values, and the theology of history has a supernatural, eschatological orientation.

This dualism pervades the entire body of his work in theory of history. But then, abruptly, we are reminded that the Scholastic conception, while requiring that nature and grace be sharply distinguished, holds equally that the two are harmoniously ordered with respect to one another as the natural-temporal to the supernatural. And that comes out unexpectedly in Marrou when he later makes the claim that in his book *De la connaissance historique* he *could not help* but "cite" Augustine at every turn.[15] We would like to see those citations from Augustine sometime! There is, however, a tendency in Marrou's writings that sheds light on this alleged agreement with Augustine. What he says about the relation of *Geschichte* (the object of theology of history) to *histoire* (the reality studied by historical science) is to him so self-evident that to his mind the historical cannot but be ordered to the spiritual-supernatural. Thus his connecting with theology of history came about at the natural-temporal level without involving theology of history or the Christian view of history.[16]

---

[14] Marrou, "Existe-t-il une vision chrétienne de l'histoire?" in *XXVes Journées Universitaires* (Paris, 1948), 48–67. [Cf. idem, *Théologie de l'histoire* (1968); Eng. trans., *Time and Timeliness* (1969).]

[15] Marrou, "La Théologie de l'histoire." Report with discussion. In *Augustinus Magister* (proceedings of the international Augustine conference, Paris, 1954); supplement of the *Revue des études augustiniennes* (1955): 3:193–212, at 196.

[16] Cf. Marrou, *L'Ambivalence du temps de l'histoire chez saint Augustin* (1950), 31.

Marrou did, of course, as we have seen, begin somewhere, namely with the question: *How do we know?* And he left aside the primary question: *How do we know that this is a legitimate point of departure?* He had perforce to follow this route, for otherwise he would have had to appeal to philosophy of history for help, or to theology of history, which for him is concerned only with the eschatological orientation of history.

Just how decisive the choice of a point of departure is for the knowledge of history becomes very clear when we place Marrou's critical philosophy next to the views of Reinhard Wittram. In Wittram we do not encounter the constant concern about human existence. To be sure, he too recognizes the value of subjectivity in the formation of knowledge about the past, and he too knows that historical existence is challenged, but—here comes the big difference—Wittram is equally concerned about *historical reality* as such, thus about the object *itself.* His main question is not: What use or what value does knowledge about the past have for my challenged and imperiled existence? but: How does history retain its dignity? [17]

The subjective elements in historical knowledge, says Wittram, must not be overestimated: personal and national antipathies and social prejudices can be eliminated. But what then, when we have succeeded in achieving "correctness," when we have discovered *"wie es eigentlich gewesen ist,"* how things really were? Historical truth, as defined by Wittram, embraces more than that. It embraces the demand of justice, and inseparable from it: an acknowledgment of the respect we owe history. Wittram means that the dignity of history does not lie in its relation to us or in its utility for us. No, history has a dignity and worth of its own, and therefore in our dealing with it all arbitrary or careless treatment is a crime. The justice that must be observed by the historian is to be viewed in the same perspective, and it will only be observed if the historian succeeds in focusing on the essence of man.[18] But with that we have made the transition to our next problem.

(2) *The relation of God and history*

The demand to do "justice" to historical persons and phenomena would seem to defy human capacity. Wittram is very much aware of this, and that is why he comes to speak in this connection of God in history.[19] Nor does he do so only to withdraw hastily again with the excuse that we must not become guilty of vain speculations about God's activity in history.

It deserves notice that not only Wittram but also Meinhold, Butterfield, Marrou and other Christian historians deal quite explicitly with the God of history—with many reservations, to be sure, and Marrou only in his theology of

---

[17] Reinhard Wittram, *Das Interesse an der Geschichte* (1958), 30.
[18] Ibid., 24, 27.
[19] Ibid., 30.

history, but still, it is done. There has even been talk of a revival of the problem of God in history. In the face of all the objections of vain curiosity, speculation, the inscrutability and mystery of God, almost all the authors mentioned assert: but God *has* revealed himself, in Jesus Christ, in history! Thus the great tension is located in what Ridderbos, speaking of Christ, once called his "self-revealment and self-concealment."[20] One of the most topical themes in contemporary theology is that of God's redemptive activity in history, and we suspect that this has some bearing on the new interest historical science is showing in the relation of Providence to the historical process. It is one thing when this theme is raised in theology, however, and quite another when it receives fresh attention in so-called profane historical science.

Perhaps someone will want to interrupt and replace 'historical science' with 'historical vision.' But that, *precisely*, will *not* do, and that is why our problem of God and history is so supremely difficult and complicated.

I have sometimes asked myself why our authors—and others as well—have ventured into this hornets' nest of difficult and ultimately unsolvable problems. Two answers can be suggested. The first has something to do with renewed concern about the unity and meaning of history. When Karl Jaspers contemplates the unity of history he knows this unity can never be realized—history itself will always cause such unity to "suffer shipwreck," he says; yet by contemplating it something of this unity can still be realized.[21] Such is also the case with the problem at hand.

Our second consideration is of an entirely different sort. Several of our authors deal with it in so many words. Butterfield, for example, goes into it extensively. Like Marrou, Butterfield is struck by the fact that history is receding from the general consciousness. The common criticism targets the critical method that has fostered widespread skepticism; people are dissatisfied with that endless establishing of facts that has caused academic history to become so anemic.[22] Christopher Dawson reports the same criticism of the impoverishment in academic history.[23] Many (including not in the last place young students) ask for bread and are given stones—*bread*, which in this case is *the meaning of life*.

Butterfield's response to this criticism is that factual research will always have a right to exist, the scientific historian can provide no elucidation of the meaning of life, the key to solving the human drama lies not in technical history but in religion: the Bible has already informed us of it. It is the Bible that

---

[20] Cf. Herman N. Ridderbos, *Zelfopenbaring en zelfverberging; het historisch karakter van Jezus' messiaanse zelfopenbaring volgens de synoptische evangeliën* [Self-revealment and self-concealment: the historical character of Jesus' messianic self-revelation according to the Synoptic Gospels] (1946).

[21] Karl Jaspers, *Vom Ursprung und Ziel der Geschichte* (1949), 305–27 [Eng. trans., 247–65].

[22] Herbert Butterfield, *Christianity and History* (1949), 20.

[23] Christopher Dawson, "The Problem of Metahistory," *History Today* 1.6 (1951): 9–12; reprinted in *Dynamics of World History*, ed. John J. Mulloy (1956), 287–93.

provides clarification of and commentary upon the ultimate meaning of life. Since that is something to which the technical, working historian as such can never attain, he may proceed directly to the study of mundane events.[24] That is where Butterfield draws the borderlines. There are two histories for him: that of the scientific, "technical" historian, and that of the Bible. And so the problems have evaporated.

Yet only apparently so. Neither Butterfield nor Wittram nor Marrou is able, while dwelling in the mundane world, to forget about the God of the Bible, the more so since they have posed yet another difficult problem. They empathically call attention to the moral dimension both in history and in the work of the historian. The ethical questions form the bridge over which God—who, it seemed, had to go—re-enters history.

In Butterfield this happens through complicated, not always clear reflections on the Providence of God. For Butterfield, an immanent nemesis rules in history. Moral judgments belong to the essence of the historical process. Thus in both German defeats, of 1918 and 1945, God pronounced his judgment on German militarism and things Prussian. (To avoid misunderstanding: Butterfield does not mean to say that other nations do not fall equally under judgment.) But then Butterfield partially retracts his verdict; ultimately, he submits, the decision whether we can speak of a judgment of God in history is not a problem for science but a matter of conscience.[25]

Fritz Wagner is quite right when he observes that there is a natural progression in Butterfield from the technical methods of history, through the existential problem, to the realm of ethics.[26] Also, Butterfield's view of man is a direct implicate of his view of history. In history there is one cardinal sin that holds man bound in all other sins: his self-righteousness. And (historical) judgment strikes precisely those who—as the prophets saw—"think themselves gods." [27]

These border crossings from historical science to ethics, anthropology, and personal faith are not made by Butterfield alone. Marrou, Wittram, Meinhold and Wagner do the same, though each in his own way. For Marrou, for instance, history is not entirely opaque after all. With respect to Spain in the Golden Age, for example, the defeat of the Armada meant that to God the cause of the City of God was not identical to what Philip II made of the idea. As a second example he cites Isaiah 45, which reveals to us the real meaning of Cyrus's victory. Yet these are exceptions. In general, history is a mystery.[28]

More important, I think, is an idea that recurs time and again in Wittram. He knows of the self-concealment of God in history, and he acknowledges that "the

---

[24] Butterfield, *Christianity and History*, 22–24.
[25] Ibid., 48–63.
[26] Fritz Wagner, *Moderne Geschichtsschreibung. Ausblick auf eine Philosophie der Geschichtswissenschaft* [Modern historiography: prospects of a philosophy of historical science] (1960), 53–65, esp. 54.
[27] Cf. Butterfield, *Christianity and History*, 60, 104.
[28] Marrou, "Existe-t-il une vision chrétienne de l'histoire?" 58.

whole truth of history is hidden from us." *However*, there is also the self-communication of God in the person of Jesus Christ, and although this yields no commentary on world history, it does provide direction of another kind: the truth about man.[29] Wittram returns to this in his essay on "Man and the Moral Dimension in History." Notice the correlation. In this essay he wants to understand man as a *creature of God*. To prevent anyone from dismissing that as a conventional idea, he adds: *the fact that man is a creature of God* entails far-reaching consequences, consequences which indeed reach much farther than is commonly recognized: as a creation of God, man possesses a uniqueness that extends beyond his spiritual and ethical worth and is expressed by the Biblical concept 'image of God.' But this concept too, says Wittram, is all too often woefully misunderstood. With Otto Weber he takes the concept to mean that humans "have received what is the quintessence of their humanity from God" and that therein lies also humanity's *destiny*, a destiny that will be upheld by God through all historical changes, from the earliest forms of humanity through the forms still to come.[30]

What does Wittram do with this extremely important insight? He falls back again upon his other thesis that no scientifically verifiable connection whatever exists between salvation history and any specific event in profane history.[31] With his view of man as creature and image of God Wittram has, I think, crossed the boundary from salvation history to profane history, but as we read on, the contents of faith turn out to be merely forms of religious experience—a subjective stance which none the less influences Wittram's assessment time and again. Thus he can only continue to see unity in history, for example, in that man lives before the face of God.

The most important reflections are those of Peter Meinhold and Fritz Wagner. It is only a pity that these authors have not gotten beyond their first outlines. We have been looking forward for some time now to Meinhold's *Prolegomena zu einer Weltgeschichte*, promised a number of years ago. The risk of wanting to infer too much from Meinhold's and Wagner's provisional insights is therefore great. However, at this stage I do believe it can at least be said that Meinhold is bent on overcoming that fatal barrier between salvation history (in the broader sense) and world history (read: profane history). No longer satisfied with a subjective religious experience of faith in the God of history, Meinhold takes a decisive next step. He confesses not only that the whole of history falls under the rule of the Redeemer in whom time is fulfilled—the historian can confess this without doing much with it—but the point that matters for him is this: *profane history does not escape the effect of the death on the cross of the Redeemer who transforms the world*—although historical science

---

[29] Wittram, *Das Interesse an der Geschichte*, 31.
[30] Ibid., 71, 72.
[31] Ibid., 145; cf. Wagner, "Zweierlei Maß der Geschichtsschreibung—eine offene Frage" [A double standard in historiography?], *Saeculum* 10 (1959): 113–15.

in its scientific methods is powerless to "grasp this adequately."[32] Meinhold does not retract with the second statement what he has said in the first, for he draws the transcendent dimension into the scientific method.[33] We have to view the preceding in the light of his image of three concentric circles: salvation history, church history, world history—the first being the core, also of profane history.[34] World history hereby loses its autonomy and finds itself constantly in a "metaphysical retro-connection."[35] To my way of thinking, in the entire discussion of a Christian historical science or a Christian perspective *no more hopeful word has been spoken*.

(3) *The individual and the universal in history*

Heeding the warning of time, I shall be brief on this topic. However sharply opposed to each other philosophy of history and historical science may be, they have common interests in the theme individual-universal (or particular-general), but again, no common insights.

This third problem can also be expressed as the relation of freedom and determinism. It is certainly not a new problem. In the struggle of nascent historical science against Hegelianism and philosophical positivism the point, in essence, was always that of rescuing the individual and safeguarding freedom. But the problems under consideration are of particular interest to historians today. In a wide circle there is concern about an overemphasis on the particular as well as a ground swell for the category of the general in history.

The search is on again for an original coherence, for a history behind the phenomena, be it a *geschehende Geschichte*, a silently operative *structure*, or an *ordo*. All have in common that they determine man and the historical phenomena at the deepest level. Other writers on history, however, are committed to resisting the determining power of a coherence, continuity, order, or whatever it may be called (world history, period, age, spirit of the age, structure, etc.). They are out to rescue the individual person and also the individual event from the determining power of the anonymous historical process or of one of its components.

The difficulty is, however, that no individual existence is possible without the all-embracing historical coherence, as also no historical order is possible without individual events.

And to make the relation individual-universal even more complicated: the problem of meaning can never be evaded. All the Christian historians under con-

---

[32] Peter Meinhold, "Grundfragen kirchlicher Geschichtsdeutung" [Fundamental problems of an ecclesiastical interpretation of history], in Asmussen and Stählin, eds., *Die Katholizität der Kirche* (1957), 133–60; discussed by Wagner, "Zweierlei Maß der Geschichtsschreibung."

[33] Thus Wagner, "Zweierlei Maß der Geschichtsschreibung," 121.

[34] Meinhold, "Weltgeschichte – Kirchengeschichte – Heilsgeschichte" [World history – church history – salvation history], *Saeculum* 9 (1958): 261–81, at 280.

[35] A "metaphysischer Rückbeziehung" [the term is found in Wagner, "Zweierlei Maß der Geschichtsschreibung," 121].

sideration here are caught up in this problem, if only because they all—the one more than the other—have been affected by the existentializing mode of thought. Thus it is not at all surprising that Marrou and Butterfield should have rejected the structuralist view of history. The world-historical perspective, on the other hand, plays a large role in Butterfield and Wittram and especially in Meinhold (leaving Marrou aside here).

The tension between the individual and the universal is greatest in Butterfield. He calls attention to the many and diverse determinants: the circumstances, the environment, the inescapable situations, and the great conflicts; broadly speaking, history goes its way according to its own laws, over people's heads.[36] Admittedly, within this interplay of empirical conditions there remains an area of free decisions, and the conscious individual always manages in the end to emerge triumphantly from the coercive forces. Yet one must wonder what remains of this ultimately rescued freedom when Butterfield is forced to admit that the individual is in turn shackled to the structure of his own personality. In short, Butterfield attempts to safeguard the individual by allowing freedom a tiny but unassailable haven of refuge.[37] Will this attempt ever succeed?

Meinhold and Wagner seek the solution in an entirely different direction. (It is not impossible that this same quest is Butterfield's underlying motive.) They relate the problem of the relations individual-universal and freedom-necessity to the meaning of history, regarding which they maintain that *world history does not bear its meaning within itself.* In this way history loses its gravity, its autonomy, and the determinants lose their coercive character. This can also be expressed in the words "metaphysical retro-connection," which is why Wagner advocates resurrecting Ranke's idea of the "God-relatedness" (*Gottbezogenheit*) in all history,[38] an idea that has become an absurdity to con-

---

[36] Butterfield, *Christianity and History*, 94, 96; Wagner, *Moderne Geschichtsschreibung*, 56. Cf. also Gerhard Ritter, *Die Dämonie der Macht. Betrachtungen über Geschichte und Wesen des Machtsproblems im politischen Denken der Neuzeit* (6th rev. ed., 1948) [Eng. trans., *The Corrupting Influence of Power* (1952)].

[37] Butterfield, "The Rôle of the Individual in History," *History* 40 (1955): 1–17 [reprinted in idem, *Writings on Christianity and History* (1979), ed. C. T. McIntire, 17–36].

[38] [For Ranke's concept of history's "Gottbezogenheit" Professor Smit was in the habit of pointing to the following passages:

From "On the Epochs of Modern History," *Weltgeschichte*, IX/2 (Leipzig, 1888), pp. 5–6: "I would maintain, however, that every age is immediate to God, and that its worth consists, not in what follows from it, but in its own existence, in its own proper self. . . . Since no time lies before Him, I picture God as surveying the whole of historic mankind in its totality and finding it everywhere of equal value. . . . From God's point of view all the generations of mankind have equal rights, and this is how the historian too must view the matter."

From *Sämtliche Werke*, vol. 53/54 (Leipzig, 1890): "God dwells, lives, must be recognized in all history. Every deed testifies to Him, every moment proclaims His Name, but most of all, it seems to me, the connectedness of history in the large. There it stands, like a holy hieroglyph, perceived in its contours and preserved, perhaps, lest it be lost from sight to future centuries. Very well, whatever may come of it, let us do our part to try to decipher this holy hieroglyph! So too do we serve God, are we priests and teachers."

temporary historical consciousness (as a result of accepting an ineluctable automatism in the determinants).[39]

One last escape seems to be that of existential freedom, of liberation from the unity of history. On this view, the conscious individual and the historically existing man receive their meaning no longer from the universal realm of world-history, nor yet from objective events, but have meaning in themselves. This appears to be Marrou's solution. But how then can there still be interconnections between events, and how can such historical monads gain understanding of each other and of historical objects? At the very best an "encounter," a "dialogue" will be possible, only fleetingly, for otherwise there is no escaping the overpowering force of the object.

This paper must come to an end. Our focus was the question, "New perspectives for a Christian conception of history?" Looking back, we can answer: Wittram, Butterfield, Meinhold and Wagner all agree that these perspectives can only be found in the "metaphysical connection." The task of the future will be to draw out the implications of this idea. Meinhold and Wagner have already begun to do that.

From a fragment of 1835, edited by Eberhard Kessel, in "Rankes Idee der Universalhistorie," *Historische Zeitschrift* 178 (1954): 295: "History recognizes something infinite in every existence: in every condition, every being, there is something eternal that comes from God; and this is their vital principle. Apart from the divine ground of its existence, how could anything be? . . . We need not give elaborate proof of the indwelling of the eternal in the individual. This is the religious basis on which our labors rest. We believe that nothing is apart from God, and nothing lives except through God."

Cf. also the published dissertations supervised by Professor Leonhard von Muralt of Zurich: Heinrich Hauser, *Leopold von Rankes protestantisches Geschichtsbild* (1950) and Gerhard Frick, *Der handelnde Mensch in Rankes Geschichtsbild* (1953).]

[39] Wagner, *Die Historiker und die Weltgeschichte* (1965), 107; see also idem, "Rankes Geschichtsbild und die moderne Universalhistorie" [Ranke's view of history and modern world history], *Archiv für Kulturgeschichte* 44 (1962): 1–26.

12/ THE VALUE OF HISTORY

THERE IS CURRENTLY an ambivalent attitude toward history.[1] For quite some time now, many people have disparaged history. To their mind it has really become time past. Such people will say: we live in an entirely different age, a new era, with other problems and concerns. Moreover, we are living at such a rapid pace that we have to be freed from our own present. The tie to the past still exists, alas. History is a burden we have to bear, a constant obstacle on our way to a better future. Just look what earlier generations have left behind: a Germany deeply infected by nationalism, a divided France, a "pillarized" Netherlands, and the list goes on. Salvation for the present and the future can therefore be expected only from a break with the past. As Alfred Weber has put it: *"Abschied von der bisherigen Geschichte"*—good-bye to the history we left behind us.

Yet we said: the attitude towards history is currently *ambivalent*. For indeed, are there not also numerous signs that point to a renewed interest in history, and precisely in circles where one would not have expected it, among people like doctors and engineers? The very ones who used to call history bunk now love history books. This is undoubtedly hopeful, but does it imply an awareness of the real value of distant and alien times?

Let us look again at this ambivalence. There is the criticism—sometimes vehement—of the history of the academic historians, and this criticism is leveled not only by outsiders or by philosophers and sociologists but just as much by the practitioners of historical science themselves. Academic historians, they charge, have only themselves to blame that history has come to stand outside life and outside culture.

Just think of it: while historians pored over their difficult sources in the tranquility of their studies and penned their volumes, unperturbed by what was going on around them, a severe economic crisis ravaged the world and Hitler gained the opportunity to prepare Germany for another war. No one less than Lucien Febvre has accused the historians in the academic tradition of being co-responsible for the defeats suffered by France in 1940. And Charles Beard, the American historian and sometime adviser to President Roosevelt, complains: the learned historian just sits in his ivory tower, is an excellent philologist, but does not concern himself with the needs and desires of modern man.

---

[1] [Paper read to the History Club in the Catholic University at Nijmegen, spring 1966. The text incorporated portions of earlier papers on "The Meaning of History" presented to the Calvinist Student Association in Delft, Dec. 1962, and to the Society of Reformed Students in Leiden, fall 1964. Subheadings have been supplied.]

The search for meaning

In contrast—again this ambivalence—there is a great deal of interest today in philosophy of history, and particularly in *the question concerning the meaning of history.*

To be sure, every age has known that search for meaning. The nineteenth century was the century of the great philosophers of history, and interest in the question of meaning was keen throughout the period. Still, the *crisis of meaning* has become graver—so grave, in fact, that within philosophy of history a separate discipline has emerged: *metahistory*, in which all attention is focused directly on the essence, goal, and meaning of history.

My sense is that people no longer expect an answer to the real question of meaning from the scientific practitioners of history and that they are now turning instead to social philosophy or to philosophy of history.

Before testing the correctness of this conjecture, however, let us take note of a third form of ambivalence with respect to history.

History versus the history of the historians

This is indeed an expression one hears often nowadays: "the history of the historians." And one knows beforehand that the opinion of it is not favorable. Most academic historians are said to be still governed by a positivistic conception, not in the sense that their historical practice still slavishly models itself after the natural sciences (as in the nineteenth century), but certainly in the sense that they still swear by the old ideal of establishing facts, the *bruta facta*: if they have but learned *wie es eigentlich gewesen ist* ("how things really were") and assigned the facts their place in the evolution of history, then they regard their task as finished.

But, so say their critics, this is where we must *begin*. A history of the *bruta facta* is irrelevant to the needs of contemporary man; he is looking for a different sort of history. — I believe we touch here upon what lies behind the current ambivalence in the appreciation of history. When people speak of the value of history the question should first be raised: *Which history do you mean?*

Two histories

A recurring theme in the last twenty years is that of two kinds of history. Most essays on history, in fact, *presuppose* some such distinction. Equally typical of the current situation, I should add, are the many attempts at overcoming this bifid unity in a genuine unity. But how is such a genuine unity to be achieved?

Just what are these two histories? There are many of these pairs, and the remarkable thing is that they are all concerned with the same historical data: Alexander the Great, for example, yet also a common Hellenistic peasant. All such data can figure in a *structural history*, but also in a *history of events*, yet in each case, characteristically, the data function in an entirely different way.

But the concept of two histories finds much broader application. There is the history in the *conception* of the present-day historian, and there is the history *as it really happened*, and the two cannot really be reduced to each other. The historian after all can never say, This is how it really happened, since he will always mix in something of his own view or his own time.

Another contrasting pair today is the history of the historians, or narrative factual history (*Historie, histoire*), and history proper, real history (*Geschichte*), the history in virtue of which I find myself in an existential relation. Thus there is the history of the philosophers, in which the *question of meaning* is central, and there are the factual accounts offered by the historians, devoid of the problem of meaning, since presumably *meaning is too far off, too high and too deep.*

Now, it is far from being the case that all these histories and all these lovers of history live in peace and harmony with each other, exchanging mutual assurances that they beautifully complement one another. No, reproaches abound and complaints are heard on all sides. Listen to them: Of what earthly use are all those facts, established so painstakingly and with so much scientific fervor? If well narrated, they are able at most to soothe the aesthetic senses and provide a pretty pastime. Or they can serve in a variety of cases (their number is declining) to resolve legal questions—perhaps that is why the jurist is sometimes a more frequently observed visitor at the archives than is the historian. However—the argument continues—if you are confronted by great problems of an existential nature, all those naked facts leave you in the lurch.

The reply from the other side is not long in coming: If you drag the problems and exigencies of our time into the past and put the question of meaning to history, you are violating history. Then you are imposing something on history or trying to wrest something from history that is *essentially* alien to it.

Or if you will: While the historians study, Saguntum (France, you fill it in) perishes. And the reply is: We have only to establish *wie es eigentlich gewesen ist,* and in so doing we fulfill our subsidiary role. — Truly, matters of no little consequence are at stake as we ponder the *value of history* this evening!

Existential interpretations

The existentializing approach insists: insight into *my* imperiled existence determines *my* approach to history. No doubt a person has the right, even the duty, to deal with history in an objective way, applying all the rules of scientific historical method. But, so says our existentially thinking contemporary, in this way history remains distant, fails to bridge the gulf between *then and now*. What we need to do is to transcend the mere historical-objective and enter into a living relationship with history. And this *happens* when I *understand myself in relation to it*: the history which was at first far off—in the form of objective knowledge about it—is now *very near* to me, through its connection with my existential self-understanding.

Historical facts—the argument continues—do not have meaning in themselves but acquire meaning solely in their connection to my self-understanding and to my imperiled existence. Myriads of facts will thus be of no relevance, and an existentialist engagement with history must be highly selective. Furthermore, facts that are existentially relevant will be so only in a particular respect, depending on the measure of my self-understanding. In short, in the interpretation of a text, in the determination of the true nature and significance of an historical phenomenon or event or complex of events, what will be decisive is *the connection to, the value for, existence.*

Let me give you an example, borrowed for objectivity's sake from one of the leading proponents of the existentialistic interpretation of history, Gotthold Hasenhüttl. Commenting on the medieval definition of truth as the *adequation of intellect and thing,* Hasenhüttl remarks: *Today* this proposition tells us very little about truth and appears devoid of any *existential* [!] significance. An objective interpretation cannot do justice to the proposition in question. This definition will take on significance only if we transpose it into the existential language of our time, and then there is no longer any essential difference from the original medieval definition.[2]

Summing up, we must draw the following conclusions:

1. The difference between the objective-historical and the existential views of the value of history is not so great after all. In either case, the *value of history is conceived and determined again and again in terms of the ego.* History is needed so that I may become myself, constitute myself. The ego is forever engrossed, like it or not, in pressing the Other into its service.

2. The value of history—and with it the importance of historical research—thus becomes problematical. When the historically other is altered and transformed until it says what historical existence knew all along, then what value can dealing with that historically other have? And when I rewrite history in terms of my own time, as the child of a time with its own special needs, whom do I then meet in it other than myself? Is dealing with history in this fashion anything more than passing time in a hall of mirrors? With a variation on the words of Jesus (*"he that loseth his life for my sake shall find it"*), we say: He that measures history by its value for himself and his own times shall lose it.

Should we then side with those who advise: the historian is to do his work objectively, solely to show *wie es eigentlich gewesen ist,* and he is not to concern himself with its usefulness? Should we follow Enklaar when he says that the historian is disposed (or has learned) to look at the course of world events, even in changing times, "with neutral resignation, as from a distance" ?[3] More importantly, in our appreciation of history how can we escape the clutches of the ego?

---

[2] Gotthold Hasenhüttl, *Geschichte und existenziales Denken* (1965), 21f.
[3] In a review of a volume of literary essays, in *Bijdragen tot de Geschiedenis der Nederlanden* 6 (1951/52): 240f.

We recall the words of Jesus: *"He that findeth his life shall lose it; and he that loseth his life for My sake shall find it."* Applying that to the appreciation of history, we realize that something important is served when we no longer proceed in terms of our own times or of ourselves, but in terms of *another*, the *other*—the *other person*, whom we meet with in history in myriads of forms, as well as the other thing: each and every historical phenomenon and event.

History demands of us that we transcend ourselves, by which I mean that we relinquish our ego and its interests and accept and care for all those *other* persons and things, strange and remote as they may be, not part of our world. These strangers want to be recognized in terms of their *own value*, apart from any connection to the present. They want to be appreciated for their *own wealth of meaning*. They want to be recognized, accordingly, in all their specific details.

He who knocks thus at the door of history, with respectful disinterest, shall find there, not himself, but the real treasure of centuries. There he shall meet with love, freedom, peace and all the other fundamental relations without which no human can live. They will all be "other" than in his own time, and he will not be able to say immediately what meaning they have for the present. They want to be recognized not only for their enduring identity but also, and equally, for their changeable, concrete historical shapes. But the moment they are assessed in terms of their meaning for a later time, or are appraised as "backward" from the perspective of 1966, they close like flowers touched by the chill night breeze and wrap themselves in inscrutable silence.

Meeting the other
Against this background, what can we say is the value of history and of being disinterestedly engaged in it?

In history we are confronted with peace, freedom, love, etc., etc., not as abstract essences but in all their unique and irreplaceable concreteness. No one has ever designed or been able to account for peace, freedom and love. Man can only think them and dwell in them (or turn against them) because they are *granted* to him, *in the origin*, in an altogether original way.

Peace, freedom, love, and so on, are *given to us in the origin, but they reach us only via history*: here lies the awesome importance of history.

Yet, here lies at the same time the limitation of history, namely, its *dependence on the origin*. History can only hand over (*tra-ditio*) what it has itself received from the origin. At the same time, however, history not only hands down or transmits but also molds what it has received, giving rise to a multiplicity of historical shapes and phenomena.

Equally real, however, is historical freedom. In essence, freedom is the act of transcending. It is the possibility of disengaging oneself from the concrete phenomena and returning to the origin.

In history we thus have two components: (1) that which is given to us in the origin and to which man in his historical freedom can return; and (2) the shaping of what has been given us in an original way: what man makes of freedom, love, peace, and so on.

A number of points can be very briefly illustrated from an historical phenomenon such as the rise of courtly love. It has not yet proved possible to account for courtly love in a satisfactory way from antecedent or contemporary phenomena. *However strongly it may be tied into history, it nevertheless has its own originality.* If it did not have this—if it were purely historically determined—then it would not even have had its "being."

"That which is far off, and exceeding deep, who shall find it?" says the Preacher in Ecclesiastes—words which describe the work of the historian exceedingly well. He shall find it. If he is prepared to forsake the ego-circle he shall find what it is to be truly free, to be truly a person, to love, to do justice, to make peace, and so on, *in their original meaning*. These things are far off and very deep. They dwell amongst remote peoples and are found in ages long past. And yet, they are *very near* to him who knows Ranke's word: *Every age is equidistant to God.*

13/ THE TIME OF HISTORY

AMONG THE COUNTLESS STUDIES dealing with history and with time, those that are devoted specifically to the "time of history" are few.[1] There are, however, signs that point to a change—take, for example, the acclaim Samuel Brandon received when he argued in his book *History, Time and Deity*[2] that the priority given for so long to history ought now to be granted to time.

Yet what difference would it make, really, if we were to give priority to time rather than history? In history are we not always dealing implicitly with time, and is philosophy of history not also philosophy of time? — Even if we answer these questions in the affirmative we may still deem it of philosophical and scientific importance to deal explicitly with historical time, since it is here that all the problems concerning the nature of history converge and can be put into much sharper focus.

Still, why is the problem of time regarded as so exceptionally difficult and why has any explicit treatment of the subject been avoided for so long and so often? Augustine wrote the well-known words: "What is time? If no one asks me, I know; if someone poses the question and I try to explain, I know no longer."[3] Yet however unfathomable time was for Augustine, this did not deter him from engaging in fundamental reflection on the temporal. Augustine's ideas indicate, however, that he was concerned less about what time is *in itself* than about the relation of time to eternity and about its inner unity that encompasses its plurality of moments.

With that, we have posed the main question regarding time: what constitutes the inner unity or coherence within and between the temporal phenomena? This is also the central theme of historical periodization: Does a period or phase have real unity, or do we simply gather a large number of facts and historical moments together under one name because a complete enumeration of the fragments is utterly impossible? Generally, historians will characterize an age or period and attach the corresponding label without first having considered the philosophical question concerning the nature of historical time. The disappointing result, as a rule, is that not all the phenomena of a particular time yield gracefully to placement in a particular, pre-conceived pattern. If, then, it is far

---

[1] [This essay was composed for use on a lecture tour of South Africa, fall 1966, and was published as "De tijd der geschiedenis" in *Bulletin van die Suid-Afrikaanse Vereniging vir die Bevordering van Christelike Wetenschap*, no. 12 (1968), 5–19. Subheadings have been added.]

[2] S. G. F. Brandon, *History, Time and Deity: A Historical and Comparative Study of the Conception of Time in Religious Thought and Practice* (1965).

[3] *Confessions*, XI, 14, 17.

from easy to approximate the "spirit" or the "structure" of a term of but limited duration, we may surmise that a conceivable unity of world history will confront us with still greater difficulties.

These introductory remarks suggest what should be given priority in any essay on the time of history. Time, it seems, works in two ways: (1) it unbinds, tears apart, disintegrates, is transient and discontinuous; (2) it binds, integrates, establishes connections, is continuous. Time—here and in what follows I mean the time of history—causes the culture of Antiquity to perish, removing it from the flux of history, yet it is this very same time that links later civilizations to it.

Perennially, attempts are made to escape the disintegrating action and meaninglessness of time by taking refuge in some immutable substance, which is then made the bearer of meaning.

Mythical and successive time

To achieve a clearer picture of the problem of time, let us go back in the history of thought. In the theological and philosophical literature of the last decades, an almost canonical significance has been attached to the contrast between cyclical and linear views of history. Presumably, there is an intrinsic connection between, on the one hand, Christian belief and the linear idea of time, and on the other hand, the cyclical idea and non-Christian thought. Criticism of this scheme has mounted in recent years, not only because mathematical symbols are deemed inadequate for representing historical reality, but also because both the Christian and the non-Christian conceptions of history are too complex to be placed under a single heading.

Although the current contrast may be an oversimplification, it has had a beneficial effect in that it has generated considerable interest in the relation between time and religious belief. This resulted in the appearance of penetrating studies devoted to the mythical experience of time and its meaning for present-day philosophical reflection on time.

If the mythical notion of time had been the only notion of time in the non-Christian cultures, then it would not be such a difficult matter to reconstruct its precise meaning. What makes it so puzzling and so intrinsically contradictory to us is the fact that, for all its cyclical character, time is still always connected somehow to successive time with its notion of 'earlier' and 'later' and its clearly distinguished temporal moments. Mythical time receives its dynamics from creation; from some primordial event; sometimes even from an historical event —all of which, however, are in principle undatable. They do belong to a (distant) past, yet they do not occur there as past moments of successive time; they are not ordinary history, yet they can enter into it, not only as recollection or re-presentation, but exactly as they were in primordial time; creation and the mythical historical event will happen again and again, in countless, unending repetition. Language is too closely bound to successive time to permit description of what is experienced in the mythical notion of time. The word "repetition" conveys the idea best, but then the word must be taken in its original, undiluted sense, for every thought of an analogy in the repetition would already shortchange the two kinds of direction in mythical temporality: on the one hand, mythical temporality means the "re-presencing," here and now, of the primordial event itself, while on the other hand it means a being transported back to that primordial past, a re-entering and participating in an undatable 'original' event.

In our attempt to clarify the mythical notion of time we have had to use concepts from successive time. This is not to be ascribed solely to *our* limited means of expression; mythical language, too, can only express the meaning of the original actuality in terms of a succession of earlier and later. Thus the two notions of time appear to interpenetrate one another even at the level of language; but they do so in another way as well: primordial time does not remain purely transcendent, since it enters into history, not of itself, as an anonymous power, but via human acts. The act of creation, for example, is repeated in the performance of rituals, in the ascending of the throne, in the conquest of the enemy. To the extent that such actions and events repeat the 'original' event, they stand outside ordinary time—and yet they can be precisely dated in terms of successive time and people take great pains to describe them concretely, right down to the minutest details. To the Egyptian, for instance, an event was more than a datable happening; he saw it also in another temporal perspective, one that to him was the most important one, for only via mythical time could a historical action partake of the wholeness (*heil*) of the origin. In this light it becomes clear to us why successive time is persistently disqualified: it is transient and fleeting and thus can have no meaning in itself; if wholeness is yet to be its portion, then the event-from-the-beginning must be actualized in it time and time again. There was a constant anxiety here about losing one's powers under the pressure of time; the endless process of becoming and perishing was experienced as a tyrant whose dominion could be rendered bearable only by the performance of sacred rituals.

Augustine on time

On our hasty excursion through the history of the problem of time we pass over a great deal, but we must pause to consider Augustine, and then not primarily because of his well-known notion of so-called psychological time: that is looked at too often for its own sake, in isolation from the rest of his thought, and then it seems a simple matter to point to analogies with modern insights. Fortunately, in many of the more recent studies of Augustine his view of time is considered in the context of the whole of his thought.

Augustine was much concerned with time, yet the result was never a definition or concept of time-in-itself. As I have already said, his interest was not time as time-unto-itself but rather time in relation to—in dependence upon, and in connection with—eternity. It was here that Augustine looked for a solution to the problem of time—to the extent that one may ever expect to find a solution, in view of the fact that temporality, in spite of all illuminating insights, will always remain a mystery.

It is only in relation to eternity that we know what time is: contingent and finite, creaturely and dependent, above all tending towards non-being. Yet it is precisely this threat of non-being and its creatureliness that keep time oriented to what is not subject to change. Thus it would appear that on Augustine's view time has a twofold orientation. In reality, however, the problem is not that simple for him. On the one hand he relates time to eternity as immutability; on the other hand he relates it to an event that is itself temporal, historical, namely, the Incarnation. This dual orientation of time in Augustine must not be taken to mean that he related so-called psychological time to the eternal and thereby isolated it from temporality in the historical sense. It has been correctly observed that already in the *Confessions* (XI, 38) time is analyzed in conjunction with the history of mankind.[4]

Nevertheless, Augustine never arrived at a harmonious conception of time; the inner tension in his mind between the modes of temporality persisted. The dualism in which he was caught can be sharply observed in his estimation of the past: on the one hand it counts as nothing, for it is no more; on the other hand that same past is the basis for salvation, for once upon a time an event took place in the past which was of decisive significance for all ages. Ultimately, Augustine overcame the dark side of time, its vanity and futility, not by discovering the eternal within time, but precisely by acknowledging meaning within the temporal, visible world.

Time in the Middle Ages

Augustine's influence on the thought of the Middle Ages has been much debated, but it is certain that it was profound. Still, we should not forget that in that middle period of a thousand years, many other intellectual currents exercised their influence. Furthermore, we should remember that medieval people did not live exclusively from what they had received: they had their own spirituality as well, certainly in their reflection upon and experience of time. Change in the temporal sense brought them, too, to an inner conflict—which they never resolved satisfactorily: everyday life and history spoke the clear language of frailty and transience, so how could they ever be meaningful! Medieval literature abounds with complaints about the vanity of things because they are subject to change. On the other hand, it could not be denied that God himself had willed change and that change therefore must have a positive meaning. A clear example of this ambivalent attitude towards time and history is found in the most important medieval philosopher of history, Otto of Freising. Even though he went so far as to put change on a par with sin, an essential part of his philosophy

---

[4] U. Duchrow, "Der sogenannte psychologische Zeitbegriff Augustins im Verhältnis zur physikalischen und geschichtlichen Zeit," *Zeitschrift für Theologie und Kirche* 63 (1966): 269.

of history is based upon a positive assessment of *mutatio* in history. It is no mean task to make clear in what way Otto of Freising, and the medieval conception of history in general, managed to see meaning in change. Medieval writers of history often baffle modern historians because they sometimes date events as precisely as they can and at other times are very careless, even to the point of placing centuries later what happened in an earlier period. What we have here is the propensity—noted also by Étienne Gilson in connection with medieval philosophy—to allow the past to be absorbed by the present, but I regard another tendency as even more important, namely, to allow the eternal to come down into the temporal. What I am referring to here is more than just a case of linking the time of history to eternity. The fact is, rather, that medieval man thought in very concrete terms about the eternal within time. He believed the kingdom of God—an eternal kingdom—was realizable on earth, although at the same time he was aware—albeit not always—that the gulf separating time from eternity never ceased to exist. I think the monastic notion of "having already in this life a foretaste of eternal life" best expresses what the medieval person had in mind: or, in more modern terms, medieval people conceived of an anticipatory relation of time to eternity, a relation which would not be of the same intensity in every period since in times of decline eternity might withdraw almost completely. In the final analysis it is not transience but the value of the eternal in the temporal that dominates in the medieval conception of time.

Time in Hegel and thereafter

However radical the differences between the medieval and the Hegelian philosophies of history may be, there is an important similarity to be noted with regard to the problem of time: Hegel's metaphysics of time also has its redoubtable antipode in eternity. The World Spirit does indeed come down into history to make its dialectical journey through time, in order thus to unfold its riches in all their fullness; but in its *Auslegung*, in the multiplicity of historical manifestations, it continues to be what it was: *eternal*. This is the root problem of Hegel's system and the source of all the difficulties that came to haunt him. For how can the Spirit, which is eternal, become one with history, which remains temporal? The dilemma would be resolved if one could agree with some current interpreters who claim Hegel temporalized and thereby historicized the Logos, but there is no evidence to support this interpretation. Granted, for Hegel history with all its infinite wealth of forms *is* an intrinsic necessity of the Spirit, but the historical development in itself is empty, deriving as it does its entire wealth of meaning from the Logos. For example, a nation, once it is abandoned by the Logos, may prolong its existence but then no longer as part of authentic history. Despite the necessary connection of the one to the other, Logos and time remain alien to each other: the former never really enters into time, but in every historical period returns to itself again, for it remains always what it was: eternal.

Dialectical trappings designed to hold the irreconcilable elements together cannot, finally, conceal the negation of time.

In the century and a half since Hegel, there has been no lack of criticism of his views. There has been a strong reaction against his devaluation of the intrinsic value of time and history. In the nineteenth- and twentieth-century mainstreams, the emphasis would come to fall on the temporality of history, on the finite character—and therefore on the restricted validity—of historical phenomena and social circumstances, of religious beliefs and philosophical worldviews. All are swept away in the current of history, yet each in its time and under its own particular historical circumstances has its unique value. Opposition to Hegel was fierce among both working historians and philosophers of history. Nevertheless, the age-old problem of the eternal in time resisted relegation to the background. The initial, and thereafter growing, emphasis on the finitude of historical phenomena made way again for a renewed awareness that radical historicizing means the end of history. The search for the solid Ground, for that which is "removed from relativity" (Dilthey), has become increasingly urgent. There must be something in history that establishes coherence that sets things in relation to each other. This is now acknowledged, though often with reluctance, so deeply rooted is the dread of dragging the banished metaphysics back into historical science. Yet neither the philosophy nor the science of history can do without an idea of a unity in historical time: some regard history as a whole composed of periods and epochs that are centered on themselves (Dilthey); others view it as a progressive development which by virtue of its inner dynamism remains the same throughout all times (e.g., positivism); still others understand authentic historical events to be a repetition of the same existential decision (existentialism); while in the last thirty years the idea of a single, continuous, *structural* historical time has rapidly gained many adherents (for example, those connected with the French periodical *Annales*).

The fabric of time directions

Meanwhile, the problem of time as I defined it above is still with us. Is it possible that in the disintegrating / integrating action of time we have two irreducible forces? Or are they themselves dependent in turn upon a higher or deeper unity?

Preparatory to dealing with these questions, we need to acquire a clearer picture of the multiformity and extreme complexity of historical time. Cyclical time presupposes, it is true, an infinite number of time movements, but in point of fact, since every later cycle is a repetition of the preceding one, nothing ever happens that is really new. Linear time, in contrast, knows but a single historical movement without repetition, so that every event appears as something unique, as something never having been before. In this perspective history is an unbroken line stretching from the beginning (Creation) through the covenant with Abraham and the center (the Incarnation), to the final goal (the consummation of all things in Christ). The linear view persisted in the modern conception of history, be it in secularized form (for example, the unfolding of the World Spirit to complete freedom; progressive evolution). This conception of time can better be called *unilinear*, in view of the fact that the many phenomena are all, without exception, included in the one historical movement of time; in fact, whenever certain events and circumstances are difficult to fit into the general development they are either placed *outside* history or else *dialectically* brought into coherence with the single world history. This reduction of things to unilinear development is not wholly arbitrary, since time—as we saw—does indeed also join the events and times; it is thanks in part to this that history does not fall apart into fragments—indeed, that there can even be a world history, and likewise that periods, times, epochs, ages exhibit a certain unity or structure. It is for this reason that we can speak of "our time," of "Antiquity," and so on; in every time there must be something that distinguishes it from every other.

If one attempts, however, to grasp that "something," that unity of a period, then it just cannot be done. Is that ascribable to the unfathomableness of time and hence also of the period in question? Or perhaps to a failure to appreciate the multiformity of time and an excessive readiness to revert to a unilinear conception of history? As I see it, the latter is the case. Still, I do not want to underestimate the difficulties that arise when we abandon the idea of a single continuous time as the reference point or connecting line for all particular developments and individual phenomena. The consequence seems to be that we are left with a chaotic plurality of facts. But let us see whether there is not another possibility of discovering unity or, at least, coherence in the diversity.

When we view history under the aspect of time, it presents an extraordinarily rich picture. The peoples, societies, and cultures all have their own movements of time, which vary in tempo, intensity, and direction. The differentiation goes still further: the temporal course of a nation or culture often undergoes change, now slowing down, now accelerating; and even the direction does not always remain constant. Moreover, not just the whole but also the religious, social, and aesthetic sectors know a diversity of "times." And the individualization goes still further: the single work of art, the distinct political event, the religious experience, etc., etc., all have their own specific, characteristic times. Nor does individual human life escape the rich diversity of time. If we proceed to analyze the time of, say, a particular work of art or of a certain person, we soon discover it is in turn integrated in various "times," for example in national, social, religious, philosophical temporality, in a fabric of time directions. I am calling it a fabric for the moment, in an attempt to convey figuratively the unique nature of each "time" as well as the interwovenness of the "times." The life of an individual, for example, is only interwoven in part with the history of a nation, with nature, and with intellectual currents; alongside these, the individual has time for himself and for many other relationships.

We have used the word "times" in another than the usual sense. People usually understand by it periods *that follow one another,* but what we mean by it is that every historical phenomenon, be it of shorter or longer duration, *participates, in one and the same phase, in different times.*

Transcendental time

That brings us to one of the key problems of temporality, namely, that in spite of the multiplicity and heterogeneity of the "times," temporality still gives the impression of an inner order. Where does this order come from and what determines it? The answer to this question is almost invariably sought in the one-dimensional historical time I described earlier. People attempt to locate the order that there is in time by discovering in the most divergent phenomena some common feature (called, for example, style, structure, spirit). This method often entails the unhappy consequence that whole complexes of events that essentially cannot be fitted into some concrete structure have to be depreciated, for example as a "reaction." Still more often, however, an "aberration" is relegated to history of a lower order. That which is common to the various facts and phenomena usually is reduced in that case to some formal aspects.

Our question concerning the inner order and coherence of time still stands unanswered. That this order is there despite the plurality of "times" is a source of profound astonishment. But the matter cannot be left at that. In many theological discussions concerned with understanding temporality, a contrast is drawn between the way theologians view temporality and the way philosophers regard it: theologians, it is said, always see time in its subjection to God's rule, whereas philosophers regard it from the viewpoint of its immanent, autonomous movement, inexorable for man.

This contrast is unacceptable. Philosophers, too, encounter in temporality more than earlier-later, more than past-present-future. They, too, cannot dispense with what I shall provisionally call trans-successive, qualitative time. Now, it is of great importance whether the concept of trans-successive time is introduced only after numerous speculations have already been made about time or whether it is drawn into the problem from the outset, as the theologians claim they do. Theologians may reproach philosophers for thinking and speaking of time as though it were an anonymous and autonomous power, but the central question to be asked is, What is the source of this power? Or in other words, where does time derive the power to be time, continuous and discontinuous? If philosophy replies that time has this power of and by itself, or that "that is simply the way things are," then I must say I find both notions inconceivable. If, however, time is recognized as deriving its power, presence, or existence from an origin, then it follows that time is what it is by virtue of that origin. The reality that time is not of itself but has *received* its existence affects it essentially, intrinsically, and for all time, holding it in permanent dependency. Both continuous and discontinuous events now lose their autonomy and neutrality in their orientation to the origin and in their pointing above and beyond themselves. In all its modalities time remains what it was, but it is governed by another time, which because of its original relation and orientation to the Transcendent One I shall call *transcendental time*—despite the many meanings the word "transcendental" already has.

From my discussion so far it may have become clear, but it needs to be emphasized again at this point, that what is at issue here is not one form of temporality alongside others. No, there is just one time, transcendental time—which is to say that the only time there is is rooted in, borders on, and stands in relation to eternity, albeit not as emanating from it, since in that case it would itself be eternal and autonomous.

What does the transcendental character of time all involve? To clarify that, we note its striking similarity to the perspective of prophecy. Essential for any prophecy are two things: it has the whole in view; and it obliterates or at least it blurs the temporal distance. Events that are said to fulfill a prophecy may occur in various times, but the prophecy speaks of them together as if they are to happen at one and the same point in time. Now, that loss of distance is also characteristic of transcendental time: past, present, and future concur and coincide yet at the same time are differentiated into earlier and later. Again, it almost seems as if prophecy rises above the world of temporality into a distant transhistorical realm, yet in reality it remains fully temporal, not only as regards its content but also with regard to the time it is uttered: it remains datable in every respect. The same is true of transcendental time: it is *comprehensive*, not in any external fashion but in such a way that all moments and centuries, all events and developments are brought into relation to it and given direction by it.

Just as theology distinguishes in prophecy between a temporally bound historical event, its continuation into a near and/or distant future, and its consummation (in the eschaton), so we meet with corresponding moments in transcendental time: it has an origin, it stretches out, and it returns again into itself. But this observation requires further comment.

Take such a thing as freedom. The historian will observe phenomena from various centuries and call them all "freedom." He inquires into the causes and influences behind their inception; in short, he investigates the "history" of the various forms of freedom. But the average historian usually does not concern himself with *the fact that there is* such a thing as freedom.

To make my meaning clear I might refer to countless other phenomena and things, such as man himself, the love between two people, concord, peace, the simple fact that there is the possibility of observation or that humans can think. To a certain extent we can explain how a particular state of peace came about, how someone arrived at a particular thought, or why someone made a particular decision, but there has never yet been anyone who by himself conceived of, designed, or called into being decision-making or freedom as such, or history, or the meaning of history. The first man perhaps? But he already *was* freedom and history, and so on, before he could even think or surmise them.

Thus in every event and act, in every thing and phenomenon there is something incomprehensible, namely the mystery of coming into existence and of existing. This mystery does not hover above history; rather, it actualizes itself anew, ever and again as it were, in every visible act and event. By the bare fact of the existence of things I do not mean some timeless essence, but it is the *meaning* of these things, the meaning of their actuality, in all their concreteness, *given* in the origin, which itself is time.

I believe that the idea of transcendental time can help point out the *vitium originis,* the original fatal flaw, of historicism. Historicism knows, indeed, of a meaning in history, notably of the meaning of a period or a single event, but it simply *assumes* this meaning without grounding it in and relating it to a meaning given in a transcendental origin. This meaning, too, does not derive from man's designing it, or assigning it; rather, it is given directly in the divine act of creation. And by virtue of the unity of the historical moments in transcendental time, every moment of human history is involved in the meaning of the whole of history—which was already present in the beginning. (It needs to be noted that the beginning is something else than the situation at the beginning.)

Now the meaning of history (and the meaning of freedom, of love, etc.) has been entrusted to man, has been placed as it were in his hands. He dwells in it—there is no escape—in face-to-face confrontation with the original freedom and love. Certainly he can turn against it, ignore it, or try to restrict and repress it, but he will never succeed, for he remains bound to what is given in the transcendental meaning. It is beyond his capacity, for example, to destroy freedom, for as long as he is man he is freedom.

Transcendental time is both unity and diversity; it goes out from the origin and returns to it again. So essential is the origin that I can even say time stretches out within its confines, for to go beyond the confines of the origin would mean for time to lose all meaning. In the discontinuous manifestations of freedom and love, for example, in all the diversity of forms and acts throughout the whole of history, there occurs both a re-actualization of and a return to the original meaning of freedom and love.

Time moves in one direction only, it is often said; in recent decades this has been said especially by the group of the *Annales.* In contrast I have several times now employed the expressions of time's going out and returning again. Man is so fascinated by the *succession* of events that he has no eye for the countermovement in history, and yet he participates in it from moment to moment, for how else would human life be possible if it were not for this act of returning, and the act of re-actualization that goes with it! How countless are the times we enter into the facts and events of a hundred or a thousand years ago!

The going out and the returning again of time is likewise the avenue by which history has meaning and value for the present. Without the convergence of the times in transcendental time there would be no access to the meaning of existence in every one of its aspects: man would be as one who has lost his memory: totally bewildered.

The question concerning the meaning of history and life has been posed countless times. The answer that Christian belief offers is simple, but let us not forget that this meaning, in order to reach us, has had to travel the long road of history. It does not just force its way into time as a stranger every now and then; it takes its departure in historical events of decisive significance. Thus the question concerning the meaning of history should also be understood to entail the question: *What end is served by the fact that history exists at all?* Our answer would be that the meaning of life needs a channel, within the confines of transcendental time, along which to come to people and things.

We must also turn very *consciously* to history, to its meaning. Doing so requires a decision on our part, the most important and most far-reaching decision we can make in this life. We evince no true sense of history if we entrust ourselves to some sort of (progressive) evolution, or if we romantically try to revive the past, or if we comb history for models and examples to help solve the problems of our own day. Let us face the fact that we live in another time and that yesterday's solutions no longer apply; let us face the fact above all that in the discontinuous-continuous flux of history as such there is no solid ground to be found. Many look for the significance of history in its ability to highlight the transience and relativity of things. But surely we do not need history to tell us that! Its value and its power are far greater. History constantly sends us *out towards* and *back to* the house of meaning; there is no other power than history —in its transcendental orientation to its Meaning-giver—to keep us in the origin and the center of life.

14/ APPROACHES TO THE REFORMATION

IN THE FIELD OF THE HISTORY of the Reformation [1] as well as of the period to which it belongs and of the fourteenth century that preceded it, many, very many topical studies and monographs have appeared in recent decades. Happily, the historiography of the fifteenth and sixteenth centuries has not been confined to specialist studies, as time after time historians have felt called to describe the Reformation in its broader and deeper connections in works of synthesis. Bernd Moeller, one of the most knowledgeable scholars of the Reformation and its antecedents, finds however that these works lack the originality and maturity of earlier histories. We ask: Is the history of the Reformation no longer manageable for any one author, or is there an absence of a broad vision, a prerequisite for the construction of any grand historical design?

Not surprisingly, philosophers and theoreticians of history have always taken a great interest in the Reformation. True, the continuous course of history does not leave philosophy of history unmoved, but its interest goes out primarily to the great events and turning points of history.

Working historians as a rule do not welcome philosophical reflection on, say, the fall of the Roman Empire, or the Renaissance and the Reformation, and the like. They fear philosophy will bring more confusion than clarification. Philosophers of history, on the other hand, claim to provide insights that elude the professional scientific researchers but that are essential none the less for an understanding of the historical phenomena. The pretension extends even further: important philosophical and theoretical issues are said to be at stake wherever deeper interrelationships are encountered in history.

From the above one might draw the conclusion that professional historians and philosophers of history are ranged against each other along sharply defined fronts. Outwardly, that is indeed the case. In reality, however, the two parties rely heavily on each other and employ each other's materials—often unwittingly—with the salutary effect that they stimulate each other to formulate new problems.

The reason why the Reformation has held such an enormous attraction for philosophers of history is not solely that it represents one of the great crises of world history. More importantly, in the Reformation there is a coming together of many of the general problems of history. For example, is the Reformation as a whole simply part of an historical trend and therefore intrinsically determined

---

[1] [Paper read at the annual meeting of the Association for Calvinist Philosophy, Jan. 1970; published as "Wijsgerige en theoretische benadering van de Reformatie" in *Mededelingen van de Vereniging voor Calvinistische Wijsbegeerte* 35.2 (1970): 3–5.]

by it, or does it have something unique about it that is related to its origin? Must the Reformation be accounted for in terms of social, economic and political factors, or is it a strictly religious phenomenon? Does the Reformation form a structural unity with the sixteenth century or with the period 1450 to 1550, or does it cut right through the reciprocal relations between the phenomena and events of this period?

We are obliged to introduce rather more difficult formulations. Does the Reformation perhaps partake of both the continuity and discontinuity of history? Is the Reformation, while essentially religious in character, nevertheless not inseparable from socio-economic and political factors? Does the Reformation —this is the main question—despite its participation in the one, continuous history as well as in the structural unity of the emerging modern period, not also have *an originality of its own*?

These are the problems that constantly reappear, if only implicitly, in the many studies and interpretations of the Reformation, a few of which we shall now look at more closely.

An approach from a philosophical position
Let us begin with Hegel. In his thought, the Reformation (along with the Renaissance) is one of the great moments in the dialectical progress of the Spirit through world history. In the fourth Age, which includes the Reformation, subjective and objective Mind or Spirit, the spiritual and the secular, arrive at a new unity, at reconciliation. Through its triumph over the Middle Ages, the Spirit takes a decisive step forward towards its goal, namely, towards coming-to-itself. It is still only an initial breakthrough, and many centuries will be required for the full realization of its freedom.[2]

In Hegel's philosophy of history the Reformation thus assumed a meaningful place, forming an inner unity not only with the sixteenth century but with the entire modern age, as well as with the Middle Ages, albeit dialectically. But whatever became of Luther? Not that he was never mentioned in Hegel's lectures on *The Philosophy of History*, but the world-historical coherence so preponderates in Hegel that both the *individual* figure of Luther and the *intrinsic* value of the Reformation are lost from sight.

Ranke saw this and reproached Hegel for it. It is not illegitimate to apply Ranke's famous dictum, "Every epoch is immediate to God," to the Age of the Reformation, but then one must also note the words that follow immediately: "and its worth is not based on what follows from it but rather on its own existence, on its own proper self."[3] This time the danger was very real—though not in Ranke personally—that the emphasis would fall so heavily on the

---

[2] G. W. F. Hegel, *Vorlesungen über die Philosophie der Weltgeschichte* (1837), Vierter Teil, Dritter Abschnitt, Erstes Kapittel; Eng. trans., *The Philosophy of History* (1899), Part IV, Section III, Chapter I.

[3] L. von Ranke, *Über die Epochen der neueren Geschichte* [On the epochs of modern history] (1854); repr. in *Weltgeschichte* (1888), IX/2:1–9, at 5.

irreducibility of the Reformation that its world-historical connections would be ignored. In Ranke's ideal of discovering "the unique value of every epoch," a whole problem comes into focus: How can recognition of the unique and intrinsic value of the Reformation be combined with a proper recognition of the world-historical coherence without which it is inconceivable?

Generally, the Reformation has been considered in more limited contexts. Its relations to the national histories, to the character of the sixteenth century, and to the Middle Ages have been painstakingly scrutinized. However interesting all this may be in connection with our subject, we shall have to leave it and go on.

An approach from a theoretical position

In the *Revue Historique* of 1929 there appeared an article by Lucien Febvre that has since become famous. The title alone is enough to suggest we are dealing with a combative author who advocates an "altogether different approach" to the Reformation; it reads: "A badly put question: The origins of the French Reformation and the problem of the causes of the Reformation." [4] It is not my intention to discuss here whether the pretension of an "altogether different approach" is historically correct. But when we try to take the writer's conception as a whole—which one will probably never quite achieve in the case of Febvre, who thinks in leaps—then we get a picture of the Reformation and the Reformation era in which all the problems I described in my introduction come together.

Febvre wrote his celebrated article in 1929. That was also the year in which the *Annales* was founded, a journal which, initially under the leadership of Marc Bloch and Lucien Febvre and later under that of Fernand Braudel, earned a position of dominance in French historical science. The "school of the Annales" is commonly characterized after the central significance it attributes to the "history of structures." Excessive use of the term *structure* did not please Febvre, however. More in harmony with his intention is the use of terms like *social ethos* or *social history*, but then it is essential to explain at length what the word *social* meant to him. That being the case, I will just use the word *structure*, since it is flexible enough to cover Febvre's intentions.

At first blush the doctrine of structure is clear and not very complex, but on delving a bit deeper one discovers that its adherents could not avoid the great problems of theory of history. The difficulty is that they proceed to deal with these problems only superficially and become entangled in numerous contradictions. One gains the impression that they are so convinced of the correctness of their own conception that they regard philosophical and theoretical reflections as superfluous.

---

[4] Lucien Febvre, "Une Question mal posée: les origines de la réforme française et le problème des causes de la réforme," *Revue historique* 161 (1929) [Eng. trans. by Keith Folca, "The Origins of the French Reformation: A Badly-put Question?"; in Peter Burke, ed., *A New Kind of History: From the Writings of Lucien Febvre* (1973), 44–107].

What, now, is the "altogether different approach" to history taken by Febvre and others? He reproaches traditional history for seeing only isolated events, at most their causal connections. Traditional history regards historical phenomena only in their short term—nor can it do otherwise because "things" interest it only "on the surface." According to the basic premise of the *Annales* school, history—thus including also the apparently isolated events—is determined by the "history of the structures," by the one "social" history, by supra-personal forces of long duration and sustained action. This "one history" in which all the elements are interrelated is operative at a deeper level, "silently and imperiously."

The "annalistic" conception of history takes the whole of history as its field of research, so it is noteworthy that it has always felt attracted in particular to the Reformation and the period 1400 to 1650.

The Reformation is for Febvre a broad historical movement that must be grasped *at the same time* and *in the same manner* on the political, economic, social, moral and cultural levels. We must understand the Reformation, he holds forth, in terms of the needs of the age that was then socially and morally in full development. The proclamation that faith alone justifies "provided a new and powerful means of satisfaction for certain deep-rooted tendencies." The Reformation was supported primarily by the middle class, the very class that had developed a new outlook and was greedy for independence. The bourgeoisie had climbed the social ladder through personal effort and were no longer prepared to accept anything that "smacked of mediation or intercession" such as by the church. Behind the Reformation there operated a crisis of exceptional proportions, which emerged even before 1517. The best people of the age were looking for a religion suited to them, a "faith adapted to their needs." [5]

The "one history" recognizes no boundaries between the nations, for the Europe of the early sixteenth century formed a unity of religious aspirations. Nor does it recognize any partitions between the Middle Ages and the Reformation, for both were incorporated in the great, uninterrupted flow of events, in the continuity of the Christian world of thought and feeling.

According to the structuralist notion, therefore, the Reformation was in a number of respects universal. But is this position tenable? As I see it, the school of the *Annales* has capitulated on at least two essential points.

First, it presupposes an inner unity between the Middle Ages and Modern Times, a structural entity that maintained itself for many centuries. But equally essential to it is another integral coherence, that of only one or two centuries—in this case, roughly the fifteenth and sixteenth centuries—and this coherent whole is clearly set off against the times before and after it. How are these two structural entities to be harmonized with each other?

Secondly, in keeping with their basic theme Febvre and his colleagues are forever concerned with the "one history," a "total world," the common "style" of a given period. Yet it is also a basic theme of theirs that a particular national

---

[5] Ibid. [cf. Eng. trans., 71, 75, 88].

identity (of France, for example) remains the same throughout all the structural differences between periods. Through the years, in fact, a nationalistic streak in Febvre's thought has grown more pronounced, especially as a result of the Second World War. Here again we must point the finger at the collision of two different structures.

The problem we have sketched around the Reformation involves the old question of the relation universal-individual (or general-particular, universal-unique). Historians have refused to treat the Reformation as an isolated movement. Yet the question must be posed: Why has this caused them so many difficulties? It has done so—let us come right out and say it—because as the result of an overemphasis on the universal, the individual event or unique phenomenon (in this case the Reformation) can no longer be *itself* and so loses its *originality*, being no more than an expression of an historical trend or a structure.

To reject this approach does not mean to drive the Reformation into an a-historical or supra-historical isolation. One of the great problems with regard to the Reformation—and with regard to every historical phenomenon—is that it is incorporated in a totality, in a comprehensive reality, and at the same time has an originality all its own.

15/ THE FIRST AND THE SECOND HISTORY

THE FOLLOWING REFLECTIONS will have a bearing not only on my lectures of last year but on all the problems I have raised for discussion in recent years.[1] These problems were not dealt with in isolation but in the context of currents in historical science and philosophy of history. Among these currents were Hegelianism, historicism, and existentialism, but also positivism, cultural morphology, structuralism, and others.

These currents as such will no longer occupy the place of central importance in my reflections. I turn rather to a number of the great questions of theory and philosophy of history. The currents I mentioned served to afford a better view of the true nature and significance of such questions as: What is history and what is historical time? Is world history possible? Is all history ultimately world history? How does history relate to its meaning? Are there structural relations in history? What is one to think of continuity and discontinuity in historical development and of the relation between the science of history and philosophy of history?

Such are the problems that will now, as I said, occupy the place of central importance. With respect to the different approaches to these problems, I shall, for the time being at least, adopt a position only implicitly. Of course I will allude to them from time to time, since controversies can indeed lead to clearer insights. In any positive exposition, the element of critique will be constantly, if tacitly, present.

Moreover, it should be taken into consideration that my reflections range over numerous problems without expressly identifying them each time. This I can do because I think history coincides with the meaning of history and historical time with history itself, and because the answer to the question concerning development and progress must be contained in the view of the meaning of life. Of course it is not sufficient simply to say this; the case should be developed through extensive demonstration, which I cannot provide here; but the relation between, for example, meaning and history ranks among the cardinal questions of philosophy of history.

What is history?

In view of the fact that this question is under constant discussion in what follows, a single remark will have to do at this time.

---

[1] [These "reflections" were first presented as lectures in the Theory of History course in the spring and fall of 1969. The text was made available in stenciled form for discussion in a special graduate seminar, which met five times in the spring of the following year.]

Karel Kuypers has pointed out that Augustine never dealt with the question.[2] And Henri-Irénée Marrou has observed that a definition is only a pedagogical device; a definition of history can never present the essence of history a priori.[3]

Why is a definition powerless in the face of the essence and meaning of history? Because history ranks among the fundamental givens and phenomena behind which man cannot penetrate and from which he can only *pro*-ceed— which is to say that history is not derivative but entirely *original*. What we can do, of course, is to make explicit what is implicitly present in history as such— and that, to be sure, is the constant enterprise of the theorists and philosophers of history.[4]

In recent decades it has become increasingly common to speak of a twofold history, of history in a primary and in a secondary sense. Writers distinguish between *Geschichte* and *Historie*; history as meaning and history as fact; "event history" and structural history. I shall work with a similar terminology, but my idea of a twofold history will have to be quite different.

The first history

It is exceptionally difficult to express in words what the essence and meaning of the first history is. It is so difficult because modern man has grown almost entirely insensible to the first history, even though he lives in it and with it every day. It is especially as a result of the rational analytical method and mind of modern science that the first history has vanished from present-day consciousness. In the process, science itself has sustained a great loss, as Erich Fromm reminds us by recounting Ibsen's story about Peer Gynt's search for his self: layer after layer is peeled off, as from an onion, until it appears he has no core, and hence no unity; like the onion, man is held together by mere cohesion.[5] Science has become a knowledge of foregrounds in their external coherences. Fortunately, science is incapable of taking a single step without taking the backgrounds (the deeper unity and coherence) at least implicitly into account.

Scholars in various fields of science have noted this. I mention only a few, starting with several natural scientists. Evert Slijper, a zoologist who passed away last year,[6] felt that all events on earth must be guided by a divine power

---

[2] K. Kuypers, "Die Frage nach dem Sinn der Geschichte" [The question of the meaning of history], *Verspreide Geschriften* (1968), 1:239. [Reprinted from *Philosophy and Christianity: Philosophical Essays Dedicated to Herman Dooyeweerd* (1965), 113, citing W. Kamlah, *Christentum und Geschichtlichkeit. Untersuchungen zur Entstehung des Christentums und zu Augustins "Bürgerschaft Gottes"* (1951), 330.]

[3] H.-I. Marrou, *De la Connaissance historique* (1954), 31ff. [Eng. trans., 32ff.].

[4] Definitions of history cannot help but involve derivation and so are self-defeating; cf. Jan Romein's: "History in one way or another embraces everything that has happened to people in community"; *In de hof der historie; kleine encyclopedie der theoretische geschiedenis* [In the nursery of history: a short encyclopedia of theoretical history] (1951), 56f.

[5] Erich Fromm, *Man for Himself: An Inquiry into the Psychology of Ethics* (1947), 73.

[6] [Everhard Johannes Slijper (1907–68) was Professor of Vertebrate Anatomy in the City University of Amsterdam.]

or fixed plan that one encounters precisely when penetrating deeper into the mysteries of matter and evolution. Walther Heitler, a physicist and natural philosopher, not only observes that an electron behaves in accordance with certain laws but also feels compelled to raise the question *why* an electron behaves like that.[7] Max Hartmann, too, is overcome by awe at the "pre-established harmony between thought and the rationally comprehensible part of nature"; it compels him to the belief in an omnipotent Meaning-giver.[8]

Thus some scientists are still very much aware of the incomprehensible fact that things and phenomena *are*. Only, this awareness is all too incidental, and—most importantly—is rarely taken into account scientifically. Very well, what appears here only incidentally must become the very cornerstone of our further reflections.

What is the cause of an electron's behaving as it does? Do physical laws accomplish this? If so, how do these laws come to be what they are, and how is it that this relation exists between the laws and the electron? By chance? Assuming that such a thing exists, it still has to work with whatever there is already. Moreover, 'chance' itself implies a remarkable convergence. To whom or what is such convergence attributable? To inner necessity? But that in turn would need to be explained.

Among the practitioners of historical science too there have been, and there are, those who have had an eye for what I have called the first history. Ranke observed that there is an unfathomable mystery to things and that the human mind is incapable of fully understanding the historical process; he professed to be conscious of an element that could not be *empirically* grasped—it was to him as if an "occult force" worked in events to establish unity, interconnections, meaningful wholes. Herbert Butterfield speaks of being keenly aware of a "*kind of history-making* which goes on so to speak over our heads"; the historian, for all his penetrating analyses, never arrives "at the bottom of the well." [9]

Ranke, Butterfield, and many others have perceived the problem of what I have called the first history, and they have also been conscious that it has a profound effect on the professional study of history. Yet, for all that, the question lingers: In virtue of what are the facts, events or phenomena what they are; what ultimately establishes inner coherence, unity, the mutual relation of things to each other, the connection between the factors, the historical order—and what accomplishes all this *without infringing upon the originality* that is proper to all events, phenomena and people in themselves? Is it Mind, the state, society? Or is it perhaps *history itself, in its totality,* for is not history more encompassing than all the others since it spans the centuries and penetrates all ages? Or is that not the whole answer, and are we obliged to introduce a crucial concept?

---

[7] Walther Heitler, "Kausalität und Teleologie in der Sicht der heutigen Naturwissenschaft" (Causality and teleology from the perspective of modern physics], *Universitas* 21 (1966): 10.

[8] Max Hartmann, *Naturwissenschaft und Religion* (1940), 11.

[9] H. Butterfield, *Christianity and History* (1949), 94.

The first history would seem to be very vulnerable and quickly brushed aside. Accordingly, I want to approach it with the utmost circumspection. To this end I shall select an eminently historical (!) category, that of justice (I might with equal justification have selected love, power, peace, or one of ever so many other fundamental concepts). I purposely speak of justice and not "right" or "law" in view of the need to avoid any restriction whatsoever to positive law. By justice I mean to refer to something that man ought to observe in all his relations. I have already said that I consider justice a *historical* category; this is in order to cut off every thought of justice as an idea outside concrete historical reality.

Now then, man can live in justice, advance the cause of justice, contemplate justice. But no one has ever succeeded in designing *justice itself* or calling it into being. Did perhaps the first man devise and establish what law is, and did his posterity build upon it for generation after generation? Impossible, for before the first man realized it he was already involved in legal relations.

Let's take another example. It is sometimes said that the supreme historical category is *decision*. Now I agree, man can make many decisions, including some of broad historical significance. But *decision itself*, in all its richness and individual variety, has not been called into being by man. All man can do is avail himself of it and work with it.

Similarly, man can *love*. But the *possibility of loving* is a gift. Love is not of man's invention. Of course, what man can do is reflect upon love, justice, and so forth—that is, upon that which already is.

And—to add no more—there is *history* itself. Man lives his life in history. Deprived of history, he is deprived of life. Yet, to history's *being there* he has been unable to make the slightest contribution. It has fallen to him in an entirely incomprehensible way.

Thus there is something in all things and phenomena which cannot be traced back to human activities and decisions, or to causes and effects, and which I therefore call incomprehensible. Nevertheless, this is the very thing which makes the life of the foregrounds possible at all and which is therefore the most precious of all, even while it is approachable only in ontological wonder.

History in the first sense is, in short, that things and phenomena *are*, that they exist. It is for this reason that we can also say that history is in everything and in every phenomenon. But why call this history? We call it history because existence ("*be*-staan") implies genesis ("*ont*-staan") and genesis implies origin (origin is not the same as original state). Things exist just as they have come forth from the origin. Their genesis, their coming into being, is not restricted to a single point in time, somewhere in the beginning; rather, it actively asserts itself in every phase, in every moment. For things remain as they were in the origin. Justice, for example, in all its richness—thus not just formally and empty of content—remains "original" in all its historical forms.

I repeat, why call all this history? It is history in the primary sense that things have come to presence, that they are *not of themselves*. And history is also *the power that keeps things related to the origin*. Remove history, and they cease to exist.

Who or what, then, is the origin? When I say *God*, I do not do so via the classic proofs of God, however much they may suggest themselves here; with proofs one never arrives at God but only at an extension of created existence. The issue will always be one of faith. Is it any less correct on that account? We are concerned with a state of affairs which in order to be truly *seen* requires the link with faith. Faith is linked in two ways: to the Origin, and to history; and as such faith enters into science.

This primary history I call transcendental history or transcendental time, because this history, or time, is oriented to the *transcendental Origin*. It is characterized by the meeting of time and eternity. (In this meeting, note well, time remains time, as history remains temporal history.) This orientation is intrinsic to time and history, and actively present throughout the whole of history, which is to say it is determinative for history to its very core.[10]

When I speak of the transcendental or original relation I do not mean something external or non-essential, or something that was there in the beginning but is now gone. I refer, rather, to that in which (historical) reality is permanently caught up and by which it is intrinsically conditioned. All our understanding and interpreting of reality must include, or at least presuppose, its *intrinsic conditionality*. In our ordinary conceptual knowledge this intrinsic conditionality is *implicitly* and necessarily present; after all, without it (the first history) the thing or phenomenon has no existence. The matter is simply one of making what is implicit explicit and putting its correctness to the test. This implicit knowledge (that of the first history) is not—the term says as much—a knowledge *alongside* but rather a knowledge *within* ordinary empirical and conceptual knowledge.

By keeping the primary or transcendental history in mind, it is possible to overcome the difficulties in which Hegel and Heidegger landed. Nevertheless, the problems that confront us here are not resolved at a single stroke by the notion of the transcendental history. For one encounters here the extremely difficult question concerning unity and coherence in history and in the whole of reality and the whole of life. I would inquire cautiously, in the footsteps of a

---

[10] To avoid misunderstanding I need to say that the attempt has been made to interpret 'transcendental' in my concept of transcendental time as 'transcendent.' In view of the fact that the transcendent as such can never become temporal or become history, this is impossible. The misunderstanding is plausible because in the 19th and 20th centuries 'transcendent' has acquired a sense that locates it within this world, and so the term 'transcendental' too has undergone (in any case since Kant) a change of meaning: beyond the boundaries of experience, lying outside the natural world, etc. One can summarize by stating that in modern usage, to transcend is to go above or beyond one area to another—yet, always intramundanely. Cf. O. D. Duintjer, *De vraag naar het transcendentale, vooral in verband met Kant en Heidegger* [The quest for the transcendental, particularly in connection with Kant and Heidegger] (1966).

number of philosophers, including Hegel: *Is it perhaps (the first) history* that establishes coherence in the myriad number of facts, events, conditions, institutions, etc.? The answer to this question must become the touchstone for the correctness of what I have said so far and of what is to follow.

Hence I return to justice (in the comprehensive and profound sense in which I took this concept above) and for the time being confine the problem of unity to it, leaving aside for the moment the coherence of history in its totality. Justice, then, though always imperfectly realized, often violated, and constantly threatened, is never absent in any age. But neither is it ever the same from one phase of history to the next. Its forms constantly alter. And yet justice retains its identity throughout all the changes it undergoes.

How is this to be grasped? It will be helpful to turn for a moment to another field of science, biology. Jules Carles has argued that organisms—plants, animals, humans—renew their energetic material many times over, sometimes a number of times a day. (And to think that the smallest detail can have repercussions throughout the entire organism!) With this in mind, Carles points out that when Heraclitus said that "one cannot step into the same stream twice" he still argued from the basis of the stability of the body, whereas we now know that the living being (including man) is itself a constantly changing stream—so that for this reason as well, one cannot step into the same stream twice. Modern physiology justifies our saying, in the words of the Comtesse de Noailles, "Never again shall we have the body we had this evening." And yet, says Carles, our organism endures, retains its identity, remains what it was, throughout all the changes it undergoes. The central question therefore is: What sustains the identity of this plant or that particular body in spite of numerous, incessant changes? Wherein resides the unity of that living thing? [11]

The problem is an ancient one. Carles looks for the unity of a living thing in its "finality," its teleological goal, end or destination. The matter bears comparison, I think, with the Scholastic notion that the individual is ineffable (*individuum est ineffabile*); for so it is, too, with the *unity* of a living organism, the unity of justice, the unity of history as a whole. Furthermore, what Carles adds is of no less importance: this *unity* can never be bypassed, because it so happens that apart from this unity the living being cannot be grasped; it is the basis from which we proceed and to which we must constantly return.

The same is true of justice and the other historical phenomena and modes of being. Justice is subject to constant change yet retains its identity. The usual bipartite terminology will not do here; we must reach beyond 'mutable-immutable' to a better way of expressing the matter. It is best to speak of the *unity* of justice, since this includes its being different again each time.

This "being different" is no inconsequential matter. It involves being different among different peoples and being different in different times. Indeed, justice even differs from one instance to the next (no two court cases, for exam-

---

[11] Jules Carles, "L'Unité du vivant," *Études philosophiques* 41 (1966): 38.

ple, are ever identical). And yet, *unity*: this is the ultimate, limiting concept of justice, and it leaves the dynamic multiformity intact. Nevertheless the question remains: What guarantees the unity throughout all the changes?

Various replies have been offered. Often it is said that the guarantee is located in the *essence* (of justice), but that is a restriction on the dynamic variety; essence is an abstraction and as such unchangeable; hence in this answer change is shortchanged: change is made subordinate and accidental. Again, it is said that the guarantee is located in the *structure*; but in this reply too, there is a narrowing of the horizon. A third reply invokes the *form*; this too is an abstraction.

What constitutes and guarantees the unity of anything is its meaning. It is meaning that expresses a phenomenon's origin, ground, rich variety, value, and orientation or direction. Meaning is only accessible, however, to our *implicit* knowledge.

Meaning is often equated with worth or purpose (finality). Wrongly so, for these are but aspects of meaning; meaning is not exhausted in them. To state it more accurately: that things have value or purpose stems from the fact that they *are* meaning.

Philosophy of history is often defined as the discipline that inquires after meaning as final purpose, whereas historical science, it is believed, seeks meaning in the sense of worth or value; hence the conflict between the two.[12] Wrong. *That concrete, individual thing or phenomenon has meaning*, not owing to a final purpose, nor yet owing to a rigid, immutable essence or being, but *owing to the transcendental relation which sustains its unity through all its dynamic mutations*.

I return to justice as one of the many historical modes of being, immune to fleeting, annihilating time, changeable, certainly, but ever retaining that most essential element: *its meaning*. And yet justice *is in time*, and *is itself time*.

Here we encounter *another time*, a time which is neither discontinuous nor continuous, a time for which neither earlier nor later obtains, a time which makes continuity and discontinuity possible in the first place: *transcendental time*. Or, to put it in other words, here we encounter the *unity of time* in which past, present, future, and all phases and periods of time coincide (not: converge); all these are present in this time in their full diversity, yet together they constitute a unity of meaning.

A comparison with prophecy may help to clarify what I mean. In ancient Israel, or in the case of Jesus, prophecies sometimes pertain to what is about to happen in the present and *at the same time* to what is going to happen in the period to come; they pertain to what is to happen during Jesus' sojourn on earth and at the same time they pertain to the "latter days" (subsequent to Pentecost). In the words of the prophets, however, these times all coincide.

---

[12] See Kuypers, *Verspreide Geschriften*, 1:241 [in *Philosophy and Christianity*, 115 (see note 2)].

Thus far I have dealt with unity and coherence mainly as they pertain to historical modes of being, separately considered. Now, do this unity (namely, unity of meaning) and coherence also obtain in the historical world considered as a whole, from the beginning right on down to the present and in any given time frame (a period or a phase)? I will have to return to these questions later, but for now I affirm the following: every thing, every mode of being, every discrete reality is woven and written into reality as a whole and can exist only by being incorporated into the encompassing reality, through which everything is so connected with everything else that if just one of the fundamental modes of being were taken away (for example, justice), the others too would no longer exist.

Now, what is the power that lends coherence to this total reality? That power is the primary or transcendental history, which is not susceptible of further definition since it is the prime given but which can be approximated as follows: *It is the state of being suspended between the origin and every later moment.* This means that each and every thing or mode of being in all its concreteness is permeated by the total historical reality. At the same time it also means that the ever different, the singular, the unique can exist only within this total unity or coherence. It is irreducible, it is unique, *and* it is interwoven with all that is.

The second history

Little can be said about the second history in itself, since in the absence of coherence with the first history it has no existence. Inversely, the same is really true of the first history as well, which for its realization is dependent upon the second history. What we have done here is simply what philosophy and science normally do: we have separated what is given as an integral whole. This procedure is necessary for gaining deepened insight, albeit such insight is gained only when what is thus separated is viewed simultaneously as an integral whole.

The first history is placed in man's hands, as it were; we can even say that it is dependent on that. It is the 'inner *dynamis*' of the first history to enter into the designs and deeds of man; and that is what constitutes the second history.

This coherence of the first and second histories—we may even speak of their being "in each other"—presents serious difficulties for our understanding and powers of expression. On the one hand, the first history is independent of man; on the other, it cannot come into being without man. (It is not the case, as in Hegel and Heidegger, that Spirit or Being imposes itself by superior force on the subjective will of the individuals.) The transcendental history is independent of the designs and deeds of man insofar as its coming into existence is concerned; yet in its existing it is ineluctably bound to these designs and deeds.

I said just now that the *original history* delivers itself up to man! Actually, this is not entirely true. The original history can be acknowledged, followed and obeyed, but it can also be ignored, transgressed, violated and fiercely combated.

In other words, this original history is of a *normative* character, which is to say that it does not impose itself deterministically or by superior force, but rather enters into the freedom and responsibility of man, imperiled by many dangers. But escape it man never can. He abides in it to all ages, because without it no life is possible.

The primary history comes towards us as the *meaning* of history, justice as the *meaning* of justice, and so on. Meaning therefore is not far away in some unassailable height or depth or in the endtime. On the contrary, it is the meaning of history etc. that *gives itself* to man, entering into the freedom of man. The converse is also true: since man can never step outside meaning, a struggle is going on within the very meaning itself of history, of love, peace, etc.

This struggle *within* the meaning and *for* the meaning of history, and within and for the meaning of individual phenomena and individual human lives—this stuggle is the *warp and woof* of history, in two respects: (1) as embarking on, or being engaged in, a quest for meaning (though one should realize that this pursuit is not an isolated activity, nor mere reflection upon it: it permeates, albeit usually unawares, all our daily thoughts and activity; in short, this quest is itself history); (2) as realizing meaning, by *going back* or *returning* to the transcendental history.

Yet what is the provenance of this struggle for meaning? The question cannot be evaded. To view man as living in meaning in all his designs and deeds—is that not a highly optimistic view? And why then must there still be struggle? To meet this objection it is essential to observe that the meaning of the primary history demands a return to *integral* justice and love, in fact a return to the *integral* meaning of history or of the individual.

What do I mean by 'integral'? Is this the integralism of Jan Romein or the integralism of structuralism? No, for that would only mean having things in their proper place or order with respect to each other. I mean integral in the term's primary sense, 'integrity,' from the classical Latin term '*integer*': 'not touched,' which in turn means 'unviolated,' in the sense, then, of 'whole,' 'complete,' or 'undiminished.' That which is integral is complete. It is whole. It possesses 'integrity or 'integrality.' Now then, I am talking about *integral* justice, *integral* love, etc., which is to say that the struggle is not just about meaning but about the *integrity* of meaning.

In this struggle there are *at least three great moving forces* at work.

(1) The positive predominates: it is the process of *returning* to meaning.

(2) The whole of the second history can be summarized as a *responding* to the first history, as a reacting to it. Try to picture it: in every moment of history, be it of the world or of the individual person, there is an *irresistible coming* of meaning, which knocks at the door of time. The great question confronts man ever anew: Should he open, should he answer—and how? Open he must, but he is free to choose *how*. Now, what one usually witnesses is this: the reaction turns into a real *counter*movement. Against meaning? We shall come to that in a

moment. At all events, the reaction becomes a countermovement to what still is and what shortly before still was.

On the one hand we say: How fortunate! for with that, absolutized objectives are removed. On the other hand we must say: Alas! for with that, people become estranged from *essential values,* which may indeed live on, but only in a pitiful state: it sometimes takes centuries before these values are rediscovered and reintegrated into a culture. The constantly renewed attempts at realizing meaning involve, among other things, a disregard for and a displacement of earlier realizations of meaning, since in the new "returning" it is not integral meaning itself but only a particular aspect of meaning that is realized.

So much is this the familiar picture of the dynamics of history that it gives us every reason to believe we are on the track of *one of the essential features of history,* including *renaissances* and *reformations* (thus not just those of the fifteenth, sixteenth, twelfth or tenth century). Renaissances and reformations occur in every age. They are "returnings" to what was once rejected as intrinsically foreign, to what thereby undergoes resurrection, sometimes repeatedly.

From theory, let us turn to practice for a moment. For my first example I go to the beginning of Modern Times.

In the Middle Ages man was so much a part of a rich variety of organic ties and relationships that very little room was left for individual worth and freedom; as Huizinga has shown, to set a personal goal for one's life remained virtually foreign to the Middle Ages. In the Renaissance, however, partly in reaction, attention came to be focused on the dignity and freedom of the individual. In every field the individual began to feel free and independent. The formation of the personality now became the supreme ideal, to such a degree in fact that there has even been talk of *la découverte de l'homme,* the discovery of man[13]—which is to say that there is dignity and worth in the human person as such, quite apart from the communities. Undoubtedly, this spelled an important gain. Yet, as a countermovement it entailed the consequence that the awakening of the self-determining personality was all too deficient, as Huizinga puts it, in *social, altruistic components*. The Renaissance saw an externalizing of numerous social relations that interrupted for more than a century what had been a hopeful progress towards a better form of society.

As a second example I refer to the history of love. In the classical Greek period, eros predominated; in the primitive Christian era, agape; in the courtly world, erotic love; in Romanticism, emotional love. This history implies not that agape vanished from courtly culture but that it became *subordinate* to eros and so suffered loss with respect to its original richness.

---

[13] [A characterization of the Renaissance first used by Jules Michelet in the introduction to his *Histoire de France,* vol. 7 (1843) and further elaborated by Jakob Burckhardt in *Die Kultur der Renaissance in Italien* (1860).]

What is worthy of note in both these examples is that the meaning of community, of personality, of love does break through, but not their integral meaning as given in the transcendental history.

My third example is taken from the world of philosophy. There are many indications today that existentialism and the philosophy of existence have passed their peak. Now, even those who reject both of them on principle must acknowledge that they have conveyed important insights, insights that are now in danger of being lost for lack of appreciation.

My fourth and final example concerns Romanticism. At the end of the eighteenth and the beginning of the nineteenth centuries, Western Europeans fell under the spell of Romanticism. Thereafter it went underground, from whence it reappears from time to time and place to place, often when least expected. Will man ever escape the tensions between intimacy, privacy, security on the one hand, and nostalgia for the infinite, the boundless horizon, the universal, on the other?

(3) Moving on to the third of the three great moving forces to which I alluded: I have already argued that the transcendental history does not go its own way, over the head of the second history, but that it realizes itself only through responsible action in the second history. This assumes that the first history remains hidden in part, that it is never fully disclosed, since there is a power at work in the second history that continually holds itself in readiness to ward off the irresistible coming of the transcendental history. That is the second *countermovement* and the third great moving force of which I spoke.

Yet why such resistance? If the second history were to allow the first history to enter unobstructed, would it not, as we have seen, stand to gain participation in the *integral meaning* of history? Is it a question of powerlessness on the part of the second history to realize integral meaning, as something beyond its capacity? No, not in the first instance. The crucial point is: the second history is ruled by a polarity. It is dependent on the first history for its existence but at the same time it tries to escape from it. The first history belongs to the essence of the second, yet the second experiences the first as the other, as a foreigner: *to the second history the first history is the transcendental stranger.*

However, we must inquire further. Why this polarization in the second history, this withdrawal into self, this countermovement against the first history, this experiencing of it as the "transcendental stranger" ? Because the second history wants to remain by itself, wants to withdraw into itself, and believes it is sufficient unto itself. Just look at historical science, for instance: whatever cannot be established according to rigorous scientific methods must remain beyond purview, since it undermines the certainty of scientific results.

Nevertheless, the *irruptive force* of the transcendental history does not allow itself to be broken—but neither does the *countermovement* of the second history. Here then is *that struggle within the meaning of history* to which I alluded above.

History can teach us what is going on here. In the Gothic we experience such a breakthrough of the first history, particularly in the classic cathedrals of Chartres, Amiens, Reims. Thereafter, this style of architecture set the trend. Attempts were made to perfect it; certain forms were elaborated and over-accentuated. No longer was there a direct returning to the origin. Instead, the form which derived from it *became the norm.*

In the Reformation, too, the counterforce of the will to self-sufficiency took hold. In the area of church and theology one need mention only the growth of rigid orthodoxy—although it must be remembered that, just as in the case of the Gothic, the first history remained present, if underground.

In summary, real history is: being constantly open to the original history, listening to it, acting on it. There is a mighty and unrelenting élan at work in the original history which perpetually threatens humans absolutizations and substantializations—including all forms of self-sufficiency—and which, in the great crises of world history, topples them.

The unrelenting dynamic force of the first history at the same time sees to it that whatever the countermovement had driven out, despite its real value, is brought back again from exile—sometimes after many years, sometimes after centuries.

Again, a few examples. Take the concept of 'misuse of the law' (*abus de droit*). Already known to the Romans, it became an important principle of law in the Middle Ages and from the sixteenth through the eighteenth centuries. Yet it was discarded in the nineteenth century, under the influence of liberalism and positivism. It was reintroduced into the legal order, however, in the twentieth century, as "law behind the law" (Scholten).[14] Similarly, in recent years there has been a marked and *rapidly growing positive reappraisal of the nineteenth century,* expressed most notably in various forms of neo-Hegelianism, neo-anarchism, neo-romanticism, the updating of positivism, and so forth. Particularly remarkable (what a contrast to just several decades ago!) is the higher rating being accorded the neo-Gothic: people are again impressed especially by its clear creation of space and its spatial unity and simplicity.

Citing examples can create a misunderstanding—namely, that the matter is one of incidental cases. The opposite is true. The first history is unrelentingly at work to bring to light what has been neglected, discarded, relegated to the subterranean stream. This does not happen, however, in a uniform way.

There are a number of general characteristics to this process of return, and they are aptly illustrated in the example of the neo-Gothic. The Gothic Revival was not so much concerned with *imitation* or restoration or a recovery of all the historical particulars as with the rediscovery of fundamental principles. Such principles, for all their genuine validity in different times, are neither timeless nor ahistorical: on the contrary, they are *fully historical*, standing *in a particular historical context*, and they acquire *historical validity again* in *another historical*

---

[14] See W. B. Helmich, *Theorie van het rechtsmisbruik* (1945).

context. Thus, in the fifteenth century Brunelleschi found his examples in the classical world and even made precise measurements for that purpose, but how severely the nineteenth-century critics rebuked him for having deviated from the classics!

So the process of return is not a simple matter, and it does not follow a uniform course. Notice, for example, the place of technology throughout history. The technological history of the early Middle Ages appears to be of little relevance for today yet is topical as it could possibly be. The present high level of technological development is bringing ever more clearly to light man's powerlessness in the face of typically human problems (including man's alienation from the world and from his next-door neighbor). I consider it a matter of the greatest importance that we immerse ourselves in a world in which technology still played an almost negligible role—not in order to adopt a negative stance but in order to get on the track of the essential relations of man and *technè*.

I would emphasize again that what returns, what is reborn, is not a timeless essence or a timeless model. It is fully and dynamically historical. It is subject to historical change; sometimes it is so much changed, in fact, that it is not immediately recognized as a historical given (as, for example, in the current evaluation of the neo-Gothic).

The following question necessarily arises: If then the return is such an important factor in the great movements of history, why is it just *this* possibility —*this* particular one, rather than one of countless others—that comes to life again? I will return to this question later but I should make one comment already now. What is surprising is that as initiative or creative moment, this return usually does not emanate from the professional historians. They do *contribute material once the irruption of the past has occurred,* but, I repeat, the irruption is usually not attributable to them. Historians are well aware that it is not they who make fresh openings to the past. How often have they themselves not declared that history must be redone and rewritten again and again from the public's new perspective on their own time!

Principal results of the preceding reflections
(1) In the first history, with which the historian usually does not work explicitly, we have found the real source and orientation point of the second history (which is the history of the historians). At the same time, it is the first history which brings to presence again that which once was.

(2) My reflections conflict with two principles which in the last centuries have become cornerstones of the "history of the historians," namely, that of *continuity*; and that of *historical causality* or, more mildly, that of *"how things came about."*

Indeed, in spite of much sharp opposition to the causality principle, a historian does not rest until he has discovered the cause or causes, origins and influences involved in a historical event or phenomenon. Courtly culture, for example, which arose in a relatively short period of time, has occasioned the production of a whole library aimed at explaining this unique historical phenomenon—whether it was a product of the West, of Catharism, or of the Arabian world, and so forth. The same is true of sundry other complex phenomena. Meanwhile, for all the recognition of the unique, what has become of the element of the origin?

The purport of my discussion, by contrast, has been *not* to explain the phenomena wholly and exclusively from the "continuous history of the historians" but to appeal equally to an *original* history which breaks through this continuous history in a twofold way: (i) by its unremitting irruptive force, and (ii) by disengagement from the context of one's own time and the immediately preceding time for the sake of harking back across the centuries to the meaning of earlier thinking and acting.

At this juncture, however, we must take into account an unavoidable complication. Continuity is not lost altogether. For example, the coming of courtly culture may have been unique and original, but changes in the social structures were already taking place as if in preparation for receiving it. Thus an event, a phenomenon, a state of affairs, etc., is embedded *in continuity* but at the same time possesses *an originality all its own* (note that this is something quite different from discontinuity). Once again we are placed before a penetrating question: How can both appear in one fact at the same time—do they not exclude each other?

The question is even more complicated than that. Facts (or phenomena) participate at one and the same time not only in both continuous and transcendental time but also in the universal, in the national, in various groups, etc. In addition, they are individual as well. And each of these has a different time and rhythm of its own.

Historians—including theorists and philosophers—are disposed to explain the facts, etc., in terms of one aspect or one 'time,' but the real question is: What datum, what time is it that integrates all this into the unity of the fact, or the unity of history as a whole; and what is it that ultimately establishes its internal coherence?

The exact same problem arises in connection with periods. Take the sixteenth century as an example. It has been rightly said that certain characteristic features of the sixteenth century are distinctly medieval; on the other hand, the century can also be viewed as a prelude to the following centuries. And there is more. Was there not a great deal in the sixteenth century that was borrowed from the time prior to the Middle Ages, from Classical Antiquity and the period of the Early Church? The Middle Ages were simultaneously perpetuated and passed over. Moreover, how much, indeed, was there not in the sixteenth century that is universally human and proper to any age in world history!

Customarily, this problem is resolved by speaking of the "structure" or the "spirit" of an age or a period in history, but this usually means that one or more specific facets are allowed to dominate while whatever does not seem to "fit" is relegated to a place of secondary importance. It is a point in favor of this method, however, that where historians decline to use it, the facts and periods seem to disintegrate beyond repair. I agree, events and times do have unity. But the real question is: Whence their unity and coherence?

Answer

I have referred again and again, as if it were a matter of course, to returning to earlier times. No one ever seems to make a problem of it. Actually, however, the matter should arouse profound astonishment. *For how can such a thing be?* By virtue of the continuity of time perhaps? Impossible, for that is broken in many ways. While temporal continuity may thus not open the way, still it must be *time* that brings us into contact with the events and circumstances of centuries ago.

Philosophers especially have a tendency to reduce past, present and future to one. Augustine, for example, attempted to overcome the disintegrating power of time in that he let all three coincide—in the soul, at least—in the present by having the present incorporate the past as remembrance and embrace the future as expectation.

I concur in this tendency. Yet an objection arises. If the time-moments past, present and future coincide in one of the three, we remain enclosed within continuous-discontinuous time with all the irresolvable difficulties this entails (witness Augustine). This continuous-discontinuous time cannot be accounted for in terms of itself. It needs a basis, which can be time, but not mathematical time. We are concerned here with another time, transcendental time, since it alone is original time. As the concentration of all meaning, transcendental time remains what it was and at the same time is different in all temporal moments. Here language fails and thought reaches its limits.

Transcendental time makes language and thought and likewise the continuous-discontinuous course of history possible to begin with. *It separates into discrete moments, phases and periods of time, and it is due to it that unity and coherence reside in the facts and times of world history.*

Transcendental time *makes history possible,* in the precise sense that history can *exist at all.* And, no less important, transcendental time also makes possible *our ability to acquire knowledge concerning history*; for, again, to be able to acquire knowledge about history, the historian requires unity and coherence.

Transcendental time accordingly has a twofold character (keeping ever in mind that it is itself fully time): (1) all temporal moments—past, present and future—*coincide* in it; or, if you like, they are all concentrated in it or participate in it; and (2) it *breaks up* time into the various temporal moments, phases and periods of history.

The meaning of transcendental time as I have thus described it is made marvelously clear, I think, by the words of the apostle Paul in the epistle to the Romans. To be "dead and buried *with* Christ" must not be understood mystically but *realistically and historically*. It means: *at that very moment to be comprehended in Christ*, sharing in what was happening to him, while at the same time recognizing the distinction, the time difference.[15]

History implies being directed not only to the origin but also to the center and to the consummation of time. These are the three great *concentration points* of world history, in which the meaning of life contracts into the integral meaning of history.

Concentration points should be distinguished from *crystallization* points. Actually, every fact and every age is a crystallization point, but some are more so than others. In crystallization points the first history lays hold of the progression of time, sometimes for centuries. The past and the future are compressed in them. Nor can they ever be eliminated again. Of course, I do not mean this deterministically, for they are ever freshly entrusted to man in a normative sense. Examples are innumerable. I mention only: 1066; Bramante's arrival in Rome; the Industrial Revolution; the Dutch struggle for independence.

The need for hermeneutics

Many important problems have been omitted here, but there is one I cannot pass over even though it can only be dealt with extensively in the context of hermeneutics. If it be granted that this first, transcendental history cannot be forced into the background but that it occupies an all-controlling position, *how does one get a view of it*? How does one discover the integral meaning of history, the meaning of justice, love, power, and so on? Also, how does one discover the *integral* meaning of irruptive events and phenomena such as the imperial coronation of A.D. 800; the Renaissance; the supranational unification of postwar Western Europe; the second Industrial Revolution? And furthermore, how is the historian supposed to deal with these questions?

To take the last question first: the historian can lay these questions aside and claim to restrict himself to the "*history of the historians*," which is to say, to the *continuous history,* to "*how things came about.*" To persist in this ideal of a so-called *objective historical development* entails the consequence that, as a historian, one adjusts oneself to it, sticking scrupulously to what history has brought to light. The historian is expected to uncover what once was and how it came about, and to derive the standards for evaluating the culture he studies from the culture itself. *But creativity is not expected of the historian*. That is assigned to philosophers, poets, sociologists, and the like.

Hence the question becomes all the more urgent: How does one get a view of the first history in its connection with the "history of the historians"? For the

---

[15] [Cf. Herman Ridderbos, *Paulus; ontwerp van zijn theologie* (1966), 58f., 181–83, 415, commenting on Rom. 6: 4, 8 [Eng. trans., 60f., 168f., 372].

first history is the source of creativity, and creativity is the constant source of what is new.

A first requirement is that historians free themselves from their isolation and their enslavement to the second history and be prepared to go where the philosophers, ethicists, theologians, jurists, etc., abide, where the representatives of all times and all nations gather, where the walls between the ages and the cultures come down, where in often emotional discussions the questions are addressed that affect all alike. The contributions of the historians to these discussions will not be any less important than those of any other group; historians in particular can know how meaning (in its contest with anti-meaning) has already for thousands of years and in countless places found its way through history.

Whom do we find there? A Plato, Augustine, Alberti, Poussin, Adam Smith, but also the Hellenistic peasant, the feudal lord, the oppressed slave, also Ranke, countless others. *In the perspective of the continuous second history it is impossible that they should all be present at the same time, yet the first history enables them to be always each other's contemporaries, even while it remains obvious from what age, what nation, town or village, what milieu they come.*

But will they find the *integral* meaning? The answer is in the first place a matter for hermeneutics—at least if hermeneutics be taken to be not a set of rules for the interpretation of texts but a philosophical discipline. Hermeneutics, after all, by way of the interpretation of texts, penetrates to the facts and to history itself.

16/ TOWARD A REORDERING OF KNOWLEDGE

PHILOSOPHY OF SCIENCE commonly distinguishes between fact and interpretation.[1] Facts are accessible to critical scientific investigation, while in interpretation subjective notions are said to play an important role. The distinction between fact and interpretation, however, has become controversial today. In particular, the question of the scientific status and objectivity of interpretation is being debated.

But with the terms fact and interpretation am I not contrasting two disparate things: facts refer to what is factually given and interpretation refers to a meaning ascribed to the facts. I have used the terms advisedly and not in imitation of current usage. When we speak in science of facts we mean that we have acquired them on the basis of objective scientific research. But, on the prevailing view, when we approach a fact along another avenue, that of interpretation, we land in uncertainty, the uncertainty that comes with intuition, empathy, vision, etc.

With that, we still have not indicated the real crux with which both the scientific method and interpretation (hermeneutics) confront us. According to the classic notion of science, philosophy and science are concerned with the universal, in the sense of what is always and everywhere valid. Modern scholarship, in contrast, has placed increasing emphasis on the individual, the unique, the changeable—the individual in the sense, not of an individuation of the universal, but in its own authentic, irreducible meaning.

Here lies the core of the problem regarding the relation between fact and interpretation, between science and hermeneutics. If the individual cannot be deduced from the universal, what is its ground? But as soon as the *question of the ground* is posed—which was done already in the Middle Ages—the relation universal-individual becomes secondary, also epistemologically.

Faith, history, and the question of the ground

My introductory comments have indicated various aspects of the faith-science relation[2] without once, curiously, using the term 'faith.' It was done deliberately. Usually when this problem is discussed people begin by opposing faith and science (or faith and knowledge), or at least by distinguishing them sharply, in order thereafter to look into the possibility of building a bridge

---

[1] [Text of a paper dated Sept. 1980. We have consulted the critical edition published in J. Klapwijk, ed., *De eerste en tweede geschiedenis; nagelaten geschriften van Meijer C. Smit.* (Amsterdam: Buijten & Schipperheijn, 1987), 180–206. Subheadings are our own.]

[2] [Allusion to the mandate of the research team 'Faith and [Theoretic] Thought,' to which this paper was presented; Philosophy Department, Free University, Amsterdam.]

between them. My approach will be different. I propose to inquire whether faith is not present in all forms of knowledge, from the very outset; and if the same cannot also be said of history, love, the social, the aesthetic, etc.

But will faith—and history, and love—not lose their true significance if involved in the complexities of knowledge? Should we not be afraid, in fact, that pure thought will lose its integrity this way? There is no reason to fear the latter, I think, since the history of science as well as of philosophy contains enough indications that if faith, love and history should try to gain entrance into the bulwark of science—an imposing edifice that has been consciously in the making for more than two millennia—they will be forcefully warded off with the aid of the most formidable weapon that science (including philosophy) has at its disposal: the rational-empirical method. The reason why science's self-defense has been so successful is that according to Western notions it would not be able to fulfill its great task if irrational elements of such potency as, for example, history and faith—faith in revelation no less—were allowed to compromise it.

With that, we have arrived at a critical juncture. On the one hand, science is threatened by the irrational. On the other hand, science itself threatens the higher values by penetrating into those areas it disparages as "irrational" and then making its judgments there according to its own "scientific" standards.

The cardinal question we have to address concerns the presuppositions of science. Do science and philosophy not *always* involve historicity, love, and so much more that is assigned to the "irrational" (we should say: a-rational) sphere?

The foregoing implies that faith and the 'question of the ground' (the ground of things and thus also of knowledge) are bound up in each other; we shall return to that later. The foregoing implies as well that historicity and this ground are intimately connected. Modern thought has had great difficulty with both implications. I shall not lose sight of that, even as I now take you on a brief tour of a long chapter in intellectual history.

Faith and history in modern thought

Modern thought has continually tried to shut out 'religious faith,' for example by transmogrifying faith into rational knowledge. Yet faith proved resistant to being shut out. Acknowledged or not, it remained a living reality in the form of the inescapable question of the ground. This is one of the main reasons why intellectual thought has become so complicated in recent centuries.

Modern thought has become complicated no less by the phenomenon of 'history.' As early as the 18th century, thinkers like Herder and others discovered a genuine connection between the formation of knowledge (including scientific knowledge) and history. And this not just in the sense that history can be an object of scientific investigation, or that history must be understood as continuous development, but especially in the sense that reason too must be intrinsically *historical*. (Modern usage prefers the term *geschichtlich* to express the historicity of reality.)

Thus the problem of history emerged unmistakably in the thought of Herder, Dilthey, Troeltsch. The odd thing is that in the major intellectual currents and some of the greatest philosophers (among whom Kant, Hegel—yes, even he— and Husserl) the real problem of history was swept under the rug. Indeed, an old antagonism exists between reason and history. Nevertheless I gladly endorse Meinecke's statement that historical thinking has been "one of the greatest intellectual-spiritual revolutions that Western thought has ever seen."[3] Historical thinking has retained its vitality to this day, despite the serious decline in historical sense. Our remarks so far, taken together, make the path of history in the life of our time seem very mysterious indeed.

The reductionism of the scientific method

Science and philosophy, clearly, are marked by ambivalence: in regard to faith (the question of the ground), and in regard to history (and the great values of human life). As we proceed with our discussion we will allow ourselves to be guided by three problems: (1) What is it, at bottom, that gives things coherence? (2) Do things (that is, concrete, unique, 'individual' things, facts, phenomena, and so on) possess an intrinsic, essential, irreducible meaning and worth? (3) Are things in that deepest sense knowable; in particular, are they accessible to scientific knowledge, and is any scientific knowledge possible without that essential value?

Obviously our three questions cannot be dealt with in isolation from each other; we can look for answers only in their mutual coherence. Just posing these questions, however, usually meets with strong opposition in the world of science: presumably, such questions threaten the "purity" of scientific research, they are superfluous, and from a functional point of view they are of no scientific consequence. Only in philosophical speculation are they not dismissed out of hand, although even here the current climate is hardly conducive to dealing with such fundamental questions.

These observations are offset, however, by a growing conviction that in science an intolerable reduction of reality has taken place. Things have lost a dimension without which they cannot exist—a dimension which therefore can never have been entirely absent from scientific knowledge, if only implicitly.

There is a point of contact between this last view and the scientific mode of thought which I advocate. Our point of contact is that scientists encounter the question of meaning not just in philosophy—at its best—or in the limiting concepts of a discipline, but at the very outset of their scientific work.

Science and dualism

But it is time we stated what we mean by 'science.' That does not appear to pose too many problems, since science has been practiced successfully for many centuries already. There also appears to be a general consensus about what

---

[3] Friedrich Meinecke, *Die Entstehung des Historismus* (1959), 1 [Eng. trans., 1].

science is; expressions like "science has shown" and "scientists have discovered" testify to continued confidence.

No sooner are we called to give an account of what we mean by science, however, than the difficulties begin. A reference to Augustine's well-known words about time[4] is not far-fetched, as will become apparent in a moment. The difficulty of forming a correct concept of science is due, I believe, to an impoverishment in the view of reality. For the close relationship of science and reality we use the term 'scientific worldview.' This is to use 'worldview' in an unusual sense. 'Scientific worldview' means, among other things, that the rational-empirical method encounters not just particular aspects of reality but the whole of reality (the world). It is no different in the mythical worldview, in the pre-scientific worldview, or in other forms of knowledge. Always, the world is experienced as an all-encompassing reality.

In this way, many worldviews have arisen in the course of time. The scientific worldview is only one of these, and is itself further differentiated. The fascinating question is, How could this great variety or contrast in worldviews have arisen, and how has it managed to survive despite the growth of human knowledge and the deepening of insight? We must confine ourselves here to just a few worldviews and cannot enter into, say, the mythical, the pre-scientific, or the aesthetic worldviews. For that matter, even with respect to science we cannot do justice here to the great differentiation of views that prevails there.

In the philosophical-scientific worldview no idea has been of more decisive significance than that of a split in reality, and a corresponding split in knowledge. The idea starts already with the awakening of the philosophic spirit in the Greek world, it gets its chief formulation in Aristotle, it is set in motion again in the Middle Ages, and then presses on from the close of the Middle Ages to the present, albeit with a different orientation. Always there is the dualism that mentally keeps reality divided into a higher, meaningful or true reality, and a lower reality. The dividing line may run differently each time, but the idea of a split world continues unabated. The split is introduced each time at the point of departure of thought or the process of knowing.

From its earliest beginnings, a dualism has been so much part of the Western worldview that the whole notion of a deeper unity of reality has come to be dismissed a priori. In light of this it is encouraging that not a few natural scientists today are raising the question: What is it that ultimately gives things coherence?

Our questions (see above) aim at overcoming this split. We certainly are not alone in this. Among various practitioners of science there is an unmistakable endeavor to return to the unity of reality, in order thus to surmount the scientific and ecological (also the spritual!) crisis. Let me just mention three instances:

---

[4] "What is time? If no one asks me, I know; if someone poses the question and I try to explain, I know no longer." *Confessions*, XI, 14, 17.

Hugo Staudinger (b. 1921) and Heinrich Beck (b. 1929) in various publications,[5] and also Otto Vossler (b. 1902) in his recent book about History as Meaning.[6] These authors endeavor to offer modern man a new orientation for his mode of thought and experience, an orientation to the essential and the meaningful. Now, terms like essence and meaning seem particularly apt to preserve the old dualism; the very terms are so much affected by the prevailing mode of thought that it will prove difficult to regain acceptance in science for a different, non-dualistic meaning of essence and meaning. Essence and meaning, however, concern the origin and ground of reality, which science usually passes over.

The question is as intriguing as it is imperative: How could the above-mentioned split have arisen and found acceptance to this day? Looking at the history of theoretical thought one might answer: it is man who, after declaring himself autonomous, places himself *over against* the world, puts himself in an exceptional position via his theoretical and religious consciousness and, forgetting where he came from, elevates himself above created reality. And indeed, the power of the human pretension to autonomy can scarcely be overestimated; but it is not enough to account for the split. Throughout the history of the West, reality itself, in its mystery and complexity, has challenged man in his thought and his experience to understand it as an integral unity in which man and things, for all that, have their own originality. Only in rare moments of history, however, has man been able to apprehend that integral unity, mystery and originality without violating its authenticity.

The individual in the scientific worldview

To proceed with our case we have to return to the worldviews that embody the almost universally accepted dualism and complexity of the world.

One of the great themes of scientific thought since the Greeks is the opposition universal-individual. It is especially among the Greeks that this theme had not only epistemological but also ontological significance. Aristotle in particular elaborated and harmonized it, and it is especially in this form that it exercised profound influence in later centuries. Science purportedly is concerned only with the universal, not the individual (or unique, variable, finite). The latter could be given scientific status, it is true, by subsuming it under the universal, but often the individual was depreciated—think only of Aristotle's attitude toward history. A positive appreciation of the individual and the finite could hardly arise in Greek thought since the universal at once constituted the permanent, essential quality of things. In direct line with this is the notion, from late Antiquity, that being is the more powerful in proportion as it is the more universal.

The depreciation of the individual and the unique—both terms taken in their authentic meaning—did not weigh heavy upon the ancients, because they

---

[5] Cf. Hugo Staudinger, *Mensch und Staat im Strukturwandel der Gegenwart* (1971), esp. 9–31; Heinrich Beck, *Kulturphilosophie der Technik* (1979).

[6] Otto Vossler, *Geschichte als Sinn* (1979).

found a way back from the individual to the essential-universal. Medieval scholastics show a similar pattern, at least in a number of important philosophers.

Things changed dramatically in the 18th century, however, in line with Augustine and a strong current in the Middle Ages. Historicity was rediscovered, and the tension between the universal and the individual would mount as never before—to this day. The individual and the unique, far from being depreciated, now enjoyed a *positive* appreciation, sometimes even in the sense of being preferred to the universal. While in Aristotle the particular was viewed as disruptive of the general order, in both modern philosophy and the modern outlook on life the universal came to be experienced as a threat to the individual.

As a result, an old polarity in the problem of knowledge has revived. Traditionally, science and philosophy are essentially connected with the universal, and knowledge of the individual and unique has less value and certainty—when that very individual is deemed of higher value for reality. This discrepancy has sparked a controversy that has dominated in significant measure the direction of philosophy of science.

The causal-genetic worldview

Here, too, the problem of the individual occupies an important place. Because so much attention is paid to the individual, the question of the ground or origin of the individual has receded far too much into the shade.

The causal-genetic worldview, no less than the scientific worldview discussed earlier, has a double layer owing to a split that can be traced to a fundamental decision made at the beginning of philosophy—a decision that has been repeated again and again in the course of the centuries. This time it is not a question of *one* polarity or tension, but of several: science and history, permanence and change, and others.

Vossler claims that in every case *meaning* is placed in the first layer.[7] Now it is certainly true that it has been much harder for thought to discover meaning in the transitory, the finite, the historical, than in the permanent, the constant. Thus it is no rarity that those who begin by affirming the concrete, the historical, nevertheless end by ascribing solidity and meaning only to some immutable essence or structure—mainly to theoretical or scientific reason. Yet on the whole I believe historical development contradicts Vossler's generalization.

Why is it that Western man has such a deep desire to demonstrate that the present forms of life (not just in an organic sense, but more broadly) owe their existence to development from other forms? The notion that things *are* what they *have* from their genesis and development, from their causal connections and 'influences,' belongs to the fixed ingredients of the present-day worldview, including that of lay people. Structuralism has arisen in opposition, but without attacking the point of departure; it has merely shifted the focus from the idea of

---

[7] Vossler, op. cit., 66.

development to the hypothesis of structure, but the causality principle remains intact in both. With my own question Why? I may seem to be conforming to causal thinking; the case I wish to demonstrate, however, is that there is a way of seeing coherence between things other than in terms of primarily causal relations.

The dawn of the Modern Age—in which I include, for the present context, the Late Middle Ages—marked the inception in both theoretical thought and the general outlook on life of a profound reorientation which, once started, would take centuries to become fully effective. A worldview in which all the emphasis had been on the universal and immutable was opened up in the direction of full recognition of the mutable and factual. On the one hand there was a conforming to reality by means of exact, empirical, objective description and by submission to its laws; on the other hand there was the endeavor to master this same reality, both scientifically and culturally, by means of emancipated, hence (supposedly) pure reason.

From the middle of the 18th century, or perhaps even earlier, the notion of change was revived in that it was given a key function in the reawakening of historical sense—to counteract the naive self-confidence of pure, unaided reason. This dualism between pure reason and the idea of a history grounded in itself has stamped the course of the last centuries. It is noteworthy that from the middle of the 18th century an ambivalence appeared in the attitude toward history which has never left it and which we also encountered when we looked at change and mutability in general. Sometimes history is seen as an autonomous entity, pressing on in spite of every man-made revolutionary innovation, obeying its own laws, either advancing roughshod over individual happiness and misery or finding time in its rapid upward progress to testify anonymously of its goodness. At other times, human individuals, mindful of history's perceived irrationality and discontinuity, conspire against its silent power and seize control, though generally leaving the action to the so-called great personalities. People acquire a new awareness of 'time,' which is translated into history in national, epochal or world-historical perspectives; it is also translated with the aid of existential motifs.

With their new, high appreciation of history, people experience history in its unpredictability, inscrutability and relativity, and they contrast it with the clarity of reason. This cannot but affect the whole of life, by virtue of the intimate connection between history and life. During the nineteenth century and during the twentieth, too, in many ways, the finitude of historical forms and phenomena has not been able to shake people's confidence in history. Expectations have run high; as one observer put it: "the nature of anything is entirely comprehended in its development." [8]

It was—and still is—entirely possible to combine historical thinking in this sense with theoretical reason. What encouraged such a "rapprochement" (I had

---

[8] Geoffrey Barraclough, *History and the Common Man* (1967), 10.

better express myself carefully, in view of what follows) was the fact that reason was increasingly being seen as dynamic and as incorporated in a progressive development[9]—thus the same discovery that the new historical consciousness had made with respect to the whole of reality. History could only become—so one would have expected—the antipode both of the universal and of truth. Amazingly, the opposite turned out to be the case. Within the universal, a profound historical individuation occurs, and truth *unfolds itself* progressively in *historical* forms.

Historical thinking
The impact of history, however, would be even greater. That brings us to one of the main problems in our discussion: the relation of (scientific) knowledge and historicity. The second half of the eighteenth century was already keenly aware of this problem, and since then it has lost none of its urgency. Time and again our problem was believed solved; time and again it proved to have lost none of its tantalizing vitality. Here the word 'historicism' should be introduced, but I will avoid that term, preferring instead to speak of 'historical thinking' in order to express my solidarity with the renewed appreciation of historicity. You expect me, of course, to state at last what I understand by historicity and history, since these and related terms have so many meanings. Well, I mean *all* those meanings. It is the inexhaustible wealth of history that finds expression in these terms and concepts—though I must add, by way of anticipation, that this wealth will not be appreciated as wealth until viewed in a certain light.

To pick up the thread of my argument: when I affirm my solidarity with modern historical thinking I hasten to add that such thinking is not proof against the criticism I must level against it in terms of my own basic conviction regarding history. In saying that, I do not, in the first place, have in mind the two kinds of historical thinking: the one in which history is understood (following Dilthey) as comprehensive historical development, and the other in which history is understood (following Heidegger) as "historicity," that is to say, as recognizing individuality and uniqueness in their full authenticity. It is in this last sense, as a rule, that historical thinking gives rise to the intense opposition between historicity and thought (philosophy, science, knowledge of whatever kind).

My concern is not with something non-essential. Let me explain. The problem of historical thinking is not in the first place an epistemological one; nor is it a question of hermeneutics. Rather, it is an ontological problem. Historical thinking may be epistemological, but its basis is ontological. In saying this I am challenging the common view; however, I am in conformity with what illustrious representatives of the historical method have shown.[10]

Why this narrowing of focus? Because what we have called the reawakening of historical sense or "historical consciousness" and the rediscovery of

---
[9] [An allusion to hegelian "Reason in History."]
[10] [Probable meaning: ultimately they all avow some ontological basis or ground.]

history cuts deeper than is usually supposed. Man becomes conscious of the finitude, mutability and uniqueness of people and things. But surely this was known *before* the breakthrough of the new experience of historicity? Of course it was, but Wilhelm Dilthey (1833–1911), one of the most important philosophers of historical thinking, pinpointed the far-reaching effect of the rediscovery of history when he wrote: In the face of the great enigma of the origin of things, the purpose of our existence, and the ultimate worth of our actions, we feel "more at a loss than at any former time in history." [11] Dilthey was acutely conscious of the twin consequences flowing from the rejection of the idea of a transmundane origin: (1) without it, one could no longer apprehend historical entities (nations, periods, 'existences') and phenomena in their inner coherence[12] ; (2) without a transmundane origin, the ultimate value of our existence and our actions had become an enigma.

Thinkers devoted to reflecting on history have restlessly occupied themselves with finding an escape from the dual impasse while at the same time maintaining the full historicity of existence. Dilthey himself led the way. Has the search resulted in a satisfactory solution?

One cannot give a simple answer. There have been some, like Meinecke, who persevered in evading both these problems. There have also been some, like Heidegger, who radicalized *geschichtlichkeit* but without doing justice to factual history. But most could not endure the absolute historicity of life for very long. The solution they came up with, as it turns out, is perfectly in line with Western thought. Historical thinking has brought about profound changes, but in the end, to overcome the most vexing problems, it has returned to the age-old dualism.

On this view, history runs on two levels. The first level is that of the near-permanent, of that which is exempt from historical change; on this level is found what is common to all times and peoples. The other level is that of historicity; this is the level of real history. On the first level the phenomena border on the universal, which allows one to apply the rules of historical reason. But on the second level? There the problem of historicity remains unsolved, although it is felt less acutely because of the possibility of taking refuge in the first level.

The main thesis in historical thinking is that man is not just incorporated or caught up in the great flux—or progressive evolution—of history but that he is indeed a thoroughly historical being, and that thought and the other forms of knowledge are therefore likewise of an historical nature. Historicism has encountered vehement opposition because of its implied relativism; but I let that rest. More importantly, historical thinking has caused great confusion in the Western conception of science on account of its emphasis on the individual and the unique.

---

[11] Wilhelm Dilthey, *Gesammelte Schriften*, 8:193.

[12] Like Dilthey, J. G. Herder (1744–1803) saw no possibility of apprehending historical individuals in more than an external coherence. Existence philosophers [e.g., Pierre Thévenaz] talk of a "dust cloud" of individuals.

A single example may suffice. Max Weber believes in a strict separation between science and the world of values: values are beyond the reach of the scientific method. But the whole distinction Weber makes here, in which he has been followed by countless others, loses credibility as soon as we notice that Weber is unable to write a single page without encountering values that make historical existence possible to begin with.

My own position: historicity and originality
Coming now to a more thetical exposition, I must clarify a few matters.

  a. Our position has been a critical one. That does not diminish the fact that it is at the same time a position of existential solidarity or engagement with what moves the Western worldview. In the first part of my paper that solidarity has been expressed in a paradoxical way; engagement *as well as* rejection is of the essence in my view of history.[13]

  b. In modern philosophy, epistemology has primacy, not metaphysics or ontology. I too acknowledge a primacy, but then in reverse order. Science and philosophy are only possible on the basis of an ontological posing of the problems; scientific knowledge not only gives *power*, to be sure, but it is pursued above all because it gives *meaning*.

Dilthey saw with great clarity the decisive significance of the origin and meaning of things. Only, he could no longer believe in them because of the new historical consciousness.[14] We are confronted here with Dilthey's rejection of the Christian idea of the origin. From the very outset he saw clearly the alarming consequences of his rejection: consigned to historical relativity, man loses his solid ground. At the same time he realized that man has an inner need to leave historical conditionality and relativity behind and be able to rely on something deeper, something that escapes relativity.[15] And then we see Dilthey continue his intellectual journey. On the one hand he lived in the permanent expectation that *historical consciousness*—precisely in its relativism—would bring healing (an expectation that was never fulfilled). On the other hand he resorted to philosophy's old solution of grafting the historical onto the rational. In so doing, he still ended up in the vicinity of Hegel.

---

[13] [Probable meaning: We cannot but react to historicism as a phenomenon of our time, in which we share; but we respond adequately only by returning to transcendental time (see the previous essay).]

[14] Has Dilthey not had his day? No doubt as a philosopher he was a child of his time. Yet he also rose above his age to entertain and experience (more than analyze) numerous fundamental problems, such as the questions of the ground of being, the ground of knowledge, and the reciprocal relation between knowledge and history. He was preoccupied especially with the deeper connection between these and other problems, working in so thorough and nuanced a fashion that in my opinion he has never been surpassed by anyone, not even Heidegger, nor by any Christian thinker. Dilthey's example shows that what is "essential" (see above) never sinks away into the silent depths of the past.

[15] Cf. Dilthey, *Gesammelte Schriften*, 8:194.

To formulate the problem even more sharply, I shall summarize the foregoing in different words. When we use the term historicity we may delude ourselves into supposing for a moment that we have avoided the relativistic consequences by taking history in a limited sense and assimilating it into a more encompassing, teleological development. But the moment we begin to speak of 'mutability'—yes of 'finitude'—without affirming the origin and ground of existence, things proceed to overwhelm us in their meaninglessness. Usually finitude is not experienced so poignantly after all, because in the last centuries man has succeeded almost every time—at least so he thinks—in finding a fixed (absolutized) point in this world, thus casting a veil over finitude in its absurdity.

But here I declare my confidence—in this I do not wish to be outdone by Dilthey and his disciples—in the *historical* nature of things. And when I next affirm that man is a *historical* being, then that is an essential, not a casual addition. I go on and add: the finite historical facts have *meaning* too! But meaning can exist only in the transcendental relation. Things, of whatever kind, have meaning—*are* meaning—not in themselves but from and in the divine origin; without meaning things have no existence. This thesis must perforce run counter to the common conception, namely, that we do not know whether there is a meaning in existence. That human existence, individual as well communal, in its various aspects has a deep intrinsic meaning we generally do not discover except in times of terror and extreme danger. As Emmanuel Levinas says somewhere: during torture the personality persists stubbornly in affirming itself.[16] In his knowing and acting, man constantly affirms himself in what he really is, that is to say, in what he is in all his originality. But in the affluent West, where life is good, the need to acknowledge meaning has devaluated into an option.

Things as they are, as they "essentially" are, or, to put it differently, things in their transcendental relation to the ground—that is also the fixed orientation point for all knowledge, including scientific knowledge. One might perhaps expect the term 'faith' here; but that term refers too much to a particular aspect. Our concern here is to show that all of existence in all of its aspects is incorporated in the relation to the origin and that this transcendental relation penetrates into scientific knowledge or any knowledge whatsoever.

The dialectic of science

After hearing all this, many will react with the following remark (and then the tone is still friendly): the idea that human existence has 'meaning' and that the question of 'essence' must be posed before all else is too ethereal and too abstract to be of any help in directing the formation of scientific knowledge. If

---

[16] Cf. Louis de Raeymaeker, "Het menselijk gelaat, uitdrukking van transcendentie, naar de filosofische opvattingen van Emmanuel Levinas" [The human face, expression of transcendence, according to the philosophical views of Emmanuel Levinas], *Tijdschrift voor Filosofie* 32 (1970): 375–454, at 410.

science seeks to know more than how things function, if it sets out to acquire a more fundamental knowledge of things, then it goes astray.

Yet this is the great misunderstanding. With respect to meaning I can provide a very concrete instance by way of reply. Both the jurist and the judge—the student of law and the administrator of law—have (if things are well) only one goal: that justice be done, that right prevail. Our system of justice, in the courts and in the law schools, is concerned with one of the highest values of human life, in a very concrete way that affects the well-being and vital interests of persons and communities. And it is no different in the other disciplines; in many of them, concepts like freedom and peace, for example, play a prominent role.

Again, what we encounter both in our experience and in the formation of our knowledge are the things, phenomena, facts in all their *originality*, in their transcendental dimension. Without that dimension they cannot have existence. Although this idea is rare in science, we are beginning to hear it talked about more often all the time. I mention only P. Groen,[17] Heinrich Beck,[18] A. M. Klaus Müller[19] and Robert Spaemann.[20]

A dialectic is at work in the practice of science. On the one hand the highest values are operative in science, for without them things have no reality. On the other hand science offers fundamental resistance to admitting those values.

Why this resistance, on principle? There are two causes or reasons, each implicit in the other.

1) The thesis that all things are grounded in the origin, hence that all values too are "original," implies that nothing that exists owes its existence to itself; everything owes its existence to a Giver of meaning. Now then, this is in absolute contradiction to the supposed autonomy of modern man, who experiences his autonomy most strongly in science.

2) The second cause or reason flows from the first. Science owes its progress and certainty to the rational-empirical method. The highest truths, however, lie beyond this method's reach.

If we follow the way of *rational thinking*, on the basis of *empirical observation*—these two concepts together constitute the norm for science—then our concepts *drain empty*. For what meaning or content can a concept still have if it captures only the rational aspect of things? Things can exist only in the indissoluble coherence of all their aspects.

---

[17] Cf. his valedictory address as professor of physics, given on 9 March 1979, published under the title *Grenzen* [Limits] (1979), 10, where he speaks of "a transcendental dimension that gives things a *meaning*, a significance of [being] more than objects." [In 1952 Professor Groen's inaugural address had been entitled *Over de grenzen der voorspelbaarheid* [On the limits of predictability.]

[18] See note 5 above.

[19] [Cf. Adolf M. Klaus Müller, *Wende der Wahrnehmung. Erwägungen zur Grundlagenkrise in Physik, Medizin, Pädagogik und Theologie* [Thoughts on the crisis in the foundations of physics, medicine, pedagogy and theology] (Munich: Kaiser, 1978).]

[20] Cf. R. Spaemann, "Über die kontroverse Natur der Philosophie," *Neue Zürcher Zeitung*, 25/26 August 1979.

Yet our concepts do not drain empty after all! For, the origin, the intrinsic value of all that is given, never allows itself to be eliminated, no matter how hard the rational-empirical method may try to shut it out. Imagine seeking to eliminate the question, What is justice? from the discipline of jurisprudence or the interpretation of the law. Think, too, of the natural sciences and the meaning of a question such as What is life? [21] Are the natural sciences not living proof that a strictly empirical and formal-rational approach just will not do? As in other disciplines, one has to distinguish in the natural sciences between the schemes and precepts of philosophy of science and the manuals, on the one hand, and the real-life practice of science itself, on the other. The latter too has its rules and norms, but they are subject to change, sometimes radical change.

But does the dialectic not ensure that it matters very little whether or not origin and meaning, for example, are known and acknowledged? Do they not play their decisive role in the broad gamut of the presuppositions of science? My reply would have to be that, in the sense in which I have used the term, of course, the dialectic has a *leveling* effect and that, accordingly, science does not simply take cognizance of what goes on in the dialectic but fights a real battle against admitting the questions of the ground. The transcendental dimension asserts itself, and scientific or philosophical analysis keeps it at bay. That is the situation. It has given rise to *definitions*. For centuries now, a definition has been considered the ideal outcome of analysis, but upon closer analysis a definition often turns out to be little more than a pale generalization or a tautology; it merely touches upon the exterior of phenomena. Imagine for a moment what an enormous difference it would make in, say, scientific peace research if a scholar, unhindered by the scientific bias, opened himself to the full, rich content of peace rather than confining himself to rational-empirical definitions of peace! In this connection I should not fail to mention the radical critique that has been leveled against the prevailing conception of science on the ground that it not only introduces intolerable restrictions in knowledge but even poses an existential threat to man. I have in mind those whom I have already mentioned with complete sympathy, but also several philosophers of existence, like Levinas and, to mention no more, Kurt Hübner.

Transcending the totality

Resonating throughout my discussion you will have heard the contrast I began with, that between science and [interpretation, *Erklären* and *Verstehen*, rational-empirical analysis and] hermeneutics. The two shade off into one another, although it must be recognized that in the current conception of science interpretation gets closer to the questions of the ground. The field of "interpretation"—to stay with the customary terminology for a moment—knows no rest; at times it resembles a battlefield. That unrest and that battle are good things and

---

[21] See also D. Dieks, *Studies in the Foundations of Physics: A Discussion of Some Relations Between Physics, the Foundations of Physics, and the Philosophy of Science* (1981), 83.

they will always be around, of that I am certain, unless a social or scientific totality takes over. When the prevailing view ascribes the turmoil to the "subjective" nature of interpretation, it betrays the primacy it gives to epistemology over ontology.

But why will *Verstehen* never come to rest? Because the individual is not the first, the essential factor. The first and essential factor is: being grounded in the Origin. And the Origin is unfathomable and unutterable. For this reason the things we handle every day and without which we cannot exist are equally unfathomable by virtue of their originality. There is an urge in man, on account of the 'first history,' [22] to draw near to the unfathomable in order to understand it better, even though it remains unfathomable. This is the *dynamis* in knowledge and in history, the *historicity* in knowledge. But no sooner do people realize that history is fully operative in knowledge, in norms, in all of reality, than they sound warnings against relativism—but what are they then talking about? History affects all these terrains, that is to say, affects them with what is most essential and most authentic. Because there is an arising from the origin and a returning to it again, knowing, and acting too, will remain in a state of unrest.

Knowledge *is* intrinsically historical. It is not only *in* history, but is itself history. Or as Hegel put it: ". . . what we are, we are at the same time historically" [23]—only to be untrue to it himself. So, too, knowledge (here I shall always include scientific knowledge) is *essential* or *original* knowledge. This implies that faith, for example, is not merely an aspect in the process of knowing; it penetrates all knowing.

In this mutual interpenetration, then, the ethical, the empirical, the rational, and so forth, all have their place. One who desires to know a thing can *conceptualize* it only as part of a complex pattern. He need not fathom it all, for in the formation of knowledge concerning just social reality, for example, one is already submerged inevitably in the depth-layer of reality.

What is it, then, that ultimately holds all this together? *It is a complex pattern of meaning.* It is when we turn to reality that we discover that complex *fullness of meaning* that we cannot step outside of for a moment, either in the formation of our knowledge or in our everyday lives. We exist, think, and act within a pattern of countless circumstances, decisions, intuitions, events, and so forth, and at every moment of history this results in an interconnectedness between things, phenomena, and so on, an integral whole of a sort that no one has designed or would ever be able to design or construct.

Even now I have not yet stated what is most essential. There is a coming-into-existence of the world that is a result of our own doing, but there is at the same time a coming-into-existence that has been—and continuously is—granted to us and that makes the former possible. This condition of being

---

[22] [For this whole paragraph, see the previous essay.]

[23] ". . . was wir sind, sind wir zugleich geschichtlich." G. W. F. Hegel, *Einleitung in die Geschichte der Philosophie*, ed. Hoffmeister (1966), 12.

granted, of being instituted, is, as Buber says, the *fundamental given of existence*.

It is within this interconnected whole that man is situated as a knowing and acting being; and—as must follow from the argument just made—in this situation he is also *overwhelmed* by the incomprehensible multiplicity and unfathomable totality.

That is the way matters are dealt with in most theories of science. For man can never be kept within the constraints of the totalitarian whole, even if this has perhaps never really been noticed. An example for clarification! On the one hand we have to affirm that history forges ahead from out the past as a mighty, uninterrupted whole, and that man is swept along in it. On the other hand this same history does not just flow simply onward; rather, there are clear differences between changing times, and even between successive days. And that does not happen *in isolation from human freedom*.

We can express these things by saying that every person transcends the totality of reality, of history, *at every moment* in the direction of the origin. Here we stand before the prime given that we *belong to* being in countless interconnections yet also *transcend* being. Well then, it is this prime given that must inform all our accounts of reality and knowledge—unless, abstracting, we presume to place ourselves outside it.

The task of Christian scholarship

To round off my reflections, one final consideration: How significant is all this, in practice, for science and philosophy? I myself have said that science in its innocence does ask, among other things, What is justice? We can hardly expect more from it. We no longer live in the age of an Augustine (the fifth century), or of a Ranke (the nineteenth century) who said that "every age is immediate to God." Since then, the process of secularization has rendered science immune to what I have defended. Ranke's dictum is of historical interest, of course, but *out of date*.

But then in Vossler, to whom I alluded earlier, I come across this remark (written in 1979!): "It is not enough to say that every age is immediate to God; the adage should be: *every act in history is immediate to God."* [24] Vossler can say this because he acknowledges history as *meaning*, which is grounded in its turn in an *absolute*. He makes this remark in the context of historical *science*— more accurately: of science in general—for he no longer has any confidence in *philosophy* of history; I will come back to this.

"Every act is immediate to God"—and that said right in a scientific treatise —that is *quite something*. For it implies that the integral, coherent pattern is broken from moment to moment by the transcendental relation. Think of it: the comprehensive pattern broken, a pattern sacred to the scientist and in the absence of which no scientific analysis is deemed possible!

---

[24] Vossler, op. cit., 158.

I have just asked what practical significance my reflections have for science. Well, that will have to appear from the following problem, which I introduce as an example. It is the problem of the causal pattern or nexus. (I take *causa* not in the Aristotelian-Scholastic but in the modern, functionalist sense.) I spoke of a *sacred* causal pattern, for according to the common view the "scientific" status of a discipline depends on its ability to explain ideas, events, phenomena, etc., in terms of their causes. On this view, ideas are the product of circumstances, or circumstances are the product of ideas—there appears to be no escaping the dilemma of idealism or materialism. Often, causal thinking is mitigated and the talk is of circumstances, influences, relations, but such thinking is no less strongly causal in its starting point!

But what, in that case, are we to think of hermeneutics with its *Verstehen*, which is intended precisely as a convincing counterweight to causal explanation? Hermeneutics is indeed friendlier, as we observed earlier, but its method is no less causal and totalitarian. Hermeneutics endeavors to understand things and phenomena in terms of the spirit of the times, the structure, the nation. But is not structuralism a reaction against that merry-go-round of factors? To be sure, but the structure is said to impose its will, silently and imperiously. Seldom has there been a time when science was as totalitarian as it is in our own day. *The socio-economic way of thinking has infected the whole of reality.* The origin of religion, the progress of philosophy, artistic expressions, psychic developments and deformations—to mention no more—are all in the grip of the anonymous power of the economic-social structure. This is all swallowed so easily because ordinary people never thought any differently: they always "knew" that an underprivileged family will inevitably produce criminal behavior.

The fight against causal thinking must be directed against its totalitarian aspect. This may sound unduly harsh, so let me remind you of the words of Geoffrey Barraclough (alas, he does not repudiate them): "the nature of anything is *entirely comprehended* in its development." [25] Barraclough makes this statement while invoking the hermeneutical method. As I said, science and hermeneutics are well matched when it comes to this paramount issue.

How could it be otherwise? From the earliest times people have posed the *why* question, and they continue to do so. Only, the question is now wrapped in a scientific cloak. With the *why* question science has been given an enormously broad field; here empiricism and rational thought rule supreme, and the coveted goal is the formulation of causal laws. The manner in which I have dealt with causality and the *why* question should have made clear, however, that I for one regard the sacred causal pattern as open to challenge.

Is there a link to be made here with philosophy? Philosophy, of course, can be mentioned only in hushed tones. Philosophy has lost its significance almost entirely and must live within the narrow confines allowed it by science. The great significance of philosophy for the sciences—I have yet to see it. I prefer

---

[25] [See note 8 above.]

to speak of the *isolation of philosophy*, for which philosophy has only itself to blame. For in its docile stance with respect to the scientific worldview, philosophy has missed a unique opportunity to bring openness to the closed causal order. The *why* question and the search for the *archè* have been its most difficult problems even in the best of times. I am therefore harking back to the essence of philosophical thought when I assert that there are givens that are inaccessible to the causal-scientific, structural mode of thought. Language and law, art and social context, economy and religion—to take just a few examples from the countless many—*are intimately interconnected*, yet *not* in terms of an autonomous causal order, for that can never exist of itself. A causal pattern points back towards the original, transcendental integral whole.

There has never been anyone who has designed or constructed, and realized, the integral whole in history. And yet all people and all things are in it, and have being and life within it alone. But surely, then, in a causally interconnected way? — To be sure, things are interconnected in reality in many ways. But there is one coherent whole that is *fundamental and original*, that grounds them all, and this we call the *fullness of meaning*.

And thus—in this given fullness of meaning—do life, culture, freedom, peace, the individual and the universal, and also scientific concepts, enter into scientific practice. The controlling starting point for scientific concept formation can be no other than the acknowledgment that these all *were* there already *before* they were taken in hand by man, and *before* they entered into human knowing— I mean this not chronologically but *ontologically*.

In the current scientific climate, this is inconceivable. Again, let me illustrate. When people inquire into the origin and essence of the Renaissance they research the factors that led to its birth and that account for its essence. In contrast, I emphasize: the Renaissance *was* there already (again, speaking ontologically) *before* the factors in question could exercise their influence. It *was*, before human forming and deforming activity could begin its work and rebel against what was given in the meaning of the Renaissance.

It is the task of philosophy both to redirect the question concerning the origin and ground of things (in this case the Renaissance) towards the divine creativity, and also to have a never flagging interest in the daily renewal in creation (of which the Renaissance is an instance).

Do you find it offensive to have the divine creativity and the Renaissance brought so near each other? To set your mind at ease, let me sum up my entire position in different words. People always say: phenomena, ideas, are *time-bound*. I turn it around: *time is bound, the times are bound, to the transcendental dimension*, and the world, the fullness of life and history, are not opened up until this dimension is laid bare.[26] To promote this insight is the task of Christian scholarship.

---

[26] Cf. H. de Jong, *Bron en norm; een bundel bijbelstudies* (1979).

BIBLIOGRAPHY

WORKS CITED IN PART ONE

Aalders, W. J. *De analogia entis in het geding.* Mededeelingen der Koninklijke Akademie van Wetenschappen, Afdeling Letterkunde, vol. 83.2 (1937).

Adam, Karl. "Jesu menschliches Wesen im Licht der urchristlichen Verkündigung." *Wissenschaft und Weisheit* 6 (1939): 111–20.

———. "Kirche und Seele. Randbemerkungen zur gleichnamigen Schrift von Ildefons Herwegen." *Theologische Quartalschrift* 106 (1925): 231–39.

———. "Le Mystère de l'Église. Du scandal à la foi triomphante." In *L'Église est Une. Hommage à Moehler*, 33–52. Paris, 1939.

———. "Das Problem des Geschichtlichen im Leben der Kirche." Festrede, gehalten auf der 50. General-versammlung der Görresgesellschaft zu Hildesheim. In *Jahresbericht der Görresgesellschaft, 1936*, 73–85. Cologne, 1937.

Angelinus, O.F.M.Cap. *Algemene Zijnsleer.* Edited by Martinianus, O.F.M.Cap. Utrecht and Brussels: Het Spectrum, 1947. Bibliotheek van Thomistische Wijsbegeerte, 3.

———. "De eenheid van het analoge zijnsbegrip." In *De Analogie van het Zijn*, 5–24. Proceedings of the Eighth General Meeting of the Society for Thomist Philosophy. Supplement of *Studia Catholica* (1941).

Allo, Ernest Bernard, O.P. *L'Apocalypse.* Paris: Gabalda, 1921.

Aubert, Roger. "Discussions récentes autour de la Théologie de l'histoire." *Collectanea Mechliniensia* 33 (1948): 129–49.

———. "Les grandes tendances théologiques entre les deux guerres." *Collectanea Mechliniensia* 31 (1946): 17–36.

———. "Quelques études récentes sur la place du Laïcat dans l'Église." *Collectanea Mechliniensia* 33 (1948): 674–91.

Badoux, B., O.F.M. "Quaestio de philosophia christiana." *Antonianum* 11 (1936): 487–552.

Bäumler, Alfred. "Bamberg und Naumburg: Über die Epochen des Mittelalters." *Zeitwende* 1 (1925): 462–80.

Bartmann, Bernard. *Lehrbuch der Dogmatik.* 2 vols. 8th ed. Freiburg im Breisgau: Herder, 1932.

Bastable, Patrick K. *Desire for God: Does Man Aspire Naturally to the Beatific Vision? An Analysis of This Question and of Its History.* London and Dublin: Burns, Oates & Washbourne, 1947.

Bauhofer, Oskar. "Abendland und christliche Kultur." *Der Katholische Gedanke* 9 (1936): 38–47.

———. *Das Geheimnis der Zeiten. Christliche Sinndeutung der Geschichte.* Munich: Kösel & Pustet, 1935.

———. *Die Heimholung der Welt. Von der sakramentalen Lebensordnung.* Freiburg in Breisgau: Herder, 1937.

Bavinck, Herman. *Wijsbegeerte der Openbaring*. Kampen: Kok, 1908.
Eng. trans., *The Philosophy of Revelation*. London: Longmans, 1909. Reprint. Grand Rapids, Mich.: Eerdmans, 1953. The Stone Lectures for 1908–09, Princeton Theological Seminary.
Belloc, Hilaire. *Europe and the Faith*. New York: Paulist Press, 1920. 3rd impr. London, 1924.
Bellon, Karel Leopold. "Vrijheid, wettelijkheid en ontwikkeling in de geschiedenis." In *Miscellanea historica in honorem Alberti de Meyer*, 68–76. Louvain: Bibliothèque de l'Université, 1946.
———. "Wijsbegeerte en theologie." In *Verslagboek van de Tweede Philosophische Week*, 17–25. Utrecht and Nijmegen, 1933.
Berkouwer, Gerrit Cornelis. *Conflict met Rome*. Kampen: Kok, 1948.
Eng. trans., *The Conflict with Rome*. Translated by H. de Jongste and David H. Freeman. Philadelphia: Presbyterian & Reformed, 1958.
———. *Karl Barth*. Kampen: Kok, 1936.
Blondel, Maurice. *L'Action. Essai d'une critique de la vie et d'une science de la pratique*. 1893. Paris: Presses universitaires de France, 1950. Bibliothèque de philosophie contemporaine, 7.
———. *L'Action*. 2 vols. Paris: Alcan, 1936–37. Vol. 1: *Le Problème des causes secondes et le pur agir*, 1936. Vol. 2: *L'Action humaine et les conditions de son aboutissement*, 1937.
———. *Le Problème de la philosophie catholique*. Paris: Bloud & Gay, 1932. Cahiers de la Nouvelle Journée, 20.
———. "Le Problème de la philosophie catholique." *Les Études philosophiques* 7 (1933): 13–32.
———. *La Pensée*. 2 vols. Vol. 1: *La Genèse de la Pensée et les paliers de son ascension spontanée*. Vol. 2: *Les Responsabilités de la Pensée et la possibilité de son achèvement*. Paris: Presses universitaires de France, 1934.
———. "La Philosophie chrétienne existe-t-elle comme philosophie?" *Bulletin de la Société française de philosophie* (Séance du 21 mars 1931): 86–92.
———. *La Philosophie et l'esprit chrétien*. 2 vols. Paris: Presses universitaires de France, 1944–46. Vol. 1: *Autonomie essentielle et connexion indéclinable*, 1944. Vol. 2: *Conditions de la symbiose seule normale, logique et salutaire*, 1946.
———. "Pour la philosophie intégrale." *Revue néoscolastique* 37 (1934): 49–64.
Bonnefoy, J.-Fr., O.F.M. "La Place du Christ dans le plan divin de la création." *Mélanges de science religieuse* 4 (1947): 257–84; 5 (1948): 39–62.
Boyer, Charles, S.J. *Handboek der Wijsbegeerte*. Dutch ed., H. Rambonnet. 2 vols., 's-Hertogenbosch (Bois-le-Duc), 1947. Vol. 1: *Algemene Inleiding, Logica, Inleiding tot de Metaphysica*. Vol. 2: *Cosmologie en Psychologie*.
Bréhier, Émile. *Histoire de la philosophie*. 2 vols. Paris: Presses universitaires de France, 1927. Vol. 1: *L'Antiquité et le Moyen Âge*.
Eng. trans. by J. Thomas, *The History of Philosophy*. Vol. 1: *The Hellenic Age*. Chicago: University of Chiago Press, 1963. The History of Philosophy, 1.
———. "Y a-t-il une philosophie chrétienne?" *Revue de métaphysique et de morale* 38 (1931): 133–62.
Broglie, G. de. "De la place du surnaturel dans la philosophie de saint Thomas." *Recherches de science religieuse* 14 (1924): 193–246, 481–96; 15 (1925): 5–53.

Casel, Odo, O.S.B. *Das christliche Kultmysterium*. Regensburg, 1932; 3rd ed. 1948.
   Eng. trans., *The Mystery of Christian Worship and Other Writings*. Edited by Burkhard Neunheuser. Westminster, Md.: Newman Press, 1962.
———. "Mysterienfrömmigkeit." *Bonner Zeitschrift für Theologie und Seelsorge* 4 (1927): 101–17.
———. "Le Sens chrétien du temps." *La Vie spirituelle* 76 (1947): 18–26.
Cerfaux, Lucien. "Le Royaume de Dieu." *La Vie spirituelle* 75 (1946): 645–56.
Chroust, Anton Hermann. "The Meaning of Time in the Ancient World." *The New Scholasticism* 21 (1947): 1–70.
———. "The Metaphysics of Time and History in Early Christian Thought." *The New Scholasticism* 19 (1945): 322–52.
Congar, Yves Marie Joseph, O.P. "Bulletin d'Ecclésiologie." *Revue des sciences philosophiques et théologiques* 31 (1947): 77–96, 272–96.
———. "Pour une théologie du laïcat." *Les Études philosophiques* 256 (1948): pt. 1: "Le Laïcat et la réalité sacrale de l'Église," 42–54; pt. 2: "Le Laïcat et l'Église dans son rapport au monde," 195–217.
   Cf. idem, *Jalons pour une théologie du laïcat*. Paris: Éditions du Cerf, 1953.
   Eng. trans. by Donald Attwater, *Lay People in the Church: A Study for a Theology of the Laity*. Westminster, Md.: Newman Press, 1957.
———. "Tendances actuelles de la pensée religieuse." *Cahiers du monde nouveau* 4 (1948): 33–50.
Conrad-Martius, Hedwig. "Schöpfung und Zeugung." *Tijdschrift voor Philosophie* 1 (1939): 801–26.
———. *Ursprung und Aufbau des lebendigen Kosmos*. Salzburg and Leipzig: Müller, 1938.
Cordovani, Mariano, O.P. "Per la vitalità della Teologia Cattolica." *Angelicum* 17 (1940): 133–46.
Cullmann, Oscar. *Christus und die Zeit. Die urchristliche Zeit- und Geschichtsauffassung*. Zurich: Zollikon, 1946.
   Eng. trans. by Floyd V. Filson, *Christ and Time: The Primitive Christian Conception of Time and History*. 1951. Rev. ed. Philadelphia: Westminster, 1964.
Daniélou, Jean, S.J. "Christianisme et histoire." *Les Études philosophiques* 254 (1947): 166–84.
———. "Christianisme et progrès." *Les Études philosophiques* 255 (1947): 399–402.
———. *Le Mystère du salut des nations*. Paris: Éditions du Seuil, 1946. Collection la Sphère de la Croix.
   Eng. trans. by Angeline Bouchard, *The Salvation of the Nations*. London: Sheed & Ward, 1949. Reprint. University of Notre Dame Press, 1962.
———. "Les Orientations présentes de la pensée religieuse." *Les Études philosophiques* 249 (1946): 5–21.
———. "Saint Irénée et les origines de la théologie de l'histoire." *Recherches de science religieuse* 34 (1947): 227–31.
Dawson, Christopher. "The Kingdom of God and History." In *The Kingdom of God and History*, 197–216. Edited by H. G. Wood, C. H. Dodd et al. London: Allen & Unwin, 1938. Church, Community and State, 3.
   Reprinted in idem, *Dynamics of World History*, 270–86. Edited by John J. Mulloy. New York: Sheed & Ward, 1956.

Dawson, Christopher. *Progress and Religion: An Historical Enquiry.* London: Sheed & Ward, 1929.
Dekkers, Eligius, O.S.B. "De mysterieleer van Maria-Laach." *Tijdschrift voor Liturgie* 22 (1942): 129–52.
———. "Het Mysterium middelpunt van het Christendom." *Tijdschrift voor Liturgie* 23 (1943). Offprint, 23 pp.
Delp, Alfred., S.J. *Der Mensch und die Geschichte.* Kolmar: Glock, 1943.
———. "Weltgeschichte und Heilsgeschichte." *Stimmen der Zeit* 138 (1940/41): 245–54.
Dessauer, Philipp. *Der Anfang und das Ende. Eine religiöse und theologische Betrachtung zur Heilsgeschichte.* Leipzig: Hegner, 1939.
———. "Wege und Abwege der Geschichtstheologie in der Gegenwart." *Die Schildgenossen* 15 (1936): 234–76.
Dialogue Théologique. Edited by M. Labourdette, M.-J. Nicolas, R.-L. Bruckberger et al. Saint-Maximin (Var), 1947.
Dooyeweerd, Herman. "De idee der individualiteits-structuur en het Thomistisch substantiebegrip: Een critisch onderzoek naar de grondslagen der Thomistische zijnsleer." *Philosophia Reformata* 8 (1943): 65–99.
———. *De Wijsbegeerte der Wetsidee.* 3 vols. Amsterdam: H. J. Paris, 1935–36. Rev. ed., in Eng. trans. by David H. Freeman et al., *A New Critique of Theoretical Thought.* 4 vols. Philadelphia: Presbyterian & Reformed, 1953–58.
Doucet, Vittorino, O.F.M. "De naturali seu innato supernaturalis beatitudinis desiderio iuxta Theologos a saeculo XIII usque ad XX." *Antonianum* 4 (1929): 167–208.
Duprécl, Eugène G. *Deux essais sur le progrès.* Brussels: Palais des Académies, 1928.
Durand, Alfred, S.J. "Incarnation et Christocentrisme." *Nouvelle revue théologique* 69 (1947): 475–86.
Feder, Alfred Leonhard, S.J. *Lehrbuch der geschichtlichen Methode.* 1919. 3rd ed. Regensburg: Kösel & Pustet, 1924.
Féret, Henricus Maria, O.P. "Apocalypse, histoire et eschatologie chrétiennes." *Dieu vivant* 2 (1945): 115–34.
———. *L'Apocalypse de Saint Jean. Vision chrétienne de l'histoire.* Paris: Corrêa, 1943. Eng. trans. by Elizabethe H. C. Corathiel, *The Apocalypse of St. John.* Westminster, Md.: Newman Press, 1958.
———. "A propos de la primauté du Christ." *Revue de sciences philosophiques et théologiques* 27 (1938): 69–72.
Feuling, Daniel. *Katholische Glaubenslehre.* Salzburg, 1937.
Flahiff, George B. "A Catholic Looks at History." *Catholic Historical Review* 27 (April 1941): 1–15.
Fortmann, H. J. H. M. "Enige gedachten over Menswording en Verlossing." *Nederlandse Katholieke Stemmen* 44 (1948): 321–25.
Freyer, Hans. "Das Problem der Einheit der Weltgeschichte." In *Philosophische Vorträge und Diskussionen. Bericht über den Mainzer Philosophen-Kongress 1948*, 180–84. Wurzach: Birnbach, 1948.
———. "Die Systeme der weltgeschichtlichen Betrachtung." In *Propyläen-Weltgeschichte*, 1:1–28. Berlin, 1931.
Garrigou-Lagrange, R., O.P. "De relationibus inter philosophiam et religionem." In *Acta secundi congressus thomistici internationalis, 1936*, 379–94. Turin, 1937.

Geiger, L.-B., O.P. *La Participation dans la philosophie de Saint Thomas d'Aquin.* Paris: Vrin, 1942. Bibliothèque thomiste, 23.
George, Brother Justus. "Transfigured Universe." *Thought* 23 (1948): 483–91.
Gilson, Étienne. *L'Esprit de la philosophie médiévale.* 2 vols. 1932. 2nd ed. Paris: Vrin, 1944. Études de philosophie médiévale, 33.
  Eng. trans. by A. H. C. Downes, *The Spirit of Mediaeval Philosophy.* London: Sheed & Ward, and New York: Scribner's, 1936. Gifford Lectures, 1931–32.
———. "The Future of Augustinian Metaphysics." In M. C. D'Arcy, Maurice Blondel, Christopher Dawson et al., *A Monument to Saint Augustine,* 278–315. London: Sheed & Ward, 1930. 2nd ed. 1945. Reprinted in *A Gilson Reader,* 82–104.
———. *A Gilson Reader: Selections from the Writings of Etienne Gilson.* Edited by Anton C. Pegis. New York: Doubleday, 1957.
———. "La Notion de philosophie chrétienne." In *Bulletin de la Société française de philosophie* 31 (1931): 37–93.
  Cf. "What is Christian Philosophy?" In *A Gilson Reader,* 177–91.
———. "Réflexions sur la controverse S. Thomas – S. Augustin." In *Mélanges Mandonnet,* 1:371–83. Paris, 1930. Bibliothèque thomiste, 13.
  Cf. "The Idea of Philosophy in St. Augustine and in St. Thomas Aquinas." In *A Gilson Reader,* 68–81.
Gilson, Etienne and Philotheus Böhner. *Die Geschichte der christlichen Philosophie von ihren Anfängen bis Nikolaus von Cues.* Paderborn: Schöningh, 1937.
Graham, Aelred. *The Christ of Catholicism: A Meditative Study.* London and New York: Longmans, 1947.
Grosche, Robert. "Natur und Geschichte." *Catholica* 4 (1935): 49–60.
———. "Reich Gottes und Kirche." *Catholica* 6 (1937): 45–61.
Grossouw, Willem K. M. *In Christus; schets van een theologie van Sint Paulus.* 2nd ed. Utrecht and Brussels: Het Spectrum, 1948.
Gurian, Waldemar. "On Maritain's Political Philosophy." In *The Thomist* 5 (1943): 7–22. The Maritain Volume of *The Thomist.* New York, 1943.
Haecker, Theodor. *Der Christ und die Geschichte.* Leipzig: Hegner, 1935.
———. "Über den christlichen Sinn der Geschichte." *Hochland* 32 (1934/35): 481–500.
———. *Vergil, Vater des Abendlandes.* 1931. 2nd ed. Leipzig: Hegner, 1934.
  Eng. trans. by A. W. Wheen, *Virgil, Father of the West.* New York and London: Sheed & Ward, 1934. Essays in Order, 14.
Heitz, A. "Dernières étapes du renouveau liturgique allemand." *La Maison-Dieu* 7 (1946): 51–73. *Documents officiels,* 97–114.
Héris, Ch.-V., O.P. "Le Motif de l'Incarnation." *Bulletin de la Société française d'études mariales* 4 (1938): 15–29.
Herwegen, Ildefons, O.S.B. *Antike, Germanentum und Christentum. Drei Vorlesungen.* Bücherei der Salzburger Hochschulwochen, 1. Salzburg, 1932.
———. "Kirche und Seele: eine Entgegnung." *Theologische Quartalschrift* 106 (1925): 239–48.
———. *Kirche und Seele. Die Seelenhaltung des Mysterienkultus und ihr Wandel im Mittelalter.* Münster (Westph.), 1926. Aschendorffs zeitgemässe Schriften, 9.
Heufelder, Emmanuel Maria, O.S.B. "Benedikt von Nursia und das Abendland." *Neues Abendland* 2 (1947): 129–34.

Hoffman, Ross J. S. "Catholicism and Historismus." *Catholic Historical Review* 24 (Jan. 1939): 401–12.
Holzer, Oswald, O.F.M. "Hamartiozentrische oder Christozentrische Theologie?" *Wissenschaft und Weisheit* 6 (1939): 265–82; 7 (1940): 19–31.
Hove, Aloysius van. *De Erfzonde*. Nijmegen: Dekker & Van de Vegt, 1936. Leerboeken der Dogmatica en der Apologetica, 16.
Huber, Max. "Zeit und Geschichte." *Neue Schweizerische Rundschau* 6 (1938): 129–51. Reprinted in idem, *Glaube und Kirche. Gesammelte Aufsätze*, 349–71. Zurich: Atlantis, 1948.
Huby, Joseph, S.J. "Apocalypse et histoire." *Construire* 15 (1944): 80–100.
———. "Autour de l'Apocalypse." *Dieu vivant* 5 (1946): 119–30.
———. Review of *Introduction à la théologie* by Charles Journet. In *Les Études philosophiques* 259 (1948): 138–39.
Hugon, Edouard, O.P. *Le Mystère de l'Incarnation*. 1913. 8th ed. Paris: Téqui, 1946.
Janssens, Aloïs. *Het menschgeworden Woord*. 1925. 2nd rev. ed. Nijmegen: Dekker & Van de Vegt, 1929. Leerboeken der Dogmatica en der Apologetica, 3.
Jolivet, Régis. "Le Christianisme et l'avènement de l'idée de progrès." *Revue thomiste* 44 (1938): 494–507.
Journet, Charles. "Définition synthétique de l'âme créée de l'Église." *Revue thomiste* 47 (1947): 197–243; 467–81.
———. "Les Destinées du Royaume de Dieu." *Nova et Vetera* 10 (1935): 68–111.
———. *Introduction à la théologie*. Paris: Desclée de Brouwer, 1947. Questions disputées, 12.
Kearney, Hugh F. "Christianity and the Study of History." *The Downside Review* 67 (1949): 62–73.
Koster, Mannes Dominikus, O.P. "Natur und Übernatur. Die christliche Gesamtordnung." *Catholica* 5 (1936): 15–29.
Kreling, [Gerardus] Petrus, O.P. "De beteekenis van de analogie in de kennis van God." In *De Analogie van het Zijn*, 31–54. Supplement of *Studia Catholica* (1941).
Lagarde, Georges de. *La Naissance de l'esprit laïque au déclin du moyen âge*. 3 vols. Paris: Presses universitaires de France, 1934–39.
Lamy, Agnès. "La Vie monastique et ses problèmes actuels. Introduction à Bios angelikos." *Dieu vivant* 7 (1946): 59–77.
Laporta, J. G., O.S.B. "Natuur en genade." *Ons geloof* 12 (1926): 433–52.
———. "Les Notions d'appétit naturel et de puissance obédientielle chez saint Thomas d'Aquin." *Ephemerides Theologicae Lovanienses* 5 (1928): 257–77.
Leeuwen, Antonius F. van, S.J. "L'Analogie de l'être." *Revue néoscolastique de philosophie* 39 (1936): 293–320.
Lefèvre, Luc-J. "Une ascétique nouvelle." *La Pensée catholique* 8 (1948): 7–21.
Lialine, Clément. "Une étape en ecclésiologie. Réflexions sur l'encyclique *Mystici corporis*." *Irénikon* 19 (1946): 129–52, 283–317.
Lousse, Émile. *Geschiedenis van de hedendaagsche beschaving*. Bruges and Brussels: De Kinkhoren, 1945.

Lubac, Henri de, S.J. *Catholicisme. Les Aspects sociaux du dogma*. 1938. 4th ed. Paris: Éditions du Cerf, 1947. Unam Sanctam, 3.
  Eng. trans. by Lancelot C. Sheppard, *Catholicism: A Study of Dogma in Relation to the Corporate Destiny of Mankind*. New York: Longmans, and London: Burns & Oates, 1950.
———. *Corpus Mysticum. L'Eucharistie et l'Église au moyen âge*. Paris, 1944. Théologie, 3.
———. "Sur la philosophie chrétienne." *Nouvelle rev. théologique* 63 (1936): 225–53.
———. *Surnaturel. Études historiques*. Paris: Aubier, 1946. Théologie, 8.
Lusseau, Henri. "L'Évolution spirituelle." *La Pensée catholique* 1 (1946): 21–41.
Luyten, N., O.P. *De Schepping*. Utrecht: Spectrum, 1940. De Katholieke Kerk, 4.
Maes, J. D. M., O.P. "De stelregels van het Blondélisme." *Tijdschrift voor Philosophie* 3 (1941): 65–96.
Malevez, Léopold, S.J. "L'Esprit et le désir de Dieu." *Nouvelle revue théologique* 69 (1947): 3–31.
———. "La Philosophie chrétienne du progrès." *Nouvelle revue théologique* 64 (1937): 377–85.
———. "La Vision chrétienne de l'histoire." Pt. 1: "Dans la théologie de Karl Barth." Pt. 2: "Dans la théologie catholique." *Nouvelle revue théologique* 71 (1949): 113–34, 244–64.
Malmberg, Felix, S.J. "Onze eenheid met den Godmensch in de Kerk." *Bijdragen der Nederlandse Jezuieten* 5 (1942): 168–204, 360–96; 6 (1943/45): 48–63, 246–67; 8 (1947): 223–55.
Mandonnet, Pierre Félix, O.P. "La Philosophie chrétienne." In *La Philosophie chrétienne* (see below), 62–72.
Maritain, Jacques. "Le Catholicisme et la philosophie." In *Verslagboek van de Derde Philosophische Week*, 27–42. Nijmegen and Utrecht, 1934.
———. *Christianisme et démocratie*. New York: Éditions de la Maison française, 1943, and Paris, 1945.
  Eng. trans. by Doris C. Anson, *Christianity and Democracy*. New York: Scribner's, 1944, and London: Bles, 1945.
———. *Distinguer pour unir, ou les degrés du savoir*. 1932. 4th ed. Paris, 1946.
  Eng. trans. by Bernard Wall and Margot R. Adamson, *The Degrees of Knowledge*. London, 1937.
———. *Humanisme intégral. Problèmes temporels et spirituels d'une nouvelle chrétienté*. 1936. 2nd ed. Paris: Aubier, 1947.
  Eng. trans. by Margot R. Adamson, *True Humanism*. London: Bles, 1938.
  A new English translation by Joseph W. Evans, *Integral Humanism: Temporal and Spiritual Problems of a New Christendom*. New York: Scribner's, 1968.
———. *De la philosophie chrétienne*. Paris: Desclée de Brouwer, 1933. Questions disputées, 9.
  Eng. trans. by Edward H. Flannery, *An Essay on Christian Philosophy*. New York: Philosophical Library, 1955.
———. *Primauté du spirituel*. Paris: Plon, 1927. Le Roseau d'or, oeuvres et chroniques, 19
  Eng. trans. by J. F. Scanlan, *The Things That Are Not Caesar's*. New York, 1930.

Maritain, Jacques. *Du régime temporel et de la liberté.* Paris: Desclée de Brouwer, 1933. Questions disputées, 11.
Eng. trans. by Richard O'Sullivan, *Freedom in the Modern World.* 1936. New York: Gordion, 1971.
——. *Religion et culture.* 1930. 2nd ed. Paris: Desclée de Brouwer, 1946. Questions disputées, 1.
Eng. trans. by J. F. Scanlan, *Religion and Culture.* London: Sheed & Ward, 1931. Essays in Order, 1.
——. *Science et sagesse. Suivi d'éclaircissements sur la philosophie morale.* Paris: Labergerie, 1935.
Eng. trans. by Bernard Wall, *Science and Wisdom.* London: Bles, 1940.
Marrou, Henri-Irenée. "Existe-t-il une vision chrétienne de l'histoire?" In *Christianisme et histoire. XXVes Journées Universitaires Aix-en-Provence 30 mars–2 avril 1948*, 48–67. Paris, 1948.
Mayer, Anton L. "Altchristliche Liturgie und Germanentum." *Jahrbuch für Liturgiewissenschaft* 5 (1925).
——. "Die Liturgie und die Geist der Gothik." *Jahrbuch für Liturgiewissenschaft* 6 (1926).
Mercier, A., O.P. "Le Surnaturel." *Revue thomiste* 10 (1902): 125–37.
Mercier, Louis J. A. "Current Crises and the Perspective of History." *Catholic Historical Review* 24 (Oct. 1938): 257–68.
Meijer, Brocardus, O.Carm. *De eerste levensvraag in het intellectualisme van St. Thomas van Aquino en het integraal-realisme van Maurice Blondel.* Roermond and Maaseik: Romen, 1940.
Michel, Albert. "Jésus-Christ." *Dictionnaire de Théologie catholique*, 8.1 (1924): col. 1108–1411.
——. "Surnaturel." *Dictionnaire de Théologie Catholique*, 14 (1941): col. 2849–59.
Michels, Thomas, O.S.B. *Das Heilswerk der Kirche. Ein Beitrag zu einer Theologie der Geschichte.* Salzburg: Pustet, 1935. Bücherei der Salzburger Hochschulwochen, 5.
Moeller, Charles. *Humanisme et sainteté. Témoignages de la littérature occidentale.* Tournai and Paris: Casterman, 1946. Bibliothèque de l'Institut supérieur des sciences religieuses de l'Université Catholique de Louvain, 1.
Montuclard, M.-I. "La Médiation de l'Église et la médiation de l'Histoire." *Jeunesse de l'Église* 7 (1947): 9–33.
Monument to Saint Augustine, A. Edited by M. C. D'Arcy, M. Blondel, Chr. Dawson et al. London: Sheed & Ward, 1930. 2nd ed. 1945.
Mounier, Emmanuel. "Le Christianisme et l'idée de progrès." In *Progrès technique et progrès moral. Rencontres internationales de Genève, 1–13 sept. 1947*, 181–223. Neuchâtel, 1948. Reprinted in *Oeuvres d'Emmanuel Mounier*, 3:391–438. Paris: Éditions du Seuil, 1962.
Noël, Léon. "La Notion de philosophie chrétienne." *Revue néoscolastique de philosophie* 37 (1934): 337–44.
"Notion, La – de philosophie chrétienne: Séance de la Société française de philosophie du 21 mars 1931." In *Bulletin de la Société française de philosophie* 31 (1931): 37–93.

O'Connor, William R. Review of *The True Life: Sociology of the Supernatural* by Luigi Sturzo. In *Thought* 18 (1943): 749–52.
O'Mahony, James E., O.F.M.Cap. *The Desire of God in the Philosophy of St. Thomas Aquinas*. Diss. Louvain, 1928. Dublin and Cork: Cork University Press, 1929.
Padovani, Umberto Antonio. *La concezione cristiana della storia e "La Città di Dio" di S. Agostino*. Milan, 1946. Vita e Pensiero, 1.
——. "Filosofia e religione." In *Filosofi italiani contemporanei*, 387–400. 2nd ed. Milan, n.d.
——. "Filosofia religiosa tomistica e agostiniana." In *Filosofia e Cristianesimo*, 247–52. Milan, 1947.
——. "La teologia della storia." *La Scuola Cattolica* 67 (1939): 481–86.
Cf. idem, *Filosofia e teologia della storia*. Brescia: Morcelliana, 1953.
Peters, J. A. S., C.ss.R. "De wijsgeerige waarde van Sint Thomas' participatieleer." In *De Thomistische Participatieleer*, 30–54. Report of the Tenth General Meeting of the Society for Thomist Philosophy. Supplement of *Studia Catholica* (1944).
Philosophie, La – chrétienne. Vol. 2 of *Journées d'études de la Société thomiste*, Juvisy, 11 sept. 1933. Paris: Éditions du Cerf, 1934.
Pinsk, Joh. "Germanentum und katholische Kirche." *Abendland* 2 (1926/27): 360–62; 3 (1927/28): 17–19.
——. *Die sakramentale Welt*. Freiburg im Breisgau: Herder, 1938.
Cf. Johannes Pinsk, *Cycle of Christ: The Mass Texts Interpreted in the Spirit of Liturgy*. Translated by Arthur Gibson. New York: Desclée, 1966.
See also Johannes Pinsk, *Towards the Center of Christian Living*. Translated by H. E. Winstone. New York: Herder & Herder, 1961.
Ploeg, J. van der, O.P. "De verlossende kracht van Jezus' Verrijzenis." *Studia Catholica* 23 (1948): 263–65.
Poschmann, Bernhard. "'Mysteriegegenwart' in Licht des hl. Thomas." *Theologische Quartalschrift* 116 (1935): 53–116.
Przywara, Erich, S.J. "Religion und Philosophie." *Wissenschaft und Weisheit* 7 (1940): 99–107.
Putte, A. van der, O.P. "De Mysterietheologie en de scholastieke opvatting van de Oeconomia Salutis." In *Verslagboek van het Internationaal Liturgisch Congres, Maastricht, 1946*, 45–64. Maastricht-Vroenhoven, 1947.
Rabeau, Gaston. "Communication, rédigée spécialement en fonction des positions de MM. J. Maritain et M. Blondel." In *La Philosophie chrétienne*, 154–63.
Raeymaeker, Louis de. "Le Climat doctrinal chrétien et la philosophie." *Revue philosophique de Louvain* 46 (Nov. 1948): 448–62.
——. *De metaphysiek van het zijn*. 1944. 2nd rev. ed. Antwerp: Standaard-Boekhandel, and Nijmegen: Dekker & Van de Vegte, 1947. Philosophische Bibliotheek.
Eng. trans. by Edmund H. Ziegelmeyer, *The Philosophy of Being: A Synthesis of Metaphysics*. St. Louis: Herder, 1954.
Rast, Maximilian, S.J. "Zur Theodizee der Geschichte." *Stimmen der Zeit* 131 (1936): 1–11.
Robbers, J. H. "De eeuwige terugkeer der dingen." *Studiën* 62/114 (1930): 369–93.
——. *Menschelijk weten over God en schepping; hoofdstukken uit een wijsgeerige theologie in den geest van S. Thomas*. Utrecht and Brussels: Het Spectrum, 1943. Bibliotheek van Thomistische Wijsbegeerte, 1.

Robbers, Johannes Henricus, S.J. *Wijsbegeerte en openbaring*. Utrecht and Brussels: Het Spectrum, 1948. Bibliotheek van Thomistische Wijsbegeerte, 3.

———. "De zin der geschiedenis." *Bijdragen der Ned. Jezuieten* 5 (1942): 233–59.

Romualdus van Delft, O.F.M.Cap. "Het wezen van het genade- en glorieleven." In *Voordrachten en Discussies van het Werkgenootschap van Katholieke Theologen in Nederland, 1947–48*, 54–68. Roermond and Maaseik: Romen, 1949.

Rooyen, Henri van, O.S.Cr. *De Genade*. Utrecht: Het Spectrum, 1939. De Katholieke Kerk, 6.

Rosenmüller, B. "Die übernatürliche Belebung der natürlichen Ordnungen." *Der Katholische Gedanke* 9 (1936): 15–27.

Rousselot, Pierre, S.J. *L'Intellectualisme de saint Thomas*. 1908. 3rd ed. Paris: Beauchesne, 1936. Eng. trans. by James E. O'Mahony, *The Intellectualism of Saint Thomas*. New York: Sheed & Ward, 1935.

Ruding, H., S.J. "Het begrip Persoon in de leer omtrent de Hypostatische Vereniging." *Bijdragen der Nederlandse Jezuieten* 7 (1946): 231–72.

Salvatorelli, Luigi. *Benedikt, der Abt des Abendlandes*. Hamburg: Goverts, 1937. German translation of *San Benedetto e l'Italia del suo tempo*, Bari, 1929.

———. *Storia d'Italia*. Vol. 3: *L'Italia medioevale*. Milan, 1938.

———. *Sommario della storia d'Italia dai tempi preistorici ai nostri giorno*. Turin: Einaudi, 1938. Eng. trans. by Bernard Miall, *A Concise History of Italy from Prehistoric Times to Our Own Day*. London: Allen & Unwin, and New York: Oxford UP, 1940.

Sassen, Ferdinand. "De opvatting van de geschiedenis bij de Scholastieken van de 12e eeuw." In *Geschiedenis; een bundel studies over den zin der Geschiedenis*, 55–78. Assen: Van Gorcum, 1944. Festschrift for Prof. Dr. W. J. Aalders.

Sawicki, Franz. *Geschichtsphilosophie*. 1920. 3rd ed. Munich and Kempten: Kösel, 1923. Philosophische Handbibliothek, 2.

Schilfgaarde, Paul van. *De Zin der geschiedenis; een wijsgeerige bespreking van den gang der menschheid*. Vol. 2: *Geschiedkundige theorieën*. Leiden: Brill, 1947.

Schmaus, Michael. *Katholische Dogmatik*. 3 vols. Munich: Hübner, 1938–40.

Schmidt, Wilhelm. *Rassen und Völker in Vorgeschichte und Geschichte des Abendlandes*. Vol. 3: *Gegenwart und Zukunft des Abendlandes*. Lucerne: Josef Stocker, 1949. Sammlung Stocker, 3.

———. "Werdendes Abendland." In Friedrich Deassauer et al., *Erbe und Zukunft des Abendlandes*, 7–17. Bern: Francke, 1948.

Schnürer, Gustav. *Die Anfänge der abendländischen Völkergemeinschaft*. Freiburg im Breisgau: Herder, 1932. Geschichte der führenden Völker, 11.

———. *Katholische Kirche und Kultur im 18. Jahrhundert*. Paderborn: Schöningh, 1941.

———. *Katholische Kirche und Kultur in der Barockzeit*. Paderborn: Schöningh, 1937.

———. *Kirche und Kultur im Mittelalter*. 3 vols. Paderborn: Schöningh, 1924–29. 2nd ed. 1927–30. Eng. trans. of vol. 1 by George J. Undreiner, *Church and Culture in the Middle Ages, A.D. 350-814*. Paterson, N.J.: St. Anthony Guild Press, 1956.

———. *Über Periodisierung der Weltgeschichte*. Rectorial Address delivered at the University of Freiburg, Switzerland, 15 Nov. 1900.

Schwartz, Balduin. "Jacques Maritain und die christliche Geschichtsphilosophie." *Schweizerische Rundschau* 37 (1937): 473–80.
Sciacca, Michele Federico. *Italienische Philosophie der Gegenwart.* Translated from the Italian by Ernst Schneider. Bern: Francke, 1948. Bibliographische Einführungen in das Studium der Philosophie, 7.
Seiller, Léon, O.F.M. *L'Activité humaine du Christ selon Duns Scot.* Paris: Éditions Franciscaines, 1944. Études de science religieuse, 3.
Sertillanges, Antonin-Gilbert, O.P. Report of his contribution in *La Philosophie chrétienne.*
Söhngen, Gottlieb. *Der Wesensaufbau des Mysteriums.* Bonn: Hanstein, 1938.
Solages, Bruno de. "La Pensée chrétienne face à l'Évolution." *Bulletin de littérature ecclésiastique,* Chronique (oct.–déc., 1947): ciii–cxvi.
Soukup, Leopold, O.S.B. "Teilnahme an Gott." *Divus Thomas* 19 (1941): 157–65.
Spiess, Emil J. *Grundfragen der Geschichtsphilosophie.* Schwyz: Maria Hilf, 1937.
Steenberghen, Fernand van. "La deuxième Journée d'Études de la Société thomiste et la notion de 'philosophie chrétienne.'" *Revue néoscolastique de philosophie* 35 (1933): 539–54.
Steins Bisschop, L., S.J. "Over het bestaan eener Christelijke Wijsbegeerte." In *Het vraagstuk der Christelijke Wijsbegeerte,* 28–55. Report of the 1st General Meeting of the Society for Thomist Philosophy. Supplement of *Studia Catholica* (1934).
Stolz, Anselm, O.S.B. *Anthropologia Theologica.* Freiburg im Breisgau, 1940. Manuale Theologiae Dogmaticae, vol. 4.
———. "Natur und Gnade." *Der Katholische Gedanke* 9 (1936): 116–23.
Sturzo, Luigi. "History and Philosophy." *Thought* 21 (1946): 45–62.
———. *Inner Laws of Society: A New Sociology.* Translated from the Italian by Barbara Barclay Carter. New York: P. J. Kenedy, 1944.
———. *La vera vita, sociologia del soprannaturale.* Rome, 1947.
Eng. trans. by Barbara Barclay Carter, *The True Life: Sociology of the Supernatural.* Washington: Catholic University of America Press, 1943.
Suenens, Leo Jozef. "Les Controverses récentes autour de la notion de philosophie chrétienne." *Collectanea Mechliniensia* 21 (1932): 393–405.
Taymans d'Eypernon, Francis, S.J. *Le Mystère primordial. La Trinité dans sa vivante image.* Brussels: Édition universelle, and Paris: Desclée de Brouwer, 1946. Museum Lessianum; Section Théologique, 41.
Teilhard de Chardin, Pierre, S.J. "La Crise présente. Réflexions d'un naturaliste." *Les Études philosophiques* 233 (1937): 145–65.
Theeuws, Paul. "Sacrale en profane Christenheid." *Collectanea Mechliniensia* 32 (1947): 257–69.
Thieme, Karl. *Gott und die Geschichte. Zehn Aufsätze zu den Grundfragen der Theologie und der Historik.* Freiburg: Herder, 1948.
Thils, Gustave. *Christendom en menschelijke instellingen.* Bruges, 1945. Sociale Studiën, 1.
———. *Naar een nieuwe voorstelling van de katholieke zedenleer.* Brussels and Amsterdam, 1947. Orig. title: *Tendances actuelles en théologie morale.* Gembloux: Duculot, 1940.
———. *Théologie des réalités terrestres.* Vol. 1: *Préludes.* Bruges: Desclée, 1946. Vol. 2: *Théologie de l'histoire.* Bruges: Desclée, 1949.

Timp, P. M., O.P. *De Verlosser.* Utrecht: Het Spectrum, 1948. De Katholieke Kerk, 5.

Toynbee, Arnold J. *Civilization on Trial.* Oxford and New York: Oxford University Press, 1948.

Tromp, Sebastianus. *Corpus Christi quod est Ecclesia.* 2 vols. Rome: Università Gregoriana, 1937. Vol. 1: *Introductio generalis,* 1937. Vol. 2, rev. ed., 1946.

Tschipke, Theophil, O.P. *Die Menschheit Christi als Heilsorgan der Gottheit, unter besonderer Berücksichtigung der Lehre des heiligen Thomas von Aquin.* Freiburg im Breisgau: Herder, 1940. Freiburger Theologische Studien, 55.

Vraagstuk, Het – der Christelijke Wijsbegeerte. Report of the First General Meeting of the Society for Thomist Philosophy. Supplement of *Studia Catholica* (1934).

Vollenhoven, D. H. T. "The Course of Plato's Development." In *Library of the Xth International Congress of Philosophy.* Vol. 2: *Philosophical Essays,* 1–16. Amsterdam: Veen, 1948.

———. "Richtlijnen ter oriëntatie in de gangbare wijsbegeerte; pt. II: Het Aristotelische Realisme." *Philosophia Reformata* 7 (1942): 9–46.

Vonier, Anscar, O.S.B. "Vom Mysterium der Verherrlichung Christi." *Der Katholische Gedanke* 8 (1935): 211–19.

Vries, Joseph de, S.J. "Christliche Philosophie." *Scholastik* 12 (1937): 1–16.

Vugts, Ant., M.S.C. "De vereenigingsgenade van Christus in de theologie van S. Thomas en diens tijdgenooten." *Bijdragen der Nederlandse Jezuieten* 5 (1942): 303–59.

Cf. idem, *La Grace d'union d'après S. Thomas d'Aquin. Essai historique et doctrinal.* Tilburg: Missiehuis, 1946. Diss., Collegium Maximum, Maastricht, 1942.

Weyers, M.-R., O.P. "In Christo Jesu." *Revue thomiste* 47 (1947): 499–516.

Windelband, Wilhelm. *Präludien. Aufsätze und Reden zur Philosophie und ihrer Geschichte.* 2 vols. 1907. 4th ed. Tübingen: Mohr, 1911.

Eng. trans. by Joseph McCabe, *An Introduction to Philosophy.* London: Allen & Unwin, and New York: Dover, 1921.

Winzen, Damasus, O.S.B. "Note complémentaire et réponse à quelques critiques." *Les Questions liturgiques et paroissiales* 24 (1939): 108–13.

Wolf, Walther, *Wesen und Wert der Aegyptologie.* Glückstadt, Hamburg and New York: Augustin, 1937.

Woltjer, R. H. *Het Woord Gods en het woord der menschen.* Utrecht: Ruys, 1913.

Zechmeister, August. *Das Herz und das Kommende. Von der Einsamkeit des Christen in dieser Zeit.* 1945. Reprint. Vienna: Amandus, 1946.

WORKS CITED IN PART TWO

Acton, Lord. "On the Study of History," Inaugural lecture, 11 June 1895. In idem, *Lectures on Modern History*, 1–17. London: Macmillan, 1906. Reprinted 1926.
Adam, Karl. "Deutsches Volkstum und katholisches Christentum." *Theologische Quartalschrift* 144 (1933): 55–64.
Algemene Geschiedenis der Nederlanden. Edited by J. A. van Houtte et al. 12 vols. Utrecht: De Haan, 1949–58.
Anderle, Othmar F. "Arnold J. Toynbee und die Problematik der geschichtlichen Sinndeutung." *Die Welt als Geschichte. Zeitschrift für Universalgeschichte* 20 (1960): 143–56.
Aron, Raymond. *Essai sur la théorie de l'histoire dans l'Allemagne contemporaine. La Philosophie critique de l'histoire*. Paris: Vrin, 1938. 2nd ed., 1950.
———. *Introduction à la philosophie de l'histoire. Essai sur les limites de l'objectivité historique*. Paris: Gallimard, 1938.
    Eng. trans. by George J. Irwin, *Introduction to the Philosophy of History: An Essay on the Limits of Historical Objectivity*. Boston: Beacon, 1961.
Aulard, François-Alphonse. *Le Patriotisme français de la Renaissance à la Révolution*. Paris, 1921.
Bakker, Jan T. "Christus en de geschiedenis." *Homiletica* 17.3 (1958): 13–20.
Barth, Karl. *Christengemeinde und Bürgergemeinde*. Zurich: Zollikon, 1938.
———. *Die Kirchliche Dogmatik*. 14 vols. Zurich: Zollikon, 1932–70.
    Eng. trans. by Geoffrey W. Bromiley, *Church Dogmatics*. 13 vols. Edinburgh: Clark, 1936–69.
Baethgen, Friedrich. "Zur geistigen Entwicklungsgeschichte Rankes in seiner Frühzeit." In Werner Conze, ed., *Deutschland und Europa. Festschrift für Hans Rothfels*. Düsseldorf: Droste, 1951.
Bandmann, Günter. *Mittelalterliche Architektur als Bedeutungsträger*. Berlin: Mann, 1951.
Barraclough, Geoffrey. *History and the Common Man*. London: The Historical Association, 1967.
Bavinck, Johann H. *Flitsen en fragmenten*. Kampen: Kok, 1959.
Beard, Charles A. and Alfred Vagts. "Currents of Thought in Historiography." *American Historical Review* 42 (1936/37): 460–83.
Beck, Heinrich. *Kulturphilosophie der Technik. Perspektiven zu Technik - Menschheit - Zukunft*. Trier: Spee-Verlag, 1979.
Bellon, Karel Leopold. "Onder welke voorwaarden is de wetenschap der geschiedenis mogelijk?" *Tijdschrift voor Philosophie* 15 (1953): 163–78.
———. *Wijsbegeerte der geschiedenis*. Antwerp and Amsterdam: Standaard-Boekhandel, 1953.
Berkhof, Hendrikus. *Christus de zin der geschiedenis*. Nijkerk: Callenbach, 1958.
    Eng. trans. from the 4th ed. of 1962 by Lambertus Buurman, *Christ the Meaning of History*. London: SCM Press, 1966.

Berkouwer, Gerrit Cornelis. *De Mens het beeld Gods*. Kampen: Kok, 1957. Dogmatische Studiën 10.
   Eng. trans. by Dirk W. Jellema, *Man, the Image of God*. Grand Rapids, Mich.: Eerdmans, 1962. Studies in Dogmatics.
——. *De Voorzienigheid Gods*. Kampen: Kok, 1950. Dogmatische Studiën 4.
   Eng. trans. by Lewis B. Smedes, *The Providence of God*. Grand Rapids, Mich.: Eerdmans, 1952. Studies in Dogmatics.
Boer, Willem den. *Benaderbaar verleden*. Leiden: Universitaire Pers, 1952.
Boogman, Johan Christiaan. *Vaderlandse geschiedenis (na de middeleeuwen) in hedendaags perspectief; enige kanttekeningen en beschouwingen*. Inaugural lecture, University of Groningen. Groningen: Wolters, 1959.
Bouman, Pieter J. *In de ban der geschiedenis*. Assen: Van Gorcum, 1961.
Brandon, S. G. F. *History, Time and Deity: A Historical and Comparative Study of the Conception of Time in Religious Thought and Practice*. Manchester: Manchester University Press, 1965.
Braudel, Fernand. "L'Apport de l'histoire des civilisations." *La Table Ronde*, 137 (May, 1959), 54–73.
   Eng. trans., "The History of Civilizations: The Past Explains the Present," in idem, *On History*, 177–218.
——. *La Méditerranée et le monde méditerranéen à l'époque de Philippe II*. Paris: Armand Colin, 1949. 2nd rev. ed. 2 vols. 1966.
   Eng. trans. by Siân Reynolds, *The Mediterranean and the Mediterranean World in the Age of Philip II*. New York: Harper & Row, 1973.
——. *On History*. Translated by Sarah Matthews. Chicago: University of Chicago Press, 1980.
——. "Les Responsabilités de l'histoire." *Cahiers internationaux de sociologie* 10 (1951): 3–18.
——. "Sur une conception de l'Histoire sociale." Review of *Neue Wege der Sozialgeschichte* (1956) by Otto Brunner. *Annales* 14 (1959): 308–19.
   Eng. trans., "On a Concept of Social History,"in idem, *On History*, 120–31.
Bredero, Adriaan H. "Een Mythe der Middeleeuwen." *Te Elfder Ure* 3 (1956): 40–55, 78–89.
Bultmann, Rudolf. "Zur Frage der Entmythologisierung. Antword an Karl Jaspers." *Theologische Zeitschrift* 10 (1954): 81–95.
Butterfield, Herbert. *Christianity and History*. London: Bell, 1949.
——. "The Rôle of the Individual in History." *History* 40 (1955): 1–17.
   Reprinted in idem,*Writings on Christianity and History*, 17–36. Edited by C. T. McIntire. New York: Oxford University Press, 1979.
Carles, Jules, S.J. "L'Unité du vivant." *Les Études philosophiques* 41 (1966): 29–41.
Chanson, Paul. *La Continuité pontificale*. Paris, 1935.
Cremers, V. *Kerk en Staat*. Antwerp and Amsterdam: Standaard-Boekhandel, 1927.
Cullmann, Oscar. *Christus und die Zeit. Die urchristliche Zeit- und Geschichtsauffassung*. Zurich: Zollikon, 1945.
   Eng. trans. by Floyd V. Filson, *Christ and Time: The Primitive Christian Conception of Time and History*. Philadelphia: Westminster, 1964.
Daniélou, Jean, S.J. "Christianisme et progrès." *Les Études philosophiques* 255 (1947): 399–402.

Bibliography: Part Two 411

Daniélou, Jean, S.J. "Essai sur le mystère de l'histoire." Paris: Éditions du Seuil, 1953.
   Eng. trans. by Nigel Abercrombie, *The Lord of History: Reflections on the Inner Meaning of History*. London: Longmans, 1958.
Dawson, Christopher. "The Problem of Metahistory." *History Today* 1.6 (1951): 9–12.
   Reprinted in idem, *Dynamics of World History*, 287–93. Edited by John J. Mulloy. New York: Sheed & Ward, 1956.
Delos, Joseph Thomas, O.P. *La Société internationale et les principes du droit public*. 1929. 2nd ed. Paris: Pedone, 1950.
Didier, Georges, S.J. "Eschatologie et engagement chrétien." *Nouvelle revue théologique* 75.1 (1953): 1–14.
Dieks, Dennis. *Studies in the Foundations of Physics: A Discussion of Some Relations Between Physics, the Foundations of Physics, and the Philosophy of Science*. Utrecht: Elinkwijk, 1981.
Dilthey, Wilhelm. *Gesammelte Schriften*. 21 vols. Göttingen: Vandenhoeck & Ruprecht, 1960–
Dooyeweerd, Herman. *De Wijsbegeerte der Wetsidee*. 3 vols. Amsterdam: H. J. Paris, 1935–36.
   Rev. ed., in Eng. trans. by David H. Freeman et al., *A New Critique of Theoretical Thought*. 4 vols. Philadelphia: Presbyterian & Reformed, 1953–58.
Duchrow, Ulrich. "Der sogenannte psychologische Zeitbegriff Augustins im Verhältnis zur physikalischen und geschichtlichen Zeit." *Zeitschrift für Theologie und Kirche* 63 (1966): 267–88.
Duintjer, Otto Dirk. *De Vraag naar het transcendentale, vooral in verband met Kant en Heidegger*. Leiden: University Press, 1966.
Duynstee, F. J. F. M. *Het glazen huis*. 2nd ed. The Hague, 1946.
Eliade, Mircea. *Le Mythe de l'éternel retour*. Paris: Gallimard, 1949.
   Eng. trans. by Willard R. Trask, *The Myth of the Eternal Return*. New York: Pantheon, 1954.
Enklaar, D. Th. Review of *Mensen en meningen* by Anton van Duinkerken. In *Bijdragen tot de Geschiedenis der Nederlanden* 6 (1951/52): 240–41.
Ennen, Edith. *Frühgeschichte der europäischen Stadt*. Bonn: Röhrscheid, 1953.
Faulhaber, Michael von. *Christentum und Germanentum*. Sermon on the feast of St. Sylvester, 31 Dec. 1933. Munich, 1934.
Febvre, Lucien. "Sur une autre histoire sociale." *Revue de métaphysique et de morale* 58 (1949).
   Reprinted in idem, *Combats pour l'histoire*. Paris: Armand Colin, 1953.
   Eng. trans. by Keith Folca, "A New Kind of History." In Peter Burke, ed., *A New Kind of History: From the Writings of Lucien Febvre*, 27–43. London: Routledge & Kegan Paul, 1973.
———. "Pro parva nostra domo. Scolies sur deux articles belges." *Annales* 8 (1953): 512–18.
———. "Une Question mal posée: les origines de la réforme française et le problème général des causes de la réforme." *Revue historique* 161 (1929): 1–73.
   Eng. trans. by Keith Folca, "The Origins of the French Reformation: A Badly-put Question?" In Peter Burke, ed., *A New Kind of History: From the Writings of Lucien Febvre*, 44–107. London: Routledge & Kegan Paul, 1973.

Ferlus, Dom François, O.B. *Le Patriotisme chrétien. Discours prêché aux États du Languedoc en 1787*. Montpellier, 1787.

Fichtenau, Heinrich. "Karl der Große und das Kaisertum." *Mitteilungen des Instituts für Österreichische Geschichtsforschung* 61 (1953): 257–334.

Finke, Heinrich. *Die Frau im Mittelalter*. Munich and Kempten: Kösel, 1913.

———. *Über Friedrich und Dorothea Schlegel*. Cologne: Bachem, 1918.

Fischer, Fritz. "Objektivität und Subjektivität – ein Prinzipienstreit in der amerikanischen Geschichtsschreibung." In Alfred Hermann, ed., *Aus Geschichte und Politik. Festschrift zum 70. Geburtstag von Ludwig Bergsträsser*, 167–82. Düsseldorf, 1954.

Freyer, Hans. "Das Problem der Einheit der Weltgeschichte." In *Philosophische Vorträge und Diskussionen. Bericht über den Mainzer Philosophen-Kongress, 1948*, 180–84. Wurzach: Birnbach, 1948.

Fromm, Erich. *Man for Himself: An Inquiry into the Psychology of Ethics*. New York: Holt, Rinehart & Winston, 1947.

Fruin, Robert J. *Verspreide Geschriften*. 10 vols. The Hague: Nijhoff, 1902–05.

Gloege, Gerhard. "Vom Sinn der Weltgeschichte. Überlegungen zum Thema 'Heilsgeschehen und Weltgeschichte.'" *Lutherische Monatshefte* 2 (1963): 112–22. Reprinted in idem, *Heilsgeschehen und Welt. Theologische Traktate*, 1:27–52. Göttingen: Vandenhoeck & Ruprecht, 1965.

Görres, Joseph. *Gesammelte Schriften*. Edited by Wilhelm Schellberg et al. 11 vols. Cologne: Gilde-Verlag, 1928. Published by the Görres Gesellschaft.

Gollwitzer, Heinz. *Europabild und Europagedanke. Beiträge zur deutschen Geistesgeschichte des 18. und 19. Jahrhunderts*. Munich: Beck, 1951. Rev. ed., 1964.

Groen, P. *Grenzen. Voordracht, uitgesproken bij het afscheid als hoogleraar in de Wis- en Natuurkunde aan de Vrije Universiteit, op 9 maart 1979*. Amsterdam: Free University Press, 1979.

Guardini, Romano. "Erscheinung und Wesen der Romantik." In Theodor Steinbüchel, ed., *Romantik. Ein Zyklus Tübinger Vorlesungen*. Tübingen and Stuttgart: Wunderlich, 1948.

Hartman, Max. *Naturwissenschaft und Religion*. Stuttgart: Gustav Fischer, 1940.

Hasenhüttl, Gotthold. *Geschichte und existenziales Denken*. Wiesbaden: Franz Steiner, 1965.

Hayes, Carlton J. H. *Essays on Nationalism*. New York: Macmillan, 1926.

Hendrikx, Ephraem, O.E.S.A. *Lekenspiritualiteit, een probleem in de geschiedenis van de Kerk*. Utrecht: Dekker & Van de Vegt, 1959.

Hegel, G. W. F. *Einleitung in die Geschichte der Philosophie*. Joh. Hoffmeister, ed. Berlin: Akademie-Verlag, 1966.

———. *Vorlesungen über die Philosophie der Weltgeschichte*. Berlin, 1837. Eng. trans. by J. Sibree, *The Philosophy of History*. London: Colonial Press, 1899.

Heitler, Walther Heinrich. "Kausalität und Teleologie in der Sicht der heutigen Naturwissenschaft." *Universitas. Zeitschrift für Wissenschaft, Kunst und Literatur* 21 (1966): 1–13.

Helmich, Werner Bernhard. *Theorie van het rechtsmisbruik*. Diss., Nijmegen, 1945.

Herzfeld, Ernst Emil. *Archeological History of Iran*. London: Oxford University Press, 1935.

———. *Iran in the Ancient East*. London and New York: Oxford University Press, 1941.

Höfler, Otto. *Der Runenstein von Røk und die germanische Individualweihe.* Tübingen: Niemeyer, 1952.
———. "Die Trelleborg auf Seeland under der Runenstein von Røk." *Anzeiger der philologisch-historische Klasse der Österreichische Akademie der Wissenschaft* (1948): 9–37.
Huizinga, Johan. *Verzamelde Werken.* 8 vols. Haarlem: Tjeenk Willink, 1948–53.
Janssen, Johannes. *An meine Kritiker.* Rev. ed. Freiburg im Breisgau: Herder, 1891.
Jaspers, Karl. *Vom Ursprung und Ziel der Geschichte.* Munich: Piper, 1949.
> Eng. trans. by Michael Bullock, *The Origin and Goal of History.* New Haven, Conn.: Yale University Press, 1953.

Jong, Henk de. *Bron en norm; een bundel bijbelstudies.* Kampen: Kok, 1979.
Kearney, Hugh F. "Christianity and the Study of History." *The Downside Review* 67 (1949): 62–73.
Köhler, Oskar. "Versuch Kategorien der Weltgeschichte zu bestimmen." *Saeculum* 9 (1958): 446–57.
———. "Was ist 'Welt' in der Weltgeschichte?" *Saeculum* 6 (1955): 1–9.
Krüger, Gerhard. *Freiheit und Weltverwaltung. Aufsätze zur Philosophie der Geschichte.* Munich: Karl Alber, 1958.
Kuyper, Abraham. *De Gemeene Gratie.* 3 vols. Leiden: Donner, 1902–05. 3rd impr., Kampen: Kok, n.d. [1931–32].
Kuypers, Karel. "Die Frage nach dem Sinn der Geschichte." In H. J. [van Eikema] Hommes et al., eds., *Philosophy and Christianity: Philosophical Essays Dedicated to Professor Dr. Herman Dooyeweerd,* 100–123. Kampen: Kok, and Amsterdam: North-Holland, 1965. Reprinted in K. Kuypers, *Verspreide Geschriften,* 1:236–49. 2 vols. Assen: Van Gorcum, 1968.
Kwant, Remy C. "De Historie en het absolute." *Tijdschrift voor Philosophie* 17 (1955): 255–305.
Lasaulx, Ernst von. *Neuer Versuch einer alten, auf die Wahrheit der Tatsachen gegründeten Philosophie der Geschichte.* Edited by Eugen Thurnher. Vienna: Verlag für Geschichte und Politik, 1952.
Lavedan, Pierre. *Histoire de l'urbanisme.* 3 vols. Paris: Laurent, 1926–52.
Leclercq, Jean, O.S.B. *L'Amour des lettres et le désir de Dieu.* Paris: Éditions du Cerf, 1957.
> Eng. trans. by Catharine Misrahi, *The Love of Learning and the Desire for God: A Study of Monastic Culture.* New York: Fordham University Press, 1961.

Le Goff, Jacques. "Au Moyen Âge: Temps de l'Église et temps du marchand." *Annales* 15 (1960): 417–33.
> Reprinted in idem, *Pour un autre Moyen Âge. Temps, travail et culture en Occident.* Paris: Gallimard, 1977.
> Eng. trans. by Arthur Goldhammer, *Time, Work, and Culture in the Middle Ages,* at 29–42. Chicago: University of Chicago Press, 1980.

Lemberg, Eugen. *Geschichte des Nationalismus in Europa.* Stuttgart: Schwab, 1950.
Lenhart, Ludwig. "Christentum und Germanentum im Werturteil der letzten Jahrhunderte." *Beiträge zur christliche Philosophie* 1 (1947): 1–39.
L'Orange, Hans-Peter. "Trelleborg - Aggersborg og de kongelige byer i Osten." *Viking* (Oslo) 16 (1953): 307–31.

Löwith, Karl. "Die Dynamik der Geschichte und der Historismus." *Eranos-Jahrbuch* 221 (1952): 217–54.

———. *Meaning in History: The Theological Implications of the Philosophy of History.* Chicago: University of Chicago Press, 1949.

———. "Natur und Geschichte." *Die Neue Rundschau* 62 (1951): 65–78.

———. *Der Weltbegriff der neuzeitlichen Philosophie.* Heidelberg: Winter, 1960.

Mackay, Ernest John Henry. *Early Indus Civilizations.* London: Luzac, 1948.

———. *Die Induskultur. Ausgrabungen in Mohenjo-Daro und Harappa.* Leipzig: Brockhaus, 1938. Trans. of *The Indus Civilization.* London: Dickson, 1935.

Maistre, Joseph Marie, comte de. *Oeuvres complètes.* 14 vols. Lyon: Vitte & Perrussel, 1884–86.

Marrou, Henri-Irénée. *L'Ambivalence du temps de l'histoire chez saint Augustin.* Paris and Montréal: Vrin, 1950.

———. "Comment comprendre le métier d'historien?" In *Encyclopédie de la Pléiade*, 11:1467–1539. Edited by Charles Samaran. Paris: Gallimard, 1961.

———. *De la Connaissance historique.* Paris: Éditions du Seuil, 1954. Eng. trans. by Robert J. Olson, *The Meaning of History.* Baltimore and Dublin: Helicon, 1966.

———. "Existe-t-il une vision chrétienne de l'histoire?" In *XXVes Journées Universitaires*, 48–67. Paris, 1948.

———. *Les Troubadours.* Paris: Éditions du Seuil, 1971.

Cf. Henri Davenson [pseud.]. *Les Troubadours.* Paris: Éditions du Seuil, 1961.

———. *Saint Augustin et l'augustinisme.* Paris: Éditions du Seuil, 1955.

———. "La Théologie de l'histoire." Report with discussion. In *Augustinus Magister.* Proceedings of the International Augustinian Congress, Paris, 1954. Supplement of *Revue des études augustiniennes* (1955). 3:193–212.

———. *Théologie de l'histoire.* Paris: Éditions du Seuil, 1969. Eng. trans. by Violet Nevile, *Time and Timeliness.* New York: Sheed & Ward, 1969.

Mayer, J. E. "Vollkommenheit in dieser Zeit." In Karl Rudolf, ed., *Seid vollkommen. Formen und Führung christlicher Aszese.* Vienna: Herder, 1955.

Meinecke, Friedrich. *Die Entstehung des Historismus.* Munich: Oldenbourg, 1959. Eng. trans. by J. E. Anderson, *Historism: The Rise of a New Historical Outlook.* London: Routledge & Kegan Paul, 1972.

Meinhold, Peter. "Grundfragen kirchlicher Geschichtsdeutung." In Hans Asmussen and Wilhelm Stählin, eds. *Die Katholizität der Kirche. Beiträge zum Gespräch zwischen der evangelischen und der römisch-katholischen Kirche*, 133–60. Stuttgart: Evangelische Verlagswerk, 1957.

———. "Weltgeschichte - Kirchengeschichte - Heilsgeschichte." *Saeculum* 9 (1958): 261–81.

Melsen, A. G. M. van. "Reflecties van een 20e eeuwse Nederlandse Katholiek over de tolerantie." *Wending* 4 (1949): 246–47.

Müller, Adam Heinrich. *Die Elemente der Staatskunst. 36 Vorlesungen.* Dresden, 1809. Reprint. Berlin: Haude & Spener, 1968.

Müller, Heinz. "Die Hand Gottes in der Geschichte. Zum Geschichtsverständnis von Augustinus bis Otto von Freising." Diss., University of Hamburg, 1949.

Münzhuber, Joseph. "Erkenntnis und Glaube." *Zeitschrift für philosophische Forschung* 3 (1948): 60–73.
Niebuhr, Reinhold. *Beyond Tragedy: Essays on the Christian Interpretation of History*. New York: Scribner's, 1937.
———. *Faith and History: A Comparison of Christian and Modern Views of History*. New York: Scribner's, 1949.
Noack, Ulrich. "Stadtbaukunst." In B. Hackelsberger et al., eds. *Kunstgeschichtliche Beiträge. Festschrift für Kurt Bauch*. Munich: Deutscher Kunstverlag, 1957.
Nørlund, Poul. *Trelleborg*. Copenhagen: Glydendal, 1948.
Pauwels, C. F., O.P. "Godsdienstvrijheid en gewetensvrijheid." *Het Schild* 26 (1948–49): 145–53.
Pernoud, Régine. *Lumière du Moyen-Âge*. Paris: Grasset, 1944.
    Eng. trans. by Joyce Emerson, *The Glory of the Medieval World*. London: Dennis Dobson, 1950.
Ploumen, P. *De Katholieke levensopvatting; het burgerschap van twee rijken, kerk en staat*. 's-Hertogenbosch (Bois-le-Duc): Malmberg, 1937. Studiën-reeks, 2.
Pompignan, Jean-Jacques Lefranc, marquis de. *Oeuvres*. 4 vols. Paris: Nyon, 1770–84.
Pope, Arthur Upham. *Masterpieces of Persian Art*. New York: Dryden, 1945.
———. *Persian Architecture: The Triumph of Form and Color*. New York: George Braziller, 1965.
———. *A Survey of Persian Art from Prehistoric Times to the Present*. 6 vols. London and New York: Oxford University Press, 1938–39.
Propyläen-Weltgeschichte. Edited by Walter Goetz. 11 vols. Berlin: Propyläen-Verlag, 1929–33. 2nd ed. by Golo Mann. 12 vols. 1961–65.
Raeymaeker, Louis de. "Het menselijk gelaat, uitdrukking van transcendentie, naar de filosofische opvatting van Emmanuel Levinas." *Tijdschrift voor Filosofie* 32 (1970): 375–454.
Ranke, Leopold (von). *Das Briefwerk*. Edited by Walter Peter Fuchs. Hamburg: Hoffmann & Campe, 1949.
———. "Über die Epochen der neueren Geschichte." 1854. Reprinted in idem, *Weltgeschichte*, XI/2:1–9. Berlin, 1888.
    Eng. trans. (excerpt) in Georg Iggers and Konrad von Moltke, eds. *The Theory and Practice of History: Leopold von Ranke*, 51–6. Indianapolis: Bobbs-Merrill, 1973.
Ranke-Heinemann, Uta. "Die Gottesliebe als ein Motiv für die Entstehung des Mönchtums." *Münchener Theologische Zeitschrift* 8 (1957): 289–94.
Read, Conyers. "The Social Responsibilities of the Historian." *American Historical Review* 55 (1949/50): 275–85.
Ridderbos, Herman N. *Paulus; ontwerp van zijn theologie*. Kampen: Kok, 1966.
    Eng. trans. by John Richard de Witt, *Paul: An Outline of His Theology*. Grand Rapids, Mich.: Eerdmans, 1975.
———. Review of *Christus de zin der geschiedenis* by Hendrikus Berkhof. In *Gereformeerd Weekblad*, 5 September – 3 October 1958.
———. *Zelfopbaring en zelfverberging; het historisch karakter van Jezus' messiaanse zelfopenbaring volgens de synoptische evangeliën*. Kampen: Kok, 1946.

Ritter, Gerhard. *Die Dämonie der Macht. Betrachtungen über Geschichte und Wesen des Machtsproblems im politischen Denken der Neuzeit*. 1940. 6th rev. ed. Munich: Leibniz, 1948. Eng. trans. by F. W. Pick, *The Corrupting Influence of Power*. Hadleigh, Essex: Tower Bridge, 1952.

——. "Zur Problematik gegenwärtiger Geschichtsschreibung." In idem, *Lebendige Vergangenheit. Beiträge zur historisch-politischen Selbstbesinning*, 255–83. Munich: Oldenbourg, 1958.

Robinson, James Harvey. *The New History: Essays Illustrating the Modern Historical Outlook*. New York: Macmillan, 1912.

Romein, Jan Marius. *In de hof der historie; kleine encyclopedie der theoretische geschiedenis*. Amsterdam: Querido, 1951.

——. "Integrale geschiedschrijving." In *Eender en anders; twaalf nagelaten essays*, 25–42. Amsterdam: Querido, 1964.

Romme, Carl P. M. *Nieuwe grondwetsartikelen. Een bijdrage tot herstel en vernieuwing*. Amsterdam: Urbi et Orbi, n.d. [1943].

Rommen, Heinrich Albert. *Die Staatslehre der Franz Suarez, S.J.* Munich: Gladbach, 1926.

Rousset, Paul. "La Croyance en la justice immanente à l'époque féodale."*Le Moyen-Âge* 54 (1948): 225–48.

Ruler, Arnold A. van. *Kuypers idee eener christelijke cultuur*. Nijkerk: Callenbach, 1940.

Salomon, Gottfried. *Das Mittelalter als Ideal der Romantik*. Munich: Drei Masken, 1922.

Sawicki, Franz. *Geschichtsphilosophie*. 1920. 3rd ed. Munich and Kempten: Kösel, 1923. Philosophische Handbibliothek, 2.

Schelven, Aart A. van. "Geschiedeniswetenschap en Voorzienigheidsgeloof."*Almanak van het Studentencorps aan de Vrije Universiteit, 1924*, 81–88. Amsterdam, 1924.

Schellberg, Wilhelm, ed. *Joseph von Görres' Ausgewählte Werke und Briefe*. 2 vols. Munich and Kempten: Kösel, 1911.

Schlegel, Friedrich von. *Sämtliche Werke*. 14 vols. 1810. 2nd impr. Vienna: Klang, 1846.

Schmidt, Erich Friedrich. *Persepolis*. 3 vols. Chicago: University of Chicago Press, 1953–69.

Schmidt, Heinrich. *Die deutschen Städtechroniken als Spiegel des bürgerlichen Selbstverständnisses im Spätmittelalter*. Göttingen: Vandenhoeck & Ruprecht, 1958. Diss., University of Göttingen, 1958.

Schoonenberg, Piet J. A. M. "Onderwerpt de aarde." *Nederlandse Katholieke Stemmen* 52 (1956): 162–65.

Schultz, Carl Georg. "Aggersborg." *Vikingelejren ved Limfjorden fra Nationalmuseets Arbejdsmark* (1949): 91–108.

Schwarz, Richard. "Die Frage nach dem Sinn der Geschichte." *Wissenschaft und Weltbild* 14.3 (1961): 161–79.

Seidlmayer, Michael. *Das Mittelalter. Umrisse und Ergebnisse des Zeitalters*. Regensburg: Pustet, 1949.

——. "Religiös-ethische Probleme des italienischen Humanismus." *Germanisch-Romanische Monatschrift* 39 (1958): 101–13.

Spaemann, Robert. "Über die kontroverse Natur der Philosophie." *Neue Zürcher Zeitung*, 25/6 Aug. 1979.
Staudinger, Hugo. *Mensch und Staat im Strukturwandel der Gegenwart*. Paderborn: Schöningh, 1971.
Tenenti, Alberto. *La Vie et la Mort à travers l'art du XVe siècle*. Paris: Armand Colin, 1952. Cahiers des Annales, 8.
Thévenaz, Pierre. "Événement et historicité." In *L'Homme et l'histoire. Actes du VIe Congrès des Sociétés de Philosophie de langue française*, 217–25. Paris: Presses universitaires de France, 1952.
  Reprinted in idem, *L'Homme et sa raison*, 121–28. Neuchâtel: Baconnière, 1956.
Thiel, Johannes H. Review of *Benaderbaar verleden* by W. den Boer. In *Tijdschrift voor Geschiedenis* 66 (1953): 249.
Troeltsch, Ernst. *Gesammelte Schriften*. 4 vols. Tübingen: Mohr & Siebeck, 1912–25.
Vossler, Otto. *Geschichte als Sinn*. Frankfurt am Main: Suhrkamp, 1979.
Wagner, Fritz. *Die Historiker und die Weltgeschichte*. Munich: Karl Alber, 1965.
———. *Moderne Geschichtsschreibung. Ausblick auf eine Philosophie der Geschichtswissenschaft*. Berlin: Duncker & Humblot, 1960.
———. "Rankes Geschichtsbild und die moderne Universalhistorie." *Archiv für Kulturgeschichte* 44 (1962): 1–26.
———. "Zweierlei Mass der Geschichtsschreibung - eine offene Frage." *Saeculum* 10 (1959): 113–23.
Wheeler, Sir Robert Eric Mortimer. *The Indus Civilization*. Cambridge: Cambridge University Press, 1953.
Windischmann, K. J. *Das Gericht des Herrn über Europa*. Frankfurt am Main, 1814.
Wittram, Reinhard. *Das Interesse an der Geschichte*. Göttingen: Vandenhoeck & Ruprecht, 1958.
Wright, John Joseph. *National Patriotism in Papal Teaching*. Westminster, Md.: The Newman Bookshop, 1943.
Woroniecki, Hyacinthus, O.P. "Qaestio disputata de nationae et statu civili." *Divus Thomas* (Freiburg) 29 (1926): 25–41.

INDEX OF NAMES

Aalders, W. J., 18, 19n
Acton, Lord, 143n, 316
Adam, Karl, 112–13, 217
Anderle, Othmar F., 309
Alcuin of York, 263
Allo, Ernest Bernard, 98n
Angelinus, 17
Anselm of Canterbury, 126
Aquinas. *See* Thomas Aquinas
Aristotle, 11, 32, 117, 125, 128, 383, 384
Aron, Raymond, 329–32
Aubert, Roger, 100, 109, 110, 154
Augustine, Aurelius, 115, 122, 125, 141, 142, 184, 225–26, 243, 333, 347, 349–50, 364, 377
Aulard, François-Alphonse, 207

Baethgen, Friedrich, 232n
Baius, 24–25, 31
Bakker, J. T., 270
Bandmann, Günter, 301n
Barraclough, Geoffrey, 315n, 386n, 395
Barth, Karl, 66, 74, 171–75, 179–81
Bartmann, Bernard, 111
Bastable, Patrick K., 25n
Bäumler, Alfred, 165
Baudoux, B., 123n
Bauhofer, Oskar, 51–54, 58, 71
Bavinck, Herman, 102n
Bavinck, Johan H., 279n
Beard, Charles A., 307, 308, 341
Beck, Heinrich, 384, 391
Becker, Carl Lotus, 308
Belloc, Hilaire, 145, 157
Bellon, K. L., 229, 244
Benedict of Aniane, 254
Benedict of Nursia, 96
Berengarius of Tours, 11
Berkhof, Hendrikus, 268–70, 274-75, 278
Berkouwer, G. C., 44, 51n, 66, 224, 276–77
Bernard of Clairvaux, 225
Bloch, Marc, 299, 360
Blondel, Maurice, 26, 27, 28–31, 130–38
Boer, W. den, 224

Böhner, Philotheus, 125n
Bonnefoy, J.-Fr., 37n
Boogman, J. C., 311, 315
Bossuet, J. B., 70, 141, 202–07, 210, 216, 316
Bouman, P. J., 322n
Boyer, Charles, 16n
Brandon, S. G. F., 347
Braudel, Fernand, 308, 309, 310, 311, 360
Brehier, Emile, 121
Buber, Martin, 394
Bultmann, Rudolf, 325
Burckhardt, Jakob, 372n
Butterfield, Herbert, 241n, 314n, 315, 335–336, 339, 365

Cajetan, 17, 18, 25, 33
Calvin, John, 276
Camus, Albert, 263
Candidus of Fulda, 302
Carles, Jules, 368
Casel, Odo, 45–47, 116, 161
Chanson, Paul, 218n
Chrysostom, John, 273
Congar, Yves, 61, 64, 72, 77, 83, 117
Conrad-Martius, Hedwig, 89
Conze, Werner, 308
Cremers, V., 193n
Croce, Benedetto, 144
Ctesias, 294
Cuervo, Mario, 25n
Cullmann, Oscar, 177–79

Daniélou, Jean, 13, 54–56, 58, 76, 82–83, 105, 109, 188, 216
D'Argenson, René Louis, 206, 207
Dawson, Christopher, 93–94, 109, 115, 335
De Broglie, Guy, 26
Dekkers, Eligius, 161n
De Lubac, Henri, 22, 26, 31–33, 134, 137
De Solages, Bruno, 106, 108
Delos, Joseph Thomas, 214
Delp, Alfred, 56–59, 71
Dessauer, Philipp, 56n, 69n

Didier, Georges, 263n
Dieks, Dennis, 392
Dilthey, Wilhelm, 92, 312, 313, 317, 329, 352, 382, 387–90
Doucet, Vittorino, 25n, 27n
Dooyeweerd, Herman, 81, 102n, 111n, 117–118, 184n, 245, 276n
Du Bos, Jean-Baptiste, 206
Duchrow, Ulrich, 350n
Duintjer, Otto Dirk, 367n
Dupréel, Eugène, 117
Durand, Alfred, 40n
Duystee, F. J. F. M., 192n

Eliade, Mircea, 234–35, 237
Enklaar, D. T., 307, 344
Ennen, Edith, 295

Faulhaber, Michael von, 219
Febvre, Lucien, 307n, 308, 309, 311, 341, 360–62
Feder, Alfred L., 152–53
Fénelon, 207
Féret, Henricus Maria, 38, 98–100
Ferlus, François, 207
Ferrariensis, Sylvester, 25
Feuling, Daniel, 37
Fichtenau, Heinrich, 305
Finke, Heinrich, 256
Fischer, Fritz, 307n
Flahiff, George B., 150n, 154
Forbes, R. J., 290
Fortmann, H. J. H. M., 40n
Francis of Assisi, 160, 272
Francis of Sales, 272
Freyer, Hans, 92n, 93, 235n
Fromm, Erich, 364
Fruin, Robert J., 223, 315–16
Funk, Philipp, 248

Ganshof, F. L., 299
Garrigou-Lagrange, Reginald, 129
George, Justus, 77
Gilson, Etienne, 121, 124–26, 134–35, 299, 351
Gloege, Gerhard, 314n
Görres, Joseph, 209, 210, 221
Gollwitzer, Heinz, 217n
Graaf, Simon Gerrit de, 6, 111n
Grassi, Ernesto, 314n
Gregory I, 159, 264, 265
Groen, P., 391

Groen van Prinsterer, Guillaume, 224
Grosche, Robert, 48, 116
Grossouw, W., 46n
Guardini, Romano, 208
Gurian, Waldemar, 61n

Haecker, Theodor, 79n, 111, 116
Hartmann, Max, 365
Hartmann, Nicolai, 236n
Hasenhüttl, Gotthold, 344
Hayes, Carlton J. H., 204
Hegel, G. W. F., 312, 321, 328, 351, 359, 367, 368, 370, 382, 393
Heidegger, Martin, 324n, 329, 331, 367, 370, 387, 388
Heimpel, Herman, 315n
Heitler, Walther Heinrich, 365
Heitz, A., 161n
Helmich, W. Bernhard, 374n
Hendrikx, Ephraem, 272
Herder, J. G. von, 209, 381, 382, 388n
Héris, Charles-Vincent, 37
Herwegen, Ildefons, 46, 161–66
Herzfeld, Ernst Emil, 294
Höfler, Otto, 291
Heufelder, Emmanuel Maria, 96
Hofbauer, Clemens Maria, 221
Hofer, Walther, 314n
Hoffman, Ross J. S., 143–45, 157
Holzer, Oswald, 38
Hove, Aloysius van, 35n
Hrabanus Maurus, 300
Huber, Max, 92n
Huby, Joseph, 100
Hübner, Kurt, 392
Hugon, Edouard, 39n
Huizinga, Johan, 97, 298, 309, 372

Irenaeus, 115

Janssen, Johannes, 209, 220
Janssens, Aloïs, 38n
Jaspers, Karl, 274n, 320, 329, 335
Jolivet, Régis, 115, 119
Jong, Henk de, 396
Journet, Charles, 49, 98n, 129

Kamlah, Wilhelm, 364n
Kant, Immanuel, 367n, 382
Kearney, Hugh F., 141, 152, 154n, 231n
Köhler, Oskar, 320
Koster, Mannes Dominikus, 27n

Index of Names

Kreling, Gerardus Petrus, 17–18
Krüger, Gerhard, 314
Kuyper, Abraham, 175, 191, 197, 275
Kuypers, Karel, 364, 369n
Kwant, Remigius C., 244

Lamy, Agnès, 85
Laporta, J. G., 26, 27
Lasaulx, Ernst von, 209
Lavedan, Pierre, 295
Leclercq, Jean, 267, 271
Leeuwen, Arend van, 17n
Lefranc de Pompignan, Jean-Jacques, 207
Lefèvre, Luc-J., 73n, 84n
Le Goff, Jacques, 299
Lemberg, Eugen, 215
Lenhart, Ludwig, 214n
Levinas, Emmanuel, 390, 392
Leo XIII, 192, 219
Lialine, Clément, 44n
Loeff, J. J., 190–201
Löwith, Karl, 314, 315
L'Orange, Hans-Peter, 294
Lousse, Emile, 153n
Loyola, Ignatius of, 272
Lucretius, 117
Lusseau, Henri, 109
Luther, Martin, 163, 359

Macarius the Great, 266n
Mackay, Ernest J. H., 284
Maistre, Joseph de, 210–11, 222
Malevez, Leopold, 64–66, 76, 77, 82, 181
Malmberg, Felix, 39
Mandonnet, Pierre, 123–24, 134, 141
Manser, G., 17n
Marcel, Gabriel, 122
Maréchal, Joseph, 26
Maritain, Jacques, 49, 55, 59–63, 72, 126–130, 134–38, 149–50, 151–53, 180, 182, 194–95
Marrou, Henri-Irénée, 78, 110, 114, 150n, 315, 328–34, 336, 339, 364
Mayer, Anton L., 164–66
Mayer, Joseph Ernst, 270–71, 272–73
Meinecke, Friedrich, 382, 388
Meinhold, Peter, 337–38, 339
Meijer, Brocardus, 25n
Melsen, A. G. M. van, 200
Mercier, A., 23
Mercier, Louis J. A., 140–41
Michalson, Carl, 314n

Michel, Albert, 23n, 24n
Michels, Thomas, 66–69, 78
Michelet, Jules, 372n
Möhler, J. A., 44
Moeller, Bernd, 358
Moeller, Charles, 107
Montuclard, M.-I., 104–05
Mounier, Emmanuel, 92n, 107, 117
Müller, Adam H., 208, 221–22
Müller, A. M. Klaus, 391
Müller, Heinz, 225n, 226
Münzhuber, Joseph, 234n

Niebuhr, Barthold Georg, 170, 328
Niebuhr, Reinhold, 170–71
Niermeyer, J. F., 315
Noack, Ulrich, 296
Noël, Léon, 124
Nørlund, Poul, 291, 292

O'Connor, William, 148
Odo of Cluny, 264
O'Mahony, James E., 26n
Otto of Freising, 225, 226, 350

Padovani, Umberto, 141–43, 154, 157
Pauwels, C. F., 193n, 194n
Pernoud, Régine, 247, 248, 257
Peters, J. A. S., 19, 21
Pius V, 25n
Pius XI, 212n
Pius XII, 185–88, 190, 195, 222n
Pinsk, Johannes, 66–68, 164–65
Plato, 11, 125
Ploumen, P., 193n
Ploeg, J. van der, 46n
Polybius, 91
Pope, Arthur Upham, 294, 295, 298
Poschmann, Bernard, 47n
Postan, Mikhail M. 315n
Przywara, Erich, 15, 122n

Rabeau, Gaston, 137
Raeymaeker, Louis de, 20, 21, 390n
Ranke, Leopold von, 97, 143, 232, 311, 328, 339, 346, 359–60, 365, 394
Ranke-Heinemann, Uta, 266n
Rast, Maximilian, 53n, 69
Read, Conyers, 307, 308
Rickert, Heinrich, 329
Ridderbos, H. N., 270, 274, 275, 335, 378n

Ritter, Gerhard, 311n, 339n
Robbers, Herman, 78, 117, 134
Robinson, James Harvey, 307n, 308
Rollin, Charles, 206, 207
Romein, Jan Marius, 309, 317n, 364n
Romme, Carel P. M., 218n
Rommen, Heinrich Albert, 205n
Romualdus van Delft, 24n
Rooyen, Henri van, 35n, 36n
Rosenmüller, B., 19
Rottenberg, Isaac, 175n
Rousseau, Jean-Jacques, 207
Rousselot, Pierre, 26
Rousset, Paul, 225n, 299
Ruller, A. A. van, 175–77

Salomon, G., 210n
Salvatorelli, Luigi, 96n
Sawicki, Franz, 78, 86–88, 227
Schelven, A. A. van, 229
Schilfgaarde, Paul van, 92
Schlegel, Friedrich von, 209
Schmaus, Michael, 37, 112
Schmidt, Erich Friedrich, 294
Schmidt, Heinrich, 300
Schmidt, Wilhelm, 95, 96
Schneider, C. M., 26
Schnürer, Gustav, 95, 101–03, 157–61
Scholten, Paul, 374
Schoonenberg, Piet J. A. M., 277n
Schultz, Carl G., 291, 292
Schwarz, Balduin, 151
Schwarz, Richard, 323
Sciacca, Michele, 122, 141
Scotus, Duns, 36, 37, 38
Seidlmayer, Michael, 251, 254, 272
Seiller, Léon, 42n
Sertillanges, Antonin-Gilbert, 26
Simmel, Georg, 329
Slijper, Everhard Joh., 364
Smaragdus of Saint-Mihiel, 254
Smith, Page, 314n
Smitskamp, Hendrik, 6, 245
Söhngen, Gottlieb, 47
Soukup, Leopold, 17n, 18n
Spaemann, Robert, 391
Spiess, Emil J., 92n
Spengler, Oswald, 92
Staudinger, Hugo, 384
Steenberghen, Fernand van, 123, 150n
Steins Bisschop, L., 134
Strabo, 283

Stolz, Anselm, 26, 27, 28, 157
Sturzo, Luigi, 145–49, 152–53
Suarez, Francesco, 204
Suenens, Leo Jozef, 135n
Suger of St. Denis, 304

Taymans d'Eypernon, François, 134n
Tenenti, Alberto, 309
Teilhard de Chardin, Pierre, 105–10, 321–22
Theodoret of Cyr, 266
Theeuws, Paul, 62
Thévenaz, Pierre, 236, 314n, 324n, 388n
Thiel, Johannes H., 229n
Thieme, Karl, 94
Thils, Gustave, 63–64, 150n
Thomas Aquinas, 11, 18, 32, 60, 62, 125, 126, 215–16
Tillemont, Louis Sebastian de, 316
Timp, P. M., 39n
Toynbee, Arnold, 92n, 309n
Troeltsch, Ernst, 92, 312, 317, 382
Tromp, Sebastianus, 44n
Tschipke, Theophil, 41n

Vagts, Alfred, 307n
Verberne, L. G. J., 190n
Vico, Giambattista, 119n
Virgil, 117
Vollenhoven, Dirk H. T., 11n, 245
Vonier, Anscar, 48
Vossler, Otto, 384, 385, 394
Vries, Joseph de, 127n, 129

Wagner, Fritz, 336, 337, 339
Walafrid Strabo, 254
Weber, Alfred, 341
Weber, Max, 389
Weber, Otto, 337
Wedgwood, Cicely V., 315n
Wheeler, Mortimer, 284
Windelband, Wilhelm 329
Windischmann, Karl J., 216–17
Winzen, Damasus, 47
Wittram, Reinhard, 334, 336–37, 339
Wolf, Walther, 119n
Woltjer, R. H., 92n
Woroniecki, Hyacinthus, 214
Wright, J. J., 213n, 218n

Xenophon, 294

Zechmeister, August, 61

INDEX OF SUBJECTS

Absolutism, 203, 205, 210, 211, 216
Alienation: from culture, 262, 264; from fellow-man, 375; from God, 271; from history, 237–41, 318, 328, 335, 341
Annales (journal, school), 308–11, 352, 356, 360–61
Analogia entis, 15
Analogical relation: in Barth, 173, 179; in Berkhof, 268–69
Antiquity, 91–97, 102, 112, 114, 115, 117, 118, 144, 158–60, 162–66, 252–54, 274, 275, 297–98
Apologetics, 11, 43
Apostasy, 195, 220, 241, 275; Berkhof on, 275; Dooyeweerd on, 118
Architecture: Near Eastern, 281–91, 294–96, 298; medieval, 252, 374; pagan, 160
Arianism, 158–59
Art, medieval, 163, 165, 166
Asceticism, 83–85, 254–56, 259, 262–80. *See also* Renunciation of the world
Augustinianism, 124–25, 215, 257
Autonomy: of cultures, 157; of historical reality, 155, 156, 182, 228–29, 240–243, 338, 339, 354, 386; of man, 324, 384, 391; of nature, the natural order, 31, 89, 130, 193, 197; of the nation, 214–16; of science and philosophy, 141, 142; of the temporal, 75, 79, 81, 85, 88, 354; of (rational) thought, 124, 132–39, 141, 187, 188. *See also* Self-sufficiency

Belgic Confession, 191n
Benedictines, 95–96, 159

Calvinism and toleration, 189–201
Calvinist philosophy, 75, 138, 169, 181–84, 188, 189–201. *See also* Reformational
Carolingians, 166, 252, 253, 254, 257, 263
Catholic philosophy, 121–39, 141
Catholic thought, shift in modern, 3, 7–12, 24, 33, 37, 80, 111, 122, 185–88, 217, 243
Causality, 144, 155–56, 239–44; intramundane, 233, 375–76, 385–86, 395, 396; supernatural, 229

Cause, the First, 20, 25, 156, 218
Chivalry, 257, 259, 272
Christendom, 209, 221, 261. *See also* Middle Ages
Christian culture, 59–63, 64, 73, 94–97, 158–60, 164, 180, 182–83, 195, 260; Van Ruller on, 175–77
Church Fathers, 10–13, 32, 185
Church, 41–44, 93–97, 102–03, 105, 112, 144, 157–65, 178, 216, 256; and kingdom of God, 48–49; and State, 189–201, 206, 218–22
Cistercian order, 265
City plans: Near Eastern, 281–90, 294–95, 297–98; medieval, 296, 298–302
Cluniac order, 257, 264–65
Corpus mysticum, 43–48, 161. *See also* Mystical Body of Christ
Counter-Reformation, 11, 166
Courtly culture, 322, 346, 372, 376
Cross (crucifixion), 38, 40, 48–50, 81–85, 171
Crystallization points, 378
Cultural mandate, 261, 265, 267, 277, 278, 325
Culture, 260–80; disclosure of, 118, 274
Cyclical thinking, 114–19, 235, 311, 348–49, 352; Berkhof on, 269, 274
Cynics, 91

Desiderium naturale, 24–34, 131, 213

Eastern Orthodoxy, 66
Edict of Milan, 85
Education, 194, 214
Encyclicals: *Divini Redemptoris*, 212n; *Ex omnibus afflictionibus*, 25n; *Humani generis*, 185–88; *Immortale Dei*, 192, 200, 219; *Inscrutabili*, 219; *Libertas*, 192, 198
Enlightenment, 206–08
Eschatology (last things, end-time), 49, 57, 65, 77, 78–79, 99–101, 110, 171, 175, 178, 182, 228, 230, 314, 320, 324, 334, 355, 378; and asceticism, 267, 271; Marrou on, 78, 334

Eucharist, 45–47, 68, 161
Evil, 142, 171, 234–38, 240, 257, 273, 275, 318, 323
Evolutionism, 105, 321, 322
Existentialism, 237, 313, 373; of Marcel, 122; of Marrou, 329–33, 339; and freedom, 324–25, 392; and history, 343–44, 352; in Butterfield, 336, 339

Fall into sin, 35–50, 154, 170, 173, 177, 183, 271, 278; Reformed theology on, 75, 174; in Teilhard, 109
Factors, 308, 395; supernatural, 152–53; Sturzo on, 145–48
Facts, 140, 147, 150, 237–43, 306, 308, 316–17, 335, 342, 343–44, 380, 390; supernatural, 152–53
Faith, 230; and history, 381; and knowledge, 381, 393; and reason, 121–39, 141, 154, 187, 188, 233; and science, 156, 223–46, 367, 380
First (primary) history, 363–79. *See also* Metahistory
Free University, 5, 223, 244, 245, 246
Freedom, 239, 269, 270, 277, 311–13, 321–325, 338–39, 345, 356, 371–72, 394
French Revolution, 207, 210, 310

Germanic: culture, 161–65; religiosity, 112, 225; tribes, 252–56
Gnosticism, 173
Gothic, 160, 164–66, 258, 259, 280, 374
Grace, divine, 183, 277
Great men (personalities), 243, 307; Hegel on, 321
Greek philosophy, 92, 94, 112, 114–19, 177, 215, 274, 383, 384
Ground: of being, 238, 320, 380–96; of history, 321, 325, 352, 356, 369. *See also* First history; Metahistory

Hellenism, 158, 164–65
Heresy (error), 185, 192, 195, 198, 221, 256
Hermeneutics, 378–79, 380, 392–96
Historians: academic, 341, 375; Catholic, 140–66; Christian, 148; concern for meaning, 319; neutrality of, 307, 344; and the Middle Ages, 247–49
Historical consciousness, 114, 312–14, 357, 382, 386–90
Historical method, inadequacy of, 261, 297, 306, 309, 329, 335, 343

Historical objectivity, 140, 147, 331, 343, 344, 378, 380; Marrou on, 331, 332
Historical outlook, 305
Historical Schools, 86, 209
Historical science, 140–66; and (presence of) God, 223–46; skepticism about, 328; turnabout in, 305–17. *See also* Historical method
Historicism, 81, 184, 313–14, 356, 387, 388; and freedom, 313, 324–25; and relativism, 80, 237, 317, 388, 390, 393; Marrou on, 331
Historicity, 184, 237–40, 313–14, 328, 363–379, 393
Historie and *Geschichte*, 179, 333, 343, 364
History, discipline of. *See* Historical science
History: as channel of meaning, 319, 326, 357; meaning of, 78–81, 151, 154, 169–184, 228, 235, 313, 316, 317, 335, 342, 343, 350, 356–57, 363–79; hand of God in, 85–90, 114, 153, 223–46; in Berkhof, 268–70, 274–75; in Romanticism, 210
Holy Roman Empire, 59, 68, 210, 215
Humanism (literary movement), 203–04, 257
Humanism (worldview), 195, 198
Human rights: Maritain on, 63, 201; Pius XI on, 213n; Pius XII on, 190, 195
Hypostatical union, 38, 39–42, 65, 67, 76, 77, 181

Image of God, 187, 276, 325, 337
Incarnation, 36–40, 47, 66, 81, 91, 93, 102, 106, 146, 155, 350
Incarnation theology, 64–65, 181–82
Integralism, 147, 308–10, 315, 317

Job, Book of, 228
Judgment in history, 225, 228, 229, 323, 336
Justice, 366, 368, 369, 391

Kingdom of God, 261, 276; and the church, 48–49, 113; and the end-time, 171; and history, 91, 182–84, 221, 242, 276, 325, 337; and human activity, 77; in the here and now, 176, 351
Kingship: Ancient Near Eastern, 282, 294, 295n, 297; medieval, 225, 251, 252, 296; Bossuet on, 205
Knowledge, 22, 144, 377, 381; historicity of, 388, 393; limits of, 226, 228, 233, 239; reordering of, 234, 380–96

Index of Subjects

Laity, 9–10, 272, 273
Liturgical Movement, 161
Love, 366, 372; of country, 205, 207; of God, 194, 262–67, 273; of learning, 254, 263, 267; of neighbor, 194, 200, 205, 263

Manicheism, 264, 270–71, 273
Meaning of life, 267–69, 313, 318–26, 335–336, 356–57, 363–79; existentialism on, 324, 339. *See also* History, meaning of
Metahistory, 235, 313, 314–17, 342
Mentalities, history of, 310
Middle Ages, 121, 129, 220–22, 247–59; culture of, 204, 272, 280, 297–304; view of history in, 225–28; Herwegen on, 161–66; Maritain on, 59–63, 73, 95–97, 180, 195, 265, 271, 372; Schnürer on, 101–03, 157–60
Missions, 217, 219; Berkhof on, 269, 270; Bultmann on, 325
Mystery, 92, 223–46, 350, 356, 365, 384
Mystery theology, 45–49, 116, 161
Mystical Body of Christ, 48, 65, 113, 193, 221

Nationalism, 202–22, 362
National Socialism, 211, 217
Nature: and grace, 9, 82, 157, 163, 169, 182, 333; and the supernatural, 14–34, 68, 70–90, 111, 141, 149, 153, 163, 180; in Barth, 74; in Blondel, 133; in Löwith, 314, in Marrou, 333
Natural law, 191, 195–96, 207, 314
Natural reason, 21, 142, 146, 148, 186, 212, 386
Natural theology, 186–88, 213, 218, 244

Origin, 154–55, 184, 322, 345, 354, 366–67, 384, 388, 390–93, 396. *See also* Ground

Participation (in the divine), 164, 183, 229, 244; doctrine of, 11, 15–16, 19, 21, 22, 23, 31, 139, 244
Peace, 355, 366, 392
Periodization, 97–103, 155, 158–60, 162–166, 243, 250, 347, 353, 376–77
Philosophy of life, 92, 237
Positivism, 143, 147, 330, 338, 342, 352
Pragmatism, 308
Presentism, 248–49, 307, 311, 341–45, 357, 375

Presupposition (point of departure), 138–39, 147, 155, 181, 187; in Teilhard, 108; of science, 152, 154, 297–98, 306, 327, 334, 381, 392, 396. *See also* Faith
Progress, 308, 316, 352, 357, 372; idea of, 91–120, 170, 181–83, 237, 246, 248, 260, 317, 318, 321, 322; Berkhof on, 269–70; Hegel on, 312, 321; Malevez on, 64, 65, 76, 82, 181–83
Prophecy, nature of, 355, 369
Providence, 70, 153, 155, 205–06, 208, 216, 223–46, 335, 336. *See also* History, hand of God in

Reason: and faith, 121–39, 150; and ethics, 191–92, 218; and human passions, 36; and progress, 387; and theology, 12. *See also* Natural reason
Reformation, 166, 195, 215, 220–21, 374; approaches to, 358–62
Reformational thought, 3–4, 74, 111, 169–170, 181–84. *See also* Calvinist philosophy
Relation to God, 276–80, 325–26, 327, 334–38, 339, 355, 367. *See also* Origin
Relativism, 313, 388, 390, 393
Relativity, 321, 352, 357, 386, 389
Religion, 241, 247, 250; Germanic conception of, 253; in pre-modern architecture, 295–304
Renaissance, the, 160, 165, 166, 195, 204, 215, 372, 396
Renaissances, 253, 254, 372
Renunciation of the world, 83–85, 160, 255, 256, 262–80. *See also* Asceticism
Restlessness, 184; medieval, 254; modern, 279–80; in Blondel, 131; of the Germanic spirit, 162, 165
Resurrection, 38, 46, 48–50, 66–67, 171, 178, 268, 270, 326
Revisionism, 249, 305, 375
Revolution: concept of, 163; spirit of, 316
Romanesque, 160, 164–65
Romanticism, 86, 203, 208–10, 216, 221, 372–73
Rule of Saint Benedict, 265, 268, 272

Sacraments, 44, 67, 161, 164
Sacred space, 281–304
Scholasticism, 14–34, 137, 138, 140, 156, 163, 166, 179, 185, 186, 215–16, 227, 228, 333, 368. *See also* Thomism

Science, method of, 239, 364, 380–96
Second history, 370–79
Secularization, 215, 216, 221, 234, 258, 314, 353
Self-sufficiency, 240–44, 374. *See also* Autonomy
Sermon on the Mount, 242, 261, 277–79
Sin, 35–50, 74, 75, 82, 104, 142, 154, 170, 173, 179, 180, 183, 259, 275, 326, 336. *See also* Fall into sin
Social history, the new, 309, 315, 360–61
Spirit of the age, 211, 216, 248, 338, 354, 377, 395
State, government, 189–201; and love of country, 210
Stoics, 91
Structuralism, 239, 308–11, 317, 338, 352, 359, 360–62, 385, 395
Subjectivity, 233, 316, 320, 330–33, 334, 337, 343, 344, 379. *See also* Faith; Presupposition
Suffering, 234–38; and asceticism, 263, 266
Supernatural, the: 142, 146; and the nation, 211–14, 216, 218–20; and nature, 22–34, 75, 110, 149; and philosophy, 126, 127, 128, 130–37; in history, 146–49, 151–153, 227–29; Teilhard on, 107, 108
Symbolism, in pre-modern culture, 298–304
Synthesis, 211, 309; medieval, 166, 252–55; in Thomism, 32, 187, 188

Technology, 269, 375
Théologie nouvelle, 8, 31, 122, 185
Theology of history: Catholic, 36–44, 48–50 51–69, 70–120, 140–57, 179–83, 313; Protestant, 170–84; on time, 114–19

Thomism, 15, 21, 31, 37, 124, 127, 185–88, 195–96, 215–16
Time, 347–57, 363–79; Cullmann on, 177–79; medieval sense of, 299–300, 350–51; transcendental, 354–56, 367–79
Toleration, 189–201
Transcendent, the, 216, 250, 251, 255, 258
Transcendent One, the, 241, 243, 355
Transcendental history. *See* First history
Trans-historical meaning of history, 235–38. *See also* Metahistory
Truth, 279, 344; Marrou on, 332; Wittram on, 334, 337

Utility of history, 249, 306, 308, 334, 357

Value of history, 306, 326, 331, 341–46, 357, 375; Fruin on, 315–16
Vatican I, 44, 66n
Vatican II, viii, 127n
Verstehen, method of, 332, 392–93, 395
Viking fortresses, 291–94
Volkish thought, 209, 217

West, western culture, 65, 94–97, 101–03, 113, 129, 158–59, 182, 221, 252, 257, 264, 265, 390
Wonder (amazement), 354, 365, 366
Wonders (miracles), 89–90, 153. *See also* History, hand of God in
World history, 91–120, 229, 235, 315, 317, 368, 376; unity (inner coherence) of, 91–95, 227, 236, 243, 335, 353, 367–70, 393; Hegel on, 321, 351, 359
World-order (creation ordinances), 227, 232, 240, 242, 243; medieval *ordo*, 257